AMERICAN

ARMIES AND BATTLEFIELDS

IN EUROPE

American Meuse-Argonne Memorial at Montfaucon, France

AMERICAN
ARMIES AND BATTLEFIELDS
IN EUROPE

A HISTORY, GUIDE, AND REFERENCE BOOK

★

Prepared by the

AMERICAN BATTLE MONUMENTS

COMMISSION

UNITED STATES

GOVERNMENT PRINTING OFFICE

1938

COPIES FOR SALE BY
THE SUPERINTENDENT OF DOCUMENTS
GOVERNMENT PRINTING OFFICE
WASHINGTON, D. C.
$2.75
PER COPY

IMPORTANT ABBREVIATIONS USED IN TEXT

A. E. F.—American Expeditionary Forces.

G. H. Q.—General Headquarters, A. E. F.

S. O. S.—Services of Supply, A. E. F.

With a few obvious exceptions, all places mentioned in the text are in France, and all dates are in 1918 unless otherwise indicated.

CONTENTS

‿∽

MAPS AND SKETCHES

ॐ

PREFACE

THIS book has been prepared as part of the project of the American Battle Monuments Commission to commemorate in a complete and lasting manner the accomplishments and services of the American forces in Europe during the World War.

It is a revision of a book entitled "A Guide to the American Battlefields in Europe" which was published by the Commission in 1927. The text, however, has been enlarged considerably to meet also the need for a concise reference book and a brief history of the American Expeditionary Forces.

Because of space limitations, practically all information concerning the Allied Armies has been omitted. This omission should not be construed as a lack of appreciation of the magnitude of their effort, but rather as a recognition of the fact that any attempt to describe the operations of their armies during four years of fighting could not, as an incident to a book of this character, do justice to their importance.

Every possible precaution has been taken to insure the accuracy of the historical statements made in this text and each one has been subjected to careful scrutiny by the Chairman of the Commission and to several independent checks by a corps of selected officers from the Regular Army. The documents and other evidence supporting the historical statements have been listed and these lists form part of the files of the Commission.

The three areas in which American troops in relatively large numbers engaged in battle are dealt with in Chapters II, III and IV. Each of these chapters consists of a short general story and a detailed itinerary which takes the tourist to the most interesting points of the terrain and describes the American operations which occurred there. Each chapter also includes a list giving places of interest not described on the tour, a summary of the services of the American divisions in that part of France covered by the chapter, and a colored map which will aid in understanding the operations and which will be of use in following the described route.

The American fighting in the Champagne region and in the battle area north of Paris is described in Chapters V and VI. In these regions the American operations were in most cases those of units not larger than a division, and the areas in which they took place are quite far apart. Chapter V contains a detailed itinerary for the Champagne region and Chapter VI a suggested route for an extended tour in the region north of Paris.

Special attention is invited to Chapters XI and XII which give information about the military cemeteries and war memorials constructed in Europe by the United States Government.

Numerous sketches and maps are used to give a graphic picture of the American fighting and its relationship to the combat services of the Allied Armies. Included among these are three large maps inside the rear cover which show the American operations in the Aisne-Marne, St. Mihiel and Meuse-Argonne regions, the three areas in France where most of the American fighting occurred.

The wartime photographs in the volume were selected with a view to giving a comprehensive pictorial story of the American war activities in Europe. Certain of the photographs were obtained from the British Imperial War Museum and the German Heeresarchiv, and cannot be reproduced without their permission. These copyright pictures are identified in the titles by the symbols © B and © G, respectively. Copies of most of the other photographs may be purchased at the usual rate from the Photographic Division, Office of the Chief Signal Officer, U. S. Army, Washington, D. C.

A large part of the interesting information in this book, including all detailed accounts of actual fighting, is given in the described tours. If the battlefields cannot be visited, it is suggested that the tours be read and followed on the maps. While doing this the panoramic sketches will be of help in obtaining an idea of the terrain.

Those who read this book from beginning to end will note some repetition. This was found necessary to meet the needs of the various classes of readers for whom the book is intended.

Many statements are made in the text concerning conditions or things which will change with the passing of time. These statements refer, of course, to 1937, the year this book was placed in the hands of the printer.

For the benefit of those who desire to make a more complete study of the American battle operations in Europe, the Commission is now preparing a series of booklets giving detailed data concerning the combat services of the American divisions. A booklet will be published for each division which will be illustrated by large maps, scale 1/20,000, showing the daily front lines of the unit. The first of the series of these booklets will be on sale by the Superintendent of Documents, Government Printing Office, Washington, D. C., during the summer of 1938.

It would be impossible here to give credit individually to all those who have made this book possible. Special mention is made, however, of Lieutenant Colonel X. H. Price, Corps of Engineers, U. S. Army, the Secretary of the Commission, under whose personal supervision the book has been prepared, and the following members of the Commission staff whose painstaking and careful work was invaluable in its preparation: Major Howard F. K. Cahill, Infantry, U. S. Army, Mr. James E. Mangum, Major Henry O. Swindler, Infantry, U. S. Army, Major Hal M. Rose, Cavalry, U. S. Army, Captain John R. Vance, Infantry, U. S. Army, Captain Richard P. Ovenshine, Infantry, U. S. Army, 1st Lieutenant Bream C. Patrick, Field Artillery, U. S. Army, and Mr. Richard A. Hansen.

It is desired also to make acknowledgment of the assistance given by other agencies of the Government in the preparation of this volume, notably the Adjutant General of the Army, who made available the World War records and furnished other essential information; the Historical Section of the Army War College, which placed its records at the disposal of the Commission and cooperated in other ways in searching out historical facts; the Engineer Reproduction Plant of the United States Army for its help in connection with the preparation of sketches and maps and the printing of the larger maps; the Signal Corps of the Army for assistance in selecting and furnishing photographs; the Quartermaster General for important information concerning medals, troop movements and burials; the Navy Department for supplying important facts from its files; the Department of State and the military attachés in Europe, who obtained from foreign countries such data as were requested; the Smithsonian Institution, which kindly loaned certain medals for reproduction in charts of this book; the library of the Army War College and the Library of Congress, which placed at the disposal of the Commission numerous official documents and works of reference; and the Government Printing Office, which actually printed the book in addition to furnishing advice concerning its make-up.

As future editions of this book will no doubt be published, suggestions for its improvement from men who participated in the activities of the American Expeditionary Forces are invited.

AMERICAN BATTLE MONUMENTS COMMISSION,

JOHN J. PERSHING,
Chairman.

AMERICAN

ARMIES AND BATTLEFIELDS

IN EUROPE

THE WORLD WAR TO MAY 28, 1918
AND THE ORGANIZATION
OF THE AMERICAN EXPEDITIONARY FORCES

THE WAR BEFORE THE ENTRY OF THE UNITED STATES

FOR some years prior to 1914 the great countries of Europe had been divided into two rival groups. One of these was the Triple Alliance, which comprised Germany, Austria-Hungary and Italy. The other was the Triple Entente, which consisted of France, Great Britain and Russia.

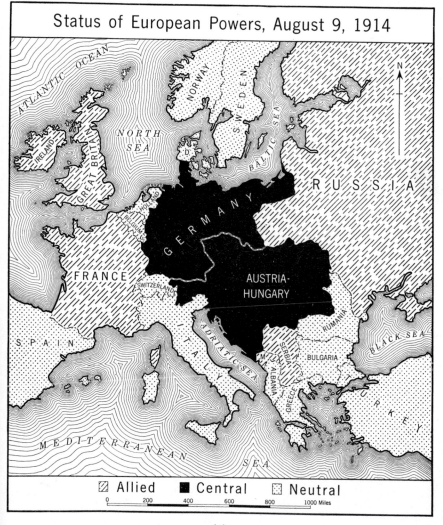

Status of European Powers, August 9, 1914

Allied   Central   Neutral

0   200   400   600   800   1000 Miles

The Triple Alliance, dominated by Germany, was the first to be formed and was initiated by Germany as a part of an ambitious plan to create a great world empire with herself at its head. In furtherance of this plan Germany had established close relationships with Turkey and some of the Balkan states, had extended her colonies by peaceful means and seizure, and had launched upon a program of military and naval expansion with the idea of becoming supreme on land and sea.

Great Britain, France and Russia, realizing their individual danger if called upon to act alone against a combination of powers such as the Triple Alliance, had formed the Triple Entente.

Belgium was not identified with either the Triple Alliance or the Triple Entente, as her neutrality had been guaranteed by all members of both groups except Italy.

Various incidents which occurred before 1914 had almost caused war between the two groups and each incident had increased to some extent the strain which existed between them.

EVENTS OF 1914

The breaking point came when the Crown Prince of Austria was assassinated on June 28, 1914, while inspecting troops in the Austrian city of Serajevo, near the Serbian border. Austria at once accused Serbia of having instigated the crime and adopted an aggressive attitude in the diplomatic negotiations which ensued. Serbia went to great lengths to prevent war with her powerful neighbor, and after submitting to practically all the demands made upon her, agreed to arbitrate the others. Austria, however, confident of the support of Germany in a war of aggression, refused to accept the Serbian proposals and declared war against her on July 28, 1914.

Austria started mobilizing her army and Russia soon thereafter did likewise. Germany demanded that the Russian mobilization cease at once, and at the same time sent an ultimatum to France requiring that nation to state immediately her intentions in case of a Russo-German war. Receiving no reply from Russia, and a statement from France that she would do what her own interests dictated, Germany declared war against Russia on August 1 and against France on August 3.

Italy asserted that her agreements as a member of the Triple Alliance did not compel her to take part in a war of aggression and announced her neutrality. Great Britain did not enter the war until August 4, when it became certain that Germany had violated Belgian neutrality by invading that country regardless of her solemn agreement not to do so.

By that date, therefore, Germany and Austria-Hungary, commonly known as the Central Powers, were at war against

German Cavalry Leaving Berlin, August 1914

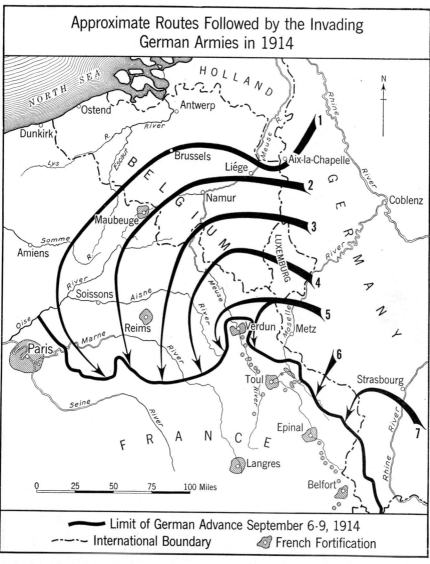

Approximate Routes Followed by the Invading German Armies in 1914

—— Limit of German Advance September 6-9, 1914
--·--·-- International Boundary   ◿ French Fortification

the Allies, consisting of France, Russia, Great Britain, Serbia and Belgium, which were joined by Montenegro a few days later. Four of these nations, France and Russia of the Allies, and Germany and Austria of the Central Powers, were able to place large, well trained armies in the field at once. Serbia, Belgium and Montenegro had relatively small armies and Great Britain's organized power was

mainly centered in her navy which at that time was the strongest in the world.

Believing that in the event of war Russia would mobilize her forces much more slowly than France, Germany, prior to the opening of hostilities, had made plans to crush the latter by a sudden and powerful offensive. According to these plans Austria and comparatively small German forces were to engage Russia on the east until France could be defeated, after which the combined strength of the Central Powers was to be sent against Russia to impose the same fate on her.

Immediately after the declaration of war the German Army began the invasion of France, using all natural avenues of approach, including that through neutral Belgium. In spite of heroic resistance by the Belgians, and the vital aid rendered the French by Great Britain's comparatively small expeditionary force, the Allies were forced back rapidly to the general line of the Marne River. Making a determined stand in early September, they withstood further attacks and so threatened the enemy's right that his armies were compelled to retire to a position behind the Aisne River.

Following this battle both sides realized that the war would not end quickly and each, knowing the supreme importance

to future military operations of the ports of northwestern France, ordered certain of their units to secure possession of these ports with all haste. If they had fallen to the Germans, not only would British military operations have been badly hampered, but Germany would have secured excellent bases for naval activities. In this famous "race to the sea" the Allies succeeded in retaining all ports southwest of Ostend.

At the end of these operations neither of the contending forces on the Western Front had sufficient superiority to undertake a major offensive, and each began to stabilize its position by the use of every artificial means available. Elaborate trench systems, defended by unprecedented numbers of machine guns and other quick-firing weapons, were built along the front and broad belts of barbed wire were constructed. These continuous

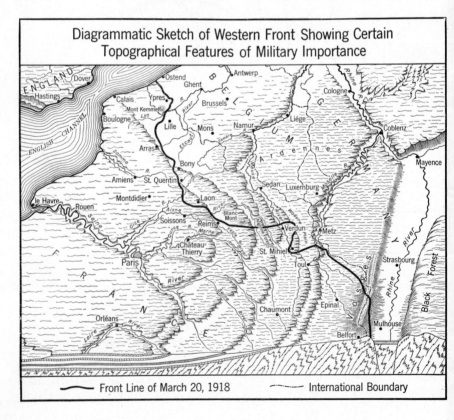

Diagrammatic Sketch of Western Front Showing Certain Topographical Features of Military Importance

——— Front Line of March 20, 1918   —·—·— International Boundary

A Gas Attack on the Western Front

defenses, with the hostile lines separated in many places by only a narrow strip of ground, resulted in the type of fighting known as "trench warfare".

During the advance of her armies toward Paris, Germany became greatly alarmed at the speed of the Russian mobilization and the progress of that country's offensive against East Prussia. This situation caused the German High Command, even before the Battle of the Marne, to weaken the force invading France by withdrawing approximately 90,000 men from its right wing—where they were so badly needed later—and starting them eastward to meet the Russian threat. The units withdrawn almost equaled in numbers the strength of the British Army in France at that time.

Generals von Hindenburg and von Ludendorff came into prominence in August when they were ordered to the German Eastern Army as Commander and Chief of Staff, respectively. The succeeding operations under their direction were characterized by rapid movements and crushing attacks, in which the losses inflicted on Russia were stupendous. The Russian Armies were hurled out of East Prussia by the decisive German victories at Tannenberg and the Mazurian Lakes, and farther south were soon thereafter pushed back toward Warsaw. Still farther south,

however, the Russians succeeded in driving the Austrian troops west of the passes through the Carpathian Mountains.

Turkey entered the war on the side of the Central Powers in November 1914, thus threatening Great Britain's communications with the East by way of the Suez Canal. As a result, many thousands of Allied soldiers, always badly needed on the French front, were employed throughout the war in operations near the eastern end of the Mediterranean Sea.

Germany was in a very strong position at the close of the year. She had inflicted staggering losses on the Russians; was in possession of practically all of Belgium and of industrial areas in France which contained about three fourths of the French coal and iron deposits; and although the German colonies were virtually lost, her home resources had not been damaged by invasion and were still intact.

EVENTS OF 1915

Italy entered the war in May 1915 on the side of the Allies. This caused a large proportion of Austria's strength to be withdrawn from the eastern and southeastern theaters of operations and be sent from there for service on the Italian front.

During the year the French and British launched several offensives against the Germans, the most important being the attacks begun in September by the French and British Armies north of Arras and by the French Army in the Champagne. These operations however did not produce any material change in the military situation on the Western Front.

On April 22, 1915, poison gas was used for the first time during the war when the Germans employed it against French troops serving in the line near Ypres.

Germany was again victorious against Russia in a series of desperate battles. Bulgaria, which entered the war on the side of the Central Powers in October, joined in the offensive that overran Serbia and Montenegro, while the Allied expedition to the Dardanelles was shattered and withdrawn immediately after the close of the year. The British Fleet held the mastery of the seas, but the submarine blockade which Germany had established in February was becoming a serious menace to Allied supply, both civil and military.

EVENTS OF 1916

The Central Powers, believing they had nothing to fear from Russia, planned a vigorous campaign in the west for 1916. In February they began intensive assaults against Verdun, which continued for months, only to dash themselves to pieces against French heroism. The German pressure at Verdun was relieved as a result of the British and French offensive on the Somme which began on July 1 and resulted in enormous losses to all armies engaged. It was during this battle that tanks were used for the first time, being employed by the British in an attack on September 15.

The German Fleet made a sortie in May and met the British on the North Sea in the Battle of Jutland, the principal naval engagement of the war. This battle resulted in the loss of several vessels on each side, but was not decisive. It terminated when the German Fleet withdrew to its fortified harbors, which it did not leave again in force during the war.

Large German Gun in Action on the Western Front. © G

British Tank Set on Fire by German Flame Thrower
Note German trench and soldiers in foreground.   © G

Russia astonished the world by her powers of recuperation, and in June practically destroyed the Austrian Army of Galicia. When the Austrian Army in Italy was defeated in August, and Rumania entered the war against the Central Powers in the same month, it became necessary that Austria be rescued without delay. Germany, quickly passing to the defensive in the west, started the eastern offensives which not only marked the beginning of the end for Russia but resulted in the elimination of Rumania before the close of the year.

In August General von Hindenburg was appointed Chief of the General Staff of the German Field Army. Offers of peace made by the Central Powers in the month of December were spurned by the Allied Governments as insincere.

EVENTS OF 1917 TO APRIL 6

The German High Command decided to remain on the defensive in the west during 1917. To further this purpose, it greatly disrupted the Allied plans by devastating a large area in the vicinity of Péronne and by withdrawing from that area to a previously-prepared defensive position of great strength.

Germany renewed unrestricted submarine warfare in February and her U-boats were making alarming inroads on Allied shipping when the United States entered the war.

Meanwhile the Allies had decided to undertake offensives on a large scale. In April, a few days after the United States declared war, the British began the Battle of Arras, and the French the Second Battle of the Aisne. These attacks gained some ground but the losses suffered by the attacking troops were very great, especially in the battle on the Aisne. The results created a serious situation in the French Army and brought grave discouragement to the Allies. With Russia's strength waning fast, this was almost final proof that without additional help the Allies would be unable to defeat Germany.

Sinking by the Germans of the American Bark *Kirby*

Sinking of the British Ship *Messanabie*—Torpedoed Twice by a German Submarine

British Hospital Ship *Gloucester Castle*—Torpedoed in the Mediterranean, April 1917

REASONS FOR THE ENTRY OF THE UNITED STATES INTO THE WORLD WAR

THE United States was in every respect a neutral nation at the beginning of the World War. The sympathies of the American citizens were naturally divided, but as the causes which brought on the conflict were considered by the mass of the people to be of no direct concern to the United States, the attitude of the country as a whole was one of neutrality.

Early in the war, however, the activities of the warring nations on the high seas began to interfere with American maritime trade. Allied interference with American commerce caused an exchange of vigorous diplomatic notes with Great Britain while differences with Germany over the use of the submarine became particularly irritating. It soon developed that Germany intended to disregard a fundamental principle of international law which up to that time in history had remained unquestioned. This was that neither merchant vessels of the enemy nor those of neutrals could be lawfully sunk without first taking steps to remove the passengers and crew.

The first serious difficulty with Germany arose when on February 4, 1915, she proclaimed that the waters surrounding Great Britain and Ireland would be regarded as part of the war zone in which enemy merchant vessels would be destroyed and in which even neutral vessels were in danger of destruction without assurance that the passengers and crew could be saved. The United States strongly protested this action which would endanger American lives and property, reminding Germany that under the conditions which existed her sole right under international law in dealing with neutral vessels on the high seas was limited to that of visit and search.

The German reply was unsatisfactory, stating in effect that the German Government would not be responsible for the consequences to neutral ships if they entered the waters announced by it as closed. The sinking of unarmed vessels soon occurred without any attempt being made to save those on board. This destruction of people innocent of any connection with the war reached its climax on the afternoon of May 7, 1915, when the British liner *Lusitania* was sunk, without warning, by a German submarine off the coast of Ireland. 1,195 lives were lost, including 124 Americans and 94 children, of which number 35 were infants.

The United States protested on May 13 and, in answer to the German Government's reply, reiterated its position on June 9, 1915, stating that the United States was contending for something much greater than mere rights of property or privileges of commerce—that it was contending for the rights of humanity.

On July 8, 1915, Germany assured the United States that American ships would not be hindered in the prosecution of legitimate shipping and that the lives of American citizens on neutral vessels would not be placed in jeopardy provided there was no contraband on board. This reply failed to meet the real issue and Germany was informed that a repetition by commanders of German naval vessels of acts in contravention to the rights of the American Government, where they affected the lives of American citizens, would be considered as deliberately unfriendly to the United States.

On August 19, 1915, the British steamer *Arabic* was sunk without warning and two American lives were lost. Germany disavowed this act but offered an indemnity.

The events up to this time had brought a gradual change in the attitude of the people of the United States toward the war. The violation of Belgian neutrality by Germany, in spite of her definite written pledges to respect it, naturally had an unfavorable reaction on the majority of the people in America and left them with the impression that the German

The *Leviathan,* Formerly the German Liner *Vaterland,*
Being Used as an American Transport

Government would stop at nothing to gain its ends. This idea was strengthened by Germany's submarine policy pursued in utter disregard of the property and lives of neutrals engaged in peaceful pursuits. Other contributing factors were the persistent reports of alleged German atrocities, acts of German sabotage in the United States, the first use of poison gas in warfare, considered at that time as an inhuman weapon, by the German Army on April 22, 1915, and patently false propaganda emanating from the German Embassy at Washington. This propaganda became so obnoxious to the press of America that they complained to the President with the result that the member of the German Embassy staff responsible for it was forced to return to Germany.

During the early part of 1916 the destruction of unarmed ships continued and on April 18 the President notified Germany that unless she at once abandoned her methods of submarine warfare against commercial vessels, diplomatic relations would be severed. Germany then promised that passenger ships would not be sunk, that due warning would be given to all other vessels which her submarines might seek to destroy, when no resistance was offered or escape attempted, and that care would be taken that the crews were given a reasonable chance to save themselves in their life boats.

This promise relieved the tension and relations between the two countries became more nearly normal during the next nine months. The situation, however, again grew critical when on January 31, 1917, Germany revoked her pledges to the United States and announced that it was her purpose to use submarines to sink every vessel which sought to approach either the ports of Great Britain and Ireland or the western coasts of Europe or any of the ports controlled by the enemies of Germany within the Mediterranean. President Wilson at once broke off diplomatic relations. He did not, however, then recommend a declaration of war, stating to Congress that he could not take such an extreme step unless the German Government should actually carry out its threat of sinking ships under the conditions to which the United States expressly objected.

Events which drove the United States into war now developed rapidly. On February 26, 1917, the President requested Congress to give him authority to equip American merchant ships with defensive arms should that become necessary. Two days later the President gave to the press the contents of a telegram which had been intercepted by the British Government late in January. This telegram had been sent by the German Secretary of Foreign Affairs, Arthur Zimmermann, through the German Embassy in Washington to the German Minister in Mexico City. It proposed that, in the event of war between the United States and Germany, an alliance be formed between Mexico and Germany and that Mexico endeavor to persuade Japan to desert the Allies and align herself with the Central Powers. Mexico was to be allowed "to reconquer her lost territory in Texas, New Mexico and Arizona". The effect of the publication of this telegram upon the American people was instantaneous and widespread. It seemed to crystallize public opinion into a strong feeling of hostility toward Germany. The House of Representatives promptly passed the bill to authorize the arming of merchant ships and, although due to a filibuster the measure failed to pass the Senate before its adjournment on March 4, it was clear that the overwhelming sentiment of Congress was in favor of the passage of the bill.

After the sinking of American ships by German submarines had actually occurred, the President addressed a special session of Congress on April 2, 1917, saying that under Germany's new policy "Vessels of every kind, whatever their flag, their character, their cargo, their

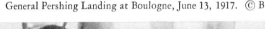

General Pershing Landing at Boulogne, June 13, 1917. © B

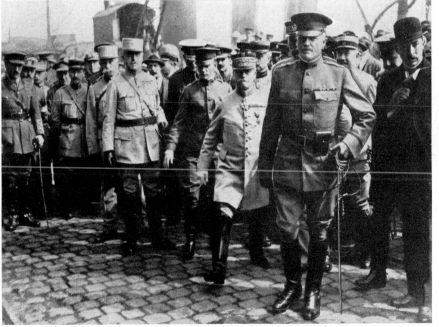

The First American Troops Arriving at St. Nazaire, June 26, 1917

German Zeppelin Forced Down at Bourbonne-les-Bains, October 1917

destination, their errand, have been ruthlessly sent to the bottom without warning and without thought of help or mercy for those on board, the vessels of friendly neutrals along with those of belligerents. Even hospital ships and ships carrying relief to the sorely bereaved and stricken people of Belgium . . . have been sunk with the same reckless lack of compassion and of principle." He further stated that he was not "thinking of the loss of property, immense and serious as that is, but only of the wanton and wholesale destruction of the lives of non-combatants, men, women, and children, engaged in pursuits which have always, even in the darkest periods of modern history, been deemed innocent and legitimate . . . " He then advised that war be declared against the Imperial German Government. Congress, with but few dissenting votes, approved this recommendation and war was declared against Germany on April 6, 1917.

Diplomatic relations were severed with Austria-Hungary two days later, but war was not actually declared against her until December 7, 1917.

The President took great care in his speech to Congress on April 2, 1917, to announce the aims and attitude of America. He said: "We have no selfish ends to serve. We desire no conquest, no dominion. We seek no indemnities for ourselves, no material compensation for the sacrifice we shall freely make. We are but one of the champions of the rights of mankind . . . We enter this war only where we are clearly forced into it, because there are no other means of defending our rights."

Both the sincerity of his statement and the correctness of his interpretation of the national aims and ideals of the United States were forcibly proved to the world, when, at the peace table in Versailles many months later, the American Government demanded neither one dollar of indemnity nor one square mile of territory from the defeated nations.

American Troops Parading in London, August 15, 1917

American Aviation Field at Issoudun

Storage Dam at Savenay Being Constructed by American Engineers

American Plant and Storage Yard at La Rochelle, Illuminated for Night Work

ORGANIZATION
OF THE AMERICAN EXPEDITIONARY FORCES
AND FORMATION OF ITS COMBAT ARMY

THE great task facing the United States when she entered the war was to place on the front as quickly as possible an American army sufficiently strong to give the combined Allied and American forces a decisive superiority over the Central Powers. It was evident that considerable time would elapse before America could actually have more than a nominal force in the battle lines, as her very small Regular Army, numbering less than 135,000 men, was scattered in weak detachments throughout her home territory and outlying possessions. There were no complete and permanent units larger than regiments, and even these units were not suitably equipped and organized for major operations.

The Allies asked, however, that immediate help be rendered by other means, and upon their request the United States loaned them huge sums of money, sent them great quantities of food, and assisted against the submarine menace both by the use of her

General John J. Pershing
American Commander-in-Chief

Navy and by building commercial ships to replace losses. The Allies also urged that an American unit be sent over at once for the effect on the morale of their armies and people. Accordingly, the 1st Division was formed from existing organizations and sent to France where most of its elements landed on June 26, 1917.

Major General John J. Pershing [1] was designated Commander-in-Chief of the American Expeditionary Forces effective on May 26, 1917, and served continuously in that capacity until the Armistice was signed and the Army was demobilized. He landed in France on June 13, 1917, accompanied by a small staff, and immediately plunged into the preliminary work of organizing the A. E. F.

After a thorough study of the situation, General Pershing cabled the War Department early in July that every effort should be made to have an American army in France of at least 1,000,000 men by the

[1] Appointed to the rank of General, October 8, 1917.

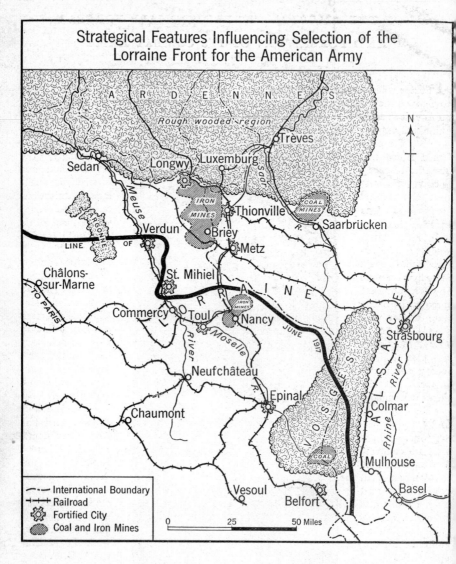

Strategical Features Influencing Selection of the Lorraine Front for the American Army

following May.   He pointed out that this figure did not represent the total number required, and recommended that plans for the further development of the military forces of the United States should contemplate placing 3,000,000 American soldiers in the field in Europe.

Decisions affecting the organization, size and equipment of various units; methods of training to be followed; the priority in which troops and supplies of various classes should be sent; and the requirements of the army in special equipment and personnel were cabled to Washington.   These cables formed the basis of the War Department's policies in mobilizing the great National Army in 1917 and 1918, and enabled the authorities in the United States to proceed with their tasks in such a way as best to meet the needs of the fighting forces in France.

One decision which had a marked

FRANCE

Legend:
- —— National Highway
- ━━ Battle Line March 20, 1918
- —·— International Boundary

0 25 50 75 100 MILES
0 50 100 KILOMETERS

ENGINEER REPRODUCTION PLANT, U.S. ARMY, FORT HUMPHREYS, D.C. 11954 1937

nfluence on the later operations of the American Army was that all training should be conducted in preparation for offensive warfare in the open. "Trench warfare", although practically the only method of combat being taught in the Allied Armies at that time, was considered by the American Commander-in-Chief only as a special phase of military operations which, if allowed to assume too great importance in training, could not fail to inculcate a defensive rather than an aggressive spirit in the army.

Another important decision was that affecting the size of the American combat division, which as organized for service in France was about twice the strength of any European division. Under the conditions then existing this resulted in giving to the American division much greater driving power in the offensive than that possessed by any other.

General Pershing's instructions from the Secretary of War upon sailing for Europe had stated that he must cooperate with the Allies "but in so doing the underlying idea must be kept in view that the forces of the United States are a separate and distinct component of the combined forces, the identity of which must

be preserved". These instructions were faithfully carried out by General Pershing who insisted throughout the war, in spite of the greatest pressure from the Allies, each of whom was influenced to some extent by its own special interests, that the forces under his command should constitute an American army under its own flag and its own commander. This basic idea was kept constantly in mind in organizing the American Expeditionary Forces and proved to be a decisive factor in the defeat of Germany.

Agreements had to be reached very quickly with the Allies as to where the American Army should be located, in order that the necessary preparations for its development and use could be initiated. With the British forces placed to cover the channel ports and the French Armies committed to the protection of Paris, the transportation systems in these regions were heavily burdened. The necessity for the supply and movement of additional forces made it essential for the American Army to choose a less crowded area where roads and railways were relatively free. The fact that there were few troops in Lorraine and that rail facilities, although extending across the

First American Troops to Land in France Parading in Paris, July 4, 1917

entire width of France, were available for transporting men and supplies from the French ports south of Le Havre to the Lorraine sector, were important considerations which finally decided its choice as the American front.

Another factor in the selection was the determination of the Commander-in-Chief to place his forces where their employment would decisively affect the outcome of the war. The coal and iron mines near Metz, the fortress itself and the essential railway systems at Sedan and to the southeast, all made the area protected by the Lorraine front of vital importance to Germany. Of the territory within striking distance of the Western Front, this was the area which she could least afford to lose, because on its retention depended her ability to maintain the German Armies west of the Rhine. The American Army in Lorraine would, therefore, be admirably located to strike at the most important German strategical area near the battle front.

The lack of vessels seriously retarded the transfer of troops to France, and the question was one of grave concern to the American Commander-in-Chief. At the beginning of 1918 agreements were made by him with the British for the use of a portion of their tonnage as they controlled most of the world's shipping at that time. It, however, took the crisis caused by the German offensive in March of that year to bring out the amount of Allied shipping that made possible the

remarkable increase of American arrival to a maximum in one month of ove 300,000 officers and men.

This crisis interrupted the formatio of an American army as the succession o German drives in the spring of 1918 re quired the use of every available Amer can and Allied division if defeat was t be avoided. It was at this time tha General Pershing went to General Foc and freely offered him the use of ever American man and gun in France.

When the American divisions had com pleted their part in the emergency an had assisted in the subsequent counter offensive which turned the tide in favo of the Allies, the American Commander in-Chief, despite renewed opposition o the part of the Allies, again insisted upo their assembly into one force, and soo thereafter this was resumed.

The American First Army was organ ized on August 10, 1918, and immediatel started preparations for the reduction o the St. Mihiel salient, which was to be it first large offensive operation.

Meanwhile, in spite of the handicap of a foreign country and language and th long line of communications to th United States, a multitude of tasks ha been accomplished in order that th American forces could begin operation when the divisions became available Staffs had been organized and trained docks, railways, roads, depots, hospitals bridges, and telegraph and telephone line had been built; ammunition and supplie

German Infantry Advancing Through Hermies
After Its Capture in March 1918. © G

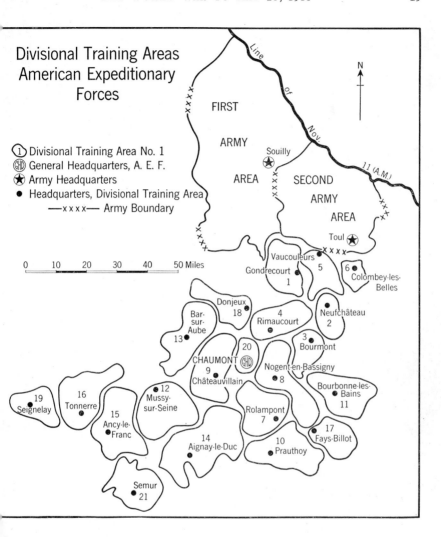

Divisional Training Areas
American Expeditionary
Forces

① Divisional Training Area No. 1
Ⓖ General Headquarters, A. E. F.
★ Army Headquarters
● Headquarters, Divisional Training Area
—x x x x— Army Boundary

0   10   20   30   40   50 Miles

FIRST
ARMY
AREA

SECOND
ARMY
AREA

Souilly
Toul
Vaucouleurs
Gondrecourt 5
1   6 Colombey-les-Belles
Donjeux
18   4
Bar-sur-Aube   Rimaucourt   Neufchâteau
13   2
20   3 Bourmont
CHAUMONT
9   Nogent-en-Bassigny
Châteauvillain   8
19   16   12   Bourbonne-les-Bains
Seignelay   Tonnerre   Mussy-sur-Seine   11
15
Ancy-le-Franc   Rolampont
7   17
14   Fays-Billot
Aignay-le-Duc   10
Prauthoy
Semur
21

d been collected; intensive training
hemes had been put into effect; and
ans for the future military operations
the American Army on the Western
ront had been studied and perfected.
The Commander-in-Chief, having fore-
en that a considerable part of the artil-
ry, airplanes and tanks necessary for a
rge force could not be obtained from
merican sources for some time to come,
d made arrangements to purchase large
antities of them from the Allies. The
isdom of this is evident when it is con-

sidered that, except for four 14-inch naval
guns on railway mounts, the American
First Army throughout its entire service
on the front did not fire an American-
made cannon or shell, and that no American-made tank was ever available in
Europe for use in battle.

Finally, after months of patient and un-
remitting labor, during which obstacles of
every nature had been met and overcome,
the American Army was ready on the
morning of September 12, 1918, for its
first great attack as an independent army.

Germans Defending Against a British Tank Attack
The tanks are under fire from field and anti-aircraft artillery and trench mortars
Middle picture shows a direct hit on a tank. © G

THE military situation in June 1917 was very favorable to Germany and her morale was high. Practically all her ffensives, with the exceptions of the Battle of the Marne in 1914 and the Verdun perations in 1916, had been crowned with

The sacrifice by France of a large proportion of her man power, and the presence of hostile armies on her soil for three years, had caused deep discouragement among her civil population. This was aggravated by the severe reverse which her

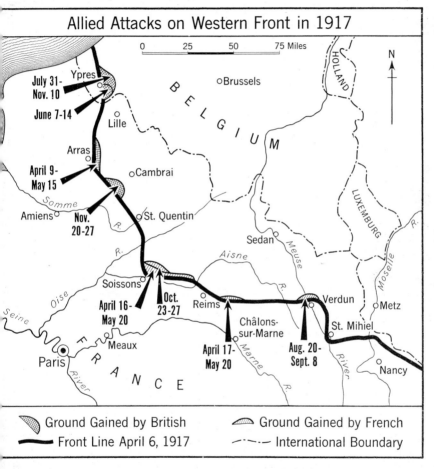

Allied Attacks on Western Front in 1917

0   25   50   75 Miles

N

July 31-
Nov. 10

June 7-14

April 9-
May 15

Nov.
20-27

April 16-
May 20

Oct.
23-27

April 17-
May 20

Aug. 20-
Sept. 8

Ypres

Brussels

Lille

Arras

Cambrai

Amiens

St. Quentin

Sedan

Soissons

Reims

Verdun

Metz

Châlons-
sur-Marne

St. Mihiel

Meaux

Paris

Nancy

BELGIUM

HOLLAND

LUXEMBURG

Somme R.

Oise

Seine

Aisne

Meuse

Moselle R.

Marne

River

FRANCE

Ground Gained by British   Ground Gained by French

Front Line April 6, 1917   International Boundary

reat success. Her battle lines, save for a mall section in Alsace, were on foreign erritory, her own resources were untouched by hostile occupation and wherever attacked by the Allies her armies ad inflicted tremendous losses upon them.

armies had suffered in April on the Aisne, which had resulted in a veritable wave of defeatism sweeping over the country and over the French military forces.

Great Britain, except for morale, was scarcely better off than France. Much of

American Troops Marching Through Neufchâteau on Their Way to the Battle Line

her best blood had been poured out on the battlefields; and like her allies, she had expended vast sums in the conflict. She retained command of the sea, but the German submarine campaign was reducing food and other supplies to the point where her very existence was threatened.

Italy was having great difficulty in financing the war, and grave deficiencies existed in her armies, as the events of the autumn of 1917 were to show.

The revolution in Russia, which had occurred in March, made it practically certain that the Allies could not count on effective help from that country.

The Germans were frankly scornful of America's ability to exercise any real military influence in the war and evidently believed it impossible for any considerable American force to be organized and transported to France before the defeat of the Allies could be accomplished. Germany, therefore, looked forward with great confidence to her armies gaining a decisive victory in 1918.

General Pershing's arrival in France, followed in two weeks by the landing of the American 1st Division, greatly improved the French morale.

The Allied conception of the critical nature of the military situation in the summer of 1917, and of the actions to be taken to meet it, are indicated in the conclusions reached by the Commanders-in-Chief of the American, French and Italian Armies, and the Chiefs of Staff of the French and British Armies at a conference held in Paris during the latter part of July. An extract from their report is given in the following paragraph:

"General conclusions reached were Necessity for adoption of purely defensive attitude on all secondary fronts and withdrawing surplus troops for duty on Western Front. By thus strengthening Western Front believed Allies could hold until American forces arrive in numbers sufficient to gain ascendency."

As far as their strength would permit the Allies sought, however, to maintain the offensive on the Western Front during the latter part of 1917 in order to hinder the conquest of Russia by Germany and if possible, to prevent an attack on the Italian front with German troops.

Accordingly, the British attacked in June capturing Messines Ridge, and near Ypres undertook a series of operations which began on July 31 and lasted until November 10. Later in November they launched an offensive near Cambrai, in which many tanks were used, and made important initial gains which were largely lost in a German counteroffensive ten days later. These British attacks though very costly in men and matériel had no decisive effect on the military situation.

The Cambrai operation was the first major offensive in which American troops participated. Three American engineer

(22)

giments were serving with the British
the time and one of these was actually
ngaged in the front-line fighting.

The French conducted carefully-pre-
ared limited attacks near Verdun in Au-
ust and near the Chemin des Dames in
ctober, both of which though compara-
vely small were successful.

Russia finally collapsed in early Sep-
mber, and the Italians suffered a dis-
strous defeat near Caporetto in October,
aking it necessary to send French and
ritish divisions to their assistance.

An analysis of these events left no
oubt in the minds of Allied commanders
at Germany would soon resume the of-
nsive on the Western Front, with her
mies there augmented by large num-
ers of divisions drawn from the Russian
eater of operations. This transfer of
oops from Russia actually started in
e month of November 1917.

Notwithstanding Germany's favorable
ilitary position at the close of 1917,
nditions within the Fatherland and the
pidly growing American Expeditionary
orces made it imperative for her to try
bring the war to a prompt conclusion.
e know now that to accomplish this her
ans contemplated the destruction of the
ritish Army in the early spring of 1918,
ter which a crushing blow was to be
rected against the French Army.

On December 31, 1917, there were
74,884 American soldiers in Europe, of
which the 1st Division alone had served
at the front. The British and French
desired to hasten the appearance of
American troops in the line if only for the
effect on the morale of their troops, and
urged that the American training be
limited to the minimum necessary for
trench fighting. They also requested
that American troops, in company and
battalion units, be assigned to their organizations, pointing out the shortage of
man power in their armies as sufficient
reason for this request. They contended
that the elimination of Russia as a factor
in the war, together with the Italian defeat, had so altered conditions for the
worse that to withstand the expected
German attacks every American soldier
in France should at once be made available for service at the front.

The American Commander-in-Chief
agreed that every combat unit in France
should be made available for front-line
service, but remained fixed in his determination to assemble all Americans into
an independent army. Any sort of
prolonged amalgamation with the Allied
Armies would have committed the for-
tunes of the American forces to alien
hands, with no responsibility to the
American Government for their proper
care, training and employment. Such a
step would have met with the decided
opposition of the American officers and
soldiers and would have been destructive

American Soldiers En Route to the Front

German Infantry Attacking Over a Mine-Crater Area at Ripont in March 1917. © G

German Cavalry Ready for a Break-Through in March 1918. © G

German Engineers Advancing Through Captured British Position, March 1918. © G

o their morale. It would have been strongly disapproved by the American people. There was, on the other hand, no doubt that the effect of aggressive American units in the battle line under their own commanders would produce far greater military results and be far more depressing to the morale of the German Armies and civil population than the presence of small American units under foreign officers in Allied regiments.

The policy of employing the American units as a single force, steadfastly maintained by General Pershing in the face of tremendous opposition from the Allies, unquestionably produced decisive results that could not have been obtained otherwise.[1] Because of this policy, the American Army, welded into one powerful body, inspired by the traditions of its own country, confident in its leaders, and sure of its ability in the offensive, was finally enabled to deliver the terrific blows at St. Mihiel, in the Argonne and along the Meuse which made possible the defeat of Germany.

The Commander-in-Chief speeded up to the utmost the use of American units in the front line. As a consequence, the 1st Division relieved a French division in a sector north of Toul in January; the 26th entered the line with the French north-

Marshal Ferdinand Foch
Allied Commander-in-Chief

east of Soissons in February; the 42d went in east of Lunéville during the same month; and about the middle of March, the 2d entered the line with the French southeast of Verdun.

On March 21, when the first great German offensive of 1918 started, there were approximately 300,000 American troops in France. Of these the 1st, 2d and 42d Divisions were in the trenches and the 26th was ready for service. The 32d and 41st Divisions had arrived in France but had been designated as replacement units, although later, in April, the 32d was redesignated as a combat division.

The German onslaught of March 21 struck the British in Picardy between the Oise and the Scarpe Rivers along a front of about 50 miles, part of which had been recently taken over from the French. Within eight days the attacking troops, sweeping all before them, practically destroyed the British Fifth Army and penetrated to a maximum depth of about 37 miles. The situation was serious and many French Divisions were rushed to aid the British.

During this period the Allies were still further annoyed and troubled when on March 23 the shelling of Paris by a large German gun from a distance of 75 miles was begun.

General Pershing, knowing the gravity of the Allied position, deferred the execution of his plan to form an American army and went to General Foch and said:

[1] Marshal Pétain declared in a public address delivered in Versailles, France, in October 1937 that General Pershing was right in opposing the amalgamation of American troops with the Allied forces.

American Soldiers Advancing to Attack at Cantigny

"I have come to tell you that the American people would consider it a great honor for our troops to be engaged in the present battle. I ask you for this in their name and my own.

"At this moment there are no other questions but of fighting.

"Infantry, artillery, aviation, all that we have are yours; use them as you wish. More will come, in numbers equal to requirements.

"I have come especially to tell you that the American people will be proud to take part in the greatest battle of history."

This message had a stimulating effect upon French morale. Its confident optimism is an indication of the splendid spirit of cooperation which characterized the personnel of the entire American Army in France throughout the war.

On March 26 General Foch was charged with coordinating the actions of the French and British Armies, and soon afterwards on April 3 was given strategic direction of the French, British and American Armies on the Western Front.

Fortunately the Germans were stopped before capturing Amiens, the loss of which would have separated the French and British Armies and enabled the Germans to operate against each of them separately. In this event the British Army would probably have had to hurry out of northern France or else run the risk of almost certain destruction.

The Germans succeeded in cutting one railroad into Amiens from the south and in seriously impeding traffic on the other; they increased the frontage which the Allies were forced to hold with diminished numbers, they proved that their force could break through the highly organized defenses of the Western Front, they enormously increased the morale of their own troops and very seriously lowered that of the British and French units.

The fighting near Amiens had scarcely died down when, on April 9, the Germans broke through the British lines in Flanders on a 12-mile front along the Lys

Cantigny After Its Capture, May 28, 1918.

River south of Ypres. Their initial advantage was not well exploited but operations were continued there until April 25 when the German troops succeeded in capturing Mont Kemmel, which at the time was defended by French units serving with the British Army.

A number of American medical, engineer and air service units with the British Army took part in the operations near Amiens and along the Lys River.

prevent their being sent later to aid the British, the Germans decided to make an attack against the French Army first.

Immediately following the battle in Flanders the American 1st Division, which had been in sector near Seicheprey, in the St. Mihiel region, took over an exceedingly active portion of the line west of Montdidier. It captured Cantigny on May 28 in a well-planned operation and held that place in spite of violent and

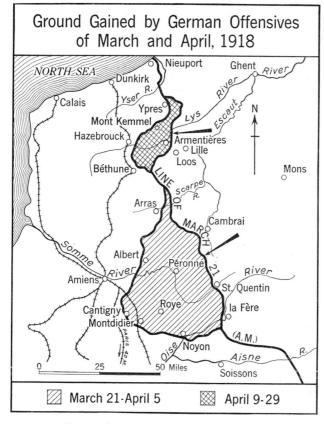

Ground Gained by German Offensives of March and April, 1918

March 21-April 5   April 9-29

The German High Command believed that one more major attack against the British Army would destroy it. However, since elaborate preparations had already been made to strike the French, an offensive against them could be launched much quicker. As such an attack would use up French reserves, and

sustained counterattacks. This fighting again demonstrated the superb caliber of the American soldier in offensive and defensive combat and since troops from the United States were at that time arriving in France in increasingly large numbers, the Allied Armies and the Allied people could still hope for final victory.

Chapter II

AMERICAN OPERATIONS IN THE
AISNE–MARNE REGION

THE German strategical plan for 1918 involved the destruction of the British Army in the early spring, to be followed immediately by a crushing blow at the French. In pursuance of this plan, German offensive operations were launched in Picardy and Flanders in March and April. Although gaining considerable ground and inflicting heavy

many French troops had been shifted from there to the British area. Consequently, when a German assault struck the Aisne front between Berry-au-Bac and Anizy-le-Château early on the morning of May 27 it came as a surprise.

The Germans carried the Chemin des Dames positions in the first dash and crossed the Aisne River about noon on

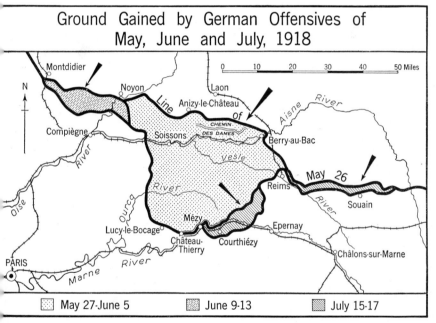

Ground Gained by German Offensives of May, June and July, 1918

May 27-June 5   June 9-13   July 15-17

losses, these operations failed in their primary purpose of destroying the British. Meanwhile preparations for a powerful drive against the French along the line of the Aisne River had been progressing.

The Allied Commanders, after the German April attack in Flanders had been checked, felt sure that a new German offensive was about to take place but were uncertain where it would fall. It was considered improbable, however, that it would fall on the Aisne front, and

bridges which the French had failed to destroy. Their progress exceeded all expectation. By evening they were south of the Vesle, and early on the 29th had captured Soissons. Advancing rapidly toward the Marne River and meeting very little resistance, they started to exploit their success toward Paris. The French people throughout the country were thrown into consternation, and the Government made preparations to flee from Paris to Bordeaux, a city much farther south.

Reserves from every quarter were ushed to the front to meet this new langer. Among these were the American 'd and 3d Divisions which had been urned over to the French by the American Commander-in-Chief. They were urried forward by forced marches and by very available means of transportation. The motorized machine gun battalion of the 3d Division reached Château-Thierry on May 31, and there gallantly ssisted in preventing the Germans from rossing the Marne. As the infantry units f the 3d Division came up they reinforced 'rench units holding the south bank of he river as far eastward as Courthiézy, 5 miles from Château-Thierry.

The 2d Division, arriving by truck on 'une 1, immediately went into position orthwest of Château-Thierry. Facing ortheast, with its center at Lucy-le-Bocage, the division established its line cross the main route to Paris, where it epulsed all attacks and effectively stopped he German advance in that direction.

With this American assistance the 'rench were able to stem the onslaught, ut only after the Germans had driven a reat salient, roughly defined by the tringle formed by Reims, Château-Thierry nd Soissons, into the Allied lines.

In addition to a 30-mile gain straight oward the heart of France, the Germans aptured 60,000 prisoners, 650 cannon nd enormous quantities of supplies, mmunition and equipment. The situaion looked very black for the Allies. 'heir rays of hope, however, were the apid arrival of American troops, which vere then pouring into France at the rate f about 9,000 per day, and their growng knowledge of the splendid dash and ombat ability of the American soldiers, hen being tested daily in battle.

These characteristics had been amply lemonstrated by the troops of the 1st Division in its capture of Cantigny, north f Paris, on May 28, and in its retention f that place despite repeated counterttacks, as well as by the brilliant fighting of the 2d and 3d Divisions near Château-Thierry. They were finally proved beyond all doubt when the 2d Division, starting on the morning of June 6, struck back at the Germans and after prolonged and bitter fighting recaptured from them the strong positions of Belleau Wood, Bouresches and Vaux.

This fighting caused a change in the German opinion which up to that time had been frankly skeptical of the fighting ability of the American soldier and the driving power of American units. This change is illustrated by the following extracts from a communication issued on June 17 by the German corps which opposed the 2d Division and which had previously issued orders that as many casualties as possible be inflicted upon the Americans: "The personnel must be called excellent . . . The spirit of the troops is high . . . The 2d American Division can be rated as a very good division . . . The various attacks of the marines were carried out smartly and ruthlessly. The moral effect of our fire did not materially check the advance of the infantry. The nerves of the Americans are still unshaken."

Although the Germans in their May attack made a deep penetration to the west and southwest of Reims, they failed in their efforts to capture that city and its important railway facilities. As a result, the 40 divisions which they had thrown into the salient were in a dangerous situation as they were mainly dependent for food, supplies and ammunition on one railroad through Soissons. This fact was realized by the American Commander-in-Chief who saw that if the heights south of that city were seized and held by the Allies the Germans would be deprived of the use of the railroad and would be compelled to retire from the Marne, thus removing the threat against Paris. He proposed that these heights be attacked and captured at once by American troops. The Allied Commander-in-Chief approved the idea of such an attack but felt that he was not yet ready to assume the offensive.

The German High Command also realized the dangerous position of its

Vincelles
Marne U
French Artill
June 1918.

German Reserves
Advancing Close
Behind the Assault
Line at Chavignon,
May 1918. © G

German T
Just Befor
Assault Near
on Terrain Un
by the W
May 1918.

Germans With a Trainload
of Provisions Which Were
Left by the French
South of the Aisne,
May 1918. © G

Part of a German
Barge Battery of Heavy
Artillery Firing on
the Western Front,
May 1918. © G

Sharing a Meal Aban
by an English Offic
on the Chemin des I
Early on May 27, 19
© G

troops in the salient, and promptly undertook operations to relieve the situation. Consequently, on June 9 two German armies started an attack toward Compiègne, for which careful preparations had previously been made, in an attempt to widen the salient and to secure the use of the railroad between that place and Soissons. They met, however, determined resistance from the French and failed to reach their objective.

The next move of the Germans was to begin preparations for a great offensive on both sides of Reims, in the general direction of Epernay and Châlons-sur-Marne. This attack was to capture Reims and the high ground to the south of it, and by so doing secure the use of another great trunk line railroad. The separation of the French forces defending Paris from those in the vicinity of Verdun was considered a possibility. A formidable array of three armies, totaling 47 divisions, and an enormous amount of artillery were assembled, and nothing was left undone to provide both the troops and matériel considered necessary to break the French battle lines.

Meanwhile, the Allies were exerting every effort to prepare for the next German attack, and to discover where it would fall. In this last they were singularly successful, for not only did they learn the front to be attacked but they were also fortunate enough to determine

Marshal Pétain,
Commander-in-Chief French Armies.
Picture taken at Chaumont,
January 1919

the exact day and hour the offensive was scheduled to commence.

There were 26 American divisions in France on July 15 and the American and Allied strength was then superior to that of the Germans. The combat training of the American divisions was progressing well and seven were ready for battle operations, while five others were holding quiet sectors of the line. Thus 12 American divisions, the equivalent in numbers of 24 French, British or German divisions, were available for service in the front line.

With this increase in strength and with many more Americans on the way, General Foch definitely decided to attack the western face of the Marne salient, as had been previously proposed by General Pershing. In view of the enemy's known intention to advance on both sides of Reims, this Allied offensive was of the greatest importance as it was to be launched against the most vulnerable part of the hostile line.

The task of drawing up the necessary plans for meeting the German assault and for the counterattack to be launched later, fell to General Pétain, the French Commander-in-Chief. He later stated that it would not have been possible to carry out the counterattack, which succeeded far beyond expectations, without the aid of the American troops.

To meet the German attack, General Pétain ordered that the front line be

German Troops Ready for an Attack North of Compiègne, June 1918. © G

The Same Troops Jumping Off a Few Minutes Later. © G

ld by weak detachments only, which
re to retire before a strong hostile
sault, and that the main resistance be
de on the intermediate position 1 to
miles in rear of the front line. When
e attack came, these tactics proved
ceptionally successful and most of the
avy German artillery and trench-mortar
eparatory fire was wasted on the aban-
ned French front-line trenches.

In addition the Allies profited by their
owledge of the hour of the German
ack by starting their artillery bom-
rdment about 30 minutes before the
rman artillery was scheduled to com-
nce firing. The Allied bombardment
used heavy losses and much confusion
the ranks of the Germans assembled
the initial assault. Certain German
its suffered so severely they had to be
placed before the attack began.

East of Reims, in the attack against
e French Fourth Army, the hostile
ops were heavily shelled upon reaching
e abandoned front line, and upon
proaching the intermediate position
re met with withering fire and fierce
unterattacks. The offensive there broke
wn all along the front. Southwest of
ims, the Germans succeeded in crossing
e Marne and advancing on both banks
the river toward Epernay. When this
ack was finally stopped, eight German
visions were 'south of the Marne in a
all area between Epernay and Mézy.

In this defensive operation, the Ameri-
n soldiers still further distinguished
emselves. The 42d Division, serving
th the French Fourth Army, took part
the battle and fully measured up
the reputation of the Americans as
endid fighting men. The 369th In-
try of the 93d Division was also with
e French Fourth Army at that time,
hough not engaged in battle on the
nt of the main German attack.

*A graphic representation of the opera-
ns now to be described is given on the
p at the end of the chapter. It should
consulted in reading this narrative.*

The 3d Division, in line along the
arne River from opposite Jaulgonne to

Phosphorus Bomb Exploding

Château-Thierry, was subjected to intense
artillery fire and repeated assaults in the
eastern part of its sector. The French
unit on its right was compelled to give
way, which made the task of the 3d
Division extremely difficult. However,
the Germans who succeeded in crossing
the Marne on its front were counterattacked and driven back and by noon of
the 16th, no enemy troops remained south
of the Marne in the division sector,
except on its extreme right flank where
the front line was bent back to connect
with the adjoining French division.

Elements of the 28th Division were in
line with the French divisions on each

A Regimental Staff of the 4th Division in
Conference Near the Vesle River, August 9, 1918

3d Division Troops Entrucking Near Moulins

side of the 3d, and some of its units encountered extremely heavy fighting. Northwest of Château-Thierry, the front of the American I Corps, held by a French division and the American 26th Division, which had relieved the 2d in the sector between Vaux and Torcy, was subjected to a heavy bombardment. The 2d, which had suffered over 8,100 casualties in the fighting near Belleau Wood, and the 4th Division were in reserve to the west of the salient. The 1st Division was northeast of Paris.

On July 17 the German High Command ordered the offensive stopped. The assaulting troops had suffered tremendous losses and none of the important results expected had been obtained.

Regardless of their terrific defeat, the German leaders were still determined to maintain the offensive, realizing that the American forces were rapidly increasing and that victory must be won quickly or not at all. The troops recently repulsed were directed to prepare to resume the attack as quickly as practicable, and plans for another offensive against the British Army were pushed.

The Allies, however, took immediate advantage of the German defeat and launched the previously prepared counter-offensive against the Aisne-Marne salient.

The French Fifth, Ninth, Sixth and Tenth Armies, in line from right to le on the front from Reims to Compiègr were engaged. The Tenth Army, ne Soissons, was designated to deliver t main attack. The spearhead of the Army was the French XX Corps, whi was to capture the high ground south Soissons. It consisted of the Americ 1st and 2d Divisions and the French 1 Moroccan Division. Its direction attack was eastward over the plate just south of Soissons and across t main railroad and road leading sou from that place. The composition of t corps was such that four fifths of numerical strength was American.

The concentration of troops was ca ried out with the utmost secrecy, the 1 and 2d Divisions going into line only the last minute. Some units of the Division marched all night and th double-timed over muddy roads in t dark in order to jump off with the ba rage. The assault was launched in t early morning of July 18 and took t German troops by surprise.

The units of the 1st and 2d Divisio with those of the 1st Moroccan Divisio between them, advanced with characte istic dash and vigor. They quickly pierc the hostile front lines, overran the fe ard artillery positions, and took many prisoners. By 8:00 a. m. they had advanced more than 3 miles and were in possession of ground which practically assured the success of the whole battle.

To the south, elements of the 4th Division attacking as a part of two French divisions in the Sixth Army, had progressed about 2 miles by nightfall. Still further south the 26th Division captured the villages of Belleau and Torcy. In the Ninth Army, the 3d Division, which was in line on the south bank of the Marne, did not attack that day. The 38th Division was near the 3d in reserve.

As a result of the deep advance of the X Corps on July 18, the situation of the German troops in the salient became most precarious and orders for a gradual withdrawal were issued by the German High Command that night. Reserves were sent to the south of Soissons with the utmost speed and orders were given to hold the ground there at all costs until the withdrawal from the salient could be accomplished. In fact, a disastrous defeat was certain if the American and French advance at that point could not be promptly and definitely checked.

The German retirement began on the night of July 19–20 with the evacuation of all ground south of the Marne. From then on, their withdrawal was conducted in successive stages, the Germans attempting to save what they could of the enormous quantities of supplies, ammunition and equipment in the salient. Intermediate positions were prepared and each one defended desperately until the pressure of the continued attacks against it forced a further withdrawal.

The 1st and 2d Divisions encountered fresh German troops on the 19th, but in spite of bitter opposition throughout the day both made important gains. The 2d Division surged forward about 2 miles to the Soissons–Château-Thierry highway but after severe fighting was forced back and established itself just west of Tigny, with the road about ½ mile away under the control of its guns. The division was relieved from the line that night by a French division. It had driven the enemy back 6 miles, captured 3,000

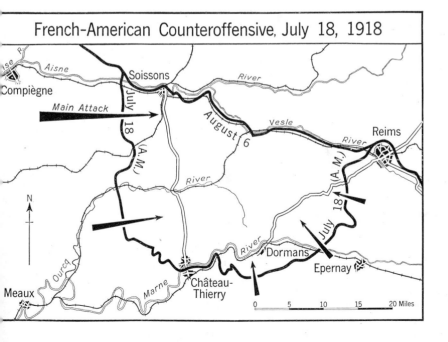

French-American Counteroffensive, July 18, 1918

2d Division Moving Up for the Attack on July 18, 1918

1st Division Artillery in Position Near Ploisy, July 20, 1918

Artillery Horses Assembled Near the Front Line Ready to Move Battery Forward, July 20, 1918

·isoners and 75 guns, and in turn had ᴅffered casualties of about 4,300 men. On the following day, the attention of the ᴛt Division was directed particularly toᴀrd Berzy-le-Sec. That town had orig-ally been in the zone of action of the ad-ᴄent French division which, after several ᴛtempts, had failed to capture it. The ᴛsk was then turned over to the Ameri-ᴀns. The fighting near the town was

and suffered a loss of about 6,900 officers and men. The 1st and 2d Divisions on this battlefield wrote a most brilliant page in American military history.

While the struggle near Soissons was going on, the American troops with the French Sixth Army continued to advance. The units of the 4th Division, whose total losses were 2,100, gained an additional 2 miles before the last of its

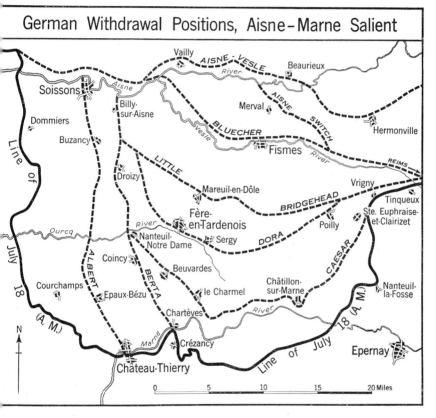

German Withdrawal Positions, Aisne-Marne Salient

aged with the greatest fury, the 1st ᴅivision capturing it on the 21st. On ᴛat same day the division crossed the ᴅissons—Château-Thierry highway which ᴀs one of the objectives of the Tenth ᴛrmy attack. The division was relieved ᴛ the night of July 22, after five days ᴛ the line. It had advanced almost 7 ᴛiles, captured 3,500 prisoners and 68 ᴛns from 7 different German divisions

troops were relieved on the morning of July 21; and the 26th Division drove the Germans through the Bois de Bouresches and beyond, after hard fighting. Assisted part of the time by the 56th Infantry Brigade of the 28th Division, it continued the pursuit until the 24th of July, when it was stopped near La Croix Rouge Farm, having made an advance of 10 miles and having suffered more

American Battery in Action Near Chéry-Chartreuve

than 5,000 casualties during its service on the front line in this region.

On July 21 the 3d Division crossed the Marne River and joined the advance, capturing Mont St. Père that day and Jaulgonne on the following day. Steadily pressing on, it took Le Charmel during the 25th, after a bitter contest, and on the 28th crossed the Ourcq River and seized Ronchères. When it was withdrawn from the line on the 30th it had taken part in three major engagements and had advanced about 10 miles. Its losses, including those in the defensive operations along the Marne River, were, all told, nearly 6,600 officers and men.

The 42d Division, which relieved the 26th near La Croix Rouge Farm, succeeded in crossing the Ourcq on July 28. Just north of that river it engaged in stubborn fighting, some points changing hands as many as four times. It captured Sergy and Seringes-et-Nesles and persistently fought its way forward until relieved on August 3 during the pursuit of the enemy toward the Vesle. The division was assisted part of this time by the 47th Infantry Regiment of the 4th Division. When taken out of the battle the 42d had advanced 7 miles and had suffered almost 6,500 casualties.

The 32d Division entered the line on July 30 on the right of the 28th Division, which had relieved a French division tw days before. These two divisions deli ered a combined attack on July 30 in whic the 28th Division captured the Bois d Grimpettes, after which it passed int reserve, while the 32d continued in th offensive covering both divisional front

On the following day the 32d too Cierges, and on August 1, after dete mined attacks, captured the importan position of Les Jomblets, holding against sustained and vicious counte attacks. On August 2 it took up th pursuit of the Germans, who had bee forced to fall back to their next prepare line north of the Vesle River.

The 4th Division, which had relieve the 42d on August 3, and the 32d were no the only American divisions in line an they pushed forward side by side. O August 4 the 32d captured Fismes, o the south bank of the Vesle. During th next few days the 4th and 32d Division and the 6th Infantry Brigade of the 3 which had entered the line to the rig of the 32d, made determined attemp to establish bridgeheads north of th river. On August 7 the 32d Divisio was relieved by the 28th. It had ad vanced 11 miles and lost almost 3,80 men. The 6th Infantry Brigade of th 3d Division was relieved on August 1 its losses having been approximately 60

Meanwhile, on August 4 the American I Corps had taken command of the ⊃oops near Fismes, thus placing two ⊓merican corps in line side by side for the ⸱st time in the war. The sectors of ⸱ese corps comprised the entire front ⸱mmanded by the French Sixth Army. The reduction of the Aisne-Marne ⸱lient was completed when the American ⸱d Allied troops reached the Vesle River. ⸱he counterattack having achieved its ⸱⸱rpose and the Germans having shown ⸱eir intention to hold the line of the Vesle ⸱force, the general attack on that front ⸱as stopped on August 6. The American ⸱oops, however, continued to exert pres-⸱re against the enemy. On August 10 ⸱e 28th Division succeeded in capturing ⸱ismette, opposite Fismes. The 4th ⸱ivision before being relieved on August ⸱2, after having suffered about 3,500 ⸱sualties, established a small force on ⸱e north bank of the Vesle River.

At the start of the counterattack, the ⸱ermans had 50 divisions between Reims ⸱d Compiègne. To withstand the Allied ⸱ssault temporarily, they had been forced ⸱ throw 27 more divisions into the salient. ⸱uring the same period the Allies had ⸱lded 8 French and 3 American divisions ⸱ the 42 French, 6 American (equivalent ⸱ 12 French divisions), 4 British and 1

Italian divisions which had previously been in line or in reserve in this region.

The results of this battle were most important. The threat against Paris was removed, important railroads were freed for Allied use, the American soldier proved to all concerned his ability as a fighter and it was obvious that the constantly increasing American forces were to be the decisive factor in the war. The attack south of Soissons completely changed the military situation. Thereafter the initiative was in the hands of the Allied Armies, and the Germans were forced into a defensive rôle and fought only to avert a serious disaster.

This situation made it possible for the American Commander-in-Chief to insist again upon the formation of an American combat army. After several conferences with General Foch an agreement was reached, and on August 10 the American First Army was organized and shortly thereafter the assembly of American divisions in the St. Mihiel region was begun.

In compliance with the desire of General Foch [1] to retain some American units with the Allied Armies, the 77th Division, which had relieved the 4th, and the 28th were allowed to remain in line

[1] General Foch was made a Marshal of France on August 6, 1918, toward the conclusion of this fighting.

Main Bridge Between Fismes and Fismette Destroyed by the Retreating Germans

on the Vesle, while the 32d was left in the area as a reserve under French orders.

With a view to continuing the pressure and giving the Germans no time to rest or reorganize, Allied operations were immediately planned against other portions of the front. The first of these, the Somme offensive, was begun by the British on August 8 against the salient immediately east of Amiens and was highly successful.

Then followed on August 18 the French Oise-Aisne offensive in the vicinity of Noyon for the purpose of flanking the German positions on the Vesle and Aisne Rivers and forcing them to be abandoned. This offensive succeeded in its purpose, aided to a large extent by the American 32d Division which attacked from August 28 to September 1, capturing the town of Juvigny in a brilliant assault and penetrating the hostile positions to a depth of 2½ miles. The division was taken out of the line during September 2 after having suffered more than 2,600 casualties.

The progress of the Oise-Aisne offensive forced the Germans to retire from the Vesle on the night of September 3–4. The American 28th and 77th Divisions, which were still in line there, advanced in pursuit and attacked the new German line near the Aisne River. After a number of local successes the 28th was relieved on September 8, its total losses on the Ourcq

and Vesle having been over 6,700 office and men. The 77th was relieved later, September 16, its casualties havi totaled nearly 4,800, and both divisio moved eastward to take part in the Meus Argonne operations of the American Fir Army which occurred shortly afterwar

During the latter part of September t 370th Infantry of the 93d Division serv in the line north of Vauxaillon, as a pa of the French 59th Division, and made substantial advance. It remained in li until about the middle of October, wh it was relieved. It reentered the battle November 5 and participated in the pursu of the German Army. The activities this regiment concluded the America fighting in the Aisne-Marne region.

During the severe battles in this are a total American force of about 310,0 men, which comprised two corps hea quarters, nine divisions, air units, hea artillery, medical troops and transport tion units, served with the Allies a suffered losses of more than 67,000.

While some American units attracte special attention due to their great experience and the importance of their o jectives, yet the reputations of all Amer can divisions which served in this regi were enhanced by their gallant condu in battle, and they received unstint praise from all, especially the Frenc

American Unit Entraining at Château-Thierry

A TOUR OF THE AMERICAN BATTLEFIELDS
IN THE AISNE-MARNE REGION

THIS tour, which is a long one, begins and ends at Paris. It can be completed ten hours if care is taken not to spend too uch time at interesting points. To save me lunch should be carried.

Soissons is suggested as a stopping place r those who desire to spend more than e day in the area. It is on the described ute and from there one can conveniatly reach the French battlefields along e Chemin des Dames, and those of the merican 32d Division near Juvigny and e 370th Infantry, 93d Division, in the cinity of Vauxaillon.

The data given on pages 520–521 will helpful to those following this tour.

The narrative at the beginning of the apter should be kept in mind and the ap at the end consulted so that the rious operations which took place in e region of this tour will be more clearly derstood by the tourist.

The speedometer distances given are r general reference and are not essential following this tour. They may, however, be helpful in a few places and for at reason it is suggested that at the idge in La Ferté-sous-Jouarre the tour set his speedometer to agree with the stance which appears in the text.

When following this itinerary, unless ntrary road instructions are given, the urist should continue straight ahead.

EN ROUTE PARIS TO NORTH OF
LUCY-LE-BOCAGE

(0 m 0 km) **Leave vicinity of the Place l'Opéra in Paris on Rue Lafayette. Follow Highway N–3 through Claye and eaux to La Ferté-sous-Jouarre.** *For a nsiderable distance beyond Paris, N–3 is dicated on street signs as the Rue de Paris.*

(18.3 m 29.4 km) **Claye** is the point arest Paris reached by hostile patrols uring the German advance in 1914.

(24.1 m 38.8 km) **About 5 miles beyond laye, near the right side of the road,** is en a monument to Marshal Gallieni

Monument Near Meaux
to Marshal Gallieni
Erected by the City of Paris

whose famous "taxicab army" hurried forward from Paris to this vicinity in September 1914 to aid in stopping the progress of the German Armies.

(27.5 m 44.2 km) **At entrance to Meaux, at main road fork, take right branch.**

Meaux was near the battle line for several days in 1914 during the First Battle of the Marne. Desperate fighting took place immediately to the north of it.

An interesting old cathedral is seen to the left of the road in the center of town.

A monument, consisting of a colossal statuary group, to commemorate the First Battle of the Marne is located a short distance northeast of Meaux. It was erected by Americans with funds raised in America. To visit, just before reaching far side of Meaux turn left on main road to Soissons (N-36) and proceed ½ mile to monument. Time required for side trip—10 minutes.

Monument Erected
Northeast of Meaux to
Commemorate the
First Battle of the Marne
in 1914

(30.9 m 49.7 km) **At Trilport** the route goes over the historic Marne River on a masonry bridge parts of which were destroyed by the French in 1814, 1870 and again in 1914 to hinder the march toward Paris of invading armies. Small plates on the right-hand wall record the dates of the destruction and reconstruction.

(39.6 m 63.7 km) **In La Ferté-sous-Jouarre, turn to the left at the large monument.**

This monument is to the unknown dead of the British Expeditionary Force which landed in France during August 1914. It was here that this British force, after its memorable retreat from near Mons, struck back with vigor at the German divisions in the First Battle of the Marne.

To the left of the bridge, on the river banks, are markers which indicate the place where British troops recrossed the river on a temporary bridge, built by the Royal Engineers while under hostile fire.

The American I Corps Headquarters was located in this town from June 18 to July 21, and from August 13 to August 18.

American First Army Headquarters was organized here on August 10, 1918. It remained but a short time, moving to Neufchâteau three days later.

(39.7 m 63.9 km) **Cross the Marne River and continue toward Château-Thierry still following Highway N-3.**

(45.5 m 73.2 km) **Montreuil-aux-Lions** was the Headquarters of the 2d Division during the early part of its fighting in the vicinity of Belleau Wood.

(47.1 m 75.8 km) **Just after leaving town, on the right** is seen a British military cemetery. A large cross of the type erected therein is the distinguishing feature of each British World War military cemetery. Most of the soldiers buried here fell in September 1914.

The infantry of the American 2d Division detrained at Montreuil-aux-Lions while hurrying forward to enter the battle line near Belleau Wood. They reported this road crowded and, in some places, blocked with French civilian and troops endeavoring to get out of the way of the German advance.

(49.6 m 79.8 km) **At the next bend in the road, about 2 miles farther on, is a** large group of buildings called Paris Farm. This farm was several miles in rear of the battle line during June and July, and was subjected to frequent bombardment by German heavy artillery.

(51.0 m 82.1 km) **About a mile farther**

Assault Unit of 26th Division in Attack on Torcy at 4:35 a. m., July 18, 1918

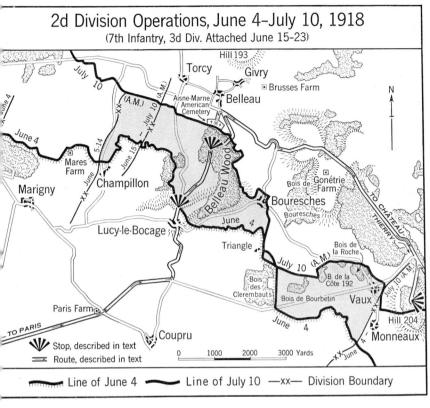

2d Division Operations, June 4–July 10, 1918
(7th Infantry, 3d Div. Attached June 15-23)

Stop, described in text
Route, described in text

0   1000   2000   3000 Yards

Line of June 4   Line of July 10   —xx— Division Boundary

n, turn to the left toward Belleau Wood.

(51.8 m 83.3 km) **In the valley just before reaching the next village, Lucy-e-Bocage,** a culvert is crossed near which medical officers of the United States Navy, attached to the Marine Brigade of the 2d Division, maintained a dressing tation. Many of the division wounded vere treated here and sent to the rear long the small valley to the left.

(52.1 m 83.8 km) **Lucy-le-Bocage** was completely destroyed by German shell-ire during the fighting near by.

The boulder marker, seen at the left ide of the road just before reaching the hurch, is one of many such markers rected by the 2d Division after the Armistice, on or near its battlefields.

(52.4 m 84.3 km) **At the crest of the irst hill beyond the village, STOP.**

Face down the road, which direction is pproximately north. (See sketch above.)

If view to the right front is obstructed for any reason climb bank at left of road.

Belleau Wood is the nearest wood seen to the right front and right. The observer is standing on the line from which the first attack against it was launched by the 2d Division.

During the last days of May 1918 a powerful German offensive had broken through the Chemin des Dames front and German troops were advancing rapidly toward the Marne River. The Allied situation was critical and reserves from all parts of the Western Front were promptly rushed to this region.

Among the troops hurriedly moved here was the American 2d Division, which included one brigade of marines. Arriving on June 1, it was assigned a battle position with its center near this point. All available men immediately began digging trenches and otherwise preparing

French Refugees Fleeing From the Germans During the Advance of May 1918

for defense, the Germans at the time being delayed by French detachments in positions on the near slopes of the line of hills seen in the distance approximately 2 miles away to the right front.

The front line organized by the division ran around the wood seen on top of the hill about 600 yards to the left front, included this point, and continued on to the right rear passing around the buildings of Triangle, seen on the hillside a mile away in that direction. It then crossed the main highway which the tour has been following from Paris, thus blocking the direct road to that important place.

Small advance groups of the enemy came in contact with that section of the American line near Triangle on June 2 and during the next day a determined assault against the left of the 2d Division position was repulsed with heavy losses. On June 4 the entire front line of the division was engaged and on that day the advance of the German forces in this region was definitely stopped.

The German High Command, upon hearing of the presence of American troops on this important battle front,

directed that they be denied any succes whatsoever and that as much damage a possible be inflicted upon them. Conse quently, as the Americans were deter mined to regain certain strong point which the Germans had captured, th fighting near here was very bitter and th casualties on both sides were out of al proportion to the amount of groun which finally changed hands.

During the morning of June 6, the firs of the many 2d Division attacks in thi vicinity was launched from its line on th far side of the wood to the left front This attack, made in conjunction wit the French, resulted in a gain of abou ½ mile. That afternoon a powerful as sault against Belleau Wood was mad from here and succeeded in obtaining foothold in that part of the wood seen t the right. While advancing across th open fields to the right front, heavy casu alties were suffered. During the course o the attack the village of Bouresches to th right at the foot of this hill, but not visibl was captured and held in spite of five de termined attempts made by the German during the next few days to recapture i

Belleau Wood, which is shaped some-
at like a distorted hour glass, with the
ver or southern section to the right of
re and the larger upper or northern sec-
n to the observer's right front, was the
ene of prolonged and bitter struggles
which the 7th Infantry of the 3d Di-
sion and engineer troops of the 2d
vision, acting as infantry, assisted for
brief period before its capture was
ally completed many days later.

Severe fighting took place in the south-
n part of Belleau Wood on June 7 and
but all efforts to advance resulted in
ly minor gains. The wood was aban-
ned on the 9th to permit the artillery
concentrate its fire on the German posi-
ns there without endangering Ameri-
n troops, and on the 10th a determined
tack was launched against the wood
m the line to the right of here. This
gained the positions previously held but
spite of every effort the troops were un-
le to progress farther. Consequently,
June 11 another attack against the
tire wood was launched from near here
the direction of the observer's right
ont. The assaulting units entered the
rthern part of the wood and took the

enemy in the flank and rear. This
resulted in many captures and hand-to-
hand combats. Elements of the attacking force reached the far edge of the
wood where they themselves were attacked in the rear. The fighting continued violently throughout the day, the
Germans making two organized counterattacks by fresh battalions. That night
no part of the northern section of the
wood was retained, although the southern section, to the right of here, was for
the first time entirely occupied.

On June 12 the northern section of the
wood was again attacked and about one
third of it taken. From that day on the
fighting in it was fierce and furious.
Counterattacks followed attacks as each
side, determined not to yield an inch,
stubbornly defended its positions. The
casualties were heavy as the artillery
executed prolonged bombardments and
the machine guns took their toll. In the
end, however, the determination of the
Americans prevailed and Belleau Wood,
after a bitter struggle on June 25, was
definitely cleared of the enemy.

On July 1, following a terrific 24-hour
bombardment, the town of Vaux, to the

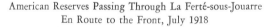

American Reserves Passing Through La Ferté-sous-Jouarre
En Route to the Front, July 1918

right rear from here beyond the large wood in the distance, was captured by the infantry and engineers of the 2d Division in a perfectly executed attack, with but few losses to themselves.

During the fighting on June 6 to the left front, Gunnery Sergeant Charles F. Hoffman, Marine Corps, 2d Division, performed the feat for which he was awarded the Congressional Medal of Honor, the highest award for bravery given by the American Government. Immediately after his company had reached its objective, several hostile counterattacks were launched against it. Sergeant Hoffman was attempting to organize the new position when he saw 12 of the enemy, armed with five light machine guns, crawling toward his group. Giving the alarm, he rushed the hostile detachment, bayoneted the two leaders, and forced the others to flee, abandoning their guns. His quick action, initiative and courage drove the enemy from a place where they could have swept the hill with machine-gun fire and forced the withdrawal of his company.

The splendid conduct of the 2d Division in fighting the enemy to a standstill on this front, in spite of a casualty list of approximately 8,100 officers and men, was widely and enthusiastically proclaimed the French Army and the people of France

EN ROUTE NORTH OF LUCY-LE-BOCAGE TO BELLEAU WOOD

(52.6 m 84.6 km) **At the road junction 200 yards ahead, turn to the right.**

(53.5 m 86.1 km) **At the flagpole in t center of Belleau Wood, STOP.**

This wood, officially called by t French the Bois de la Brigade de Mari in honor of the unit mainly responsib for its capture, is now owned by t United States Government. It is bei maintained as a memorial to all Americ troops who fought in Europe during t World War. It is the only place on tl tour where evidences of the fighting st exist to any extent, as the other battlefiel of this section of France again have be placed under intensive cultivation.

The remains of trenches and vario relics of the war may be seen by walki through the wood, and a visit to the sm museum will disclose many interesti

Belleau Wood
Note the field crossed by the 2d Division in its first attack against the wood

German Combat Group Working Its Way Forward,
May 1918. © G

eapons and articles of equipment a large
umber of which were found near by.

The large cleared space near the mu-
•um and that part of the wood beyond
te clearing were captured on June 25 in
1 assault launched at 5 o'clock in the
'ternoon. An artillery bombardment of
4 hours preceded this attack, during
hich many thousands of shells of all cal-
•ers were poured into this small area.
'he fighting lasted well into the night
efore this part of Belleau Wood, the last
•ction of the wood to be captured, was
nally in the hands of the 2d Division.

The importance of the American success
a this region is indicated by the following
xtract from a statement which a German
ivision commander published to his
•oops who were engaged in the fighting:

"Should the Americans on our front
ven temporarily gain the upper hand, it
ould have a most unfavorable effect for
s as regards the morale of the Allies and
1e duration of the war. In the fighting
1at now confronts us, we are not con-
erned about the occupation or non-
ccupation of this or that unimportant
•ood or village, but rather with the ques-
.on as to whether Anglo-American prop-

aganda that the American Army is equal
to or even superior to the German, will
be successful."

EN ROUTE BELLEAU WOOD TO AISNE-
MARNE AMERICAN CEMETERY

(53.6 m 86.2 km) **While proceeding
through Belleau Wood,** note the uneven
character of the terrain and the tangled
undergrowth which greatly hindered the
advance of the American troops.

(54.0 m 86.9 km) **Soon after leaving the
wood** another 2d Division boulder marker
is passed and shortly thereafter to the
left is seen the Aisne-Marne American
Cemetery. The church passed near the
corner of the cemetery is one restored by
an association of veterans of the 26th
Division as a memorial to that division.

(54.5 m 87.7 km) **Beyond the church,
turn to the left into the cemetery.**

The building on the right of the drive-
way contains a reception room for the
convenience of visitors and the office of
the superintendent in charge of the cemetery. Inquiries concerning the location
of a particular grave should be made at this
office. The building on the left is the
residence of the cemetery superintendent.

Airplane View of Aisne-Marne Cemetery

This cemetery, laid out in a sweeping curve at the foot of the hill upon which stands Belleau Wood, contains 2,288 graves. The majority of those buried here are from units which fought in the immediate vicinity and along the Marne River. Some hundreds of bodies, however, were moved here in 1922 from wartime cemeteries in the general vicinity of Lyon and Clermont in central France.

From the center of the hillside rises the memorial chapel, a striking example of French Romanesque architecture. Over its entrance is carved the figure of a Crusader in armor, flanked by the shields of the United States and France. The decorative sculpture of the door and window openings is of trench scenes and articles of military equipment. Around the top of the tower runs a frieze of shields upon which are carved the insignia of the American corps and divisions which participated in the operations that took place in the Aisne-Marne region.

The crowning feature of the interior is the exquisitely carved and gilded altar,

Altar of Chapel

Door of Chapel

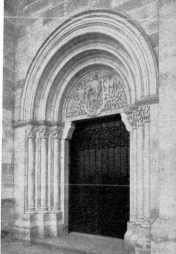

Entrance to Cemetery

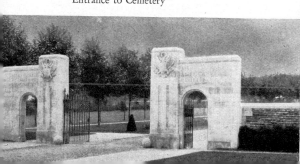

Machine Gun Unit of the 26th Division Going into Action
Near Belleau, July 19, 1918

the solemn beauty of which is heightened by the effect of the three beautiful stained-glass windows above it. These represent St. Michael triumphing over the powers of evil, St. Louis the great crusader, and St. Denis the patron saint of France. The transept windows are decorated with coats of arms of the United States and Allied nations and the insignia of American divisions and higher units that fought in the Aisne-Marne region. The walls are inscribed with the names of American soldiers and marines who are carried on the rolls as missing in the operations of the vicinity.

A door in the chapel gives access to a circular stairway leading to the tower from which an excellent view of the surrounding country may be obtained.

Climb the chapel stairs and go to the front window of the upper landing, which faces approximately north.

The general view of the cemetery obtained from this point is superb.

The direction arrows on the window ledges should be used to locate the places mentioned below. The map at the end of the chapter should also be consulted.

The chapel stands directly over front-line trenches dug by the 2d Division as part of the defenses of Belleau Wood after it was captured on June 25.

The ground in front of here to the foot of the high ridge, Hill 193, and to the right as far as the eye can see was cap-

tured by troops of the American 26th Division during July in severe fighting.

The 26th Division relieved the 2 Division on a line passing through the point on July 10. Its front line was the about 5 miles long. On this part of the front it faced in the direction the observe is now facing but to the right of here followed around the edge of Belle Wood, as the crosses do now, and th changed direction so as to face approx mately east. The division while servi here was with the American I Corps.

When the great French-America counteroffensive against the Mar salient started on July 18, the 26th w

Hunting Lodge in Belleau Wood

(52)

26th Division Memorial Church at Belleau

on the right flank of the attack. It advanced on the first day in spite of terrific fire from Hill 193, which was in the zone of action of the French division on its left, and captured Torcy, seen in the trees to the left front, Belleau just outside the cemetery gate, and Givry, just beyond the church. The Germans on Hill 193 held out against the French attacks for three days and during this time poured a deadly fire into the American troops below them. The precarious and difficult position of these troops is evident from here and too much credit can not be given to the men of the division for holding to their gains.

Go to right (east) window of tower.

The isolated group of buildings to the left front is called Les Brusses Farm.

It is situated near the end of a long ridge which runs to the right and gradually increases in height until La Gonétrie Farm, seen to the front on the top of the hill, is reached. The near slopes and wooded areas on that ridge were such as to afford ideal positions for the German troops who were defending it.

In the assault of July 18, units of the 26th Division reached the valley on this side of the ridge but severe fire from it and Hill 193 forced them back to Belleau Wood. It was during that attack that Private First Class George Dilboy of the 26th Division won the Congressional Medal of Honor. After an advance he was reconnoitering the ground in front with his platoon leader when a machine gun suddenly opened fire on them from 100 yards. From a standing position, fully exposed to view, he returned the fire at once. He then rushed forward, with bayonet fixed, falling within 25 yards of the gun with his right leg nearly severed and other wounds in his body. With undaunted courage and gallantry, he continued to fire from a prone position killing part of the machine gun crew and dispersing the rest. Private Dilboy died on the field of his exploits.

On July 20 the division attacked along its entire front and captured, after fierce fighting, La Gonétrie Farm and the Bois de Bouresches, the wood seen to the right of the farm. The ridge between Les Brusses Farm and La Gonétrie Farm was not taken on that day due to heavy machine-gun fire from

German Prisoners Captured at Belleau Wood

it and enfilade fire from the top of Hill 193.

That night the Germans withdrew to a new line, and on July 21 the division advanced over the ridge which had caused them so much trouble and continued on about 5 miles, meeting for the most part but little opposition. A severe two-day struggle then followed near Epieds before the enemy again withdrew to a new position.

On July 25 the 26th Division was relieved by the 42d Division. During the 15 days it had served in line on this front the casualties of the division were approximately 5,000 officers and men.

Go to opposite (west) window of tower.

The village to the right front on top of the ridge is Hautevesnes and to the right of it also on the ridge is Courchamps. Elements of the American 4th Division assisted in the capture of both of those places in bitter fighting on July 18.

The 4th Division, except for its artillery and one infantry brigade, was attached to the French 164th Division for the July 18 assault. In addition to the elements which fought at Hautevesnes and Courchamps, other units beyond Hautevesnes vigorously advanced about 2 miles.

Still farther along the front, about 7 miles beyond Hautevesnes, the 7th Infantry Brigade of the 4th Division was serving with the French 33d Division. Units of it attacked with the French on

Part of Belleau Wood Soon After Its Capture by the 2d Division

July 18, cleaned out the strong German positions in the wood, Buisson de Cresnes, and by nightfall had captured Noroy-sur-Ourcq which was about 2 miles within the hostile lines.   (See map on next page.)

On July 19 the elements of the 4th Division which were still in line attacked against heavy machine-gun resistance and extended the gains of the previous day. These units were relieved from the battle during the early morning of July 21. The total casualties of the division, whose units had efficiently performed their missions during this fighting, were 2,100.

The center of the front of attack of the American 1st and 2d Divisions in the July 18 counteroffensive was about 14

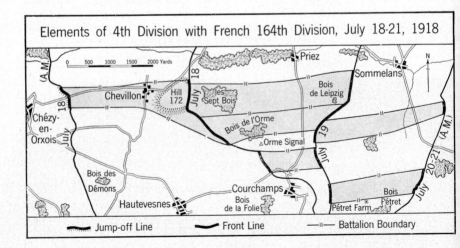

Elements of 4th Division with French 164th Division, July 18-21, 1918

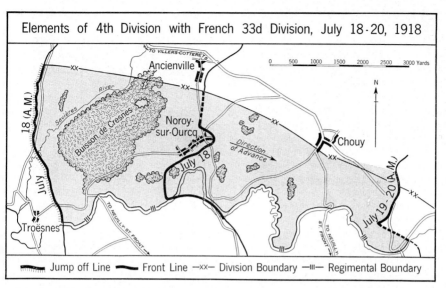

Elements of 4th Division with French 33d Division, July 18-20, 1918

━━━ Jump off Line   ━━ Front Line —xx— Division Boundary —ııı— Regimental Boundary

miles beyond Courchamps, the attack being made across the observer's line of vision in the direction from left to right.

Belleau Wood is the wood close to the chapel in rear and on both sides of it.

EN ROUTE AISNE-MARNE AMERICAN
CEMETERY TO MONUMENT
ON HILL 204

Opposite the cemetery gate is seen a form of marker which has been placed on most of the roads of France and Belgium to indicate the farthest advance of the German Armies in 1918. This one is incorrectly placed, the Germans having

Band, 5th Marines, 2d Division

been in possession of all of Belleau Wood.

(54.7 m 88.0 km) **Turn right at cemetery gate and continue straight ahead.**

(55.1 m 88.7 km) **Bouresches,** captured by the 2d Division on June 6, is soon visible to the right front.

(55.4 m 89.1 km) **When road starts to dip into deep valley, to the left across the valley** is seen a closer view of the Les Brusses Farm–La Gonétrie Farm ridge mentioned at the last stop. The Germans on part of this ridge held out for three days in spite of the determined assaults of the 26th Division.

(55.8 m 89.8 km) **On far side of valley,** the road climbs up a slope stormed by troops of the 26th Division on July 20.

(57.0 m 91.7 km) **After ascending hill, the first buildings seen to the right** are those of La Gonétrie Farm, captured by the 26th Division as the result of hard fighting during July 20.

(57.4 m 92.4 km) **Beyond the farm,** the advance of the 26th Division on July 21 was generally from right to left across this road. Its zone of action extended as far as the next main road crossing, now marked by the entrance pylons to the American monument on Hill 204.

(59.3 m 95.4 km) **Cross main highway and proceed to the site of the monument**

Airplane View of East Face of Aisne-Marne American Memorial Near Château-Thierry

West Face of Aisne-Marne American Memorial

This impressive memorial was erected by the United States Government to commemorate the American fighting in the Aisne-Marne region and the friendship and cooperation of the French and American forces during the war.

The two sculptured figures at the center of the colonnade are symbolic of France and the United States. The names inscribed above the columns are those of places where important American fighting occurred. Inside the colonnade at the closed ends are marble tablets upon which appear inscriptions giving a brief résumé of all of the American fighting in this general vicinity.

From the terrace of the monument, a wonderful view of the Marne River valley is obtained. On this terrace is located an orientation table giving distances and directions to various places and above it is an ornamental map of the region showing the ground gained by American troops on July 18 and thereafter. Along the walls on each side of the map are carved the names and wartime insignia of the corps and divisions whose services are commemorated at this place.

Jean de la Fontaine, who was born in Château-Thierry, is said to have written a number of his fables on this hill. Napoleon, just prior to the battle of

Symbolic Eagle and Ornamental Map
Aisne-Marne Memorial

Montmirail, camped his army in this neighborhood. The old main highway to Paris passed through this spot.

The following description of the American fighting in this vicinity has been written to be read while on the main terrace of the monument.

The large town which is seen about a mile away, located on both sides of the Marne River, is Château-Thierry.

Face its tall, square church tower, which direction is approximately east.

Just beyond and to the left of the church are the tree-covered ruins of the old château which gave the town its name.

During the critical days of late May 1918, when the German troops were advancing rapidly in this direction, the American 3d Division was training in an area some distance to the southeast of here. As the hostile rush continued and the gravity of the situation became more apparent, this division, which had had no front-line experience, was hurriedly moved up and thrown into the line in scattered detachments near Château-Thierry, to assist in preventing the Germans from crossing the Marne River. The 7th Machine Gun Battalion of

that division arrived late in the evening of May 31, about the time the German troops were entering the northern (left) outskirts of Château-Thierry, and took up a position along the south (right as seen from here) bank of the river to defend the crossings in town. Two guns of that unit were sent to assist French detachments fighting just beyond the château and, though orders for their withdrawal had been issued, they were still there when during the night of June 1 the highway bridge was blown up by the French to prevent the Germans from crossing. Arriving at the bridge just after it had been destroyed, the men who had manned these two machine guns resolutely fought their way to the railroad bridge where they and their French comrades, after a hand-to-hand conflict with German infantry, succeeded in recrossing.

This machine gun battalion of the 3d Division, assisted by French troops, prevented the Germans from crossing the river in town and inflicted exceptionally heavy losses on them.

It was due to this spirited defense, to the gallant stand of the 2d Division in the area just visited and to the desperate

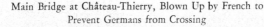

Main Bridge at Château-Thierry, Blown Up by French to
Prevent Germans from Crossing

American Troops in Public Square of Château-Thierry After Its Capture, July 1918

efforts of the French units that the German advance on this front was definitely stopped on June 4. The hostile front line at that time did not cross the Marne River but did include all of this hill.

On June 6 and 7 the French 10th Colonial Division with the 30th Infantry of the 3d Division attached, starting about 1½ miles to the right of here, launched two attacks against this hill and succeeded in gaining a foothold on top of it. The 4th Infantry, 3d Division, later in June, held a front-line position in the wood behind here for a few days.

The 3d Division held the south bank of the river from Château-Thierry on as far as the eye can see during part of June and July, the German lines being on the other bank. Its activities until July 15 consisted mainly in preparing its own position for defense and in sending an occasional patrol across the river to capture prisoners and attempt to secure information concerning the enemy troops.

On July 1 small units of the 111th Infantry, 28th Division, and on July 6 elements of the 111th and 112th Infantry Regiments, 28th Division, assisted the French in local attacks which gained some ground in front of here. On July 6 the small wood, Bois de Courteau, seen directly ahead on this slope, was captured. On the night of July 8–9, the Germans recaptured that wood in an attack during the course of which four companies of the 28th Division became engaged.

As a result of the French-American counteroffensive which began on July 18 south of Soissons, the Germans withdrew from this vicinity during the night of July 20–21. They were immediately pursued by the troops on this front.

EN ROUTE MONUMENT ON HILL 204 TO NEAR MÉZY

(61.0 m 98.1 km) **Return to main highway, turn sharply to the right and continue into the town of Château-Thierry.**

3d Division Monument at Château-Thierry

(63.0 m 101.4 km) **Just before reaching the main bridge in Château-Thierry, on the left** is a building containing a small museum of war relics, and near it is a monument erected by the 3d Division.

(63.1 m 101.5 km) **Cross the river.**

From bridge, to the right in the distance can be seen the monument on Hill 204.

(63.6 m 102.3 km) **Beyond the viaduct over the railroad, turn to the left.**

(65.0 m 104.6 km) **Beyond the town, for the next few miles** the tour runs near the Marne River, which winds its way in the valley to the left of this road.

(65.2 m 104.9 km) **The high ridge seen to the left** is on the opposite side of the river. German observation posts there kept close watch of the American activities near this road. All suspicious movements were communicated to German batteries concealed in woods and ravines in rear of the ridge and the places concerned on this side were generally subjected to immediate shellfire.

(67.0 m 107.8 km) **Near first sharp left bend in road** is the village of Fossoy. This was close to the west flank of the last

Machine Gun, 3d Division, in Position at
Château-Thierry, June 1, 1918

great German offensive of the war, which started on July 15. That part of the 3d Division in the area seen to the left front was caught by the full force of the assault units of the powerful German attack.

(67.6 m 108.8 km) **From top of first hill beyond Fossoy, to the left about 1/2 mile away** are seen two farms. The troops of the 3d Division defending those places on July 15 fought to the last man. The few Germans who then advanced beyond this road were later either killed or captured by the American troops.

The area where units of the 28th Division assisted the French in stopping the German advance on July 15 lies about 4 miles southeast of the next village, Crézancy. To visit, at second street in Crézancy turn right and travel via St. Eugène, Monthurel, Celles-les-Condé to St. Agnan. Consult map on page 65 before starting. To complete a loop and to visit the sectors held by units of the 28th Division along the Marne continue through St. Agnan toward Dormans. Upon joining main highway near Dormans turn left and follow it to Crézancy. Rejoin the tour there. Length of detour about 18 miles. Amount of time required—1 hour.

(68.7 m 110.5 km) **Soon after entering the next town, Crézancy, turn sharply to the left on the road to Mézy.**

Crézancy was never captured by the Germans although the other side of Surmelin Creek valley, seen to the right, was in their possession for four days, and during two days fighting occurred in rear (south) of the town on the high ground across the creek from it.

(69.6 m 112.0 km) **At first crossroads beyond the village cemetery, STOP.**

In this vicinity occurred some of the most desperate fighting of the war.

Face down the road which direction is approximately north.

Except for Moulins Ridge, seen directly to the right, all other hills on the horizon to the front and sides are on the opposite bank of the Marne River and were in German hands on July 14.

The German attack of July 15, their last great offensive, involved a 50-mile front from near here to beyond Reims.

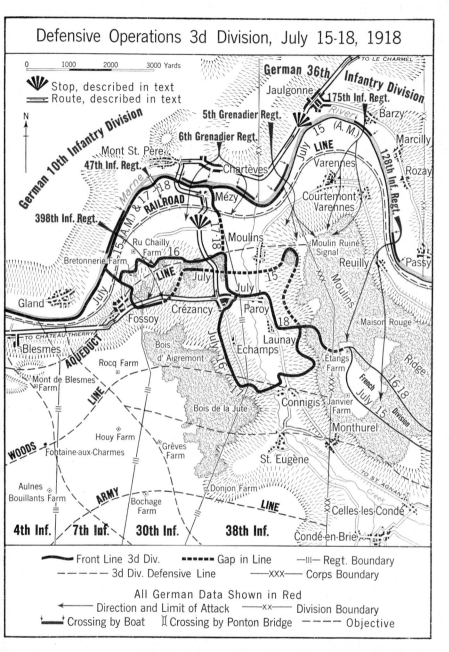

Defensive Operations 3d Division, July 15-18, 1918

0   1000   2000   3000 Yards

WV Stop, described in text
═══ Route, described in text

N

TO LE CHARMEL

German 36th Infantry Division

Jaulgonne   175th Inf. Regt.

5th Grenadier Regt.   Barzy

German 10th Infantry Division

6th Grenadier Regt.   Marcilly

Mont St. Père   River   15 (A.M.)

47th Inf. Regt.   Chartèves   Varennes   Rozay

Marne   LINE   128th Inf. Regt.

Mézy   Courtemont-Varennes

398th Inf. Regt.   RAILROAD   15 (A.M.) & 17 & 18

Ru Chailly Farm   16   Moulins   Moulin Ruiné Signal

Bretonnerie Farm   LINE   July   Reuilly   Passy

Gland   July   July   15   Moulins

Crézancy   Paroy

Fossoy   Maison Rouge

TO CHÂTEAU-THIERRY   18   Launay   Ridge

Blesmes   AQUEDUCT   Bois d'Aigremont   Echamps   Etangs Farm   16-18

Rocq Farm   French July 15 Division

Mont de Blesmes Farm   LINE   Bois de la Jute   Connigis   Janvier Farm

Houy Farm   Monthurel

WOODS   Fontaine-aux-Charmes   Grèves Farm   Surmelin

Aulnes Bouillants Farm   ARMY   St. Eugène   TO ST. AGNAN

Bochage Farm   Donjon Farm   LINE   Celles-les-Condé

Creek

4th Inf.   7th Inf.   30th Inf.   38th Inf.   Condé-en-Brie

─── Front Line 3d Div.   ▪▪▪▪▪▪ Gap in Line   ─ⅠⅠⅠ─ Regt. Boundary
── ── ── 3d Div. Defensive Line   ──xxx── Corps Boundary

All German Data Shown in Red
◄─── Direction and Limit of Attack   ──xx── Division Boundary
Ⅱ Crossing by Boat   Ⅱ Crossing by Ponton Bridge   ── ── Objective

In this vicinity the 3d Division held the line of the river from Moulins Ridge to Château-Thierry, 5 miles away to the left. On the evening of July 14, prisoners were captured east of Reims from whom it was learned that the long-expected German offensive would begin shortly after midnight. Taking full advantage

German Anti-Aircraft Shells Exploding Near American Observation Balloon Stationed in the Vicinity of Château-Thierry

of this information, at 11:45 p. m. every gun on this side of the river blazed forth in an intensive bombardment which caused great havoc in front of here in the German masses forming up for the attack. The support trenches and other points where German troops would naturally assemble for an assault were so heavily shelled that some of their units had to be replaced before the attack began.

At 12:10 a. m. on July 15 the German artillery opened up, and about 2:00 a. m. there was a sudden increase of machine-gun and rifle fire along the river as the enemy started his attempts to cross by means of ferries and ponton bridges. One of the six German regiments which attacked the 3d Division crossed in front of here. It was badly cut up by American artillery fire, and the troops who reached the railroad near Mézy, the village seen ahead, were counterattacked and forced back over the river, the remnants reaching the far bank about 5:00 a. m. Another regiment which crossed to the left of here suffered heavily from artillery and machine-gun fire. However, it wiped out the American troops on the riverbank and advanced about 5:00 a. m. in the face of rifle and machine-gun fire from Americans in the woods above them. The attack was stopped near the edges of the woods to the left rear of here. A third regiment, after several disastrous attempts, crossed near Mont St. Père, seen

on the hillside to the left of Mézy, about 8:45 a. m. and in spite of heavy casualties a considerable part of it reached the railroad and the field in front of here, in both of which places large numbers of German soldiers later surrendered.

Early in the morning, the Germans succeeded in advancing over ground held by the French on the far side of Moulins Ridge. This exposed the right of the American line, and detachments on the ridge had to withstand several attacks against their front and flank during the day. The fighting there and near this point was of the greatest severity, involving repeated attacks and counterattacks until the units concerned were almost destroyed.

On the entire front of attack this side of Reims, the Germans succeeded in advancing about 4 miles on July 15 at all places except near here where they were opposed by American troops. At midnight of that day the Germans to the front and left front were retreating across the Marne while the front line of the 3d Division was about 600 yards behind this point in the woods.

On the 16th the detachments of the 3d Division still on Moulins Ridge, being almost cut off from neighboring units, were withdrawn to a line about 1 mile to the rear. On that same day the 111th Infantry of the 28th Division relieved that part of the 3d Division in rear of here and on July 17 that regiment reestablished its part of the front line along the riverbank to the left of Mézy.

The Germans made no organized attacks in this vicinity on the 16th, but farther to the right their advance continued although slowed up to a large extent by a French counterattack.

Of the two regiments of the 3d Division which were caught by the full force of the initial German attack, the 38th Infantry on the right was eventually forced to meet assaults from the front and from both flanks. In this precarious position it gallantly fought the storm troops of the enemy to a standstill. The 30th Infantry on the left, in a different but no less difficult situation, performed its task with equal determination and bravery, and consequently on the front of these units the Germans gained nothing to compensate them for their careful preparations and heavy losses. The conduct of the American troops in this action gave further impetus to the rapidly increasing reputation of the American divisions.

By July 17 the German offensive had been definitely stopped on the whole front, and the next day the French and Americans began their great counteroffensive south of Soissons. As a result of the Allied counteroffensive, the German High Command promptly ordered a withdrawal from this part of the Aisne-Marne salient, which began during the night of July 19.

On July 21 a regiment of the 3d Division crossed the river near Château-Thierry and occupied Mont St. Père from which place it protected the crossing of the remainder of the division.

From here to Fismes, about 19 miles away, the American divisions advanced along the axis of the Marne salient. The ground passed over on the tour is part of that which they restored to France during the period July 20 to August 6.

EN ROUTE NEAR MÉZY TO NEAR COURMONT

(70.0 m 112.6 km) **To the right of the bridge on which this road passes over the railway in Mézy,** an American detachment held out until late in the afternoon of July 15 in spite of all efforts of the Germans to capture them.

(70.1 m 112.8 km) **Beyond bridge, at curve in road, in the excavations seen to the left,** a small group of Americans held their position on the first day of the offensive long after the German lines had swept beyond them on both their flanks.

(70.4 m 113.3 km) **Upon approaching the river** note the open fields on this side of it. Reports of German officers state that their troops suffered heavy losses on those flats from the accurate rifle fire of the American soldiers.

During the night of July 21 and the next morning a large part of the 3d Division crossed the river on a temporary

German Anti-Balloon Gun in Action. ©️ G

Le Charmel Château, Captured by the
3d Division, July 27, 1918

bridge built by the division engineers
near the site of the present structure.

(70.8 m 113.9 km) **After crossing bridge,
at first junction bear to the right.**

(71.2 m 114.6 km) **Pass through the
village of Chartèves,** which was occupied
by the 3d Division on July 22.

(71.4 m 114.9 km) **At far side of village,
by looking to the right across the river a**
view of the American position as seen by
the attacking German troops on July 15 is
obtained. Detachments of Americans
with machine guns were in the underbrush

along the riverbank while stronger forces
were along the railroad seen beyond it.
The division orders prescribed that the
main line of resistance on the high wooded
ground in rear be held at all costs.

(72.7 m 117.0 km) **Just before entering
the next village, Jaulgonne, STOP without leaving car.** (See map on next page.)

To the right front, on the other side of
the bridge, the course of the river bends
abruptly, its valley being visible for some
distance extending to the right. Four
companies of the 28th Division, attached
to French units, were stationed along that
part of the river when the enemy launched
the July 15 attack. One of them was on
the opposite bank with its nearest flank
at the bridge, while the other three were
up the valley just beyond the next bend.
The Germans forced a crossing between
these two groups and also advanced past
their outer flanks for a considerable distance, but were unable to cross the river
in their immediate front. Shortly after
daybreak, when the full power of the
German attack developed, the French
fell back without advising the Americans
or ordering their retirement, thus abandoning the four American companies
on the riverbank. Although surrounded,

Ponton Bridge Near Mézy Built by Engineers of
the 3d Division

these companies maintained their positions until 8:00 a. m., when they started to fight their way back to regain the French lines which had been reestablished, with the help of other units of the 28th Division, about 3 miles to the rear. The survivors reached these new French lines during the afternoon.

On July 16 and 17 the French units and those of the 28th Division on these new lines launched counterattacks which succeeded in recovering some of the lost ground. During July 18 the elements of the 28th Division were withdrawn from the front line, its losses in this area from July 15 to 18 having been about 1,200 officers and men.

Continue.

(73.2 m 117.8 km) **Straight through Jaulgonne,** which was captured by the 3d Division on July 22.

(73.7 m 118.6 km) **Beyond town, in the ravine along this road,** a part of the division

Defensive Operations of 28th Division
July 15-18, 1918

Stop, described in text
Route, described in text

American Front Line   French Front Line   - - - Gap July 16
—xx— Boundary French Division with which Elements
of 28th Division Were Serving
Arrows show counterattack of 109th Inf. July 16

advanced on July 22 to the far edge of the next village, Le Charmel. Threatened with isolation, these units, which were then several miles ahead of the troops on both sides of them, withdrew to the general vicinity of Jaulgonne.

During the next few days bitter struggles took place near this road as the German Army fought for time to withdraw the great quantities of supplies and ammunition which had been brought to this front but which had not been used, due

to the sudden unsuccessful ending of their offensive which started early on July 15.

(74.3 m 119.5 km) **Some distance farther on, to the right front up the valley,** can be seen Le Charmel Château. That château, now rebuilt, was the scene of intense fighting, ♦ Germans holding it against severe attacks until July 27.

(75.1 m 120.8 km) **At next main road junction, keep straight ahead passing through Le Charmel,** which although stubbornly defended was captured by the

la Croix Blanche Farm   la Cense   Villers-sur-Fère   Oise-Aisne American Cemetery   Seringes-et-Nesles

Panorama From Stop

3d Division during daylight hours on July 25 after an extremely hard fight.

For the next few miles the American advance encountered only slight resistance as the main German forces had been withdrawn to the Ourcq River during the night of July 26–27.

The operations, described later, of the 28th and 32d Divisions on the Ourcq were directed from their division headquarters located in Le Charmel.

(78.1 m 125.7 km) **About 3 miles beyond the town of Le Charmel,** Courmont is seen to the right of the road.

(78.5 m 126.3 km) **After passing the village of Courmont, a few yards before reaching the next main crossroad, STOP.**

The panoramic sketch on these pages will be of great help in case difficulty occurs in locating the places mentioned below.

The Ourcq River lies in the valley to the right and right front. The far slopes of it had been organized by the Germans into a formidable position by the time the American and French troops arrived here on the evening of July 27 and began the series of attacks which finally drove the German troops from it.

This fighting was of the most severe character and although most of the American divisions were participating in an offensive for the first time the natural courage and fighting spirit of the American soldiers carried them forward to

German Trench-Mortar Bombardment of Allied Strong Point, July 15, 1918. © G

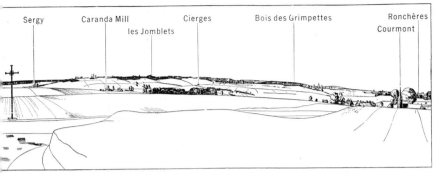

Sergy   Caranda Mill   Cierges   Bois des Grimpettes   Ronchères
les Jomblets   Courmont

West of Courmont

accomplishments which could not have been excelled by veteran assault divisions.

From this point many of the attacks made against the German defenses were visible. Long thin lines of khaki-clad American soldiers could be seen advancing up the slopes across the valley, preceded by bursts of smoke as the artillery barrage moved forward to prepare the way for them. Hostile fire took heavy toll from the attacking units, and counterattacks launched from the wooded heights often forced the Americans back. Such setbacks, however, were but signals for new assaults, which were bravely and persistently repeated until all of the heights were finally in American hands.

The nearest village to the front in the Ourcq River valley is Sergy. To the right front a road is seen, in the distance, entering a large wooded area.

Face that point, which direction is approximately northeast.

Courmont, the nearest town seen to the right, was captured by a French division on July 27. That night the 28th Division relieved the French, taking over a line the center of which was near this point and which changed direction so as to run along the far side of Courmont. The 3d Division had the zone of action to the right of Courmont.

On July 28 Ronchères, seen on the hill beyond Courmont, was captured by the

German Heavy Machine Gun Unit Advancing Through Captured Village,
July 15, 1918. © G

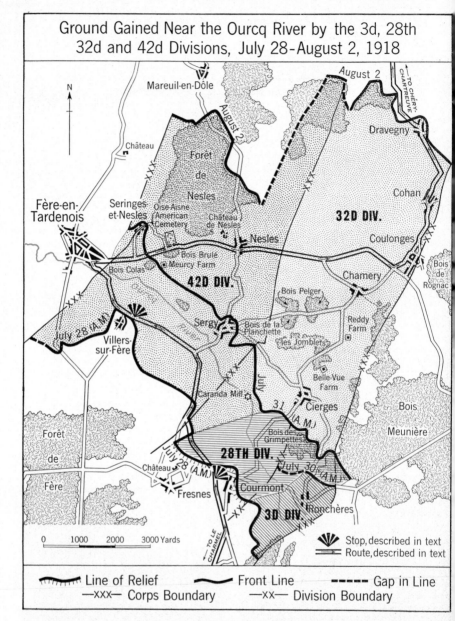

Ground Gained Near the Ourcq River by the 3d, 28th 32d and 42d Divisions, July 28-August 2, 1918

3d Division, and the 28th Division advanced its lines to the other side of the Ourcq River all along its front. During the fighting that day the German resistance was such that it became evident they intended to make a determined stand on the opposite side of this valley.

About a mile from here, on the nearest hill seen to the left of and beyond Courmont, is the Bois des Grimpettes, a key point of the German position. Although in the zone of action of the 3d and later of the 32d Division, it commanded the 28th Division front to such an extent that it had to be captured before any appreciable advance could be made. On both July 28 and 29 it was attacked, but not captured, by the 3d Division from near Ronchères and by the 28th Division from its position in front of here.

On the night of July 29 the 3d Division was relieved by the 32d, after having been in line since early June and having made an outstanding record in combat. Its casualties were nearly 6,600.

On July 30, as the result of two attacks supported by brief but intense artillery preparations, the 28th Division succeeded in taking the Bois des Grimpettes in the afternoon, after a savage hand-to-hand fight in which it was assisted by the 32d Division. It also occupied for a short time part of the village of Cierges, whose church tower, which looks like a small house from here, can be seen to the right of and below the point the observer is facing. A German counterattack was repulsed about dark of that day.

During the night of July 30–31 the 32d Division relieved the 28th Division, whose casualties had totaled more than 1,400 officers and men, thus extending its front to the left as far as Caranda Mill, the building partially seen in the small clump of trees at the foot of this hill about midway between Cierges and Sergy.

The wood which covers the crest of the ridge to the right of and beyond Caranda Mill is Les Jomblets. It lay in the German main line of defense and was an important strong point. On July 31 the 32d Division, in an attack launched about 2:00 p. m., captured Cierges and reached Les Jomblets, but was forced by heavy hostile fire to fall back from that wood. On the next day, in an attack made in the early morning, the division captured Les Jomblets and established itself about ½ mile farther on. There the troops repulsed a counterattack made shortly after daybreak. About 9:00 a. m., however, they were driven back by a fierce German counterattack supported by artillery. That afternoon Les Jomblets

42d Division Artillery Passing Through Sergy, August 3, 1918

was finally taken and held by the 32d Division as the result of two separate regimental assaults, made about the same time, which converged close to the point which the observer is now facing.

Sergy, in the valley to the left front, and Seringes-et-Nesles seen well to the left of it, are both located beyond the Ourcq. Villers-sur-Fère in the distance to the observer's left, is on this side of the river. These towns were captured by the 42d Division in operations which will be described at the next stop.

To the left front in the distance, the Oise-Aisne American Cemetery, which is distinguished by its field of white headstones, is seen slightly to the right of and below the village of Seringes-et-Nesles.

Street Barricade at Northern Edge of Le Charmel, July 1918
Built by the Germans in their retreat

Soissons: Fighting in Villages was Fierce After Its Capture by the 2d Division, July 27, 1918

The route now follows closely the south bank of the Ourcq River and a better view of many of the places just mentioned will be obtained. The natural strength of the German positions across the river will also be more evident at that time.

EN ROUTE NEAR COURMONT TO NEAR VILLERS-SUR-FÈRE

(79.5 m 127.9 km) **While ascending the next ridge, Cierges** is seen to the right, about a mile away.

(80.4 m 129.4 km) **The next village seen to the right is Sergy.** That town

led a platoon in an attack which resulted in the capture of that wood, and although again hit several times during the assault, he broke up a hostile counterattack mainly by his own accurate automatic rifle fire. He remained in charge until the position had been made secure, after which, suffering from nine wounds in various parts of the body, this gallant soldier dragged himself to shelter.

(81.8 m 131.6 km) **Just before reaching the next town, Villers-sur-Fère, about 100 yards from top of hill, where a clear view to right is obtained, STOP.**

German Dressing Station Near Château de la Forêt
Being Used by Americans Soon After Its Capture

and the steep slopes on both sides of it were stubbornly defended by the German troops who were holding them.

(80.9 m 130.2 km) **A short distance farther on, to the right on the hillside across the valley,** is seen a small triangular-shaped wood where Private Sidney E. Manning, 42d Division, performed the deeds on July 28 for which he was awarded the Congressional Medal of Honor. Private Manning, who had been severely wounded shortly before,

The village of Seringes-et-Nesles and the Oise-Aisne American Cemetery to the right of it are seen across the valley.

Face the cemetery, which direction is approximately northeast.

The Ourcq River is located in the valley at the foot of this slope.

The 42d Division captured Villers-sur-Fère on the 27th and continued its attacks on the 28th gaining a foothold on the other side of the Ourcq. Sergy, seen to the right, which was strongly held by

42d Division Infantry in Position Near Seringes-et-Nesles, July 29, 1918

the Germans, was entered by patrols that day but not captured although ground was gained in its immediate vicinity.

Across the river in front of here an unusual exploit was performed on July 28 by Sergeant Frank Gardella, Jr., of the 42d Division. Two enemy airplanes were flying parallel to the American infantry lines and pouring machine-gun bullets into them, driving everyone to cover. Sergeant Gardella, noting the situation, rushed to his machine gun and took aim at the upper of the two machines. Although he was constantly subject to a storm of bullets from the planes and from enemy snipers on the ground, he nevertheless coolly sighted his gun and riddled the upper plane, causing it to collapse and fall in flames. In falling it struck the lower plane and brought it to the earth also. For his coolness and bravery he was awarded the Distinguished Service Cross.

Part of the 47th Infantry, 4th Division, was attached to the 42d Division and, with this additional strength, Sergy was captured on July 29 and other advances made. In the valley to the front, the nearest wood in line with the cemetery,

Bois Colas, which was literally bristling with hostile machine guns, and the town of Seringes-et-Nesles were captured on that day in brilliant attacks. Although the gains at Seringes-et-Nesles and Sergy formed pronounced salients in the line and the troops in them were subjected to fire from three sides, the Germans were unable to retake that ground.

On July 30 the attacks were continued but in spite of determined efforts no substantial gains were made. A strong German counterattack near Meurcy Farm, identified by the buildings seen to the right of the cemetery, was repulsed.

In the bitter fighting around that farm, Sergeant Richard W. O'Neill, 42d Division, advanced ahead of the assaulting line and attacked an enemy force of about 25 men. In the ensuing hand-to-hand encounter he sustained pistol wounds but heroically continued in the fight, during which he received additional wounds. With great physical effort he remained in active command of his detachment until he was again wounded and was forced by weakness and loss of blood to be evacuated. He insisted upon being taken first to the battalion commander in order to transmit to him valuable information relative to the enemy positions and the disposition of his men. For his conspicuous bravery above and beyond the call of duty Sergeant O'Neill was later awarded the Congressional Medal of Honor.

On July 31, after a very heavy bombardment in which smoke and thermite shells were used, the tiny Bois Brulé, which covered the ground near this end of the cemetery, was abandoned by the Germans and the 42d Division occupied it and Meurcy Farm, thus forming another salient in the German lines. By the evening of August 1 the 42d and 32d Divisions were in secure possession of a large portion of the high ground on the other side of the river, from Seringes-et-Nesles to beyond Les Jomblets.

These successes, and those of the French farther to the left, caused the Germans to withdraw during the night of August 1–2 to their next prepared position at the Vesle River, 10 miles in front of here. The pursuit, which was begun by the Americans and French on the morning of August 2, had to overcome

many hostile machine-gun nests cleverly placed in mutually supporting positions throughout the entire area between the Ourcq and the Vesle Rivers.

The 42d Division on August 2 advanced over the ground on which the cemetery stands and through the Forêt de Nesles, the large wood seen beyond the cemetery. On August 3 the division, having suffered nearly 6,500 casualties, was relieved by the 4th Division which, together with the 32d Division on its right, continued to push forward until the Vesle River was reached.

EN ROUTE NEAR VILLERS-SUR-FÈRE TO OISE-AISNE AMERICAN CEMETERY

(82.6 m 132.9 km) **Cross Ourcq River.** Note its extremely small size.

(83.0 m 133.5 km) **Turn sharply to the right on the first street in the next town, Fère-en-Tardenois.**

The American I Corps Headquarters was located here from August 5 to 13 after the Germans had been driven back from their position near the Ourcq.

(84.3 m 135.6 km) **Beyond town, at the large cemetery near the road, STOP.**

German Ammunition Train Destroyed by American Shellfire at Cierges

This is the Oise-Aisne American Cemetery, the second largest American military cemetery in Europe. It contains 6,012 graves. The majority of the battle dead who rest here were killed in the fighting along the Ourcq River and in the territory between here and the Oise River. In 1922, American soldiers then buried in France in the general area west of the line, Tours–Romorantin–Paris–Le Havre were moved to this cemetery.

The building across the road contains a rearranging themselves into a succession of symmetrical geometrical designs.

The chapel is a harmony of color, with its pink and gray sandstone walls and variegated marble columns. It is semicircular in form and from its terrace a fine view of the cemetery and the surrounding country can be obtained.

The decorative sculpture of the chapel is Romanesque in style but modern in subject. On each front wall appears the coat of arms of the United States,

Oise-Aisne Cemetery Chapel
Note the exterior altar in the foreground

reception room for visitors and the office of the superintendent, where inquiries for information or concerning the location of a particular grave should be made.

The cemetery is entered through an ornamental wrought-iron gateway. Rows of trees and beds of red roses line the central paths. The chapel overlooks the cemetery from the rear and as the visitor walks toward it the fields of white marble headstones constantly change pattern, the crosses apparently arranging and beneath a frieze of shields which display the insignia of branches of the Army. The column capitals are carved with the insignia of the American divisions which took part in the battles in this region and with various military weapons and articles of equipment. In the four medallions above the columns the modern soldier is contrasted with the medieval crusader.

The simple lines of the interior are softened by the subdued light from the windows whose panes are thin slabs of

Field Artillery During a Lull Between
Engagements, July 1918

Joyce Kilmer, the poet, was killed in the fighting near here and now rests in this cemetery with so many other of his brave friends and comrades.

As the inscription which is seen above the columns of the chapel states:

"THESE ENDURED ALL AND GAVE ALL THAT HONOR AND JUSTICE MIGHT PREVAIL AND THAT THE WORLD MIGHT ENJOY FREEDOM AND INHERIT PEACE."

EN ROUTE OISE-AISNE AMERICAN CEMETERY TO NEAR FISMES

(85.5 m 137.6 km) **The next village, Nesles**, was taken by the 42d Division on August 2. Near it can be seen the ruins of a 13th Century château.

(86.0 m 138.4 km) **Beyond Nesles, about ¹/₂ mile**, the zone of action of the 32d Division is entered.

During an aerial combat on July 14, First Lieutenant Quentin Roosevelt, son of ex-President Theodore Roosevelt, was shot down near Chamery. The Germans buried him where he fell, and marked his grave with the wheels of his plane and a rough cross bearing the inscription "ROOSEVELT, AMERICAN AVIATOR". On

Algerian onyx. The chapel contains a beautiful altar of carved stone, and upon the walls appear in carved and gilded letters the names of American soldiers who fought in this region and who sleep in unknown graves. The museum room across the terrace from the chapel proper contains flags of the United States and France and a beautifully carved and decorated wall map, upon which are shown the areas in this region captured by the different American divisions.

While visiting the cemetery it is only with effort that the visitor can bring his imagination to picture the scenes of bitter combat which took place on these slopes when the 42d Division was fighting for them, and on the various other battlefields of the Ourcq River valley which were fought over by soldiers of the American 3d, 4th, 28th, 32d and 42d Divisions.

4th Division Troops on Way to Front,
Seringes-et-Nesles, August 4, 1918

Camouflaged Road Just North of Dravegny
Road followed by tour

August 2 the grave was found by advancing troops of the 32d Division, who held appropriate services and built a fence protecting the spot. Since that time it has been more permanently marked.

To visit grave, turn right at crossroad indicated in next paragraph. At next village, Chamery, take first road to the left (impassable in wet weather) and go 800 yards to grave, which is 100 yards to left of road. Total length of side trip—2 miles. Amount of time required—30 minutes.

(88.2 m 141.9 km) **At next main crossroad at foot of long slope, turn left toward the village of Coulonges.**

(88.6 m 142.6 km) **In next village, Coulonges, beyond bridge turn left.**

This village and the next one, Cohan, were captured on August 2 by the 32d Division. The right boundary of the division was just to the right of the road which the tour is following.

(89.6 m 144.2 km) **Continue through the town of Cohan.**

(90.9 m 146.3 km) **In the next village, Dravegny, at the church turn to the left, at the next corner turn to the right toward the village of Chéry-Chartreuve.**

Dravegny was captured by the 32d Division on August 2. The front line of the division on that night was established in the north edge of the town.

The 28th Division Headquarters directed operations from this village during the period August 4–14, while the division was fighting along the Vesle.

(91.7 m 147.5 km) **Beyond the next hill, the town seen in front across the valley is Chéry-Chartreuve.** The 4th Division, after relieving the 42d Division during the early morning, advanced on August 3 to the wood seen just to the right of and beyond that town.

(93.7 m 150.8 km) **At small monument near entrance to Chéry-Chartreuve turn right. Note speedometer reading.**

(97.3 m 156.6 km) **3.6 miles farther on, when the large town, Fismes, comes in full view to the right front, STOP.**

Face the church, the right one of the

Observation Balloon Trucks Passing Through
Coulonges, August 4, 1918

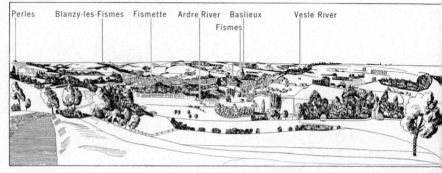

Panorama From Stop Near Fismes

two buildings with a tower, which direction is approximately northeast.

The stream at the foot of this hill is the Ardre River, which joins the Vesle River at a point to the left front in the valley. The German troops fought stubbornly to hold Fismes and the slopes which are seen beyond it.

On the afternoon of August 4 the 32d Division attacked Fismes from this hill, suffering severe losses from hostile artillery and machine-gun fire before the town was finally captured.

On August 6, the 6th Brigade of the 3d Division was placed in the line to the right of Fismes. Although worn out by its heavy fighting on the Marne River, the brigade on August 7 and 10 made valiant efforts to cross the river but did not succeed in establishing a foothold on the far bank. On August 11 the brigade was relieved, its losses in this general vicinity being about 600 officers and men.

On the night of August 6–7 the 28th

Ruins of the City Hall of Fismes, August 14, 1918

Division relieved the 32d Division, which had advanced 11 miles and whose casualties had been almost 3,800 since entering the battle on the Ourcq River.

The 28th Division on August 7 launched an unsuccessful attack upon Fismette, which is beyond the Vesle River, adjoining Fismes on its left side. The next day, after two attacks with heavy artillery preparation, parts of Fismette were captured and held. The town was completely occupied on August 10, but because of the German efforts to retake it, desperate fighting took place in the streets of the town almost daily during the next two weeks.

In the fighting in Fismette on August 10 Sergeant James I. Mestrovitch, 28th Division, performed the act of gallantry for which he was awarded the Congressional Medal of Honor. Seeing his company commander lying wounded 30 yards in front of the line after his company had withdrawn to a sheltered position behind a stone wall, Sergeant Mestrovitch voluntarily left cover and crawled through heavy machine-gun and shell fire to where the officer lay. He took the officer upon his back and crawled back to a place of safety where he administered first aid treatment. His exceptional heroism saved the life of his company commander.

During the early morning hours of August 27, the Germans inclosed Fismette in a heavy barrage and attacked in force with flame throwers, capturing or killing all Americans holding it except a few who escaped by swimming across the river.

On August 12 the 77th Division relieved the 4th to the left of here and on the 13th changes were made in the division boundaries so that the 28th Division held Fismes and the riverbank for about 2½ miles to the right of it, while the 77th Division held the line along the river from Fismes to the left for about 3 miles.

The American III Corps directed active operations for the first time on this front, holding a sector immediately alongside that of the American I Corps.

On the night of September 3–4, as a result of the Oise-Aisne offensive, which began north of Soissons on August 18, the German lines here were turned and the enemy troops along this front withdrew toward the Aisne River. This movement was covered by rear guards composed mainly of machine gun organizations.

On September 4 the divisions here started in pursuit, and by September 6 the 28th had pushed its front line about a mile north of Baslieux, partially seen in the little valley 3 miles away beyond the church in Fismes. There the division again faced a prepared German position and had severe fighting in front of it until relieved on the night of September 7–8 by one of the French divisions.

The 77th Division was stopped on September 6, south of the Aisne River, after an advance of 5 miles. From that day

Engineers Exploding Mine Trap Left by Germans in a Dugout Near Blanzy-les-Fismes, September 5, 1918

until September 16, when it was relieved by an Italian division (of which there were two serving on the Western Front), its line remained approximately in the same place. A brief description of its service on the Aisne is given at the next stop.

In these operations the casualties of the 28th Division were about 5,300 and those of the 77th Division nearly 4,800. By their repeated efforts to cross the river and by their energetic pursuit after the Germans had retired, both divisions brought great credit upon themselves and upon the American forces.

The State of Pennsylvania has built a memorial bridge over the Vesle between Fismes and Fismette. To visit it, bear

Fismette, Scene of Hard Fighting by the 28th Division

right at road junction indicated in the next paragraph, go to open plaza in town, turn left and cross railroad to bridge. Total length of side trip—1 mile. Amount of time required—15 minutes.

EN ROUTE NEAR FISMES TO
NEAR BAZOCHES

(98.2 m 158.0 km) **At the near edge of Fismes, beyond the small bridge turn sharply to the left toward Soissons.**

The American advance passed from the left to right across this road.

(98.8 m 159.0 km) **After crossing the Vesle River and the railroad,** a densely wooded area is seen on the left. Part of it surrounds a château called, on war time maps, the Château du Diable (Castle of the Devil). Troops of the 4th, 28th and 77th Divisions, who engaged in many hot fights with the Germans near this château, agree that the place was well named.

(99.4 m 160.0 km) **Beyond the far end of the wooded area,** a 4th Division monument is passed on the right.

(100.3 m 161.4 km) **At the second crest, when the next village is plainly seen down the road ahead, STOP.**

Face to the left, which direction is approximately south.

From this point a good view is obtained of the ground fought over by the 4th and later by the 77th Division.

The 4th Division, advancing in this direction over the line of hills in front of here, on August 4 captured St. Thibaut, seen on the hillside to the right front, and Ville-Savoye, seen to the left front. The next day the division repulsed a counter-attack and began attacks to gain a foot-hold on this side of the river. Small detachments succeeded in crossing to the

4th Division Monument
Near Bazoches

left front of here and also near Bazoches, seen in the valley to the right, but they were later withdrawn to the far bank.

On August 6 the division attacked in force, after a 4-hour artillery preparation, with this road as its main objective. It forced a crossing opposite Ville-Savoye and reached this highway about ½ mile to the left of here. The line was maintained there, in spite of strong counterattacks, until August 8, when it was withdrawn to the railroad which runs in the valley near this side of the river.

From August 7 to 9, the 4th Division launched several attacks near Bazoches. Hostile fire preventing the building of suitable footbridges, many of the men courageously attempted to swim the river or crawl over on fallen trees. Those who succeeded were insufficient in number to establish themselves on this bank. Between August 3 and 12, when it was relieved by the 77th Division, the 4th Division lost approximately 3,500 men.

For the next ten days this sector, like others along the front where troops of neither side were trying to advance, was comparatively quiet except at night. During the daytime all troops remained well concealed to escape the vigilance of snipers and hostile observers searching for favorable artillery targets. After nightfall, however, the hillside swarmed with men busily strengthening the positions, while patrols from each side, trying to discover the dispositions and intentions of the other, frequently clashed along the banks of the river and engaged in small but desperate battles in the dark.

On August 22 the Germans attacked the Château du Diable, located to the eft in the trees, and drove the 77th Division troops holding it across the river. Early the next morning, the 77th counterattacked and in desperate fighting lasting into the night regained part of the wood.

Bazoches was the objective of a carefully prepared assault by the 77th Division launched early on August 27. The Château du Diable was also attacked and in each case the objectives fixed for the day were reached after severe combats, but in the end could not be retained.

Two German attacks were repulsed during the night of September 1-2. On September 4 the division crossed the river, occupied Bazoches, and advanced

lead his company in making a hazardous attack on a commanding trench position near the Aisne Canal, which other troops had previously attempted to take without success. His company immediately met with intense machine-gun fire, against which it had no artillery assistance, but Captain Miles preceded the first wave and assisted in cutting a passage through the enemy wire entanglements. In so doing he was wounded five times by machine-gun bullets, both legs and one arm being fractured, whereupon he ordered himself placed on a stretcher and had himself carried forward to the enemy trench in order that he might encourage and direct

Street in Soissons, September 1918

in pursuit of the Germans who had withdrawn during the previous night. The division reached the Aisne River valley on September 6 and established its front line close to this side of it.

The next few days were marked by frequent local actions bitterly fought but with only minor results. On September 14 the division attacked as part of a general assault and made some gains in spite of stubborn resistance.

It was during the fighting of this day that Captain L. Wardlaw Miles, 77th Division, performed the heroic services for which he was awarded the Congressional Medal of Honor. He volunteered to

his company, which by this time had suffered numerous casualties. Under his inspiration the men held the hostile position and consolidated their front line after an action lasting two hours. This gallant officer was then carried against his will to a first-aid station for treatment.

On September 15, after repulsing a German counterattack, the division was relieved from the line and was sent to the Meuse-Argonne region to take part there in the great offensive of the American First Army later in the month.

The tour now follows the Vesle River valley as far as near Sermoise and then continues along the Aisne River valley to

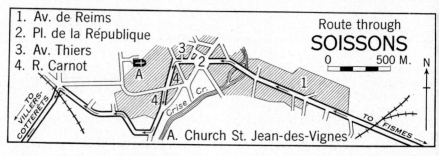

1. Av. de Reims
2. Pl. de la République
3. Av. Thiers
4. R. Carnot

Route through
SOISSONS
0   500 M.   N

A. Church St. Jean-des-Vignes

Soissons. No American fighting took place in the area which will be passed over.

EN ROUTE NEAR BAZOCHES TO NEAR MISSY-AUX-BOIS

In its long and eventful history Soissons has been destroyed and rebuilt many times, and no less than 32 sieges and major battles have occurred there or in the immediate vicinity. Among the points of interest in town are the cathedral and the church of St. Jean-des-Vignes.

The American battlefields at Juvigny and near Vauxaillon may be reached by following the main highway from Soissons to St. Quentin. See pages 91–93.

An American 14-inch naval gun on a railroad mount, manned by men of the United States Navy, fired from a position in St. Christophe Cemetery, ½ mile west of Soissons, from September 10 to October 24. Its target was the railroad junction in the town of Laon, about 19 miles away.

(116.5 m 187.4 km) **Upon reaching the large monument in Soissons, continue straight ahead toward church for one block. Bear left onto Rue Carnot and take second street to right. Continue to railroad, then turn sharp left across the tracks toward Villers-Cotterêts.**

(120.1 m 193.2 km) **After leaving the valley, the large cemetery passed** contains French, British and German graves.

(121.2 m 195.0 km) **Beyond cemetery 1.1 miles, Missy-aux-Bois is seen to the right front. When the village is in full view, on top of the next rise in the road (beyond the kilometer post), STOP.**

Face Missy-aux-Bois, which direction is approximately west.

The reader is now on ground swept over by the main attack of the French-American counteroffensive of July 18 which marked the turning point in the succession

Advance Command Post and Aid Station, 1st Division,
Near Missy-aux-Bois, July 20, 1918

of dramatic military events that so closely followed each other in the year 1918. Up to the time of this attack, the Allies had been compelled to withstand a series of powerful German offensives which almost gained a decisive victory. It was in this region that the tide definitely turned in favor of the Allies, and this battle was the first of a series of offensives, made possible by the rapid arrival of American troops, which, within less than four months, forced the enemy troops back and compelled Germany to sue for an immediate armistice.

It is difficult to imagine this peaceful countryside as the scene of such a bitter struggle. The fields were covered with wheat, breast high, ready for harvest. The Germans had dug here no elaborate system of trenches, but every little rise in the ground had its group of individual rifle pits and nests of machine guns, while along the farm roads and ravines and hidden by banks of earth and the tall grain, were batteries of German artillery. The farm buildings and villages, largely of stone construction, afforded admirable protection, and each constituted a strong point which could be taken only after the most desperate fighting.

The 1st Division attacked toward this road from a line about 3 miles in front of here, this point being near the center of its zone of action. The zone of action of the French 1st Moroccan Division, one regiment of which was the famous Foreign Legion, included Cravançon Farm, the group of buildings a mile down the road to the left, and the zone of action of the 2d Division (to be visited later) lay beyond. These three divisions formed the spearhead of the attack which started at

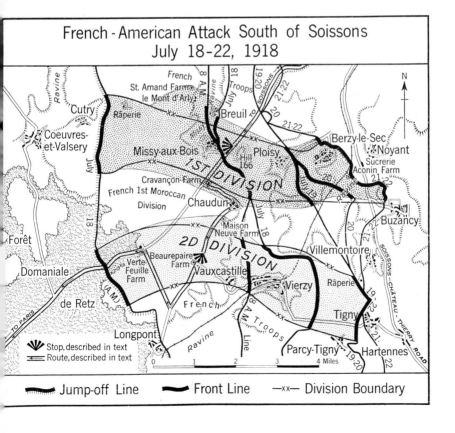

French - American Attack South of Soissons
July 18-22, 1918

4:35 a. m. on July 18. This assault was made without artillery preparation but behind a rolling barrage, and quickly overran the forward German positions.

About 7:00 a. m. the 1st Division reached Missy-aux-Bois and the far edge of Missy Ravine, which extends to the right from that village. By that time the resistance had greatly stiffened, and Missy-aux-Bois and the ravine itself were full of enemy troops. The assaulting units at once pushed on into the ravine in the face of point-blank fire from many batteries of German artillery located therein. These guns, whose removal

French division. During the attack hostile fire from there held up the advance of part of the 1st Division, where upon a support battalion of the division attacking in conjunction with the French captured the place in a hard fight. St Amand Farm, seen on the hill above L Mont d'Arly, had been previously cap tured by the 1st Division although als situated in the French zone of action.

After the leading troops of the 1s Division had reached this side of th valley, a large hostile force came out o a cave on the far slope near Le Mon d'Arly and formed up to attack th

Infantry of 1st Division Near Berzy-le-Sec, July 21, 1918

had been prevented by the rapidity of the American advance, destroyed a majority of the tanks which accompanied the brigade of the 1st Division on that flank. However, after a terrific struggle the Germans in the ravine were killed or taken prisoner, and the guns emplaced in it were captured.

The little group of buildings called Le Mont d'Arly, seen 1½ miles to the right front in the trees below the edge of the ravine, was in the zone of action of a

American troops in rear. This force however, was driven back into the cav by an American support unit. Afte futile attempts to bomb this Germar force out of its cave, late in the after noon an officer appeared at the mouth o it waving a white flag and surrendere his entire command, consisting of approxi mately 600 officers and men.

While the advance to Missy Ravin was being made, other troops of the 1s Division captured Cravançon Farm, an

he artillery placed a heavy barrage upon
he German positions along this highway
ind on Hill 166, which slopes up to the
eft rear from this point. When the
)arrage moved forward at 7:53 a. m., the
nfantry continued the attack, meeting
lesperate resistance. To the left of here,
he far slope of Hill 166 was reached and
ield. Soon thereafter the troops which
idvanced from Missy Ravine toward
his locality encountered heavy fire from
he top of the hill and from points to the
)bserver's right along this road. A few
Americans reached the highway near
.ere, but not in sufficient numbers to
ıold the gains they had made.

The 1st Division captured most of its
)bjectives by 10:00 a. m. and spent the
ifternoon in preparing to renew the
ittack. Fresh troops were brought up,
he artillery moved forward, telephone
ines were strung and food and ammuni-
ion distributed. The enemy during this
)eriod became increasingly vigilant and
very movement in the American lines
)romptly drew machine-gun fire.

The division front line that night
vas established along the near edge of
Missy Ravine. It crossed this road
ıbout 300 yards to the left of here and
ontinued on from there, in the direction
)f the observer's left rear, for about one
nile to where it joined with the French.
Face to the rear.

After the loss of their original position
nd most of the artillery in it on July 18,
he Germans rushed every available re-
erve to this area. An enormous number
f machine guns were set up in front of
ıere; new artillery was placed on the hills
)ordering the Soissons–Château-Thierry
)ad, 3 miles away; and the troops were
)ld to hold the ground then occupied
egardless of cost. Machine guns were
rdered to be sacrificed, if necessary, but
vere not to be withdrawn.

About 4:00 a. m. on July 19 the 1st
)ivision, supported by tanks, attacked
II along its front behind a rolling barrage.
'he troops who jumped off from Missy
.avine advanced, in the face of devastat-
ıg machine-gun fire, up the bare exposed

1st Division Artillery Changing Position
Near Missy-aux-Bois, July 19, 1918

slopes of Hill 166, seen to the right front,
and captured the top of it. Those attacking to the left of this point reached
this road where they were stopped by a
withering fire from the front and left
flank. All tanks which accompanied the
assault units were disabled. The troops
attacking from the right of the division
line which was to the right front from
here, made an advance of about ½ mile
in spite of intense opposition.

At 5:30 in the afternoon, that part of
the 1st Division near here attacked in
conjunction with the French. It started
from this road, advanced over the fields
seen ahead, which were being swept by
severe hostile machine-gun fire, and captured the town of Ploisy, about 1 mile
from here just to the right of the direction
the observer is facing. Against obstinate
resistance the troops on the right of the
division advanced that part of its line
another ½ mile during the afternoon.

The next day the attacks of the 1st
Division were continued. In addition
to terrific machine-gun and artillery fire,
many hostile airplanes flew low over the
area, machine-gunning and bombing the
troops, as the Germans frantically tried
to stop the American advance. In spite

Captured German Field Gun
Near Missy-aux-Bois

f this the right part of the division front
ne was advanced an additional ½ mile
▸ the other side of the main railroad
·ading south from Soissons.

On the 21st the fighting continued
·ith much fury. Berzy-le-Sec was cap-
·ured that day, the division reaching
·uzancy, beyond the Soissons–Château-
·hierry highway, thereby cutting the most
·nportant road of the German communi-
·ation system within the salient.

The 1st Division, after its remarkable
·emonstration of fighting ability in this
·ttack, was relieved from the line on the
·ight of July 22–23. The casualties of the
·ivision, an indication of its exceptional
·ervices during the five days of fighting
·ere, reached the total of 6,870 offi-
·ers and men. Three fourths of all the
·fantry field officers of the division were
·ther killed or wounded and one regiment
·as at the end commanded by a captain
·f less than two years' service.

N ROUTE NEAR MISSY-AUX-BOIS TO NEAR
BEAUREPAIRE FARM

(122.4 m 196.9 km) **Just beyond the
·ext group of buildings, Cravançon Farm,
·urn sharply to the left.**

The right boundary of the 1st Division
·uring the advance was 200 yards to the
·ft of and parallel to this road.

(123.3 m 198.4 km) **Immediately after
·ntering the next village, Chaudun, turn
·harply to the right.**

This town, although in the zone of ac-
·on of the Moroccan division, was cap-
·ured on July 18 in an attack in which the
·d Division participated. The attack

Large Cave South of Soissons
Many similar caves are in this vicinity

French Tank With American Forces South of
Soissons, July 18, 1918

was launched from the direction opposite
to the one the tourist is now traveling.

(124.2 m 199.8 km) **The next large
group of buildings, La Maison-Neuve
Farm,** was in the zone of action of the
Moroccans but was captured on July 18
by troops of the 2d Division.

(125.0 m 201.1 km) **About 3/4 mile beyond La Maison-Neuve Farm, where a
good view is obtained of the group of
buildings directly ahead, STOP.**

Face down the road, which direction is
approximately southwest.

After some of its units had marched all
night and double-timed over muddy roads
in a driving rain in order to jump off at
the time designated, the 2d Division
attacked at 4:35 a. m., July 18, in this
general direction from a line about 2 miles
to the right front. The initial attack was
made without the machine gun companies, as they had been unable to reach
the line of departure in time to partici-
pate, and without the full support of the
tanks, which were late in arriving.

About 5:45 a. m. the French tanks
which had caught up with the front line
circled around La Verte-Feuille Farm,
partially visible through the trees to the
right front, while troops of the Marine
Brigade charged out of the woods seen
beyond it and overpowered the German
garrison after a sharp encounter.

Beaurepaire Farm, which the Germans
had converted into a veritable fortress,
is seen straight down the road. It was
near the center of the 2d Division zone of
action and was captured early on the
morning of July 18 by the Infantry Brigade

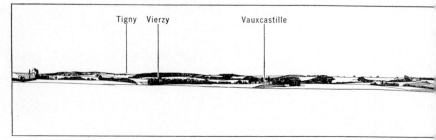

Tigny   Vierzy   Vauxcastille

Panorama From Sto

of the division. At least 100 prisoners were captured in or near the farm.

Batteries of German artillery in the wheat fields in this general vicinity fired point-blank at the Americans as they advanced, and before they could be silenced these guns had destroyed many of the tanks accompanying the attack.

Adding to the confusion caused by these terrific bombardments, low-flying airplanes, both Allied and German, machine-gunned and bombed the troops of their opponents. The Americans crawled or darted through the wheat, steadily advancing against the Germans, who were often unseen until the infantry practically stumbled on them or until the rapidly moving tanks drove the German soldiers from their cover into the open.

La Verte-Feuille Farm After Its Capture by the 2d Division, July 18, 1918

Across the open field to the left, on th low ground a mile away, is Vauxcastill and running toward the left from it, a proximately parallel to this road, is deep wooded ravine. Attacking fro right to left across this road in the ear morning of the first day of the offensiv troops of the 2d Division swarmed int that ravine, where a desperate confli raged until about 7:00 a. m., when th Germans were driven beyond it. A larg number of the enemy who had been su rounded at Vauxcastille took refuge the caves in that vicinity. They r ceived a message dropped from a Germa airplane directing them to retire, and la in the afternoon were captured whi attempting to fight their way back fro the town to their own lines.

Vierzy, situated in a ravine to the le of and beyond Vauxcastille, is about miles from here on this side of the neare heavily wooded hill in that directio It was reached by American troops abo 7:00 a. m. The town was entered abo 9:30 a. m. but the American soldiers we later compelled to retire on account the presence of persistent gas.

Early in the evening the 2d Divisio attacked from the vicinity of Vau castille, and after a hard fight in Vierz where a large number of Germans we made prisoner, pushed on and by mi night was about a mile beyond tha place. Desperate counterattacks launche against the 2d Division during the nig of July 18 were unsuccessful.

On July 19 the division attacked abo 9:00 a. m. The Germans were drive back steadily until 10:00 a. m. when th

Beaurepaire Farm   la Verte-Feuille Farm

North of Beaurepaire Farm

American troops were near Tigny, which can be seen on a clear day 4 miles away from here, beyond Vierzy. There a German counterattack against the division's exposed left flank was repulsed.

The 2d Division was relieved by a French division during the night of July 19–20, after brilliantly accomplishing, during two days of continuous attacks, almost every mission assigned to it. Its losses were over 4,300 officers and men.

✦

This is the last stop of the tour. Every important area of American fighting in the region has been visited or pointed out except that of the 32d Division near Juvigny and the 370th Infantry (93d Division) near Vauxaillon. The operations of these units are described in detail a few pages farther on in this chapter.

The battle areas were visited very closely in the chronological order of the fighting, except for the one here. The reader should remember that the counteroffensive just described occurred after the defensive fighting of the 2d, 3d and 28th Divisions near Château-Thierry and before any of the American divisions had gained any appreciable amount of ground in the Aisne-Marne region.

Although the American divisions in this region served with French units and not as part of an American army, they supplied the numbers which made it possible to attack and contributed greatly to the strength of the offensive and to the Allied morale. The American part in the actual fighting is evident when it is realized that 310,000 American soldiers were engaged in battle and that 67,000 were casualties.

✦

Those desiring to complete a loop in this area or who started the tour at a place other than Paris or Belleau, should proceed to the Aisne-Marne American Cemetery either by way of Vierzy, Tigny and Château-Thierry or via Longpont and Neuilly-St. Front. The route through Château-Thierry is easier to follow and will take less time. The other is more picturesque and goes through the area where elements of the 4th Division fought. For information concerning this fighting see page 54.

About 1 mile from road junction beyond Beaurepaire Farm is Longpont, location of interesting ruins of a large Cistercian abbey which was built in the 12th Century. A visit to the town is worth while if time is available. Length of side trip—2 miles. Time required for side trip—20 minutes.

Beaurepaire Farm, July 19, 1918

EN ROUTE NEAR BEAUREPAIRE FARM
TO PARIS

The Headquarters of the 2d Division was established in the ruins of Beaurepaire Farm after it was captured on July 18, and remained there until the division was relieved from the front line.

(126.6 m 203.7 km) **Beyond Beaurepaire Farm, at the first road junction turn sharply to the right.**

Compare the present appearance of La Verte-Feuille Farm, at the next corner, with the picture on page 88.

(128.3 m 206.4 km) **Upon reaching the next road crossing, turn to the left.**

The advance of the 2d Division on July 18 was in the direction opposite to that which the tourist is now following.

In the woods to the right of this road were performed early on the morning of July 18 the deeds for which Sergeants Louis Cukela and Matej Kocak, Marine Corps, 2d Division, were later awarded Congressional Medals of Honor.

Sergeant Cukela was near this road when his company met with heavy fire from an enemy strong point in the wood. Disregarding the warnings of his comrades, he crawled out from the flank and made his way toward the German line in the face of heavy fire. He succeeded in getting behind the enemy position and rushed a machine-gun emplacement, killing or driving off the crew with his bayonet. With German hand grenades he then bombed out the remaining portion of the strong point, capturing four men and two machine guns.

About the same time Sergeant Kocak, who was in the wood about 500 yards from this road, went forward alone against another machine-gun nest that, hidden in the underbrush, had checked the American advance. Without the protection of fire from his own men, he worked his way in between the German positions in the face of fire from hostile covering detachments. Locating the machine-gun nest, he rushed it and with his bayonet drove off the crew. Shortly thereafter he took command of 25 French colonial troops who had become separated

Captured Weapons in Public Square at Villers-Cotterêts, July 27, 1918

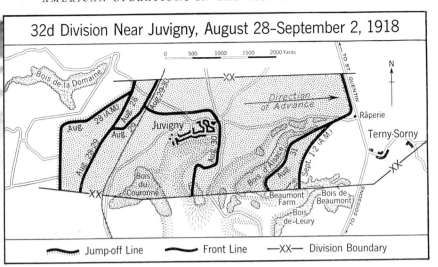

32d Division Near Juvigny, August 28–September 2, 1918

0   500   1000   1500   2000 Yards

N

Bois de la Domaine

TO ST QUENTIN

Direction of Advance

Juvigny

Râperie

Terny-Sorny

Aug. 28 (A.M.)

Aug. 29–30

Aug.

Aug.

Aug. 29–30

Bois du Couronne

Font d'Aboss.

Sept. 1–2 (A.M.)

Beaumont Farm

Bois de Beaumont

Bois de Leury

TO SOISSONS

XX

Jump-off Line   Front Line   —XX— Division Boundary

from their company and led them in an attack which succeeded in wiping out another machine-gun nest.

(129.4 m 208.2 km) **Beyond the farm about 1 mile** are a 2d Division boulder marker and a marker indicating the farthest advance of the German Army in 1918. They are on the left near the road. The jump-off line of the 2d Division ran near the location of these markers and was at right angles to this road.

(134.9 m 217.1 km) **From Villers-Cotterêts there are three main roads to Paris—via Senlis, or La Ferté-Milon and Meaux, or Nanteuil and Dommartin.**

32D DIVISION NEAR JUVIGNY, AUGUST 28–SEPTEMBER 2

The 32d Division, after its relief on the Vesle River early in August, was assigned on August 23 to the French Tenth Army. That Army was then engaged in the Oise-Aisne offensive northwest of Soissons which, if successful, would force the Germans to withdraw from their positions along the Vesle and Aisne Rivers.

The division was held in reserve until August 28, when it entered the line about 1 mile west of Juvigny. That day it launched local attacks and gained some ground in spite of heavy hostile fire.

On August 29 a general assault was made by the entire Tenth Army. This attack met with severe enemy fire and the net result was only slight gains.

During the afternoon of August 30 the 32d Division flanked the town of Juvigny from the south and captured it in a skillful attack, after some vicious street fighting. That evening two strong German counterattacks were repulsed. The American line that night formed a small salient projecting into the German lines.

The attacks were resumed on the 31st, during which the artillery supporting the attack fired a double barrage, instead of a single barrage, as was customary. The Germans, who had been in the habit of remaining in the numerous caves during the artillery bombardments and then manning their trenches and machine-gun nests when the barrage moved on, were caught by the second barrage and suffered heavy casualties from it.

By the end of the day the 32d Division had reached in hard fighting the important Soissons–St. Quentin road at a point northwest of Terny-Sorny. The next day local efforts to advance met with determined resistance. The division was relieved by the 1st Moroccan Division on the night of September 1–2, having made a total advance of 3 miles and having suffered over 2,600 casualties.

The success of the 32d Division in this operation was of great assistance to the

French Tenth Army, whose pressure caused the Germans on this front to retreat from the Vesle River on September 4 to a new position on the Aisne River, east of its junction with the Vesle.

370TH INFANTRY, 93D DIVISION, SEPTEMBER 15–NOVEMBER 11

The 370th Infantry, which had served during the summer in both the St. Mihiel

Participating in the attack of the 59th Division, which began on September 28, the 370th Infantry succeeded in advancing its lines to the Ailette River valley by September 30. The Germans withdrew from this front on the night of October 11, and the American regiment crossed the Ailette and advanced into Bois de Mortier on the 12th. Thereafter, acting as division reserve, it participated in the pursuit

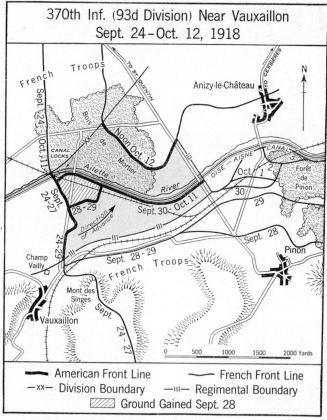

370th Inf. (93d Division) Near Vauxaillon
Sept. 24–Oct. 12, 1918

━━ American Front Line   ── French Front Line
─xx─ Division Boundary   ─⫫─ Regimental Boundary
▨ Ground Gained Sept. 28

and Argonne regions with units of the French Army, moved into the Vauxaillon area on September 15 as part of the French 59th Division. Four of its companies assisted French troops in unsuccessful attacks against Mont des Singes between September 17 and 20, and on the 24th the regiment as a unit took command of that part of the front line just north of the small village of Vauxaillon.

as far as Cessières. The losses in these operations were about 500 officers and men.

The French 59th Division was then relieved, only to reenter the battle near Grandlup-et-Fay on October 30, the American regiment being placed in support near Chantrud Farm, about a mile southwest of Grandlup-et-Fay. There, on November 3, it suffered a loss of 41 men from the explosion of a single shell.

The Germans made a general retirement in early November, and the 59th Division took part in the pursuit. Although spasmodic fighting occurred, the

leading the advance of the 59th Division.

At the time of the Armistice the forward battalion of the regiment was at Le Gué d'Hossus, having marched about 40 miles

French Tanks With the 32d Division at Juvigny, August 29, 1918

370th Infantry moved forward mainly in march formation. Battalions of the regiment alternated with French units in

during the last week of the war. There were 65 casualties in the regiment during the fighting which has just been described.

ADDITIONAL PLACES OF INTEREST IN THE
AISNE-MARNE REGION

IN addition to the places whose World War history has been described in the itinerary, there are a number of other places in the Aisne-Marne region where interesting war events occurred, where there now exist features of special interest, or which are of sufficient importance in pre-World War history to warrant special mention. For reference purposes and for the benefit of the tourist who travels in the area on roads other than the described route, these places with some of their history have been recorded here.

The map on the next page indicates the general location of the places mentioned. At those places indicated by a star there is some existing interesting object such as a memorial, ancient ruins or World War feature of an outstanding character in excellent state of preservation.

Arcis-le-Ponsart. 28th Div. Hdqrs. during the period Aug. 14–20.

Belle-Vue Farm, north of Cierges. Scene of heavy fighting by the 32d Division on both July 31 and August 1.

★ **Beugneux.** About halfway between Soissons and Château-Thierry, south of Beugneux, on the road to Wallée is located a large French monument to com-

memorate the Second Battle of the Marne. It consists of a statue near the road symbolizing France and a sculptured group on a hillside representing eight phantom spirits. The monument has a beautiful location and commands a fine view of the surrounding country.

Beuvardes. Location of 42d Div. Hdqrs., during the period July 28–Aug. 12.

★ **Blérancourt.** In a 17th Century château, which has been partially restored, is displayed in this town an interesting collection of paintings, engravings and other articles relating to the historical cooperation of America and France. The establishment, financed by Americans, is called the "Musée de Coopération Franco-Américain" and is one of the national museums of France. A visit, if in the neighborhood, is recommended.

Bois de Bourbetin; Bois de la Côte 192; Bois de la Roche. These woods near Vaux were the scenes of hard fighting by the Infantry Brigade of the 2d Division. On June 6 the division captured the Bois de Bourbetin and the Bois de la Côte 192 in spite of heavy hostile fire, and then defeated an enemy counterattack close to the last-named wood. The positions

Museum at Blérancourt

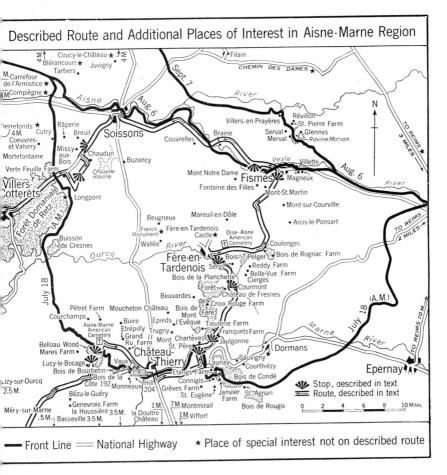

Described Route and Additional Places of Interest in Aisne-Marne Region

— Front Line   === National Highway   ★ Place of special interest not on described route

were ordered evacuated that night. In the late afternoon of July 1 an attack was launched on Vaux and the near-by Bois de la Roche. During the course of this attack the Bois de Bourbetin and the Bois de la Côte 192 were taken. All objectives were gained within two hours and many machine guns were captured. A German counterattack early in the morning of July 2 was repulsed with heavy losses. In all, over 400 prisoners and much matériel were captured.

Bois Pelger; Bois de la Planchette. These adjoining woods northeast of Sergy were strongly held by the Germans after their retreat to the Ourcq River. The 32d and 42d Divisions, and elements of the 4th attached to the latter, were heavily engaged in the vicinity of these woods from July 29 to August 1. The woods were finally captured by the 32d Division during August 2.

Bois de Rognac Farm, one mile southeast of Coulonges. III Corps Hdqrs., Aug. 8–19, while directing operations on the Vesle. 28th Div. Hdqrs. during the period Aug. 20–Sept. 5.

Breuil. This village was captured in severe fighting early on July 18 by the combined efforts of the 1st Division and the adjoining French troops.

Buire. I Corps Hdqrs., July 22–28, during part of the time that its troops were moving forward to the Ourcq River.

Buisson de Cresnes. This wood was captured on the morning of July 18 by units of the 4th Division which were serving with the French 33d Division.

Buzancy. Near this town the Soissons–Château-Thierry highway was cut by the 1st Division on July 21 and hostile counter-attacks were repulsed in heavy fighting. At the château near the village several hundred prisoners were captured. A small 1st Division monument is located alongside the main highway.

★ **Carrefour de l'Armistice.** The place in the Forêt de Compiègne where the Armistice was signed is now marked by several interesting monuments. Marshal Foch's headquarters car is housed there in a building donated by an American.

Château de Fresnes, west of Courmont. III Corps Hdqrs., Aug. 19–Sept. 6.

Chazelle Ravine, east of Chaudun. Scene of bitter fighting by the 1st Division during its attack on July 19.

★ **Chemin des Dames.** The terrain in the vicinity of this road was fought over by the French and Germans many times during the war. A number of French war monuments are to be seen alongside it.

Coeuvres-et-Valsery. 1st Div. Hdqr during the period from July 18 to 2

★ **Compiègne.** This city was occupie for a short time in 1914 by the Germa and the Armistice was signed near i Joan of Arc was captured at Compièg in 1430 by the Burgundians, who sold h to the English. The city contains a fir historic château which is open to visitor

★ **Coucy-le-Château.** Location of i teresting ruins of a large ancient castl partly destroyed by Germans during th war. The massive concrete emplacemer of a large German railroad gun is still t be seen a short distance across the track from the railroad station.

Courthiézy and **Sauvigny.** Front-lir positions on the south bank of the Marn River near these villages were held b elements of the 3d Division from June 3 t 8 and by units of the 28th Division fro July 9 to 15. The 28th Division unit due to the retirement of the French o their flanks, were surrounded and nearl annihilated in the German attack July 15. (See sketch on page 65.)

Couvrelles, about 2 miles west Braine. Location of 26th Div. Hdqr

Marshal Foch's Train Arriving at Compiègne
The Armistice was signed in the car in the foreground

Ruins of Old Castle at Coucy-le-Château

for a six weeks' period in February and March, 1918, while the division received front-line training with troops of the French XI Corps then occupying the Chemin des Dames Sector. At various times during this period elements of the 26th Division held portions of the corps front which extended to the westward from Filain for about 11 miles.

Croix Rouge Farm. The 26th Division, whose front line at the time was composed entirely of troops of the 56th Brigade, 28th Division, attached to it, was held up near this farm on July 24 by heavy resistance in the Forêt de Fère. The farm was captured two days later, after severe hand-to-hand fighting by the 42d Division which had relieved the 26th.

★ **Dormans.** An interesting World War memorial church has been constructed on the hill in rear of this town.

★ **Fère-en-Tardenois Castle.** An interesting medieval castle built about 1200 A.D. is located about 1½ miles northeast of Fère-en-Tardenois, close to the road to Fismes. The 77th Div. Hdqrs. was located in the adjoining château for the period from August 13 to September 4.

Fontaine des Filles, west of Mont-St.

Martin. In a cave north of this point was located the 77th Div. Hdqrs. from September 4 to September 16.

Franquets Farm, about ½ mile north of Jaulgonne. Scene of heavy fighting by the 3d Division on July 22 and 23. The farm was finally captured on July 24.

Genevrois Farm, near Bézu-le-Guéry. 2d Div. Hdqrs., June 10–July 10. 26th Div. Hdqrs., July 10–15, and on July 20.

Glennes. On the plateau south of this village the 28th Division engaged in severe fighting on September 6, capturing four enemy strong points and holding them against a counterattack.

Grand Ru Farm, southeast of Etrépilly. 26th Div. Hdqrs., July 21–30.

Grèves Farm, 1½ miles west of St. Eugène. On July 15 a battalion of the 3d Division advanced from near this farm to counterattack the advancing Germans. It was heavily shelled by hostile artillery and suffered severe losses.

Close to this farm First Lieutenant George P. Hays, Field Artillery, 3d Division, rendered the gallant services for which he was awarded the Congressional Medal of Honor. At the outset of the terrific enemy artillery bombardment on

German Troops Advancing Across the Chemin des Dames, May 1918

the night of July 14–15, his telephone line was destroyed beyond repair. He immediately set out to establish contact with the neighboring command post and while so doing established liaison with two French batteries, visiting their positions so frequently that he was mainly responsible for the accurate fire therefrom. While thus engaged he was severely wounded. His deeds were an important factor in checking the advance of the enemy troops on this front.

During the same battle and also near this farm, Second Lieutenant Jay F. Hostetter, Field Artillery, 3d Division, having discovered that two French guns on his left had lost their crews during the heavy German bombardment, requested and obtained permission to use them. Securing eight volunteers from his ranks, he pressed the guns into action, and for several hours poured an effective fire into the advancing enemy. For this action he and the eight men were awarded Distinguished Service Crosses.

Janvier Farm, about ½ mile east of Connigis. Near this farm a battery of the 3d Division on July 15 fired at point-blank range against German infantry until its ammunition was exhausted. The guns were then disabled and the gunners retired to the infantry lines.

La Doultre Château, near Viffort. 3d Div. Hdqrs., June 11–July 22.

La Houssière, east of Bassevelle. 28th Div. Hdqrs., July 15–18.

Launay. In the vicinity of this village and Etangs Farm troops of the 3d Division on the afternoon of July 15 repulsed a strong German attack.

Lizy-sur-Ourcq. 4th Div. Headquarters during the period from July 5 to 23.

Large German Gun Emplacement at Coucy-le-Château in 1934

(98)

German Batteries in Position Near the Marne River, June 1918. © G

★ **Longpont.** In this town are the ruins of a large Cistercian abbey, said to have been built in the 12th Century.

Magneux. Near this place on August 16 and 25, the 28th Division launched attacks to advance its lines closer to the Vesle River. These attacks resulted in heavy fighting although no permanent gains of ground were made.

Mares Farm. About noon on June 2 a marine battalion of the 2d Division hurried into a second-line position at this farm, which is about 2 miles northwest of Lucy-le-Bocage. Late the next day, the Germans pushed through the French troops and reached the farm where their advance was stopped by the American battalion after a severe fight.

Mareuil-en-Dôle. 4th Div. Hdqrs., Aug. 4–12, and 77th Div. Hdqrs., Aug. 12–13. The town was captured by the 42d Division on August 2 after a battle with German machine gun units but was voluntarily abandoned the same day. It was reoccupied on August 3 by the 4th Division, which had relieved the 42d.

Merval and **Serval** were occupied on September 5 by the 77th Division while it was moving its front line forward from the Vesle toward the Aisne River.

Méry-sur-Marne. 26th Div. Hdqrs. during the period July 15–20.

Missy-aux-Bois. During the fighting in the ravine north of Missy-aux-Bois a gap had developed between the American 1st Division and the French division on its left, thus exposing the left of the 1st Division to terrific fire from several German machine guns located in a rock quarry. Second Lieutenant Samuel I. Parker, 1st Division, observing this serious situation, ordered his depleted platoon

Artillery of I Corps on the March Near Vaux, July 1918

8-Inch Austrian Howitzer Captured by the 26th Division at Epieds, July 24, 1918

to follow him in an attack upon the strong point. Meeting a disorganized group of French soldiers wandering about in the ravine, he pursuaded them to join his platoon. This consolidated group followed Lieutenant Parker through direct enemy rifle and machine-gun fire to the crest above the ravine and, rushing forward, took the quarry by storm, capturing six machine guns and about 40 prisoners. Lieutenant Parker remained in the combat the following day and, although painfully wounded, led the battalion he then commanded to its objective. For this example of conspicuous gallantry and spirit of self-sacrifice he was later awarded the Congressional Medal of Honor.

Monneaux, on the western slope of Hill 204. This town was captured on June 6 by elements of the 3d Division serving with the French 10th Colonial Division.

Montmirail. The non-motorized units of the 3d Division detrained at this town early in June when the division was hurrying forward to enter the battle near Château-Thierry. Near Montmirail important battles were fought by Napoleon on February 11 and 14, 1814.

Mont Notre Dame. The large church located here replaces one destroyed by the Germans and stands on a site occupied by historic churches since the 9th Century.

Mont-St. Martin. On August 3 this village was occupied by the 32d Division after a sharp fight in the vicinity with German machine gun units.

Mont-sur-Courville. 28th Div. Hdqrs. during the period Sept. 5–9.

Mortefontaine. 1st Div. Hdqrs., just before the offensive of July 18. III Corps Hdqrs., July 24–30, prior to its assuming active direction of operations. The 1st Division assembled in the vicinity of this village before it started its attack early on the morning of July 18.

German Gun Firing Near Reims, June 1917. © G

Americans Marching to Attack Near Beuvardes, July 24, 1918
The men are in gas masks, the road having recently been gassed by the Germans

Moucheton Château, north of Epieds. I Corps Hdqrs., from July 28 to Aug. 5.

Pétret Farm, 1 mile east of Courchamps. A battalion of the 4th Division attached to the French 164th Division captured this farm and the near-by wood during the day of July 20.

★ **Pierrefonds Château.** This magnificent castle is a fine example of French medieval military architecture. Originally built in 1390, the castle was restored in 1862. During the war, while used as a hospital, it was shelled several times.

Râperie, about 1 mile east of Cutry. In the vicinity of this mill, the 1st Division had a short but bitter fight early on the morning of July 18. During this engagement, Private First Class Daniel R. Edwards, 1st Division, who had been under treatment for several weeks for numerous and serious wounds and was suffering intense pain from a freshly shattered arm, crawled alone into an occupied German trench. He killed four men and captured four more. While conducting them to the rear a shell completely shattered one of Private Edwards' legs but he continued to the rear, forcing one of the prisoners to carry him. The bravery of Private Edwards, then a tradition in his battalion because of his previous gallant acts, again raised the morale of his comrades to a high pitch. For his exceptional bravery during this fighting, Private Edwards was later awarded the Congressional Medal of Honor.

Ravine Marion, southwest of Glennes. Scene of sharp fighting by the 77th Division on September 8, 9 and 14.

Reddy Farm, northeast of Cierges. The vicinity of this farm was the scene of heavy fighting by the 32d Division on August 1. It was captured by that division during August 2 after a sharp fight.

The Repairing of Roads Was a Problem
for the Engineers

Troops of the 2d Division En Route to a Rest Camp During a
Temporary Relief from the Front Line, June 17, 1918

★ **Reims,** one of the historic cities of France, was badly damaged by German bombardments during the war. Objects of interest in it are its Roman ruins and the world-famous cathedral where many of the kings of France were crowned. A visit to one of the vast champagne cellars at Reims will prove interesting.

St. Agnan. In the near-by Bois de Rougis and Bois de Condé, the 55th Brigade of the 28th Division assisted the French in checking the German July 15 offensive. It sustained heavy losses in two counterattacks launched by it from the Bois de Rougis on July 16. (See the sketch which appears on page 65.)

St. Pierre Farm, southwest of Révillon. Intense local fighting by the 77th Division occurred near this place on September 8, 9 and 14. On the latter date positions near the farm changed hands as many as three times before they finally remained in the possession of the Americans.

Tartiers. 32d Div. Headquarters during the period Aug. 27–Sept. 6.

Tieulerie Farm and the near-by Bois de Mont l'Evêque, about 1½ miles north of Chartèves. This farm and wood were the scenes of bitter fighting on July 22 and 23 by the 3d Division. They were both finally captured on the latter date.

Trugny and **Epieds.** The 26th Division engaged in severe fighting for the possession of these two villages, which were part of a strong German defensive position. In four different attacks made during July 22 and 23 the towns changed hands a number of times.

Verte-Feuille Farm. Southwest of Soissons, on the main road to Villers-Cotterêts, about 1 mile northeast of Verte-Feuille Farm is located a French monument "TO THE GLORY OF THE FRENCH AND ALLIED SOLDIERS WHO FOUGHT VICTORIOUSLY ON THIS PLATEAU FROM MAY 29 TO JULY 25, 1918." Among the many units listed are British divisions and the American 1st and 2d Divisions.

Villers-en-Prayères. Captured by the 77th Division on September 6.

Villette. The 6th Brigade of the 3d Division held the front line northwest of the village of Villette near the Vesle River from August 6 to 11 and during this period made two determined attempts to establish a bridgehead north of the river.

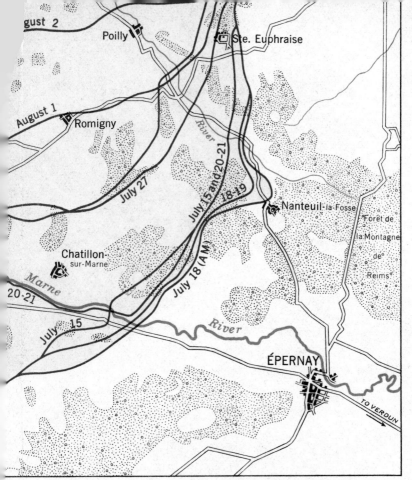

ENGINEER REPRODUCTION PLANT, U. S. ARMY, FORT HUMPHREYS, D. C. 12703
1937

Colored areas except as otherwise indicated show ground gained by
American units in the Aisne-Marne Offensive July 18–August 6

Ground gained by American units June 4–July 17

Ground gained by American units in the Oise-Aisne
Offensive August 18–October 12

Ground gained by French divisions July 18–October 12

Large circled numeral in a colored area indicates the
American division which fought there

Small circled numeral indicates part of American division
which fought attached to another division

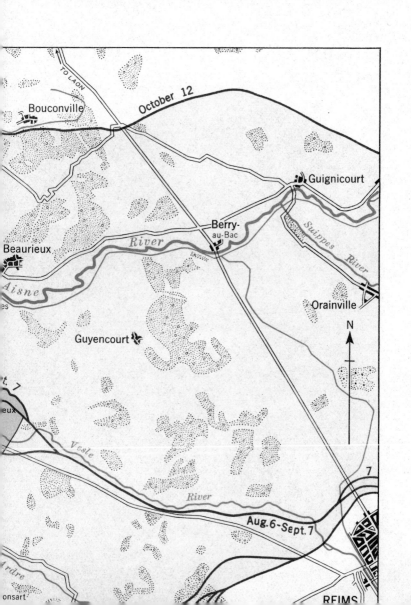

TO LAON

Bouconville

October 12

Guignicourt

Berry-
au-Bac

River

Beaurieux

Suippes

River

Aisne

es

Orainville

N

Guyencourt

t. 7

eux

Vesle

7

River

Aug. 6-Sept. 7

rdre

onsart

REIMS

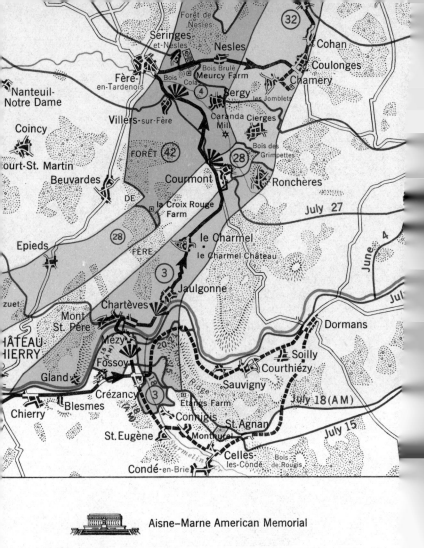

Nanteuil-
Notre Dame

Coincy

ourt-St. Martin

Beuvardes

Epieds

zuet

Mont
St. Père

HÂTEAU
HIERRY

Gland

Chierry

Séringes-
et-Nesles

Fère-
en-Tardenois

Villers-sur-Fère

FORÊT ㊷

Courmont

DE

la Croix Rouge
Farm

FÈRE

Chartèves

Mézy

Fossoy

Crézancy

Blesmes

St. Eugène

Condé-en-Brie

Forêt de
Nesles

Nesles

Bois Brûlé

Bois Cola

Meurcy Farm

Bois

㋪

Bergy
les Jomblets

Caranda
Mill

Cierges

Bois des
Grimpettes

㋘

Roncheres

le Charmel

le Charmel Château

Jaulgonne

Soilly

Courthiézy

Sauvigny

Étangs Farm

Connigis

Monthurel

St. Agnan

Celles-
les-Condé

Bois
de Rougis

Cohan

Coulonges

Chamery

㉜

㋞

㊷

July 27

㋓

Dormans

July 18 (AM)

July 15

June 4

Jul

Jul

Scale $\frac{1}{200000}$

0   5   10 Miles

0   5   10 Kilometers

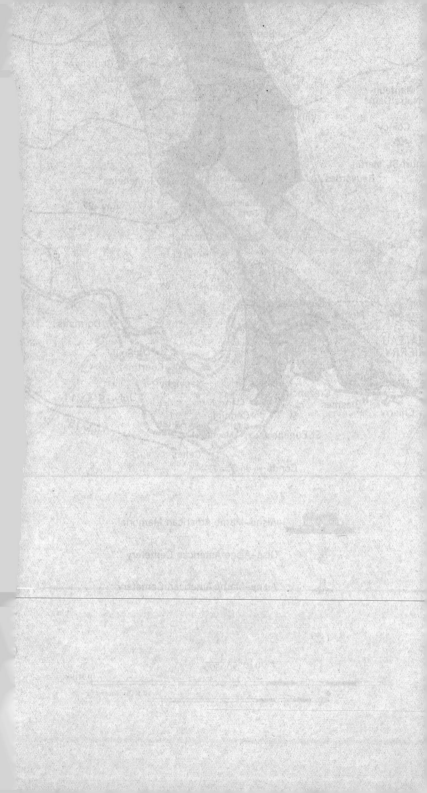

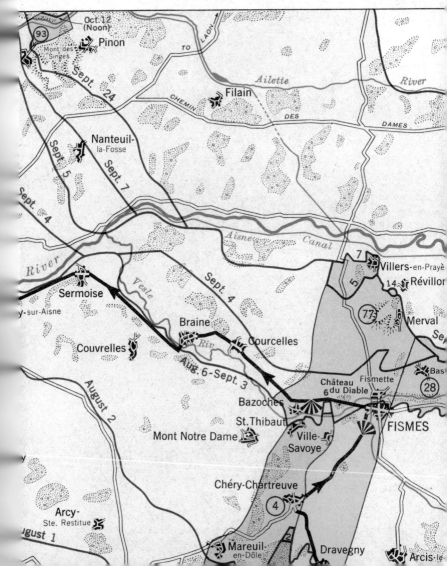

Oct. 12
(Noon)
93
Mont des
Singes
Pinon
TO LAON
Sept. 24
Ailette
River
CHEMIN
Filain
DES
DAMES
Sept. 5
Nanteuil-
la-Fosse
Sept. 7
Sept. 4
Aisne
Canal
River
7
Villers-en-Prayè
5
14
Révillor
Sermoise
Vesle
77
Sept. 4
Merval
y-sur-Aisne
Braine
Se
Couvrelles
Riv
Courcelles
Aug. 6-Sept. 3
Bas
Château
Fismette
6 du Diable
28
Bazoches
St. Thibaut
FISMES
Mont Notre Dame
Ville-
Savoye
August 2
Chéry-Chartreuve
4
Arcy-
Ste. Restitue
August 1
Mareuil-
en-Dôle
2
Dravegny
Arcis-le

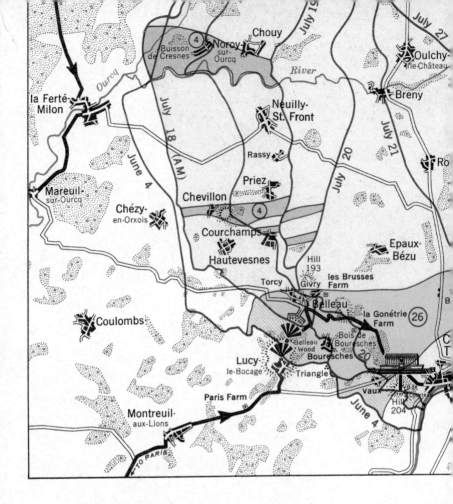

Route, described in text

- - - - - - - Side trip

Stop, described in text

Highway

Front line for date shown

All front lines are as of midnight for dates shown unless otherwise
noted; thus July 18 on a line indicates the line held at midnight
July 18/19.   The dates July 21–22 on a line indicate
that the line was located at the same place at midnight of both
July 21 and July 22

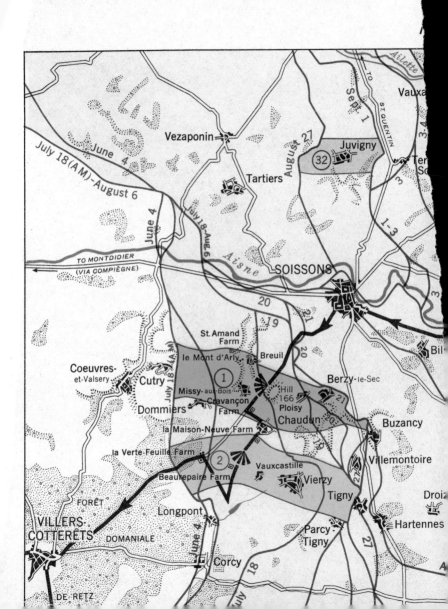

VILLERS-COTTERÊTS

FORÊT

DOMANIALE

DE RETZ

Coeuvres-et-Valsery

Cutry

Dommiers

la Verte-Feuille Farm

Beaurepaire Farm

Longpont

Corcy

June 4

July 18

July 18(AM)-August 6

July 18-Aug.6

TO MONTDIDIER
(VIA COMPIÈGNE)

June 4

Vezaponin

Tartiers

August 27

Sept. 1

Juvigny

(32)

Aisne

SOISSONS

20

19

21

20

St. Amand Farm

le Mont d'Arly

Breuil

Missy-aux-Bois

Cravançon Farm

(1)

Hill 166

Ploisy

Chaudun

Berzy-le-Sec

21

la Maison-Neuve Farm

Vauxcastille

(2)

Vierzy

Buzancy

Villemontoire

Tigny

Parcy-Tigny

Hartennes

27

Bil

Ter Sc

Vauxa

Ailette

TO ST. QUENTIN

3-4

3

1-3

3

Droi

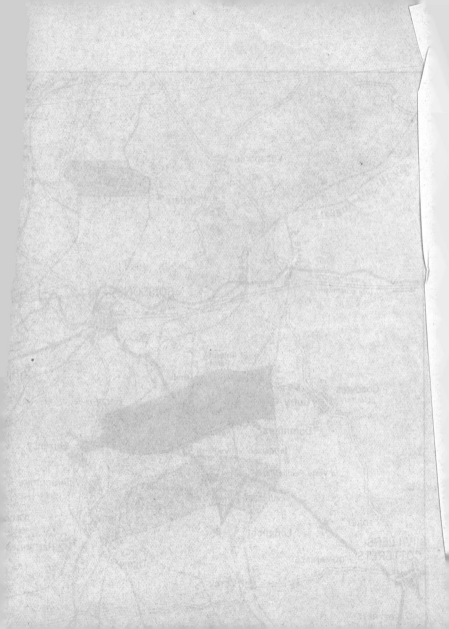

Name of Div.	Period of Service 1918	Character of Service	Location of Service General vicinity of—	Army to Which Attached [1]	Corps to Which Attached [1]	Casualties [2]
1	July 18–22	Battle	Missy - aux - Bois and Berzy-le-Sec.	Tentn	XX	6,870
2	June 2–5	Battle	Lucy-le-Bocage	Sixth	XXI	546
	June 6–July 10	Sector	Belleau Wood and Vaux.	Sixth	XXI until June 21, then III until July 4, then Am. I.	7,225 (363)
	July 18–20	Battle	La Verte-Feuille Farm and Vierzy.	Tenth	XX	4,319
3	May 31–June 5	Battle	Château-Thierry and along the Marne River to Courthiézy.	Sixth	XXXVIII	65
	June 6–July 14	Sector	Château-Thierry and along the Marne River to Courthiézy.	Sixth	XXXVIII	432
	July 15–30	Battle	Mézy and Ronchères	Sixth until July 17, then Ninth until July 20, then Sixth.	XXXVIII	5,964 (92)
(6th Brig. only)	Aug. 6	Battle	Vesle River east of Fismes.	Sixth	Am. III	32
(6th Brig. only)	Aug. 7–11	Sector	Vesle River east of Fismes.	Sixth	Am. III	574 (2)
4	July 18–21	Battle	Noroy-sur-Ourcq and Chevillon.	Sixth	II and VII	2,100
	Aug. 3–6	Battle	Mareuil-en-Dôle and St. Thibaut.	Sixth	Am. I	1,625 (33)
	Aug. 7–12	Sector	St. Thibaut	Sixth	Am. I	1,761 (59)
26	Feb. 6–Mar. 19	Training in Line	Chemin des Dames	Sixth	XI	404
	July 10–14	Sector	Belleau Wood	Sixth	Am. I	213
	July 15–25	Battle	Belleau and Epieds	Sixth	Am. I	4,644 (149)
28	July 1–14	Training in Line	Château-Thierry and along the Marne River to Courthiézy.	Sixth	XXXVIII and III	178
	July 15–18	Battle	Château-Thierry and along the Marne River to Courthiézy.	Sixth until July 17, then Ninth.	III and XXXVIII	1,233
	July 28–31	Battle	Bois des Grimpettes	Sixth	XXXVIII	1,416
	Aug. 7–17	Sector	Fismes	Sixth	Am. III	1,899 (124)
	Aug. 18–Sept. 8	Battle	Baslieux	Sixth	Am. III	3,277 (25)
32	July 30–Aug. 6	Battle	Cierges and Fismes	Sixth	XXXVIII until Aug. 4, then Am. III.	3,662 (49)

See footnotes on page 104.

Name of Div.	Period of Service 1918	Character of Service	Location of Service General vicinity of—	Army to Which Attached[1]	Corps to Which Attached[1]	Casualties[2]
	Aug. 7	Sector	Fismes	Sixth	Am. III	42
	Aug. 28–Sept. 2	Battle	Juvigny	Tenth	XXX	2,633 (13)
42	July 25–Aug. 3	Battle	Sergy and Seringes-et-Nesles.	Sixth	Am. I	5,476 (975)
77	Aug. 12–17	Sector	St. Thibaut	Sixth	Am. I until Aug. 13, then Am. III.	1,407 (135)
	Aug. 18–Sept. 16.	Battle	Bazoches, Merval and Villers-en-Prayères.	Sixth until Sept. 8, then Fifth.	Am. III until Sept. 9, then XVI.	3,200 (13)
93 (370th Inf. only)	Sept. 17–Oct. 12.	Battle	Northeast of Vauxaillon.	Tenth	XXX until Oct. 6, then XVI.	504
(370th Inf. only)	Nov. 5–11	Battle	Northeast of Laon and Rocroi.	Third	XVIII until Nov. 10, then XVI.	65

[1] All armies and corps are French unless otherwise indicated. In this table Am. = American.

[2] Casualties are for period in line only. Figures in parentheses give casualties for units temporarily attached. Add figure in parentheses to the one above in order to obtain the total casualties during entire operation.

32d Division Troops Resting Near Mont-St. Martin, August 6, 1918

Chapter III

AMERICAN OPERATIONS IN THE ST. MIHIEL REGION

THE St. Mihiel offensive, which began on September 12, 1918, was the first operation in the World War carried out by a complete American army under the separate and independent control of the American Commander-in-Chief.

The plan to develop an army near St. Mihiel when sufficient troops were avail-

of the American Headquarters in France. This plan was constantly kept in mind by the American High Command and beginning in January 1918 the battle front near St. Mihiel was used to give front-line experience to American divisions and to acquaint them with the region in which they would later attack.

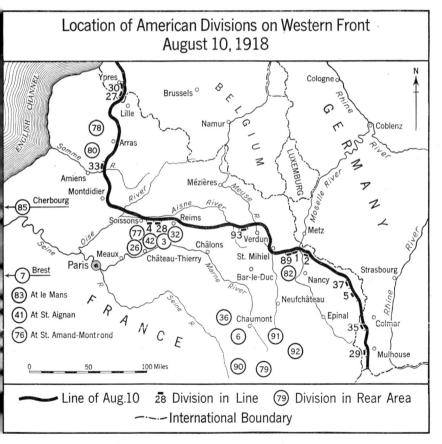

Location of American Divisions on Western Front
August 10, 1918

━━ Line of Aug.10 (28) Division in Line (79) Division in Rear Area
—·—·— International Boundary

able, and to reduce the salient there as a preliminary to a more decisive operation in the same vicinity, was proposed by General Pershing and was agreed to by General Pétain at the first conference between them shortly after the arrival

The succession of German drives in the spring of 1918 made it necessary to postpone the original plan, as all available troops were urgently needed at other places on the front. Consequently, although there were more than 1,200,000 American

Wartime View From Top of Montsec
Arrows indicate successive barriers of wire

soldiers in France in July, the American combat units were widely distributed along the entire front, either serving in line with the French and British Armies or undergoing training in rear areas.

When the reduction of the Aisne-Marne salient was assured General Pershing pointed out to the Allied Commander-in-Chief that the improved situation made possible the concentration of American units, and insisted that the formation of an American army be resumed. Although the French but more especially the British urged that American units be left with their forces, an understanding was reached that most of these units should soon be assembled into an independent army in the neighborhood of St. Mihiel.

The American First Army Headquarters began to function on August 10 and on that day started vigorous preparations for the reduction of the St. Mihiel salient. The assembling of units commenced soon thereafter and on August 30 the First Army took command of the battle front from Port-sur-Seille, 5 miles east of the Moselle, to Watronville, 7 miles southeast of Verdun.

The St. Mihiel salient was shaped roughly like a triangle with its points near Pont-à-Mousson, St. Mihiel and Verdun. It was 25 miles wide at its base, extended 16 miles into the Allied lines and had remained almost un-

changed in shape for four years. Its western face ran diagonally across the wooded heights east of the Meuse River, and its southern face extended from St. Mihiel to the Moselle River, traversing the Heights of the Meuse, the Heights of the Môselle and the intervening Woëvre Plain. This plain is cut by small streams and dotted with woods of varying size. It is comparatively low ground containing many large ponds and swampy areas, thus making cross-country travel difficult especially in wet weather.

Within the German lines at the south face of the salient were the high isolated hills of Loupmont and Montsec. These were not only strong natural defensive positions but in addition afforded the enemy excellent observation of much of the ground behind the Allied lines.

Two strong German positions had been prepared in front of the one across the base of the salient, and all had been strengthened by elaborate systems of trenches, barbed-wire entanglements, concrete shelters and machine-gun emplacements. The salient was therefore a veritable field fortress against which the French in the preceding years had made a number of unsuccessful attacks.

The value of the salient to Germany lay in the fact that it protected the strategic centers of Metz and the Briey iron basin; interrupted traffic on the main

Paris–Nancy railroad; cut the Verdun–Toul railroad; and threatened the Allied territory in its vicinity, especially west of the Meuse. Its reduction was imperative before any great Allied offensive could be launched against the Briey and Metz region or northward, between the Meuse River and Argonne Forest, toward the general area around Sedan.

The preparations for the attack against the salient were well along when, on August 30, the Allied Commander-in-Chief suggested to General Pershing that the offensive be reduced greatly in scope, that most of the American divisions be used for an attack about September 15 between Verdun and Reims and that in the new attack some of the American divisions be assigned to operate under certain of the higher French commands.

General Pershing felt that the St. Mihiel offensive should be carried out as planned and definitely stated that the American divisions would fight in the future only as part of an independent American army. After a series of conferences with Marshal Foch it was finally agreed, on September 2, that the St. Mihiel attack would be carried out, but that its objectives would be strictly limited so that the American Army could undertake another major offensive about ten days later on the front between the Meuse River and the Argonne Forest.

This agreement put a great burden upon the American First Army as under it the Army was called upon to carry to a conclusion the important offensive at St. Mihiel which was scheduled to start on September 12, to concentrate an enor-

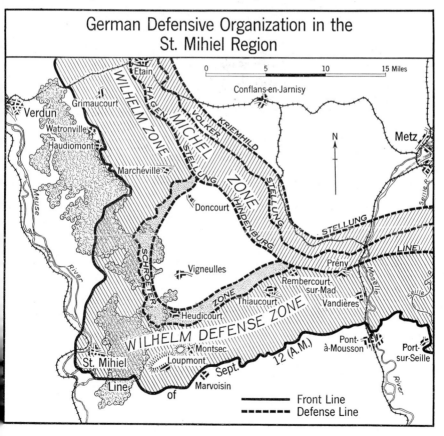

German Defensive Organization in the St. Mihiel Region

Reserves Moving Forward During the St. Mihiel Offensive

mous force on the Meuse-Argonne front, and to initiate a still greater operation there, all within the brief space of two weeks. In other words, at the time the agreement with the Allied Commander in-Chief was made the American Army undertook the mission of launching within the next 23 days two great offensives on battlefields 40 miles apart. Never before on the Western Front had a single army attempted such a colossal task,

I Corps, extending from Port-sur-Seille westward, had the 82d, 90th, 5th and 2d Divisions in line from right to left, and the 78th in reserve. The IV Corps continued the line to the west as far as Marvoisin, with the 89th, 42d and 1st Divisions in line, and the 3d in reserve.

The American V Corps, composed of the 26th Division, the French 15th Colonial Division and part of the 4th Division, in line from right to left, and

Plan of Attack of First Army, September 12, 1918

| Jump-off Line Sept. 12 (A.M.) | Front Line Actually Reached |
| —xxxx— Army Boundary | —xxx— Corps Boundary |

Numerals indicate divisions   Arrows indicate direction and weight of attacks

and its successful accomplishment reflects great credit on all those concerned.

The final plans for the St. Mihiel operation provided for a main drive against the southern face of the salient, a secondary blow against the western face, and holding attacks and raids against the tip. The American I and IV Corps were designated to deliver the main attack. The

the remainder of the 4th in reserve, was to make the secondary attack on and from that part of the Heights of the Meuse to the south of Haudiomont.

The French II Colonial Corps, composed of three French divisions, each occupying large sectors of the front line around the tip of the salient, was to support the left of the main attack and the

Road Near Sanzey Just Before the
St. Mihiel Offensive

Note its muddy, torn-up condition typical of
most roads in the region at that time

More than 550,000 Americans and about 110,000 French were involved in the offensive. The air force concentrated for it, 1,481 airplanes, was the largest ever brought together up to that time and consisted chiefly of French and British planes. The Army had about 400 French tanks available of which 350 were light ones and 144 were manned by Americans. About 3,000 pieces of artillery were used and approximately 3,300,000 rounds of artillery ammunition were brought into the area in preparation for the offensive.

The secret movement of such a large number of troops to the battle front and the many details involved in planning the operation and in providing the necessary special troops put a tremendous strain upon the Army Staff which it successfully met. Finally, after weeks of effort, on the night of September 11–12 all preparations had been completed, and the First Army was in position ready for battle.

Opposing it, holding the salient, was an enemy force known as Army Detachment "C". It was composed of 8 divisions and 2 brigades in line and 5 divisions which were held in the rear areas in reserve.

The Germans suspected that an attack was being prepared but believed that it would not take place until late in September. In anticipation of this attack, and to shorten their front line because their reserves on the Western Front were being depleted, the German High Command issued orders on September 11 for a gradual withdrawal from the salient and the destruction of all things of military value which could not be moved. The execution of this order, however, had

right of the secondary attack and to hold the enemy at the apex of the salient while the other attacks were being made.

Of the three American corps and the nine American divisions which took part in the attack two of the corps and four of the divisions had never before been engaged at the front in offensive combat.

The First Army had the 35th, 80th and 91st Divisions in reserve for use in case of necessity. The Army's needs for additional aviation, artillery and tanks, to round out the normal proportions of these arms in the higher units, were largely met by the French and British.

Wrecked Bridge at Flirey

Note double line of traffic, continuous for three days after the attack of September 12, 1918

German 21-Centimeter Mortar Battery Firing on Western Front, October 1918. © G

not begun when the American attack burst upon the defenders of the salient.

The bombardment of the hostile positions began at 1:00 a.m. on September 12 and was so intense and overpowering that the German guns could not make effective reply. At 5:00 a.m. the infantry of the main attack jumped off. Despite the lack of tanks, only a few of which came up in time to assist the troops through the wire entanglements, the entire advance proceeded according to schedule.

The plan provided that the greatest initial penetration should be made by the IV Corps and the left of the I Corps, the objectives for September 12 requiring a 5-mile advance. In its execution the 1st Division, on the left flank of the main attack, captured Nonsard and entered the woods to the north; the 42d Division pushed on beyond the towns of Essey and Pannes; while the 89th seized Bouillon-ville. In the I Corps, the 2d Division captured Thiaucourt, and the 5th drove through Viéville-en-Haye, with its eastern flank bent back to connect with the 90th Division, which was at the pivot of the main attack on the first day.

On the western face of the salient the artillery preparation was continued until 8:00 a.m., when the infantry of the V Corps launched its assault. By nightfall the corps had advanced about 2 miles.

While the attacks on the two faces were progressing reports indicated that the Germans were retiring from that part of the salient in front of the French troops, although raids into the opposing lines made by the French near the town of St. Mihiel met with considerable opposition principally from machine gun units.

With the idea of cutting off the retreat of as many Germans as possible, General Pershing, early on the evening of the 12th, directed that troops of the IV and V Corps be rushed with all speed to the vicinity of Vigneulles. Part of the 26th Division marched along a narrow forest road directly to the heart of the salient, and soon after 2:00 a.m. Vigneulles was in its possession. About dawn on the 13th it met patrols of the 1st Division just northeast of that town. This marked the closing of the salient and the German soldiers who had not retired beyond that vicinity were cut off and captured.

Practically all objectives had been gained by the evening of September 13,

American 75-Millimeter Gun Firing Toward Montsec From a Position Near Beaumont, September 12, 1918

(111)

Supplies Moving Forward and Prisoners Marching to the Rear at St. Baussant,
September 12, 1918

and the organization of the new position, roughly along the line joining Vandières and Haudiomont, was begun. Deep raids and local attacks were pushed, especially on the eastern part of the front of attack, until September 16, by which time the whole of the Bois des Rappes and much adjoining territory had been captured.

Although the new front was 21 miles shorter than the former battle line, by September 17 the enemy forces had been increased to 10 divisions and 2 brigades in line, and 10 other divisions in reserve, an actual increase of seven divisions during the period of the offensive. The First Army had placed the 78th Division in line during the same period and had withdrawn from the line the American 1st, 2d, 4th, 5th and French 26th Divisions.

The complete success of the American Army in its first offensive greatly stimulated the morale of the Allies and depressed that of the Germans. The American casualties were less than 9,000, yet

German Prisoners at Beaumont,
September 12, 1918

more than 15,000 prisoners and about 450 cannon had been captured, and over 200 square miles of territory, with its remaining French population, had been restored to France. The railroads in the vicinity of St. Mihiel had been freed for Allied use, the threat of the salient against the surrounding country had been removed and one of the most important obstacles to an advance toward the vital Briey–Metz region or Sedan had been overcome. American staffs had shown their ability to maneuver and control large masses, and the whole Army had developed added self-confidence and a sense of power which was to be of great value in helping it to surmount the difficult tasks ahead.

The battle was the first large Allied offensive of the year against a carefully prepared trench system, the previous Allied attacks of 1918 having been made against salients created by the Germans in their spring and summer offensives and which were only partially organized for defense. The clean-cut victory of the American Army at St. Mihiel indicated that no longer could any German positions on the Western Front be considered strong enough to be impregnable.

The ability displayed by the Americans in penetrating formidable wire entanglements so favorably impressed the French High Command that selected groups of officers and enlisted men were sent from neighboring French armies to view the strength of the obstacles through which the American soldiers had made their way. The French official comments at the time characterized the conduct of the American divisions in this battle as "magnificent".

Gas Alarm for an American Unit on Western Face of the St. Mihiel Salient,
April 30, 1918

The transfer of American units to the Meuse-Argonne region, their next great battlefield, was begun even before the completion of the St. Mihiel offensive, and by the 20th of September only the 26th, 42d, 78th, 89th, 90th and four French divisions were left to serve on this front.

These divisions, and those which entered the line from time to time as relieving units, continued to strengthen the positions and to conduct local attacks to secure points of vantage. Artillery bombardments by both sides were of frequent occurrence. On October 12 Major General Robert L. Bullard, the Commanding General of the newly organized American Second Army, took command of the front between Fresnes-en-Woëvre and Port-sur-Seille, then held by the 7th, 37th, 79th, 92d and two French divisions. The 28th American Division was in Army reserve.

At that time the First Army offensive in the Meuse-Argonne region had been in

Lieutenant General Robert L. Bullard
Commanding General of the
Second Army from October 12, 1918,
to April 15, 1919

progress for more than two weeks, and the situation there demanded that every American division be used to the limit of its endurance. The Second Army, therefore, had for the time being the rôle of holding its front principally with tired divisions while they rested and prepared for another tour of duty in the Meuse-Argonne fighting. Active patrolling and raiding were continued, however, and the artillery carefully registered on targets in anticipation of a possible major offensive to be undertaken later.

Early in November it became evident that the Allied and American attacks, covering almost the entire front from the Meuse to the North Sea, were producing great disorganization within the German armies, and on November 5 the American Commander-in-Chief ordered the Second Army to begin advancing its lines in preparation for an offensive in the direction of Briey. The Army planned to

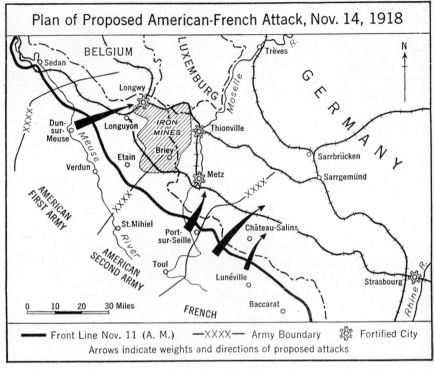

Plan of Proposed American-French Attack, Nov. 14, 1918

Front Line Nov. 11 (A. M.)   —XXXX— Army Boundary   🕸 Fortified City
Arrows indicate weights and directions of proposed attacks

launch these attacks on November 11 but on the evening of November 9 a message was transmitted from the Allied Commander-in-Chief which directed that vigorous pressure be applied immediately along the whole front.

The 7th, 28th, 33d and 92d Divisions, then on the Second Army front, began at once the attacks already planned. The scarcity of troops prohibited strong concentrations but in spite of this and of stubborn resistance encountered, the Army made a considerable advance, recovering a total of approximately 25 square miles of French territory.

In the meantime the Allied Commander-in-Chief had decided upon an offensive east of the Moselle River, and requested that six American divisions be designated to take part in it. General Pershing had long favored an attack in that direction and had planned to launch one there following the St. Mihiel offensive. He therefore selected the 3d, 4th, 28th, 29th, 35th and 36th Divisions for

the task, with the stipulation that these units should operate under the command of the American Second Army.

The plans prepared by the Second Army for its part in this offensive provided for a powerful drive in a northeasterly direction from the vicinity of Port-sur-Seille, east of the Moselle River. On its right flank a French army group was to attack at the same time and the American First Army from its location in the general vicinity of the Meuse River was to drive eastward in the direction of Longwy, as shown on the sketch at the top of this page.

The date for the commencement of this combined offensive, which without doubt would have produced far-reaching results, was fixed by the French High Command as November 14. The American divisions directed to take part on that section of the front east of the Moselle River were already in movement toward their new positions when the Armistice became effective on the morning of November 11.

THIS tour begins and ends at Verdun. It is 96.1 miles (154.6 kilometers) ong and can be completed in eight hours f care is taken not to spend too much ime at the interesting places. It is suggested that lunch be carried.

The data given on pages 520–521 will e helpful to those following this tour.

The narrative at the beginning of the hapter should be kept in mind and the nap facing page 164 consulted so that the operations which took place in this region will be more clearly understood.

The speedometer distances given on the ollowing pages are mainly for general reference purposes and, except for a few places at the beginning and near the end f the tour which are specifically noted in he road instructions, these distances re not essential in following this tour.

When following this itinerary, unless contrary road instructions are given, the tourist should continue straight ahead.

EN ROUTE VERDUN TO CÔTE DE SENOUX

Speedometer distance is measured from the Victory monument in Verdun.

(0 m 0 km) **At large World War monument near center of city (Monument à la Victoire et aux Soldats de Verdun), with the flight of steps up to the monument on the right-hand side of automobile, set speedometer at zero. Proceed straight ahead, at the second street turn left and cross the Meuse River.**

Beyond town, follow the road signs toward the city of Metz.

(6.1 m 9.8 km) At road fork 6.1 miles (9.8 kilometers) from starting point, bear

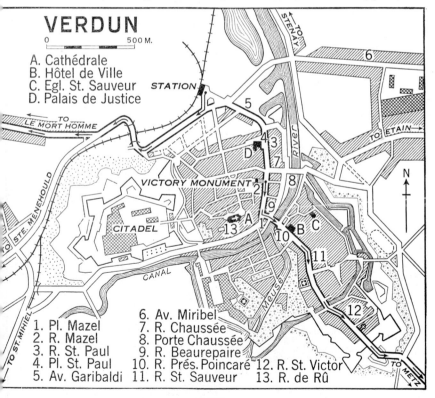

VERDUN

0   500 M.

A. Cathédrale
B. Hôtel de Ville
C. Egl. St. Sauveur   STATION
D. Palais de Justice

VICTORY MONUMENT

CITADEL

CANAL

1. Pl. Mazel
2. R. Mazel
3. R. St. Paul
4. Pl. St. Paul
5. Av. Garibaldi
6. Av. Miribel
7. R. Chaussée
8. Porte Chaussée
9. R. Beaurepaire
10. R. Prés. Poincaré
11. R. St. Sauveur
12. R. St. Victor
13. R. de Rû

) the right toward the village of Hatton-
hâtel. Note the speedometer reading.

The tour now goes on a narrow road
long the wooded Heights of the Meuse
River directly to Hattonchâtel.

This road is called the Grande Tranchée
e Calonne. It is said to have been built
y direction of M. de Calonne, Minister
f Finance under Louis XVI, as a means
f access to his château at Hattonchâtel.

During the war it was of great im-
ortance as an avenue of supply and
ommunication. Near it, concealed in
he trees, were hundreds of shacks, under-
round shelters, artillery emplacements,
emporary roads, narrow-gauge railway
racks and supply depots of all kinds.

In the periods of intensive fighting on
he front ahead this road was the scene
f great activity as motor trucks and
ther vehicles moved thousands of tons
f ammunition, supplies and equipment
o the front lines, and innumerable men
sed it in going to and returning from
attle. This activity was carried on
nainly at night and consequently during
he hours of darkness the road was
acked with continuous streams of traffic
noving in both directions.

On August 30, 1918, the American First
Army took command of the front which
ncluded the St. Mihiel salient. Its
rders for the offensive on September 12
rovided for a main attack by six divi-
ions against the southern face, a sec-
ndary drive by one American and one
rench division against the face in front
f here, and a holding attack by a French
orps around the tip of the salient. The
nain attack was to be made by the
American I and IV Corps at 5:00 a. m.
nd the secondary attack by the American
Corps at 8:00 a. m.

The V Corps at the time of the offensive
vas composed of the 4th and 26th Divi-
ions and a French division.

As an additional help in locating the stop-
ing point indicated in the next paragraph,
t should be noted that a small monument
o Lieutenant Robert Guillie, a French
fficer, is located on the crest immediately
receding, alongside the left of the road.

Changing the German Name of a Street
in Vigneulles From "Hindenburg Strasse"
to "Wilson, U. S. A."

(12.6 m 20.3 km) **At top of crest, 6.5
miles (10.5 kilometers) from road fork
where speedometer reading was noted,
STOP.**

This is the Côte de Senoux.

Face down the road, which at this point
runs approximately south.

The American 2d Division received its
first training in the battle line near here
during March, April and May of 1918.

The French front-line trenches which
ran through this point at right angles to
the road had been located here for nearly
four years when on September 8 the 26th
Division took command of this part of the
front. The German trenches were then
about 100 yards ahead, the intervening
ground being no man's land.

Only a faint idea can now be obtained
of the scene of appalling destruction
which existed here at that time. The
land was a grayish-white waste with but
little vegetation. Thick masses of barbed
wire and other debris covered the ground
and shattered and splintered trees dotted

Maneuvering a Balloon Near Haudainville

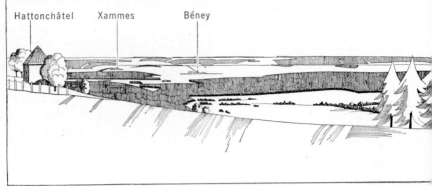

Hattonchâtel   Xammes   Béney

Panorama From St⸱

the landscape. Trenches furrowed the area in all directions and interlocking shell holes were everywhere.

Taking part in the great offensive of the First Army against the St. Mihiel salient, the 26th Division from its sector astride this road attacked at 8:00 a. m. on September 12, after a seven-hour artillery bombardment. In spite of considerable resistance and the difficult nature of the terrain, it had advanced by nightfall more than 2 miles along this road.

The main attack from the other side of the salient started at 5:00 a. m. and progressed so rapidly in this general direction that by afternoon the success of the entire offensive was assured. In order to reap the full benefits of the victory and to prevent the escape of German units still remaining in the salient, General Pershing early in the evening directed that the 26th Division rush troops to the vicinity of

Hattonchâtel, about 8 miles from thⁱ point, to meet the advanced elements ⸱ the American troops in the main attacⱪ

In compliance with this order a brigadᵉ of the division, reinforced by artillery anⱱ machine gun units, formed a column oⱱ this road some distance ahead, and shortlⱪ after dark boldly marched forward to aⱪ complish its mission. Although the Geⱳ mans were considerably disorganized bⱪ the American successes of that daⱪ nevertheless the night march was danⱻ gerous and difficult. After having capⱻ tured a considerable number of prisonerⱼ the brigade reached Hattonchâtel abouⱴ 2:00 a. m. and by daybreak had estabⱼ lished contact below that village witⱨ the troops of the main attack.

After leaving this point the tour noⱳ enters the area captured by the Ameriⱼ can First Army in its September 12 offenⱼ sive and goes to the heart of the salienⱴ

German Cavalry Regiment Deployed for Counterattack, September 1918. © G

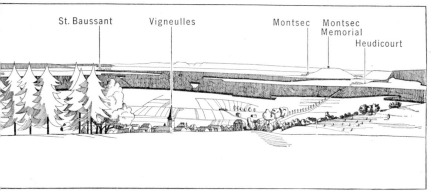

St. Baussant   Vigneulles   Montsec   Montsec Memorial   Heudicourt

Near Hattonchâtel

EN ROUTE CÔTE DE SENOUX
TO HATTONCHÂTEL

Note the speedometer reading.

(15.0 m 24.1 km) **2.4 miles (3.8 kilometers) farther on, near the kilometer post seen to the left of the road,** is the place from which the night march of the 26th Division began. During the advance small detachments were placed to guard each road and trail leading off to the right with the object of trapping the Germans who had not already retreated to the left across this road.

(20.6 m 33.1 km) **About 80 yards this side of next village, Hattonchâtel, STOP.**

Face the town of Hattonchâtel, which direction is approximately east.

This point is near the center of the St. Mihiel salient. When the troops of the 26th Division reached here during the night of September 12–13 they saw the Woëvre Plain below ablaze with burning buildings and supply dumps which the retreating Germans were destroying. The leading elements promptly moved down from these heights and occupied Vigneulles, the village seen to the right not far from the foot of this hill.

The isolated hill seen to the right in the distance, 7 miles away, is Montsec. The memorial on its summit was built by the United States Government to commemorate the St. Mihiel and other American operations in this part of France.

The main attack on September 12 was launched in this general direction by the American I and IV Corps from a line to the left of and beyond Montsec. The blow fell with crushing effect on the surprised defenders and the victorious troops on the first day swept forward approximately 5 miles. The Germans, realizing that they could not hold the salient in the face of this tremendous

American Narrow-Gauge Train Bringing Up Rations Near Ménil-la-Tour

Vigneulles Soon After Its Capture

advance, began quickly to withdraw and to destroy all supplies and other articles that could not be taken with them.

By dark on September 12 the 1st Division, the nearest flank unit of the main attack, was in the center of the large wood seen to the right front. Contact between these troops and the 26th Division was established about dawn on September 13, at the foot of these slopes, thus closing the salient.

On September 13 the rapid advance of the main attack continued and all divisions moved up to a line approximately straight ahead from this point. By nightfall practically all objectives of the offensive had been gained.

On that day the 26th Division moved into Viéville-sous-les-Côtes and Billy-sous-les-Côtes, the two villages to the left close in at the foot of this hill. It was at and near those towns that a composite squadron of the American 2d Cavalry reconnoitered on September 13. This is of interest as it is one of the few times that American cavalry was used as combat units during the war and gives a good indication of the extent of the breakthrough during the St. Mihiel attack.

The village to the left front, some dis-tance away, is Woël. On September 14 the troops of the First Army captured it and that night the front line of the Army was established just beyond Woël, running generally at right angles to the observer's line of vision when facing in the direction of that place.

One brigade of the American 4th Division was in line along the edge of the heights about 8 miles to the left of here, at the pivot of the attack on this face of the salient. On September 12 and 13 its activities were confined to reconnoitering but on September 14 it moved forward capturing considerable ground.

For several days after September 14 fighting took place at a number of points along the First Army front as the divisions repulsed counterattacks and made local attacks to determine definitely the new enemy line of resistance and to establish their own lines in the most advantageous positions. The area in which this fighting occurred is passed through toward the end of this tour.

At the far side of Hattonchâtel is a picturesque château to which visitors are admitted. It was restored soon after the war and from its grounds an excellent view of the surrounding country is obtained.

ROUTE HATTONCHÂTEL TO MONTSEC

(20.7 m 33.3 km) **Immediately after entering Hattonchâtel, turn sharply to the right and descend the hill.**

(21.9 m 35.2 km) **In the center of Vigneulles where road ends abruptly, turn to the right; then to the left.**
In Vigneulles the 26th Division captured a considerable number of prisoners, including a regimental band, and a great quantity of military supplies.

(22.3 m 35.8 km) **Beyond town, at first road junction, to the right of the road** was located one of the many big supply depots which the Germans had constructed along the Western Front during the war. These depots consisted of a large number of storehouses so arranged in a network of railroad lines and roads that supplies delivered to them from Germany by standard-gauge railway could be reshipped with a minimum of labor to units in the front lines by narrow-gauge railroads, motor trucks and wagons.

(22.4 m 36.0 km) **To the right up the** small valley is seen the town of Creuë, which was entered early on September 13 by patrols sent out by the 26th Division. **Continue through Heudicourt, which**

was captured by a patrol of the 26th Division early on the morning of September 13.

Straight through the villages of Buxières and Buxerulles which were occupied by a French division on September 13. In the wooded ravines to the right of these towns were located many German war establishments. These included a large hospital camp, a dressing station and extensive supply dumps for food, engineer materials and ammunition.

(28.8 m 46.3 km) **In next village, Woinville, turn sharp left toward Montsec.**
This village was the location of the headquarters of the American IV Corps after the St. Mihiel offensive, from November 3 to the Armistice.

(29.2 m 46.9 km) **Beyond town, to the right** is seen Loupmont Ridge. It is a long narrow ridge which lay in rear of the German front line and was an important part of their defensive system. Numerous deep underground shelters had been dug into this side of it.

(31.9 m 51.2 km) **At far side of the next village, Montsec, turn right toward the village of Loupmont.**

(32.1 m 51.7 km) **At the next road junction, bear to the right up Montsec hill.**

(33.1 m 53.2 km) **At flagpole, STOP.**

Anti-Aircraft Gun in Action

This imposing monument is one of the three principal memorials erected by the United States Government in France. Its site upon this high isolated hill, dominating the surrounding country in nearly all directions, cannot be surpassed.

The hill of Montsec is well known to the soldiers of the American Expeditionary Forces as a large number of American divisions had their first service in the battle line near this place.

The following description of the combat operations should be read by the observer when standing upon the upper terrace of the monument in the space between the first columns to the south (right as flagpole is faced) of the steps.

This hill was close to the south face of the St. Mihiel salient. Because of its natural strength and height it was an exceptionally important point in the German defensive system. On this side it was protected by numerous trenches, machine-gun emplacements and barbed-wire entanglements. On the other side tunnels led to large underground shelters in the hill and to observation posts along this crest from which the German artillery fire was directed and controlled.

Except for the weakness inherent to all salients, which is the danger of attack from both sides at once, the St. Mihiel salient was exceptionally strong. Proof of this is that it projected into the Allied lines for four years. In 1914 the Germans had established themselves near here on strong natural positions and had spent the following years in constructing elaborate trenches, vast masses of barbed-wire entanglements, concrete machine-gun emplacements and other field works in an endeavor to make these positions impregnable. It was feared by many that attacking the salient would prove to be a difficult and costly undertaking.

The plan of the offensive consisted of a main attack by the I and IV Corps on a 14-mile front on this face of the salient, a secondary attack a few hours later by the V Corps, whose zone of action we have already visited, and a diversion and exploitation by the French II Colonial

(123)

Church at Montsec

German Artillery Telephone Exchange at Montsec

German Dugout Entrance on Montsec
The hill was honeycombed with dugouts

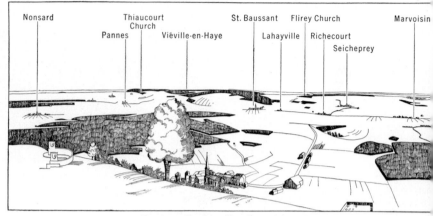

Panorama Looking East From Montsec

Corps which held the tip of the salient.

The places mentioned below should be identified by means of the direction arrows located between the columns.

Spread out before the observer like a huge relief map is part of the ground over which the main assault of the First Army swept on September 12, 1918.

The jump-off line extended from Marvoisin, the small village seen to the right front just beyond the nearest wood; passed between Richecourt and Seicheprey; ran this side of Flirey, whose church steeple is seen to the left of Seicheprey; and continued on to the Moselle River, which is about 15 miles away.

The divisions in the initial assault were, in order from the observer's right to left, the 1st, 42d, 89th, 2d, 5th and part of the 90th. The rest of the 90th Division and that part of the 82d Division beyond it on this side of the Moselle did not attack until the second day of the offensive.

German Communication Trench Between Montsec and Richecourt

The battle started at 1:00 a.m., dotting the countryside in front of here with flame as about 3,000 pieces of artillery of all calibers commenced a violent bombardment. In the next few hours thousands of shells crashed into the hostile battery emplacements, observation posts, communication centers, trenches and other vital points, while a smoke screen was placed around this hill to prevent the German observers on it from seeing and reporting details of the advance.

The infantry assault in front of here began at 5:00 a.m., in a drizzling rain and mist. The strength and suddenness of the attack completely disrupted the German defense and the divisions advanced steadily. Within a few hours sufficient ground had been gained to assure the success of the entire operation.

Richecourt and Lahayville, the town seen to the left of Richecourt, promptly fell to the 1st Division while St. Baussant the large village seen to the front, was captured by the 42d Division.

Before noon the 1st Division had captured Nonsard, the nearest village to the left front, and by night was advancing in the large wood seen to the left of and beyond that village. The 42d Division seized Pannes, seen to the right of Nonsard, and advanced several miles beyond it while the 89th Division reached a line near Thiaucourt, which town can be seen

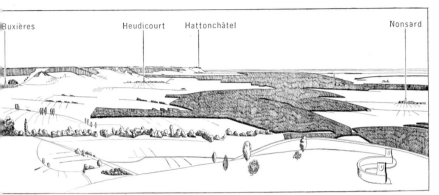

Buxières   Heudicourt   Hattonchâtel   Nonsard

Panorama Looking North From Montsec

o the left front on a clear day. The 2d Division captured Thiaucourt and the 5th captured Viéville-en-Haye, the village seen some distance to the right of Thiaucourt just below the sky line in an open space between two large woods.

Go to space between first columns on opposite side of the steps.

The village seen to the front on the nose of the hill is Hattonchâtel. About dawn on September 13 patrols of the 1st Division met the advanced elements of the 26th Division below that place, thus actually closing the salient.

During September 13 the advance was continued with the right of the 90th and the 82d Division on this side of the Moselle River joining in the attack. By late evening of the 13th practically every objective of the offensive had been secured.

On that day this hill and the villages seen to the left along the base of the heights were evacuated by the Germans.

The main attack terminated on the 13th although during the next three days local operations continued and numerous small advances were made at various places as the American units attempted to improve their positions.

The offensive here was launched at a most propitious moment. The German High Command had decided to abandon the St. Mihiel salient so as to shorten the line held by its forces, and orders had been issued on September 11 for a gradual and orderly withdrawal. The plans for this withdrawal and the laying waste of the country in the salient were completely frustrated, however, by the suddenness and strength of the American attack.

As a result of this offensive a large number of prisoners and great quantities of matériel and supplies were captured, and several important roads and railroads south of Verdun were released for Allied use. The successful conclusion of the operation had a marked adverse psychological effect upon the enemy and greatly improved the morale of the Allies.

Before leaving this spot the tourist should step to the right and from the space between the next columns note the St. Mihiel American Cemetery near Thiaucourt, identified by its white stone chapel and field of white headstones, which can be seen in the distance on a clear day on a line just to the right of the round plaza at the flagpole. At that cemetery are buried more than 4,000 American soldiers among which are many of those who so gallantly gave their lives in the battle which has just been described.

German Trench Southwest of Montsec

Within the circle of columns, resting upon a stone platform decorated with carvings of military equipment carried by American soldiers, is a large bronze relief map of the St. Mihiel salient. Upon it are shown the front lines before and after the American offensives in this region. By lining up the monument on the map with any feature on the map, that feature on the ground, if visible, will be seen in the distance on the same line and thus can be identified.

To aid the visitor in understanding the military operations illustrated by the bronze map, and to permit identification by name of the villages shown on it, three round porcelain maps of Sèvres manufacture have been placed in the border.

The names of the American and French units whose brilliant services are commemorated here have been recorded on the inside attic wall. The inscription which appears below them is from the final report of the Commander-in-Chief of the American Expeditionary Forces.

Other interesting features of the uppe terrace are the insignia of the principa arms and branches of the American force which have been carved on the shield below the eagles of the pilaster capitals the compass included in the inlaid desig of the floor; and the inscription on th stone base of the relief map which give a brief record of the accomplishments o the American Army near here.

The dedicatory inscriptions, in Frenc on one side and in English on the othe are on the large inclined stones at th sides of the steps descending from th upper terrace. Included in these inscrip tions is a tribute to the friendship an cooperation of the French and America Armies during the World War.

The names on the outside frieze abov the columns are those of villages in thi general region which were captured b American troops. These places whe considered as a whole give a good ide of the large area covered by the America combat activities in Alsace and Lorraine

Close-Up View of St. Mihiel American Memorial

Distant View of American Memorial on Montsec

The coats of arms carved on the stone pillars near the flagpole are those of France and the United States, whose divisions fought side by side in this region; and of Alsace and Lorraine, the two French provinces in which occurred the fighting commemorated by this memorial.

EN ROUTE MONTSEC TO EAST
OF SEICHEPREY

Descend hill to the village of Montsec. (34.3 m 55.2 km) **In town, turn sharp right on the descending road.**

(34.8 m 56.0 km) **Beyond town, by looking to the rear,** can be seen the view of Montsec most familiar to the American soldiers who served in this region.

(36.0 m 57.9 km) **Just before reaching the next sharp RIGHT bend in road,** the zone of action of the 1st Division during the main attack is entered.

(36.5 m 58.7 km) **The next village, Richecourt,** was just within the enemy front line. The Germans had elaborately organized it as a strong point and the immediate surroundings were a maze of trenches and wire entanglements. The town itself was completely obliterated by Allied shellfire during the war.

At the far edge of the town the Rupt de Mad is crossed. This small stream, which ran obliquely across a considerable part of the zone of attack, was a serious obstacle to the tanks and transportation of the First Army until its destroyed bridges were replaced by the engineers.

(36.7 m 59.0 km) **Beyond town, at first crossroad, continue straight ahead.**

(36.8 m 59.2 km) **At top of next crest, where a good view to the left front is obtained, STOP without leaving the car.**

The German front-line trench ran at right angles to this road and passed through this point. Near the bottom of the shallow valley ahead was located the American front line, the intervening ground being that of no man's land.

Sectors in this vicinity were held for considerable periods of time by the 1st, 26th, 82d and 89th Divisions before the concentration for the St. Mihiel attack.

The village seen to the front is Seicheprey and the wood in the valley to the left of it is the Bois de Remières.

Early on the morning of April 20 Seicheprey was the scene of a German raid against the 26th Division, which was then holding this part of the front. The Germans placed a heavy "box barrage" around Seicheprey and the Bois de Remières to prevent supporting troops from entering that area. Then, screened by a dense fog, about 1,200 picked German assault troops, starting from near here, quickly overran the American front lines and entered Seicheprey. They destroyed the dugouts, battalion first-aid station and kitchen, and captured a considerable number of prisoners. Soon thereafter the Germans withdrew from the town and remained most of the day in the American front-line trenches. They retired to their own lines shortly before an American counterattack could be launched to drive them out.

Continue.

(37.4 m 60.2 km) **The railroad which is next crossed** is a strategic railroad which has been constructed since the war.

The ridge seen on the sky line ahead was the location of the Allied main line of resistance. That position had been

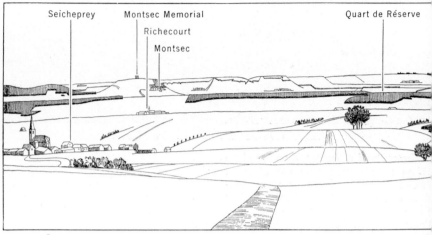

Seicheprey   Montsec Memorial   Quart de Réserve

Richecourt

Montsec

Panorama Looking North

elaborately prepared for defense by the French Army during the preceding years.

(38.1 m 61.3 km) **At near edge of next village, Seicheprey,** the sector which was held by the 42d Division is entered.

In Seicheprey, alongside the church, is a small memorial fountain presented to the village by men and women of the State of Connecticut. To visit it, turn to the left in the town. Time of side trip—3 minutes.

Fountain at Seicheprey
Erected by Inhabitants of Connecticut

(38.3 m 61.5 km) **In town turn right, at first road turn to the left toward Flirey.**

(39.2 m 63.0 km) **About 50 yards from the next large wood, STOP.**

To the left rear the nearest wood which is seen is called the Bois de Remières.

Face its center, which direction is approximately north.

Montsec is visible to the left front.

From observation posts located near here a large part of the ground within the German lines could be seen. In these posts, which were carefully concealed, observers continuously watched the enemy positions during daylight hours and reported at once all signs of unusual activity. This work was supplemented by the use of captive balloons stationed several miles in rear of the forward trenches at intervals along the entire front. The occupants of these balloons also studied the hostile positions through powerful glasses and telephoned immediately to the ground forces all information gained. The balloon observer, his helpers on the ground, and the protecting anti-aircraft artillery had to be constantly on the alert for German airplanes, as a successful airplane attack on the inflammable balloon invariably caused it to burst into flames and be destroyed.

A large amount of important information was also obtained by the Air Service

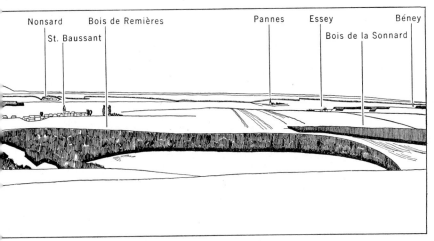

Nonsard   Bois de Remières   Pannes   Essey   Béney
St. Baussant   Bois de la Sonnard

From Stop Near Seicheprey

which periodically sent airplanes over the enemy lines to reconnoiter and to take photographs of the hostile battle lines. These photographs, when compared with others previously taken, gave valuable indications of changes in the enemy defensive organization and in his plans.

This point is near the center of the zone of the IV Corps, which attacked on September 12 with the 1st, 42d and 89th Divisions in line from left to right.

The German front line at that time ran just this side of Richecourt, the second village between here and Montsec; just beyond the Bois de Remières; and along the near edge of the Bois de la Sonnard, the large wood which is seen to the right of the Bois de Remières.

The troops here jumped off at 5:00 a. m. in a rain and fog, closely following a heavy rolling barrage. The 1st Division promptly captured Richecourt but encountered considerable resistance in the Quart de Réserve, the wood seen just beyond the left side of the Bois de Remières. Overcoming this before noon, it captured Nonsard, the village seen beyond and to the right of the Quart de Réserve, and was advancing at dark in the wood seen beyond that place.

The 42d Division, in front of here, met stubborn resistance from machine gun units at St. Baussant, the village seen to

the front, and in the Bois de la Sonnard. It drove forward aggressively, however, capturing Essey, the first village seen over the right side of the Bois de Remières, about noon, and Pannes, whose church is seen to the left of Essey, about 2:00 p. m. Lamarche, seen in the distance to the left of Pannes, was beyond the first day's objective. It was, how-

Flare Used at Night to Call for an
Artillery Barrage

ever, entered by a patrol of the 42d Division in the afternoon and occupied by the 1st Division that night.

The 89th Division, to the right of here, advanced rapidly through the large wood, Bois de Mort-Mare, in front of its jump-off line and that night established itself about a mile this side of Béney, the village seen on a clear day in the distance to the right of and beyond Essey.

The rapid advance of the IV Corps on this front made certain the success of the whole attack of the First Army.

EN ROUTE EAST OF SEICHEPREY TO EAST OF REGNIÉVILLE

(39.7 m 63.8 km) **At the next road junction, turn to the left.**

Beyond the road junction, the front trenches of the Allied main line of resistance ran immediately alongside this road for the next several miles.

(40.8 m 65.3 km) **Before reaching the next village, Flirey,** the sector held by the soldiers of the 89th Division is entered.

(41.0 m 66.0 km) **At entrance to town** are seen the embankments of a large railway bridge which formerly spanned the road. This bridge was destroyed by the French Army early in the war.

The 89th Division Headquarters during the attack was located in dugouts at the embankment nearest the road.

(41.3 m 66.4 km) **In center of town, on the right** is seen a monument erected by the people of Lorraine to commemorate the services of the American Army in this region. On it are listed the American divisions which fought near here.

(41.4 m 66.6 km) **At far edge of town** are seen the ruins of the old village, Flirey having been rebuilt on a new site.

(41.5 m 66.8 km) **To the left of this road, about ¾ mile,** was the location of a successful raid made on August 4 by the 82d Division, which occupied this sector for about one month before the St. Mihiel offensive. Two companies of the division penetrated the German lines to a depth of more than 600 yards, inflicting a number of casualties on the enemy forces and capturing three machine guns before returning to their own trenches.

(131)

French Monument at Flirey Listing American Units Which Fought in the Vicinity

(42.1 m 67.7 km) **Beyond town, at top of first crest,** was the scene of a strong German raid early on August 31 against the 89th Division, which was then occupying this sector. The Germans passed through the American front line between two regiments, crossed this road and in a trench along the right side of it moved in the direction the tourist is traveling, at the same time calling out in English that they were from the adjoining American regiment. This ruse failed to mislead the American platoon commander, who

Church at Limey

Air Photograph of Bridge Near Flirey

Dugouts in Rear of the 89th Division Jump-Off Line Near Flirey

View of Flirey on September 13, 1918

Ruins of Remenauville, October 1918

repulsed the raiding party by a courageous and well executed defense. The
Germans were forced to abandon two of
their dead within the American lines.

(42.6 m 68.5 km) **While approaching
the next village, Limey, to the left** is seen
a ridge upon which were located jump-off
trenches of the 89th Division.

(43.5 m 70.0 km) **Near this side of
the town,** the sector of the 2d Division
before the offensive is entered.

(43.8 m 70.5 km) **Just before reaching
the far end of Limey, turn sharply to the
left toward Remenauville.**

(43.9 m 70.6 km) **Beyond town, to the
front** is seen Ansoncourt Farm, which was
near the boundary line between the zones
of action of the 2d and 89th Divisions.

That farm, which was a strong point
in the German lines, was captured by the
89th Division on September 12. During
the attack on it Second Lieutenant J.
Hunter Wickersham of the 89th Division
won the Congressional Medal of Honor.
Severely wounded in four places by a high-
explosive shell, and with his right arm
disabled, he declined aid for himself
until he had dressed the wounds of his orderly, who had been wounded at the same
time. Leading his men forward again
he continued fighting, using his pistol
with his left hand until exhausted from
loss of blood he finally fell and died.

(44.5 m 71.5 km) **On far side of first
valley,** a 2d Division boulder marker, one
of a number erected after the Armistice
by that division on its former battlefields,
is passed near the road.

(44.7 m 71.8 km) **Near the top of the
next crest** were located the front-line
trenches of the 2d Division. They are
still (1937) plainly to be seen.

(45.0 m 72.4 km) **The church seen to
the left of the road** marks the site of the
former village of Remenauville which
was completely destroyed during the
war. That town was just within the
German front line. On September 12
it was captured by the 2d Division
which met determined resistance in
the Bois du Four, the large wood seen to
the left. After a severe fight the enemy
troops were driven out, and by 1:00 p. m.
the division had advanced about 5 miles.

(45.2 m 72.7 km) **Upon reaching the
next road junction, turn to the right.**

(45.4 m 73.0 km) **At the bottom of the
valley** the zone of action of the 5th Division during the attack is entered.

(45.7 m 73.5 km) **At the top of the next
hill** are seen (1937) traces of the trench
system held by the 5th Division before it
jumped off for the main attack.

(45.9 m 73.8 km) **The church seen
ahead** marks the site of Regniéville, which
was just within the American lines. The

town was totally demolished during the four years of fighting in this vicinity.

At the road junction ahead is a 5th Division marker, one of many erected by that division shortly after the Armistice; also a French marker indicating the farthest advance of the German forces during the last year of the war.

(46.2 m 74.3 km) **Upon reaching the road junction, turn to the right.**

The road running to the left at this point is the most direct route to Thiaucourt.

(46.7 m 75.1 km) **Just before reaching the top of the next crest, when a good view is obtained to the rear, STOP.**

If the growth of trees has obstructed the view go off the road or back down hill in order to obtain the best view possible.

Face so that the church just passed, which marks the site of the former village of Regniéville, is seen to the left front. The direction which the tourist is now facing is approximately north.

This point is close to the center of the jump-off line of the I Corps.

The church which is seen to the left is the one passed a short time ago in the former village of Remenauville.

The German front line in this vicinity ran from the observer's left of Ansoncourt Farm, seen beyond and to the right of the church of Remenauville; included Remenauville; passed on the other side

of Regniéville; ran along the near slopes of the ridge seen ahead; and continued on to the right crossing the Moselle River, which is about 5 miles away.

On September 12 the 2d, 5th and the left of the 90th Division attacked at 5:00 a. m. and made rapid and deep penetrations into the hostile positions.

The 2d Division promptly captured Remenauville and advanced quickly to the Bois du Four, the wood seen to the left front, where considerable resistance from machine-gun nests was encountered. This was overcome by 7:00 a. m. and Thiaucourt (not visible), 4 miles away beyond the right edge of the Bois du Four, was captured about noon. The 2d Division dug in that night on a position north of Thiaucourt, which was one of the main objectives of the offensive.

The 5th Division jumped off from near Regniéville and made steady progress through the German trenches and thick wire entanglements on its front. Determined resistance from machine guns in the wood, Bois de la Rappe, seen fringing the ridge ahead, was overcome about 6:15 a. m. and from then on the advance was rapid until that night, when the front line of the 5th Division was established about 3 miles ahead of this point.

The left of the 90th Division, which attacked to the right of this point, met

Regniéville in October 1918

SECTION OF WAR MAP SHOWING
TRENCH SYSTEM NEAR REMENAUVILLE

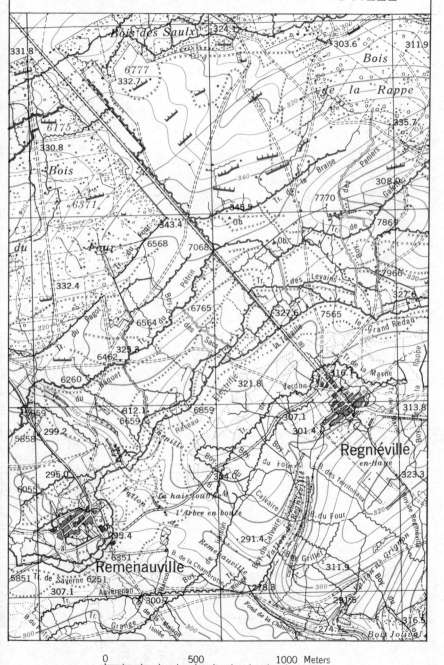

0   500   1000 Meters

obstinate resistance from machine-gun nests and snipers in the wood, the treetops of which can be seen in the distance to the right front. That resistance was cleared out during the morning and by 1:30 p. m. the division had reached its objective. The position consolidated that night was 2 miles from here, at about right angles to the observer's line of vision when looking in the direction of his right front.

The masses of barbed-wire entanglements on this front were very formidable but the extensive preparations which had

EN ROUTE EAST OF REGNIÉVILLE TO NORTH OF PONT-À-MOUSSON

(47.8 m 76.9 km) **The next village, Fey-en-Haye,** has been rebuilt on a new site. The site of the old town, which was destroyed, is about a mile to the left of this road, on the 90th Division jump-off line.

(48.9 m 78.6 km) **Beyond the town, at the next crossroad, turn to the left.**

The opposing front lines between here and the Meuse River ran about a mile to the left of this road. They traversed the Forêt du Bois-le-Prêtre, a dense wood in

Pont-à-Mousson, October 1918

been made by the American divisions to pass through them without loss of time proved to be unexpectedly effective.

The fighting after September 12 of the divisions which attacked from this part of the front will be discussed later when the area of that fighting is visited.

On the preceding page is a section of a wartime map, scale 1/20,000 (about 3″=1 mile), showing Remenauville and Regniéville. This map, which is of the type most commonly used by American front-line units, gives a good idea of the extent of the trench system existing in this region before the American attack.

which the Germans had established themselves early in the war and from which the French had made several unsuccessful attempts to drive them out.

When the 90th Division took over a sector in this vicinity on August 24 the opposing positions in some places were only 20 yards apart, each of them being composed of wide zones of deep trenches, bristling with machine guns in concrete emplacements and strongly protected by numerous thick bands of barbed wire.

(50.0 m 80.5 km) **After leaving the wood, to the left front across the valley** is seen a French World War cemetery.

Memorial Fountain of the American Field
Service in Pont-à-Mousson

The 1st and 2d Divisions held adjoining
sectors near here for a short time in August.

(50.5 m 81.2 km) **While approaching
the next town, Montauville,** over it is seen
Mousson Hill, upon which is located the
village of Mousson. That place served as
an excellent observation point for the
French and American units on this front.
The ruins of an 11th Century
castle and a church tower, upon
which stands a statue of Joan of
Arc, are visible on the hill.

**After passing through Montau-
ville and the adjoining village,
Maidières, the tour enters Pont-
à-Mousson** which was captured by
the Germans in 1914. It was retaken by French troops shortly
thereafter and remained in the
hands of the Allies from then on.
Pont-à-Mousson being near the
front line was often heavily
shelled by the German artillery.
The churches of St. Laurent and
St. Martin are places of interest.

(52.5 m 84.5 km) **After entering the
town, cross over the railroad tracks.**

**In center of town, at large plaza with
the arcades, to the right** is seen a Renais-
sance fountain reconstructed by the
American Field Service as a memorial to
its war dead. That Service was composed of a number of American ambulance sections, organized in the fall of
1914, and truck units, formed in the
spring of 1918. It served with the French
Army both before and after the United
States entered the war, although it was
made part of the American Army in 1917.

(52.7 m 84.8 km) **At center of the large
plaza with the arcades, turn to the left
toward Pagny-sur-Moselle.**

The tour now goes north down the
Moselle valley and for approximately the
next 4 miles follows in the direction of
advance of the American Army.

(54.5 m 87.5 km) **Beyond the town,
after crossing the railroad, at the first
crest where a good view of the hill to the
front is obtained, STOP.**

Face down the road, which, at this
point, runs approximately north.

The Moselle River is to the right in the
valley. The high peak, seen to the right
on the other side of it, is Xon Hill.

On September 12 the 82d Division was
holding a line, astride the river, which ran
through this point and included Xon Hill.
Its right connected with the French at
Port-sur-Seille, a town about 6 miles

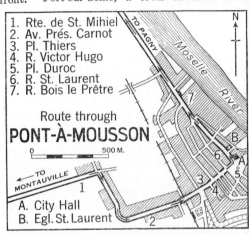

1. Rte. de St. Mihiel
2. Av. Prés. Carnot
3. Pl. Thiers
4. R. Victor Hugo
5. Pl. Duroc
6. R. St. Laurent
7. R. Bois le Prêtre

Route through
PONT-À-MOUSSON

0   500 M.

A. City Hall
B. Egl. St. Laurent

away to the right rear, and its left joined the 90th Division, at a point which is about ½ mile to the left of here.

No attack was made on this front on September 12, the mission of the 82d Division being to exert pressure on the enemy by raiding and patrolling, but not to make a permanent advance. At this particular place, in carrying out this mission, an enemy strong point at the house seen down the road was raided.

On September 13 the 90th Division was ordered to advance its right about 1 mile and the 82d was directed to protect its flank. The 90th Division attacked at 9:30 a. m., drove the enemy in determined fighting out of the woods and quarries in its zone of action and by 5:00 p. m. had reached its objective which it held in spite of a severe gas and high explosive bombardment. The 82d Division attacked after dark, advanced across the valley ahead under heavy hostile fire from the other side of the Moselle and reached a line just beyond the crest of Hill 324, seen ahead. Its position was then abreast of the line of the 90th Division.

On the 15th the 90th again drove forward, early in the morning, and advanced to a ridge 1½ miles farther on. Shortly after noon the 82d passed through Vandières, about 2 miles down this road, to a

German Front-Line Trench and Barbed Wire Near Fey-en-Haye, September 1918

position alongside that of the 90th. The ground held by the 82d Division was exposed to artillery fire from the north and from across the river so, after many casualties, it was given up. Vandières will be passed through and the position just mentioned will be seen later in the tour.

One of the outstanding deeds of daring in the fighting near here was that of Lieutenant Colonel Emory J. Pike, 82d Division, on the far slopes of Hill 324. Going beyond the call of his own duties as division machine gun officer he volunteered to assist in reorganizing advanced units under a terrific bombardment. Although seriously wounded while going to the aid of an injured soldier in the outpost line he continued in command and remained in the position until it was prepared for defense, encouraging everyone

Light Tank Manned by Americans Crossing a Trench During the St. Mihiel Operation

90th Division Detachment Coming Out of Line Near Vilcey-sur-Trey,
September 15, 1918

with his cheerful spirit, courage and confidence. This gallant soldier died from his wounds. For his heroic actions in this fighting he was posthumously awarded the Congressional Medal of Honor.

On September 18 that part of the 82d Division on this side of the river was relieved by the 90th Division and on the 20th the remainder of the division was replaced in the line by French troops.

On October 9 the 92d Division took over a sector just beyond the Moselle River and on October 26 its front was extended for a short distance on this side. On November 10 the division attacked and captured the Bois Fréhaut, the wooded area seen to the left of Xon Hill, held it under heavy bombardment and made other minor gains farther to the right.

In the region of the Vosges Mountains, lying to the right rear from here, many American divisions had their first service in the battle lines. The nature of that country was such that large operations were practically impossible, and the sectors there were ordinarily held by tired or newly formed divisions. (See Chapter VII for information of that region.)

EN ROUTE NORTH OF PONT-À-MOUSSON
TO SOUTHEAST OF THIAUCOURT

(55.0 m 88.5 km) **Upon reaching the road fork on the next low crest, bear right.**

(55.2 m 88.8 km) **Up the valley leading to the left** is seen Norroy, which was occupied by troops of the 82d Division during the evening of September 13.

The next village, Vandières, was captured by the 82d Division on September 15. Due to intense hostile artillery fire the division withdrew from the village early the next day. The 90th Division, after relieving the 82d on September 18, advanced its front line beyond the town.

(56.7 m 91.2 km) **In Vandières, turn to the left toward Villers-sous-Prény.**

The tour turns west at this point and from now on runs generally across the zone of action of the American First Army.

American Officers at a Captured German Canteen,
Nonsard, September 13, 1918

Light Railway Operated by the American Army, Moving Civilian Property From
the Vicinity of the Front Line

(57.1 m 91.9 km) **Beyond town, leading up from the right of the road,** are the slopes of the hill captured by the 82d Division on September 15, and from which it later withdrew because of intense hostile artillery bombardments.

(57.6 m 92.7 km) **At next group of farm buildings seen to the left near the road,** the zone of action of the 90th Division during the attack is entered.

The high bald ridge with the irregular crest seen to the left is Hill 324, which was mentioned at the last stop. The village of Norroy is located just the other side of it. The front line of the 82d Division on both September 13 and 14 was just beyond the crest of that ridge.

Road Work
The silk hat was found in Thiaucourt

(58.3 m 93.7 km) **Some distance farther on to the right** is seen a high wooded ridge, captured on September 15 by the 90th Division. In the Bois des Rappes, the dense wooded area on its summit, considerable fighting occurred.

(58.7 m 94.4 km) **Continue through the village of Villers-sous-Prény.**

The valley which the road now follows received a continuous bombardment of gas and high explosive shells after its capture on September 15, from German batteries on the hills seen to the rear beyond the Moselle River. On account of this shelling it received the name of the "Valley of Death" from the American soldiers who served near here.

(59.4 m 95.6 km) **While approaching the next village, Vilcey-sur-Trey, to the right front** is seen the edge of the wood, Forêt des Venchères, along which the 90th Division line rested on September 13. That line crossed this road at right angles just this side of the town.

(60.1 m 96.8 km) **Continue through the village of Vilcey-sur-Trey.**

(61.0 m 98.1 km) **In the large wood, Forêt des Venchères, next entered,** the 90th Division encountered stubborn resistance from the Germans who were driven out of it on September 13.

In this wood was located a large German rest camp for troops waiting to enter

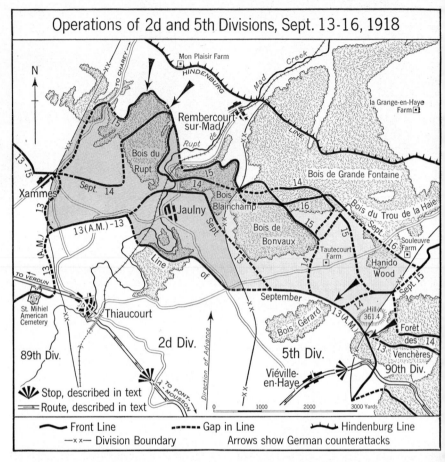

Operations of 2d and 5th Divisions, Sept. 13-16, 1918

Mon Plaisir Farm

TO CHAREY

HINDENBURG

Creek

Mad

la Grange-en-Haye
Farm

N

Rembercourt-
sur-Mad

LINE

de

Rupt

Bois du
Rupt

Bois de Grande Fontaine

Sept. 14

Xammes

13-15

13

Jaulny

Blainchamp
Bois

Bois du Trou de la Haie

Souleuvre
Farm

13(A.M.)-13

Bois de
Bonvaux

Sept

Tautecourt
Farm

Hanido
Wood

(A.M.)

TO VERDUN

Line

of

September

Sept 15

Bois Gérard

Hill
361.4

Forêt
des

St. Mihiel
American
Cemetery

Thiaucourt

2d Div.

5th Div.

Venchères

89th Div.

Direction of Advance

TO PONT-
À-MOUSSON

Viéville-
en-Haye

90th Div.

Stop, described in text

Route, described in text

0   1000   2000   3000 Yards

Front Line   Gap in Line   Hindenburg Line
—x x— Division Boundary   Arrows show German counterattacks

the front lines. Hundreds of huts had been constructed under the trees, where they were concealed from the view of hostile aviators, and many facilities for the comfort of the soldiers were provided.

(61.1 m 98.3 km) **On the far side of the small valley which the road follows** was located the front line of the 90th Division on the evening of September 12.

(62.1 m 99.9 km) **After leaving wood, just before reaching sharp bend in road,** the front line of the 5th Division on the first day of the attack is crossed. It ran almost at right angles to the road and at this point faced in the direction opposite to that which the tourist is traveling.

(62.4 m 100.4 km) **Beyond bend, at the first crest, STOP without leaving car.**

The village seen ahead is Viéville-en-Haye, one of the objectives of the I Corps in the St. Mihiel offensive. In an attack launched from the edge of the wood, Bois de St. Claude, seen to the left, the 5th Division captured that town about noon on September 12. Its front line was then established about a mile to the right of this road and included the Bois Gérard, located just over the ridge seen to the right. The upper parts of several of the highest trees of that wood can be seen topping the ridge to the right front.

Due to this deep penetration by the 5th Division, parts of two fresh German divisions were put into the line on this front. These launched a strong counterattack on the afternoon of September 13 and although small hostile units succeeded in entering the Bois Gérard, the division line at midnight was not materially changed.

On the 14th the 5th Division once again attacked and after severe fighting, during which another German counterattack was repulsed, advanced its line a mile in the left part of its zone of action and approximately 800 yards in the right part.

During September 15 and 16 further fighting occurred but the division line remained practically unchanged except on its extreme right where an advance of approximately 800 yards was made.

Its mission having been efficiently accomplished the 5th Division was relieved on September 17 by the 78th Division.

Continue.

(62.8 m 101.0 km) **Straight through the village of Viéville-en-Haye.**

(63.1 m 101.5 km) **Beyond village cemetery, to the right front on the sky line** is seen the American monument on Montsec hill, visited earlier in the tour.

(63.9 m 102.8 km) **Near first pronounced LEFT bend in road,** the zone of action of the 2d Division is entered.

(64.1 m 103.1 km) **In the wood, Bois d'Heiche, seen to the right,** taken by the 2d Division about 9:30 a. m. on September 12, a large number of prisoners and great quantities of supplies were captured.

(64.2 m 103.3 km) **Upon approaching the next crossroad, to the left front** can be seen (1937) the remains of a German concrete machine-gun emplacement.

In a building, called Loge Mangin, near the edge of the wood seen to the left front, the 2d Division Headquarters was established on September 12. When that division was relieved from this front the building was used as the 78th Division Headquarters until October 5.

(64.4 m 103.5 km) **Upon reaching the next crossroad, turn to the right.**

(64.5 m 103.8 km) **Beyond crossroad, to the left** is seen the large wood, Bois du Beau Vallon, taken by troops of the 2d

No Man's Land Along Southern Face of St. Mihiel Salient
Shows character of the terrain advanced over

Thiaucourt Being Shelled by the Germans After
Its Capture by the 2d Division

and 89th Divisions on the morning of the first day of the offensive of September 12.

(65.3 m 105.1 km) **At the next road crossing, turn to the right.**

(65.4 m 105.3 km) **Immediately beyond the next crossroad, STOP.**

Face down the road, which direction is approximately northwest.

From this point on a clear day may be seen to the left and left front a wonderful panorama of the Woëvre Plain over which the American troops advanced.

To the left in the distance is seen Montsec, crowned by the American monument, with the village of Montsec at its base. The jump-off line of the main attack on September 12 was approximately parallel to the observer's line of sight when facing Montsec and about 3 miles to the left of that line. Between here and the hill of Montsec the line of vision cuts directly across part of the zone of action of the 2d Division and through the zones of action of the 89th, 42d and 1st Divisions in that order.

To the left front Hattonchâtel with its picturesque château is plainly visible just below the sky line, perched on one of the prominent heights which rim the plain in

that direction; and to the left of it, strung along the forward slopes of the confining heights, are the villages of Vigneulles, Heudicourt, Buxières, Buxerulles and Woinville which were passed through earlier in the tour.

The observer is near the middle of the 2d Division zone of action. That division reached this vicinity about 9:00 a. m. on September 12 and by early afternoon had captured Thiaucourt, the town seen in the valley ahead, and had established its line on the Army objective about 2 miles to the right front from here. Later in the afternoon the division repulsed two strong hostile counterattacks.

Thiaucourt was an important point in the German supply system, and with its capture there fell into American hands 11 field guns loaded on railroad cars, numerous empty railway cars, and vast quantities of food, lumber and military supplies and equipment of all kinds.

The St. Mihiel American Cemetery, identified by its white chapel and field of white headstones, can be plainly seen to the left of and beyond Thiaucourt.

The 89th Division drove forward on September 12 through the wooded areas in front of its jump-off line and about noon captured Euvezin, identified by the nearest building between here and Montsec. Later in the day it captured the ground upon which the American cemetery now stands. It dug in that night with its front line running near the right edge of the present cemetery area.

The prominent church tower with the slate colored roof, seen some distance to the right of Euvezin, is in Pannes which lay within the zone of action of the 42d Division and was captured by it early in the afternoon on September 12.

Slightly to the right of and beyond the church tower in Pannes is seen the church steeple of Nonsard. That village lay within the zone of action of the 1st Division and was taken by it about noon on the first day of the attack.

On September 13 the 89th Division captured the Bois de Xammes which can be seen on the sky line immediately above and beyond the church steeple in Thiaucourt, and the 2d Division drove forward in the direction of the observer's right front for approximately three fourths of a mile in the right of its zone of action.

During the 14th and 15th, the 2d Division pushed strong reconnaissance patrols to the front and on the 15th several hostile counterattacks were broken up. The division line was advanced slightly along all of its front during these days.

The 2d Division was relieved from the line on September 16 by the 78th. The 89th Division remained on this front until October 7 when it was relieved by the 37th. Both divisions had brilliantly performed their battle assignments.

EN ROUTE SOUTHEAST OF THIAUCOURT TO ST. MIHIEL AMERICAN CEMETERY

(65.9 m 106.0 km) **While approaching Thiaucourt, along the right side of the road** is seen a German military cemetery.

Thiaucourt is well known to troops of the 7th, 28th, 37th, 78th and 89th Divisions, which served in the line north of it at various times between September 16 and the Armistice. It was subjected to heavy German shelling soon after its capture by the Americans.

(66.6 m 107.2 km) **In town, cross right-hand bridge over the Rupt de Mad.**

(66.8 m 107.5 km) **Near the church, passed on the left,** is the village monument upon which are named the American units that fought in this vicinity during the St. Mihiel offensive.

(66.9 m 107.6 km) **At the small monument farther on, bear to the left.**

(67.1 m 108.0 km) **At far edge of town** the zone of action of the 89th Division during the attack is entered.

(67.5 m 108.5 km) **Beyond town, at the large cemetery at left of road, STOP.**

Street in Thiaucourt After the German Bombardment

Entrance, St. Mihiel Cemetery

This is the St. Mihiel American Cemetery. It is the third largest of the eight American military cemeteries in Europe and contains 4,152 graves. Most of the men buried here gave their lives in the St. Mihiel offensive. The majority of the others died while serving in sectors in this region or in the divisional training areas which were located to the southwest.

The architecture of the cemetery is classic in design and the entire development has been made along formal lines. A harmonious and beautiful effect has thus been obtained which can not fail to impress the visitor from America with the fitness of this as a final resting place for these gallant soldier dead.

The formal entrance, with its gem-like pavilions and ornamental black and gilded grill fence, is of striking beauty. Through it an excellent view of the cemetery can be obtained from the main highway.

As the cemetery is entered, the pavilion to the right contains the superintendent's office. Inquiries concerning the location of a particular grave or requests for other information should be made there. The pavilion to the left contains a well-appointed reception room and other facilities for the convenience of visitors.

Although the flower beds and roses and the large green lawns which carpet the grave areas are now in their final beauty, visitors during the next few years will have to draw upon their imaginations to visualize the greater beauty that will

come when the trees and shrubbery have reached their full growth. In time the cemetery will be sheltered on all sides by masses of vegetation outside the stone walls, and the main paths will pass through leafy canopies formed by overhanging boughs of the trees along them.

The white marble headstones, which are the same in all the American military cemeteries in Europe, are of a cross design for those of the Christian faith and a six-pointed star design for those of the Jewish faith. The changing beauty of these fields of crosses when seen at various times throughout the day and in different lights is unusually impressive.

At the center of the cemetery is a large sundial of attractive design surrounded by beautiful beds of flowers. Carved around the top of its base appears the prophetic inscription "TIME WILL NOT DIM THE GLORY OF THEIR DEEDS."

From this point the beautiful perspectives along the cross axes of the cemetery catch the eye. Between the trees and flower beds along one axis is seen a small monument depicting a typical American soldier in his wartime uniform, standing in front of a stone cross. Behind this and framing it is a stone hemicycle intended ultimately to be set off by a high square-trimmed tree hedge. At the end of the other axis there is seen an ornamental urn on a semicircular platform from which a fine view of Thiaucourt and the terrain in that direction may be obtained.

From the center of the cemetery there
a splendid view of the chapel, a building of great simplicity and dignity, which
has been built of fine white stone.

The two flags flying in front of the
chapel bring a feeling of patriotism to
American visitors and a sense of gratifica-
tion that the brave men who rest here will
always sleep beneath their country's flag.

Carved inscriptions in French and
English on the front of the chapel state
that it has been dedicated "TO THOSE
WHO DIED FOR THEIR COUNTRY", and this
thought has been repeated in the main
inscription inside the peristyle which
reads: "THIS CHAPEL HAS BEEN ERECTED
BY THE UNITED STATES OF AMERICA IN
GRATEFUL REMEMBRANCE OF HER SONS
WHO DIED IN THE WORLD WAR."

These words, carved in stone, emphasize
the fact that the chapel stands not to
commemorate the glory of battles won
or the triumph of victory achieved, but
as a direct tribute of America to those who
made the supreme sacrifice for it.

The large rose-granite urn with its
carved drapery at the center of the peristyle recalls to mind an ancient funereal
vase.   One of the decorative features on
it is a winged horse, which is intended to
symbolize the flight of the immortal soul
to its resting place in the life beyond.

The bronze door to the left, decorated
with stars and two miniature bronze
soldier heads, leads to the impressive
interior of the chapel. As the visitor
enters, his attention is first attracted to
the carved, ivory-tinted altar, with its
beautiful cross and the rich mosaic above
it, portraying an angel sheathing his
sword. The mosaics on the end walls
have as their main features large shields
displaying the national colors of the
United States and of France.

The coffered ceiling is decorated in gold
and blue, while the floor and lower wall-
paneling are of inlaid marble with light
and dark green markings. Disposed
about the chapel in appropriate places are
graceful candelabra and bronze-decorated
seats and kneeling-benches.

On the other side of the peristyle is a

View at St. Mihiel Cemetery Chapel

room upon the end walls of which are recorded, in carved and gilded letters on
black marble panels, the names of all
American soldiers who are carried on the
rolls as missing in the operations in this
vicinity. The wall opposite the door
displays an inlaid marble map, to a
scale of 1/10,000, upon which the ground
gained by the American divisions is
shown in various colored marbles.

Behind the chapel, corresponding in
position to the flagpoles in front, are two
weeping willows and filling the four
corners of the chapel terrace are large
masses of trimmed evergreen trees.

From the rear of the peristyle, the
American monument on Montsec is plainly
visible in the distance on a clear day.

EN ROUTE ST. MIHIEL AMERICAN CEME-
TERY TO WEST OF WOËL

From this cemetery the tour follows
the main road to Verdun. For most of
the distance to Haudiomont, 20 miles
away, the front line held by the American troops at the end of the war lay generally from 1 to 3 miles to the right of
and approximately parallel to this road.

(67.8 m 109.1 km) **Beyond first crest, to
the right,** the nearest village is Xammes,
which was close to the final objective of
the First Army in the St. Mihiel offensive.
It was occupied by the 89th Division
early on the morning of September 13.

On September 16 the front line of the
First Army was established about a mile
beyond Xammes. It was located there
when the American Second Army took
over this front on October 12.

(68.2 m 109.7 km) **To the left front,
in the distance, Montsec** is clearly visible.

(68.5 m 110.2 km) **Continue through
Béney,** which was captured before dawn
on September 13 by the 89th Division.

(69.0 m 110.9 km) **At far edge of the**
village the zone of action of the 42d Di
sion during the attack is entered.

(69.1 m 111.2 km) **Beyond town, to
left** is seen the wood, Bois de Thiaucou
near the left end of which, approximate
parallel to this road, was located the fr
line held by troops of the 42d Division
the evening of September 12.

(69.6 m 111.9 km) **To the left front**
seen the Bois de Béney, at the near ed
of which during most of the war the G
mans maintained and flew an observati
balloon. In that wood was captured
large German supply depot.

(70.9 m 114.0 km) **While approachi
the next village, St. Benoît, in its ri
edge** is seen a château where a briga
headquarters of the 42d Division w
located after the capture of the town
September 13. Several times after th
date it was heavily shelled.

(71.4 m 114.9 km) **Continue throu
the village of St. Benoît.**

As part of a general forward moveme
of the 42d Division early on Septemb
13, one of its battalions drove out sm
hostile units in the woods near this roa

A Battalion Headquarters of the 89th Division Near Béney,
September 16, 1918

42d Division Patrol Near Hassavant Farm,
September 14, 1918

ptured Hassavant Farm, the next oup of buildings, organized a position eyond the farm, and sent patrols still rther along down the road.

The 42d Division was relieved by the th Division during October 1.

(73.0 m 117.5 km) At Hassavant Farm, the left is seen Hattonchâtel which was sited earlier in the tour. In the area the left of that place the 1st Division as assembled on September 14, having een pinched out of the front line due to he meeting of the two forces advancing om the sides of the salient. Its moveent to the Meuse-Argonne region was arted from there on September 20.

(76.1 m 122.4 km) Continue through ext village, Woël, which was occupied by French division on September 14.

(77.0 m 123.9 km) Beyond town, at far ide of crest where the next village, Donourt, comes in full view, STOP.

Face to the right, which direction is pproximately northeast.

After September 16 this part of the ont became stabilized and the activities ere from then on were mainly those of

patrolling, with an occasional raid into the German lines to find out information concerning the dispositions of their troops and their future plans of action.

On September 26, when the Meuse-Argonne operation began, the troops here were ordered to make demonstrations with the idea of confusing the enemy as to the exact point of the American attack. Consequently, artillery bombardments lasting as long as nine hours were laid down and strong patrols were sent to attack the enemy lines. These maneuvers served to hold the German reserves behind this front much longer than would otherwise have been the case.

On October 12 the American Second Army took command of this part of the front. Its sector extended from Port-sur-Seille, on the other side of the Moselle River, to Fresnes-en-Woëvre, about 5 miles to the left from here. The front line at that time was practically in the same place as it was at the termination of the main St. Mihiel attack.

Comparatively little activity occurred on this front during the month of October.

Crossroads at St. Hilaire

Early in November the Allied attacks, covering almost the entire front from the Meuse River to the North Sea, produced great disorganization in the German forces. The Second Army was therefore ordered to keep close watch of the enemy for any indications of a withdrawal.

At that time the Second Army front was held, in order from right to left, by the VI Corps with the 92d Division in line, the IV Corps with 7th and 28th in line, and the French XVII Corps with the American 33d Division in line.

The 33d Division held this part of the front and its sector included the towns of Woël, seen to the right; the far edge of Doncourt; and Wadonville, seen to the left of and beyond Doncourt.

The nearest part of the sector held by the 28th Division was at the woods seen in the distance to the right.

On November 9, while the Armistice negotiations were in progress, urgent orders were issued by Marshal Foch, the Allied Commander-in-Chief, directing that the enemy be pushed all along the Western Front and that he be given no time to rest or reorganize his troops.

In carrying out these instructions all divisions on this front, following some local operations on November 9, launched attacks on November 10 and 11 in the general direction the observer is facing. This American offensive is generally referred to as the Woëvre Plain operation.

These attacks resulted in substantial gains and by the time of the Armistice the front line had been advanced to includ the large wood, seen to the right fron the first wood, Bois de Warville, seen t the left front; and St. Hilaire, the villag whose church steeple may be seen at ce tain seasons of the year beyond Doncour

Jonville, whose church is seen to th front, was never captured although th ground between here and that village wa the scene of numerous severe combat

EN ROUTE WEST OF WOËL TO EAST
OF HAUDIOMONT

(77.5 m 124.7 km) **Straight throug the village of Doncourt.**

The 79th Division held a sector in th vicinity during most of the month of Oct ber. It was relieved by the 33d Divisio which assumed command on October 2

(79.1 m 127.3 km) **The next village, S Hilaire,** was occupied on September 13 b a French division and was taken ove from it by the 26th Division on the sam day. It was abandoned on September 1 after an enemy attack had been repulse because by its retention a sharp salier was created in the American line.

The town was raided by America troops a number of times before its ca ture on November 10 by the 33d Divisio The front line at the time of the Armistic was near the far edge of the village.

(80.3 m 129.2 km) **The next villag Marchéville,** had been elaborately o ganized for defense by the Germans befor September 1918. After the salient wa eliminated the village was strongly hel

(152)

y German troops and was the scene of
much vicious fighting until November 11.

On September 26, as part of the demon-
stration on this front at the time of the
opening of the Meuse-Argonne offensive,
a battalion of the 26th Division made an
attack against the town and entered it at
5:00 a. m. after stubborn fighting; a
counterattack by a German unit was
beaten off about noon, and the town
changed hands four times before the
troops of the 26th Division were ordered
to withdraw that evening.

On November 10 the village was attacked in force by the 33d Division which
inflicted heavy losses in overcoming the
stubborn resistance of the enemy. Sharp
hostile counterattacks from the front and
tanks and heavy artillery fire caused a
withdrawal to the higher ground seen to
he left of the village. On November 11
another attack was launched and fighting
was going on in the streets when notifica-
tion of the Armistice was received.

(80.9 m 130.2 km) **Beyond town, at
the road fork, bear to the right.**

(82.3 m 132.4 km) **While approaching
the next town, Fresnes-en-Woëvre,** on
the right are seen (1937) several concrete
machine-gun emplacements which were
part of one of the main German defensive
lines which ran near here.

(82.8 m 133.2 km) **Straight through
Fresnes-en-Woëvre,** captured on September 14 by the 4th Division. The front
line remained near this town until the
morning of November 11 when the 33d

Division advanced it ¾ mile to the right
of the road which the tourist is following.

(83.2 m 133.9 km) **Beyond town, about
500 yards,** was located the boundary
between the American First and Second
Armies at the close of hostilities.

(84.5 m 136.0 km) **At next road junction**
is seen a monument erected by the 4th
Division after the Armistice.

(84.7 m 136.3 km) **Continue through
next village, Manheulles,** captured by
the 4th Division on September 14.
During October and the early part of
November it was just within the American lines. Its exposed location made it
subject to frequent and intense bombardments from hostile artillery.

(85.5 m 137.5 km) **Beyond town, just
beyond second bend in road, before
reaching the railroad, STOP.**

Face down the road, which direction is
approximately west.

On November 7 the 81st Division
relieved the 35th on a line which ran
along the edge of the heights seen ahead.
It was at that time the right flank division
belonging to the American First Army.

On November 9 the division attacked
as part of the general forward movement on this front. It advanced to the
right of this road well into the wood,
Bois de Manheulles, seen in that direction. Only two isolated groups, however,
remained in the wood during the night.
The smaller of these withdrew about
10:00 a. m. the next day to the road on
which the observer is standing. The

On Front of 81st Division Near Manheulles, November 10, 1918

Troops of the 81st Division in Manheulles, November 10, 1918

other group, a company, was attacked by the Germans early on the morning of the 10th and about half of its men were captured. The remnants, however, about 40 men, bravely fought their way back to the American position at Haudiomont, which is the village seen ahead.

No attack was made here on November 10 but on the 11th the 81st Division met resistance in its efforts to advance in the Bois de Manheulles. Its front line was in the wood at the time of the Armistice.

About 4 miles to the right front from here the left of the 81st Division made successive advances during November 9, 10 and 11, for a total gain of about 3 miles.

✦

As this is the last stop on the tour, a brief summary of the events connected with the reduction of the St. Mihiel salient will serve to fix them more definitely in the mind of the reader.

Shortly after the American Expeditionary Forces reached France in 1917 General Pershing decided that the American Army should be built up and enter the battle line in this region, and that the reduction of the St. Mihiel salient should be its first major operation of the war.

In the spring of 1918 the formation of

the American Army was postponed because of the great demand for divisions to meet critical situations created on other parts of the front by the successful German offensives at that time.

Early in August of that year the situation became such that General Pershing felt free to insist that the creation of an American army be no longer delayed. As a result the First Army was formed and took over on August 30 all of the front line around the St. Mihiel salient.

The original plans for the attack provided for exploiting toward Metz and the Briey iron region if the situation became favorable. These plans, however, were

Captured Burros Carrying Water Near Haudiomont, November 1918

Effect of a Direct Hit on a German
Concrete Shelter

depressed, as the superb fighting qualities of the American soldier had again been demonstrated and the American high commanders and their staffs had successfully proved their ability to conduct large operations, an ability previously doubted by the Germans.   The Allies were greatly encouraged and all Americans were elated at the victory, which was far more rapid and clear-cut than even the most optimistic had a right to expect.

Before leaving this stop the speedometer reading should be noted.

EN ROUTE EAST OF HAUDIOMONT TO VERDUN

changed in order to fit in with those for an offensive in the Meuse-Argonne region and it was finally decided that the St. Mihiel operation should be limited merely to the reduction of the salient.

After almost superhuman efforts on the part of all concerned the First Army was in place on this front ready to attack early on the morning of September 12.

The main attack was carried through with dash and precision and ended on the evening of September 13, all major objectives having been gained.

The effect upon morale of this striking victory of the American Army in its initial major offensive is almost beyond evaluation.   The Germans were greatly

(86.5 m 139.1 km) **Straight through the village of Haudiomont.**

(87.0 m 139.9 km) **Beyond town, while ascending hill, to the rear** may be seen a fine view of the Woëvre Plain.

(90.7 m 145.9 km) **5.2 miles (8.4 kilometers) from the last stop; at top of hill where Fort du Rozellier is to the right of the road; to the right front** on a clear day may be seen the shaft of the Meuse-Argonne American Memorial at Montfaucon, approximately 18 miles away.

(96.1 m 154.6 km) **Continue to the Victory monument in the center of Verdun.**

Verdun is the starting point for the tour of the American battlefields in the Meuse-Argonne region described in Chapter IV.

German Command Post at Manheulles Captured by the 4th Division on September 14, 1918

IN addition to the places whose World War history has been described in the itinerary, there are a number of other places in the St. Mihiel region where interesting war events occurred, where there now exist features of special interest, or which are of sufficient importance in pre-World War history to warrant special mention. For reference purposes and for the benefit of the tourist who travels in the area not on the described route, these places and parts of their history have been recorded on the following pages.

The sketch which appears on this page shows the general location of the places

mentioned. At those indicated by a sta on the sketch and in the text there is som interesting object such as a memoria ancient ruins or outstanding World Wa feature in a good state of preservation.

Abaucourt. Captured on November 1 by the 81st Division after severe fighting

Ancemont. Location of V Corps Head quarters, September 10–16.

Ansauville. Location of 42d Div Headquarters, September 9–14.

Apremont. This village, just within the German front lines, was completel demolished by French and America artillery fire. In town, near the church

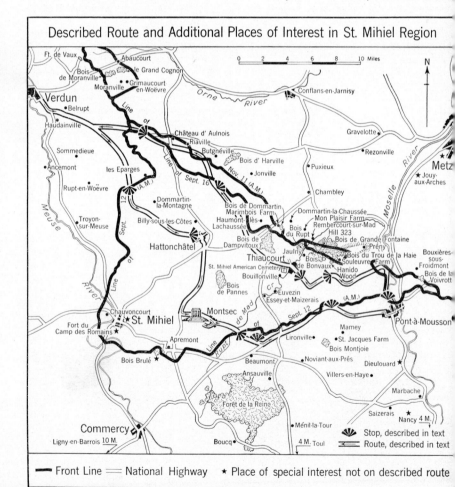

Described Route and Additional Places of Interest in St. Mihiel Region

Allied Prisoners Returning to American Lines at Abaucourt,
November 13, 1918

s a memorial fountain to the American
soldiers who fell at Apremont, donated
y the city of Holyoke, Massachusetts.

Beaumont. 1st Div. Hdqrs., Sept. 11–13.

Belrupt. 81st Div. Hdqrs., Nov. 9–11.

Billy-sous-les-Côtes. While alone on
voluntary air patrol near this place on
eptember 25, First Lieutenant Edward
. Rickenbacker, Air Service, encoun-
ered a hostile formation of seven planes.
Disregarding the odds against him he
ived on them and shot one down out of
ontrol. He then attacked a second which
vas likewise shot down. For this con-
picuous gallantry and intrepidity above
nd beyond the call of duty, Lieutenant
Rickenbacker was later awarded the Con-
ressional Medal of Honor.

Bois de Bonvaux. This wood was
eached by patrols of the 5th Division
n September 12. It was the scene of
ard fighting on September 14 when the
Germans were driven from it.

★ **Bois Brulé.** Scene of bitter fighting
between the French and Germans in 1915.
The 26th Division engaged in severe local
ombats in the vicinity during April 1918.
Many interesting trenches and German
ugouts are being preserved there (1937).

Bois de Dampvitoux. Near this wood

the Germans had an important aviation
field and a group of barracks. The wood
was occupied during September 13 by the
troops of the 42d and 89th Divisions.

Bois de Dommartin. Located about
600 yards in front of the American lines
after the St. Mihiel operation, this little
wood was the scene of many small but
bitter fights in which at different times
the 89th, 37th and 28th Divisions, in that
order, participated. It was occupied by
the 28th Division on November 10 and
held until after the Armistice.

Bois de Grande Fontaine. Scene of
severe local fighting by the 5th, 78th and
7th Divisions at various times from September 14 on. During November 1 the
southern part of this wood was captured
and held by troops of the 7th Division.

Bois d'Harville. The 33d Division attacked and gained a foothold in this wood
on November 10 in spite of heavy machine-gun and artillery fire. The wood
was abandoned that night, however, because of hostile gas-shell bombardments.

Bois Montjoie, about ½ mile southeast
of Lironville, was the location of the 2d
Div. Headquarters, September 10–12.

Bois de Pannes. The 42d Div. Hdqrs.
was located here from Sept. 25 to Oct. 1.

Bois du Rupt. A counterattack of the German 31st Division, launched from this wood during the afternoon of September 12, was repulsed by the 2d Division, which inflicted heavy losses. The wood was occupied by the 2d Division on September 14 and remained in American hands until after the Armistice.

Bois du Trou de la Haie. Considerable hard fighting occurred in this wooded area both before and after November 1, on which date the 7th Division established its front line well into it.

Bois de la Voivrotte. The 92d Division captured this wood early on November 11 and from it launched two attacks against Bouxières-sous-Froidmont.

Boucq. Location of 26th Div. Hdqrs., Mar. 31–June 20, and IV Corps Hdqrs. for the period Oct. 10 to Nov. 3.

Bouillonville. Sergeant Harry J. Adams, 89th Division, won the Distinguished Service Cross in this town for an act of great coolness and daring on September 12. Discovering a group of Germans in a building he promptly fired his remaining pistol bullets through the door and demanded the instant surrender of the occupants. Some 300 German emerged and Sergeant Adams, althou alone and armed only with an emp pistol, made prisoners of them all.

Butgnéville. A 33d Division attack November 11 made against this villa was repulsed with severe losses.

Chambley. Site of an important Ge man ammunition depot.

Château d'Aulnois. Captured by t 33d Division on November 11. It h; been the objective of active patrolling various American units before then.

Chauvoncourt. This town, situat across the Meuse River from St. Mihi and the flat-topped hill near it, were ca tured by the Germans in 1914 and he as a bridgehead until the American atta of September 12 forced their evacuatio

Conflans-en-Jarnisy. Headquarters the German Army Detachment "C which was holding the St. Mihiel salier The town was an important communic tion center and the objective of many the American aviation bombing raids.

★ **Dieulouard.** In the northern ou skirts of this town, along the main roa are (1937) the remains of a large concre

Wartime View of German Support Trenches Near Apremont

nplacement for an Allied railroad gun.

Dommartin-la-Chaussée. Site of a rge German supply depot. The town as in the main line of resistance of the indenburg Line. Attempts of the 28th ivision to capture it on November 10 ere defeated with considerable losses.

Dommartin-la-Montagne. Fire from his village halted the advance of the left nits of the 26th Division on September 2. It was captured the next morning.

Essey-et-Maizerais. Location of the 2d Div. Headquarters, Sept. 14–25.

Euvezin. Captured by the 89th Division. Before the St. Mihiel offensive a erman artillery camp was located in the ivine south of the town. The camp was he 89th Div. Hdqrs., Sept. 14–Oct. 7; 7th Div. Hdqrs., Oct. 7–16; 28th Div. Idqrs., Oct. 16–29; and 7th Div. Hdqrs., ct. 30 to after the Armistice.

★ **Fort du Camp des Romains.** This rt near St. Mihiel was built by the rench about 1879 upon the site of an old oman camp. It was captured in 1914 y the Germans and retained by them ntil the attack of the American First rmy forced its evacuation. The fort is ot used now and is in ruins.

Gravelotte. This village was the scene f an important German victory in 1870 uring the Franco-Prussian War.

Grimaucourt-en-Woëvre. Captured by he 81st Division on November 10 but ot held that night. The next day the ivision pushed forward through the own and about 1 mile beyond it.

Hanido Wood and **Souleuvre Farm.** These places were occupied on the afteroon of September 12 by the German axon 123d Division which had entered he battle to check the American advance. counterattack by that division from the ood the next day was repulsed by the th Division after severe fighting.

Haudainville. Location of 4th Div. Ieadquarters, September 9–19.

Haumont-lès-Lachaussée. This village as lightly held by the Germans folowing the St. Mihiel attack. The 42d, 9th and 37th Divisions raided it several imes and the 28th Division occupied it on

Château d'Aulnois, November 1918

two different occasions; from October 24 to 29, and again from November 9 to 11.

Hill 323, south of Rembercourt-sur-Mad. This hill was strongly held by the Germans following the St. Mihiel offensive. It was the scene of numerous severe combats by the 5th, 78th and 7th Divisions prior to its capture by the latter on November 10. Several determined German attempts to retake it were repulsed.

Jaulny. This town was captured by the 2d Division about 1:00 p. m. on September 12. A German ammunition train and a completely equipped hospital train were captured there. Because the village lay beyond the objective of the American Army it was abandoned later in the day. The Germans reoccupied it but on the next day the 2d Division again drove them from the town and the American lines were then established beyond it.

Mon Plaisir Farm in the Winter After the Armistice

Jonville. On September 14 a group of American tanks, operating considerably ahead of the infantry lines, engaged in a severe fight near this town.

★ **Jouy-aux-Arches.** At this place there are still standing several arches of a large aqueduct built by the Romans to bring water across the Moselle River to Metz.

Le Grand Cognon. This wooded area was captured by the 81st Division on November 10 after a hard fight.

Les Eparges. Scene of bitter fighting between the French and Germans in 1914 and 1915. The remains of large mine craters are still (1937) to be seen there.

Ligny-en-Barrois. Location of First Army Hdqrs., Aug. 28–Sept. 21. Advance G. H. Q., A. E. F., Oct. 25–Dec. 3.

Lucey. 82d Div. Hdqrs., June 27–Aug. 10; 89th Div. Hdqrs., Aug. 10–Sept. 10.

Mamey. Location of 90th Div. Hdqrs., for the period September 11–19.

Marbache. 2d Div. Hdqrs., Aug. 9–19; 82d Div. Hdqrs., Aug. 18–Sept. 20; and 92d Div. Hdqrs., Oct. 9–Nov. 10.

Marimbois Farm. This farm was in German hands at the close of the St. Mihiel offensive. From September 16 on patrols of the 42d and, later, of the 89th and 28th Divisions frequently clashed with the enemy there. It was occupied by the 28th Division on November 9 and held until the Armistice.

Ménil-la-Tour. 1st Div. Headquarters, from January 18–April 3, and IV Corps Headquarters, September 10–October 10.

★ **Metz.** This city, which is strategically located on the Moselle River, has

been a fortress of importance since the time of the Romans, who called it Divodurum. The city was plundered by Attila the Hun in the 5th Century. It was ceded by France to Germany after the War of 1870 and became one of the principal fortified places in the German line of frontier defenses. It was returned to France after the World War by the provisions of the Treaty of Versailles.

Mon Plaisir Farm. A strongly organized place in the Hindenburg Line which was attacked at different times after the St. Mihiel offensive by the 78th and 7th Divisions. The 28th and 89th Divisions sent patrols to it. The farm was still in the hands of the Germans when the Armistice became effective.

Moranville and the **Bois de Moranville.** These places in the outpost zone of the Hindenburg Line were captured by the 81st Division on November 9 in spite of determined hostile resistance.

★ **Nancy.** The Kaiser is said to have come to view the German attacks north of Nancy at the beginning of the World War, expecting to make a triumphal entry into the city. Although it was shelled all attempts to capture the town were repulsed. Nancy contains many beautiful buildings and other works of art. It is well worth a visit.

Noviant-aux-Prés. In a dugout along the railroad north of this town was located the 89th Div. Headquarters, for the period September 10 to 12.

Prény. This town, picturesquely situated on a long ridge in the Hindenburg

St. Mihiel Soon After Its Capture

Line, was the objective of frequent raids by the 90th and 7th Divisions. Many hand-to-hand fights took place near it. The interesting ruins of an ancient fortified château are to be seen there.

Puxieux. An important German aviation field and a large munitions depot were located near this town.

Rembercourt-sur-Mad. This village, situated in the valley of the Rupt de Mad, and the wooded heights south of it were hastily occupied on September 12 by the German 31st Division which had entered the battle line to check the American advance. The German division launched a counterattack that afternoon which was repulsed by the 2d Division.

Rezonville. Scene of a desperate battle in the Franco-Prussian War of 1870. This battle and that of Gravelotte prevented Marshal Bazaine from retreating toward Paris and forced his army into Metz, where it later surrendered.

Riaville. Captured by the 33d Division on the morning of November 11.

Rupt-en-Woëvre. Location of 26th Division Headquarters, Sept. 6–16.

St. Jacques Farm, about 1 mile southwest of Mamey. 5th Division Headquarters during the period, Sept. 10–17.

★ **St. Mihiel.** This town, at the tip of the St. Mihiel salient, gave the salient its name. The town was captured on September 24, 1914, by the Germans. Several thousand French civilians lived in it during the entire war and for that reason, though near the front line, it was never heavily bombarded by the Allies. St. Mihiel was not attacked during the offensive of September 12 but was hastily abandoned by the enemy troops when the American divisions broke through the battle line on both sides of it. The town was occupied on September 13 by a French division attached to the American First Army. Soon after its occupation the President of the French Republic sent a message to the United States Government in which he expressed the deep gratitude of the French nation because of the restoration to France of that place.

Among the points of interest in or

Searching Prisoners at Headquarters, 5th Division, St. Jacques Farm, September 12, 1918

near the town are the churches of St. Etienne and St. Mihiel, and at the northern edge of the town on the road to Verdun are located seven great rocks near which have been found many interesting relics of prehistoric man.

The 370th Infantry, 93d Division, while attached to the French 34th Division had front-line service to the south of this town during the month of June 1918.

St. Mihiel–Apremont Road. Alongside

Off Duty

this road are to be seen many interesting examples of wartime military construction. The large concrete shelter extending into the roadway is well worth a visit. It was built by the Germans as a first-aid station. In the wood near by are many other German field works constructed

face of the St. Mihiel salient. Location of 35th Div. Hdqrs., Oct. 15–Nov. 7, and 81st Div. Hdqrs., Nov. 7–9.

Toul. This city was the American Second Army Headquarters during the entire time that Army served at the front. IV Corps Hdqrs., Aug. 13 to Sept. 10.

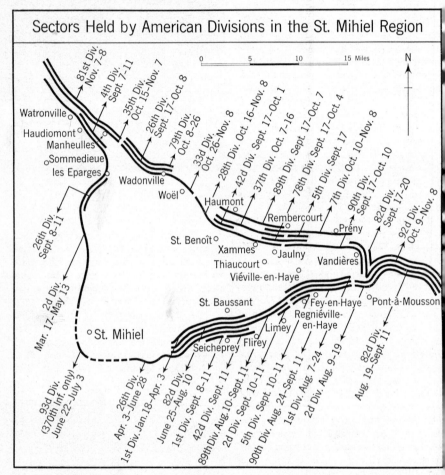

Sectors Held by American Divisions in the St. Mihiel Region

during the four years of trench warfare.

Saizerais. Location of 1st Div. Hdqrs., Aug. 7–24; I Corps Hdqrs., Aug. 21–Sept. 18; and VI Corps Hdqrs., from Sept. 15 until after the Armistice.

Sommedieue. 2d Div. Hdqrs., during most of the period, Mar. 16–May 9, while the division was training in the front line with the French on the western

Troyon-sur-Meuse. Location of 26th Div. Hdqrs., Sept. 16–Oct. 8; 79th Div. Hdqrs., Oct. 8–26; and 33d Div. Hdqrs., Oct. 26 to the Armistice.

Villers-en-Haye. Location of 90th Div. Hdqrs., Aug. 24–Oct. 10, except from September 11 to 19 when it moved forward to Mamey for the St. Mihiel operation. 7th Div. Hdqrs., Oct. 10–30.

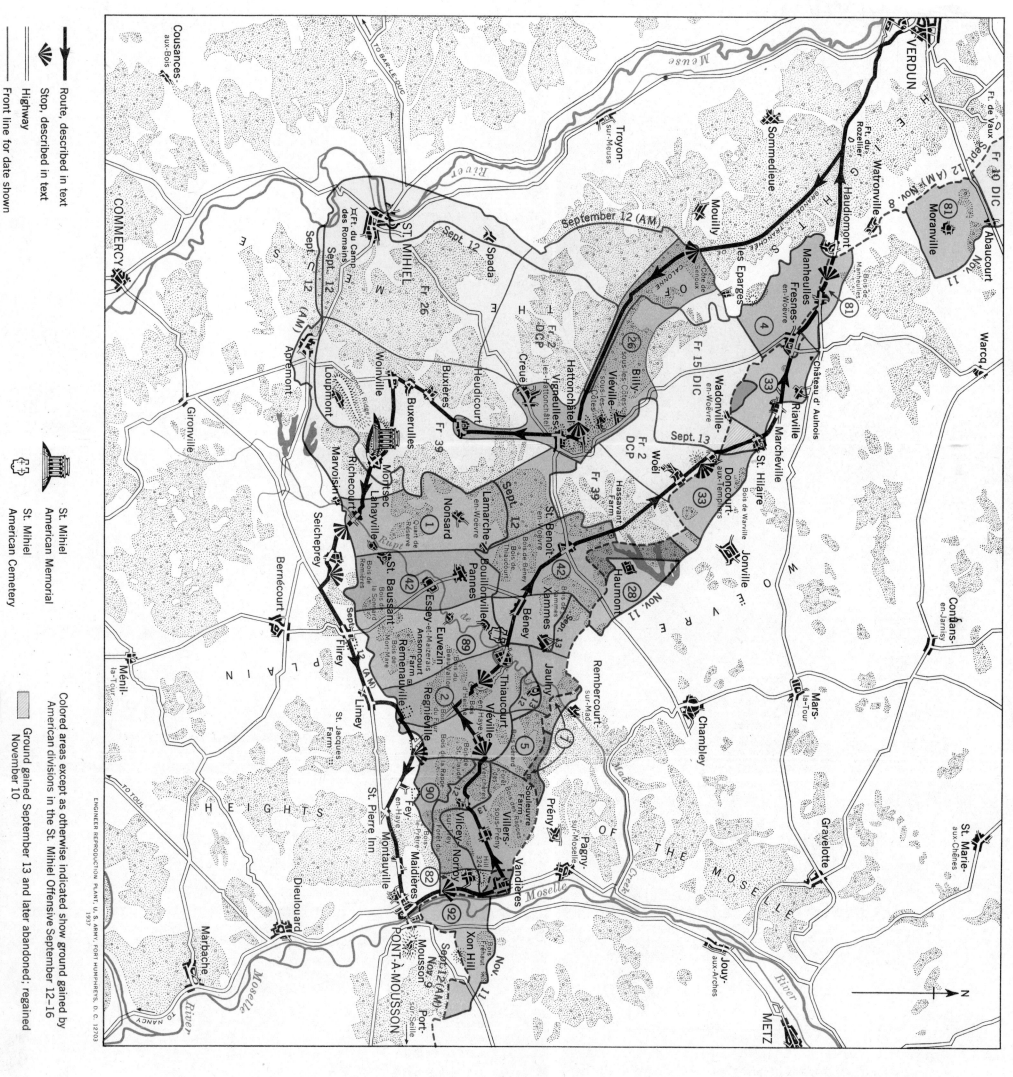

American Battle Operations in the St. Mihiel Region

Route, described in text

Stop, described in text

Highway

Front line for date shown

Front line of September 16

All front lines are as of midnight for dates shown unless otherwise noted; thus September 12 on a line indicates the line held at midnight September 12/13. The dates September 12-13 on a line indicate that the line was located at the same place at midnight of both September 12 and September 13

St. Mihiel American Memorial

St. Mihiel American Cemetery

Ruins

Colored areas except as otherwise indicated show ground gained by American divisions in the St. Mihiel Offensive September 12-16

Ground gained September 13 and later abandoned; regained November 10

Ground gained by American divisions Sept. 17-Nov. 8

November 9-11 Operation of American Second Army and 81st Division American First Army

Ground gained by French divisions attached to American Army

Circled numerals indicate American divisions

Scale 1:200000

0   5   10 Kilometers

0   5   10 Miles

ENGINEER REPRODUCTION PLANT, U. S. ARMY, FORT HUMPHREYS, D. C. 12703 1937

American Battle Operations in the St. Mihiel Region

SUMMARY OF COMBAT SERVICE OF AMERICAN DIVISIONS IN THE ST. MIHIEL REGION

Name of Div.	Period of Service 1918	Character of Service	Location of Service General vicinity of—	Army to Which Attached [1]	Corps to Which Attached [1]	Casualties [2]
1	Jan. 18–Apr. 3...	Training in Line and Sector.	Seicheprey............	Fr. First until Mar. 27, then Fr. Eighth.	Fr. XXXII.......	654
	Aug. 7–24.......	Sector.......	Forêt du Bois-le-Prêtre and Regniéville.	Fr. Eighth......	Fr. XXXII until Aug. 22, then I.	75
	Sept. 8–11........	Sector.......	Seicheprey............	First............	IV..............	13 (1)
	Sept. 12–14......	Battle.......	Richecourt and Nonsard.	First............	IV...............	467 (18)
2	Mar. 17–May 13.	Training in Line.	Northwest of St. Mihiel and Watronville.	Fr. Second until May 11, then French Group of Armies of the Reserve.	Fr. X until Apr. 17, then Fr. II CAC.	881
	Aug. 9–19.......	Sector.......	Port-sur-Seille and Pont-à-Mousson.	Fr. Eighth......	Fr. XXXII.......	38
	Sept. 10–11......	Sector.... ..	Limey................	First...........	I..............	22
	Sept. 12–16......	Battle...... .	Thiaucourt and Jaulny.	First............	I...	1,477
4	Sept. 7–11.......	Sector.......	Haudiomont...........	First............	V...............	17
	Sept. 12–15......	Battle.......	Fresnes-en-Woëvre....	First............	V...............	60
5	Sept. 10–11......	Sector.......	Regniéville-en-Haye...	First............	I...............	23
	Sept. 12–16......	Battle.......	Viéville-en-Haye......	First............	I...............	1,449
	Sept. 17.........	Sector.......	North of Viéville-en-Haye.	First............	I...............	86
7	Oct. 10–Nov. 11.	Sector.......	South of Rembercourt-sur-Mad.	First until Oct. 12, then Second.	IV..............	1,676 (85)
26	Apr. 3–June 28..	Sector.......	Seicheprey............	Fr. Eighth......	Fr. XXXII.......	2,194 (7)
	Sept. 8–11.......	Sector.......	Côte de Senoux.......	First............	V...............	24 (1)
	Sept. 12–16......	Battle.......	Côte de Senoux and Vigneulles-lès-Hattonchâtel.	First............	V until Sept. 16, then Fr. II CAC.	479 (4)
	Sept. 17–Oct. 8.	Sector.......	Wadonville............	First............	Fr. II CAC.......	738
28	Oct. 16–Nov. 11.	Sector.......	Haumont.............	Second..........	IV..............	1,059 (117)
33	Oct. 26–Nov. 11.	Sector.......	Woël and Marchéville.	Second..........	Fr. II CAC until Nov. 6, then Fr. XVII.	825 (78)
35	Oct. 15–Nov. 7..	Battle.......	Manheulles and west of Moranville.	First............	Fr. XXXIII until Nov. 1, then Fr. XVII until Nov. 6, then Fr. II CAC.	422

[1] All armies and corps are American unless otherwise indicated. In this table Fr.=French.

[2] Casualties are for period in line only. Figures in parentheses give casualties for units temporarily attached. Add figure in parentheses to the one above in order to obtain the total casualties during the entire operation.

SUMMARY OF COMBAT SERVICE—*Continued*

Name of Div.	Period of Service 1918	Character of Service	Location of Service General vicinity of—	Army to which Attached [1]	Corps to which Attached [1]	Casualties [2]
37	Oct. 7–16	Sector	Xammes	First until Oct. 12, then Second.	IV	269 (9)
42	Sept. 11	Sector	Bois de Remières	First	IV	8
	Sept. 12–16	Battle	St. Baussant, Pannes and Hassavant Farm.	First	IV	901 (7)
	Sept. 17–Oct. 1	Sector	North of St. Benoit-en-Woëvre.	First	IV	309
78	Sept. 16	Battle	North of Jaulny	First	I	58 (7)
	Sept. 17–Oct. 4	Sector	North of Jaulny	First	I until Sept. 18, then IV.	1,848 (109)
79	Oct. 8–26	Sector	Wadonville	First until Oct. 12, then Second.	Fr. II CAC	369 (210)
81	Nov. 7–11	Battle	Moranville and Bois de Manheulles.	First	Fr. II CAC	974 (5)
82	June 25–Aug. 10	Training in Line and Sector.	Forêt du Bois-le-Prêtre and Marvoisin.	Fr. Eighth	Fr. XXXII	374
	Aug. 19–Sept. 11.	Sector	Port-sur-Seille and Pont-à-Mousson.	Fr. Eighth until Aug. 30, then First.	Fr. XXXII until Aug. 22, then I.	99 (1)
	Sept. 12–16	Battle	Norroy	First	I	816
	Sept. 17–20	Sector	Port-sur-Seille and Xon Hill.	First	I until Sept. 18, then IV.	146
89	Aug. 10–Sept. 11.	Sector	Limey and Marvoisin	Fr. Eighth until Aug. 30, then First.	Fr. XXXII until Aug. 20, then IV.	212 (7)
	Sept. 12–16	Battle	Bois de Mort-Mare and Xammes.	First	IV	833 (24)
	Sept. 17–Oct. 7	Sector	Xammes	First	IV	1,351 (11)
90	Aug. 24–Sept. 11.	Sector	Forêt du Bois-le-Prêtre and Regniéville.	Fr. Eighth until Aug. 30, then First.	I	137 (19)
	Sept. 12–16	Battle	Vilcey-sur-Trey and Bois des Rappes.	First	I	1,972 (35)
	Sept. 17–Oct. 10.	Sector	Vandières and west of Souleuvre Farm.	First	I until Sept. 18, then IV.	1,830 (51)
92	Oct. 9–Nov. 11	Sector	Port-sur-Seille and Vandières.	First until Oct. 12, then Second.	IV until Oct. 23, then VI.	959 (12)
93 (370th Inf. only)	June 22–July 3	Training in Line.	Southwest of St. Mihiel	Fr. Second	Fr. II CAC	0

[1] All armies and corps are American unless otherwise indicated.   In this table Fr. = French.

[2] Casualties are for period in line only.   Figures in parentheses give casualties for units temporarily attached. Add figure in parentheses to the one above in order to obtain the total casualties during the entire operation.

Chapter IV

AMERICAN OPERATIONS IN THE
MEUSE–ARGONNE REGION

ONE of the most far-reaching effects of the rapid increase of American troops in Europe, and the resulting Allied and American successes during the summer of 1918, was that it became possible to undertake in September a gigantic convergent offensive movement against the German forces on the Western Front. The final plans for this movement were agreed upon and as a formality of coordination were promulgated by the Allied Commander-in-Chief on September 3. Under these plans the American Army was to advance northward between the Meuse River and the Argonne Forest, supported on its left by the French Fourth Army west of the Argonne. Northeast of Paris the center of the French Armies was to renew its efforts to force the Germans back from the Aisne, while farther north the British were to continue operations in the direction of St. Quentin and Cambrai, and the Allies were to attack near Ypres to free the Belgian coast.

The significance of the American Army's part in the general plan lay in the fact that its attack was to be directed against a most vital point of the German system of railroad communications.

Within the German lines were two important railways which ran to the northwest from the area around Metz and roughly paralleled the battle front. These railroads were practically the Germans' only lateral communications between their forces east and west of the Meuse, and were therefore essential to their supply system and for the transfer of troops back and forth along the front. Northwest of Mézières these railways were rather widely separated and were at a considerable distance from the front lines, but in the vicinity of Sedan and to the southeast of that city they converged and ran through a narrow strip of territory lying within 35 miles of the battle line.

To the north of Sedan, as far as Liége, the country, including the Ardennes Forest, was of a wooded and difficult character, and no important east and west railways had been built through it.

The network of railways which radiated to the west and southwest from Liége passed through a restricted zone near that place, which was bounded by the rough terrain on the south and neutral Holland on the north. These railroads were the principal lines of supply and evacuation for the German troops along the entire front northwest of Reims.

It was apparent that an Allied attack in the vicinity of the Meuse River, if carried far enough to gain control of the lateral railways, would divide the German Armies. Once this was accomplished Germany would be unable to maintain her forces in France and Belgium because communications between the two wings would be practically impossible except by the long and circuitous route through Liége and the Rhine River valley.

Furthermore, the capture cr defeat of the German northern armies would be practically certain because, under the stress of the powerful attacks which the Allies were then prepared to deliver, these armies could scarcely effect an orderly withdrawal through the congested bottle neck at Liége. It was evident, therefore, that in the sector covering the communications near Sedan, and to the southeast of that place, the German forces could least afford to lose ground. This was clearly appreciated by the German High Command which had made elaborate preparations to prevent any Allied advance on that part of the battle front.

Along most of the Western Front the

German Tank Attack, October 1918. © G

German Tank and Observation Plane Cooperating in an Attack, September 1918. © G

German Troops Mopping Up a Trench, October 1918. © G

Germans had prepared several defensive lines in rear of their first position. West and northwest of the Meuse-Argonne region, where loss of ground would have no decisive effect on the situation, these

about 10 miles in rear of the front lines.

The nature of this region was such as to make it ideal for defensive fighting. The heights just east of the Meuse River constituted not only a formidable natural

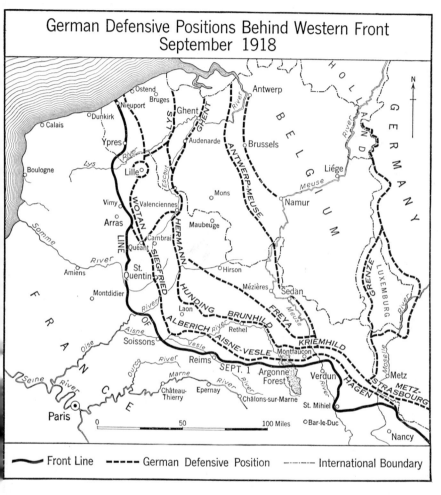

German Defensive Positions Behind Western Front
September 1918

— Front Line   ----- German Defensive Position   —·—·— International Boundary

different positions were separated by relatively great distances. In the Meuse-Argonne region, however, where the important railways lay comparatively close to the battle line, the second and third lines were very close to the forward position, forming a practically continuous zone of trenches, barbed wire and other field fortifications extending for a depth of

barrier but furnished splendid sites from which the country to the east and west could be observed and covered by artillery fire. These heights and the broken hills of the Argonne Forest had been organized into almost impregnable positions by the addition of machine guns, artillery, trenches and obstacles of all kinds. Between these two great natural bulwarks

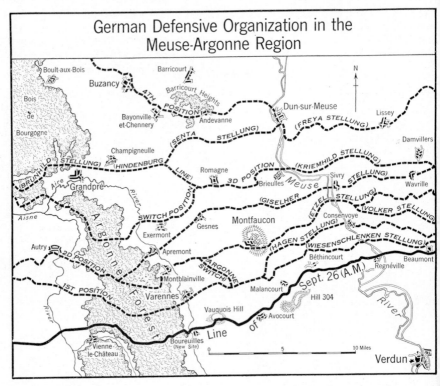

German Defensive Organization in the Meuse-Argonne Region

lay the dominating hill of Montfaucon which afforded the Germans perfect observation, and whose inherent strength had been greatly increased by the elaborate use of field fortifications of all kinds.

The numerous east and west ridges in this area lent themselves admirably to the construction of defensive lines which connected the Heights of the Meuse with the Argonne Forest. In organizing these lines the Germans had made elaborate use of barbed-wire entanglements, trenches, concrete machine-gun emplacements and prepared artillery positions, all so placed as to be mutually supporting and to cover by cross and enfilade fire the ground between the features of natural strength.

The comparatively narrow front of this natural defile and the great depth of the German defensive organization made the task of the American Army extremely difficult. The only feasible method of advancing was to drive salients into the enemy lines by frontal assaults and to exploit these penetrations by attacking the flanks of the salients thus created

American Supply Dump During the Meuse-Argonne Operation

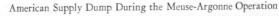

While the difficulties to be encountered in an offensive on the Meuse-Argonne front were clearly appreciated by the Allied High Command, it realized that an advance there would have far-reaching effects and that it would be essential to the success of the general plan.

In view of the strength of the German positions, the stubborn opposition that would undoubtedly be met with at that point and the vital importance of the front, the American Army could well feel that in the coming combined Allied offensive it had been given the place of honor.

When the decision was made to attack in the Meuse-Argonne region the American First Army was busily engaged in preparations for the St. Mihiel offensive, planned for September 12. However, because of the limited time available, the assembly of American divisions not scheduled for the St. Mihiel attack was begun immediately and detailed plans for the larger battle were at once prepared.

Two of the American divisions designated for the attack west of the Meuse, the 33d and 79th, were sent to that front before the middle of September and took over large sectors. Soon thereafter other American units were sent to the region and secretly concentrated behind them. The movement of men and matériel was made entirely under cover of darkness, all activity being suspended and the men kept in concealment during daylight hours. Consequently, at night the roads leading into the area were the scenes of great activity as troops and artillery, ammunition and supplies moved steadily forward. On most of the Meuse-Argonne front French soldiers remained in the outpost positions until the last minute to prevent the Germans from seeing or otherwise securing information of the presence of large numbers of American soldiers in the region and thus receiving advance warning of the impending offensive.

In all, about 220,000 Allied soldiers were moved out of the area and approximately 600,000 Americans were moved into it. The planning and execution of this gigantic movement of concentration was an intricate and arduous task. The fact that it was done with smoothness and precision, and without the knowledge of the enemy, is in itself a striking tribute to the ability of the American Army and to the skill of its staffs.

Finally, on the night of September 25–26 the First Army stood on its new front ready for the momentous battle that was to begin at dawn the next day.

The American corps and divisions in line were in position as shown on the

Road Scene at Esnes, an Important Road Center,
During the Meuse-Argonne Operation

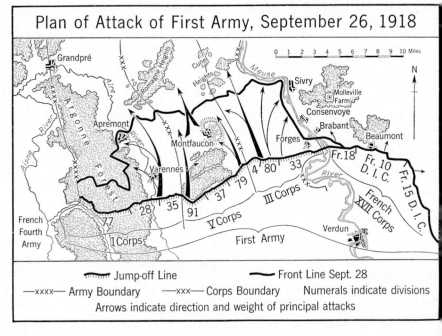

Plan of Attack of First Army, September 26, 1918

Jump-off Line   Front Line Sept. 28
—xxxx— Army Boundary   —xxx— Corps Boundary   Numerals indicate divisions
Arrows indicate direction and weight of principal attacks

above sketch. The III Corps was on the right with the 33d, 80th and 4th Divisions in line, in that order from right to left, and the 3d Division in reserve. The V Corps was in the center with the 79th, 37th and 91st Divisions in line and the 32d Division in reserve. The I Corps was on the left, with the 35th, 28th and 77th Divisions in line and the French 5th Cavalry Division and the American 92d Division, less one regiment, in reserve. The 1st, 29th and 82d Divisions composed the Army reserve. Opposing the American First Army were the German Fifth and Third Armies.

The general plans provided first for an advance of 10 miles which would break through the hostile first, second and third positions and force the Germans to give up the Argonne Forest. This was to be followed by a further penetration of about the same distance which would outflank their defenses in the Bois de Bourgogne [1] and along the Aisne in front

of the French Fourth Army, and thus open the way toward Sedan and Mézières. These attacks of the First Army were to be coordinated by General Pershing and General Pétain with those of the French Fourth Army west of the Argonne.

The difficulty of capturing Montfaucon was fully realized, and it was planned to drive deep salients into the German lines on each side of that stronghold and then, by threatening its rear, to force the retirement of the garrison. By these tactics the troops in front of the hill would be enabled to carry it without encountering too severe opposition.

The V Corps, whose zone of action included Montfaucon near its eastern boundary, was to drive vigorously forward to the left of that place and without waiting for the adjacent corps was to penetrate the German third position near Romagne. The main mission of the III Corps was to support the advance of the V Corps by turning Montfaucon from the east and by protecting the right flank of the advancing troops. The I Corps was to protect the left of the V Corps and

[1] In this text the name Bois de Bourgogne has been used to designate the entire large continuous wooded area which lies to the north of the Argonne Forest.

flank the Argonne Forest from the east. The artillery of the III Corps was especially charged with suppressing the enemy guns located on the dominating heights east of the Meuse, while the artillery of the I Corps was to silence the German guns firing from the Argonne Forest.

A brigade, under French command, which included the 368th Infantry, 92d Division, and one French regiment, had the mission of maintaining contact between the flanks of the American First Army and the French Fourth Army.

Of the nine American divisions which took part in the initial assault only five had seen service in offensive combat and four of the nine were supported by divisional artillery with which they had never served. Moreover, time had not been available in which to train the many units of the First Army in the teamwork so essential to success in battle. Despite these handicaps, however, the ability of the commanders and their staffs, and the unbounded strength, courage and will-to-win of the soldiers, carried the Army rapidly forward from the very beginning.

The artillery preparation for the attack began in full force at 2:30 on the morning of September 26. Two thousand seven hundred guns kept up an intense bombardment of the hostile positions until 5:30 a.m., at which time the assaulting infantry jumped off, protected by a rolling barrage. The dense fog during the morning, the networks of wire, myriads of shell craters, deep ravines and thick woods presented great difficulties, but, except in front of Montfaucon, the progress made that day was considered entirely satisfactory.

In the center, the left of the V Corps made a splendid advance to the west of Montfaucon but its right was held up in front of that place. The III Corps drove forward vigorously to the east of Montfaucon and by early afternoon its left flank was a mile beyond that hill. During the advance its right flank wheeled toward the Meuse and took up a defensive position along the bluffs of the river. The I Corps, on the Army's left, made a deep penetration along the Aire River while its left flank fought its way forward about one mile in the Argonne Forest.

German Narrow-Gauge Railroad Equipment Captured in the Argonne Forest

American Troops Marching Toward the Front, Montfaucon, October 2, 1918

On the evening of September 26 the strong German first position was all in American hands. Montfaucon, in the German second position, had held out, but deep salients driven into the German lines on both sides of that hill made its capture a question of merely a few hours.

On the second day the infantry assaults were continued vigorously, Montfaucon being carried about noon. The Germans' brief stand there, however, had enabled them to reinforce their strong positions north of the hill, and as the American advance of the day before had

by severe artillery concentrations and strong counterattacks by fresh German troops. Gains were made by the Americans at a number of places but most of these were isolated and had to be given up. As a result of the increased resistance and of conditions incident to the deep and rapid advance, the First Army on September 29 ordered that the positions then held be organized for defense and that vigorous preparations be started for a prompt renewal of the battle. During this period certain of the inexperienced divisions which had been in the initial

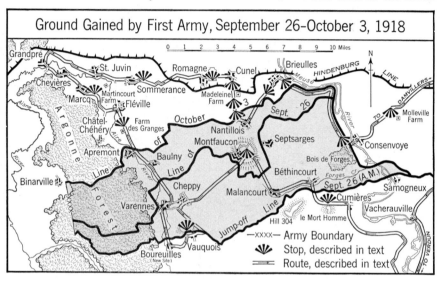

Ground Gained by First Army, September 26–October 3, 1918

been so rapid as to outrun much of its artillery support, the amount of ground captured and held by the First Army on September 27 was not as great as that secured on the preceding day.

On September 28, however, with more artillery and tank support, the American units again surged forward, gaining about 1½ miles all along the front of attack. Except in the Argonne Forest, the line held that evening was beyond the German second position and the III and V Corps faced the outpost defenses of the German third position in this region, commonly known as the Hindenburg Line.

During the next day the determined efforts of the Army to advance were met

assault were replaced in line by other divisions with previous battle service.

During the initial stages of the offensive the Army had under its control 821 airplanes, which rendered valuable service. The Army keenly felt the need of tanks. The total number with the Army was reduced during the first two weeks of the offensive from 415, of which 141 were operated by Americans, to about 94.

While the attack on the first day had surprised the Germans and resulted in important gains at comparatively small cost, the fighting all along the front from that time on was of the most desperate character. Each foot of ground was stubbornly contested, the hostile troops

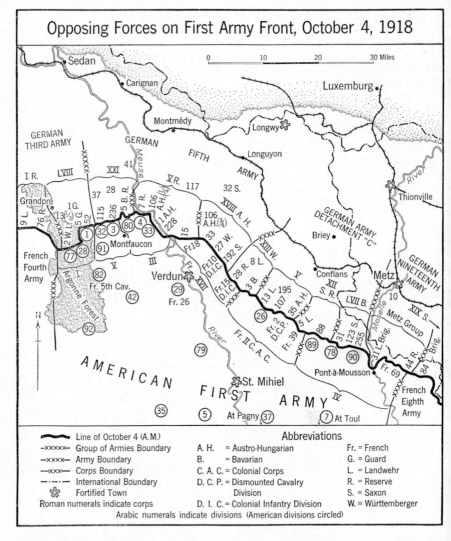

Opposing Forces on First Army Front, October 4, 1918

taking advantage of every available spot from which to pour enfilading and cross fire into the advancing Americans.

In their efforts to stop the progress of the American units, the Germans quickly began drawing reinforcements from other parts of the Western Front to strengthen their forces in the Meuse-Argonne region and by the end of the fifth day seven more German divisions had been rushed to this crucial region and had entered the battle.

The great progress of the First Army

attack and Allied pressure on other parts of the front caused the German High Command on September 29 to urge its Government to forward immediately an offer of peace to the Allied Governments and this was done on October 6.

The area near the former front lines had been torn to pieces by shellfire during the preceding four years and the few roads leading across it were almost entirely obliterated in what had been no man's land. In order to move troops, food and mmunition forward, and the wounded to he rear, these roads had to be practically ebuilt while in use. The difficulty of he task was increased by inclement veather, frequent hostile artillery bom-ardments, and the limited number of engineer and pioneer troops available.

The resumption of the attack was ordered for October 4. At that time, on most of its front east of the Argonne, the Army faced the outpost zone of the Hindenburg Line. That line, which included the Bois de Forêt, Cunel Heights and Romagne Heights, had been organized with great skill so as to take full advantage of the natural defensive features of the ground. In the Argonne Forest the First Army was in front of the German second position which extended across it to the west from Apremont.

The III and V Corps were to attack the Bois de Forêt, Cunel Heights and Ro-magne Heights, while the I Corps was to assist the V Corps by capturing the western end of Romagne Heights, neutralize the hostile artillery fire from the Argonne Forest and maintain liaison with the French Fourth Army.

Many changes had been made in the front-line divisions and on October 4 the Army order of battle from the Meuse River to the west was as follows: the 33d, 4th and 80th Divisions in line in the III Corps; the 3d and 32d Divisions in line and the 91st Division in process of with-drawal from line to reserve in the V Corps; and the 1st, 28th and 77th Divisions in line with the 82d, 92d (less the 183d Brigade) and French 5th Cavalry Divisions in reserve in the I Corps. The 35th and 42d Divisions and the 183d Brigade of the 92d Division were in Army reserve.

The attack was launched with great force about daybreak. The resistance

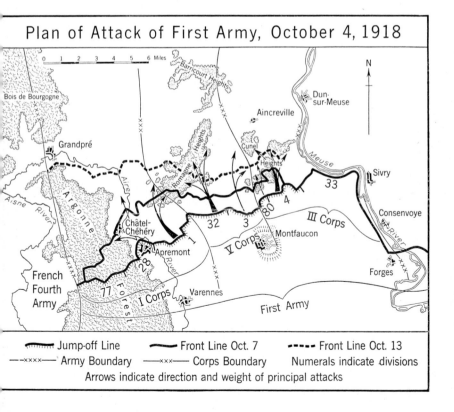

encountered was desperate in the extreme as the Germans were rapidly pouring their best troops into this battle.   Not all the assigned objectives were taken, but important gains were made, outstanding among them being the capture by the 4th Division of the Bois de Fays in the Hindenburg Line southeast of Cunel and a deep advance immediately east of the Aire River by the 1st Division.

To exploit this latter gain it became necessary to make a flank attack against the Heights of the Argonne, near Châtel-Chéhéry, from which the fire of in-

creasingly large concentrations of hostile artillery was causing severe casualties and hampering the American operations to the east of the forest.   Consequently on the morning of the 7th an assault was made by the 28th and 82d Divisions against Châtel-Chéhéry, in rear of and near the left flank of the German second position in the Argonne.   At the same time the 77th Division advanced from the south.   The flank attack was successful and freed the heroic survivors of the "Lost Battalion".   (See Chapter V.)

The advance was continued on the 8th

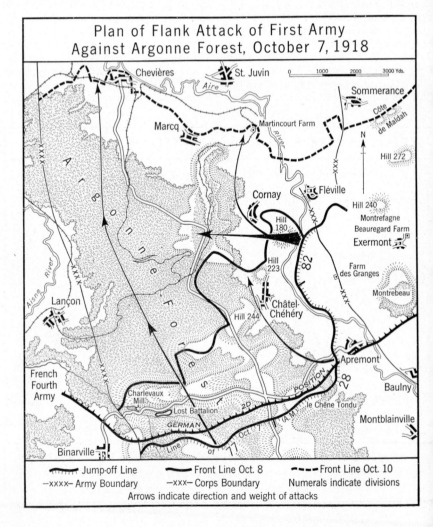

Plan of Flank Attack of First Army Against Argonne Forest, October 7, 1918

ith further valu-
ble gains. As a
esult the Germans
n October 9 started
withdrawal from
he Argonne, and
he menace to the
'irst Army of their
resence in the for-
st was removed.

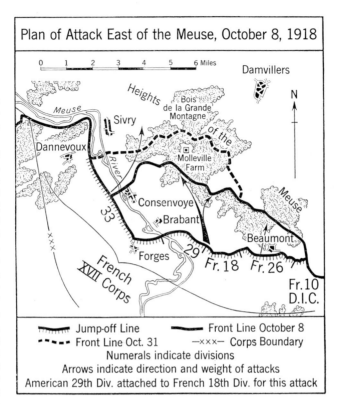

Plan of Attack East of the Meuse, October 8, 1918

0 1 2 3 4 5 6 Miles

Damvillers

Heights
Meuse
Bois de la Grande Montagne
Sivry
N
Dannevoux
Molleville Farm
of the
River
33
Consenvoye
Meuse
Brabant
Beaumont
XXX
Forges
French XVII Corps
29
Fr. 18   Fr. 26
Fr. 10
D.I.C.

Jump-off Line   Front Line October 8
Front Line Oct. 31   —xxx— Corps Boundary
Numerals indicate divisions
Arrows indicate direction and weight of attacks
American 29th Div. attached to French 18th Div. for this attack

The success in the
Argonne Forest on
October 7 was fol-
owed on October 8
y an attack east of
he Meuse by the
'rench XVII Corps
f the American
'irst Army. The
Corps was composed
f three French divi-
ions reinforced by
he American 29th
nd 33d Divisions,
making it almost
wo-thirds American
n strength. It
leared the enemy
rom an important
art of the heights
ast of the Meuse, captured approxi-
nately 3,000 prisoners and eliminated
nuch of the serious flanking fire which
ad been directed against the troops
rest of the river. This operation created
new threat against the enemy main
ateral line of communication through
edan and caused the Germans to
ncrease the number of their divisions
ngaged in the active fighting.

To reap the full advantage of the two
successful attacks in progress on the
anks, the V Corps, at the center of the
rmy, on October 9 again vigorously re-
umed the offensive, and on that day the
d and 80th Divisions penetrated the
Iindenburg Line in and near the Bois de
'unel and the 32d Division penetrated it
o the south of Romagne.

On the 10th the attacks were general
long the Army front from Beaumont,
ast of the Meuse, to the Argonne. By

the 11th the 4th Division had deepened
its penetration in the Hindenburg Line
and had gained a foothold in the Bois de
Forêt. On that day the 82d Division
came in close contact with the outpost of
the Hindenburg Line east of St. Juvin.
These operations involved fighting of the
most vicious sort, many places changing
hands several times in a single day.

The battle died down on the 12th as
the First Army again drew its breath
preparatory to a resumption of the offensive on October 14. At that time the
Army faced the Hindenburg Line, the
last fully-prepared German position,
along most of its zone of attack and had
penetrated it on a front of about 3 miles.

The plan of attack for October 14 and
the units which took part are shown on
the sketch on the following page.

For this attack the order of battle on
the Meuse-Argonne front was, from right

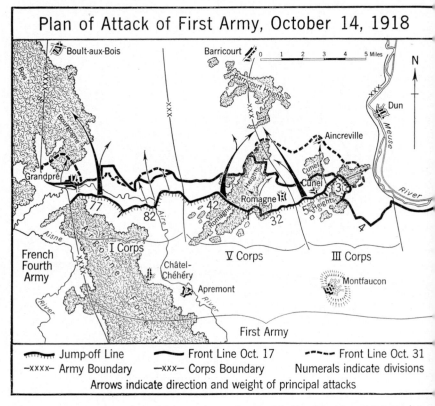

Plan of Attack of First Army, October 14, 1918

Boult-aux-Bois
Barricourt
0 1 2 3 4 5 Miles
N
Barricourt Heights
Dun
Aincreville
Grandpré
Cunel
Cunel
Romagne Heights
77
82
42
Romagne
Romagne
Cunel Heights
32
5
Meuse River
Aire
Aisne
French Fourth Army
I Corps
Châtel-Chéhéry
Apremont
V Corps
III Corps
Montfaucon
Aisne River
Aire River

First Army

Jump-off Line	Front Line Oct. 17	Front Line Oct. 31
-xxxx- Army Boundary	-xxx- Corps Boundary	Numerals indicate divisions

Arrows indicate direction and weight of principal attacks

to left, as follows: east of the Meuse—the French XVII Corps with the French 10th Colonial, 26th and 18th Divisions and the American 29th and 33d Divisions in line and the American 26th Division in reserve; west of the Meuse—the III

German Trench Mortar Used for Anti-Tank Defense, October 1918. © G

Corps with the 4th, 3d and 5th Division in line, the V Corps with the 32d an 42d Divisions in line and the 89th i reserve, and the I Corps with the 82 and 77th Divisions in line and the 78t and French 5th Cavalry Divisions i reserve. The 1st, 80th, 90th and 91s Divisions were in Army reserve. Oppos ing this front the Germans had 1 divisions in the front line and 6 in reserve

It was hoped that the III and V Corp could drive salients through the Hinden burg Line and then force the enemy fror the ground between the salients. The Corps was to protect the left of the Corps. The French XVII Corps was t continue its offensive east of the Meuse.

The offensive was to be started at th same time as one by the French Fourt Army, in an attempt to advance simu taneously on both sides of the difficu ground in the dense Bois de Bourgogn

The attack was launched with great
gor on October 14 and met with violent
sistance. Its weight, however, proved
verwhelming and positions of tremendous
rength in and near the Hindenburg Line
ere carried, the most notable being the
ois de la Pultière taken by the 3d and 5th
ivisions, the dominating Côte Dame
arie seized by the 32d Division, St.
vin captured by the 77th, and the
dge to the east of it taken by the 82d.
The offensive was pushed on the 15th
d 16th, resulting in the capture of the
ôte de Châtillon, a stronghold in the
indenburg Line, by the 42d Division and
e hill north of St. Juvin by the 82d.
lthough the ground gained in these three
ys was not so great in area, it was of
ceptional importance as it opened the
ay for further advances.

East of the Meuse, in the French XVII
orps, both the 29th and 33d Divisions
ined some ground during this period.

On October 21 General Pershing di-
cted the First Army to prepare for a
neral offensive, the date for which was
ntatively set as October 28. Prior to
e day of the attack, local assaults were

German Plane Forced Down Near Cierges,
October 4, 1918

to be made to secure favorable jump-off
lines and operations were to be initiated
on the left of the Army to clear the
wooded area north of Grandpré.

The local attacks were highly successful
in spite of severe opposition. The 3d,
5th, 26th (which had entered the line east
of the Meuse), 29th and 32d Divisions
and the 89th and 90th (which had entered
the line near Romagne) were all engaged.
By the 22d of the month the 3d Division
had completed the capture of the Bois de

Supply Train Passing Through Cuisy, October 11, 1918

Forêt; the 5th Division, Cunel Heights; and the 89th, the northern and eastern part of Romagne Heights. The American troops on the heights east of the Meuse River gave the enemy no respite and continued to advance despite the opposition of fresh German divisions.

The operations at Grandpré were pushed with great resolution, the 78th Division attacking almost continuously. Important ground was gained and by

American Second Army was formed i the Woëvre. After the reapportionmer of the American front between the tw Armies, the First extended from Fresne en-Woëvre to the western edge of t Argonne, a distance of about 49 mile The French XXXIII and XVII Corp and the American III, V and I Cor were in line from right to left.

General Pershing relinquished person command of the American First Army c

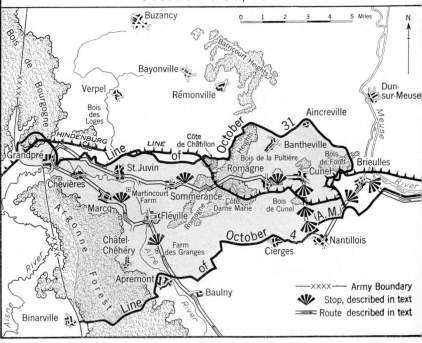

Ground Gained by First Army West of the Meuse River
October 4-31, 1918

October 27 sufficient progress had been made on that flank to enable the right of the French Fourth Army to advance. This activity had a material effect on the success of the final offensive, as it drew the hostile attention away from the center of the First Army at which point the main attack was finally delivered.

During the severe fighting in October several events of importance to the First Army occurred. On October 12 the

October 16 to Major General Hunt Liggett, and from that time on becam Commander of the American Group Armies, in addition to his duties as Con mander-in-Chief of the A. E. F.

In his report, covering the period of t Argonne battle from its beginning October 16, he paid a glowing tribute the enlisted men and junior officers the American Expeditionary Forces. said in part: " . . . attended by co

American Airplanes Ready to Start on Patrol Duty

nd inclement weather and fought largely y partially trained troops: the battle as prosecuted with an aggressive and eroic spirit of cour-ge and fortitude hich demanded even-al success despite all bstacles. The morale the American soldier uring this most trying eriod was superb. hysically strong and irile, naturally coura-eous and aggressive, spired by unselfish nd idealistic motives, e guaranteed the ictory and drove a eteran enemy from is last ditch. Too uch credit cannot e given him; his atriotism, courage, nd fortitude were eyond praise.

"Upon the young ommanders of pla-oons, companies, and attalions fell the eaviest burden. hey not only suffered ll the dangers and igors of the fight but arried the responsi-ility of caring for and irecting their men, ften newly arrived and ot fully trained . . . uick to learn, they oon developed on the field into skilled eaders and inspired their men . . ."

Although a pressing need existed during

Lieutenant General Hunter Liggett
Commanding General of the
First Army from October 16, 1918,
to April 20, 1919

the offensive for additional combat troops on the Meuse-Argonne front, the Allied Commander-in-Chief made many de-mands on General Pershing for American divisions to assist the attacks at other points. While reluctant to have his divisions op-erate away from the American Army, Gen-eral Pershing neverthe-less gave his consent in certain cases where he felt that by so doing the general situation would be improved.

The divisions which served with the Allies during this period had a very favorable effect upon the morale of the Allied soldiers, and the military accomplish-ments of these Ameri-can divisions were out-standing. The 2d and 36th were assigned to the French Fourth Army west of the Ar-gonne and early in October vitally assisted it to advance at a criti-cal period. (See Chap-ter V.) The 27th and 30th Divisions oper-ated with the British Army throughout the entire duration of the Meuse-Argonne operation. Their most striking achievement was on Sep-tember 29 when, as part of the American

First Aid Station at Main Road Junction in Montfaucon, October 1918

German Prisoners, Headed by Their Officers, Being Conducted to the Rear

German 21-Centimeter Mortar Being Withdrawn From Position, October 1918. © G

German Reserves Being Moved to the Front, October 1918. ⓒ G

I Corps, they broke the Hindenburg Line orth of St. Quentin. (See Chapter VI.) The 37th and 91st Divisions were sent to Belgium during October to assist the Group of Armies of Flanders, and late in he month attacked near Audenarde and made important gains. (See Chapter I.) The four infantry regiments of the 3d Division fought with great credit s integral parts of French divisions, and three American divisions, the 6th, 81st and 88th, held sectors for a time with the French Seventh Army in the Vosges Mountains, thus releasing French troops for service elsewhere.

On the Meuse-Argonne front a number of changes were made in the front-line units between October 22 and 31 as the worn-out divisions were relieved for rest and

recuperation and other divisions in better condition were placed in the battle line.

The American Army during this period was for the first time able to prepare for an offensive under reasonably normal conditions. It was already on the front from which the assault was to be made and sufficient time for careful and deliberate planning was available. Other favor-

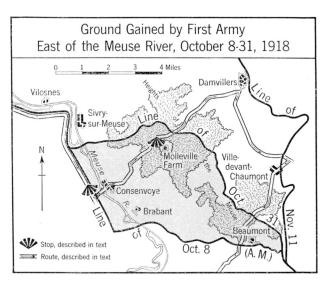

Ground Gained by First Army East of the Meuse River, October 8-31, 1918

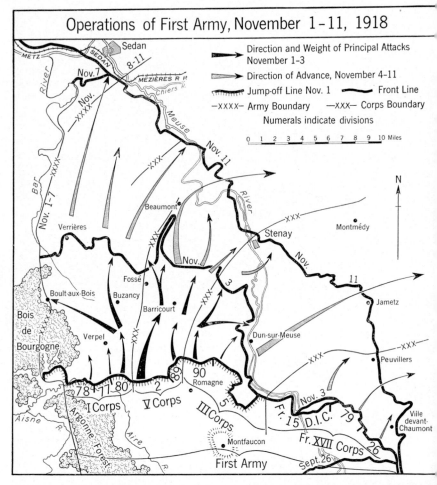

Operations of First Army, November 1–11, 1918

Direction and Weight of Principal Attacks November 1-3

Direction of Advance, November 4-11

Jump-off Line Nov. 1   Front Line

–XXXX– Army Boundary   –XXX– Corps Boundary

Numerals indicate divisions

0 1 2 3 4 5 6 7 8 9 10 Miles

able factors were that the majority of the Allied artillery and aviation units had been replaced by Americans and that the weather in the preparatory period took a turn for the better thus greatly relieving the hardships of the troops.[1]

Upon the request of the French the date of the attack was postponed until November 1, at which time the divisions of the First Army were in line as shown on the accompanying sketch. The order of

battle, from the Meuse River to the west was: the III Corps with the 5th and 90th Divisions in line and the 32d in reserve the V Corps with the 89th and 2d Divisions in line and the 1st and 42d in reserve and the I Corps with the 80th, 77th and 78th Divisions in line and the 6th and 82d in reserve. The 42d Division was transferred to the reserve of the I Corps soon after the beginning of the attack. The 3d, 29th and 36th Divisions in the rear areas composed the Army reserve.

The general mission of the First Army remained the same, to cut the Metz-Sedan–Mézières railroad. The detailed plan for the attack contemplated a deep

---

[1] During the course of the Meuse-Argonne operation, rain was reported in the official reports by at least one American division of the First Army on every day from September 26 to November 11, except for seven days, which were October 2, 3, 24, 25, 27, 28 and 29.

enetration by the V Corps in the center o secure Barricourt Heights, followed by , drive by the I Corps to connect with he French near Boult-aux-Bois. The apture of Barricourt Heights, which contituted a formidable natural obstacle, vould compel a German retirement across he Meuse, so the III Corps, while assisting the main attack in the center, was lirected to be prepared to force a crossing f the river if the enemy withdrew. There vas to be no attack by the French XVII Corps then on the heights east of the Meuse until this crossing was started. The eastern edge of the Bois de Bourgogne vas to be neutralized by heavy artillery oncentrations of persistent gas.

With conditions generally favorable, it vas a splendid force of veteran American oldiers which jumped off west of the Meuse at daybreak on November 1.

The assault was preceded by a terrific wo-hour artillery preparation which effec-

tively bombarded the sensitive points of the enemy positions. The progress of the attack exceeded all expectations. In the center, the V Corps crushed all opposition and by early afternoon had advanced about 6 miles and captured Barricourt Heights, thus assuring the success of the whole operation. On its right, the III Corps made a deep advance, wheeling toward the Meuse River to protect that flank of the Army. On the left, the I Corps, which faced the unbroken Hindenburg Line on most of its front, attacked and made an average gain of about $\frac{1}{2}$ mile. Its extreme right flank made a rapid and deep advance, keeping up with the left flank of the V Corps.

This deep penetration of the hostile lines, which overran the enemy artillery positions, caused the German High Command to issue orders on the night of November 1 for a withdrawal from the First Army front west of the Meuse.

Buzancy on the Day After Its Capture

he decision was a momentous one as ich a withdrawal required a general re-rement along the whole battle line as r as Holland, if the Germans were to void a decisive military defeat.

The First Army continued to drive for-ard on November 2 and 3. The III Corps rced the enemy across the Meuse River, e V Corps made a maximum advance 7 miles, and the I Corps gained 10 iles. By November 4 the Germans were full retreat west of the Meuse, although ill vainly trying to check the rapid ad-ance of the First Army by means of rear-iard actions and the use of machine guns

placed in strong commanding positions.

The pursuit continued until November 7, when units of the I Corps reached the heights overlooking the city of Sedan. The occupation of these heights effec-tively cut the lateral railroad through Sedan, which was the main objective of the Meuse-Argonne offensive.

During the period from November 4 to 7 the 1st Division relieved the 80th and the 42d Division relieved the 78th.

Between September 26 and November 6 the French, British and Belgians to the west and north had gradually increased the vigor and strength of their attacks

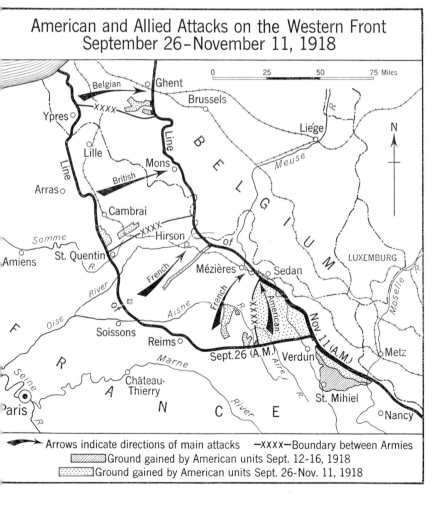

American and Allied Attacks on the Western Front September 26–November 11, 1918

Arrows indicate directions of main attacks   —xxxx—Boundary between Armies
Ground gained by American units Sept. 12-16, 1918
Ground gained by American units Sept. 26-Nov. 11, 1918

and had made substantial inroads into the hostile positions. Damaging as these drives were to the German cause, and valuable as they were in the Allied plan for victory, such was the importance to the Germans of protecting their main railroad at Sedan that they brought reserves from almost every portion of the Western Front to throw in the path of the American advance. (See the sketch below.)

When the American Army, in spite of increasing enemy reinforcements and a well-nigh impregnable hostile defensive system, had driven forward to a position dominating the German railroad communications in the vicinity of Sedan, the termination of the war in 1918 was assured.

While the pursuit was going on, the western boundary of the First Army was shifted several times by the Allied Commander-in-Chief, the notice of the las change being received on November when the American troops were on th heights south of Sedan preparing to attac the city. It limited the left of the Arm to Mouzon instead of to near Sedan. Th topography of the ground and thes modifications in its boundary caused th gradual withdrawal of the I Corps fro the battle line on the left flank of th First Army and a change from north t east in the general direction of advanc of the American Army.

Meanwhile the crossing of the Meus by the III Corps began on November when bridgeheads were established by th 5th Division south of Dun-sur-Meus These gains were exploited, assisted b

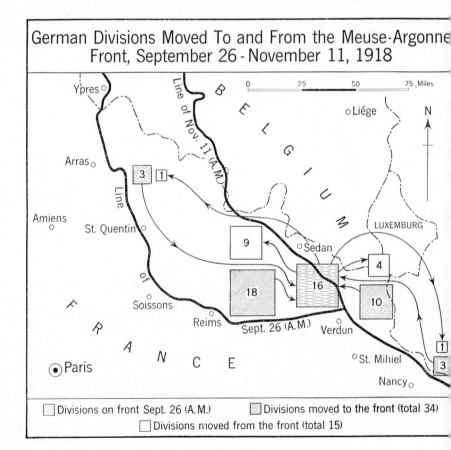

German Divisions Moved To and From the Meuse-Argonne Front, September 26 - November 11, 1918

Divisions on front Sept. 26 (A. M.)   Divisions moved to the front (total 34)
Divisions moved from the front (total 15)

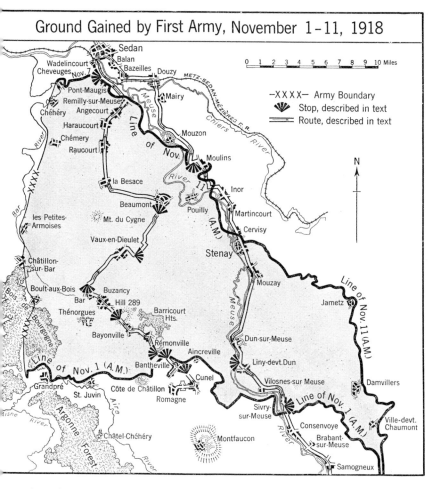

Ground Gained by First Army, November 1-11, 1918

northward movement of the French XVII Corps which was farther up the river on the heights to the east of it. This fighting gradually cleared the enemy from the heights east of the Meuse as far as Stenay. All divisions of the III Corps and French II Colonial Corps, which latter corps had relieved the French XVII Corps on November 6, were involved. These attacks, participated in by the 26th, 79th, French 15th Colonial, 2d, 5th and 90th Divisions, in order from right to left were so successful that by November 10 an excellent line of departure for an advance in the direction of Montmédy had been secured.

The American Commander-in-Chief issued instructions on November 5 directing both American Armies to prepare for an advance in the direction of Longwy and the Briey iron basin, and for the First Army to conduct an offensive with the object of driving the enemy beyond Theinte Creek and the Chiers River.

Late on November 9 Marshal Foch, then in conference with the enemy concerning the Armistice, issued instructions to all armies directing that attacks be initiated and sustained along the whole front in order to take full advantage of the demoralization of the German forces.

The First Army executed these attacks

HOW TO STOP THE WAR

Do your part to put an end to the war! Put an end to your part of it. Stop fighting! That's the simplest way. You can do it, you soldiers, just stop fighting and the war will end of its own accord. You are not fighting for anything anyway. What does it matter to you who owns Metz or Strassburg, you never saw those towns nor knew the people in them, so what do you care about them? But there is a little town back home in little old United States you would like to see and if you keep on fighting here in the hope of getting a look at those old German fortresses you may never see home again.

The only way to stop the war is to stop fighting. That's easy. Just quit it and slip across «No Man's Land» and join the bunch that's taking it easy there waiting to be exchanged and taken home. There is no disgrace in that. That bunch of American prisoners will be welcomed just as warmly as you who stick it out in these infernal trenches. Get wise and get over the top.

There is nothing in the glory of keeping up the war. But think of the increasing taxes you will have to pay the longer the war lasts the larger those taxes at home will be. Get wise and get over.

All the fine words about glory are tommy rot. You haven't got any business fighting in France. You would better be fighting the money trust at home instead of fighting your fellow soldiers in grey over here where it doesn't really matter two sticks to you how the war goes.

Your country needs you, your family needs you and you need your life for something better than being gassed, shot at, deafened by cannon shots and rendered unfit physically by the miserable life you must live there.

The tales they tell you of the cruelties of German prison camps are fairy tales. Of course you may not like being a prisoner of war but anything is better than this infernal place with no hope of escape except by being wounded after which you will only be sent back for another hole in your body.

Wake up and stop the war! You can if you want to. Your government does not mean to stop the war for years to come and the years are going to be long and dreary. You better come over while the going is good.

German Propaganda Dropped Behind the
American Lines

The First Army, which reache— a strength in early October c about 900,000 Americans, rein— forced by more than 100,00 French, was approximately eight times the size of the arm with which General Gran opposed General Lee at the en of the American Civil War.

Its total losses from all causes excluding those of the Frenc troops serving with it, wer about 117,000. It had inflicte— approximately 100,000 casualtie on the enemy and had capture— 26,000 prisoners, 874 cannon 3,000 machine guns and vas quantities of supplies, ammuni— tion and other matériel.

The American First Army i 47 days of continuous fightin had advanced steadily in spit of all obstacles, and the most des perate resistance, and had playe— a vital part in bringing th war to a successful conclusion

Allied Propaganda Being Floated
to German Lines

on November 10 and 11, making assaults along most of its front. These resulted in substantial gains, including, in addition to those mentioned above, the forcing of a crossing of the Meuse River south of Mouzon by the 2d and 89th Divisions of the V Corps, and a 1½-mile advance east of Verdun by the 81st Division, the right division of the French II Colonial Corps.

On the morning of November 11 word was received and sent to the American troops as quickly as possible that the Armistice had been signed, and that hostilities would cease at 11:00 a. m.

Thus ended the Meuse-Argonne battle, the greatest one in American history.

A VISIT TO THE AMERICAN BATTLEFIELDS
IN THE MEUSE-ARGONNE REGION

THIS itinerary of the Meuse-Argonne battlefield is divided into two tours, each requiring a day. The first, which is the shorter, traverses the area that was fought over between September 26 and November 1, 1918; the second covers principally that part where the fighting occurred between November 1 and the Armistice. The first day's tour is recommended to all tourists who can spend but one day on this battle front.

For those who have not sufficient time to follow the first day's tour, it is recommended that a special effort be made to visit the American memorial at Montfaucon and the American cemetery near Romagne-sous-Montfaucon and that pages 203–214 and 247–253 of the first day's tour be read while there. Besides being objects of great sentimental interest to Americans, these places are in areas of severe American fighting and afford excellent observation points. The combat operations described at the monument and cemetery in the first day's tour, to which the above page references refer, give a good résumé of all the fighting of the American Army in the Meuse-Argonne region.

No Man's Land South of Malancourt

FIRST DAY'S TOUR OF THE AMERICAN
MEUSE-ARGONNE BATTLEFIELDS

THIS tour begins and ends at Verdun and is about 95 miles (153 kilometers) long. It can be completed in eight hours. To save time lunch should be carried.

The data given on pages 520–521 will be helpful to those following this tour.

The narrative at the beginning of the chapter should be kept in mind and the map at the end consulted, so that the operations described in this chapter will be more clearly understood.

When following this tour of the battle-fields, unless contrary road instructions are given, continue straight ahead.

EN ROUTE RAILROAD STATION VERDUN TO NORTHERN SLOPE OF LE MORT HOMME

Speedometer distance is measured from the plaza in front of the railroad station.

(0.0 m 0.0 km) **At railroad station, with the station on right-hand side, set speedometer at zero. Proceed by the road seen straight ahead.**

(0.3 m 0.5 km) **A short distance farther on, bear right and cross the viaduct which runs over the railroad tracks.**

(0.6 m 1.0 km) **At the road junction beyond viaduct, bear to the right and continue on the road toward Montfaucon.**

(1.2 m 1.9 km) **Near far side of town at large barracks passed on the left, t the right front** can be seen glimpses of th open field in which three American 14 inch naval guns, mounted on railwa carriages and manned by personnel of th United States Navy, went into action o October 13, 1918. These guns fired a important enemy communication center about 20 miles away. Two of them wer later moved to positions near Charny several miles ahead, where they joined third that had been on duty with th French near Soissons. As a result c direct hits made by these guns on thei targets, the movement of enemy troop and supplies was considerably hampered

(2.9 m 4.7 km) **Beyond town, abou 1½ miles, at the first road junction, tur to the right toward Charny.**

To the left on top of the hill is seen on of the ring of forts constructed aroun Verdun about 1880 for its defense.

(4.7 m 7.6 km) **In next village, Charny at first road junction, turn sharp left.**

This road was an important suppl route for the American First Army in th fall of 1918. During the first part of th Meuse-Argonne battle it was seldom use in daylight hours because of the incessan

United States 14-Inch Naval Gun Firing From Railway Mount Near Charny, October 1918

(194)

33d Division Troops Passing Through Chattancourt,
October 1918

activity of hostile airplanes and artillery. Consequently, during the hours of darkness it was filled to capacity as men, ammunition and supplies were moved to the front and wounded were carried to the rear. Motor trucks, ambulances, wagons and troops had to move without lights, and much confusion and many traffic jams occurred here in spite of all precautions and constant supervision. The difficulties were greatly aggravated by the enemy artillery which at night periodically shelled the important road crossings.

(7.5 m 12.1 km) **At church in the next village, Marre, bear to the right.**

(8.7 m 14.0 km) **Near the next cross-road,** a 33d Division dressing station, which gave first aid to the wounded, was located during the early days of the American operations on this front.

(9.4 m 15.1 km) **A short distance farther on, the monument seen on the right alongside the road** marks the site of the former village of Cumières. This village was literally blown away by shellfire during the fighting in the vicinity.

(9.7 m 15.6 km) **Where the road starts to climb the hill ahead, turn sharp left on the narrow road which leads off from it.** *If narrow road is closed continue straight*

ahead and stop on far side of next ridge where a good view of the valley to the left front is obtained. At this point read itinerary to paragraph 1 of the second column on page 200. From here can be identified most of the places seen from the stop at Le Mort Homme if the map is consulted and it is remembered that the wood on the hill across the valley to the left front is the Bois de Forges. After reading itinerary, continue straight ahead. At next road fork turn left, cross bridge and again turn left. The described route is rejoined at the road crossing just beyond the next village, Béthincourt. Reset speedometer at that point.

(10.5 m 16.9 km) **Beyond the first hill, a sign is seen (1937) on the right** which indicates a path to a tunnel built by the Germans during the war. In this region were constructed many such elaborate tunnels which afforded shelter and a means of transferring troops and supplies from one place to another underground, free from hostile observation and fire.

(10.6 m 17.1 km) **The monuments seen to the left front** are French monuments on the hill called Le Mort Homme.

(10.8 m 17.4 km) **At the top of the hill which the road is climbing, where a good panorama to the right is obtained, STOP.**

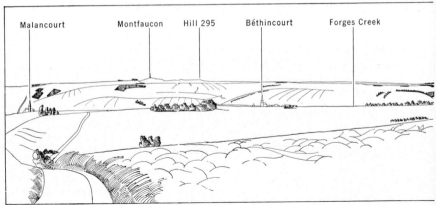

Malancourt   Montfaucon   Hill 295   Béthincourt   Forges Creek

Panorama From Stop

This point is on the northern slope of Le Mort Homme. Forges Creek runs in the valley to the right front and right. The large wood seen to the right on the hill across the valley is the Bois de Forges. The left portion of it is to the north.

Face north.

Along the slopes in front of here ran part of the battle line from which an army of 600,000 American soldiers, on the morning of September 26, 1918, started a great drive that finally reached the vicinity of Sedan, 35 miles away, after 43 days of continuous fighting.

This area at that time was a scene of indescribable desolation. Thousands of shells had churned up the surface of the

33d Division Troops in Front-Line Trench Near Forges, October 3, 1918

ground and the autumn rains had made it a sea of mud, littered with battlefield wreckage. Innumerable bands of barbed wire zigzagged their way across the hills and valleys, while the few shattered trees that remained stood lonely sentinels over the bleak landscape. Nature has done much to heal this battle-scarred area but even now (1937) the marks of trenches and shell holes are plainly visible.

The assembly of troops and supplies for the attack commenced early in September when the American 33d Division arrived in this region and on September 10 took over a large sector of the line. It was followed by the 79th, which on September 16 occupied an adjoining sector. Soon thereafter numerous other American units secretly concentrated behind this front and made preparations for the assault.

The front of attack of the American First Army ran from the Meuse River on the right, along the forward slopes of the low ridge seen directly ahead, and passed just this side of Béthincourt, whose church is plainly visible to the left front beyond the ridge. It continued on, passing to the left of Malancourt, seen on a clear day down the road to the left over the second ridge, and ended about 16 miles from here near the far edge of the Argonne Forest.

This point lay in the sector of the III Corps which had the 33d, 80th and 4th Divisions, in that order from right to left, in the initial assault. The 79th Division

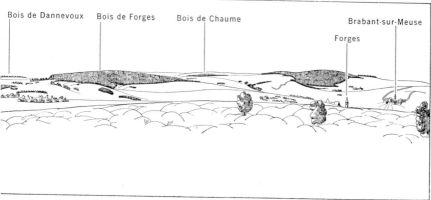

Bois de Dannevoux   Bois de Forges   Bois de Chaume   Brabant-sur-Meuse

Forges

on Le Mort Homme

of the V Corps was next in line with the commanding hill of Montfaucon, marked by the monument on the sky line to the left, in its zone of action.

Beyond the 79th Division, and also in the V Corps for the initial assault, were the 37th and 91st Divisions. The I Corps was on the left of the Army with the 35th, 28th and 77th Divisions in line.

The German positions on this front were extremely formidable, having been strengthened to the highest degree during the preceding years of fighting. In rear of their front line, they had constructed a series of positions, one behind the other, which formed a continuous defensive zone for a depth of about 10 miles. Progress here was considered so difficult that General Pétain, the Commander-in-Chief of the French Army, gave it as his opinion that the American advance would not get farther than Montfaucon before winter.

The battle began at 2:30 a. m. on September 26 when approximately 2,700 pieces of artillery opened fire on the German trenches, strong points, wire entanglements, observation posts and communication centers on the front of attack. This bombardment lasted continuously until daybreak when the infantry, protected by a dense barrage of shellfire, began its assault. A thick fog aided in concealing the movements of the American troops from the enemy but also made more difficult their tasks of

mopping up, keeping contact with adjoining units and advancing in the proper direction through the myriads of trenches, mazes of barbed wire and tangled masses of trees and underbrush.

On this part of the front, the divisions of the III Corps crossed the swampy Forges Creek valley and broke into the strong German positions to a depth of 5 miles on the first day. The 33d Division, starting from this vicinity, quickly captured the Bois de Forges, and before noon had established a line along this side of the Meuse River valley beyond the Bois de Forges as a protection for the flank of the advancing forces. The 80th Division to the left of this point took Béthincourt,

Camouflaged Road Near Forges,
October 1918

Shell Holes and Mine Craters
Good illustration of type of ground in no man's land on the Meuse-Argonne front

drove ahead several miles and by midnight had reached the Meuse River in the right part of its zone of action. The next day in severe fighting it captured the Bois de Dannevoux, the wood seen in the sky line to the right of and beyond Béthincourt. The 4th Division, passing just this side of Montfaucon, made a rapid and spectacular advance which will be described at the next stop.

The successes here were largely due to the courage and fighting spirit of the individual American soldier. Illustrative of these are the exploits of Captain George H. Mallon, First Sergeant Sydney G. Gumpertz and Sergeant Willie Sandlin of the 33d Division. All of these men were awarded Congressional Medals of Honor, the highest decoration for bravery given by the American Government, for the important part they played in the capture of the Bois de Forges.

Becoming separated from his company in the fog, Captain Mallon, with nine men, pushed forward and attacked nine hostile machine guns, capturing them all without the loss of a man. Continuing, he led his men against a battery of howitzers in action and captured the guns and their crews. Captain Mallon personally attacked one of the enemy with his fists. Later, in assaulting two other machine guns he sent his men to the flanks, while he himself rushed directly forward in the face of the fire and silenced the guns. The exceptional gallantry and determination displayed by Captain Mallon resulted in the capture of eleven machine guns, four 155-millimeter howitzers, and one anti-aircraft artillery piece.

When the advancing lines were held up by severe machine-gun fire First Sergeant Gumpertz left the platoon of which he was in command and started with two other soldiers through a heavy barrage toward the machine-gun nest. His two companions soon became casualties from the bursting shells, but Sergeant Gumpertz continued on alone in the face of direct fire from the machine gun, jumped into the nest and silenced the gun, capturing nine of the crew who were manning it.

Sergeant Sandlin showed conspicuous gallantry by advancing alone on a machine-gun nest which was holding up the progress of his unit. He killed the crew with a grenade and enabled the advance to continue. Later in the day he attacked alone and put two other machine-gun nests out of action, setting a splendid example of coolness and bravery.

Before leaving this stop the reader should fix in his mind the general appearance of the tall shaft of the monument on Montfaucon, which is visible from many places on this tour. Because it is located near the center of the area fought over by the American Army between September 26 and November 1, 1918, it will be pointed out from time to time as an orientation aid to the tourists who are following the described route.

Cumières–Forges Road, 1918

Section of Avocourt–Montfaucon Road Showing Plank Construction

EN ROUTE NORTHERN SLOPE OF LE MORT HOMME TO MONTFAUCON

(11.5 m 18.5 km) **Beyond next hill, while descending long slope, to the left front the high wooded hill marked by a monument** is Hill 304. Severe French and German fighting occurred there in 1916. It was within the American lines before the attack of September 26.

(12.0 m 19.3 km) **When Béthincourt comes into plain view to the right front,** a small marker is seen alongside the road. This is a type of marker that has been placed throughout France and Belgium to indicate the farthest advance of the German Armies in 1918. The center of the jump-off line of the 80th Division, which attacked on the morning of September 26 in the direction of Béthincourt, was approximately at this point.

(12.7 m 20.4 km) **After crossing the bridge over the creek, at the next road junction, turn left toward Malancourt.**

(13.3 m 21.4 km) **Beyond first crest, where road crosses center of shallow valley leading off to the right** the zone of action of the 4th Division is entered. It was from this part of the American front that one of the deepest and most rapid advances of the attack was made.

The valley of Forges Creek, which the road now follows, was in no man's land when the American Army arrived on this front. These slopes were covered with thick bands of barbed wire which protected the main German trenches located near the crest of the ridge to the right. The Allied trenches were close to the top of the ridge across the valley, with an enormous area of wire entanglements and other obstacles in front of them. The whole countryside was a white, desolate waste covered with interlocking shell craters and great quantities of débris.

Road Constructed With Sandbags Across No Man's Land

On September 26 the center of this valley was a spongy shell-torn morass. The infantry crossed it on boards which were carried from the American trenches and laid end to end across the mud. Later the engineers and pioneer infantry units accomplished the colossal task of building roads and bridges over it for the artillery and supply trains. To give an idea of the magnitude of the task, it may be stated that the construction of but one of these roads required the use of 40,000 sand bags.

(14.5 m 23.3 km) **Beyond place where road passes through a cut, in the next**

in advancing up the valley which the road follows beyond Malancourt. This was due to the uneven character of the ground and the fact that the first waves of the division attack passed by many German strong points in the thick fog.

(16.4 m 26.4 km) **About 1½ miles farther on, at top of first hill**, was a large, powerful field fortification called on French war maps the "Ouvrage du Démon" (Strongpoint of the Devil). By looking to the rear from the road near the top of the hill, its commanding position is evident. Heavy machine-gun fire from

German Plane Brought Down by Machine-Gun Fire Near Malancourt, October 3, 1918

shallow valley, the zone of action of the 79th Division during the attack is entered.

(14.9 m 24.0 km) **Straight through Malancourt**, which was a heap of ruins in 1918. It was captured by the 79th Division early on the morning of September 26. The town was the III Corps Headquarters, October 26–November 3.

The tour from this point on to Montfaucon generally follows the direction of advance on September 26 of the attacking units of the American First Army.

The 79th Division had great difficulty

it stopped the advance of the 79th Division troops during September 26.

(16.5 m 26.6 km) **To the left front** is seen a fine view of the American monument on top of Montfaucon.

(16.8 m 27.0 km) **To the right front considerably beyond and to the right of Montfaucon** was located the line reached by the 4th Division on the first day of the attack. The line of the 37th Division at that time was just to the left of the hill.

(18.0 m 29.0 km) **At monument in the ruined town of Montfaucon, STOP.**

The Meuse-Argonne American Memorial at Montfaucon
The shaft is 180 feet high

This imposing monument, rising from the ruins of the former village of Montfaucon, commemorates the brilliant victory of the American First Army in the Meuse-Argonne offensive and the heroic services of the Armies of France before that time on this important battle front. It was erected by the United States Government and is the largest of the American war memorials in Europe.

Montfaucon is supposed to date back to the 6th Century when it grew up as a market town around a monastery. Numerous battles have taken place in its vicinity. In one, fought against the Normans about 888 A. D., 19,000 dead are said to have been left on the battlefield. During the Hundred Years' War the district was frequently ravaged by bands of robbers; during the Religious Wars of the 16th Century, it was taken and burned; while in 1636 the town was again destroyed. In 1792, it was captured by Prussian troops taking part in the Valmy campaign.

While making excavations for the foundations of the monument, an old underground passage, hollowed out of the soft rock, was found running from the ruins behind the monument to the foot of the hill. To the left of the shaft as seen from the parking plaza, about 12 feet underground, was found a cemetery probably dating from the Middle Ages, and under the front end of the wall on the right side of the main terrace were three old cellars, one below the other, the lowest one evidently having been used as a dungeon. A small pot containing a few gold and silver pieces dated about 1750 was also discovered on the site.

The monument has the form of a Doric column surmounted by a figure representing Liberty. It faces the First Army jump-off line of September 26. From the observation platforms at the top, a large portion of the Meuse-Argonne battlefield is plainly to be seen.

Across the front of the monument appear in large letters the names of the four most important areas, from a military point of view, in the territory captured

Interior of Church at Montfaucon in 1914

by the American troops. The two large words at the sides, Meuse and Argonne, were placed in that order as the American fighting in this vicinity is officially known as the Meuse-Argonne offensive.

On the wall around the main terrace are listed the divisions which formed the First Army and under each name are given three places, now famous in American military history, where hard fighting of the division concerned occurred.

Church at Montfaucon in 1917

Corner of Observation Terrace, Meuse-Argonne Monument
Showing Direction Arrows

Inside the entrance door is a small vestibule, dec orated with flags cf the United States and France Carved on its walls are a brief description in French and English of the American operations, a colored map illustrating the American offensive in this region, and a tribute by General Pershing, the Com mander-in-Chief of the American Expeditionary Forces, to his officers and men who served here.

The observation platforms, from which superb views are obtained, are reached by the circular stairway leading up from the base of the shaft It is a climb of 234 steps. Eleven of the thirteen landings are provided with benches where those ascending the tower may stop to rest.

The following is written to be read from the observation platforms. Those not climbing the tower should read Part I from the terrace in front of the monument and Part II from the large crucifix, on the other side of the hill, 400 yards from here along the road toward the village of Nantillois

Church at Montfaucon in 1927

Map and Inscription Carved
on Interior Wall

PART I

Climb tower, go to platform overlooking plaza in front of monument and face so as to look along the center of the approach steps, which direction is south.

Spread out below the observer in a magnificent panorama is the ground over which the American Army attacked on the first day of the Meuse-Argonne offensive. The trenches and fields of barbed wire that criss-crossed this area are no longer visible, the shell holes and concrete emplacements that gave it the appearance of a desolate waste are gone, but the woods, hills and streams are still here and the names of the farms and towns, which have been rebuilt, recall the glories and sacrifices of the troops who fought near them.

This hill, an extremely important feature in the German second position, had looked down upon the fighting in front of here since 1914. Located as it is, mid-

way between the Meuse River (6 miles to the left of here, just beyond the large wood, Bois de Forges, seen on the long hill in the near distance) and the Argonne Forest (the wooded plateau near the sky line to the right), its dominating height afforded the enemy excellent observation. Inherently strong, it had been carefully prepared for defense and was a veritable fortress organized with deep shelters, concealed observation posts and obstacles of all kinds. Its strength, almost a legend to those who had served in the region, constituted a formidable mental as well as physical obstacle to any advance. In view of the strength of the German position on this front, it was perhaps fortunate that it was assigned to the young and virile American Army.

The direction arrows on the parapets of the observation platforms should be used to aid in locating the places mentioned in the following description of the operations.

American Memorial at Montfaucon Viewed From an Airplane,
Looking North

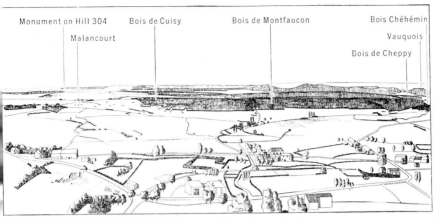

Panorama Looking South From Upper Platform,
Montfaucon Monument

The line taken over by the First Army in September and from which it jumped off on the morning of September 26 was generally parallel to the front of this monument. It ran from a point on the Meuse River beyond the right edge of the Bois de Forges; passed this side of Hill 304, the hill with a monument on its summit to the left front just beyond the first town, Malancourt; and over Vauquois Hill, the large isolated oval-shaped hill 6 miles away to the right front.

The III Corps, whose operations were described at the last stop, jumped off on the front from the Meuse River to Hill 304; the V Corps from Hill 304 to Vauquois Hill; and the I Corps, whose operations will be described further at the next stop, from Vauquois Hill to near the far edge of the Argonne Forest. Each corps had three divisions in line for the attack. In order from the observer's left to right, they were the 33d, 80th and 4th of the III Corps, the 79th, 37th and 91st of the V Corps, and the 35th, 28th and 77th of the I Corps. Montfaucon was in the zone of action of the 79th Division.

The preparations for the attack here had necessarily been hurried, as the offensive of the First Army in the St. Mihiel region had been completed only ten days before. In spite of the short time, however, on the evening of September 25 the American troops were in place on this front and the Army was ready for battle.

At 2:30 a. m. on September 26, the horizon in front of here lit up with a flash as thousands of cannon blazed into action. Explosions of all sorts followed each other with deafening noise like continuous peals of thunder. About 5:30 a. m. the noise slackened somewhat as most of the cannon prepared to fire on new targets. Some of the heavier guns had already started to shell with high explosives this hill and other known observation points. Now, just before dawn, the smaller ones were set to perform the new mission of creating a barrage of exploding shells, which would move forward in front of the infantry who, at this time, were tensely watching and waiting for the coming hour of attack in their jump-off positions.

Soon thereafter a new note was added to the din as innumerable machine guns, automatic rifles and rifles along the front went into action. This was evidence to the surprised Germans on this hill that a general offensive had started.

It was not long before the rifle and machine-gun fire to the left front was heard getting closer and closer. About 10:00 a. m. the fog lifted and small groups of khaki-clad soldiers of the 4th Division were observed moving near Septsarges, the nearest village seen to the

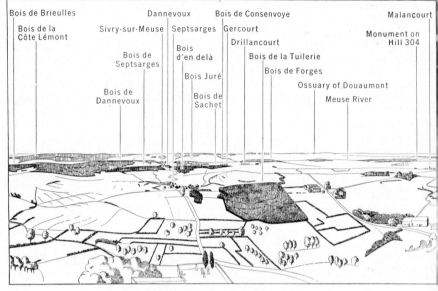

Bois de Brieulles		Dannevoux		Bois de Consenvoye		Malancourt
Bois de la Côte Lémont	Sivry-sur-Meuse	Septsarges	Gercourt			Monument on Hill 304
		Bois de Septsarges	Bois d'en delà	Drillancourt	Bois de la Tuilerie	
			Bois Juré		Bois de Forges	
		Bois de Dannevoux	Bois de Sachet		Ossuary of Douaumont Meuse River	

Panorama Looking East From Upper Platform,
Montfaucon Monument

left, where they captured an undamaged battery of German artillery which was later used effectively against its former owners. (See picture on page 211.)

Farther away to the left, troops of the 80th Division could be seen near the Bois de Sachet, the large wood beyond and to the right of Septsarges, and still farther away those of the 33d Division near Drillancourt, the village on the open ground to the right of that wood.

About 11:00 a. m., to the front and right, the leading lines of the 37th Division emerged from the Bois de Montfaucon, the large wood in that direction. They crossed the open ground this side of the wood and after capturing a German trench system in the field near the road, seen running to the right front from this hill, started changing it into an American position. Still farther to the right, soldiers of the 91st Division were on the open ground to the right of the large wood, Bois Ché-hémin, seen to the right front, having made an advance of more than 3 miles.

The 79th Division promptly captured Malancourt, seen to the left front, but had difficulty in advancing in this direction up the valley from that village, as well as through the left part of the large wood in front of here. Consequently, no assault was made by that division on Montfaucon until about 6:00 p. m., when the 79th and 37th Divisions launched an attack across the machine-gun-swept ground on this side of the wood, seen to the front. Assisted by tanks, but without artillery support, the slopes of this hill were reached in the face of heavy fire, but as night was coming on, the attack was given up.

Although Montfaucon remained in German hands, the achievements of the American Army on September 26 were more than had actually been expected. Advances of about 5 miles from the jump-off line had been made on both sides of this hill and its capture was almost a certainty within a very short time. The highly-organized German forward positions were all in American hands, in addition to thousands of prisoners, many cannon and vast stores of supplies and ammunition.

The battle for Montfaucon was renewed in a rainstorm at dawn on September 27, he hill being attacked by the 37th Division from the observer's right and by the 9th Division from the front. The ast machine-gun nest was finally wiped ut and the hill cleared of the enemy about oon by troops of the 79th Division.

Henceforth Montfaucon served as an American observation point.

PART II

After visiting the side platforms,[1] go to he rear one and read the following:

The assault on September 26 surprised he Germans and disrupted their defense, ut this situation was only momentary. rom that day on the fighting was prob- bly unsurpassed during the World War or dogged determination on both sides. ach foot of ground was stubbornly con- ested and the hostile troops took advan- age of every available spot from which o pour enfilade and cross fire into the dvancing American troops.

The line reached on the first day of the ttack included Dannevoux, seen to the ight about 5 miles away in the cup-shaped alley, and the Bois de Septsarges, the ong narrow wood to the right front, about

---

[1] The panoramic sketches on these pages show ost of the ground seen from the side platforms.

halfway between here and the nearest large wood in that direction. It then bent back sharply, passing the other side of this hill, curved forward again to near Epinonville, the third village seen to the left, and continued on to include Varennes, the village seen to the left rear below the wooded heights on the sky line.

The First Army on September 27 continued its assaults, which were met by frantic resistance from German infantry and machine gun units that had taken up new positions during the night and by unusually heavy artillery concentrations.

A large part of the American artillery had been unable to move forward because of the absence of roads over the torn-up ground of the old no man's land and, therefore, was not in a position on that day effectively to support the initial infantry assaults or to keep down the enemy shellfire. In spite of this and the shortage of tanks, the assault units attacked energetically and substantial gains were made during the day although many of them could not be retained.

On September 28, with better artillery support, the Army surged forward about 1½ miles. After severe fighting it reached that day a line marked generally by

Panorama Looking West From Upper Platform,
Montfaucon Monument

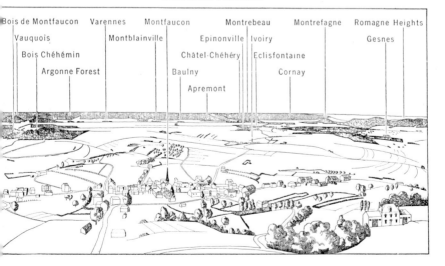

Bois de Montfaucon   Varennes   Montfaucon   Montrebeau   Montrefagne   Romagne Heights

Vauquois   Montblainville   Epinonville | Ivoiry   Gesnes

Bois Chéhémin   Châtel-Chéhéry   Eclisfontaine

Argonne Forest   Baulny   Cornay

Apremont

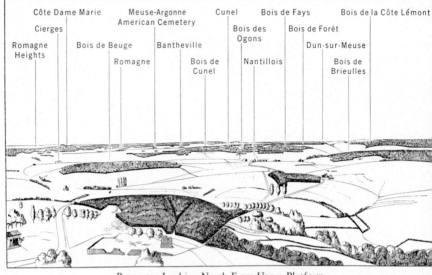

Côte Dame Marie		Meuse-Argonne American Cemetery		Cunel	Bois de Fays		Bois de la Côte Lémont
Cierges				Bois des	Bois de Forêt		
Romagne	Bois de Beuge	Bantheville		Ogons		Dun-sur-Meuse	
Heights		Romagne	Bois de Cunel		Nantillois		Bois de Brieulles

Panorama Looking North From Upper Platform,
Montfaucon Monument

the far edges of the Bois de la Côte Lémont and the Bois de Brieulles, the two nearest adjoining large woods to the right front; the slopes beyond Nantillois, the nearest town to the front; the Bois de Beuge, the first isolated wood to the left front; and Apremont, the village seen to the left in the distance near the foot of the heavily wooded heights.

On September 29 the attacks of the First Army were energetically pushed against stiffer resistance, as the enemy had reinforced his front line near here by six fresh divisions. This fighting was exceptionally bitter, the Germans making many severe counterattacks and concentrated artillery bombardments. During the day the ground gained and lost on this front by both sides was about equal.

For a few days after these attacks the Army devoted its efforts toward preparing for a renewal of the offensive. Its troops in the line were worn out by four days of terrific fighting and the advance had been so rapid that much of the heavy artillery and many of the supplies could not be brought up until the roads were rebuilt. During this pause, which was normal in every general attack, the 35th,

37th and 79th Divisions were replaced by the 1st, 32d and 3d, while the 33d extended its front and relieved the 80th Division. In all, a movement of more than 125,000 officers and men in and out of the line was made. As the roads and transportation facilities on the newly captured ground were improved, the wounded were taken to hospitals in the rear and large quantities of supplies, ammunition and artillery were moved forward.

The American casualties up to this time had totaled over 23,000. The First Army had penetrated the formidable hostile positions for more than 6 miles and included among its captures 9,000 men and 100 pieces of artillery.

The progress on this front threw consternation into the German High Command, who realized that the American Army here could not long be held in check. It urged its Government, therefore, to make peace at once before disaster overcame the German forces in the field.

The First Army on October 1 faced the outpost zone of the famous Hindenburg Line along a considerable part of its front to the east of the Argonne Forest.

The Hindenburg Line in front of here

included the long high wooded area, Bois de Forêt, to the left of and just this side of Dun-sur-Meuse, which is seen on a low pointed hill to the right of front in the distance; a large portion of the wood, Bois de Fays, seen on this side of the right part of the Bois de Forêt and apparently connected with it; the open ground just this side of Cunel, the village to the front in the distance between the woods; and Côte Dame Marie, the prominent hill to the left front. It ran through the large wooded area dotted with hills, called Romagne Heights, seen in the near distance to the left front, and continued on to the North Sea. In advancing to and gaining a foothold in that line, the First Army had its hardest fighting and the officers and men passed through their most terrific ordeal.

The battle was renewed with full vigor on October 4. The attacking divisions of the III Corps were: the 4th Division in line to the right of Nantillois, the first village seen on the open ground directly ahead, and the 80th, which had reentered the line, just beyond that town. In the V Corps, the 3d was in front of and to the right of Cierges, the nearest village to the left front; and the 32d Division, which had relieved the 91st, jumped off from a line which included the wood seen to the left of Cierges. In the

I Corps, the 1st Division faced the large isolated wooded area called Montrebeau, visible in the distance to the left well beyond the nearest towns seen in that direction; the 28th was to the left of the 1st with its left flank in the Argonne Forest; and the line of the 77th Division was entirely within the forest. The initial assault was a success and splendid advances were made all along the front, including a foothold in the Hindenburg Line in the Bois de Fays.

The progress of the First Army from October 5 to October 22 was slow but steady. In spite of the fact that it was fighting against an enemy with his back to the wall, who fully realized that this front must be held at all costs, and over terrain favorable for defense, almost daily gains were made. In the face of all obstacles and hardships and the most desperate resistance, the American Army during this period doggedly and persistently fought its way forward.

On October 7 a flank attack was launched against the Argonne Forest by the 28th Division and the 82d Division, which had entered the line for that purpose. This attack was directed against Châtel-Chéhéry and Cornay, the two villages seen to the left in the distance on the wooded heights beyond and to the right of Montrebeau, and was made in

Battery of German Guns Being Used by the 4th Division
Near Septsarges, October 1918

the direction of the reader's line of vision when facing those places. The maneuver was unusually effective and within the next three days the enemy had been driven from the Argonne Forest, which ends at the gap on the sky line to the left of the isolated peak, Montrefagne, seen in the distance to the left front.

On October 8 an attack was made on that part of the Army front beyond the Meuse River. The American 29th and 33d Divisions and two French divisions drove forward a distance of 2½ miles on that day, capturing a large part of the heights from which German artillery had been firing on the flank and rear of the troops on this side of the river. The 29th Division captured the wedge-shaped wood, Bois de Consenvoye, seen beyond Gercourt, the village to the right of and beyond Septsarges, and the 33d Division reached the Bois de Chaume, the line of woods extending down to the left from near the Bois de Consenvoye. The attacks there were pushed vigorously for several days and additional substantial gains were made, including the capture of the Bois de Chaume.

On October 9 the V Corps in front of here attacked with great force and the next day all divisions on the Army front from Beaumont, beyond the Meuse River,

to the Argonne Forest launched powerfu assaults. This fighting was extremel, bitter, positions of the Hindenburg Lin being carried on a front of 2 miles jus this side of Cunel and Romagne, the vi lage seen to the left of Cunel and abou the same distance away. The genera attacks were continued on the 11th an that day the Army, along most of th remainder of its front on this side of th Meuse, fought its way forward muc closer to the Hindenburg Line.

Another general attack was made o October 14, and after fighting of th most desperate character on that and o the days immediately following, man more strong positions in or beyond th Hindenburg Line were torn from th enemy. Among these were the Bois d la Pultière, just beyond Cunel, capture by the 3d and 5th Divisions, and th dominating Côte Dame Marie taken b the 32d Division. By October 22, all the Bois de Forêt, Cunel Heights an Romagne Heights were in American pos session and the First Army was we beyond the last prepared German posi tion at the center of its front. At tha time the units of the Army started care ful preparations for a finishing blow.

During the fighting between Octobe 1 and 31, the American losses totale

German Guard Division Returning From Hard Fighting, September 1918
This division opposed the American attack on September 26, 1918. © G

German Reserves Being Brought Up for a Counterattack,
October 1918.   © G

ver 75,000 officers and men. The 5th,
ith, 42d, 78th, 82d, 89th and 90th Divi-
ons, in addition to those previously
entioned, joined in the battle, relieving
red divisions. During this period 36
fferent German divisions were employed
a this front west of Fresnes-en-Woëvre,
veral having been engaged twice. The
ea of this fighting will be visited later,
hen a more detailed account will be given.
   The last great American offensive of the
ar was launched on November 1, com-
letely breaking through the enemy lines.
ll troops of the Army in front of here
ashed forward. The formidable Barri-
ourt Heights, the wooded heights seen
a the horizon just to the left of the
oserver's front, were carried on the first
ay and by November 6 the American
ght artillery was firing on the Metz–
edan–Mézières railway, the primary
ojective of the First Army. On the
orning of November 7 American units
ere on the hills overlooking Sedan, 31
iles away. On that very day, the
erman representatives crossed the battle
nes to ask for an immediate armistice.
From November 7 on to the Armistice
, 11:00 a. m., November 11, the First
rmy advanced in the direction to the
ght front from here. By the Armistice
had forced its way across the Meuse
iver, captured the heights on the far

side and had progressed about 10 miles
beyond the river onto the Woëvre Plain.
   Thus the war ended. The German
Army had been driven back 35 miles on
this the most vital part of its front. The
natural energy, ability and efficiency in
battle of the American soldiers and officers had prevailed against one of the
finest military forces of the world. Although the Germans were fighting with
desperation and all the skill they possessed
to deny any progress whatsoever to the
American forces, and were throwing onto
this front fresh reserves drawn from many
other parts of the Western Front, the
tremendous thrusts of the First Army at
this point could not be withstood.
   The battle here was the greatest in
American history. Its successful conclusion is a great tribute to the American
soldiers, their leaders and those behind
the lines and at home who so whole-
heartedly and efficiently supported the
combat armies in the field.
   Before leaving this observation platform, the long gray stone building to the
left front in the near distance should be
noted. It is the chapel of the Meuse-
Argonne American Cemetery, which
stands on a hillside above the graves of
more than 14,000 American soldiers whose
final resting place is there. No more
fitting site could have been chosen for

these battle dead than the gentle slopes of the valley joining Cunel and Romagne, where deeds of daring, devotion and heroism were unsurpassed.

Montfaucon was the 3d Division Headquarters, October 3–14 and October 26–31. The 79th Division Headquarters was located 600 yards south of Montfaucon from September 27 to October 1. The ground surrounding this monument is being maintained as far as practicable in its wartime state. Many relics of the war, including machine-gun posts, concrete shelters and dugouts still exist. A walk over it will prove most interesting.

Beyond the ruins of the church, about 300 yards from this monument, on the road to Nantillois are located the foundations of a house with several inscription plaques on the posts of the front fence which is still standing. In this house, which was repaired from time to time by the Germans, was built a heavy concealed concrete tower, equipped with a large periscope. It is said that in 1916 the German Crown Prince watched his troops battle for Verdun from that observatory. The periscope is now in the United States Military Academy Museum at West Point, New York.

EN ROUTE MONTFAUCON TO VAUQUOIS

Leave plaza at same side as entered, turn right immediately; 80 yards farther turn sharply to the right toward Cheppy.

37th Division Engineers Repairing Road Near Montfaucon, September 28, 1918

37th Division Memorial at Montfaucon

In the new village of Montfaucon is an almshouse constructed for this community by the State of Ohio as a memorial to the 37th Division, many of whose soldiers came from that state. To visit, turn right at next crossroad and go to main square of town. Time of side trip—15 minutes.

(18.3 m 29.5 km) **Just before reaching road crossing at foot of hill,** the zone of action of the 37th Division is entered.

In the fighting near here on September 27, First Lieutenant Fred Kochli, Sergeant Orum B. Lee and Corporal Ernest R. Rumbaugh, 37th Division, took an important part, for which each was awarded the Distinguished Service Cross. When the right of the division was held up by machine-gun fire early that morning, two combat patrols were sent to clean out the machine guns on the slope of Montfaucon to the right of this road. One patrol was unsuccessful and the other was stopped by heavy fire soon after it started. Lieutenant Kochli then asked for and received permission to lead the latter patrol which comprised 24 men. Under his bold leadership the patrol attacked and captured 14 heavy machine guns, 3 officers and 23 enlisted men. He put most of his patrol on guard over the prisoners and continued on over 200 yards farther up the hill with Sergeant Lee and Corporal Rumbaugh, under heavy fire. These three then captured three 77-millimeter field guns and two light machine guns in the orchard close

the near edge of the old town. The
stile fire was so heavy that the three
nericans were forced to take cover in a
ell hole, where they held out practically
rrounded by the enemy for a consider-
le time until reinforcements arrived.

(18.7 m 30.1 km) **Beyond road cross-**
, at first crest, to the rear is seen a fine
ew of the hill of Montfaucon.

(18.9 m 30.4 km) **To the right, near top**
ridge beyond the wide valley, was
ated a strong German trench line
ich was captured by the 37th Division
September 26. The next morning an
tack was launched from there against
oiry, beyond the ridge. That town was
ptured and the front line was moved
rward about ¾ mile in spite of heavy
stile fire and a determined German
unterattack. During the afternoon
e ground gained was given up because
heavy enemy shelling and the failure
the rest of the division to advance.
During the fighting there Second Lieu-
nant Albert E. Baesel, 37th Divi-
n, was killed while trying to rescue a
unded comrade lying about 200 yards
front of the assault line. Working his
ay through severe artillery, rifle and
achine-gun fire and a deluge of gas, he
d just placed the wounded man on his
oulder when both he and the man were
lled by the enemy fire. For this brave
ploit he was posthumously awarded

A Typical Scene in the Argonne Forest,
Southwest of Varennes

the Congressional Medal of Honor.

(20.4 m 32.8 km) **In next wood, Bois**
Chéhémin, just this side of road junction,
the zone of the 91st Division is entered.

(20.6 m 33.2 km) **After leaving wood,**
in the distance to the left front is seen
La Neuve Grange Farm, which was captured by the 91st Division on the morning
of September 26 after a hard fight. Near
that farm Sergeant Chester H. West of
the 91st Division dashed through the
fire of two German machine guns that
had suddenly opened up on his company
and killed the crews in hand-to-hand
combat. By this prompt and decisive
action his unit was enabled to advance
without losses. For it he was awarded
the Congressional Medal of Honor.

(20.7 m 33.3 km) **To the left front in**
the distance is seen Vauquois Hill.

(21.0 m 33.8 km) **In the vicinity of this**
road the 91st Division encountered strong
resistance from enemy machine gun
groups on September 26. It overcame
them before noon and drove forward
about 2 miles farther that day.

(22.3 m 35.9 km) **Immediately after the**
road starts to descend into a valley, at
the first small ravine leading off to the
right from it the zone of action of the 35th
Division during the attack is entered.

The 35th Division, which jumped off
from near Vauquois, reached the German
main line of resistance on top of the hill

155-Millimeter Tractor-Drawn Gun of the
First Army After Being Hurled 40 Feet
by a Direct Hit Near Charpentry

Street in Cheppy, October 6, 1918

to the left of this road about 8:30 a. m. There a severe struggle took place and it was not until 12:30 p. m. that, with the assistance of tanks, the strong enemy positions on that hill were captured.

(23.1 m 37.2 km) **In the next village, Cheppy,** the troops who had stormed the powerful main line of resistance of the German first position near here assembled and reorganized before renewing their attacks at 3:30 p. m.

It was during the fighting in this vicinity that Captain Alexander R. Skinker, 35th Division, won the Congressional Medal of Honor. When his company was held up by terrific machine-gun fire from "pillboxes" in a strong German position, he personally led an automatic rifleman and a carrier in an attack on the guns. The carrier was killed instantly, but Captain Skinker seized the ammunition and continued through an opening in the barbed wire, feeding the automatic rifle until he, too, was killed.

A former German command post in town was used as the 35th Division Headquarters, September 28–October 2; the 1st Division Headquarters, September 30–October 13; the 42d Division Headquarters, October 11–19; and the V Corps Headquarters, October 21–November 6.

A monument erected by the State Missouri in honor of her sons who die in the World War is located at the roa

Missouri Monument Near Cheppy

nction beyond town.   Many Missouri-
ns served in the 35th Division, which
ad very hard fighting near here.

(23.4 m 37.7 km) **Beyond bridge, at road
nction near monument bear left.**

*The tour now goes to Vauquois Hill, 1
ile away, from the top of which can be
btained a fine view of the Aire River valley
nd where unusually large mine craters can
e seen.   The climb up the steep hill must
e made on foot.   Those who can not make
ich an ascent may turn sharp right at next
ad junction and rejoin the described route
t the church in Varennes.   That part of
e itinerary not followed should be read.*

(23.6 m 38.0 km) **Beyond next road
nction, to the left front on far side of
mall valley,** is seen the locality of the
eroic exploits of Private Nels Wold, 35th
Division.   Assisted by one other soldier,
e silenced several machine-gun nests and
aptured 11 prisoners.   He then gallantly
sked his life to aid a comrade, after
hich he himself was killed in an attempt

to capture a fifth machine-gun nest.   For
his great courage and devotion to duty
he was later posthumously awarded the
Congressional Medal of Honor.

(24.1 m 38.8 km) **To the right front is**
Vauquois Hill.   Openings of underground
passages dug by the Germans can be seen
(1937) on its near slopes.

(24.8 m 40.0 km) **At first junction
where a road enters sharply from right,
turn right on it towards Vauquois.**

(25.3 m 40.7 km) **At the next road fork,
turn to the right.**

(25.8 m 41.5 km) **In next village,
Vauquois, 60 yards beyond church, just
before reaching road junction, STOP.**

**Follow path, 300 yards, to summit of
hill.**   For most of the way the path is in
an Allied communication trench.   It is a
hard climb but well worth while.

The monument on top of the hill is a
French one in memory of the soldiers who
fought in the vicinity and of the soldiers of
Vauquois who died during the World War.

Vauquois Hill From the Air, Looking Northeast

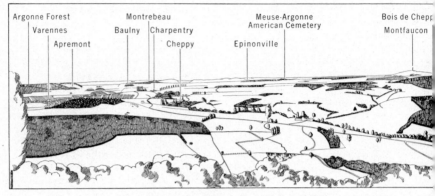

Panorama Looking North From Vauquois Hill

Cross craters to rim of hill opposite monument and face Cheppy, the nearest village marked by the scattered houses. (Note the above panoramic sketch.) The direction faced is approximately north.

Montfaucon is seen to the right front. The first large village which is plainly visible to the left front is Varennes.

In 1914 the village of Vauquois stood on this hill. It was of great military importance because of its dominating height and the facilities afforded by it for viewing the surrounding country.

Before the United States entered the war, this place was the scene of large-scale military mining operations by the French and the Germans, during which the town located here was blasted away. In these operations, deep tunnels were built under the opposing lines and vast quantities of explosives were set off in them. The huge craters thus formed are still to be seen behind the reader.

The First Army front line on the morning of September 26 ran across this hill and through the Argonne Forest, the large wooded area seen to the left. The I Corps with the 35th, 28th and 77th Divisions in line from right to left, attacked from this part of the front.

The German front line at the time of the attack was on this part of the hill, the line held by the 35th Division being on the opposite side of the crater. Five hours before the infantry assault, all American trenches on the hill were abandoned and a heavy concentration of artillery fire, including gas and smoke shell was placed on it. This forced the German troops here to remain in their bombproof shelters and so blinded their observers that when the attack took place the 35th Division was able to make rapid progress in the valleys to the right and left. Those advances isolated the hill which was then cleared of the enemy by units especially designated for the purpose. After severe fighting the division front line was established that night about 1 mile beyond Cheppy.

The 35th Division continued its attack during the next three days. By noon of September 28, after having repulsed a German counterattack that morning, it had captured Charpentry, the first village beyond Cheppy; Baulny, the village immediately to the left of Charpentry; and the large wooded area called Montrebeau seen beyond and between them in the distance, 5½ miles away. That night it dug in on the far edge of that wood. The next day the division attacked twice and had made further substantial gains when a vicious German counterattack by fresh troops, supported by large artillery concentrations from the Argonne Forest forced it back to Baulny. Its lines were there on October 1 when the division was relieved by the 1st Division.

The 28th Division, whose zone of action was half in the Argonne Forest, jumped off on the other side of the Aire River, which ins in the valley to the left of here. On eptember 26 the division drove forward igorously and captured part of Varennes. n the Argonne it made an advance of bout 1 mile. It continued to advance uring the next few days and by September 29, after severe fighting, had reached line beyond Apremont, the second village seen in the distance to the right of nd beyond Varennes.

The zone of action of the 77th Division, which was the left flank unit of the Corps and of the First Army, was entirely within the Argonne. That forest s a formidable natural obstacle, almost mpossible to walk through, with deep brupt-sided ravines, heavy underbrush nd many rock outcrops. During the preceding four years on this front, the Germans had skillfully prepared it for defense with concealed bands of barbed vire, machine guns placed so as to fire own lanes cut through the undergrowth, machine-gun nests in trees, and many ngenious traps to impede the progress of or inflict death on an advancing enemy.

In spite of all obstacles, the 77th Division drove forward in the initial assault bout 1 mile. From then on it continued o push its way forward, each day's close

finding hard-won ground behind it, until by October 1 the division was practically abreast of the other divisions of the I Corps, having made a total gain of 4 miles over the difficult ground on its front.

Outstanding among the deeds of valor in the Argonne Forest, were those of First Lieutenant Dwite H. Schaffner of the 77th Division on September 28. On that day he led his men in an attack against St. Hubert's Pavilion, about 5 miles to the left front from here, captured a strongly entrenched position after severe hand-to-hand fighting and by his bravery and contempt of danger inspired his men to hold fast in the face of three determined enemy counterattacks. He personally discovered and put out of action a machine gun that was causing heavy casualties in his company. The third counterattack made by the enemy was initiated by the appearance of a small detachment calling "Kamerad", the word used by German soldiers when they wanted to surrender. When they were almost within reach of the American front line, the attacking wave behind them appeared and assaulted vigorously, causing heavy casualties in the American platoon holding the advanced position. Lieutenant

Tanks Manned by Americans Going Forward Near Boureuilles, September 26, 1918

American Artillery in Action Near Varennes

Schaffner mounted the parapet of the trench, killed a number of the enemy and finally reached and shot the captain leading the attack. Dragging this wounded officer back into the company trenches, Lieutenant Schaffner secured valuable information about the enemy strength and position. As his company was surrounded on three sides for five hours by strong enemy forces, the undaunted bravery, gallant soldierly conduct and leadership displayed by Lieutenant Schaffner undoubtedly saved the survivors of his company from death or capture. For these acts he was awarded the Congressional Medal of Honor.

The rapid advance made on the first day by the 91st Division of the V Corps to just this side of Epinonville, the village seen to the right of and beyond Cheppy;

by the 35th Division to beyond Cheppy; and by the right of the 28th Division to the other side of Varennes partially outflanked the Argonne Forest and greatly helped the American troops to advance through that difficult area.

During this fighting the airplanes under control of the American Army to a large extent kept down the German aircraft and secured valuable information concerning the enemy. The Army badly needed tanks which in the first two weeks of the offensive, due to casualties and the transfer away of some French units, were greatly reduced in number.

On the following page is reproduced a section of a wartime map, scale 1/20,000, showing Vauquois and its vicinity. This type of map was the one generally used by American front-line units during the war.

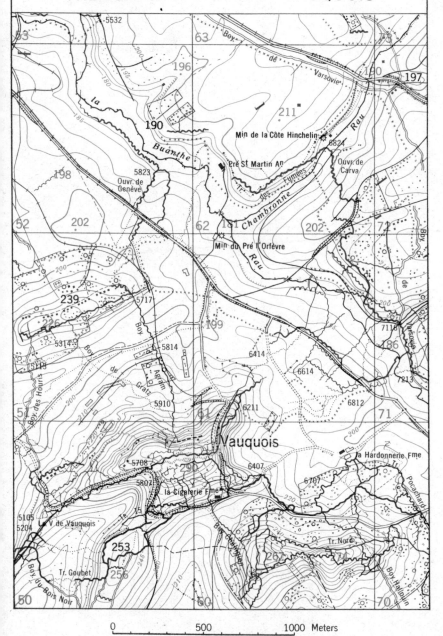

SECTION OF WAR MAP SHOWING
TRENCH SYSTEM NEAR VAUQUOIS

0   500   1000 Meters

Before leaving Vauquois Hill a walk to
e left around the top of it will disclose
any large craters, additional evidences
the war and interesting panoramas.

EN ROUTE VAUQUOIS TO NORTH
OF FARM DES GRANGES

Leave Vauquois by road to left front.
(26.3 m 42.3 km) **From the end of**
auquois Hill to the next town, Boureuilles,
is road generally runs parallel to the
rmer French front-line trenches.

(27.2 m 43.8 km) **Just before reaching**
ureuilles, the zone of action of the 28th
vision during the attack is entered.

The village of Boureuilles has been re-
ilt on a new site.   The old town, which
is one of the most advanced points in
e German lines, was located just to the
ght (north) of the new village.   It was
bjected to severe bombardments during
e four years of war and was completely
stroyed.   In 1916 the French exploded
large mine under the road just south of
wn to impede an anticipated German
vance.   Later the Germans exploded a
ine north of the village.   The enormous
aters thus formed greatly hindered the
merican operations in 1918 after the

town was captured by the 28th Division.
Temporary roads were first built around
the craters by American Army engineers
and as soon as possible thereafter bridges
were constructed across them.

(27.5 m 44.3 km) **At the church in the**
town turn to the right.

The tour here turns northward along
the Aire River and follows the general
direction of advance of the I Corps from
September 26 to October 30.

This road was one of the few main roads
in the area of the American advance.   It
was of inestimable value in supplying the
soldiers in the front lines with the food,
ammunition, supplies and equipment necessary to continue the attack.

In anticipation of further advances, the
construction of a standard-gauge railroad,
generally following this road, was rushed
from a place 5 miles south of here to the
next town, Varennes.   It was later extended to Grandpré, 11 miles farther on.
Needless to say it proved of tremendous
value to the American Army.

(27.9 m 44.9 km) **Beyond Boureuilles,**
the prominent nose of the Argonne Forest
seen to the left front is called the Côtes
des Perrières.   The front line of the left

German Dugouts in the Argonne Forest, 1918.   © G

Pennsylvania Memorial at Varennes, 1927

brigade of the 28th Division on September 26 and 27 was along the near side of that nose and on September 27 the 77th Division was abreast of the 28th Division farther over in the forest.

A large German wartime headquarters named "Champ Mahaut" on French war maps and now (1937) indicated on road signs as the "Abris du Kronprinz" is located 2 miles to the left front. Excellent examples of German concrete dugouts are preserved there. To visit, turn left at entrance to Varennes on road to Le Four de Paris. About 2 miles farther on turn right and follow small road for 800 yards. Length of side trip—5 miles. Time required—30 minutes. (See page 316.)

(29.7 m 47.8 km) **After entering the next village, Varennes,** a memorial park is seen to the left. This park was improved by the State of Pennsylvania in honor of all of her soldiers who served in the World War, a large number of whom were members of the 28th Division.

During the fighting at Varennes on September 26, Corporal Donald M. Call, Tank Corps, won the Congressional Medal of Honor. He was driver of a tank operating against enemy machine-gun nests on the western edge of the town when half of the tank turret was knocked off by a direct artillery hit. Choked by fumes from the high-explosive shell, he left the tank and took cover in a shell hole 30 yards away. Noticing that the other member of the tank crew, an officer, had not followed him, and thinking that he might be alive, Corporal Call returned to the tank under intense machine-gun and shell fire and gallantly assisted the officer to reach a place of safety.

Varennes is famous in French history as the place where Louis XVI and Marie Antoinette were captured in their attempt to escape into Belgium at the beginning of the French Revolution. The house in which they spent the night prior to their capture is the last one of the row on the right beyond the Pennsylvania monument.

This part of Varennes was captured by the 28th Division about noon on September 26, shortly before the troops of the 35th Division captured that part of the village on the other side of the river.

28th Division Engineers Repairing a Destroyed Bridge at Boureuilles, September 26, 1918

Bridge at Boureuilles After Repairs Had Been Made, September 28, 1918

28th Division Troops in Varennes, September 26, 1918

The 28th Division Headquarters was located here, September 27–30, and the 3d Division Headquarters, from October 4 to 9.

(29.9 m 48.1 km) **At bottom of hill turn right and cross the Aire River.**

(30.4 m 48.9 km) **Beyond town, at first road junction, turn to the left.**

(32.0 m 51.5 km) **After descending hill, beyond next main roadfork, at second small crest,** the line reached by the 35th Division on September 26 is crossed. The 28th Division was across the valley from it.

Varennes, Looking West Across the Aire River, September 27, 1918

(32.2 m 51.8 km) **The first village seen to the left front on the other side of the river** is Montblainville, captured by the right brigade of the 28th Division early in the morning of September 27. The division was held up by heavy machinegun fire during that entire day on the slopes beyond the town. It repulsed a hostile counterattack at that place about noon.

(32.5 m 52.3 km) **After passing Montblainville, the village seen on the hill down the road** is Baulny, taken soon after dark on September 27 by troops of the 35th Division.

(33.4 m 53.8 km) **Beyond Baulny, at first road junction, in the little valley leading off to the right** was located the front line upon which troops of the 1st Division relieved the 35th Division on October 1.

(33.6 m 54.1 km) **To the left is seen a projecting ridge of the Argonne Forest plateau,** called Le Chêne

35th Division Artillery Near Varennes, September 27, 1918

Tondu. The strong German second position had been organized along that ridge and across the Argonne in a direction approximately at right angles to this road. Le Chêne Tondu was the scene of prolonged and intense fighting by the 28th Division for ten days from September 28, the date the division first obtained a foothold on the ridge, until its capture was finally completed in an attack on the morning of October 7.

The position held by the so-called "Lost Battalion" was in the Argonne Forest to

was driven back after bitter fighting

During the fighting there Major Joseph H. Thompson, 28th Division, performed the heroic acts for which he was awarded the Congressional Medal of Honor. When his battalion was counterattacked on September 29, although wounded, he encouraged his men by constantly braving the heavy fire of machine guns and artillery. His courage was largely responsible for the severe repulse of the enemy. Again on October 1, after his battalion once more had met a strong

An American Brigade Headquarters Was Located
in These Ruins in Apremont

the left of here. To visit that area, at next road junction turn left to Apremont. At far edge of Apremont bear right on narrow road toward Binarville. Length of side trip—8.4 miles. Time required—1 hour. (For exact location and description of the position, see pages 362 to 365.)

(34.0 m 54.7 km) **The next village across the valley is Apremont.** It was captured by the 28th Division on September 28, the division line that night being established around the hill seen extending to the right from the town. Twice on September 29 strong German attacks penetrated the American lines near Apremont but each time the enemy

German counterattack, the advance of his assaulting companies was held up by fire from a hostile machine-gun nest. All but one of six accompanying tanks were disabled when Major Thompson with great gallantry and coolness, rushed forward on foot three separate times in advance of the assaulting lines and under heavy machine-gun and anti-tank gun fire led the one remaining tank to within a few yards of the enemy where it was successful in putting the machine-gun nest out of action. This brave deed permitted the infantry to advance.

(35.5 m 57.1 km) **At top of next hill, the Farm des Granges is passed on the left.**

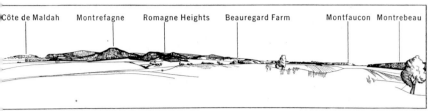

Côte de Maldah   Montrefagne   Romagne Heights   Beauregard Farm   Montfaucon Montrebeau

Panorama Looking Northeast From Stop Near Farm des Granges

(35.7 m 57.5 km) **Beyond the farm, at the next small crest, where a clear view is obtained to the front and right, STOP.**

If the trees along the road obstruct the view walk off from the road sufficiently to see the places pointed out in the following text.

Face down the road, which direction is approximately north.

The American monument on Montfaucon is on the sky line to the right rear.

The area around this point was the scene of prolonged fighting in late September and early October 1918 during which the Germans were driven from carefully prepared defensive positions, constructed with the idea that they would be impregnable. All ground within the range of vision was captured by the First Army.

The wooded hills to the right front, which were known collectively as Romagne Heights, are a natural terrain feature that had been organized by the Germans into a powerful fortified area.

The Argonne Forest, seen across the valley to the left, had been similarly prepared for defense so that troops who attempted to advance down the valley of the Aire in the direction the observer is facing, or over the open ground in front of this point, were not only subjected to frontal fire but were caught by enfilade fire from these two strong positions on their flanks.

On the hillside about a mile to the right are seen the buildings of Beauregard Farm. The most prominent peak to the right front is called Montrefagne.

Montrebeau, the large timbered area to the right rear, was captured on September 28 by troops of the 35th Division.

On September 29 the division attacked from the edge of Montrebeau under extremely heavy hostile fire and succeeded in occupying Beauregard Farm and the southern slope of Montrefagne as well as Exermont, which, invisible from here, lies in the valley near Beauregard Farm. A severe counterattack on that afternoon by fresh German troops, supported by a heavy and well-directed artillery fire from the Argonne Forest, forced the

Battery of 155-Millimeter Artillery of the First Army in Action Near Baulny, October 7, 1918

units of the 35th Division back again to a position the other side of Montrebeau.

On that same day the 28th Division had unusually severe fighting to the left rear of this point beyond the Aire River. Early in the morning it advanced about ¾ mile

which were too exposed to hold, to it former lines near Apremont. There, dur ing the course of the evening, the divisio repulsed another strong German attack

After September 29 the efforts of th First Army to advance ceased for a fev

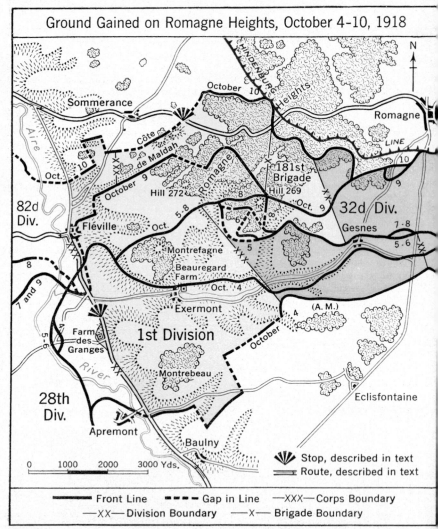

Ground Gained on Romagne Heights, October 4-10, 1918

along the river toward Châtel-Chéhéry, the village seen to the left across the val ley, and on the open fields near the river to the left of that place beat off a severe Ger man counterattack. That afternoon it withdrew from its advanced positions,

days, except for local attacks in the Ar gonne Forest, as it prepared for a renewal of the offensive on a larger scale.

After repulsing a German counterattack on the 30th, the 35th Division, which in four days had fought its way forward

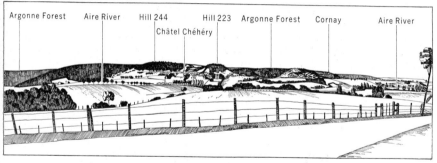

Argonne Forest   Aire River   Hill 244   Hill 223   Argonne Forest   Cornay   Aire River

Châtel Chéhéry

Panorama Looking West From Stop Near Farm des Granges

approximately 6 miles, was relieved from the line on October 1 by the 1st Division.

The First Army resumed the offensive by a general attack on October 4. The 1st Division on that day advanced in this direction from beyond Montrebeau, while the 28th drove forward along the near bank of the river. The boundary between the two divisions ran along this road.

Supported by tanks and a concentrated artillery fire, the 1st Division in a vigorous advance captured Montrebeau, Farm des Granges, Exermont and Beauregard Farm, after which it attacked Montrefagne, but was unable to take and hold that hill until the following morning. The 28th Division pushed forward about ¾ mile beyond this point, driving the enemy from most of the ground between this road and the river. The fighting during October 4 and 5 on the terrain near here was terrific, the 1st Division alone losing nearly 3,500 men.

The hill rising above the town of Châtel-Chéhéry across the valley is Hill 244. The high, round peak seen immediately to the right of the town is Hill 223. The village which is plainly seen to the left front is Cornay.

After the deep advance of the First Army near here on October 4 and 5, the Germans continued to hold the edge of the Argonne Forest in this vicinity and from it kept up a continuous artillery fire directly along and in rear of the lines of the American units on this side of the river, inflicting heavy casualties.

In order to exploit the gains of the 1st

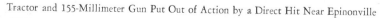

Tractor and 155-Millimeter Gun Put Out of Action by a Direct Hit Near Epinonville

and 28th Divisions on this side of the Argonne, to stop the artillery fire from the forest and to relieve a detachment of the 77th Division (the "Lost Battalion") which had gone ahead of the rest of its division on October 2 and had been surrounded for several days in the Ar-

German second position (see the sketch on this page) about 3 miles to the left rear of this point, and if successful would force the enemy to withdraw from that position and all of the Argonne Forest.

On the night of October 6 the 82d Division took over a portion of the 28th

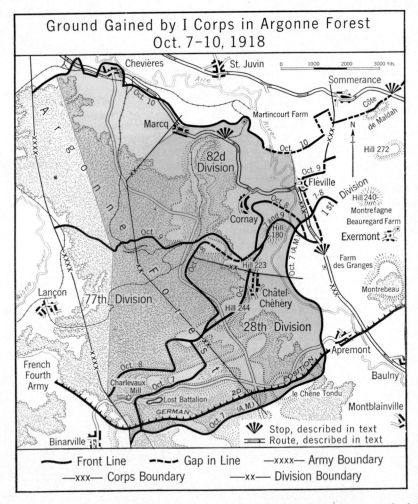

Ground Gained by I Corps in Argonne Forest
Oct. 7–10, 1918

gonne Forest to the left rear of here, it was decided to launch an attack from this vicinity straight at the German positions near Châtel-Chéhéry and Cornay. An attack in that direction would threaten the flank and rear of the hostile forces which were then holding the strong

Division line along the river, to the left front of here. The next morning both divisions attacked toward the Argonne Forest, the boundary line between them passing just north of Châtel-Chéhéry.

This daring attack was remarkably successful in spite of desperate resistance.

The 28th Division promptly captured Châtel-Chéhéry and Hill 244, and the 82d Division took Hill 223 and the high ground beyond the river between here and Cornay. Because of this advance the Germans in the Argonne Forest began a retirement during that day to a line extending to the reader's left from Cornay, approximately at right angles to the line of vision when facing that place. While the attack was progressing, the 77th Division advanced from the south and effected the rescue of the survivors of the "Lost Battalion", whose prolonged defense of an isolated position entirely within the enemy lines was an extraordinary and thrilling exploit. (See pages 337 and 362.)

On October 8 the 28th and 82d Divisions again attacked. They reached and held against a vicious counterattack positions controlling a road and light railway at the top of the ridge beyond Hill 223, thus cutting the most important north and south communications available to the German Army in the forest. That night the 82d Division took over the front of the 28th, and in the next two days pushed the retreating Germans from the wooded heights seen just beyond and to the right of Cornay, while the 77th Division, on its left, advanced rapidly northward, meeting slight opposition.

In the course of the fighting on October 8 occurred the extraordinary exploits of Private First Class Alvin C. York, 82d Division. The advance of his regiment across the valley beyond Hill 223 being held up by heavy fire from machine guns on the wooded slope at the left end of the valley, Private York was one of a patrol of 17 men who were sent out to get behind and silence the machine guns.

Carefully working their way through the woods behind the enemy line, the patrol surprised a battalion commander and a large group of men in a clearing. The Americans attacked and most of the Germans had thrown up their hands to surrender when a number of German rifles and machine guns, on a hillside a short distance away, opened fire killing and wounding nine of the patrol. From

28th Division Artillery Firing While Under a Gas Bombardment

this time on, Private York, who was nearest the firing, assumed command. The other members of the patrol took cover and fired only a few shots in the fighting which followed, as they occupied themselves in guarding the German soldiers who had previously surrendered.

Sheltering himself to some extent behind the prisoners who were flat on the ground Private York, in the face of the

Sergeant Alvin C. York, 82d Division, February 7, 1919

terrific fire, opened rapid fire with his rifle and later with his pistol. He maintained this fire until he, alone, had killed more than 15 of the enemy and had forced the remainder of them to surrender.

Forming the prisoners in a column Private York distributed the seven remaining men of his patrol along it and started back to the American lines with the German battalion commander in front of him. More Germans were encountered on the way and were forced to surrender. Private York brought back to the American lines three wounded members of the original patrol and 132 prisoners, including five German officers. Largely on account of Private York's exceptional coolness, skill with firearms, bravery and leadership his regiment was able to continue its advance on this day. For his exceptional exploits he was awarded the Congressional Medal of Honor.

Meanwhile, the 1st Division had consolidated its gains made on October 5 and had carried on active patrolling. It was assigned to the V Corps on October 7 preparatory to making a general attack with that corps. On October 8 considerable fighting took place on the hills seen to the right of Montrefagne, one of the hills, Hill 269, being captured on that day by a battalion of 1st Division engineers.

In the fighting there the next day, Sergeant Wilbur E. Colyer, Engineers, 1st Division, won the Congressional Medal of Honor. Volunteering with two other soldiers to locate machine-gun nests, Sergeant Colyer advanced on the hostile positions to a point where he was half surrounded by the nests, which were in ambush. He killed the gunner of one machine gun with a German grenade and then turned this machine gun on the other nests, silencing all of them before he returned to his platoon. He was later killed in action against the enemy.

On October 9 the 1st Division attacked with the V Corps and stormed the long wooded ridge seen to the left of and beyond Montrefagne. On the next day it seized Côte de Maldah, the double-crested ridge seen to the left of the wooded ridge. The taking of these ridges completed the capture of this end of Romagne Heights.

1st Division Infantry on Montrefagne, North of Exermont,
October 11, 1918

1st Division Artillery in Fléville, October 12, 1918

During these two days the 181st Brigade of the 91st Division was attached to the 1st Division and fought on its right flank, gaining considerable ground.

In the desperate fighting near here the 1st, 28th, 77th and 82d Divisions and the brigade of the 91st Division suffered a total of almost 18,000 casualties. Constantly attacking, undaunted by almost insuperable obstacles and the incessant demands on their strength, the American soldiers on these fields rose to supreme heights of sacrifice and heroism.

Illustrative of these characteristics are the deeds performed by Private Michael B. Ellis, 1st Division, on October 5 on the slopes to the north of Exermont. During the entire day's engagement he operated in advance of the first wave of his company, voluntarily undertaking most dangerous missions, attacking and reducing machine-gun nests singlehanded. Flanking one emplacement he killed two of the enemy with rifle fire and captured 17 others. Later he advanced under heavy fire and captured 27 prisoners, including two officers, and six machine guns. Soon thereafter he captured four other machine guns and their crews, at all times showing marked heroism and fearlessness. For his outstanding bravery and great accomplishments he was awarded the Congressional Medal of Honor.

EN ROUTE NORTH OF FARM DES GRANGES
TO NEAR MARTINCOURT FARM

(35.9 m 57.8 km) **While descending the hill, to the right in the valley, the town of Exermont** can be seen.

The next village, Fléville, after having been taken but not held by units of the 1st Division on October 4, was finally captured by the division on October 9.

(37.1 m 59.7 km) **In town turn to the left and cross the Aire River valley.**

(37.6 m 60.5 km) **While ascending the next hill, Cornay** is seen ahead. Troops of the 82d Division entered that town before dark on October 8 and after mopping up part of it withdrew about midnight. On October 9, after a hard fight, they drove the Germans from the village about 11:00 a. m. Shortly after noon the enemy launched a counterattack with artillery preparation and recaptured Cornay, surrounding in it a small force of Americans who fought desperately from house to house before being killed or captured. The town was finally taken and held during October 10.

(38.0 m 61.2 km) **At the top of the hill, turn sharply to the right.**

(39.1 m 62.9 km) **Beyond the next road junction at the top of the first crest, where an extensive panorama is obtained to the right front and right, STOP.**

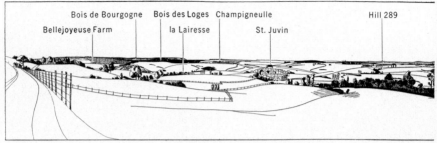

Bois de Bourgogne   Bois des Loges Champigneulle   Hill 289

Bellejoyeuse Farm   la Lairesse   St. Juvin

Panorama From

The nearest village is St. Juvin which is on the other side of the Aire River.

Face that town, which direction is approximately north.

Montfaucon is visible to the right rear, just to the left of Montrefagne, the wooded peak in that direction.

Note that the Aire River, which the tour has been following in a general way since leaving Boureuilles, changes direction not far from St. Juvin and runs approximately west in front of here, toward the left directly across the line of vision of the observer. (See sketch on page 234.)

The Hindenburg Line in this region was just to the observer's right of Côte de Châtillon, the conspicuous isolated wooded peak with the abrupt side seen to the right; passed just this side of Champigneulle, the village seen on top of the hill to the left of St. Juvin; and extended along the heights seen to the

left of that place. That position had been thoroughly studied and surveyed earlier in the war, and locations for artillery and machine guns had been carefully selected and indicated on the ground. Some shelters and trenches had been constructed, others were traced, and much barbed wire had been laid before October 1918. The great strength of the position lay, however, not so much in the works constructed on it as in the natural features of the ground and the thorough coordination of the fire power of all weapons, planned in accordance with the highest art of defensive warfare perfected by the German Army during their previous four years of intensive fighting.

St. Juvin was included in the outpost position of the Hindenburg Line which had also been strongly organized for defense.

When the I Corps arrived in this vicinity on the afternoon of October 10, its attempt to cross the Aire River disclosed that the bridges had been destroyed and that the enemy was strongly holding the Hindenburg Line and its outpost line on the far side of the valley. The corps was therefore faced, in front and to the left of here, with the almost impossible task of crossing the valley and storming the formidable positions there.

The front line established by the Army on October 10 was to the reader's right of Côte de Châtillon; just to the right of Sommerance, the village seen to the right across the valley; included Martincourt Farm, seen in the trees to the right front; and continued to the left on this side of the Aire River for approximately 4 miles.

1st Division Artillery, With Machine Gun Mounted for Anti-Aircraft Defense, Moving Toward the Front

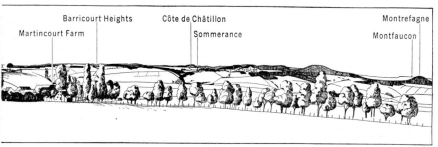

Barricourt Heights   Côte de Châtillon   Montrefagne

Martincourt Farm   Sommerance   Montfaucon

Stop Near Marcq

On October 11 the 1st Division, the left division of the V Corps, sent patrols into Sommerance. The 82d Division, whose zone of action ran from that town to just beyond the nose of the hill seen to the left, launched determined attacks that same day. The right of its line, which was beyond the river, was advanced to the open ground seen just over the roof of Martincourt Farm. The left of the division started from this vicinity in an attempt to capture St. Juvin. The assault units crossed the river in a fog on bridges which the engineers had repaired. Unfortunately the fog lifted while they were still close to the far bank and they were caught on open ground by severe machine-gun fire. After suffering heavy casualties, they were forced to return to their lines on this side of the river.

There were no American attacks in this vicinity on October 12 and 13 as the units reorganized and consolidated their positions. During that period of time the 42d Division relieved the 1st. On the afternoon of October 13 a strong German counterattack against that part of the 82d Division line to the right front across the river was driven back.

On October 14, in conjunction with the French Fourth Army on its left, the First Army launched a vigorous assault. On this part of the front the I Corps attacked with the 82d and 77th Divisions in line, the boundary between the divisions passing just to the right of St. Juvin.

The 82d Division, on the right, in a dashing attack advanced about ¾ mile, reaching the Hindenburg Line to the

right of St. Juvin and holding most of its gains in spite of a counterattack. Some of its units fought in the right part of the town. The 77th Division captured St. Juvin and many prisoners in the town but all its efforts to cross the river in force to the left front were unsuccessful until after dark. Then it reached and held as a salient in its line the last building, named La Lairesse on wartime maps, seen in the valley to the left of St. Juvin. That night the front line of the division was on the other side of St. Juvin and close to it.

The next day the assault planned for early in the morning was delayed by a strong German attack with heavy artillery preparation, made about 6:45 a. m., in the vicinity of St. Juvin. This was beaten off, the American troops, particularly a machine gun company of the 82d Division which had seized a part of the

Tank and Supply Wagon Blown Up by a German Road Mine North of Fléville, October 12, 1918

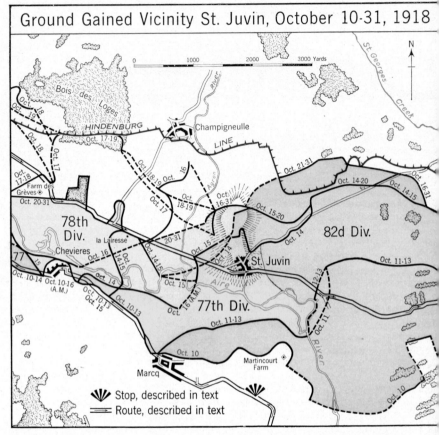

Ground Gained Vicinity St. Juvin, October 10-31, 1918

Stop, described in text
Route, described in text

hill north of St. Juvin just before the attack, inflicting severe losses on the enemy. Later in the day the left of the 82d Division advanced about 500 yards to a position on the hill north of St. Juvin in contact with this company. The 77th Division attacked Grandpré, a village to the left 3 miles away which will be passed through later in the tour, but its attempts to gain a foothold in the town were unsuccessful until next day.

The 77th Division was relieved by the 78th Division on October 16, after having been in the line since September 21 and having advanced about 11 miles through the dense terrain of the Argonne.

On October 16 after having tried to capture the hill on the two previous days the 42d Division in a brilliant assault stormed and captured Côte de Châtillon,

seen to the right. During that day the 78th and 82d Divisions in vigorou attacks reached the near side of Champigneulle, the village seen to the left o St. Juvin, but due to heavy hostile shell fire could not hold their gains.

The attacks of the 78th and 82d Divisions in front of here were continued from October 17 to 19. This fighting was of a desperate character, the attacking forces suffering many casualties from the incessant fire of the German batteries in the Bois de Bourgogne, the large wooded area on the sky line to the left front.

One of the attacks on October 17 gained a foothold in the Bois des Loges, the wood extending over the nearest high hill seen to the left front, which was a strong position in the Hindenburg Line fairly bristling with machine guns, and another assault on October 19 reached Bellejoyeuse Farm, seen to the left front just below the near edge of the Bois de Bourgogne. By October 20, however, it had been proved that the German defenses across the river were too strong to be taken without further preparations so, on that day, the 78th Division was ordered back from its advanced positions and established its line to the left front along the road across the valley marked in places by the row of trees. The line of the 82d Division remained beyond St. Juvin, and on October 21 that part of it to the right of St. Juvin was advanced about 500 yards with little opposition.

Although the battle died down in front of here on October 22, the 78th Division attacked continuously in the vicinity of Grandpré until the 27th, advancing its lines in bitter fighting more than 1 mile. Because the American efforts to advance there were so persistent and the place on the front was such an important one, the Germans opposed the attacks with their best troops. Consequently, the success of the last major offensive of the First Army on November 1 was greatly aided as the German attention in this region had been drawn to the front near Grandpré, rather than that near Côte de Châtillon at which point the vital thrust of the Army was actually made.

The casualties of the 77th, 78th, 82d and 42d Divisions in this region from October 11 to the end of the month were in excess of 13,000 officers and men.

The Army prepared for its attack of November 1 with great care and made full use of the lessons learned in its previous fighting in this region. The various combat organizations which composed it were by that time well-coordinated fighting units, fully tested in battle, and formed together a superb fighting force.

All three corps of the First Army on this side of the Meuse River were involved in the attack. The V Corps, in the center, which was already beyond the Hindenburg Line, was expected to make the greatest advance. Its immediate objective was Barricourt Heights, the high ground seen on the sky line just over and to the right of Martincourt Farm. The III Corps on the right was to pivot toward the Meuse River. The I Corps on this flank was to protect the left of the V Corps and to move forward as rapidly as possible. Its objective for the first day was the high ground 4 miles away, seen just over the center of St. Juvin.

The attack was launched at 5:30 in the morning and was an outstanding success from the start. The V Corps, with the 2d Division in line on this side of Côte de Châtillon and the 89th on the other side of it, drove forward rapidly and by early afternoon had captured the Barricourt Heights, thus making certain an extensive German retirement in this region.

Champigneulle After Its Capture by the 77th Division, November 2, 1918
Note destruction caused by American artillery fire

The I Corps, in front of here, jumped off with the 80th, 77th and 78th Divisions in line from right to left, the 80th and 77th having relieved the 82d to take part in the attack. The 80th Division was on that part of the front located in the area seen over Martincourt Farm, the 77th Division was beyond St. Juvin, and the front of the 78th ran from the building, La Lairesse, previously pointed out in the valley to the left front, on to the left for approximately 4 miles.

On November 1 the I Corps met stubborn resistance. The 80th Division was held in the left of its zone of action but its right drove forward rapidly in conjunction with the 2d Division and captured part of the wooded hill, Hill 289, seen on the sky line halfway between St. Juvin and Martincourt Farm. That hill can be easily identified (1937) by the high isolated tree on its summit. The 77th Division gained some ground on the ridge to the right of Champigneulle while the 78th captured Bellejoyeuse Farm and a small section of the nearest part of the Bois des Loges.

Due to the deep penetration by the V Corps, the Germans withdrew most of their troops on this part of the front during the night of November 1–2, leaving behind machine gun units to delay the American advance. On November 2 that resistance was overcome and all divisions of the I Corps moved rapidly northward.

The Bois de Bourgogne and the adjoining woods form a large forest area similar in character to the Argonne. On November 1 strong attacks were not made against that area but its eastern edge was heavily shelled with persistent gas. Its evacuation was forced by the advance in front of here and the advance of the French Fourth Army on the other side of it. From the time when, on November 3, the 78th Division made contact with a French division at Boult aux-Bois, about 9 miles to the left from here, the Bois de Bourgogne was definitely in Allied hands.

The Army continued to push forward vigorously until November 7 when American troops were on the hills dominating Sedan, 24 miles directly to the front of here. It then changed the direction of its attacks and on November 11, the day of the Armistice, it was driving forward to the reader's right beyond the Meuse River.

The tour now goes west to Grandpré and at that place reverses its direction and turns to the east along the far bank of the Aire River, traversing as far as the Meuse River ground captured during the month of October. The tourist must be careful from now on to note the dates of the various events as at this stop the operations on this part of the Army front have been described up to the end of the war.

Terrain Near Marcq; Note the Barbed Wire

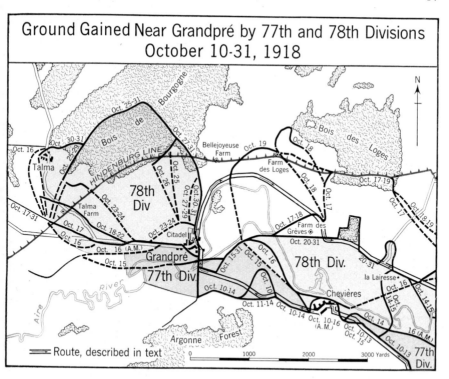

Ground Gained Near Grandpré by 77th and 78th Divisions October 10-31, 1918

EN ROUTE NEAR MARTINCOURT FARM TO EAST OF SOMMERANCE

(39.9 m 64.2 km) **Continue through the next village, Marcq,** which was captured on October 10 by soldiers from both the 77th and 82d Divisions.

(40.2 m 64.7 km) **At the far edge of the village** the zone of action of the 77th Division during its advance is entered.

(41.1 m 66.1 km) **While approaching the next village, Chevières, to the right front on the ridge across the valley** is seen the road, marked by the row of trees, from which the 78th Division jumped off for the attack on November 1.

(41.6 m 66.9 km) **Continue through Chevières,** which was captured on October 10 by troops of the 77th Division.

(42.6 m 68.6 km) **Beyond the next hill, the village seen ahead** is Grandpré. It was the scene at different times of stubborn fighting by the 77th and 78th Divisions, the 77th entering the town just before its relief by the 78th on October 16.

Most of the town is situated against a steep bluff upon which was located a citadel of great strength. This citadel, which was part of the outpost position of the Hindenburg Line, was captured by the 78th Division on October 23, after it had been attacked on previous occasions by troops of that division as well as by those of the 77th Division.

It was for deeds performed on the 23d while a member of the assaulting party which stormed and captured the citadel, that Private Edward Rischmann, 78th Division, was awarded the Distinguished Service Cross. He scaled the wall and alone entered a dugout in which he captured 45 Germans, holding them prisoners until assistance arrived.

The Germans clung desperately to the remainder of the bluff for the next four days. It was finally captured after sufficient ground had been gained to its left and rear (as seen from here) to permit an assault to be made from the rear.

On October 26 during the operations at Grandpré, Sergeant William Sawelson, 78th Division, performed the heroic act for which he was given the Congressional Medal of Honor. Hearing a wounded man in a shell hole some distance away calling for water, Sergeant Sawelson, upon his own initiative, left shelter and crawled through heavy machine-gun fire to where the man lay, giving him what water he had in his canteen. He then went back to his own shell hole, obtained more water, and was returning to his wounded comrade when he was killed by a bullet from a machine gun.

(43.2 m 69.5 km) **In the center of the village of Grandpré, turn to the right.**

(43.3 m 69.7 km) **While proceeding to exit of town, to the left on the high bluff** may be seen glimpses of the massive walls of the citadel. Its extreme strength and that of the German positions near by are more evident from this point.

(44.0 m 70.8 km) **To the left front is** seen the Farm des Loges, captured by the 78th Division on October 19 after severe hand-grenade fighting. It was given up the next day as the position was too isolated to hold without excessive losses.

Rising above the farm is the Bois des

A Street in Grandpré, October 1918

Grandpré is on one of the two main passes traversing the plateau upon which are located the Argonne Forest and the Bois de Bourgogne. Throughout the ages these passes have been natural routes of travel. Grandpré itself is reported to have been founded by followers of Clovis about 500 A. D. The village has been subjected to much severe fighting during its long and eventful history.

(42.9 m 69.0 km) **After crossing the railroad near Grandpré turn to the right.**

Loges which was an ideal defensive position for the Germans. The smooth regular slopes on the lower part of the hill afforded an excellent field of fire and the wood at the top served to give fine protection and concealment for the German movements. The hill was attacked by the American forces on a number of occasions but was never captured until after the German troops had started their withdrawal from this part of the front during the night of November 1–2.

80th Division Marching Through St. Juvin After Relief From the Front Line

(45.5 m 73.2 km) **Beyond crest of
ext hill, to the right front across the
alley** is seen Marcq and to its left Mar-
ncourt Farm. These were just within
ne American lines on October 10. The
ifficulty of advancing across the valley
nd up these steep slopes in the face of
fle, machine-gun and artillery fire is
etter appreciated from here.

(46.4 m 74.7 km) **While approaching
ne next village, St. Juvin, extending to
ne left from it** is seen the hill, in the out-
ost position of the Hindenburg Line,
hich was captured by the 82d Division
n October 15 after a hard fight.

(47. 1 m 75.8 km) **Continue through
t. Juvin,** captured on October 14 by the
7th Division after a severe struggle.

(47.4 m 76.3 km) **Beyond town, the
ailroad seen to the right crossing the
alley** was not there during the war.

*At road junction mentioned in the next
aragraph is located a monument erected
y the 1st Division listing those of the divi-
on who were killed in the fighting in its
ne of action which was near here.*

(48.0 m 77.2 km) **At the next road
nction, turn to the left.**
This road and the next village, Som-
nerance, were captured by the 82d Divi-
on on October 11. The division front
ne from that date to October 13 was
long the top of the ridge seen to the left.

(49.4 m 79.5 km) **At main road junc-
on in town, bear right toward Romagne.**
After the battle had progressed beyond
ommerance, the partially destroyed
nurch in the village was used by the
mericans as a first-aid station.

(50.4 m 81.1 km) **Beyond town, at the
est where a clear view is obtained of
ne ground to both sides, STOP.
Face to the left,** which direction is
pproximately north.
Landres-et-St. Georges, invisible from
re, is in a valley 1½ miles to the front.
The 1st Division, the left division of the
Corps, fought its way forward to this
oint on October 10, the same day that
e 82d Division of the I Corps reached the
cinity of Martincourt Farm, the place
ear which we have recently stopped.

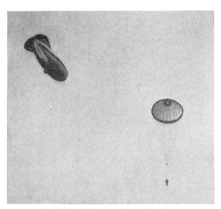

American Observer Jumping From
Captive Balloon

The high ground immediately in rear
of here, which is part of the west end of
Romagne Heights, was captured by the
1st Division in a series of well executed
attacks. The fire of all available artillery
of the division was concentrated upon
each hill individually, while the infantry
pushed close up, prepared to assault. At
a fixed time the artillery shifted to a new
target and the infantry charged the hill,
occupying it before the remaining Germans had time to leave their shelters and
offer sufficient resistance to stop the
progress of the American troops.

Côte de Maldah, the ground sloping up to the left rear from here, was
taken on October 10, about the same
time that the division advanced through

Machine Gun Unit in Position at St. Juvin,
November 1, 1918

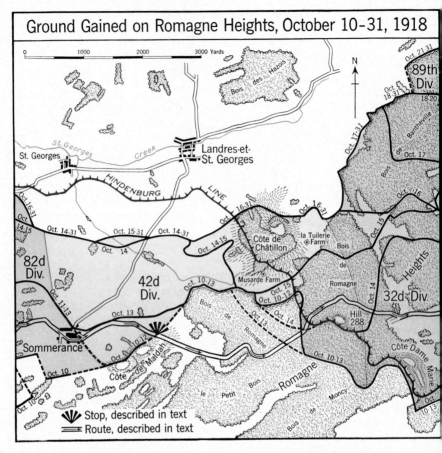

Ground Gained on Romagne Heights, October 10-31, 1918

Stop, described in text
Route, described in text

the nearest part of the Bois de Romagne, the large wood seen to the right front.

The 1st Division was relieved by the 42d Division on October 12. In its 12 days of battle near here it had driven forward more than 4 miles through the difficult terrain of Romagne Heights. Its casualties, to some extent a measure of its exceptional accomplishment, reached the heavy total of over 8,200 men, the greatest casualties of any division in the Meuse-Argonne offensive.

When the 42d Division took over the 1st Division sector it faced the Hindenburg Line which on this front included Hill 288, the left one of the three hills seen to the right; Côte de Châtillon, the prominent oval-shaped hill to the right front;

and the low bare ridge sloping off to th left from the woods on Côte de Châtillor The task of the division was to penetrat that line; and this, after repeated at tempts, it successfully accomplished.

In the general attack of the First Arm on October 14, the 42d Division jumpe off all along its front. On the right, afte overcoming stubborn resistance, it reache the crest of Hill 288. Determined as saults made against Côte de Châtillo from the far edge of the Bois de Romagn were stopped at the thick bands c barbed wire located on the open slope below the wood seen on that hill. I front and to the left front from here, th division advanced in spite of heavy ar tillery fire and dug in that night at th r side of the shallow valley, marked by e few scattered trees, about ½ mile away. During the fighting on October 14 ivate Michael A. Donaldson, 42d Divi-on, won the Congressional Medal of onor. The advance of his regiment ving been checked by intense machine-n fire of the enemy, who were en-enched on the open ridge beyond the lley in front of here, his company re-ed to reorganize, leaving several ounded near the enemy lines. Of his vn volition, in broad daylight and with ter disregard for his own safety, he ad-nced to the crest of the hill, rescued e of his wounded comrades, and re-rned under intense fire to his own lines. e repeated this heroic act until he had ought in all the men, six in number.

On October 15 the attacks were contin-d. On the right the division front line s advanced through the woods to a int about midway between Hill 288 d Côte de Châtillon. Substantial ins were made in front of here but the ound captured was so exposed to hostile e that it had to be given up. The hting on that day was very bitter, the emy making many counterattacks.

During the attacks on October 14 and in the direction of Landres-et-St. orges, Lieutenant Colonel William J. onovan, 42d Division, personally led e assault wave of his regiment. When s troops were suffering heavy casualties encouraged all near him by his daring ample, moving among his men in ex-sed positions, reorganizing decimated atoons and accompanying them for-rd in assaults. When he was wounded the leg by a machine-gun bullet, he used to be evacuated and continued th his unit until it withdrew to a less posed position. For this gallant action eutenant Colonel Donovan was award-the Congressional Medal of Honor.

On the next day, October 16, as a result persistent efforts and skillful maneu-ring, the formidable defenses of Côte Châtillon were penetrated and the hill s captured and held in spite of the most sperate efforts on the part of the Ger-mans to retake it. Taking that domi-nating strong point marked the climax of the splendid services of the 42d Division on this particular battle front.

In this fighting Private Thomas C. Neibaur won the Congressional Medal of Honor for his heroic exploits. Soon after the crest of Côte de Châtillon was reached he was sent out with an auto-matic rifle squad to enfilade enemy machine-gun nests. Just as he set up his gun he was shot through both legs by fire from a machine gun supporting a German counterattack. The German wave came on, all but surrounding the squad, and although every man in it was either killed or wounded, Private Neibaur continued to operate the gun. Due to his fire and that from the skirmish line of his company, 100 yards behind him, the Germans halted and took cover. Four of them, who attacked Private Neibaur at close quarters, he killed. Then moving out alone among the enemy lying near by, he captured 11 men at the

German Machine Gun and Observation Post Near Grandpré

point of his pistol and brought them into the American lines. The defeat of this counterattack was due to a large extent to the individual efforts of Private Neibaur, whose exploits greatly improved the morale of his battalion as they took place against the sky line in full view of it.

Among the men who were awarded Distinguished Service Crosses for their bravery at Côte de Châtillon on this day was Corporal Joseph E. Pruett of the 42d Division. After a daring dash with his platoon across open ground swept by machine-gun fire, he saw an enemy machine gun crew preparing to open fire upon the flank and rear of his position. Singlehanded he attacked, using enemy grenades, drove the crew into a dugout and by bombing the entrance to the

A Trench of the Hindenburg Line in the Bois de Bantheville, November 3, 1918

dugout, he effected the capture of fou German officers, 64 men and four heav machine guns. With remarkable galla try this soldier had thus put out of actio an enemy force that would have critical threatened a success already gained.

After October 16 the positions capture were consolidated and no further effor to advance were made by the 42d Div sion. Its front line then extended fro the far side of Côte de Châtillon to point about the same distance away fro this point to the left front.

Early on the morning of November the 2d Division passed through the 42 Division, and taking part in the Arm offensive of that date attacked straig ahead. Supported by heavy artiller fire, it quickly overcame the Germa resistance in front of here, capture Landres-et-St. Georges and by nightf had advanced approximately 6 miles.

The road followed from here to R magne runs generally east and west an was entirely within the front lines of t American Army before October 15.

EN ROUTE EAST OF SOMMERANCE TO TH MEUSE-ARGONNE AMERICAN CEMETERY

(52.2 m 84.0 km) **After entering larg wood, at second abrupt right bend in roa** the tour is passing over the northern slo of Hill 288, whose crest lies to the righ On October 14 the summit of the hill wa reached by the 42d Division which, the next day, advanced about ½ mile the left of this road in the general dire tion of Côte de Châtillon.

(52.6 m 84.7 km) **Beyond next sha right bend in road,** the zone of action the 32d Division is entered.

(53.2 m 85.6 km) **After entering fir clearing, to the right** is seen the rear si of Côte Dame Marie, a highly-organiz and important strong point of t Hindenburg Line. It was encircled a captured by the 32d Division in seve fighting on October 14. During th day the division fought its way forwa to a line about ¾ mile to the left of t road we are now traveling. Its sign victory here is described at the next sto

Top: Romagne, October 1918

Right: Romagne Church Set on Fire by an Artillery Bombardment, October 29, 1918

(54.3 m 87.4 km) **While descending the next steep hill, to the right front** may be obtained glimpses of the chapel and flagpoles located in the Meuse-Argonne American Cemetery, which is the next stop.

Beyond village cemetery at entrance to next town is a large German military cemetery. To visit, bear left at road fork at village cemetery. Rejoin tour at church in Romagne, which can be seen from cemetery entrance. Time of side trip—10 minutes.

The next town, Romagne, was captured by the 32d Division before noon on October 14. A large German supply depot located there fell into the hands of the advancing Americans. The town was the 90th Division Headquarters, October 31–November 3, and III Corps Headquarters from November 3 to 10.

(54.6 m 87.9 km) **At the church in Romagne-sous-Montfaucon, turn to the left.**

(54.7 m 88.0 km) **Beyond the bridge in the center of the town, turn to the left.**

American Cemetery at Romagne, May 1919

Entrance to the Meuse-Argonne
Cemetery Chapel

(55.6 m 89.5 km) **Enter the cemetery,
proceed slowly to far entrance, turn right,
ascend hill to chapel and STOP.**

This is the largest of the American
military cemeteries in Europe. It is
fittingly located near the center of the
area where the hardest American fighting
of the war occurred. More than 14,200
soldiers are buried on this hillside, most
of whom fell during the operations of the
First Army between September 26 and
November 11. In 1922 bodies were
brought here from the Vosges Mountains,
from the area on the other side of the
Argonne Forest, and from occupied Germany. Many of those who died at Archangel, Russia, were later moved to this
place. Almost every unit of the American Expeditionary Forces is represented
by one or more burials in this cemetery.

The permanent improvements of the
cemetery were completed in 1931. The
buildings across the valley from the grave
area contain a reception room for the convenience of visitors, the office of the superintendent, where inquiries concerning the
location of a particular grave and for

other information may be made, and a
few rooms which have been furnished
so that the relatives of those buried in
the cemetery can spend the night.

An attractive development has been
made at the center of the cemetery, and the
pools there with their flowers and gold-
fish are a never-failing source of interest
to visitors from the surrounding region.

An idea of the size of the cemetery is obtained when it is realized that the distance between the two main entrances is
600 yards and that the stone wall around
the cemetery is more than 1½ miles long.

The chapel is a splendid example of
modern architecture of the Romanesque
style. The imposing main entrance is
surmounted by a sculptured bas-relief in
which the figures represent Grief and

Interior View of the Meuse-Argonne
Cemetery Chapel

Chapel at the Meuse-Argonne Cemetery

Remembrance. Carved heads of American soldiers are included in the design of the column capitals alongside the door and at the same height across the front of the building are names of places famous in the history of the American fighting in this general region.

The chapel is entered through doors of unusual size. Within, the attention is first attracted to the apse, in the center of which is the altar, backed by a semicircle of flags of the United States and the principal Allied nations.

The insignia of the American divisions and higher units which served in Europe are worked into the patterns of the stained glass windows. Through these a soft and subdued light, which blends with the deep colors of the marble floor, is diffused throughout the interior. The impression made upon the visitor is such that he can not help but feel that this beautiful and holy place is fittingly appropriate "as a sacred rendezvous of a grateful people with its immortal dead".[1]

On the walls of the loggias are carved the names of all American soldiers who fought in this region and who now rest in unknown graves. The unknown dead of the

[1] This quotation is from the dedicatory inscription which is carved on the interior walls of the chapel.

Services of Supply are recorded on the front panel of the east loggia and the corresponding panel of the west loggia displays an ornamental map in colors showing the ground captured by each of the American divisions during the Meuse-Argonne offensive. The names of the unknown dead of the American expedition to Northern Russia are also carved on a panel of the west loggia.

On the floors of the pavilions at the end of the loggias are direction arrows pointing out the prominent features of the landscape. After enjoying the visit to the chapel and its surroundings, go to the pavilion nearest Romagne and read the following description of the fighting which took place in this vicinity.

The reader should make use of the direction arrows on the floor, and move in and around the pavilion so as to identify the various features of the landscape as they are mentioned in the text.

In the description of the operations all designations, such as right, left, front and rear, are with reference to the direction the chapel faces, which is north.

The famous German defensive position known as the Hindenburg Line ran along the ridge seen behind the chapel. It included the high wooded hill, Côte Dam-

Marie, the highest hill seen to the left rear over the buildings of the town of Romagne.

The jump-cff line cf the American First Army on September 26, 1918, was about 0 miles from here, beyond Montfaucon, een in the distance to the right rear. By the end cf the third day the Germans ad been driven back in this direction to he outlying defenses of the Hindenburg Line, which were located about midway etween here and Montfaucon.

On October 4 a second general attack was launched by the First Army and vigorously pushed, during the course of which many important gains were made.

On October 7 the flank attack against he Argonne Forest near Châtel-Chéhéry was started and the next day the drive ast of the Meuse was begun. These

were so successful that the Army ordered the V Corps on this immediate front to join in and to attack on October 9. This it did and, after some of the most heart-rending fighting of the war, it gained a foothold in the Hindenburg Line.

The 32d Division on October 9 pushed forward part way up the slopes of Côte Dame Marie and to the ridge in rear of the chapel, where it established itself in a trench of the Hindenburg Line, called on French wartime maps the Tranchée de la Mamelle. Romagne was reached in that attack but a strong German counterattack drove the advancing forces back. Isolated groups of the 3d Division, whose zone of action included the ground upon which this cemetery stands, entered the valley which runs

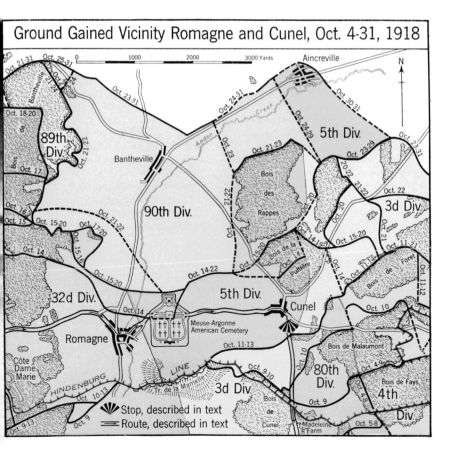

Ground Gained Vicinity Romagne and Cunel, Oct. 4-31, 1918

through the cemetery and also entered Romagne. The hostile fire was so severe, however, that these groups did not attempt to hold on but took up a position in the Tranchée de la Mamelle alongside the 32d Division. The remainder of the 3d Division, to the right rear from here, made a substantial advance also, and after dark the 80th Division on the right of the 3d entered Cunel, the village seen to the right when looking along the front of the chapel. Elements of the division were fighting in the town at midnight but it was not captured on that night.

The First Army ordered a general attack on the 10th and the fighting continued fiercely on that day all along this front. The 32d Division penetrated the trenches of the Hindenburg Line near the top of Côte Dame Marie. A counterattack caused some withdrawal but at the end of the day the division had made a total gain there of about ½ mile. Romagne was attacked but not captured. The left of the 3d Division advanced at 7:00 a. m. but was held up by fire from the front and flanks. During the day elements of the division established themselves in German trenches, located to the right rear not far from this chapel, but they were withdrawn after dark. The right of the division made two attacks which resulted in no permanent gains but in a third, begun at 9:45 p. m. and continued through most of the night, it advanced about 600 yards. During the day the 80th Division pushed its line forward about ½ mile nearer to Cunel.

The general attack was pressed with great vigor on the 11th, all divisions in line here taking part. The 32d Division made only minor gains which were not held. The left unit of the 3d Division

attacked at 7:15 a. m. but was stopped by hostile machine-gun fire from that part of this ridge to the right rear of the chapel. Shortly after 1:00 p. m. it advanced as far as the valley in the cemetery and established a position about 100 yards to the right rear of the site of the chapel but withdrew after dark. The right of the division repulsed a German counterattack at dawn, jumped off at 7:00 a. m. and made a substantial gain attacked about noon with the 80th Division and captured Cunel but did not hold the town that night. The 80th Division during the day advanced its lines about 700 yards. The 4th Division, in line beyond the 80th, captured this end of the Bois de Forêt, the wood seen above the right side of Cunel. That wood, a highly organized and strong part of the Hindenburg Line, extends to the valley of the Meuse River about 4 miles away.

On October 12 and 13 the divisions consolidated their gains. On the 12th Cunel was entered though not held by a battalion of the 5th Division, that division having relieved the 80th. On the 13th the 3d Division extended to the right, relieving parts of the 5th and 4th Divisions. During the day it was subjected to heavy hostile artillery concentrations on its front lines, particularly in the Bois de Forêt where a determined enemy attack was repulsed.

On the morning of October 14 the Army launched a general attack, the 5th and 42d Divisions having entered the line to take part. The 3d Division attacked from just beyond Cunel; the 5th from in front of Cunel and along the ridge in rear of the chapel; the 32d from the front to the observer's left of Romagne and Côte Dame Marie; the 42d from the line facing

Results of Traffic on the Avocourt–Malancourt Road Built Over No Man's Land

Observer Dropping Message for 5th Division Headquarters at Bois de la Tuilerie
(Insert)   White Panels Being Displayed as Signals to an Airplane

Côte de Châtillon (the operations there were described at the last stop) and the 82d and 77th from the front line beyond the 42d Division (the operations of the 77th and 82d Division were described at the top near Martincourt Farm).

In this attack the German defenses crumbled before the onslaughts of the terrific American assaults. The 5th Division captured Cunel and with the 3d Division stormed the strongly fortified Bois de la Pultière, seen on the hill just to the left of Cunel, and by that night had practically cleared it of the enemy. The 5th Division just before jumping off suffered heavy casualties on the ridge behind the chapel from a two-hour concentrated enemy artillery bombardment and again from an intense concentration of hostile fire just after leaving its trenches. The troops doggedly advanced, however, capturing this hill about 10:00 a. m. and, in spite of savage cross-fire from machine guns located at the edge of the Bois de la Pultière near Romagne, stormed the ridge across the valley about 10:40 a. m.   Upon arriving at that ridge,

which was devoid of trees at that time, their positions were so exposed and the sweeping cross-fire was so intense that the men could not dig in but secured what shelter they could in the shell holes and captured trenches until after dark.

The 32d Division, in spite of severe counterattacks, by a brilliant enveloping maneuver, captured Côte Dame Marie and advanced its front lines a total distance of approximately $1\frac{1}{2}$ miles. It also captured the village of Romagne and held it through a heavy German gas bombardment during that night.

The day was a momentous one for the First Army, for by its close the Hindenburg Line was in American hands on all this part of the battle front.

In this immediate vicinity the American troops organized themselves that night on a line which included the village of Romagne and ran from there along the valley to a point near the pool at the center of the cemetery. It then went diagonally to the right up the ridge across the valley and followed the top of that ridge to the Bois de la Pultière near Cunel.

90th Division Troops Passing Through Cunel, October 27, 1918

The Bois des Rappes, on the horizon to the right front, was the scene of terrific fighting for eight days before it was finally captured and cleared of the enemy on October 21 by the 5th Division. The 90th Division relieved the 5th on October 22 at the edge of the Bois des Rappes and on the ridge across the valley. The next day it captured Bantheville, seen in the valley to the left of and beyond the reception house. The 32d Division made almost daily gains until October 20 on which date it was relieved by the 89th Division. By that time it had driven a deep salient into the German lines by capturing most of the Bois de Bantheville, the very large wood which covers the tops of the hills to the left front, and which ends near Le Grand Carré Farm, seen just below the horizon to the left of front.

History records no more sustained and severe fighting than that on this front during October. The highly-organized positions of the Germans were defended with desperate tenacity by experienced troops. The ground was ideal for defense, and that the necessity of holding it was evident to the Germans is clea from the following sentence of an orde which the opposing German genera issued to his men on October 1: "Th fate of a large portion of the Wester Front, perhaps of our nation, depends o the firm holding of the Verdun Front."

The American Army attacked in cessantly and such lack cf experience a existed in its divisions in the beginnin was more than counterbalanced by th individual bravery and unbounded energ of its soldiers. Their constant pressur gradually forced the enemy back so tha by the end of October the First Arm faced the last German line on this par of its front. The bitterness of this fight ing is attested by the 27,000 casualtie suffered by the American 3d, 4th, 5th 32d, 80th, 89th and 90th Divisions in th general vicinity of this cemetery.

On November 1 the First Army agai drove forward, in what proved to be it last great attack, from a jump-off lin which ran just this side of Le Gran Carré Farm. The zone of action of th 90th Division included that farm nea s left boundary. In line on its left was the 89th Division and then the 2d Division. The immediate objective of the attack was Barricourt Heights, seen on the horizon to the right of the wood just beyond Le Grand Carré Farm, and the more distant objective was the lateral railroad running near Sedan.

The attack was a signal success and Barricourt Heights were captured by the 2d and 89th Divisions on the first day. Hill 343, the wooded hill seen to the right of front was captured by the 90th Division on November 2. By November 4 the German Army was in full retreat on his front, and by the morning of November 7 the troops of the First Army were on the heights of the river across from Sedan, 25 miles from here.

By November 11, the day of the Armistice, the Meuse River had been crossed in several places and the American Army was pushing rapidly on beyond it.

Thus the war ended with a glorious victory for the American Army. Those who sleep on this hillside and their comrades in death who now rest in the cemeteries of America had not fought in vain.

Go to the reception building on the opposite side of the valley. From its terrace a beautiful view of the cemetery and its fields of crosses is obtained.

EN ROUTE MEUSE-ARGONNE AMERICAN CEMETERY TO SOUTH OF MADELEINE FARM

(56.5 m 90.9 km) **Leave the cemetery by the gate opposite to the one entered.**

The next village, Cunel, was the scene of many desperate conflicts between October 9 and 14, in which the 80th, 3d and 5th Divisions participated. The town was captured several times but not held because it was dominated by the German positions in the Bois de la Pultière above it. The town and the wood, which was defended with the greatest tenacity, were finally captured on October 14; the town by the 5th Division and the wood by troops of the 3d and 5th Divisions.

(57.5 m 92.5 km) **At church in Cunel, bear right.** This town was the 5th Division Headquarters, November 4–7.

(57.6 m 92.7 km) **At next road fork, bear right and STOP without leaving car.**

"Cornwilly" for Breakfast in a Quarry Near Cunel, October 29, 1918

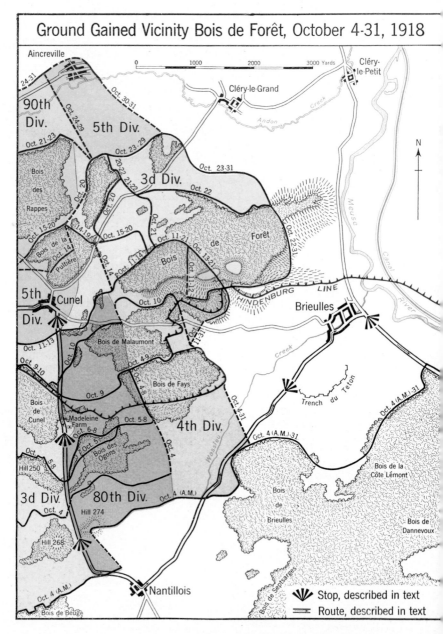

The wood seen to the left rear is the Bois de Forêt. That part of it closest to here was captured by the 4th Division on the morning of October 11 after terrific fighting. It was held in spite of several determined counterattacks, one of which was launched from the Bois de la Pultière, the wooded area seen to the rear.

The ground in this immediate vicinity was captured by the 5th Division on

October 14 and near this point is seen one of the many pyramidal markers erected after the Armistice by the 5th Division on or near its former battlefields.

The terrain to the left and rear of here was, on October 12, the scene of the heroic exploits of First Lieutenant Samuel Woodfill, 5th Division, for which he was awarded the Congressional Medal of Honor and later selected by General Pershing as an outstanding hero of the American Expeditionary Forces. Lieutenant Woodfill was leading his company in an attack toward the Bois de la Pultière from the small wooded areas to the left of here when it encountered heavy enemy fire. Followed at some distance by two soldiers, he immediately advanced toward a machine-gun nest, which was at the edge of the wood in rear of here, and worked his way around its flank. Four of the enemy emerged, three of whom were shot by Lieutenant Woodfill and the fourth, an officer, was killed in hand-to-

A Typical Scene in the Bois de Forêt

hand combat. The company then continued to advance through the wood until another machine-gun nest was encountered. Again Lieutenant Woodfill rushed ahead of his command in the face of heavy fire from the nest and when several of the enemy appeared, he shot them, captured three other members of the crew and silenced the gun. A few minutes later, this officer, for the third time, demonstrated conspicuous bravery by charging another machine-gun position and by employing in turn a rifle, a pistol, and finally a pick, killed seven of the enemy.

From here to the next town, Nantillois, the tour goes opposite to the direction of the American advance. The view of the terrain is, therefore, that which was seen from the various German positions.

The difficult character of the ground over which the American Army forced its way forward is illustrated by the country between here and the next village, Nantillois; and the bitter nature of the fighting is indicated by the comparatively small yet numerous American gains made along this road. In the next 2½ miles there are six pronounced ridges which run almost at right angles to this road. It took the First Army 14 days of nearly continuous fighting to capture them. Each time the Germans lost a ridge they had one equally good for defensive purposes just behind it.

The line reached on October 11 by the 3d and 80th Divisions was along this side of the crest in front of here. The other front lines which crossed this road will be pointed out while approaching them.

Captain Samuel Woodfill, 5th Division, July 1919

Madeleine Farm, Captured by the 3d Division on October 9, 1918
Note character of wooded areas in 1918

From the next crest on to near Nantillois, this road was the boundary between the zones of action of the 3d and 80th Divisions, the 3d Division zone of action being that to the reader's right.

Continue.

(58.0 m 93.3 km) **Beyond next crest, by looking down the valley to the right** a fine view is obtained of part of the heavily-wooded Romagne Heights.

(58.2 m 93.7 km) **At next crest, to the right front on the ridge ahead,** is seen the Bois de Cunel. Along its near edge was located the front line of the 3d Division on October 9 and 10. The Hindenburg Line crossed the road close to this side of that wood. (See map page 254.)

(58.9 m 94.8 km) **At the far side of the wood, when a clear view of the valley to the right is obtained, STOP.**

Face down the road, which direction is approximately south.

The buildings just passed are those of Madeleine Farm, famous in the history of the American Expeditionary Forces. The old building, formerly used by the Germans as a hospital, was marked with a large red cross on the roof. It had been carefully prepared for defense, however, and was the scene of desperate fighting from September 28 to October 9 when the battered ruins of the farm were finally captured by troops of the 3d Division. The first attacks against it, made by units of the 4th and 79th Divisions, supported by tanks, were repulsed on September 28. From then on the 3d, 4th, 79th and 80th Divisions all engaged in bitter fighting in its vicinity.

The large wood seen to the left is the Bois des Ogons. Troops of the 4th and 79th Divisions advanced through it on September 28, but were forced back by counterattacks. The following day elements of both divisions penetrated into it, but were again forced to fall back. It was attacked on October 4 by the 80th Division, which made frontal and flank assaults against it without success until dark when the far edge of it was reached. Attempts to capture the wood by infiltration that night were unsuccessful. On October 5, in spite of desperate efforts during the daytime, no progress could be made. About 6:00 p. m., however, the division reached this edge, which it outposted, and organized a position across the center of the wood.

The wood seen to the right front is on a ridge called during the war Hill 250, which was an exceptionally strong feature of the German defenses. It was reached by the 79th Division on September 28 and on the following day was captured but not held because it formed a sharp salient in the line. It was finally captured on the night of October 5–6 by units of the 3d Division, after a hard fight.

Hill 253, the high bare hill seen to the right, was a powerful German strong point that dominated a large part of the zone of advance of the 3d Division. It was attacked on October 4 without success and again on October 5 when a foothold was gained on its southern slopes. It was taken on October 9 by the 3d Division after a bitter struggle.

This point and the valley on each side of it were in no man's land from October 5 to 8. The American front line was along the edge of the wood to the right front and the German line was facing it from the wood across the valley.

As an illustration of the continuous fighting in this vicinity it might be noted that between midnight and dawn on October 7, the 3d Division made three determined efforts to cross this valley. Each attempt failed because of the alertness of the Germans, who illuminated the area with flares and raked it with severe machine-gun, rifle and artillery fire.

The American positions in the Bois des Ogons and on Hill 250 were subjected to many terrific artillery bombardments and counterattacks during this period.

It was during counterattacks on October 7 against Hill 250 that Private First Class John L. Barkley, 3d Division, won the Congressional Medal of Honor. He was stationed in an observation post near the edge of the wood seen to the right front. On his own initiative he repaired a captured enemy machine gun and mounted it in a disabled tank which was near his post. Shortly afterward, when the enemy launched a counterattack from the edge of the wood across the valley, Private Barkley got into the tank, waited under the hostile barrage until the enemy line was abreast of him, and then opened fire, completely breaking up the attack and killing and wounding a large number of the enemy. Five minutes later an enemy artillery piece opened point-blank fire on the tank from the opposite wood. Although one shell made a direct hit, Private Barkley stuck to his improvised "pillbox" and broke up a second counterattack several minutes later.

The fighting in this valley ended on October 9 when the 3d and 80th Divisions, attacking from the woods ahead, captured this clearing and Madeleine Farm, the Bois de Cunel, seen to the rear, and advanced their front line to the far side of the ridge directly in rear of here.

Madeleine Farm was the 3d Division Headquarters from October 14 to 26.

EN ROUTE SOUTH OF MADELEINE FARM TO NORTHWEST OF CONSENVOYE

(59.4 m 95.6 km) **At the next bend in the road** the American monument on Montfaucon is seen directly ahead.

In the small wood at this point the bodies of seven American soldiers were discovered as late as 1927 buried in the same unmarked shallow grave. They were all without shoes, probably indicating that these articles were in demand by the Germans who buried them.

(59.5 m 95.8 km) **The wood to the right front** is on Hill 268. On October 4 the American front line was about 100 yards this side of that wood and ran close to the edge of the wood seen to the left rear.

"Fox Holes" South of Bois des Ogons

Hill 274, seen to the left front, was captured on September 28 by the 4th and 79th Divisions but due to the total lack of cover and the intense enemy artillery fire, the troops of the 79th Division on that part of it nearest this road withdrew about ½ mile the next day.

(59.9 m 96.4 km) **Upon reaching the next crest proceed about 100 yards and STOP without leaving automobile.**

In this general vicinity the German reserves of men and artillery, which were rushed to this front after the attack of September 26, entered the battle and desperately strove to stop the American advance by counterattacks and heavy concentrations of artillery fire.

The crest of the ridge seen to the left front on the sky line was reached by the 4th Division early on the afternoon of September 26. The near end of the division line was just this side of Hill 295, the highest part of the ridge as seen from here. Three enemy counterattacks against that part of its line were repulsed during the course of the afternoon.

The 79th Division at that time was held up on the other side of Montfaucon but part of the 37th Division and the 91st Division had progressed almost as far as Epinonville, seen in the distance just to the right of the Bois de Beuge, the large wooded area to the right front.

On September 27 the 4th Division attacked but encountered such severe resistance that it could not advance its lines to any extent. On that same day the 79th Division, after occupying Montfaucon about noon, attacked the Bois de Beuge, which was reached by a few men but not held. The division that night dug in along the lowest well-defined line of vegetation seen on Montfaucon. The village of Epinonville was repeatedly attacked by troops of the 91st Division during the day but was not captured.

On September 28 the Bois de Beuge was taken in a vigorous assault by the 79th and 37th Divisions, the latter taking the far side of it. The 37th Division after passing the Bois de Beuge was stopped by a German counterattack. The left of its line, which had advanced over 2 miles, was driven back about ¾ mile by the same counterattack. On that day Nantillois, in the deep valley ahead, was taken by the 79th Division, it having been entered but not held by the 4th Division the day before. Being an important road center, that town, after its capture, was subjected to heavy shelling by German artillery.

In Nantillois are (1937) a building erected by a 315th Infantry association in memory of the dead of that regiment, which was a part of the 79th Division, and a memorial fountain constructed by the State of Pennsylvania as a tribute to the achievements of the 80th Division, which had a number of men in it from that state. The building is seen on the right, set back from the road, soon after entering town. The fountain is passed at the main road junction in the center of the village.

Continue.

(60.7 m 97.7 km) **At the center of Nantillois, turn sharply to the left.**

(61.2 m 98.5 km) **Beyond town, the little valley which the road follows** was the scene of desperate fighting on September 27 and 28 before it and the ridge to the left were finally taken by the 4th Division.

(63.1 m 101.5 km) **Beyond the first farm buildings located to the LEFT of the road, at second pronounced crest, STOP without leaving the automobile.**

A 4th Division monument is located alongside the road near this stopping point. (Consult the map on page 254.)

The hills seen ahead in the distance are on the other side of the Meuse River. Fire from German artillery positions located on those hills enfiladed the lines of the American units on this side of the river and caused many casualties. The hills were not taken until November 5, six days before the Armistice.

The large wood seen fringing the top of the ridge to the left and left front across the valley is the Bois de Forêt and that on the hillside seen to the left rear is the Bois de Fays. The Hindenburg Line included all of the Bois de Forêt and most of the Bois de Fays. The first penetration of the Hindenburg Line made by the First Army was on October 4 when in a dashing assault troops of the 4th Division captured the Bois de Fays.

The Bois de Forêt was the scene of many desperate conflicts, in which the 4th and 3d Divisions were engaged, before its capture was finally completed on October 22 by the 3d Division.

Because of the enfilade fire of the German artillery up this valley, no attacks were launched from this vicinity against the Bois de Forêt. The capture of that wood was finally brought about by an enveloping movement through the Bois de Fays. This movement, which involved fighting of the most vicious character, was initiated by the 4th Division on October 4 and continued by it until October 11, when the left half of the Bois de Forêt was captured. The 3d Division relieved the 4th there on October 13 and on October 22 occupied the rest of the wood.

On top of the bare hill rising to the right from here was an exceptionally strong German position called the Trench du Téton. It was occupied by the 4th Division on October 10 and soon thereafter the Germans abandoned Brieulles, seen in the valley ahead, because the town was dominated by the newly organized American positions on that hill.

During the severe fighting in the Bois de la Côte Lémont, to be pointed out later in the tour, and in the Bois de Fays, First Lieutenant William R. Arrants, Medical Corps, 80th Division, performed the heroic services for which he was awarded the Distinguished Service Cross. He accompanied his battalion into action on September 28 in the Bois de la Côte Lémont, and promptly opened his aid station within 100 yards of the front line where he worked all night under continuous fire, giving aid to the wounded. When there was a shortage of stretcher bearers he assisted in bringing in the wounded. Under intense fire he undertook to locate the ambulance station and personally directed the evacuation of wounded to it. In the attack from the Bois de Fays on October 5 he again went with the attacking troops and opened a first aid station in an old cellar. Under an intense barrage of shrapnel and high explosive shells, he performed the most devoted service in attending the wounded, working continuously until after his unit had been ordered to retire.

Continue.

(63.2 m 101.7 km) **To the left front across the valley,** is seen a large French World War military cemetery.

(63.9 m 102.8 km) **Immediately after entering Brieulles, turn to the right.**

(64.4 m 103.6 km) **Where the road ends at the railroad, turn right and STOP without leaving the automobile.**

This point is at the west side of the Meuse River valley. The river winds its way through the valley and a canal is at the foot of the nearest hill to the left.

During the progress of the last great

33d Division Troops in Drillancourt, October 4, 1918

A 79th Division Aid Station in the Bois de Consenvoye, November 8, 1918

ffensive of the First Army, one of the most difficult military feats, that of crossing a river under hostile fire, was accomplished by the 5th Division near here.

Soon after midnight on November 2–3, a footbridge was placed by the engineers over the river about 300 yards in rear of here and a patrol followed by one infantry company crossed to the flats between the river and canal. About dawn the enemy discovered the movement and laid down a heavy fire in the area. The troops on the flats were driven to the cover of the high bank along the canal, in which precarious position they remained throughout the day.

That night the canal was bridged about 300 yards to the left rear from here with two footbridges. An attempt to rush over one of the bridges at 2:00 a. m. on November 4 was defeated by enemy machine-gun fire and several other attempts to cross before daybreak were repulsed. However, after dark (the sun set at 4:19 p. m.) by a sudden rush over the footbridges the enemy was surprised and two companies quickly established themselves on the far side. These immediately extended their lines for a considerable distance along the river. Profiting by the confusion caused in the German ranks by this crossing, another battalion of the 5th Division crossed the river and canal, to the left front from here, in boats. This battalion promptly captured Hill 252, seen to the left, and organized a position on it that night.

On November 5 the division made another crossing of the river about 2 miles to the left rear from here and still further extended its gains in this vicinity, among its captures being the Bois de Châtillon, a large wooded area part of which is seen to the left front.

The successful crossing here turned the German lines on the Heights of the Meuse, to the left front beyond the river, and greatly facilitated the progress of those units of the American Army which were attacking the German lines from the front.

From now on to the village of Consen-voye, where the river is crossed, the tour goes along the Meuse River valley.

Continue.

(65.3 m 105.1 km) **At the place where large wood, Bois de la Côte Lémont, ex-tends immediately alongside road,** the 80th Division reached this valley on September 28 and established its front line along the railroad track. The opposing lines faced each other across the valley from that time on to November 6.

(66.0 m 106.2 km) **The village to the left front across the valley** is Vilosnes, captured on November 6, and beyond it on the ridge in the distance, Haraumont, captured on November 7, soon appears. These were taken by the French 15th Colonial Division which was attached to the American Army. It was assisted in the crossing of the river and the capture of Vilosnes by the 5th Division, which, after crossing at Brieulles, attacked the town from the heights seen above it.

German Observation Post Captured by the 29th Division in the Bois de Consenvoye

From here to the next sharp bend i the road, the tour runs generally eas and west, that is, at right angles to th direction of advance of the First Army.

(67.0 m 107.8 km) **Opposite Vilosnes on this side of the valley** a large Germa supply depot was captured.

(67.9 m 109.3 km) **While approachin next sharp bend in road,** there is see straight ahead a bald-topped hill marke by a small monument. That hill i the Borne de Cornouiller, called by ou men "Cornwilly Hill". The slopes of th hill to the observer's right were reached b, the 33d Division on October 9 and agai on the 10th, its front line remaining ther until the 12th. The top of the hill wa captured on November 7 by the 79t Division after parts of it had change hands several times during bitter fightin on the preceding days. The advanc was from right to left as seen from here.

The monument on the hill is a small on in commemoration of the services of th American soldiers who fought in tha vicinity. No road runs near it.

(68.9 m 110.9 km) **In the next valle leading to the right** is seen Dannevoux That village, which lay in the Germa second position, was taken after dark o September 26 by the 80th Division. O this side of Dannevoux a large depot con taining valuable military supplies wa captured by the 33d Division.

(69.1 m 111.2 km) **At next crest,** th zone of action of the 33d Division on Sep tember 26 is entered. The division estab lished its line just to the left of this roa before noon of that day.

(69.3 m 111.5 km) **In the next littl valley, after crossing the stone bridge, t the left** are seen (1937) several large con crete shelters built by the Germans.

On October 7 a French airplane wa shot down near here and crashed on th flats across the river near the enemy lines Seeing that the French aviator was in jured, Corporal Ralyn Hill, 33d Division voluntarily dashed over the river on footbridge and carried the wounded ma to this side under heavy hostile fire For his gallant exploit he was awarde

79th Division Water Service Train in Brabant-sur-Meuse, November 3, 1918

ter the Congressional Medal of Honor.

(70.4 m 113.3 km) **About 1 mile farther on, at top of the hill to the right** is seen a distant view of Montfaucon.

(70.9 m 114.1 km) **Beyond next road junction, where a good view is obtained of the valley ahead, STOP.**

Face down road, which direction is approximately southeast.

The nearest town across the valley is Consenvoye. The first buildings seen up he valley beyond it are in Brabant.

In this region, the Meuse River is followed on its far side by a comparatively narrow and rough plateau, about 4 or 5 miles wide, called the Heights of the Meuse. This forms a formidable military obstacle, being heavily wooded and indented by many deep valleys.

The German positions on those heights were not attacked on September 26, although the First Army contemplated that an advance would have to be made north along them in the near future.

This proved to be the case, because, as the offensive on this side of the river progressed, the hostile artillery fire from the heights seen to the left began to strike the flank and rear of the advancing forces and inflicted many casualties. Consequently, the French XVII Corps, which was holding that part of the front just across the river, was ordered by the First Army to attack on October 8.

The operation was executed by the American 33d and 29th Divisions and three French divisions. The main assault was made by a brigade of the 29th attached to the French 18th Division, a brigade of the French 18th Division and the French 26th Division, in line in that order from Brabant on to the observer's left. The French 10th Colonial Division protected the right flank of the corps.

The 33d Division, which held this bank of the river from Brabant to the Bois de la Côte Lémont, recently passed on the tour, was to cross at Brabant after the main attack had progressed a certain distance. It was to be notified by the French 18th Division when to cross and after crossing it was to attack toward the Bois de Chaume, the wood seen fringing the summit of the hill to the left rear.

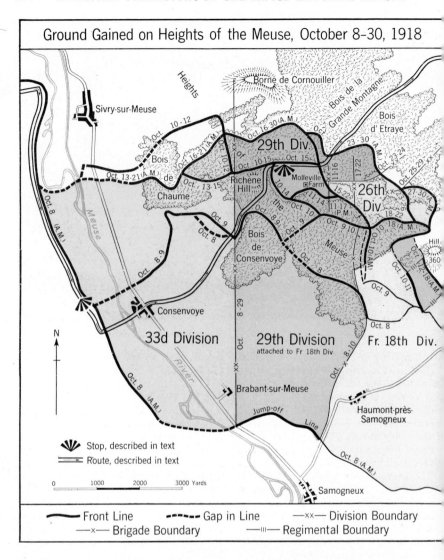

Ground Gained on Heights of the Meuse, October 8–30, 1918

The troops of the main attack jumped off at 5:00 a. m. behind an intense rolling barrage. The advance of the 29th Division was rapid for about a mile until its intermediate objective, marked roughly by an extension of the line from this point through the center of Consenvoye, was reached. From there on it was subjected to severe machine-gun fire, a large part of which came from the Bois de Consenvoye, the wedge-shaped wood seen over the left edge of Consenvoye. That wood was reached about noon and captured by the 29th Division during the afternoon.

At 9:00 a. m. the 33d Division was ordered to cross the river and at 11:00 a. m. it began its advance from Brabant. Consenvoye was captured about noon and a pause was made near there. The attack was continued soon after 4:00 p. m. against artillery and machine-gun fire. The most advanced part of the division

ne was established that night in a Ger-
uan trench which was located just to the
bserver's right of the Bois de Chaume.

On October 9 the 33d Division attacked
bout 6:40 a. m. in a thick fog. It made
n advance of about 1½ miles, well beyond
he Bois de Chaume, but withdrew that
fternoon because the 29th Division, ad-
oining it, had not advanced and the German units had begun to work their way
n behind its exposed flank. These
nemy units cut off and surrounded about
00 American soldiers near the far edge
f the Bois de Chaume, but the Americans
eld out and were rescued by the advanc-
ng troops during the next morning.

It was during this fighting on October 9
hat Private First Class Berger H. Loman,
3d Division, won the Congressional Med-
l of Honor. When his company was
pproaching its objective under terrific
ostile fire, Private Loman voluntarily
nd unaided made his way forward after
ll others had taken shelter from the di-
ect fire of an enemy machine gun. He
rawled to a position on the flank of the
un and, after killing or capturing the
ntire crew, turned the machine gun and
sed it on the retreating German troops.
On this same day Private Felix Bird of

the 33d Division advanced alone against
a German dugout and captured 49 of the
enemy, killing one officer who attempted
to escape. For this courageous and gallant deed, Private Bird was awarded the
Distinguished Service Cross.

The 33d Division attacked early on
October 10 and by 10:00 a. m. had again
captured the Bois de Chaume. On that
day the 29th Division captured Richène
Hill, the first wooded hill seen to the left
of the wedge-shaped Bois de Consenvoye.
The zone of action of the 29th Division
is visited later in the tour and the fighting
of that division is described in considerable detail at the next stop.

The 33d Division moved its front line a
short distance to the rear on October 13
to a better defensive location. On October 16 it advanced the right of its line
about ½ mile in support of an attack by
the 29th Division. This advance ended
its active fighting on this front as it was
relieved from the line on October 21.

EN ROUTE NORTHWEST OF CONSENVOYE TO NEAR MOLLEVILLE FARM

(71.4 m 114.9 km) **At road junction
opposite the village of Consenvoye, turn
to the left and cross Meuse River valley.**

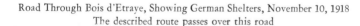

Road Through Bois d'Etraye, Showing German Shelters, November 10, 1918
The described route passes over this road

Illustrates Character of Terrain Advanced Over by the American First Army
on September 26, 1918

Soon after its capture on October 8, this road was heavily camouflaged along its left side to conceal movements over it from German observation posts located on the high ridge to the left, 4 miles away.

During the early morning of October 8 the engineers, in spite of heavy hostile artillery fire, built a bridge over the river to the right of here upon which part of the division crossed about 4:30 in the afternoon to join in the attack.

(72.1 m 116.0 km) **Continue on straight through the village of Consenvoye.**

During the attack on Consenvoye on October 8 First Sergeant Johannes S. Anderson and Private Clayton K. Slack, 33d Division, performed the acts for which they were awarded Congressional Medals of Honor. While his company was held up by intense artillery and machine-gun fire, Sergeant Anderson, armed with a shotgun, voluntarily worked his way alone to the rear of the machine-

German 21-Centimeter Howitzer Captured
by the 80th Division Near
Vaux-en-Dieulet on November 4, 1918

gun nest that was offering the mos stubborn resistance. Although his ad vance was made through an open are under constant hostile fire, he not onl silenced the gun but captured it an brought back with him 23 prisoners.

Private Slack, observing German so diers under cover 50 yards away to his le flank, upon his own initiative rushed the with his rifle and singlehanded capture ten prisoners and two heavy machin guns, thus saving his company and i adjoining units from heavy casualties.

(72.5 m 116.7 km) **Beyond town, abou 500 yards,** a German bombproof shelte is seen (1937) just at the left of the roac

In the attack on October 8 the 33d Divi sion advanced across this road from righ to left and established its front line in German trench on the near slope of th hill seen across the valley.

(73.0 m 117.5 km) **Beyond second le bend in road, by looking to the left rea down the valley** is seen the village of Con senvoye and a large part of the groun beyond the river which was captured b the First Army on September 26.

The American monument erected o Montfaucon is visible in the distance t the left on the sky line.

(73.8 m 118.8 km) **The large wood see ahead** is the Bois de Consenvoye. Th front line of the 29th Division was estab lished on October 8 along the near edge o that part of it to the right of this road. I remained there throughout the next day

Steel Observation Turrets at Fort Douaumont

(74.2 m 119.4 km) **While approaching the wood, to the left front the wooded hill nearest the road** is Richène Hill which was pointed out at the last stop.

(74.4 m 119.7 km) **After entering wood, to the right of the road** was the scene on October 8 of the heroic deeds of Sergeant Earl D. Gregory, 29th Division. Sergeant Gregory seized a rifle and trench-mortar shell, which he used as a hand-grenade, advanced ahead of the infantry and captured a machine gun and three of the enemy. Advancing still farther on beyond the machine-gun nest, he captured a 75-millimeter mountain howitzer and entering a dugout in its immediate vicinity he singlehandedly captured 19 of the enemy soldiers. For these acts of valor and outstanding gallantry he was awarded the Congressional Medal of Honor.

(75.1 m 120.9 km) **Beyond next crossroads, where a good view is obtained of valley to the right front, STOP.**

Face to the right, which direction is approximately south.

In the valley to the left front are seen the buildings of Molleville Farm.

Consult the map on page 264.

When the heights east of the Meuse were attacked on October 8, a brigade of the 29th Division, operating with a French division, drove forward aggressively in this direction from a jump-off line about 3 miles in front of here. Elements of the brigade reached the ravine seen beyond Molleville Farm on that day

(267)

but, having no contact with the troops on their flanks, they withdrew about 1 mile.

On October 9 the brigade repulsed a hostile attack and advanced its line in the woods in front of here and on October 10 units of it reached the edge of this clearing to the right front.

It was during this fighting that Second Lieutenant Patrick Regan and Private First Class Henry G. Costin, 29th Division, won Congressional Medals of Honor. While leading his platoon against a strong enemy machine-gun nest which was holding up the advance, Lieutenant Regan divided his men into three groups, sending one group to each flank, he himself attacking the nest from the front with an automatic rifle team to which Private Costin had been first to volunteer. Two of the team were killed outright, while Lieutenant Regan and Private Costin were seriously wounded, the latter being

Headquarters Constructed by the French
at Bras, Occupied by the 26th Division
October 18–November 11, 1918

unable to advance. In spite of his injury Lieutenant Regan dashed with empty pistol into the machine-gun nest, capturing 30 Austrian gunners and four machine guns, Private Costin continuing to fire his rifle in support until he collapsed. These gallant deeds permitted the advance to continue. Private Costin died as a result of his wounds but Lieutenant Regan gallantly continued to lead his platoon forward until ordered to the rear by his commanding officer.

Early on October 11 the 29th Division took command of the zone of action immediately in front of here. One brigade of it, however, still continued to operate with the French 18th Division.

On the 11th the 29th Division advanced its line in front of here to the far side of this clearing. It made three determined efforts to cross the clearing, each time being driven back by severe fire from Germans in trenches along this road.

The brigade of the 29th Division still with the French made several determined attacks on October 12 and succeeded in gaining a foothold in the Bois d'Ormont on Hill 360, the hill seen to the left front with the patch of wood on its summit.

On October 15, after a severe fight, the division finally captured this clearing and established its front line along this road to the left of here. The next day its attacks were continued and in spite of intense opposition the division pushed forward about ½ mile into the Bois de la Grande Montagne, the large wooded area immediately behind this point.

The brigade of the 29th with the French was returned to its own division on October 18, and on that day the relief of the French division to the observer's left of the 29th was completed by units of the American 26th Division.

On October 23 the 26th and 29th Divisions attacked in the direction of the observer's left and in a spirited assault advanced their lines about ¾ mile, gaining all objectives. Several hostile counter attacks made during the afternoon and evening of that day were driven back.

The 26th Division made determined efforts to capture Hill 360 on each of the three days, October 24, 25 and 27, but no permanent gains resulted.

It was during the fighting on October 2 that Private First Class Michael J. Perkins, 26th Division, voluntarily and alone

Main Street in Ville-devant-Chaumont,
November 1918

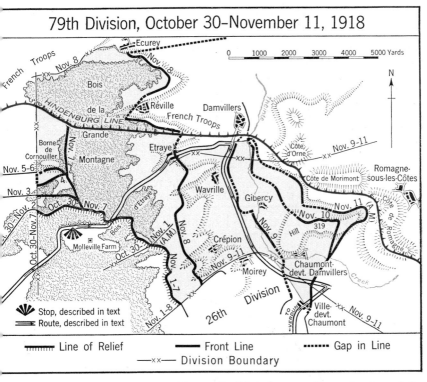

79th Division, October 30–November 11, 1918

Stop, described in text
Route, described in text

Line of Relief   Front Line   Gap in Line
—xx— Division Boundary

awled to a German concrete machineun emplacement from which grenades
ere being thrown at his platoon. Await-
g his opportunity, when the door of
ne emplacement was opened by a German
o throw a grenade, Private Perkins threw
bomb inside which burst the door down.
Then, drawing his trench knife, he rushed
to the emplacement and in a hand-to-
and struggle killed or wounded several
f the occupants, captured about 25
risoners and silenced seven machine
uns. He was killed in the operations of
hat day but was posthumously awarded
he Congressional Medal of Honor for the
ourageous feats recorded above.

The 29th Division after its hard fight-
g here was relieved from the line on
ctober 30 by the 79th Division.

On November 1 the 79th Division
xtended its sector to the observer's left,
s shown on the above sketch, so that it
eld a total frontage of about 4 miles.
The capture of Barricourt Heights by

the First Army on November 1, and the
resulting German withdrawal on the other
side of the river, caused the Army to sus-
pect a retirement was contemplated near
here. Consequently, the 79th Division
was ordered to test out the situation by
sending out strong patrols near the Borne
de Cornouiller, a high bald hill located
about 1 mile to the right rear from here,
recently pointed out from across the river.
These patrols advanced early on November 3, and in severe fighting pushed the
division line forward about 500 yards.

During November 4 and 5 the 79th
Division after further desperate fighting
reached a line near the crest of the Borne
de Cornouiller. This success and the
progress made by other divisions to the
north forced the German troops to withdraw from the heights in this vicinity.

A deep advance was made on November 7 and the next day the division moved
rapidly forward, toward the observer's
left, to the eastern edge of these heights.

Substantial daily gains were made there-after until the Armistice on November 11.

The total casualties of the 33d, 29th, 79th and 26th Divisions during their fighting on and near the Heights of the Meuse were almost 15,000 officers and men.

Molleville Farm was the 79th Division Headquarters from November 9 to 11.

Beyond this clearing for about 3 miles the tour follows the direction of advance on this front during November 8 and 9.

EN ROUTE NEAR MOLLEVILLE FARM
TO VERDUN

(75.2 m 121.0 km) **To the right in the distance** is seen the tower of the Ossuar of Douaumont, a French war memoria

(76.2 m 122.6 km) **After entering woo the valley which the road follows** was concentration place for German reser units. In the woods on both sides of th road were many elaborate shelters an dugouts, constructed by the Germans f the protection and comfort of the troop who were waiting to support the fro line or to relieve units serving in it.

(77.7 m 125.0 km) **Straight throug** next village, Etraye, which was capture by the 79th Division on November 8, an was just within its front line that nigh

From here to the ne road junction, this road w close to the left boundar of the 79th Division zor of action on November A French division was a joining it on the left.

(78.8 m 126.8 km) **Ju before reaching road jun tion, the second nose heights seen to the left** near where the 32d Div sion entered the line on th afternoon of November That afternoon some of i units reached the main roa running to the left from th village, Damvillers, seen t the left front. One of i regiments attacked fro there in a heavy fog on th morning of November 1 advanced about 2 miles an when the fog lifted foun itself isolated. It withdre in good order to its jum off line. The left of th division on that day pushe forward about 2 miles.

(79.0 m 127.1 km) At roa junction, turn sharp rigl

(79.6 m 128.1 km) **Th next town, Wavrille, w** captured by the 79th D vision about 10:00 a. m. o November 9. The hosti resistance then stiffene

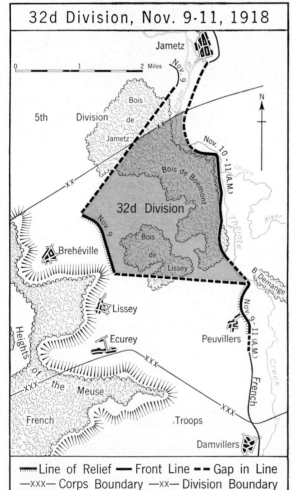

32d Division, Nov. 9-11, 1918

nd progress was difficult due mainly to
ostile fire from the hills seen to the left.
'he division established its line that night
o the left of this road and generally paral-
el to it. On the 10th it again pushed
orward despite considerable opposition
nd at the time of the Armistice the sol-
iers of the division were fighting on the
ear slopes of the hills seen to the left.

(80.1 m 128.9 km) **The bare hill seen to
he left front** was captured by the 79th
)ivision early on November 10.

(81.0 m 130.4 km) **The next town,
Ioirey, seen to the right near the road,**
vas near the boundary between the 79th
nd 26th Divisions. It was entered by
lements of both of those divisions during
he morning of November 9.

(81.3 m 130.8 km) **Soon after Moirey
ppears in view, alongside the road** are
een (1937) two large reinforced concrete
osts which were built by the Germans.
Ieavy chains suspended between them
vere intended to prevent the advance of
rmored cars along this road.

(82.0 m 132.0 km) **The village seen to
he left, part way up the hill,** is Chaumont-
evant-Damvillers. It was captured by
he 79th Division on November 10.

(82.8 m 133.2 km) **Beyond Chaumont,
ake the first road to the right.**

The tour now goes in a direction gen-
rally contrary to the direction of advance
f the Army on this part of its front.

(83.4 m 134.2 km) **Straight through
he village of Ville-devant-Chaumont,**
aptured by the 26th Division late in the
fternoon of November 10.

(83.6 m 134.5 km) **Upon leaving the
illage, to the left of the road** is seen a
ierman World War military cemetery.

(84.1 m 135.3 km) **Beyond town, along
he foot of the slopes seen to the right
ront,** the 26th Division was held up on
Iovember 9 by heavy machine-gun fire.
'he division dug in there that night,
acing in this direction. Its front line
y the time of the Armistice had been
dvanced across this road and was es-
ablished along the slopes to the left of it.

(85.4 m 137.4 km) **Near top of long
ill, just beyond the road junction,** was

Near 79th Division Headquarters at
Vacherauville, October 31, 1918

located the front line of the 26th Division,
November 3–7, from which it advanced
on the afternoon of November 8.

(85.5 m 137.6 km) **At the right side of
the road** is seen a monument, surrounded
by graves, commemorative of a heroic
defense in 1916 by a French officer,
Colonel Driant, and his unit.

(85.8 m 138.1 km) **While descending
hill, to the left front** are seen a small
chapel and monument. These mark the
site of the former village of Beaumont,
which was completely destroyed during
the severe fighting in 1916.

The battle line on September 26 was
located just the other side of Beaumont.
The attack in this region on October 8
was made from that line on a front of
about 4 miles extending from the vicinity
of Beaumont to the Meuse River.

The tour now passes through one
of the few remaining areas which give
an idea of the devastation at the front

Gate at Verdun, Said to Have Been the Inspiration for the Insignia
of the U. S. Corps of Engineers

during the war. To obtain a better picture of its wartime condition, this desolate country should be visualized as being devcid cf all vegetation.

(89.9 m 144.7 km) **In Vacherauville,** the main road to Verdun is joined. This town was the 29th Division Headquarters, October 7–30, and 79th Division Headquarters, October 29–November 9.

The route leading east from the next town, Bras, shown in broken lines on the map at the end of the chapter, is a tour of the French forts near Verdun. It will take the visitor to the Trench of Bayonets, Fort Douaumont, the Ossuary of Douaumont and other places and monuments of general interest.

(90.9 m 146.3 km) **At Bras, the next village,** was located the 26th Division Headquarters, October 18–November 11.

(91.1 m 146.6 km) **Beyond the town, on the right side of the road,** is located a French World War military cemetery.

(94.9 m 152.7 km) **Continue to Verdun. The mileage ends at the railroad station.**

The city of Verdun was severely damaged by the German heavy artillery and by numerous air bombardments during the prolonged fighting in this vicinity.

Points of interest are the underground part of the citadel, the cathedral and house of the bishop, and the Hôtel-de Ville (City Hall). The citadel is located on the western edge of the city. It underground compartments served to house various French headquarters and thousands of reserves during the great battles near here in 1916–17. In the house of the bishop, which adjoins the cathedral, is a museum which contains battlefield souvenirs as well as ancient relics of the city. The cathedral and cloister, badly damaged during the war, are of interest. The Hôtel-de-Ville, located on Rue de l'Hôtel-de-Ville, contains an excellent museum, and in the building are the many beautiful tokens of esteem given to the city by various nations in appreciation of its heroic defense in 1916.

SECOND DAY'S TOUR OF THE AMERICAN
MEUSE-ARGONNE BATTLEFIELDS

THIS tour starts at the Meuse-Argonne American Cemetery near Romagne and ends at Verdun. It is about 93 miles (150 kilometers) long and can be completed within approximately eight hours. To save time lunch should be carried.

The greater part of the tour is in the area captured by the American First Army between November 1 and 11, 1918. It is recommended to persons who have been over the first day's tour and to others who are especially interested in the last part of the Meuse-Argonne offensive.

The data given on pages 520–521 will be helpful to those following this tour.

In case the first day's tour has not been followed, it is suggested that the tourist in going to the starting point of the section day's tour follow the first day's tour from Verdun to Montfaucon and from there proceed via Nantillois and Cunel.

The narrative at the beginning of the chapter should be kept in mind, and the map facing page 326 should be consulted, so that the combat operations which took place in the region of this tour will be more clearly understood by the tourist.

Upon arriving at the Meuse-Argonne American Cemetery, go to chapel and read pages 248–253, giving information about the American fighting in the vicinity. If first day's tour has not already been followed, read also pages 247–248 which give a description of this cemetery.

When following this itinerary, unless contrary road instructions are given, the tourist should continue straight ahead.

EN ROUTE CHAPEL MEUSE-ARGONNE AMERICAN CEMETERY TO NORTH OF CUNEL

Speedometer distance is measured from the plaza immediately in front of the chapel.

(0.0 m 0.0 km) **Leave the chapel and cemetery by the road to the right.**

(0.6 m 1.0 km) **Down the road, to the left of the next village, Cunel,** is seen the Bois de la Pultière, an exceptionally strong point in the German defensive organization. It was taken on October 14 by the 3d and 5th Divisions after hard fighting.

(1.4 m 2.3 km) **At the church in the village of Cunel turn to the left.**

(1.6 m 2.6 km) **Beyond town, by looking to the left,** may be had a fine view of the exposed slopes and ridges over which the American troops advanced. The commanding situation of the many German machine-gun positions located near the edge of the Bois de la Pultière, which is seen to the right, is evident from here.

German Anti-Tank Gun in Firing Position, October 1918. © G

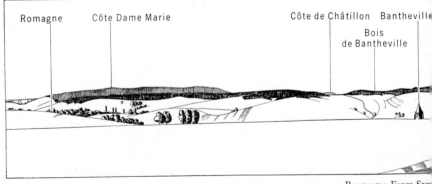

Romagne   Côte Dame Marie   Côte de Châtillon   Banthevill

Bois
de Bantheville

Panorama From Sto

(2.4 m 3.9 km) **Beyond the village cemetery, on the second crest, where a good panorama is obtained of the terrain to the front and right front, STOP.**

The town ahead in the valley is Bantheville. The village marked by the scattered houses to the right of Bantheville and some distance from it is Andevanne.

Face Andevanne, the direction to which is approximately north.

Beyond Andevanne is Sedan, 25 miles from here, through which ran the lateral railroad which was the main goal of the American Meuse-Argonne offensive.

For dauntless courage and the overcoming of seemingly impossible obstacles, the fighting of the American soldier up to and immediately beyond this point is unsurpassed in the history of the war.

On the ridges behind here was located the famous Hindenburg Line, the German defensive position constructed with the hope that it would be impregnable. Along the heights in front of here was the German Freya position, planned with the idea that it would be held, in case portions of the Hindenburg Line were broken through, until those portions could be regained by counterattacks.

A glance at the landscape with its ridges, woods and open fields will give some idea of the difficulties which the American units had to overcome. Each patch of woods was skillfully organized as a strong point and numerous enemy machine guns in them and in other concealed positions often were not discovered until

their fire started to cut down the advanc ing lines. The conduct of the America troops in overcoming the resistance i this vicinity and in forcing their way for ward is beyond all praise.

If we consider with the above the fac that the Germans were using every energ and means at their command to check th advance on this front and thus protec their vital railroad at Sedan, the tas performed by the American Army will b clearer and much better appreciated.

Positions in the woods near here fre quently changed hands several times o the same day and the opposing lines a night were sometimes but a few yard apart. The situation was so balance that a moment's relaxation by either sid risked immediate loss of men and groun

90th Division Ration Party Going Forward
Through the Bois des Rappes,
October 25, 1918

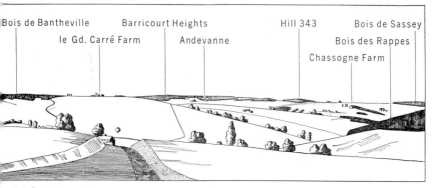

Bois de Bantheville   Barricourt Heights   Hill 343   Bois de Sassey
    le Gd. Carré Farm   Andevanne   Bois des Rappes
                                                          Chassogne Farm

orth of Cunel

After the capture of Romagne, seen in
ne valley to the left, and Côte Dame
Iarie, the high wooded peak just beyond
, the 32d Division continued to advance
ntil it had overrun most of the Bois de
antheville, the large wood which covers
ne tops of the hills to the left and left
ont.   The 89th Division relieved the
2d on October 20, on a line which in-
uded the wooded hill on the sky line seen
ust to the right of the church in Banthe-
ille.   It later succeeded in capturing the
emainder of that wood and in advancing
arough it to near Le Grand Carré Farm,
ne group of buildings seen on the hill
eyond the village of Bantheville.

The 5th Division after eight days of
ntense and bitter fighting finally com-
leted, on October 21, the capture of the
ois des Rappes, the large wood which

is seen just to the right of this road.

On October 23 the 90th Division, which
had relieved the 5th Division on the preceding day, attacked from the ridge to
the left rear and from the Bois de
Bantheville, captured Bantheville and
established itself beyond that town.   The
division front line on that night extended
across the open fields from the Bois des
Rappes to the end of the wood seen to the
left of Le Grand Carré Farm.

The wooded ridges on the sky line to
the left of Andevanne are Barricourt
Heights, and the most prominent wooded
hill seen some distance to the right of
that village is Hill 343.

The Freya position in front of here ran
along Barricourt Heights, passed through
Andevanne, included Hill 343 and continued on through the Bois de Sassey,
which is partially visible on the horizon
beyond the Bois des Rappes.

The date fixed by the First Army for
the general assault against this strong
German line was November 1.   The III,
V and I Corps, in that order from right
to left, were to take part in the attack.
The V Corps, which was to make the
main advance, was in the center of the
Army zone of attack and had the 89th
Division in line to the left of Le Grand
Carré Farm, and the 2d Division on the
far side of the 89th, with its front line
just beyond Côte de Châtillon, the
wooded hill seen to the left front in the
distance peeping up over the Bois de
Bantheville.   The immediate mission of

Machine Gun Firing at German Plane Near
Cunel, October 1918

the V Corps was to capture the dominating Barricourt Heights, the accomplishment of which was certain to cause the Germans on this front to retire in haste across the Meuse River toward Germany.

The III Corps, in front of and to the immediately in front of here, and the 5t Division, which had reentered the lin the one beyond the Bois des Rappes.

The I Corps, on the left of the Arm; was to cover the flank of the V Cor; and was given an objective in the rigl

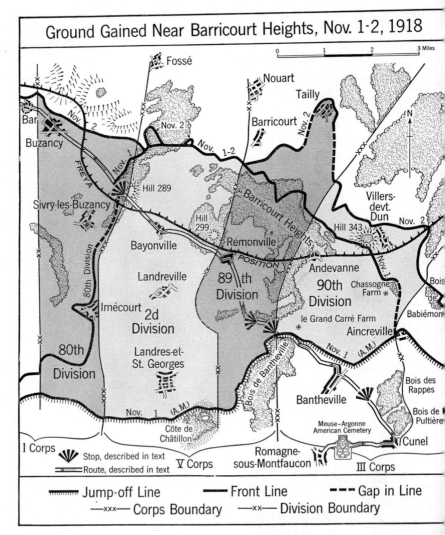

Ground Gained Near Barricourt Heights, Nov. 1-2, 1918

Jump-off Line   Front Line   Gap in Line
—xxx— Corps Boundary   —xx— Division Boundary

right of here, was to assist in the main attack and be ready to force its way over the Meuse River, which is about 3½ miles away to the right and runs just the other side of the Bois de Sassey. In this corps, the 90th Division had the zone of attack

part of its zone of action which wa about 4 miles in advance of its front lin

After an extremely heavy artiller bombardment lasting two hours, the a tack was launched on the morning (November 1. When the infantry jumpe

German Machine Gun Unit Going Into Position. © G

at 5:30 a. m. all available artillery fire s concentrated in a rolling barrage out 1,100 yards in depth, which pro- ssed immediately in front of the ad- ncing lines. This intense and ex- mely effective fire and the severity of e infantry assault so overwhelmed the rman defenders that the attack was a narkable success from the outset. The 2d and 89th Divisions, to the left here, captured Barricourt Heights by ·ly afternoon; while in front of here the th Division took Andevanne, the oded ridge seen to the right of and yond Andevanne, and Chassogne Farm, n to the right front below the sky line. e fighting was severe but the dash of e American troops was irresistible. ll 343, an exceptionally strong position, d out until the afternoon of Novem- r 2, when it was captured by soldiers of e 90th Division after a bitter struggle. The 5th Division swung toward the

Meuse River during its advance and reached the banks of that stream to the right of the Bois de Sassey on November 3; the same day the 90th Division reached the river by fighting its way forward through that dense wood.

The I Corps, on the left of the Army, which faced the unbroken Hindenburg Line on most of its front, met stubborn resistance during the first day of the attack but in spite of this drove forward an average distance of ¾ mile. That night, due to the deep advance of the V Corps, the German troops in front of the I Corps retired and from then on its progress was exceptionally rapid.

The battle soon became a pursuit, the enemy fighting a delaying action. All American divisions pushed forward rapidly until they reached the Meuse River, which flows obliquely across the direction of advance of the Army and passes through Sedan. From November 1 on

German Artillery Being Hauled Into Position by Oxen, 1918. © G

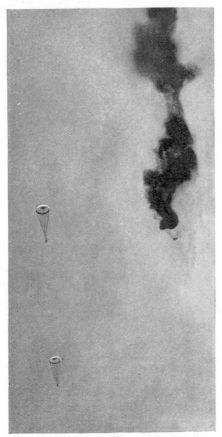

Observation Balloon Hit by German Shells
Coming Down in Flames
The balloonists are descending by parachute

the progress of the American Army was continuous until halted by the Armistice.

From here to Bar, which is 10 miles away to the left front, the described route runs generally northwest traversing in succession the zones of action of the American 90th, 89th, 2d and 80th Divisions.

EN ROUTE NORTH OF CUNEL TO HILL 289

(2.7 m 4.3 km) **While descending hill, to the right in the valley** is seen the village of Aincreville which was captured on October 30 by the 5th Division.

(2.8 m 4.5 km) **The small wood which is seen just above Aincreville** is the Bois

de Babiémont. In spite of two dete mined assaults on November 1 the 5 Division was unable to take that wo until the morning of the next day.

(2.9 m 4.7 km) **Before reaching ra road (which was not here in 1918) right of road,** is a 5th Division mark one of many erected by that division aft the Armistice on or near its battlefiel

(3.0 m 4.8 km) **While crossing the ra road, to the right down the valley is se** an isolated bald-topped hill, called Cô St. Germain, which is situated on t other side of the Meuse River. That h will be passed close up later in the tour

(3.3 m 5.3 km) **In Bantheville, whe the road ends turn to the right; at ro fork at edge of town, bear left.**

After capturing Bantheville on Octob 23, the 90th Division established front line near the crest of the hill whi is seen to the right of this road.

It is reported that on that hill a 90 Division soldier, of Italian descer charged a machine-gun nest manned six Germans. After killing three of t enemy he made prisoners of the others a marched them nearly 8 miles to divisi headquarters where, in broken English, insisted upon telling the division co mander about his experiences.

(4.5 m 7.2 km) **Near top of hill, the wo seen ahead** is the northern end of t

Tender of an Observation Balloon Mounte
with Two Machine Guns for
Anti-Aircraft Defense

ois de Bantheville.   After its capture on ctober 22, the Germans bombarded it most continuously with high explosive ells and mustard gas projectiles.

(4.6 m 7.4 km) **At top of hill, to the ght front is seen Le Grand Carré Farm,** aptured on November 1 by the 90th ivision; and beyond it to the right, Hill 43, taken by that division the next day.

were then along the edge of the wood to the left rear, under continuous machine-gun fire and rescued two wounded officers. For conspicuous gallantry and utter disregard for their own safety while performing this deed of mercy these men were awarded Congressional Medals of Honor.

In the wood seen on the hill ahead occurred the heroic act of First Lieutenant

Road Between Bantheville and Rémonville, November 1918
This road is passed over on the described tour

(5.1 m 8.2 km) **At the road fork in the** ext valley, bear right and STOP near the ad junction without leaving automobile. Note the wartime condition of this valy as shown by the above photograph aken after the American advance.   In he photograph the road climbing the hill the one the tourist has just descended. This road junction was on the First rmy jump-off line of November 1 and so was on the boundary line between the nes of the 89th and 90th Divisions.

It was to the left of here that on ctober 31 Private First Class Charles . Barger and Private Jesse N. Funk, th Division, upon their own initiative, ade two trips as stretcher bearers 500 rds beyond the American lines, which

Harold A. Furlong, 89th Division, which is illustrative of the many individual feats of bravery performed by the American soldiers during the November 1 attack. In this wood Lieutenant Furlong, finding his company held up on that morning by withering machine-gun fire which killed his company commander, moved out alone and worked his way into the German position. He succeeded in getting behind the line of machine guns and closed in on them one at a time, killing a number of the enemy with his rifle, putting four machine-gun nests out of action, and driving 20 German prisoners into the American lines. For his exceptional daring this courageous officer was later awarded the Congressional Medal of Honor.

Bois de Bantheville

Panorama From Stop No⌐

(5.6 m 9.0 km) **Continue to the top of the next crest, where a few buildings can be seen to the left front in the valley, STOP without leaving the automobile.**

The above panorama is from this point.

The nearest buildings are those of La Dhuy Farm. To the right of them in the valley can be seen a few houses of the village of Landres-et-St. Georges.

At this point can be obtained a good view of a large part of the jump-off line of the First Army on November 1.

From the road junction just passed, the line followed the edge of the large wood, seen to the left across the valley, and included Côte de Châtillon, the nearest prominent wooded hill seen to the left. From there it ran approximately parallel to this road and included St. Juvin, which

can be seen at the foot of the wood heights on the sky line to the right of a beyond the buildings of La Dhuy Far From St. Juvin it continued on for abo 4 miles and joined the French line ne the edge of the wooded heights on t sky line, which to the left of St. Juvin the Argonne Forest and to the right that town are the Bois de Bourgogne.

The 89th Division jumped off from t line to the left of here. The center of zone of action passed through the wo seen down the road ahead. The 2d Di sion started from Côte de Châtillon a beyond. Landres-et-St. Georges near the center of its zone of acti These divisions, which had fought side side in the St. Mihiel offensive, were t assault divisions of the V Corps whi

American Tanks Beside a Machine-Gun Nest Which They Put Out of Action on November 1, 1918, South of Bayonville

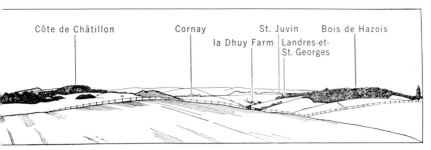

Côte de Châtillon   Cornay   St. Juvin   Bois de Hazois
la Dhuy Farm   Landres-et-
St. Georges

Bois de Bantheville

as expected to make the greatest initial penetration of the corps on the Army front. The 80th Division was beyond the 2d; e line of the 77th included St. Juvin, hich was near the center of its sector; d the 78th was still farther on, the near lge of the wooded heights being the far oundary of its prescribed zone of attack. **Continue.**

(6.6 m 10.6 km) **While approaching the** ext village, **Rémonville, beyond it to the** ght and left are seen Barricourt Heights, e first main objective of the American rmy in its November 1 attack. Hill 99, seen beyond the town, was in the one of action of the 2d Division. Rénonville and the heights to the right of ill 299 were in that of the 89th Division. The natural defensive strength of the German Freya position, which ran along those heights, is evident from here. Note the steep exposed slopes up which the American troops had to advance and the woods along the tops of the hills which afforded the enemy good concealment and excellent protection for his troops.

Near this road on November 1, Sergeant Arthur J. Forrest, 89th Division, won the Congressional Medal of Honor. When the advance of his company was held up by fire from a nest of six enemy machine guns, Sergeant Forrest worked his way alone to a point within 50 yards of the machine-gun nest. Charging the nest singlehanded, he drove the enemy out in disorder, killing one with the butt of his rifle. This gallant exploit permitted the advance of his company to continue.

Rémonville Soon After Its Capture by the 89th Division on
November 1, 1918

Reloading Artillery Ammunition in Rémonville, November 2, 1918

80th Division Troops Passing Through Imécourt, November 3, 1918

(7.3 m 11.7 km) **In the village of Ré-nonville, at the place where the road ends, turn to the left; at the far edge of the village, turn to the right.**

(7.5 m 12.1 km) **A short distance beyond town** the zone of action of the 2d Division during the advance is entered.

(7.7 m 12.4 km) **While ascending hill, to the left in the valley** is seen Landreville,

afternoon of November 1. The 89th was abreast of the 2d on its right. On November 2 the 89th Division advanced the right of its line about 2 miles farther.

(8.9 m 14.3 km) **At entrance to village, take the road to the right and continue through town toward Buzancy.**

Bayonville was captured in the morning of November 1 by the 2d Division.

German Warning Against Airplanes at Bayonville

where the 2d Division about 9:00 a. m. on November 1 encountered strong resistance from numerous machine guns. These guns were finally overcome and the advance was continued on over this hill.

(8.7 m 14.0 km) **While approaching the next village, Bayonville, to the right** are seen the wooded heights upon which the 2d Division established its lines on the

(9.3 m 15.0 km) **Beyond town, while ascending hill, to the left in the valley** is seen Imécourt which was captured about 11:00 o'clock in the morning of November 1 by the 80th Division, after which a severe counterattack against the troops in the village was repulsed.

(10.1 m 16.3 km) **Beyond next high crest, continue 80 yards, then STOP.**

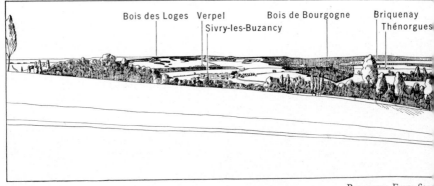

Bois des Loges   Verpel   Bois de Bourgogne   Briquenay
                  Sivry-les-Buzancy   Thénorgues

Panorama From Sto

The large tree on this crest (1937) can be seen from the monument on Montfaucon and is a conspicuous landmark from many other places in this region.

Face down the road, which at this place runs approximately northwest.

This point is on Hill 289 and was near the boundary line between the zones of action of the 2d and 80th Divisions.

The tour has just entered the area captured by the I Corps, the left corps of the First Army in its November offensive. The other boundary of its zone of action ran close to the far edge of the Bois de Bourgogne, the large wooded area seen on the sky line to the left and left front.

The I Corps objective during the November 1 attack was a line running near Verpel, the second village seen to the left

On the first day of the attack the I Corps met great resistance at the Hindenburg Line and the progress of its units was slow, except for the right of the 80th Division which captured the small wooded areas on this slope, including those seen in the foreground to the right front. The front line of the division that night ran from near here to the left rear for approximately 4 miles, almost parallel to the direction of advance of the Army.

On November 2, due to the withdrawal of the Germans on the previous night, the progress in the I Corps was rapid and by that evening all its divisions had reached a line beyond this point, the 80th Division having captured the bald-topped hill seen

German Artillery Position Near Landreville Soon After Its Capture

n Hill 289

 the left front, and the right of the 77th eing abreast of it. The left of the 77th)ivision was to the observer's right of 'hénorgues, the first village seen to the ft front over the ridge, and the 78th)ivision was to the right of Briquenay, 1e village seen beyond Thénorgues.

The nearest town seen to the left is ivry-les-Buzancy, captured by the 80th)ivision on November 2. The town just eyond it is Verpel, occupied by the 77th)ivision the same day. The towns seen eyond Verpel, near the foot of the ooded heights, were in the zone of action f the 78th Division, which had been held p on November 1 in front of the Bois des oges, the first prominent wooded hill seen the left of and beyond Verpel. That

wood was one of the strongest points of the Hindenburg Line and proved impossible to capture by direct assault. It was occupied early in the morning of November 2 by the American soldiers after the German troops had been withdrawn.

EN ROUTE HILL 289 TO NORTH OF BAR

(11.0 m 17.7 km) **While approaching the next town, Buzancy, to the right across the valley** are seen the heights to which the Germans withdrew their main forces on the night of November 1–2. The 80th Division, on November 2, established its lines to the right in the valley at the foot of this hill, facing the German position.

(11.3 m 18.2 km) **Before entering town,** a German military cemetery is passed.

German Prisoners Captured by the 2d Division

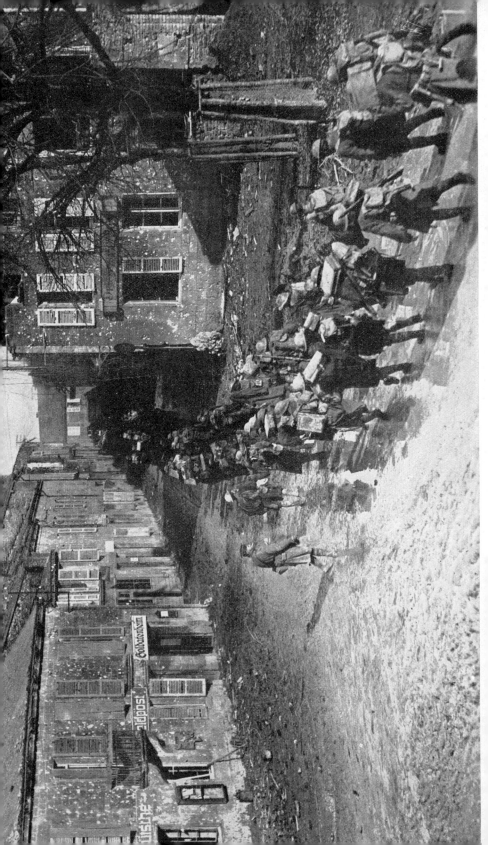

Troops West of Bar, Compelled to Pass
Around Bridge Being Repaired,
November 3, 1918

Below: At Bar, November 4, 1918
Engineer soldier having fun with passing troops
over the name of the town

Buzancy was formerly a fortified town.
n the War of 1870 between Prussia and
'rance cavalry fighting took place near it.

(11.9 m 19.2 km) **After entering town,**
ote that many of the walls and buildings
n the right side of the street are still
1937) marked by rifle and machine-gun
ullets from the fighting in the vicinity.

(12.3 m 19.8 km) **In center of Buzancy,**
ear right; pass church, then bear left.
'his town was captured by the 80th Divi-
on early on the afternoon of November 2
fter brisk fighting. Shortly thereafter it
as under heavy hostile artillery and
aachine-gun fire, and in flames.

After the Americans had advanced
eyond it, the only roads available for the
7th and 80th Divisions passed through
uzancy. Knowing that these would
e crowded, the Germans shelled and
ombed the crossroads in town for several
ays, thus making the movement of
oops and supplies through this village a
azardous and difficult undertaking.

Buzancy was the 80th Division Head-
uarters during the period November 4–7.

(13.0 m 20.9 km) **At the near edge of**
ae next village, **Bar,** the zone of action
f the 77th Division is entered.

(13.2 m 21.2 km) **Pass through Bar,**
hich was captured during the afternoon
f November 2 by the 77th Division.

(287)

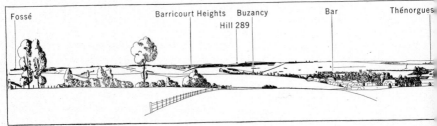

Fossé   Barricourt Heights Buzancy   Bar   Thénorgues
                    Hill 289

Panorama From

(13.5 m 21.7 km) **Beyond the town, at the first road crossing, turn to the right.**

(14.0 m 22.5 km) **Just before reaching the first LEFT bend in the road, STOP.**

To the right rear in the valley is Bar. **Face just to the right of Bar,** which direction is approximately south.

To the left front is Buzancy. Beyond and to the left of it, the most prominent wooded hill is Hill 289, which was the last stop on this tour. To the left of it, in the distance, there is visible the near end of the wooded Barricourt Heights.

When the Germans facing the I Corps withdrew during the night of November 1–2, they established new temporary positions on these slopes with their front line running close to this point. Machine gun units and detachments of other troops had been left behind to delay the American advance as much as possible.

Overcoming the resistance on their front in sharp fighting in the morning, the divisions of the I Corps advanced rapidly. The 80th and 77th Divisions reached the wide valley in front of here during the afternoon and established positions on

American 34-Centimeter Gun
on Railroad Mount

this side of it. The 80th Division front line ran from near Bar to the observer's left for about 2½ miles. Part of the 77th Division was at the foot of these slopes, its line including Bar. The rest of that division was just this side of Thénorgues, the village seen directly ahead in the distance. The valley between here and there was in many places knee deep in water and impassable. The front line of the 78th Division was located to the observer's right of and some distance on this side of the village of Thénorgues.

On November 3 the German position here were attacked and carried by the American troops, the main enemy force having retired during the night. This procedure—in which the Germans retired their main forces to a new position at night but left machine gun units scattered in strong defensive positions to hinder pursuit, and in which the Americans advanced the next day, overcame the determined machine gun resistance and fought their way forward toward the new position until stopped in front of it—was repeated almost daily until November at which time all German troops on the First Army front had been withdrawn to the east of the Meuse River.

The village of Fossé, seen on top of the hill to the left rear, was near the boundary line between the 2d and 80th Divisions It was taken by troops of the 2d Division about 6:00 a. m. on November 3.

The village seen on the sky line to the right is Belleville-sur-Bar. On the hillside some distance to the left of it is seen Boult-aux-Bois, near which, on the morning of November 3, the 78th Division joined with a unit of the French Fourth

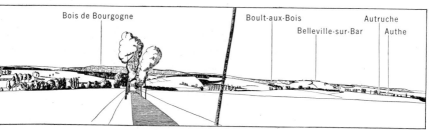

Stop Near Bar

Army which had advanced on the far side of the Bois de Bourgogne, thus pinching out that strong defensive feature.

The first town, Autruche, seen to the right rear, was taken by the 77th Division about noon on November 3. The village seen beyond it, Authe, had been occupied just before noon by the 78th Division.

To the right of Autruche, on the sky line, is seen a patch of woods which marks the ridge just beyond the village of Verrières. After a sharp fight that town was captured by the 78th Division about 5:00 p. m. on November 3. The troops of the division then established their front line on the ridge located beyond the town.

For the next 10 miles the tour goes with the direction of advance of the American First Army and passes over territory captured by the 80th and 2d Divisions.

EN ROUTE NEAR BAR TO SOUTH OF BEAUMONT

(14.5 m 23.3 km) **Beyond next crest to the right front** is seen the valley up which the 80th Division advanced on November 3. Strong resistance was encountered near the upper part of that valley.

(15.0 m 24.1 km) **At the first road fork, keep to the right.**

(15.4 m 24.8 km) **At first crest, to the left front in the distance** is seen the high wooded hill, Mont du Cygne, taken by the 77th Division on November 5. Montfaucon, 16 miles away, can be seen in the distance to the right on the sky line.

(17.1 m 27.5 km) **Beyond first sharp S-bend in road, on the next crest** the 80th Division line of November 3 crossed this road approximately at right angles to it.

(17.3 m 27.8 km) **At next main road fork, turn to the right and descend toward Vaux-en-Dieulet,** which is seen ahead in the valley. That town was captured on November 4 by the 80th Division.

(17.5 m 28.2 km) **While descending hill, to the right front** is seen a large high hill, Hill 308, fire from which stopped the advance of the right flank units of the 80th Division on November 3.

(18.1 m 29.1 km) **In Vaux-en-Dieulet, at the church, bear to the left.**

(18.4 m 29.6 km) **At road junction beyond the town, bear to the right.**

(19.0 m 30.6 km) **Where large hill descends to road,** the zone of action of the 2d Division and V Corps is again entered.

(19.6 m 31.5 km) **Just before reaching the first road junction, STOP without leaving the automobile.**

The large buildings seen to the right up the valley are those of Château de Belval, captured by the 2d Division before 9:00 a. m. on November 3. The progress of the units of the division was then stopped by heavy fire from the woods which are seen ahead and to the left of this road.

The infantry regiments of the division

German Monument to Their Dead in the Operations Near Beaumont in 1870

t had two regiments of infantry and two
marines) were ordered to make a vigor-
us advance that evening. Soon after
ark these regiments started forward in
olumn in advance-guard formation, led
y German-speaking soldiers, with the
igh ground near Beaumont, about 3
iles to the left front, as their goal. After
reaking through the hostile front line,
ne two regiments, with a battalion of
narines between them, moved forward
apidly; and as the night was extremely
ark the marching troops passed practi-
ally unnoticed. Such resistance as was
net was eliminated as quietly as possible
y having the head of the column stop
while detachments from the rear worked

2d Division column reached here the farm
was full of sleeping Germans who were
captured without difficulty and sent to
the rear under a strong guard.

(21.1 m 34.0 km) **Just beyond the farm,**
the American troops routed a hostile battalion engaged in digging trenches.

A short distance farther on, an enemy
machine gun company that had halted
along the road was captured.

(23.1 m 37.2 km) **Beyond the wood, at
the first group of buildings, La Tuilerie
Farm,** approximately 40 German soldiers
were surprised and made prisoners.

The monument across the road from
this farm is a monument in commemoration of German dead in the War of 1870.

Interior of Beaumont Church

heir way around the flanks of the oppos-
ng units and overcame them. Hostile
artillery that was seen firing from the
woods at objectives within the American
ines was left unmolested so as not to
alarm the enemy as its capture would be
assured by the success of the march.

Continue.

(19.6 m 31.5 km) **At the road junction,
turn sharp left toward Beaumont.**

(20.7 m 33.3 km) **After entering wood,
at road junction where road bends sharply to left,** the tour joins the route followed
by the units of the 2d Division at the
time of their daring night maneuver.

(20.9 m 33.6 km) **The first group of
buildings is La Forge Farm.** When the

(23.5 m 37.8 km) **Continue beyond the
next buildings, which are La Petite Forêt
Farm, about 300 yards, then STOP.**

Emerging from the woods in rear of
here shortly after midnight, the 2d Division column deployed, at right angles to
this road, on a line passing near this point.
The units of the column were then about
4 miles ahead of the adjoining divisions.

It is an interesting fact that the route
taken by the 2d Division coincided with
that used by the Germans on August 30,
1870, when they surprised and defeated
the French who were camped near Beaumont. The German monuments located
near La Tuilerie Farm and the village of
Beaumont commemorate that operation.

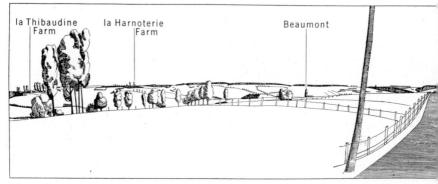

la Thibaudine Farm   la Harnoterie Farm   Beaumont

Panorama From Sto

Face down the road, which direction at this point is approximately northeast.

The Meuse River is only 2 miles away; the wooded hill which is seen straight ahead on the sky line is on the other side of it.

Shortly before noon on November 4 the 2d Division attacked from its line near here toward Beaumont, whose church is seen in the valley to the left front. Intense hostile fire was immediately encountered from the front and flanks and after heavy losses the attempt to advance was given up. The division front line was then established across this road about 100 yards ahead, and along this side of the ridge seen to the right front.

By the evening of November 4 the 80th Division had established itself along the edge of the large wood partially seen to the left rear, and the 89th Division, to the right of here, had come up abreast of the 2d Division. There were, however wide gaps in the front line in the interval between the zones of these three divisions

On the next day the 89th and 2d Divisions advanced to the bluffs of the Meuse the 89th Division occupying the Forêt de Jaulnay, the large wood seen on the horizon to the right front, while the 2d Division moved to the top of the wooded hill which is seen almost directly ahead

Beaumont was mopped up about dawn on November 5 by troops of the 2d and 80th Divisions. The 80th Division front line that night ran from near Beaumont to the vicinity of the buildings, La Thibaudine Farm, seen to the left in the trees on top of the hill across the valley

42d Division Troops Resting in Front of Cheveuges,
Near Sedan, November 7, 1918

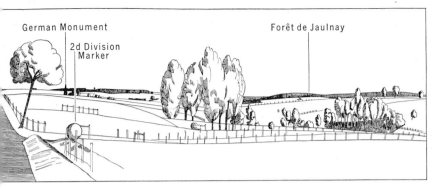

German Monument

2d Division
Marker

Forêt de Jaulnay

South of Beaumont

The farm seen to the left front across the valley is La Harnoterie Farm, occupied by the 80th Division early on the 6th.

About dawn on November 6 the 1st Division relieved the 80th Division and during the morning advanced to the Meuse River. At approximately 7:30 in the evening it moved toward Sedan, 10 miles away to the left front. The 2d Division took over the zone thus vacated.

EN ROUTE SOUTH OF BEAUMONT TO NORTH OF PONT-MAUGIS

(23.5 m 37.8 km) **Fifty yards farther on, to the right of the road** is seen a 2d Division boulder marker, one of many erected by that division on its former battlefields.

(24.4 m 39.3 km) **At the near edge of the village of Beaumont, turn to the left.**

(24.7 m 39.8 km) **Near the center of the village, beyond the church, bear left.**

The tour has now turned west, away from the Meuse River, and for 4 miles runs about at right angles to the direction of advance of the First Army.

(24.9 m 40.1 km) **At the far edge of town,** the zone of action of the 80th Division during the advance is again entered.

(25.6 m 41.2 km) **At top of next high hill to the left rear across the valley** is seen La Petite Forêt Farm, which is situated in the vicinity of the last stop.

To the right front near the edge of the nearest wood, the buildings barely visible because of the trees are those of La Harnoterie Farm. Machine-gun fire from that farm on the afternoon of November 5 stopped the advance of the 80th Division.

German Infantry Firing With Telescopic Sights,
November 1918. © G

From this crest on for about 2½ miles the front line of the 80th Division, which had been advanced from the left on November 5, was close to this road.

(26.5 m 42.6 km) **The buildings passed next** are those of La Thibaudine Farm, which was captured by the 80th Division during its advance on November 5.

(27.6 m 44.4 km) **At next group of buildings,** there is seen straight down the road a high prominent ridge upon which is the village of Stonne, captured on November 5 by the 77th Division.

The 42d Division, which relieved the 78th Division on November 5, had advanced by evening so that its front line was about in prolongation of this road on the other side of the village of Stonne.

(28.8 m 46.3 km) **At the next crossroad, turn to the right.**

From here until the Meuse River is reached the tour follows along the zone of action of the 77th Division.

(29.5 m 47.5 km) **The next village, La Besace,** was captured by the 77th Divi-

sion on November 5. The division me determined resistance just beyond tow which could not be overcome during tha day. On the next day, however, it advance units moved rapidly forward t the Meuse River, 5¾ miles away.

(31.2 m 50.2 km) **About 1¾ miles far ther on, at sharp S-bend in road, to th right up the valley** is seen Flaba nea which the 77th Division encountere machine-gun resistance on the morning o November 6. It also met with resistanc on the slopes seen to the left of this road

(32.7 m 52.6 km) **Continue throug Raucourt,** captured about 2:10 p. m. o November 6 by the 77th Division.

The boundary between the 42d an 77th Divisions during the advance wa just beyond the small stream in the valle which the tour is now following.

It is reported that the inhabitants o some of the towns displayed white flag at the approach of the American forces to prevent the advancing troops from firing on places which were not defende

77th Division Anti-Aircraft Post at Raucourt, November 10, 1918

French Peasants Expressing Their Joy at Liberation by the Americans,
November 6, 1918

by German soldiers. As the advance guards entered the villages, the joy of the people at being liberated after four years of German occupation knew no bounds.

(34.2 m 55.0 km) **The next village, Haraucourt**, was entered at about the same time on November 6 by units of both the 42d and 77th Divisions.

(34.9 m 56.2 km) **Beyond town, at first high crest**, the hills seen down the valley are on the far side of the Meuse River. The line of the 42d Division on November 6 ran to the left up the slopes seen across the valley, it having advanced from near Stonne, recently pointed out, on that day.

(35.6 m 57.3 km) **Continue through Angecourt**, captured during November 6 by the troops of the 77th Division.

(36.4 m 58.6 km) **Beyond the town of Angecourt to the left on the crest of the high hill** was where part of the front line of the 42d Division was located during the period from November 7 to 9.

(36.5 m 58.7 km) **Just before reaching next town, Remilly-sur-Meuse, to the left front** is seen the city of Sedan.

(36.8 m 59.2 km) **Remilly**, which is on the Meuse River, was occupied about 4:30 on the afternoon of November 6 by a battalion from the 77th Division.

(37.0 m 59.5 km) **At the far side of Remilly-sur-Meuse, turn to the left.**

(38.3 m 61.6 km) **While approaching first bend in road, to the right front** is seen the steel bridge over which the Metz–Sedan–Mézières railway crosses the Meuse River. The cutting of this railroad was the main objective of the American First Army in the Meuse-Argonne offensive. As soon as the advancing troops reached a

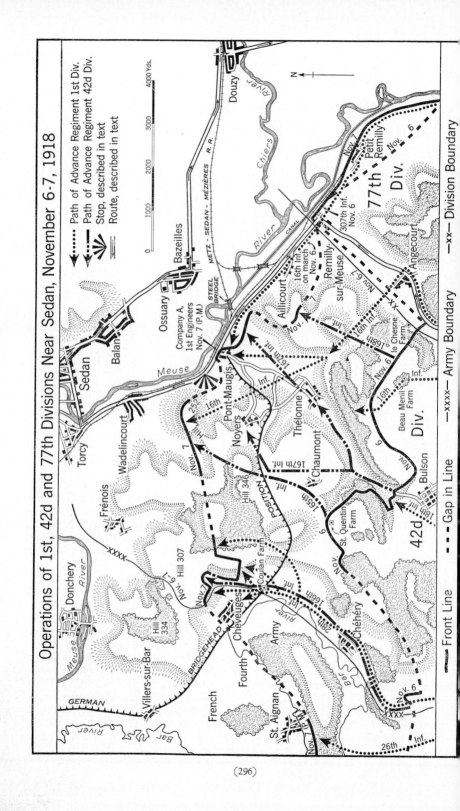

Operations of 1st, 42d and 77th Divisions Near Sedan, November 6-7, 1918

Path of Advance Regiment 1st Div.
Path of Advance Regiment 42d Div.
Stop, described in text
Route, described in text

4000 Yds.
3000
2000
1000
0

Douzy
Chiers River
River
METZ - SEDAN - MÉZIÈRES R. R.

77th
Div.
Petit Remilly
Nov. 6
Angecourt
307th Inf.
Nov. 6
Nov. 7
Remilly-
sur-Meuse
16th Inf.
on march
Nov. 6
Nov. 6-7
16th Inf.
le Chesne
Farm
189th
Nov. 6
16th
Inf.
Beau Menil
Farm
Div.
Bulson
16th Inf.

Bazeilles
Ossuary
Company A,
1st Engineers
Nov. 7 (P.M.)
CANAL
STEEL
BRIDGE
Ailliicourt
167th Inf.
Pont-Maugis
Noyers
16th Inf.
Thélonne
Chaumont
167th Inf.
St. Quentin
Farm

Sedan
Balan
Torcy
Meuse
Wadelincourt
Frénois
Hill 252
Hill 346
Hill 307
POSITION
Coulan Farm
165th Inf.
Nov. 7
Nov. 7

Donchery
Meuse River
Villers-sur-Bar
Hill 334
XXXX
Nov. 6-7
Nov. 7
BRIDGEHEAD
Cheveuges
28th 166th Inf.
Chéhéry

GERMAN
Bar River
French
Fourth Army
St. Aignan
Nov. 7
Nov. 6
XXXX
26th Inf.

42d
Div.
16th Inf.

Front Line
xxxx — Army Boundary
Gap in Line
xx — Division Boundary

(296)

oint from which long-range guns could re on the railway, it was subjected to eriodic bombardments by American rtillery in order to prevent traffic over it. 'hen on the morning of November 7, merican units captured a commanding osition on the hills to the left of this road, ue great value of this railroad to the Ger-man Army was destroyed. It is a striking oincidence that on this same day the -erman representatives crossed the battle ne to ask the Allied Commander-in-hief to grant an immediate armistice.

Germans established a bridgehead posi-tion to protect Sedan. It ran from Pont-Maugis, just passed through, included Noyers, the village which can be seen to the left up the valley, and extended, in the direction the reader is facing, from there on over the hill beyond Noyers. (See the sketch on the opposite page.)

On the afternoon of November 5 the I Corps was directed to capture Sedan, assisted on its right by the V Corps. As a result of a misconception in the V Corps of the exact intent of the orders, the 1st

1st Division Troops Advancing Through Thélonne Under Machine-Gun Fire,
November 7, 1918

(38.7 m 62.3 km) **Beyond the bend, long the left side of this road overlook-ng the bridge** was the location during 'ovember 7 of the battle position of one egiment of the 42d Division.

(39.6 m 63.7 km) **Beyond next village, 'ont-Maugis, at the bottom of the first ttle valley running to the left, STOP. Face to the left front,** which direction s approximately west.

The large city which is seen to the right bout 2 miles down the river is Sedan. During the night of November 6–7 the

Division crossed the zone of action of the 77th Division and entered that of the 42d Division. This resulted in both the 1st and 42d Divisions operating in this general region on November 6 and 7.

Before daylight on November 7 a column of troops of the 1st Division cap-tured a German wagon train in Pont-Maugis, partially mopped up the town in hand-to-hand fighting and then moved up a little valley towards Thélonne, not visible, about a mile to the left over the hill. En route there it suffered heavily from fire from that hill, from across the Meuse River and from the south, but most of the column succeeded in joining other troops of its division near Thélonne. Pont-Maugis was reentered by German troops but was retaken again about 2:00 o'clock in the afternoon by an engineer company of the 1st Division.

During the morning of November 7 the 1st and 42d Divisions attacked the German bridgehead positions on the hills to the front and left of here. After intense fighting, they succeeded in capturing these positions shortly after midday, and forced the German troops to retire still closer to Sedan. The American front line was then established on the Sedan side of Hill 252, seen to the front, after which patrols of the 42d Division advanced to within 100 yards of Wadelincourt, the next village down the road.

The French desired, probably for sentimental reasons, to be the first to enter Sedan; so during the night of November 7-8 the positions on the hills in front of here were turned over to them. The left boundary of the First Army was at that time changed by the Allied Commander-in-Chief so that it ran in a northeasterly direction passing near Pont-Maugis.

The efforts of the American First Army were then directed toward forcing the Germans back from the Meuse River, rear of here, preparatory to a general offensive in the direction of the town Longwy and the Briey iron mines.

In Sedan the tour changes direction and follows the other side of the Meuse River valley back to Verdun. The American operations described from now on are mainly efforts to cross the valley. general idea of the size and character of the Meuse River may be obtained at the stop. It should also be noted that for large part of the way there is a canal in the valley and that during the time of the American operations the valley was in places flooded by the autumn rains and by obstructions in the river. The crossing of such a valley in the face of an energetic enemy could, of course, only be accomplished by surprise and with superior concentration of forces.

EN ROUTE PONT-MAUGIS TO NEAR MOULINS

(40.0 m 64.4 km) A short distance farther on, to the left of the road is seen a 1st Division monument upon which is a list of its dead in the fighting in this region.

Railway Station at Sedan

War of 1870 Museum at Bazeilles

(40.6 m 65.3 km) **Continue on main road through the village of Wadelincourt.**

(41.4 m 66.6 km) **In Sedan, at the railroad station turn sharply to the right.** This part of the city is known as Torcy. t was entered by joint patrols of the 'rench and the 42d Division during the ight of November 8–9. This was the arthest north that any American unit actively cperated during this offensive.

(41.5 m 66.8 km) **Cross Meuse River.** Sedan has a prominent place in French istory. Here, in 1870, Napoleon III nd the Army of Marshal MacMahon urrendered to the Prussians. It contains n old château-fort, built about 1430, uring the time of Joan of Arc, which is n impressive example of the massive eudal construction of that period.

(42.4 m 68.2 km) **Where the street ends t a monument, turn to the right.**

(42.9 m 69.0 km) **Pass through Balan.**

(43.9 m 70.6 km) **Beyond town, to the ight across the Meuse River valley,** can e seen the town of Pont-Maugis, Noyers n the hill above it, and the heights beond and to the right of that place which ere captured on November 7 by American soldiers after determined fighting.

(44.1 m 71.0 km) **Just before entering** the next town, **Bazeilles, on the left** is an interesting museum of the War of 1870, called "La Maison de la Dernière Cartouche". The scene of Neuville's famous painting "Les Dernières Cartouches" ("The Last Cartridges") is laid in this building, which in 1870 was an inn called, of course, by a different name.

By bearing right at road junction at this point a large ossuary of the War of 1870 will be found on the right a few hundred yards farther on. Amount of time required for side trip—20 minutes.

(44.5 m 71.6 km) **In Bazeilles, turn to the left, keeping on the main road.**

(46.8 m 75.3 km) **While approaching next town, Douzy, to the right of the road** is seen again the railroad which the First Army had as its objective. Its importance lay in the fact that the railroads which served the German forces on the Western Front were so located that without the use of this double-tracked road Germany could not supply and maintain its armies in northern France and Belgium.

(47.7 m 76.8 km) **In center of town, turn sharp right** and cross over the Chiers River, a tributary of the Meuse River.

From here on the described route follows the main highway to the city of Verdun.

(47.9 m 77.1 km) **To the right front across the valley** is seen the line of hills on which the front line of the 77th Division rested at the end of the war.

(49.2 m 79.2 km) **After passing next village, Mairy, to the right front across the river** is seen Villers-devant-Mouzon, where, although under heavy fire, a small detachment of the 77th Division succeeded in crossing the river on November 7. It was forced to withdraw the following day as the temporary bridge upon which the detachment had crossed was destroyed by enemy artillery fire, thus preventing reinforcements from joining it.

(50.4 m 81.1 km) **The next village which is seen to the left is Amblimont.**

The American units on the other side of the valley sent many patrols to this side at night to find out the location and strength of the hostile troops. One of the most successful of these patrols, consisting of an officer and a non-commissioned officer of the 77th Division, crossed over near Villers-devant-Mouzon on a raft about midnight on November 8. It reconnoitered Amblimont, reached Hill 345, the high bare hill seen above that town, and returned with valuable information concerning the enemy forces.

(52.3 m 84.2 km) **At entrance to next town, Mouzon, bear left up the hill.**

Corporal L. M. M. Van Iersel, 2d Division, won the Congressional Medal of Honor for an outstanding exploit near this town. When his division reached the river opposite here, Corporal Van Iersel volunteered to reconnoiter the hostile positions on this side of it. While attempting, in the face of intense machine-gun fire, to crawl across on the timbers of a ruined bridge at night he was thrown into the river by a German trap. In spite of the swift current he swam the river, continued on his dangerous mission regardless of the enemy fire and obtained information of the greatest value.

(53.7 m 86.4 km) **Beyond Mouzon, to the right in the valley** are seen two farms which were captured by the 2d Division on the morning of November 11.

(54.2 m 87.2 km) **While ascending high hill, to the right on the far slopes of the**

Engineers Building a Bridge Across the Meuse Near Pouilly After the Armistice

valley, can be seen Villemontry, captured by the 1st Division during November 6.

(55.3 m 89.0 km) **Beyond the large woods where a good view of the country to the right is obtained, STOP.**

On the right side of the road are monuments erected by the V Corps and the 2d Division shortly after the Armistice.

V Corps Marker, South of Mouzon

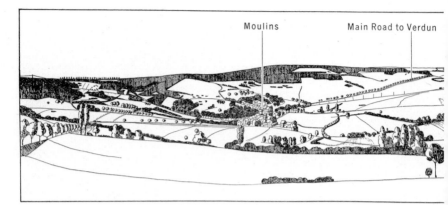

Panorama Looking South

Face the buildings, Farm St. Rémy, seen in the valley to the right rear. That direction is approximately south.

The town of Beaumont, through which the tour recently passed, is 4 miles from here beyond the edge of the large wood, Bois des Flaviers, which is seen extending off from this point to the right front.

The above sketch and the map on page 304 will aid in making the following description clearer. The map and sketch have been so drawn that they are oriented with the tops of them pointing south, the direction which the observer is facing.

About 3 miles away to the left front the Meuse River, flowing this way, changes its direction sharply. It runs on the far side of Pouilly, whose church is seen directly ahead, and, again curving abruptly, follows an irregular course, passing just to the right of the hill upon which the observer is standing. In the large bend thus formed, the 2d and 89th Divisions on the night of November 10 accomplished the difficult military feat of crossing a river under hostile fire.

During the night of November 7, in anticipation of a crossing by the Americans at Mouzon, the enemy burned oil on the surface of the river for illumination and swept the remains of the destroyed bridge by an intense cross fire from machine guns located on or near the river bank. Under cover of darkness during November 8 troops of the 2d Division attempted to cross over the ruined bridge

Pouilly and Létanne Viewed From the South
The 89th Division crossed the Meuse near the left edge of this terrain on November 10, 1918

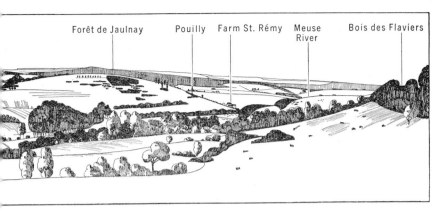

Forêt de Jaulnay   Pouilly   Farm St. Rémy   Meuse River   Bois des Flaviers

From Stop Near Moulins

there. Some of them were thrown into the water by traps placed on the bridge by the Germans for that purpose but others continued on until they reached a gap in the bridge, too wide to be passed without further preparation, at which place the attempt had to be abandoned.

On November 10 a second effort to make a surprise crossing, this time by means of footbridges constructed near Mouzon, was defeated as the enemy discovered the point at which the crossing was to be attempted and smothered it with shell and machine-gun fire. That same night, however, a crossing was forced, after heavy losses, on the far side of the Bois des Flaviers, and by the time of the Armistice troops of the 2d Division

had advanced as far as Moulins, seen to the left. Other units of the division were at Farm St. Rémy, and still others had advanced about halfway between this point and the town of Mouzon, capturing the two farms recently pointed out.

An effort of the 89th Division to construct footbridges across the river beyond Pouilly met with failure because of heavy hostile artillery fire. The division, however, crossed to the right of that town as seen from here, on large rafts holding 75 men each which had been built on a tributary stream and floated down to the main river. It captured Pouilly before daylight on November 11. Continuing its advance, it crossed this highway about 2 miles from here, just beyond where the

Flooded Meuse River Near Stenay,
November 11, 1918

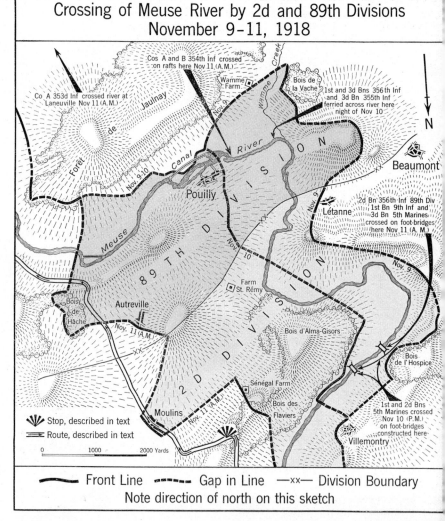

Crossing of Meuse River by 2d and 89th Divisions
November 9-11, 1918

Cos A and B 354th Inf crossed on rafts here Nov 11 (A. M.)

Wamme Farm

Bois de la Vache

Co A 353d Inf crossed river at Laneuville Nov 11 (A. M.)

1st and 3d Bns 356th Inf and 3d Bn 355th Inf ferried across river here night of Nov 10

N

89TH DIVISION

Beaumont

Pouilly

2d Bn 356th Inf 89th Div 1st Bn 9th Inf and 3d Bn 5th Marines crossed on foot-bridges here Nov 11 (A. M.)

Létanne

2D DIVISION

Farm St. Rémy

Bois de Hâche

Autreville

Bois d'Alma-Gisors

Bois de l'Hospice

Sénégal Farm

Moulins

Bois des Flaviers

1st and 2d Bns 5th Marines crossed Nov 10 (P. M.) on foot-bridges constructed here

Villemontry

Stop, described in text

Route, described in text

0   1000   2000 Yards

━━━ Front Line   ━ ━ ━ ━ Gap in Line   ─xx─ Division Boundary
Note direction of north on this sketch

highway, identified by the line of trees, can be seen to the left front disappearing over the hill which is to the right of and beyond the village of Moulins.

During the operations near Pouilly, Sergeant M. Waldo Hatler, Private First Class Harold I. Johnston and Private David B. Barkeley, all of the 89th Division, volunteered to make reconnaissances of the hostile position on this bank of the river, although there were no means of crossing except by swimming. In carrying out their dangerous missions, Private Barkeley while returning to the American lines with the desired information which he had obtained, was drowned. The others succeeded after the greatest difficulty in securing and taking back valuable information concerning the enemy forces. For these daring acts the three were awarded Congressional Medals of Honor.

EN ROUTE NEAR MOULINS TO SOUTH OF DUN-SUR-MEUSE

(56.3 m 90.6 km) **Continue through**

le village of **Moulins,** which was in possession of troops of the 2d Division when the Armistice became effective.

(57.0 m 91.7 km) **Beyond town, while scending hill, to the right in the valley** seen Autreville. That village and the igh hill to the right of it were captured y the 89th Division about 8:00 o'clock n the morning of November 11.

(57.4 m 92.4 km) **Before reaching top f hill, to the right in the valley in the istance** can be seen on a clear day the illage of Beaumont, the fighting near 'hich was recently described on the tour.

(57.7 m 92.9 km) **Beyond hill, the first ood growing to left edge of road** is the ois de Hâche, where the leading elements f the 89th Division continued fighting r a short time after 11:00 a. m., November 11, not having previously received ord concerning the Armistice.

Continue through Inor, Martincourt nd Cervisy. The Armistice line of the 9th Division was along the other bank f the Meuse River opposite these towns.

(63.7 m 102.5 km) **Continue through tenay,** where the zone of action of the 0th Division and the III Corps is en-

tered. Early on November 10 units of the 90th Division captured the far (south) side of this town but were not in sufficient strength to drive the Germans out of the rest of it. The remainder of the town was captured on November 11, before the Armistice became effective, by troops of the 89th and 90th Divisions.

(64.3 m 103.5 km) **Beyond town, the military barracks seen to the left of the road** were captured by the 90th Division. They were comparatively little damaged and were used by the Americans after the Armistice. The facilities for bathing, as well as the shelter from the cold, rainy weather were very welcome to the men who had undergone the hardships of a November campaign in this region.

(64.5 m 103.8 km) **Beyond barracks, to the left of the road** is seen the large wood, Bois de Chénois, in which the 90th Division had a severe struggle on November 10. The Division was fighting at the village of Baâlon, 2 miles away to the left, at the time of the Armistice.

The far side cf the valley opposite here was reached by the 90th Division on November 6. The division immediately

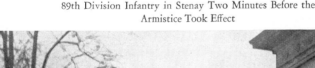

89th Division Infantry in Stenay Two Minutes Before the
Armistice Took Effect

egan assembling bridge material pre-
aratory to a crossing and from time to
me sent patrols over the river to obtain
formation. The crossing of the river
y the division was finally carried out on
ovember 9 farther up the valley.

(65.9 m 106.1 km) **Straight through
ouzay**, captured about 1:45 p. m. on
ovember 9 by the 5th Division.

(68.4 m 110.1 km) **After passing first
onounced left bend in road (about 2
iles farther on), to the right front at
ot of hill across the river** is seen Sassey-
r-Meuse. It was near there that a
rge part of the 90th Division on Novem-
r 9 crossed the river by means of a foot-
idge which had been constructed across
e demolished stone bridge.

During the afternoon of November 7
ve American ambulances lost their way,
tered the German lines near here and
ere captured. Observing their plight,
patrol of the 90th Division, which was
ar the river to the right of this road,
tacked and recaptured the ambulances.
hey were then sent to the rear loaded
ith German prisoners taken near there.

(68.6 m 110.4 km) **To the left is seen
e long, sparsely wooded ridge, Côte St.
ermain**, captured by the 5th Division
November 6 and 7, after severe fight-
g. The village on this side of it, Lion-
vant-Dun, was attacked on the 6th
it not taken until the next day.

On the other side of Côte St. Germain
Murvaux near where Second Lieu-
nant Frank Luke, Jr., Air Service, on
ptember 29, performed his last heroic
ed. After having previously destroyed
number of enemy aircraft, he voluntarily
arted on a patrol seeking German obser-
tion balloons. Though pursued by eight
erman planes which were protecting
emy balloon line, he attacked and shot
wn in flames three German balloons.
this engagement Lieutenant Luke was
posed to heavy fire from ground bat-
ries as well as hostile planes. Severely
ounded, he descended to within 50 yards
the ground, and flying at this low alti-
de near the town of Murvaux he fired
on enemy troops, killing six and wound-
g as many more. Forced to make a land-

Second Lieutenant Frank Luke, Jr., Air Service,
September 19, 1918

ing and surrounded on all sides by the
enemy, who called upon him to surrender,
he drew his automatic pistol and defended
himself until he fell dead from a wound in
the chest. For his conspicuous gallantry
in the performance of his last flight Lieutenant Luke was posthumously awarded
the Congressional Medal of Honor.

*In the next town, Dun-sur-Meuse, the
veterans of the 5th Division have erected a
wrought-iron railing on a bridge to commemorate the crossing of the Meuse River
by their division. To visit, in center of
town stop at village monument passed on the
right. The bridge adjoins the monument.*

(72.0 m 115.9 km) **Continue through
Dun-sur-Meuse**, captured after a hard
fight by the 5th Division on November 5.

The Headquarters of the 5th Division
was located here, during the period
November 7-10, and the Headquarters
of the III Corps, during November 10-11.

Engineers Relaxing in Ruined House After
Working Under Fire, Dun-sur-Meuse

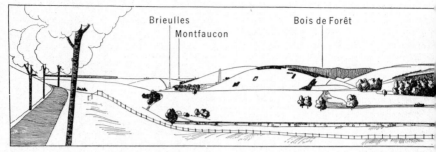

Brieulles
Montfaucon

Bois de Forêt

Panorama From Sto

(73.7 m 118.6 km) **Beyond town, from point where canal turns away from road, continue halfway up hill and STOP.**

A 5th Division marker monument is seen (1937) alongside the road.

Face to the right, which is west. Note that both the above panorama and the sketch on page 310 are oriented when the upper part is held in the direction being faced.

The Meuse-Argonne American Cemetery, where the tour started, is about 5 miles away. It is beyond the large wood, Bois de Forêt, which is seen to the left front on the other side of the river.

To the left in the distance is seen the American monument on Montfaucon.

Dun-sur-Meuse is plainly visible on the hill to the right. To the left of Dun-sur-Meuse, about a mile away from the river, is seen Doulcon. The ridge beyond that town surrounds it on three sides and the dish-shaped valley thus formed was called the "Punch Bowl" by American soldiers.

When the 5th Division attacked on No-

vember 1, it pivoted near Brieulles, see to the left up the valley, and swung toward Doulcon. By November 3 it had reached the other bank of the river as far as this point, cleared the rim of the "Punch Bowl" and captured Doulcon.

A crossing of the Meuse River valley was attempted about 1:00 a. m. on November 3 just this side of Brieulles. The river was crossed there before daylight but attempts to bridge the canal failed with heavy losses, a number of men being forced to seek shelter on the exposed flat between the river and canal all during the next day. That night desperate efforts to cross the canal, on two footbridges which the division engineers had been able to construct over it, were repulsed.

After dark on November 4 an infantry force rushed across the footbridges and gained a foothold on this bank. While the enemy's attention was engaged with this operation, another force farther up the valley came over in boats. After these

Ponton Bridge Constructed by 5th Division Engineers Near Dun-sur-Meuse

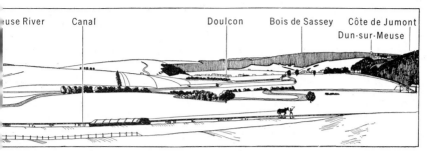

use River   Canal   Doulcon   Bois de Sassey   Côte de Jumont
                                                        Dun-sur-Meuse

uth of Dun-sur-Meuse

rprise attacks, the enemy was driven
ck far enough to enable a large part of
e division to cross during the night.
rly on the 5th some of those troops at-
cked toward this point over the low
dge seen to the left down the road.

A determined though unsuccessful at-
mpt to construct two ponton bridges
ross the river about halfway between
ere and Dun was made about 4:00 p. m.
November 4. The enemy discovered
e bridges before they were finished and
stroyed them by shellfire.

That night the river was bridged where
runs close to the hill on the other side
the valley, and the canal was bridged
ar here. At dawn, when the enemy
scovered the operation and opened fire
maging the bridges, part of a company
as on this bank and a large force was
the swampy ground between the river
d canal. The men on this bank found
emselves in a difficult position as they
d no means of retreat and were sub-

jected to severe enfilade fire from Côte
de Jumont, the hill seen down the road
to the right. To relieve the situation,
Captain Edward C. Allworth, 5th Division, called upon the remainder of his
company to follow him, plunged into
the canal, swam over under a hail of
bullets and joined his hard pressed units
near here. He then led his men in a
vigorous assault against the ridge behind
here, about the same time that it was
being attacked by the troops who had
crossed near Brieulles. The ridge was
captured after a hard fight and many
prisoners were taken. For his daring
act, Captain Allworth was awarded the
Congressional Medal of Honor.

Other troops of the division who crossed
at this point pushed down the river and
took Dun. By dark of November 5 the
Germans had been driven back more
than a mile to the rear of here.

It was during the crossing in front of
here that Sergeant Eugene P. Walker,

Division Ration Dump Near Montfaucon, October 5, 1918

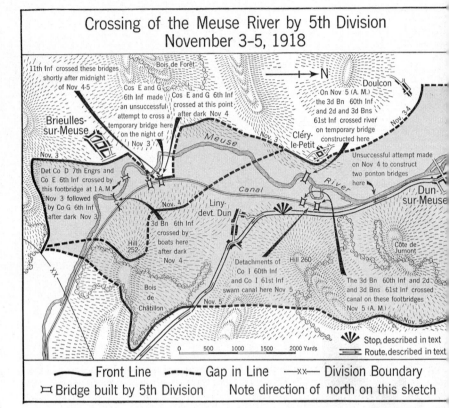

Crossing of the Meuse River by 5th Division
November 3-5, 1918

11th Inf crossed these bridges shortly after midnight of Nov 4-5

Bois de Forêt

Cos E and G 6th Inf made an unsuccessful attempt to cross a temporary bridge here on the night of Nov 3

Cos E and G 6th Inf crossed at this point after dark Nov 4

N

Doulcon

On Nov 5 (A. M.) the 3d Bn 60th Inf and 2d and 3d Bns 61st Inf crossed river on temporary bridge constructed here

Brieulles-sur-Meuse

Meuse

Cléry-le-Petit

Nov. 3

Det Co D 7th Engrs and Co E 6th Inf crossed by this footbridge at 1 A. M. Nov 3 followed by Co G 6th Inf after dark Nov 3

Unsuccessful attempt made on Nov 4 to construct two ponton bridges here

Canal

River

Dun-sur-Meuse

Nov. 4

Liny-devt. Dun

3d Bn 6th Inf crossed by boats here after dark Nov 4

Hill 252

Côte de Jumont

Hill 260

Detachments of Co I 60th Inf and Co I 61st Inf swam canal here Nov 5

The 3d Bn 60th Inf and 2d and 3d Bns 61st Inf crossed canal on these footbridges Nov 5 (A. M.)

Bois de Châtillon

Nov. 5

Nov. 5

0   500   1000   1500   2000 Yards

Stop, described in text
Route, described in text

Front Line ----- **Gap in Line** —xx— **Division Boundary**
🚪 **Bridge built by 5th Division**   Note direction of north on this sketch

Corporal Robert E. Crawford and Privates Noah L. Gump, John Hoggle and Stanley T. Murnane, all members of the 7th Engineers, 5th Division, won Distinguished Service Crosses. When three boats in a ponton bridge across the river were destroyed by artillery fire, these men voluntarily entered the icy river and, standing in water up to their armpits and under heavy shell-fire, held up the deck until new boats were launched and placed in position. This timely and courageous act permitted the crossing of the infantry units.

The 5th Division continued to advance in the direction to the right rear from here during the following days. It was assisted by one regiment of the 32d Division from November 6th to the 9th; and by the time of the Armistice had pushed the enemy back about 10 miles

from the river, onto the Woëvre Plain. During the last days of the war, the 32 Division went into the line south of th 5th Division and advanced rapidly with i

EN ROUTE SOUTH OF DUN-SUR-MEUSE TO SOUTH OF SIVRY-SUR-MEUSE

(74.4 m 119.7 km) **Continue throug the village of Liny-devant-Dun.**

(75.0 m 120.7 km) **Beyond town, th large wood which extends along the roa on the right for a considerable distan** is the Bois de Châtillon. It was ca tured by the 5th Division on Novemb 5, the front line of the division on th night resting along this edge of it.

(76.4 m 123.0 km) **Beyond wood, first crest, to the right at foot of hill** seen Vilosnes-sur-Meuse. The 5th Div sion aided the French 15th Colonial Div sion to cross the river there on November y attacking in rear, from this hill, the Germans who were defending the village.

(76.6 m 123.3 km) **While descending hill, the ridge seen to the right front** is on the other side of the Meuse. It was taken by the 80th Division on September 26 and from then on to November 6 the opposing lines faced each other across this valley.

(78.7 m 126.7 km) **Continue through the town of Sivry-sur-Meuse.**

(79.3 m 127.6 km) **Beyond far edge of own, about 80 yards, STOP.**

The monument on Montfaucon can be seen on the sky line to the right front.

Face to the left, which direction is east. The 79th Division on October 30 took over a portion of the front line, about 2 miles away, which ran in the direction the leader is facing. It attacked, from the leader's right to left, daily on November , 4 and 5, by which time, after severe fighting, a line near the crest of the bald-topped hill seen to the left front had been reached. That hill, designated on French maps as the Borne de Cornouiller, was nicknamed "Cornwilly Hill" by the American soldiers who fought on this front.

On November 7 the division took the remainder of the hill, its direction of advance then changing to the direction which the reader is now facing.

The 26th Division on November 8 advanced alongside the 79th Division on its right and at the time of the Armistice both divisions were on a line about 8 miles from here, beyond Theinte Creek.

On the right of the 26th Division were the French 10th Colonial Division and the American 81st Division. The latter division advanced about 3 miles in the period between November 9 and 11.

Face down the road, which direction is approximately south.

As this is the last stop of the tour, a brief résumé here will aid in fixing in the reader's mind the events which took place in this region during the fall of 1918.

On September 26 a smashing surprise attack by the First Army, between the Meuse River and the Argonne Forest, overran the strong German forward positions and captured the heights to the right across the valley. In four days of bitter fighting an advance exceeding 6 miles was made by the American assault units.

On October 4 the general attack was renewed and continued almost without pause until October 22, by which time the Hindenburg Line had been carried on most of the First Army front beyond the river. This period was characterized by almost daily attacks and terrific fighting during which the German reserves were used up. It included a flank attack against the Argonne Forest on October 7, an advance on this side of the Meuse River on October 8, and a general assault against the Hindenburg Line on the other side of the river on October 14.

From October 23 to the end of that month only local attacks were made as the Army prepared for an offensive on November 1 that proved to be its last one. The results of this offensive exceeded all expectations and a complete break-through of the last prepared German position occurred. As the Germans did not have sufficient reserves to stop such a strong attack, they started a withdrawal to this side of the Meuse River.

The First Army then conducted an energetic pursuit. It brilliantly forced crossings of the river at several places, and exerted terrific and continuous pressure until the Armistice became effective.

The twelve American divisions that participated in the fighting between November 1 and November 11 suffered more than 18,000 casualties. The total American losses during the entire Meuse-Argonne offensive were close to 117,000.

5th Division Troops on the Armistice Line
Near Rémoiville

Vacherauville, October 31, 1918

EN ROUTE SOUTH OF SIVRY-SUR-MEUSE
TO VERDUN

(79.9 m 128.6 km) **At next crest, running at right angles to this road, was** located the First Army front line of November 1. No attack, however, was made on this side of the river that day.

(80.6 m 129.7 km) **To the left, crowning the ridge,** is the Bois de Chaume captured by the 33d Division on October 10.

(81.6 m 131.3 km) **The next village, Consenvoye,** was captured by the 33d Division during the general attack of October 8 on this side of the river. The division advanced in the direction opposite to the one the tourist is traveling.

(82.3 m 132.4 km) **Beyond the town, to the left alongside the road** is a German World War military cemetery.

(82.5 m 132.8 km) **To the right front** is seen Forges, which was just in front of the jump-off line of the American Army in its first great attack in this region on September 26. Le Mort Homme hill is seen on the sky line beyond it.

(83.1 m 133.7 km) **Continue through** next village, Brabant-sur-Meuse.

(83.2 m 133.9 km) **From first bend in road and for about a mile farther on,** the 29th Division used this road to form on for the attack of October 8. It advanced up the slopes to the left. During the next few days it was opposed by Austrian troops, of which only three divisions ever served in line on the Western Front.

(84.9 m 136.8 km) **The next villag** Samogneux, was just within the fro line of the American Army on Septemb 26. The town was entirely obliterate during the severe fighting on this fron

(86.6 m 139.4 km) **Beyond town, tl** road climbs a steep hill called the Cô de Talou. It was captured by the Ge mans in hard fighting during 1916 ar recaptured by the French in 1917.

(87.9 m 141.5 km) **Continue throug** Vacherauville, which town was complete destroyed by shellfire during the war.

(88.5 m 142.4 km) **Beyond the tow after passing the first bend in the roa to the left front** the Ossuary of Doua mont with its tower can be seen.

The road leading east from the ne village, Bras, is the one generally follow by tourists who visit the French battlefiel near Verdun. A suggested route for th trip is shown in a broken black line on t map at the end of the chapter. This mak an interesting side trip and can be con pleted in approximately 1½ hours if no lor stops at interesting points are made.

(89.1 m 143.4 km) **Just beyond Bra** which also was completely destroye to the right of the road is a large Fren World War military cemetery.

(92.9 m 149.5 km) **Continue to Verdu** *The mileage ends at the railroad statio*

A few points of interest in Verdun ha been indicated on page 272 which is tl concluding page of the first day's itinerar

(312)

ADDITIONAL PLACES OF INTEREST IN THE
MEUSE-ARGONNE REGION

IN addition to the places whose World War history has been described in the itinerary, there are a number of other places in the Meuse-Argonne region where interesting war events occurred, where there now exist features of special interest, or which were of sufficient importance in history before the World War to warrant special mention. For reference purposes and for the benefit of the tourist who travels in the area not on the described route, these places and some of their history have been recorded here.

The map on the next page indicates the general location of most of the places mentioned. At those indicated both in the text and on the sketch by a star there is some existing interesting object such as a memorial, ancient building or ruins or outstanding World War feature which is still in a good state of preservation.

Argonne Forest. While the 77th Division was engaged in heavy fighting about 2¼ miles southeast of Binarville on September 29, Lieutenant Colonel Fred E. Smith of that division performed his last heroic act. When communication with the leading battalion of his regiment was interrupted by the infiltration of small parties of the enemy, Lieutenant Colonel Smith personally led a party of two other officers and ten soldiers forward to reestablish runner posts and carry ammunition to the front line. The party, straying

to the flank beyond supporting troops, suddenly came under fire from enemy machine guns only 50 yards away. Shouting to the members of his party to take cover, Colonel Smith disregarding his own danger opened pistol fire on the Germans. About this time he fell, severely wounded, but regaining his footing he continued to fire on the enemy until most of the men of his party were out of danger. Refusing first-aid treatment, he made his way to a hand-grenade dump and returned under heavy machine-gun fire for the purpose of making another attack on the enemy machine guns. As he was attempting to determine the exact location of the nearest nest, he fell mortally wounded. This gallant and brave soldier was later posthumously awarded the Congressional Medal of Honor.

In this same part of the Argonne Forest, Sergeant Benjamin Kaufman, 77th Division, won the Congressional Medal of Honor on September 29. He took out a patrol for the purpose of attacking an enemy machine gun which had checked the advance of his company. Before reaching the gun he became separated from his patrol and a machine-gun bullet shattered his right arm. Without hesitation he advanced on the gun alone, throwing grenades with his left hand and charging with an empty pistol, taking one prisoner and scattering the crew. He then

View Near the Jump-Off Line of the 77th Division, September 26, 1918

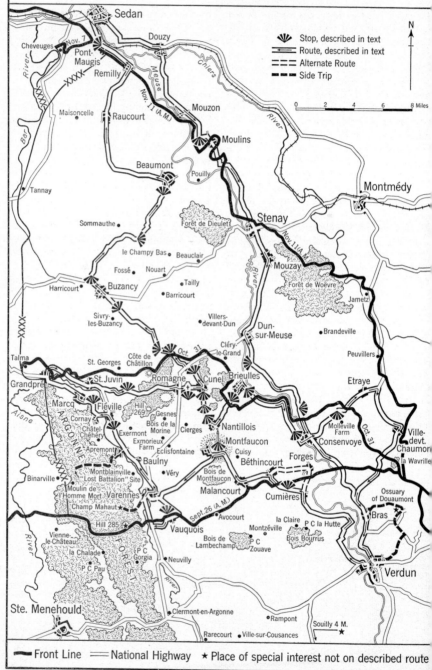

Described Routes and Additional Places of Interest in Meuse - Argonne Region

Legend:
- Stop, described in text
- Route, described in text
- Alternate Route
- Side Trip

0   2   4   6   8 Miles

N

Sedan
Cheveuges
Pont-Maugis
Remilly
Douzy
Maisoncelle
Raucourt
Nov. 11 (A.M.)
Mouzon
Moulins
Beaumont
Pouilly
Tannay
Montmédy
Sommauthe
Forêt de Dieulet
Stenay
le Champy Bas
Beauclair
Fossé
Nouart
Mouzay
Buzancy
Tailly
Forêt de Woëvre
Harricourt
Barricourt
Jametz
Sivry-les-Buzancy
Villers-devant-Dun
Dun-sur-Meuse
Brandeville
Talma
Côte de Châtillon
Oct. 31
Cléry-le-Grand
Peuvillers
St. Georges
St. Juvin
Romagne
Cunel
Brieulles
Etraye
Grandpré
Marcq
Fléville
Hill 269
Gesnes
Cierges
Nantillois
Molleville Farm
Ville-devt.-Chaumont
Cornay
Bois de la Morine
Montfaucon
Cuisy
Consenvoye
la Wavrille
Châtel-Chéhéry
Exermont
Exermont Farm
Eclisfontaine
Béthincourt
Forges
Apremont
Baulny
Bois de Montfaucon
Ossuary of Douaumont
Binarville
Montblainville "Lost Battalion" Site
Véry
Malancourt
Cumières
Bras
Moulin de l'Homme Mort
Varennes
Champ Mahaut
Hill 285
Vauquois
Avocourt
Montzéville
la Claire
P C la Hutte
Bois Bourrus
Verdun
Vienne-le-Château
la Chalade
P C Gorgia
Neuvilly
Bois de Lambechamp
P C Zouave
P C Pau
Ste. Menehould
Clermont-en-Argonne
Rampont
Souilly 4 M.
Rarecourt
Ville-sur-Cousances

ARGONNE FOREST

Meuse River
Chiers River
Bar River
Aisne River

Nov. 7
Nov. 11 (A.M.)

Front Line   **National Highway**   ★ Place of special interest not on described route

rought the machine gun and prisoner ack to the first-aid station where he went o have his wounded arm treated.

Slightly to the east of the scene of the above exploit, Private Archie A. Peck, 7th Division, also won the Congressional Medal of Honor. While engaged with two other soldiers in patrol duty on October 6, he and his comrades were subjected to the direct fire of an enemy machine gun which wounded both of his companions. Returning to his company, he obtained another soldier to assist in carrying in the wounded men. Although his assistant

Barricourt. Strong resistance was encountered in this village on November 2 before it was captured early the next day by troops of the 89th Division.

Beauchamp Farm, 1½ miles southwest of Clermont-en-Argonne. Location of 92d Div. Hdqrs., September 24–30.

Beauclair. Captured by the 89th Division on November 3 after a sharp fight.

Béthincourt. Location of 80th Div. Headquarters, October 1–12.

Bois Emont, ½ mile southwest of Cierges. Captured by the 37th Division early on September 28 after a hard fight.

Engineers Working on Road Near Barricourt, November 4, 1918
Note condition of road

was killed and Private Peck was constantly under terrific machine-gun fire he made the round trip twice, bringing in each time one of the wounded men.

Ariétal Farm, 1 mile northeast of Exermont. A tank attack on September 29 was broken up near this farm by hostile artillery fire. The farm was captured by the 1st Division on October 5.

Avocourt. This village was an important road junction just in rear of the 37th Division jump-off line on September 26.

Bois de Gesnes. This wood which is located on the Romagne Heights just west of Côte Dame Marie was the scene of heavy fighting at various times from October 10 to 14 by the 32d and 42d Divisions, and the 181st Brigade of the 91st Division while with the 1st Division.

Bois de Lambechamp. In a ravine at the east edge of this wood was located the 79th Div. Hdqrs., September 24–26.

Bois de Montfaucon. German concrete dugouts located at the crossroads

1st Division Marching Into Bantheville Just After the Armistice

on Hill 269 in the Bois de Montfaucon were occupied by the 37th Div. Hdqrs., Sept. 27–Oct. 1, and by the 32d Div. Headquarters, September 29–November 2.

Bois de la Morine and **Bois du Chêne Sec.** These woods witnessed heavy fighting on October 4 and 5 when they were attacked several times by the 32d Division. They were finally captured on October 5 after a four-hour battle.

Bois de Taille l'Abbé, 1 mile west of Apremont. At daybreak October 1 a German counterattack from this wood met a 28th Division attack supported by tanks. The Germans were driven back. The wood was finally captured by troops of the 28th Division during October 7.

Concrete Dugout in Champ Mahaut

Bois de la Tuilerie, east of Montfaucon. 5th Div. Hdqrs. from Oct. 12 to Nov. 4.

Bois de Valoup, on the southeastern slope of Côte Dame Marie. Captured October 9 by the 32d Division in heavy fighting. Attempts of the 32d Division to advance from this wood on October 10 and 11 were unsuccessful.

Bois de Ville, ¾ mile south of Ville-devant-Chaumont, was captured by the 26th Division during November 10.

Brandeville. German resistance near this place held up the advance of part of the 5th Division on November 7. The village was captured on November 8 by the 5th Division, to which the 128th Infantry Regiment of the 32d Division was attached at the time.

Camp Drachen, ¾ mile north of Apremont. At this balloon camp, captured from the Germans, was located the 42d Div. Hdqrs., Oct. 19–Nov. 3.

★ **Champ Mahaut.** At this place are (1937) a large number of wartime concrete shelters and dugouts said to have been used as a headquarters by the Crown Prince of Bavaria. The place was captured by the 28th and 77th Divisions after hard fighting on September 26, 27 and 28. The 77th Div. Hdqrs. was located there Oct. 2–12 and Oct. 16–31. To visit Champ Mahaut, leave Varennes on road to the south. Beyond town, at first road junction, take road to the right toward Vienne-le-Château. About 3

German Shells Exploding Near Cuisy, October 7, 1918
A man was severely wounded by the shell exploding in the foreground

ilometers (1.8 miles) from road junction urn right and travel 800 yards to shelters.

Châtel-Chéhéry. 77th Div. Hdqrs.,)ct. 12–16; 78th Div. Hdqrs., Oct. 16– 1; and 80th Div. Hdqrs., Oct. 30–Nov. 1.

Chaudron Farm, in a ravine 1 mile .orth of Baulny. This farm was cap- ured during September 28 by the 35th)ivision after severe fighting.

Chéhéry, 1 mile south of Fléville. In his town was located the I Corps Hdqrs., Nov. 2–5. The near-by château was the 2d Div. Hdqrs., October 13–31.

Cheveuges. Positions on the hills east .nd north of this place were occupied on November 7 by the 1st and 42d Divi- .ions. These positions were turned over o the French early on November 8.

Cierges. This town was reached by he 37th Division on September 28 but . German counterattack drove the Amer- can troops from the village. On the 29th t was attacked twice, once with tank upport, but the heavy artillery fire of the nemy was so severe that it could not be .eld. It was finally captured by troops f the 32d Division on October 1.

Clairs Chênes Wood, northeast of unel. Scene of heavy fighting by the d Division on October 14–16. It was aptured on October 20 and a German ttempt to recapture it on the 21st was epulsed. To the east are Hill 299 and .a Mi-Noël Wood, at both of which .laces severe fighting took place on Octo-

ber 14, 15 and 21. They were captured by the 3d Division on the last-named date.

Clermont-en-Argonne. This historic town, because of its position on one of the two principal passes through the Argonne Forest, has been the scene of numerous battles and sieges. The Church of St. Didier, dating from the 16th Century, is of architectural interest. The town was an important point in the supply and communication system of the American First Army during the offensive.

Cléry-le-Grand. Captured early on November 1 by the 5th Division.

Cléry-le-Petit, near Cléry-le-Grand, was captured by the 5th Division on Nov. 2.

Cuisy. Location of 4th Div. Hdqrs.

Temporary American Cemetery Near Cierges, January 1919

during the period Sept. 26–Oct. 19, and 90th Div. Hdqrs. from Oct. 19 to Oct. 31.

Dhuy Farm, 1½ miles northeast of Landres-et-St. Georges. This farm was a German strong point captured on November 1 by the 89th Division.

Eclisfontaine. In this village and in Bouleaux Bois west of it the 91st Division had bitter fighting from September 26 to 28. Both places were captured on September 27, abandoned the same day and recaptured on September 28.

In the general attack toward Eclisfontaine on September 26, First Lieutenant Deming Bronson, 91st Division, was struck by fragments of an enemy hand grenade, receiving deep cuts on the head. He nevertheless participated under hazardous conditions in the capture of an enemy dugout from which a large number of prisoners was taken. That afternoon he was painfully wounded in the arm by an enemy rifle bullet and after receiving first-aid treatment was ordered to the rear. Disregarding these instructions, Lieutenant Bronson remained on duty with his company throughout the night although suffering from severe pain and shock. On September 27 when the attack was resumed, Lieutenant Bronson's company was in support. Nevertheless, he gallantly joined the assaulting line and took part in the capture of Eclisfontaine. Later he participated in the capture of a hostile machine gun, himself killing the enemy gunner. Shortly after this encounter, when the troops were compelled to retire because of the heavy enemy artillery barrage, Lieutenant Bronson, who was the last man to leave the advanced position, was wounded in both arms by an enemy high-explosive shell. He was then assisted to cover by another officer who applied first aid. Although bleeding profusely and faint from the loss of blood, Lieutenant Bronson remained with the front line that night refusing to go to the rear for treatment. His conspicuous gallantry was an inspiration to the members of his command and for his deeds he was awarded the Congressional Medal of Honor.

During the 91st Division advance between Véry and Eclisfontaine, on September 26, Corporal Philip C. Katz performed the heroic service for which he was awarded the Congressional Medal of Honor. After his company had withdrawn about 200 yards to a line about 1 mile south of Eclisfontaine, Corporal Katz learned that one of his wounded comrades had been left in an exposed position. Voluntarily crossing an area swept by heavy machine-gun fire, he advanced to where the wounded soldier lay and carried him to a place of safety.

Epinonville, ¾ mile east of Eclisfontaine, was the 91st Div. Hdqrs., Sept. 28–Oct. 4, and 89th Div. Hdqrs., Oct. 14–24.

During the severe fighting near Epinonville, Sergeant Lloyd M. Seibert, 91st Division, won the Congressional Medal of Honor. Suffering from illness, he led his men with the highest courage and leadership under heavy shell and machine-gun fire. On September 26, with two other soldiers, he charged a machine-gun emplacement in advance of his company, he himself killing one of the enemy with a shotgun and capturing two others. In this encounter he was wounded but continued in action, and when a withdrawal was ordered he returned with the last unit, assisting a wounded comrade. Later in the evening he carried in wounded until overcome with exhaustion. On September 27, when his organization captured Epinonville, Sergeant Seibert was one of about ten soldiers who went through their own barrage into the village, where, according to his citation, he chased a group of 30 or more Germans along the main road until he dropped from exhaustion.

Exermont. In the severe fighting near here on October 4, Private Sterling Morelock, 1st Division, won the Congressional Medal of Honor. While his company was held up by heavy fire, Private Morelock voluntarily led three other men, who were acting as runners, as a patrol through his company's front line. Under intense rifle, machine-gun and artillery fire they penetrated a wood in which the German front line was located. The

A Dangerous Corner in Exermont,
October 7, 1918

patrol encountered a series of five hostile
machine-gun nests, containing from one to
five guns each, cleaned them all out, and
held control of the situation until the arrival of reinforcements, even though all
except Private Morelock had become
casualties. He rendered first aid to the
injured and evacuated them, using as
stretcher bearers ten German prisoners
whom he had captured. Soon thereafter
his company commander was wounded
and while dressing his wound Private
Morelock was severely wounded in the
hip, which forced his evacuation. His
heroic action and devotion to duty were
an inspiration to the entire regiment.

In the same attack of the 1st Division,
Corporal Berte L. Kinkade, Private First
Class Stanley Gancaz and Private George
W. Garner took an important part. When
a German 77-millimeter field gun, supported by numerous machine guns, broke
up the tank attack and held up the infantry
advance, Corporal Kinkade, with Privates
Gancaz and Garner, both of whom were
scouts, made an encircling movement on
their own initiative under heavy fire and
put the gun out of action, capturing the
entire crew. They cleaned out the enemy
dugouts in the vicinity and returned with
40 prisoners, including one infantry officer.
All three men were awarded the Distinguished Service Cross for their bravery.

Exmorieux Farm and the near-by Les
Epinettes Bois. This farm and wood
were captured by the 91st Division on
September 28 against desperate resistance.

Forêt de Dieulet. Patrols of the 89th
Division pushed through this wood on
November 4 and reached the Meuse

River that same day. The engineers o
the 89th Division built rafts in the Forê
de Dieulet which were floated dow
Wamme Creek to the Meuse where the
were used in forcing a crossing of th
river near Pouilly on November 10.

Forêt de Woëvre. This wood wa
cleared of the Germans by the 5t
Division during November 9 and 10.

Fossé. This village was the location o
the 2d Division Hdqrs., November 4–11

Gesnes. In the vicinity of this village
situated at the foot of Romagne Heights
occurred some of the most desperat
fighting of the war. The town itself wa
captured by the 91st Division on Septem
ber 29 after two previous attacks that da
had failed, but was abandoned the sam
night because it formed a sharp salient i
the line. Soon after the war a smal
marker was erected near the church b
the 362d Infantry, 91st Division, in com
memoration of its fighting at Gesne
during this period. The town was recap
tured by the 32d Division in savag
fighting during October 5.

South of this village Major Oscar F
Miller, 91st Division, performed the ex
ploits for which he was awarded th
Congressional Medal of Honor. Althoug
exhausted by two days of intense physica
and mental strain, he reorganized hi
battalion and ordered an attack during
September 28. Upon reaching the open
ground, the advancing line commenced to

A Haircut Near the Front Lines

waver in the face of machine-gun fire from the front and flanks and from direct artillery fire. Personally leading his command group forward between his front-line companies Major Miller inspired his men by his personal courage and they again moved ahead. During this advance he was shot in the leg but he staggered on in front of his command.

vision on November 2. Location of the I Corps Hdqrs. from Nov. 5 to Nov. 10.

Hill 255, northwest of Gesnes. This hill was attacked by the 32d Division on October 4 and 5. On October 9 the 181st Brigade of the 91st Division, while attached to the 1st Division, reached a position just south of the crest in heavy fighting and occupied the hill the next day.

Brabant-sur-Meuse, November 3, 1918

Soon afterwards he was shot in the arm, but continued the charge, personally cheering his men on through the heavy machine-gun fire. Just before the objective was reached, he received a wound in the abdomen, which forced him to the ground, but he continued to urge his men ahead, telling them to push on to the next ridge and leave him. He died from the effects of his wounds a few days later.

The 89th Div. Hdqrs. was located at Gesnes during the period Oct. 24–Nov. 1.

Grange-aux-Bois Farm, ½ mile west of Cierges. Scene of heavy fighting by the 37th Division on September 28 and 29 and by the 91st Division on September 29. From the road near it is obtained an excellent view of the ground captured by the 3d and 32d Divisions during the severe fighting in this vicinity in early October.

Harricourt. Captured by the 77th Di-

Hill 263, in Le Petit Bois. This hill was captured by the 1st Division on October 9 after severe fighting.

Hill 269, in the Bois de Moncy. Elements of the 1st, 32d and 91st Divisions fought on this hill at various times between October 5 and 9. The crest was captured on October 8 by the 1st Engineers, a part of the 1st Division.

In the advance on October 7 First Lieutenant Edmund P. Arpin, 32d Division, won the Distinguished Service Cross for voluntarily leading a platoon of 41 men in an attack on Hill 269. Although all but four of his men became casualties, this small group under the leadership of Lieutenant Arpin continued on its mission, capturing a position on the hill and holding it for some time although there was no hope of his receiving reinforcements.

Hill 272, two miles east of Fléville.

Heavy fire from this strong position held up the advance of the 1st Division on October 5. A hostile counterattack stopped an attempt to outflank it on October 8, but it was stormed and captured by the 1st Division, in spite of terrific hostile artillery fire, in a brilliant assault on October 9. It is reported that more than 50 German machine guns were captured during the advance up its southern slope.

★ **Hill 285,** in the Argonne Forest. This was on the American jump-off line of September 26. It was the scene of hard fighting in 1914–15 and is marked by many deep mine craters. A French ossuary monument, called the Ossuaire de la Haute Chevauchée, which mentions the American units that served in the vicinity, is on the hill. To reach it from Varennes, go southwest on road leading toward Vienne-le-Château. After entering woods take first turn to the left and proceed 1½ miles to the monument.

Hill 304, 1 mile north of Esnes. This hill was just behind the American jump-off line on September 26. It was the scene of severe French and German fighting in 1916 and 1917. A monument on its summit commemorates the French defenders of the hill and French soldiers who died on it. The monument is difficult of access (1937) and is reached from the Esnes–Malancourt road. The 79th Div. Hdqrs. was located near this road at PC Zouave, 2 miles south of Malancourt, on September 26 and 27.

Jametz. Captured after dark on November 9 by troops of the 5th Division who waded one stream and swam the Loison River under hostile fire to attack the town. The troops could not hold it that night, but reoccupied it the next day after a short fight. A German aviation field was located near there.

La Besogne, in the Argonne Forest 2 miles west of Cornay. Location of 78th Div. Headquarters, Oct. 31–Nov. 3.

La Claire, 200 yards north of Bois Bourrus. Location of 80th Div. Hdqrs. during the period Sept. 26–Oct. 1.

La Forge, ½ mile southeast of Montblainville. Captured by the 28th Division on September 27. Location of 28th Div. Hdqrs., Sept. 30–Oct. 9, and 82d Div. Hdqrs., Oct. 9–13.

La Wavrille. The French 26th Division engaged in heavy fighting on this wooded height from October 8 to 11

Salvation Army Workers Near Varennes Giving Fresh Doughnuts to Soldiers
Just in From the Front Line, October 1918

he height was captured by troops of the
American 26th Division on November 9.

Le Champy Bas. This village was
captured by the 89th Division on November 3. In this attack, Captain
Marcellus H. Chiles took a heroic part.
When his battalion, of which he had
just taken command, was halted by
machine-gun fire, he picked up the rifle
of a dead soldier and calling on his men
to follow, led the advance across a stream
waist deep. Upon reaching the opposite
bank this gallant officer was seriously
wounded, but before permitting himself
to be evacuated he made complete arrangements for turning over his command to the next senior officer. Under
the inspiration of his fearlessness, Captain
Chiles' battalion reached its objective.
He died shortly after reaching the hospital for treatment and was later awarded
the Congressional Medal of Honor.

Le Champy Haut, ½ mile southwest of
Le Champy Bas. In an unsuccessful
attack on this place on the morning of
November 3, the 2d Division sustained
heavy losses. The town was later occupied by the division without opposition.

Le Houppy Bois, east of Molleville
Farm, was captured on October 23 by the
26th Division. That night it was violently
bombarded by the German artillery.

Les Côtes de Forimont, 1¼ miles north
of Neuvilly. In a dugout near the
southern edge of the woods on these hills
was located the 35th Division Hdqrs., for
the period Sept. 25-28, and the I Corps
Hdqrs., Sept. 29-Nov. 2.

Maisoncelle. Captured by the 42d
Division on November 6. Location of
the 42d Div. Hdqrs., November 7-10.

Montrebeau, ¾ mile south of Exermont.
In the attack on this wood on October
5, Corporal Harold W. Roberts, Tank
Corps, was driving his tank into a clump
of bushes to afford protection to a disabled tank when his tank slid into a water-
filled shell hole, ten feet deep, and was
immediately submerged. Knowing that
only one of the two men in the tank could
escape, Corporal Roberts said to the
gunner "Well, only one of us can get
out, and out you go," whereupon he

American Soldiers Constructing Heavy Timber
Bridge at Dun-sur-Meuse, November 1918

pushed his companion through the back
door of the tank and was himself drowned.
He was later posthumously awarded the
Congressional Medal of Honor.

In the same attack Sergeants Harold J.
Ash and Harley N. Nichols, Tank Corps,
took a gallant part. Driving their tank
in the face of direct 77-millimeter gun fire
into the extreme eastern part of Montrebeau, it was put out of action by an
enemy shell. These men continued for
some minutes to fire on a machine-gun
nest which was firing on them, then dismounted and attacked the nest. They
killed the two gunners and disabled the
guns, and then drove the crew from
another machine gun. Under the protection of another tank, they started to
their own lines, nearly a mile away. On
the way back, they encountered two
Germans with anti-tank rifles and captured the rifles. Both men were under
heavy machine-gun and artillery fire
throughout this operation. They were
awarded Distinguished Service Crosses.

Montzéville. Location of III Corps Headquarters during the period from September 29 to October 26.

Moulin de l'Homme Mort. Four companies of the 77th Division succeeded in penetrating the German lines in the Argonne Forest on September 28, reaching a position about 200 yards south of this mill. The units on the flanks of this force had not kept abreast of it, and soon the Germans succeeded in infiltrating behind this group, cutting it off from the remainder of the division. These four companies remained thus surrounded by the enemy until the evening of September 30. On September 29 First Lieutenant Arthur F. McKeogh, accompanied by Privates First Class Jack Herschkowitz and John J. Monson, attempted to reestablish communications with regimental headquarters, in order to obtain ammunition and food. In the afternoon they were attacked by a hostile force. Killing one of the enemy, they eluded the others. When night came they crawled unknowingly into the center of a German camp, where they lay for over three hours, undetected. Finally discovered, they made a dash to escape, each drawing hostile fire. They succeeded in getting through the enemy lines and delivered valuable information to regimental headquarters, which helped in the relief of the beleaguered group. For this daring exploit each of the three men was

awarded the Distinguished Service Cros[s]

Musarde Farm, near the southern tip [of] Côte de Châtillon. Scene of heavy figh[t]ing by the 42d Division from October 1[1] to 16, when it was finally captured.

Neuville-le-Comte Farm, ½ mile eas[t] of Exermont. Captured by the 35t[h] Division on September 29, in an attac[k] made under severe artillery fire, but n[o]t held due to a heavy German countera[t]tack launched that noon. On October [2] it was recaptured by the 1st Division i[n] spite of desperate hostile opposition.

Nouart. V Corps Hdqrs., Nov. 7–1[1]

★ **Ossuaire de la Haute Chevauché[e]** See the account given under Hill 285.

★ **Ossuary of Douaumont.** 4 mile[s] northeast of Verdun, near Fort Douau[mont, stands the Ossuary of Douaumon[t], a large memorial to the French dead [of] the Verdun battles of 1916 and 1917. [A] French military cemetery adjoins it.

The "Trench of Bayonets", where [a] number of French soldiers are supposed t[o] have been buried standing up, is locate[d] about ½ mile away on the road to Bra[s.] It is sheltered by a concrete structu[re] donated by an American citizen.

PC Gorgia, 3¾ miles north of Clermon[t.] 28th Div. Headquarters, Sept. 24–27.

PC La Hutte, in the Bois Bourrus. 33[d] Div. Headquarters, Sept. 25–Oct. 21.

PC Pau, near Fontaine des Emerlot[s,] 1¼ miles southwest of La Chalade. 77t[h] Div. Headquarters, Sept. 25–Oct. 2.

Peuvillers. Early on November [1] troops of the 32d Division attached to th[e] 5th Division relieved units of the Frenc[h] 15th Colonial Division who had occupie[d] this village the previous day. East [of] the village on November 10 the 32d Div[i]sion had considerable fighting.

Polka Farm, 1 mile northwest of Son[-] mauthe. Heavy resistance near this far[m] checked the advance of the 77th and 80t[h] Divisions on November 4. The farm wa[s] captured on the 5th by the 80th Divisio[n.]

Rampont. Location of the III Corp[s] Hdqrs., Sept. 14–29, during the initi[al] attack of the Meuse-Argonne offensive.

Rarécourt. Location of the I Corp[s] Hdqrs., Sept. 18–29, during the initi[al] attack of the Meuse-Argonne offensive[.]

Town Hall at Souilly Where First Army
Headquarters Was Located

Signal Corps Photographer Taking Pictures in St. Juvin

Raucourt. Location of the 77th Div. Hdqrs. during the period from Nov. 7–11.

Ravine aux Pierres, northeast of St. Juvin. The 82d Division engaged in bitter fighting near this ravine from October 14 to 16 and occupied it on October 21. On November 1 the 77th and 80th Divisions suffered heavy losses in an attack launched from the ravine.

St. Christophe, ⅜ mile east of Cunel. An entrenched German position there was attacked twice by the 80th Division on October 10 without success but on the next day, as the result of two attacks, part of it was captured. On the 12th the 5th Division fought in the vicinity and on October 14 the area was finally captured by the troops of the 3d Division.

St. Georges. Elements of the 42d and 82d Divisions fought severe actions with the Germans south and west of this place on October 14 and 15. It was captured by a joint detachment of the 2d and 80th Divisions on November 1 after a determined fight during the main attack.

Sérieux Farm, 1 mile west of Eclisfontaine. The 91st Division overcame strong resistance here on September 28.

Sivry-les-Buzancy. This village was captured by the 80th Division on November 2. It is reported that while 45 American officers were discussing plans in an old stable that night for the next day's attack, a large shell came through the roof, causing casualties among them.

Sommauthe. Captured on November 4 by the 80th Division. Stiff resistance was encountered on the hill south of town and in the woods to the north.

★ **Souilly.** Location of First Army Headquarters from September 21 to the end of hostilities. The United States Government has placed a bronze plaque on the town hall recording this fact.

Tailly. Captured on November 2 by the 89th Division after overcoming strong machine-gun resistance. The town formed a salient in the line that night. 89th Div. Headquarters, November 4–11.

Talma, farm and village, about 1½ miles northwest of Grandpré. These were in the Hindenburg Line. French troops captured them on October 16 but were driven out the next day. From October 18 to 27 the 78th Division engaged in heavy fighting in their vicinity, capturing the farm on October 18 and the hill east of the village on October 25. This outflanked the hostile position on the hill north of Grandpré, which was captured on the 27th in desperate fighting. Talma village was occupied by the 78th Division on October 30.

During the attack by the 78th Division on October 23 against the hill east of Talma, Private Parker F. Dunn won the Congressional Medal of Honor. When his battalion commander found it necessary to send a message to a company in the attacking line and hesitated to order a runner to make the trip because of the extreme danger involved, Private Dunn, a member of the intelligence section, volunteered for the mission. After advancing across a field swept by artillery and machine-gun fire, he was wounded but continued on, falling wounded a second time. Still undaunted, he persistently attempted to carry out his mission until he was killed by a machine-gun bullet before reaching the advance line.

Tannay. Entered early on November 5 by patrols of the 78th Division. Later that day elements of the 42d Division passed through the 78th Division about ¾ mile northeast of the village and continued the advance to the north.

Transvaal Farm, on the southern slope of Côte Dame Marie. Scene of heavy fighting on October 9 and 10 by soldiers of the 32d Division. The farm was finally captured by the division on October 10.

Tronsol Farm, 1¼ miles southwest of Gesnes. Captured by the 91st Division after a hard fight on September 28 and held against a vigorous German counter-attack the next afternoon. The 32d Division had heavy fighting north of the farm.

Tuilerie Farm, near the eastern end of Côte de Châtillon. Scene of severe fighting, October 15–16, by the 42d Division.

Verrières-en-Hesse Farm, 2½ miles southeast of Avocourt. Location of the 37th Division Hdqrs., Sept. 23–26, and of the V Corps Hdqrs., Sept. 29–Oct. 21.

Véry. Captured about noon September 26 by the 91st Division. The head quarters of the division was located at a road junction ½ mile southwest of Véry during the period September 26–28.

Ville-aux-Bois Farm, ¾ mile southeast of Cunel. Scene of heavy fighting by the 80th Division on October 5, 9 and 10

Villers-devant-Dun. Captured by the 90th Div. during November 2. 90th Div Headquarters from November 3 to 10

Ville-sur-Cousances. Location of the V Corps Hdqrs. from September 18 to 29

Church Services at Verdun, October 18, 1918

FACTS CONCERNING GERMAN DIVISIONS WHICH SERVED ON THE MEUSE-ARGONNE FRONT, SEPTEMBER 26–NOVEMBER 11, 1918

Divisions moved to Meuse-Argonne front	3
Divisions moved from front	1
Divisions on front September 26 (a.m.)	1
Divisions in line twice	1
Divisions in line three times	
Divisions which came from British front	3
Divisions sent to British front	
Divisions which came from French fronts other than Vosges	18
Divisions sent to French fronts other than Vosges	
Divisions which came from Vosges	
Divisions sent to Vosges	
Divisions which came from St. Mihiel region	1
Divisions sent to St. Mihiel region	

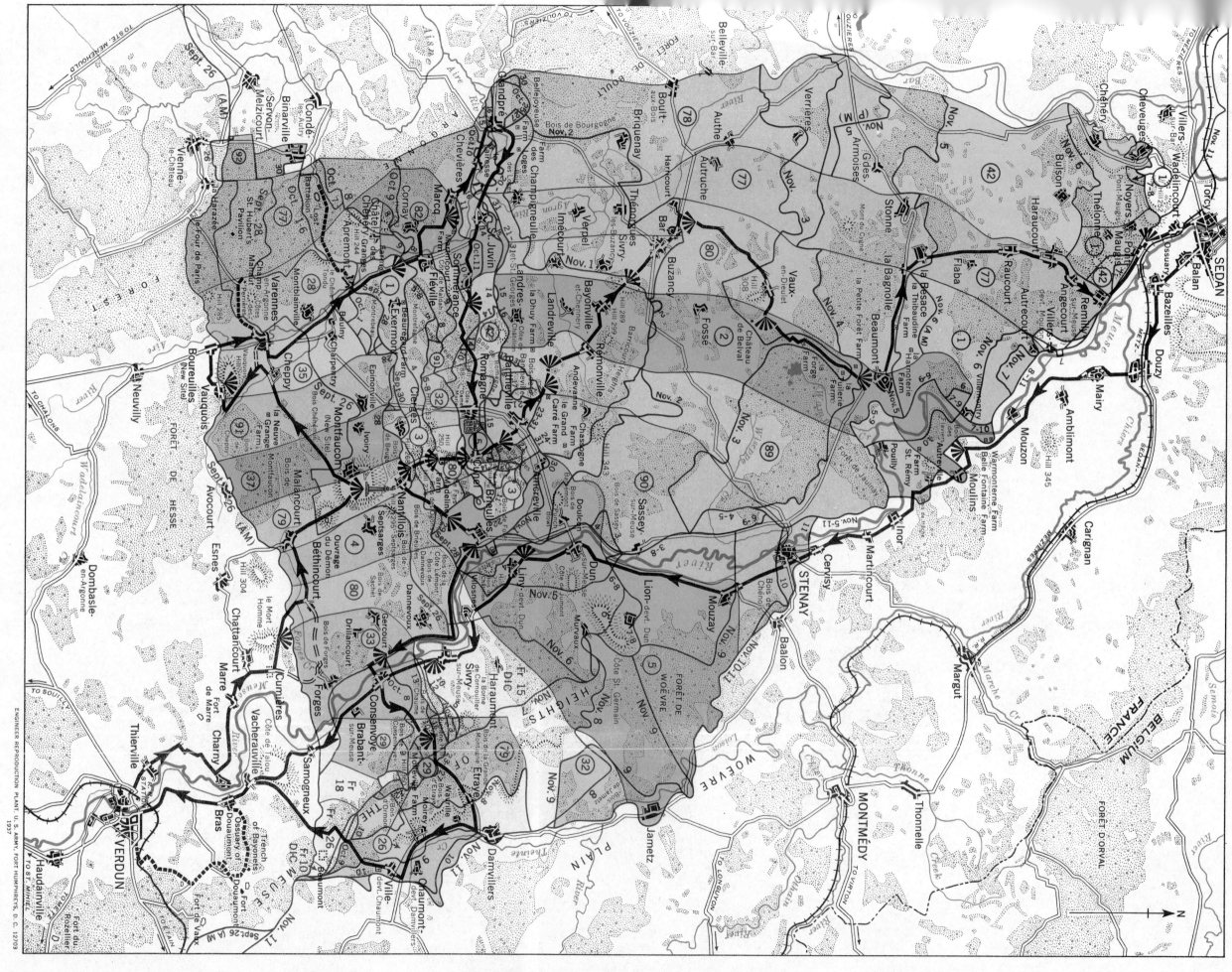

American Battle Operations in the Meuse-Argonne Region

ENGINEER REPRODUCTION PLANT, U.S. ARMY, FORT HUMPHREYS, D.C. 1937

Scale
1
200000

Route, described in text
Alternate route
Side trip
Stop, described in text
Highway
Front line

All front lines are as of midnight for dates shown unless otherwise noted; thus September 26 on a line indicates the line held at midnight September 26. The dates September 26-27 on a line indicate that the line was located at the same place at midnight of both September 26 and September 27.

Meuse-Argonne American Memorial
Meuse-Argonne American Cemetery
Ruins

Ground gained by American divisions shown by large circled numerals and colored areas
Small circled numeral indicates part of American division which fought attached to another division
Ground gained by French divisions shown by numerals and yellow areas attached to First Army

SUMMARY OF COMBAT SERVICE OF AMERICAN DIVISIONS
IN THE MEUSE-ARGONNE REGION

Name of Div.	Period of Service 1918	Character of Service	Location of Service General vicinity of—	Army to Which Attached [1]	Corps to Which Attached [1]	Casualties [2]
1	Oct. 1-12	Battle	Exermont and Côte de Maldah.	First	I until Oct. 7, then V.	7,772 (459)
	Nov. 6-8	Battle	South of Sedan	First	V.	583
2	Oct. 31-Nov. 11	Battle	Landres-et-St. Georges, Beaumont and Moulins.	First	V.	3,282 (61)
3	Sept. 30-Oct. 27	Battle	Madeleine Farm and Bois de Forêt.	First	V until Oct. 12, then III.	7,708 (165)
4	Sept. 26-Oct. 19	Battle	Septsarges and Bois de Fays.	First	III.	5,820 (396)
5	Oct. 12-22	Battle	Cunel	First	III.	4,184 (159)
	Oct. 27-Nov. 11	Battle	Dun-sur-Meuse and Jametz.	First	III.	2,083 (267)
26	Oct. 14-Nov. 11	Battle	Ville-devant-Chaumont.	First	Fr. XVII until Nov. 6, then Fr. II CAC.	4,666
28	Sept. 20-25	Sector	Boureuilles	Fr. Second until Sept. 22, then First.	Fr. IX until Sept. 21, then I.	97
	Sept. 26-Oct. 9	Battle	Côtes des Perrières, Apremont and Châtel-Chéhéry.	First	I	4,131 (106)
29	Oct. 8-30	Battle	Bois de Consenvoye and Molleville Farm.	First	Fr. XVII	4,746 (219)
32	Sept. 30-Oct. 20	Battle	Côte Dame Marie and Romagne-sous-Montfaucon.	First	V.	5,148 (370)
	Nov. 9-11	Battle	Bois de Jametz	First	III.	476 (11)
33	Sept. 10-25	Sector	Béthincourt	Fr. Second until Sept. 22, then First.	Fr. XVII until Sept. 14, then III.	48 (24)
	Sept. 26-Oct. 21	Battle	Forges and Consenvoye	First	III until Oct. 7, then Fr. XVII.	3,904 (82)
35	Sept. 21-25	Sector	Vauquois	Fr. Second until Sept. 22, then First.	I	100
	Sept. 26-Oct. 1	Battle	Cheppy and Baulny	First	I	6,006
37	Sept. 23-25	Sector	Avocourt	First	V.	40 (5)
	Sept. 26-30	Battle	Bois de Montfaucon and Ivoiry.	First	V.	3,060 (14)
42	Oct. 12-31	Battle	Côte de Châtillon and east of Sommerance.	First	V.	3,679 (91)
	Nov. 5-10	Battle	Grandes Armoises and south of Sedan.	First	I	357

See footnotes, end of table.

Name of Div.	Period of Service 1918	Character of Service	Location of Service General vicinity of—	Army to Which Attached [1]	Corps to Which Attached [1]	Casualties [2]
77	Sept. 21–25	Sector	Argonne Forest	Fr. Second until Sept. 22, then First.	I	93
	Sept. 26–Oct. 16	Battle	Argonne Forest and St. Juvin.	First	I	4,061
	Oct. 31–Nov. 11	Battle	Champigneulle, Bar and Villers-devant-Mouzon.	First	I until Nov. 10, then V.	897
78	Oct. 16–Nov. 5	Battle	Grandpré and Verrières	First	I	4,876
79	Sept. 16–25	Sector	Avocourt	Fr. Second until Sept. 22, then First.	III until Sept. 21, then V.	103 (1)
	Sept. 26–30	Battle	Malancourt, Montfaucon and Nantillois.	First	V	3,529 (65)
	Oct. 30–Nov. 11	Battle	Borne de Cornouiller and Wavrille.	First	Fr. XVII until Nov. 6, then Fr. II CAC.	2,347 (96)
80	Sept. 26–29	Battle	Béthincourt and Dannevoux.	First	III	790 (1)
	Oct. 4–12	Battle	Southeast of Cunel	First	III	2,767
	Oct. 31–Nov. 6	Battle	Imécourt, Buzancy and Beaumont.	First	I	1,219 (69)
82	Oct. 7–31	Battle	Cornay and Marcq	First	I	6,369 (8)
89	Oct. 20–Nov. 11.	Battle	Rémonville, Barricourt and Stenay.	First	V	3,864 (267)
90	Oct. 22–Nov. 11.	Battle	Bantheville, Andevanne and Stenay.	First	III	3,492 (267)
91	Sept. 20–25	Sector	East of Vauquois	First	V	39
	Sept. 26–Oct. 4	Battle	Bois de Cheppy and Epinonville.	First	V	4,568 (131)
92 (368th Inf. only)	Sept. 25	Sector	Northeast of Vienne-le-Château.	Fr. Fourth	Fr. XXXVIII	4
	Sept. 26–Oct. 1	Battle	Binarville and to the south.	Fr. Fourth	Fr. XXXVIII	266
93 (370th Inf. only)	July 23–Aug. 15	Sector	Vauquois	Fr. Second	Fr. XIII	10
93 (371st Inf. only)	June 22–Sept. 14	Training in Line and Sector.	Avocourt	Fr. Second	Fr. XIII until Aug. 21, then Fr. XVII.	40
93 (372d Inf. only)	June 6–July 14.	Training in Line.	Boureuilles	Fr. Second	Fr. XIII	15
	July 25–Sept. 9	Sector	Béthincourt	Fr. Second	Fr. XIII until Aug. 21, then Fr. XVII.	16

[1] All armies and corps are American unless otherwise indicated. In this table Fr. = French.

[2] Casualties are for period in line only. Figures in parentheses give casualties for units temporarily attached. Add figure in parentheses to the one above in order to obtain total casualties during the entire operation.

Chapter V

AMERICAN OPERATIONS IN THE
CHAMPAGNE REGION

N this chapter are described the American military operations which took place during the World War on that part of the battle front in the Champagne region between the city of Reims and the western part of the Argonne Forest. They include combat services of the 2d, 36th and 42d Divisions; the 369th, 371st and 372d Infantry Regiments of the 93d Division; the so-called "Lost Battalion" of the 77th Division; and the 368th Infantry Regiment of the 92d Division.

region are shown on the general map at the end of the chapter and each operation is illustrated by a sketch which accompanies the text of the itinerary.

The described tour begins at Reims and ends at Le Four de Paris, near the western edge of the Argonne Forest. It takes the visitor to each of the areas where American fighting occurred and to the monument constructed by the United States Government north of Sommepy to commemorate the achievements of American

German Troops Attacking Village Behind Smoke Screen, July 15, 1918. © G

The operations of the "Lost Battalion" were part of the Meuse-Argonne offensive of the American First Army but because the area concerned is near the west side of the Argonne, and therefore more easily reached from the direction of Reims, the detailed description of them is included in this part of the book.

This chapter also includes a described tour of the American battlefields. The locations of all American operations in the

and French troops who fought in the Champagne region during the World War.

This itinerary differs from those in the preceding chapters in that it does not form a complete loop. Such a change was considered advisable because it is believed this tour will be used mainly by tourists passing through the Champagne region on their way to visit the American Meuse-Argonne or St. Mihiel battlefields or other places still farther to the east.

EARLY in July the French secured information indicating that the next enemy attack would be launched near Reims. As part of the preparations to meet it the American 42d Division was sent to reinforce the French Fourth Army, which was then holding the front line from a point about 7 miles east of Reims to the edge of the Argonne Forest.

General Pétain, the Commander-in-Chief of the French Army, on June 24 had prescribed in considerable detail the plan to be followed in defending against the expected attack. Under this plan the front lines were to be held by but few troops, who were to withdraw in case of a determined assault, and the main defense was to be made at a position, intermediate between the then-existing first and second positions, about 1½ miles from the front line. The preparation for defense of this intermediate position and the existing second position in rear of it was an emergency task requiring immediate attention. Consequently, when the 42d Division arrived all available units were immediately assigned to work to strengthen these two positions.

The 42d Division was attached to the French XXI Corps, which was charged with the defense of that part of the fro[nt] including Perthes-les-Hurlus, Souain an[d] St. Hilaire-le-Grand. (See map page 343[.]) The intermediate position ran just nor[th] of these towns and the second positi[on] about 1 mile south of them. The 4[2d] Division was given the mission of prepa[r]ing for defense and holding that part [of] the second line south of Souain and S[t.] Hilaire, and, in addition, three of i[ts] battalions were placed on the intermedia[te] position in front of those places. A[ll] troops on the intermediate and secon[d] positions were directed to maintain the[ir] ground "in any event and at all costs[."]

The French Intelligence Service di[s]covered further details of the impendin[g] attack, and by July 11 was able to for[e]cast its direction, the frontage it wou[ld] cover and the probable day it woul[d] take place. As a final stroke of goo[d] fortune it was learned during the evenin[g] of July 14, from prisoners captured b[y] the French east of Reims, that th[e] German artillery bombardment woul[d] start about midnight of that day an[d] that the German infantry assault woul[d] be launched several hours later.

Thus forewarned, the French were ab[le] to complete their plans to break up t[he]

German Infantry Mopping Up a Destroyed and Still Burning Village, July 1918. © G

German Anti-Aircraft Battery in Position Near the Champagne Front.   © G

xpected attack. They had previously noved a large quantity of artillery into he sector and, shortly before the German ombardment began, the French and American guns placed an intense bombardment on the German artillery emplacements and assembly points for roops. This caused severe casualties in the hostile ranks and resulted in the replacement of several German units before the infantry assault was even started.

The Germans likewise had concentrated a great mass of artillery for the battle, and soon after midnight on July 4–15 such cannon as had not been put ut of action by the French bombardment deluged the French and American positions with a tremendous concentration of gas and high-explosive shells. While there were many casualties, the osses were much less than in the previous German offensives, as a large part of this ombardment was on the first position rom which most of the French troops had een previously withdrawn.

The few troops manning the front line ad the mission of giving warning of the ttack to the units in the intermediate position and of delaying the enemy as long as possible. They sent back information mainly by telephone, rockets and flares. The story of these men, exposed to almost certain death under the heavy shelling, is an epic of heroism. Among them was a group comprising one officer and 25 men of the 42d Division who were posted ½ mile in front of the main line of resistance to defend an anti-tank gun. This entire group was sacrificed, not one returning to the division after the attack.

The infantry assault began at 3:50 a. m. on a battle front extending east of Reims to Tahure and southwest of Reims to a point about 4 miles east of Château-Thierry. Because the Germans progressed rapidly through the French front line their first reports were highly favorable and reserve troops were rushed forward in the belief that the shock of the initial onslaught had been irresistible.

On the front of the French XXI Corps, the Allied and American artillery was kept informed of the progress of the German infantry attack by watchers in the forward positions. Consequently, the gunners were able to shorten their range progressively so that the German troops from the time the attack started

German Infantry Advancing on the Western Front, 1918. © G

were constantly under a rain of Allied shells, with no shelter available, the French having previously destroyed or made untenable by poison gas all dugouts in front of their intermediate position. Under this deluge of fire the Germans approached the intermediate position where the French and Americans were waiting. They repeatedly attacked that position during the first day, suffering terrific losses, but were everywhere repulsed, except at two places. In those places the hostile troops who penetrated the French and American lines were promptly driven out by counterattacks.

During this fighting six more American infantry companies were sent forward to the intermediate position, now become the front line, and the 150th and 151st Machine Gun Battalions and the artillery brigade of the 42d Division all actively participated in driving the enemy back.

The Germans continued their attacks on some parts of this front on July 16, but made no gains of importance.

In the sector of the French Fifth Army southwest of Reims the Germans on July 15 pushed several divisions across the Marne River and advanced a short dis-

tance in the direction of Epernay. Ha fighting continued there until the 17 when the advance was definitely stoppe

Although this powerful and ambitio drive was made by the enemy in a de perate effort to win the war, it lacked t. quality of surprise which had cha acterized most of the other Germ. attacks of 1918. The Allies not on avoided exposing their men to much the devastating effects of the host: preliminary artillery bombardment, b they fought the battle on a position their own choosing, inflicting hea losses and a serious repulse on the enem

The 42d Division, which suffered mo than 1,600 casualties, was enthusiastical commended by General Gouraud, com manding the French Fourth Army, for i gallant conduct in the defense. It w withdrawn from the line on July 19 pr paratory to moving westward to tal part in the Franco-American offensi against the Marne salient which ha begun with great success the day befor

The exact locations of the infantry uni of the 42d Division are shown on the sket on page 343 and further details of the figh ing will be found in that part of the tex

German 15-cm. Howitzer Battery Firing While Infantry Is Moving Forward, October 1918. ©

2D AND 36TH DIVISIONS WITH THE FRENCH FOURTH
ARMY, SEPTEMBER 29–OCTOBER 28, 1918

THE French Fourth Army, holding most of the front between the Argonne Forest and Reims, attacked on September 26, in conjunction with the northward drive of the American First Army between the Meuse River and the Argonne. By September 30 the Americans east of the Argonne Forest had progressed more than 6 miles, whereas the French Army near Sommepy, after an advance of about 3½ miles, met with desperate resistance just south of Blanc Mont Ridge and were unable to take that position. (See map on page 349.)

On October 2 the 2d Division took over a zone of action north of Sommepy, as part of the French XXI Corps, preparatory to launching an attack against Blanc Mont Ridge. If this ridge could be captured the enemy would be compelled to retire to the Aisne River on the entire French Fourth Army front. The American troops had therefore the most important assignment in the attack and were expected to lead the advance, which they succeeded in doing in a splendid manner.

Prior to the general attack on October 3 the 2d Division, with characteristic

German Airplane Shot Down by American Anti-Aircraft Gun

Blanc Mont Ridge was the key point of the German defenses in the region, being on the last natural defensive line south of the Aisne River, 16 miles away. It had been greatly strengthened by an elaborate system of trenches, underground shelters and barbed-wire entanglements. The capture of the ridge was essential to further progress in the region; so, at the request of the Allied Commander-in-Chief for two American divisions, General Pershing sent the 2d and 36th Divisions from the American First Army to assist the French Fourth Army in its efforts to take the ridge.

energy, captured certain sections of the hostile trenches which were necessary to provide a suitable jump-off line. It formed for the general assault with its Infantry Brigade on the right, to drive forward from the southeast against the eastern end of Blanc Mont Ridge, and its Marine Brigade on the left, to strike the western part of the ridge from the south.

Early on October 3 the 2d Division jumped off and in spite of desperate resistance within three hours had the crest of Blanc Mont Ridge firmly in its grasp. The French divisions on its flanks were left far behind. The one on

German Machine-Gun Emplacement, Blanc Mont
Ridge, Captured by the 2d Division,
October 3, 1918

its left made no progress, and the western slopes of Blanc Mont remained in the possession of the Germans. This enabled them to keep up a deadly enfilade fire against the 2d Division, and the Marine Brigade was compelled to deploy part of its forces facing to the west to cover that exposed flank. While facing in that direction these American units repulsed a determined German counterattack.

During the afternoon the Infantry Brigade again pushed forward. It reached a point about 1 mile from St. Etienne-à-Arnes where it remained that night with its flanks temporarily unsupported.

The deep advance of the 2d Division on October 3 caused the Germans to initiate at once preparations for a hasty withdrawal to the Aisne River valley.

On October 4 the Marine Brigade pushed its front lines abreast of the Infantry Brigade, while some of its troops continued to hold off the Germans on the left where the French still found it impossible to advance. It attacked again about noon but was not able to hold all of its gains. The Infantry Brigade, after defending its position against a number of vicious

counterattacks early in the mornin[g] launched an assault in the afternoon b[ut] after heavy losses retired to its jump-o[ff] position. The fighting on this day was [of] exceptional severity, the Germans launc[h]ing many counterattacks in an effort [to] regain the ground which they had lost.

During most of October 5 it was nece[s]sary for the 2d Division to wait until t[he] French divisions on its flanks had a[d]vanced farther. The Marine Briga[de] cleared the enemy from the western slo[pe] of Blanc Mont, thus enabling the Fren[ch] troops on that flank to progress, and lat[er] in the day pushed on several hundr[ed] yards in conjunction with them. On t[he] 6th both brigades again moved forward.

The 71st Brigade of the 36th Divisi[on] went into the line with the 2d Divisi[on] during the night of the 6th, and on the 8th the attacks were renewed. St. Etienne-Arnes was captured that day, and sever[al] heavy counterattacks were repulsed.

The 2d Division, except for its artille[ry] brigade and engineer regiment, whi[ch] continued on with the 36th Division, w[as] relieved by that division on October 1[0].

In the operations up to this time the 2[d] Division had lost about 6,300 officers a[nd] men. It had broken into the Germa[n] lines to a depth of about 4 miles, and ha[d] captured over 2,000 prisoners and t[he] vitally important Blanc Mont Ridg[e.] The accomplishments of the 2d Divisi[on] in this operation were responsible for t[he] advance of the entire French Four[th] Army, and for its brilliant exploits it w[as] commended in the highest terms by t[he] French Corps and Army Commander[s.]

German Tanks Disabled on the Western Front. Ⓒ G

German Trench Mortar Detachment in the Assault, July 15, 1918. Ⓒ G

For further details of this 2d Division ghting see pages 351–355 of the itinerary.

The 36th Division, which was entering he front line for the first time, took immediate advantage of the favorable condiions created by the successful advance of he 2d Division, and attacked east of St. Ctienne-à-Arnes on the 10th. After coniderable fighting it made some gains. See the sketch on page 356.)

That evening information was received rom the French XXI Corps, with which he division was serving, that the Germans vere retiring, and the Corps directed a igorous advance. As a result the 36th Division attacked the next morning, and fter overcoming machine-gun resistance, rove the Germans back about 3 miles to eyond Machault. Its aggressive adance, in conjunction with the French, vas continued on the 12th when Dricourt nd Vaux-Champagne were captured. 'he division front line was established hat night on the high ground just to the orth of the latter place. On the 13th the 6th Division again moved forward and hat day took up a defensive position long the canal near the Aisne River.

During the next few days it extended s flanks to take over sectors from French nits leaving the line. On the 18th it was laced under the French XI Corps and on he 23d it assumed control of the front cing the bend of the Aisne in which are ocated Rilly-aux-Oies and Forest Farm. t that point enemy troops had remained outh of the Aisne River and had organ-

(335)

ized a strong position across the base of the bend which a French division had assaulted unsuccessfully on October 16.

On the afternoon of October 27 the division attacked that position, drove the Germans beyond the river and organized its line north of Forest Farm.

The operations of the division, which were begun in the vicinity of St. Etienne-à-Arnes about 12 miles to the south, were terminated on October 28, and on that date the division passed into reserve, having lost close to 1,100 men. (For further details consult pages 355–357.)

This successful operation was the only one in which the 36th Division participated, although when the Armistice was signed it was again preparing to enter the battle line as part of the American Second Army for an attack near the Moselle.

German Troops Combatting Tanks With Flame Throwers, October 1918. Ⓒ G

369TH, 371ST AND 372D INFANTRY REGIMENTS
93D DIVISION WITH THE FRENCH FOURTH ARMY
SEPTEMBER 26–OCTOBER 8, 1918

WHEN the French Fourth Army advanced northward in the Champagne region on September 26, three infantry regiments of the American 93d Division [1] were serving in that Army as integral parts of French divisions. These French divisions were with the French IX Corps, which attacked from a position on the battle front lying a few miles to the west of the Argonne Forest.

The 369th Infantry had entered this general area on April 8 with the French 16th Division and was slightly engaged on July 15 during the German offensive of that date. Reassigned to the French 161st Division it was in support when the attack of September 26 started. (See the map on page 359.) On that day it entered a gap in the line, took the town of Ripont, captured a number of prisoners and several pieces of artillery, and continued forward during the 27th and the 28th. On the latter day it gained a foothold on the side of the Bellevue Signal Ridge after a stubborn fight.

On October 28 the 371st and 372d Infantry Regiments entered the line as part of the French 157th Division and attacked at once, advancing about 600 yards against machine-gun resistance.

During the morning of September 29 the 371st Infantry captured Ardeuil and Montfauxelles and the 372d made an unsuccessful assault against Séchault from the west. Although patrols entered the

[1] The units of the 93d Division were composed of colored troops from all sections of the United States.

town the units of the regiment became so intermingled that it was withdrawn for reorganization. The town of Séchault was finally taken that afternoon by the 369th, in an attack launched from the heights to the south of it.

On September 30 the 369th Infantry advanced about ½ mile and was relieved from the line that night, after having suffered heavy casualties. On the same date the 371st captured Trières Farm.

On October 1 the 372d Infantry relieved the 371st and on October 2 advanced about ¾ mile to a point south of Monthois where it was subjected to enfilade fire from the high ground to the southwest of that town. It repulsed a strong enemy counterattack on the 5th and held its position about ½ mile south of the village of Monthois until it was relieved on October 7.

All three regiments won the praise of the French authorities for their conduct in the attack. The 369th Infantry suffered 785 casualties during the fighting in this region and the 371st and 372d Infantries, 882 and 579, respectively.

For further details of the operations of these regiments consult pages 358–360.

While this fighting was going on, the other infantry regiment, the 370th, of the 93d Division was serving with a French division northeast of Soissons.

Soon after October 8 these three regiments of the 93d Division entrained with their French divisions to enter sectors of the front line in the Vosges Mountains

Troops of the 369th Infantry, 93d Division,
in the Front-Line Trenches

ON October 2 the 77th Division, attacking northward in the Argonne Forest as the left division of the I Corps and American First Army, encountered heavy resistance and made little progress except in the zone of action of the 308th Infantry. Six companies of that regiment and parts of two companies of the 306th Machine Gun Battalion, which were operating under orders to proceed without regard to the progress on their flanks, penetrated the enemy lines by following a small valley and established themselves, just before dark, on the northern slope of the ravine to the east of Charlevaux Mill. (See map page 363.) Communication had been maintained with the troops in rear during the day, and late in the evening one company of the 307th Infantry succeeded in moving forward to join this advanced force in the ravine.

The Germans, however, pushed troops between the main body of the division and these companies, with the result that by daybreak on October 3 the companies were completely surrounded.

This little force, holding a position about ½ mile in advance of the front line of the division, was subjected to repeated assaults and exposed to incessant machine-gun and minenwerfer fire from all sides. Food was exhausted on the second day, water could be procured only with difficulty from the muddy creek, which was exposed to hostile fire, and suffering from hunger and thirst became more and more acute. Ammunition soon became scarce and to defend themselves the men in the position were forced to salvage rifles and ammunition from the German dead. The Air Service did not succeed in its attempts to deliver messages or to drop food, medical supplies and ammunition into the position, and the efforts of the 77th Division to push forward to relieve its isolated troops were also unsuccessful. Disdaining any thought of surrender, however, the detachment maintained its unequal fight day and night.

Finally, on October 7, the right of the American I Corps launched an attack from the east against the flank and rear of the hostile position in the Argonne Forest and at the same time the 77th Division renewed its attacks.

This flanking movement forced the Germans to withdraw, and that evening the troops of the 77th Division advancing from the south rescued the "Lost Battalion", which that afternoon had beaten off the last and fiercest attack against it.

When relieved on the night of October 7, after having been cut off for five days and nights, only about one third of the more than 600 men who had entered the position were able to walk from it.

The American First Army at the time this operation started was engaged in the Meuse-Argonne offensive and, in the Argonne Forest, was facing the German second position, a strongly-organized defensive line. The "Lost Battalion" penetrated that line at a place temporarily unoccupied by German troops. When reoccupied by the Germans the defenses were so strong that, in spite of the greatest efforts, the 77th Division could not break through until the flank attack of the I Corps forced the enemy to retire.

For additional information concerning this "Lost Battalion", refer to pages 362–365 of the itinerary in this chapter.

Scene of the "Lost Battalion", 77th Division, in the Argonne Forest
The American troops occupied the slope below the road identified by the white gash
on the hillside near the right side of the picture

N September 26 the connecting force
between the French Fourth Army,
cking northward from the Champagne
t, and the American First Army,
cking from the Meuse-Argonne front,
composed of the 368th Infantry, 92d
sion,[1] and the French 11th Cuiras-
-à-pied, and operated under the com-
d of the French 1st Cavalry Division
mounted) which was the right ele-
t of the French XXXVIII Corps.
nese units went into line on September
The next day part of the 368th
ntry advanced about 1 mile but with
exception of one company which spent
night about 200 yards in front of its
ing point, the rest of the units re-
l during the evening to behind their
o-off positions. (See map on page 366.)
n the 27th the connecting force moved
ard an average distance of 1 mile,
untering little opposition.
n the 28th the 368th Infantry, re-
ced by two companies of the 351st
hine Gun Battalion of the 92d Divi-
French artillery units and a squadron
e French 10th Dragoons, attacked in
direction of Binarville and although
iderable movement backward and for-
l took place during the day the total
nd gained was quite small.
e American First Army placed the
inder of the 92d Division, less its
lery, engineers and 183d Brigade, at
disposal of the French XXXVIII
s on September 29. The corps re-
d the width of the zone of action of
368th Infantry at that time and the
nent spent most of the day in rear-
ing and reorganizing its units.
n the 30th a French regiment, the 9th
assiers-à-pied, was directed to cap-
Binarville. Seeing this unit advanc-
and having failed to receive the
rs to stand fast which had been sent
ements of the 368th attacked with

e 92d Division was composed of colored soldiers
various parts of the United States and all of the
ny officers of the 368th Infantry were colored.

the French. Binarville was captured and
the front line was established beyond it.

During the morning of October 1 the
American regiment was relieved from the
front line, and it passed into reserve with
other organizations of the 92d Division.

The division was returned to the con-

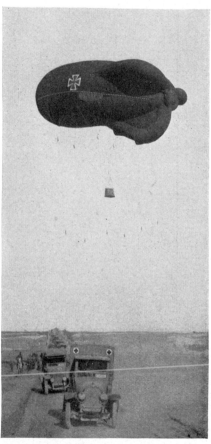

German Balloon Detachment Advancing Along
Road, 1918. © G

trol of the American First Army on
October 4, after having suffered casualties
which totaled 270 officers and men.

For further information of the fighting
of this detachment consult pages 366–367.

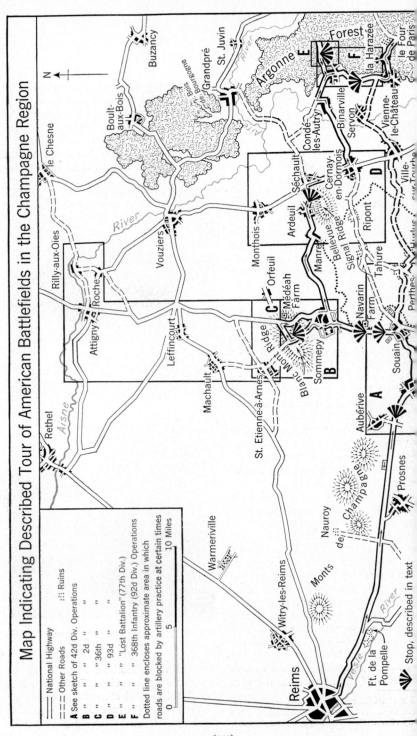

Map Indicating Described Tour of American Battlefields in the Champagne Region

National Highway
Other Roads
Ruins
A See sketch of 42d Div. Operations
B " " 2d " "
C " " 36th " "
D " " 93d " "
E " " "Lost Battalion" (77th Div.)
F " " 368th Infantry (92d Div.) Operations

Dotted line encloses approximate area in which roads are blocked by artillery practice at certain times

0   5   10 Miles

Stop, described in text

A TOUR OF THE AMERICAN BATTLEFIELDS
IN THE CHAMPAGNE REGION

HIS tour begins at Reims and ends at Le Four de Paris. It is 68 miles (109 meters) long and can be completed in hours if care is taken not to spend too h time at the interesting points. he described tour is only slightly ter in mileage than the direct route ss the area, and for that reason it is following this tour and it should be read by the tourist before he starts on his trip.

The mileage figures in the text are given merely as an aid to the reader and are not essential in following the itinerary.

When following the described route, unless contrary road instructions are specifically given, continue straight ahead.

Reims Cathedral During the War
Note the sandbag protection

ected that it will be used most often by se who cross the region from west to en route to other places. An interest-return road is suggested for those desir-to visit other battlefields in this region le going back toward Reims or Paris. he information which is given on pages -521 will be helpful to those who are

EN ROUTE REIMS CATHEDRAL TO NORTH-WEST OF ST. HILAIRE-LE-GRAND

Speedometer distance is measured from the statue of Joan of Arc which is located on the plaza in front of the cathedral.

(0.0 m 0.0 km) **With automobile facing cathedral, set speedometer to read zero.**

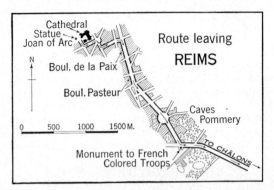

Leave plaza by street to the right front and follow the route to the exit of town shown on the above sketch.

(1.5 m 2.4 km) **Near edge of town, at road junction where street ends,** is located a small monument to the colored troops who fought in the French Armies.

(4.3 m 6.9 km) **Beyond town, after crossing railroad, on the sky line just to the right of the road ahead** are seen the battered ruins of the Fort de la Pompelle, a French fort built many years before the World War for the defense of Reims. It was captured by the Germans early in September 1914 and recaptured by the French soon thereafter. During the fighting in 1918 it was encircled by the German troops but not captured. Severe fighting took place all around it.

Across the road from the fort is a monument to the defenders of this part of the front during the World War.

At road junction near fort, close to the right side of the road, is one of a number of small markers erected at various points along the roads of France and Belgium to indicate the line from which the German forces were hurled back by the Allied Armies in the summer and fall of 1918.

(5.6 m 9.0 km) **At the road junction near Fort de la Pompelle, bear to the left.**

(6.1 m 9.8 km) **Beyond junc** about ½ mile, alongside the **r** are seen (1937) the remains large British tank. It was tured by the Germans in Pica used by them here on July in their last great offensive, put out of action at this spo French artillery fire.

The road for the next 14 n follows the trace of an old Ro road and for the greater pa the next 20 miles was eithe or just in rear of the French f line during most of the war. For a l part of the way a trench followed the side of it. Many traces of other A and German trenches are still vi (1937) in the fields along this road.

(6.3 m 10.2 km) **To the right and r rear in the distance** is seen the Monta de Reims. It is a high wooded plat forming a very strong natural defen position, and was the main objectiv the last great German offensive. portant French observation posts v located along its near edge.

(10.8 m 17.4 km) **About 4½ n farther on, while approaching main cr roads, to the left front** are seen shattered crests of the Monts de Ch pagne. These were in the hands of Germans until April 1917 when a ger French attack launched from near road pushed the enemy from them.

The French Government is attemptir preserve there a number of trenches, con machine-gun emplacements and tun To visit some of them, turn left at next c road toward Nauroy and proceed to high crest. Length of detour—3 m Time required—30 minutes.

(11.4 m 18.4 km) **Just before reac the main crossroads, to the left along the road,** are seen two small markers,

Fort de la Pompelle, Part of the Eastern Defenses of Reims

:ating the farthest advance of the man Armies in this region during 1918 the other commemorating the 27th ntry Regiment of the French Army. 2.8 m 20.6 km) **The next village seen e right** is Prosnes. At its near edge en a small monument which commem- es a French infantry regiment.

6.7 m 26.9 km) **About 4 miles farther along left side of road,** is seen a large d War cemetery, containing in differ- sections the bodies of 6,424 French, 'olish and 5,333 German dead.

7.1 m 27.5 km) **2½ miles to the left is road** is located the scene of the by the French 366th Infantry, 132d sion, IV Corps, French Fourth y, about 8:00 o'clock on the evening ily 14 which resulted in the capture ' prisoners from whom were obtained time schedule and other priceless mation concerning the great Ger-

man offensive which was made later that same night along this entire battle front.

(19.0 m 30.6 km) **Beyond next main crossroad, about 200 yards, just over the first slight crest, STOP.**

Face down the road, which direction is approximately east.

The last large German offensive of the war which was launched on July 15, was stopped in this vicinity with terrific losses to the attacking forces.

The tourist has now reached that part of the front where elements of the American 42d Division fought. The operations of that division have been previously described in this chapter. The following should be read with that description in mind and with frequent references to the map of the 42d Division operations which appears at the bottom of this page.

The intermediate position selected to be defended at all costs against the

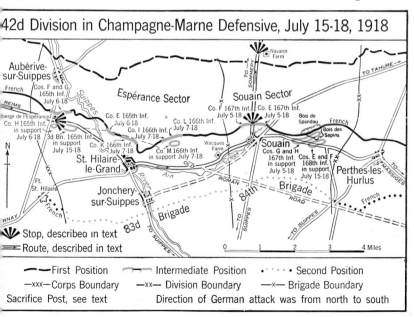

42d Division in Champagne-Marne Defensive, July 15-18, 1918

German Assault Detachment Advancing Under Enemy Fire During the Attack of
July 15, 1918. © G

expected German attack included this road near here. The forward trench of the position ran approximately parallel to this road about 300 yards away to the left. Some of the support trenches were along this road and others approximately 150 yards to the right of it.

One battalion of the 42d Division held a sector here, about ½ mile long, with two companies in the forward line and one company in support in the trench system just to the right of this point. The remaining company of this battalion held a position in the forward line about 1½ miles away in the direction the tourist is facing. Another battalion was in the position defending St. Hilaire-le-Grand, about 2 miles to the right front but invisible from here, and still another was near the village of Souain, which is passed through later in the tour.

During the night of July 14–15 the excitement at this point was intense. With full knowledge of the German plans the American and French artillery, located a mile or more to the right of this road, opened fire about 11:20 p. m. upon the German masses forming for the attack. Exactly on scheduled time, 12:10 a. m., the German artillery commenced firing. Some of its fire was directed against the positions here but most of it pounded the trenches and wire of the first line, which ran about 1½ miles away, beyond Aubérive-sur-Suippes, seen to the left, and along the top of the ridge seen to the left front. As that line had been practically abandoned, except for the

so-called "sacrifice posts", much of German fire which fell upon it was was

At 3:50 a. m. the German infa assault was launched, this fact b signalled to those near here by roc sent up by men in the "sacrifice po who then attempted to disorganize first enemy assault waves by macH gun fire while retreating slowly to lines near here. At that time the A ican soldiers near this point prep to receive the assault, but so effec was the delay caused by the small p in the front line that it was not shortly before 8:00 a. m. that the Ger troops succeeded in reaching the posi just to the left of this road. The waves were beaten off and by 10:00 a the French and Americans in this vici had repulsed, with terrific losses the Germans, seven separate assa About 11:00 a. m. the attack lost impetus and the enemy was compe to withdraw for reorganization.

Further attacks by the enemy in afternoon and early evening were pulsed, and during the night and battalion of the 42d Division was forward to support the lines near It took up a position in trenches run immediately along the right side of road with the center of the batt approximately 800 yards ahead.

At 10:30 a. m. on July 16, after h artillery preparation, the Germans newed their efforts to break through line near St. Hilaire. In spite of peated attacks, however, continued

p. m., their assaults were everywhere
ᴧlsed with severe losses. These at-
ᴋs were probably launched in an
ᴧt to conceal from the Allies the
ᴧsiveness of the defeat suffered by the
ᴧman Armies on the previous day and
ᴧ marked the end of the German
ᴧmpts to advance on this front.

ᴧn July 16 and 17 American and
ᴧch patrols operated as far as the
ᴧer French first line, then held by the
ᴧmans, and on the morning of July 18
ᴧ American troops made a successful
ᴧ on a German position to the left of
ᴧ as a result of which information and
ᴧmber of prisoners were secured.

ᴧn July 19 the 42d Division was
ᴧved from the trenches on this front,
ᴧparatory to moving westward to join
ᴧ fighting in the Aisne-Marne region.

ᴧhe headquarters of the 42d Division
ᴧng the operations on July 15 and 16
ᴧ located at Crête Niel about 6 miles
ᴧy to the right of this road.

ᴧrom here to Souain the intermediate
ᴧtion from which the German attack
ᴧ repulsed ran approximately parallel
ᴧhe road followed by the tour. It was
ᴧted from ¼ to ¾ mile to the left of it.

ROUTE NORTHWEST OF ST. HILAIRE TO
THE NAVARIN FARM MONUMENT

ᴧ1.5 m 34.6 km) **In the next village,**
Hilaire-le-Grand, immediately beyond
church, turn to the left.

ᴧn July 15 and 16 the troops of the
ᴧ Division played a prominent rôle
ᴧ the defense of St. Hilaire-le-Grand.

(23.8 m 38.3 km) **Approximately ¾**
mile to the right of this road was located
the second position, organized and held
by the greater part of the 42d Division.
That position was heavily shelled during
the attack but no active fighting took
place there as the Germans were unable
to force their way through the intermediate position to the left of this road.

Beyond next town, Souain, on road to
Tahure are a monument and cemetery of
the French Foreign Legion, the funds for
which were furnished by an American. It
is easily reached and well worth seeing.
To visit, turn right at church in Souain,
cross creek and then turn left. At road
fork near edge of town take left-hand branch
and proceed about 1 mile to monument and
cemetery which are on right side of road.
Length of side trip—3 miles. Amount of
time required—30 minutes.

(25.5 m 41.1 km) **Where road ends in**
the next village, Souain, turn left.

(25.7 m 41.4 km) **Beyond town, to the**
left of the road is seen a large World
War military cemetery containing 29,507
French and 13,708 German dead.

(25.9 m 41.7 km) **About 300 yards far-**
ther on, at small crest marked (1937) by
two concrete shelters to the left of the
road, STOP without leaving automobile.

Through this point, running at right
angles to the road and extending about
600 yards on each side of it, were located
trenches held by two companies of the
42d Division from July 15 to 19.

Early on the morning of July 15 when
the isolated groups in the front line,
which were on the ridge 2 miles ahead,

German Assault Against Village After an Artillery Preparation, July 1918. © G

German Artillery and Infantry Observers at
Berry-au-Bac, 1918. © G

retired before the German onslaught the
American troops here were caught by the
full force of the attack. After vigorous
assaults the Germans penetrated the
American lines in this vicinity about 7:50
a. m., but were thrown back at 8:30 a. m.
after vicious hand-to-hand fighting. Further attacks by the enemy during the
afternoon and early evening were so
decisively repulsed that the German
efforts to advance in this vicinity were
not renewed the following day.

The following are verbatim extracts
from an account written by an officer of
an American company in line immediately
to the left of this road:

"Just before midnight . . . our artillery opened up and the sky was red for
miles, at midnight the enemy opened up
with artillery and I could see hundreds of
trench mortar shells being thrown into
the first position where the French were
holding the lines with a skeleton force.
The shelling lasted until just before dawn.
Tanks were heard during the night, these
were put out of action before reaching
our lines. The enemy infantry and light
machine gunners . . . reached our wire
at dawn, some of these broke through into
our trenches but were killed . . . all
attacks were beaten off.

" . . . Some Germans attacked near
the road in French overcoats but were
detected in time. Before the second
attack, the Germans could be plainly
seen coming over the hill and down the
Sommepy-Souain road in the distance in
small groups and moving off to the east
of the road to form. This attack when
it came did not hit our line head on but
struck us on a slant from right to left as

a result of which large numbers of
enemy passed in front of our wire
were exposed to our fire at close ra
One German under officer stood o
little rise out in front of us and gave
signals until he was picked off, the ene
withdrew in good order when the att
ceased. I could see a group on a hill
at a considerable distance send up a ro
signal, a parachute with what appe
to be a triangle suspended from it,
attack ceased shortly after this.

"Our planes brought down a numbe
enemy observation balloons directly
front of us. The enemy planes w
numerous and active. On July 16t
counted 36 Red Nose planes in one
mation which passed over us firing on
trenches with machine guns."

Continue.

(26.2 m 42.2 km) **About 600 y**
farther on, to the right of the road
located Wagram Dugout, occupied by
2d Division Headquarters, October
during the fighting for Blanc Mont Ri

(28.0 m 45.1 km) **On the next hill, at**
large monument with the sculptured gr
on top, seen to the left of road, STOP.

This monument is across the road f
the site of Navarin Farm, which was c
pletely obliterated during the war.
takes its name from that place. F
September 1915 to July 1918 the Ger

A Brigade Headquarters of the 42d Divi
Near Suippes, July 10, 1918

French Monument Near Navarin Farm

nt-line trenches which ran at right gles to the road crossed it at this point. e French front-line trenches were about 0 yards back toward Souain.

The monument, erected by the French, mmemorates the dead of the armies of ampagne. One of the three sculptured ures on top represents an American tomatic rifleman. The inscription mes the American units which fought le by side with the French in this region. In defending against the German of- sive of July 15 the French held their nt-line trenches only lightly and nsequently the main fight in this vicinity s made near Souain at the place where e tourist recently stopped.

After the German attack in July had led, the French lines on this ridge were t reoccupied and their front line was ated about 1¼ miles from here in the rection of Souain. On September 26 e French troops in this vicinity attacked conjunction with the Meuse-Argonne ensive of the American First Army. September 30 they had advanced to yond Sommepy, seen down the road in e valley ahead, where they were held up in front of strong German positions on Blanc Mont Ridge just beyond that town.

The ground in the vicinity of this monu- ment has not been restored and a walk around it will prove most interesting.

On a clear day the square tower of the American monument, on the ridge beyond Sommepy, can be seen on the sky line by looking in a direction some distance to the left of that followed by the road ahead.

EN ROUTE NAVARIN FARM MONUMENT TO
AMERICAN MONUMENT NORTH OF
SOMMEPY

In the next village, Sommepy, under the church are (1937) German dugouts which were used by the American 2d Division Headquarters, October 6–10, and by the 36th Division Headquarters, October 10– 12. The town hall of the village was reconstructed with funds raised by a committee of American women.

(30.3 m 48.8 km) **In Sommepy, after crossing the railroad, when church steeple is seen to the LEFT front, turn left.**

(30.6 m 49.3 km) **At the road junction about ⅓ mile farther on, turn to the left.**

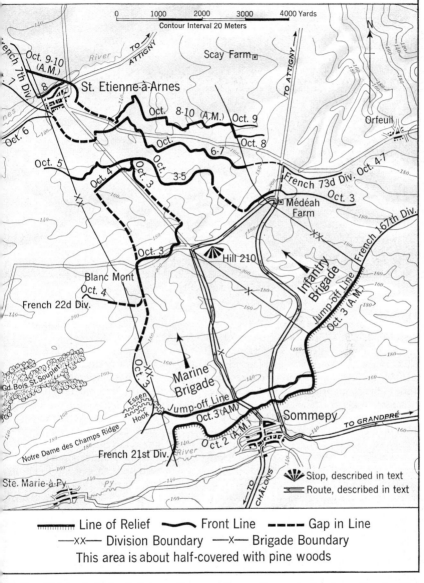

2d Division with French Fourth Army, Oct. 2-10, 1918
(71st Brigade, 36th Division, Attached October 6-9)

0   1000   2000   3000   4000 Yards
Contour Interval 20 Meters

Scay Farm

Oct. 9-10 (A.M.)

French 7th Div.

St. Etienne-à-Arnes

Oct. 6

Oct. 5

Oct. 8-10 (A.M.)

Oct. 9

Orfeuil

Oct. 8

Oct. 6-7

Oct. 4

Oct. 3

Oct. 3-5

French 73d Div. Oct. 4-7

Oct. 3

Médéah Farm

French 167th Div.

Hill 210

Blanc Mont Oct. 4

French 22d Div.

Infantry Brigade

Jump-off Line Oct. 3 (A.M.)

Gd.Bois St.Souplet

Oct. 3

Marine Brigade

Jump-off Line Oct. 3 (A.M.)

Essen Hook

Oct. 3 (A.M.)

Sommepy

TO GRANDPRÉ

Oct. 2 (A.M.)

Notre Dame des Champs Ridge

French 21st Div. River

Ste. Marie-à-Py   Py

TO CHÂLONS

Stop, described in text
Route, described in text

Line of Relief   Front Line   ---- Gap in Line
—xx— Division Boundary —x— Brigade Boundary
This area is about half-covered with pine woods

(31.1 m 50.1 km) **A short distance far-
er on, near the left side of road,** is seen a
Division boulder marker. It is located
ar the right flank of the jump-off line of
e Marine Brigade early on October 3.

Down the road ahead on the sky line
can be seen the American monument on
a high point of Blanc Mont Ridge.
(31.2 m 50.3 km) **To the left of the
road** is seen a fine view of the ground

American Memorial Near Sommepy
Commemorating the Fighting in the Champagne Region

advanced over by the Marine Brigade on October 3. The direction of advance of the brigade was approximately parallel to that which the tourist is now traveling.

(33.2 m 53.3 km) **At next crossroads, turn to the right, proceed to the site of the monument and STOP.**

This monument was erected by the United States Government to commemorate the achievements of her soldiers and those of France who fought in this region during the World War. It stands on the crest of Blanc Mont Ridge which was captured by the American 2d Division on October 3, after terrific fighting.

The memorial has the form of a tower and its sturdy, though graceful, shape harmonizes with the bleak and desolate landscape. The golden brown stones, of different shades, give an unusually attractive effect to the exterior and the monument as a whole is representative of a fine type of American architecture.

Between the road and the monument is a German trench and beyond it in the open field are the entrances to seve German dugouts. The neighborhood co tains many trenches and other indicatic of the war. A walk in the vicinity v prove to be most interesting.

On the exterior walls of the monume are carved the dedicatory inscription a the names of the American divisic which the monument commemorat their insignia, the inclusive dates tl they served in this region and four pla where each division had hard fighting.

The tower is now (1937) open to visit only on Sundays. Inside the door, o stone panel visible through the bro grille, is a brief description of the Am ican operations in the vicinity.

The following details of the fighting written to be read from the top of tower. If read from the lower terr a large part of the description will be cl and many of the places can be identifi

The direction arrows on the upper p apet walls will be of help in locating places mentioned on the following pag

The American monument on Mont-
con, 27 miles away, can be seen when
atmospheric conditions are favorable.
Climb tower, go to side of terrace over
rance door and face out with line of
on at right angles to the parapet wall.
Sommepy is in the valley ahead.

f the tourist is not familiar with the
ount of the operations of the 2d and
h Divisions, given previously in this
pter, it should now be read.

This monument is near the center of
dominating Blanc Mont Ridge. The
ge is crescent-shaped, Blanc Mont be-
that end about 1 mile away to the
nt and Hill 210 the end about the same
tance to the left front. On an offshoot
this ridge was located Médéah Farm,
ich is about 1 mile to the left.

The ridge has great natural defensive
ength due to its height above the sur-
nding country and the many wooded

ription on the American Sommepy Memorial

Entrance to the American Memorial
Near Sommepy

and cleared places on its summit. The
chalky character of its soil made the construction of field fortifications comparatively easy and many trenches, dugouts
and obstacles had been constructed.

The offensive of the French Fourth
Army, which started on September 26
from a line about 1 mile beyond the
location of the Navarin Farm monument,
the pyramid-shaped monument seen to
the right of and beyond Sommepy, was
shattered against the German positions
at the foot of this ridge. The repeated
French assaults were without avail and
the French advance had been definitely
stopped when the American 2d Division
on October 2 took over the front line
just this side of Sommepy.

A general offensive was fixed for October 3. The 2d Division's task was to
force the enemy from this ridge and thus
open the way for the French Fourth
Army to advance to the Aisne River,
about 14 miles to the rear of the observer.

The division plan of attack, though
hurriedly drawn, was cleverly conceived.
An assault was not ordered for its entire
front, but the Marine Brigade was directed to advance from the low ridge seen just
this side of and to the right of Sommepy,
and the Infantry Brigade was directed to
jump off from a line just beyond the far
edge of the wood seen to the left of front.
The direction of advance of this last
attack was directly against the eastern
end of Blanc Mont Ridge and then along
it. The zones of action of the two attacks

Tank Preparing the Way for a German Assault, September 1918. © G

converged at the crossroads seen to the right rear near this monument. No assault was made from this side of Sommepy thus avoiding a frontal attack against a very strong part of the ridge.

The attack was launched at 5:50 a. m. on October 3, after a brief but heavy artillery bombardment. It was accompanied by tanks and was preceded up these slopes by an artillery barrage. The Infantry Brigade found its jump-off line, which was in the zone of action of a French division, occupied by Germans who had made a local attack and had advanced there the day before. In spite of this and heavy enemy shellfire, the assault units lined up farther to the rear and attacked with overpowering force on scheduled time. Hill 210 was soon captured and the advance progressed rapidly along the ridge. By 8:30 a. m. the brigade objective, that part of the road in rear of the observer extending to the left from here as far as Médéah Farm, was reached and a defensive position along it was promptly organized.

The Marine Brigade, attacking from the right of Sommepy, drove forward vigorously and about 8:30 a. m. reached its objective, that part of the road in rear of the observer from the crossroads near here to the right as far as Blanc Mont. Its greatest troubles then began, as the French division alongside it had made no appreciable gain and the brigade flank, about 1 mile to the observer's right, was 2 miles ahead of the French line and entirely exposed. The Germans, realizing the critical situation of the unit, drove in heavily against the exposed flank but

were repulsed with severe losses b company on that flank which had pr ously faced in the direction of the obs er's right in preparation for such a c tingency. Other support units face that direction also and thus filled the v gap which had existed in the line.

To the right front, just to the righ the line of the direction arrow poin out St. Hilaire, is the high, parti wooded ridge called Notre Dame Champs, which was holding up the Fre On the left end of that ridge was a po ful German position called Essen H That strong point had been unsucc fully attacked by the French several tir the last attack having been repulsed the Germans early on October 3. Du the morning of October 3 the posi was taken by the marines in a flank tack and turned over to a French divis which lost it later in the day when German troops counterattacked.

Go to opposite side of terrace.

St. Etienne-à-Arnes is the village wl is seen to the left front.

The 2d Division at 2:00 p. m. on O ber 3 ordered an advance from its ne won positions along the road runnin front of here. The marine units, in beyond the road junction seen to the l between 6:00 and 7:00 p. m. received order to attack but being heavily enga on the division's left flank the batta commanders agreed among themselve attack early the next morning. The fantry Brigade, in front of and to right of here, jumped off late in the af noon of the 3d and advanced more tha mile, well beyond the units on each sid

In spite of its precarious position th both flanks exposed, the brigade naciously held to its gains.

At the end of its first day of attack the est of Blanc Mont Ridge was firmly in e grasp of the 2d Division and both of s flanks were far ahead of the adjoining rench units. Its main mission had been complished and as a result the German igh Command that day decided to reeat to the Aisne River on all the Champagne battle front. This decision caused) great change in the severity of the ghting in this region as from then on ie Germans fought even more desperely to gain time to make the withdrawal good order and thus avoid excessive sses of men, supplies and matériel.

Illustrative of the aggressive spirit and eroism of the individual soldier during ie intense fighting on October 3 are the eeds for which Corporal John H. Pruitt, rivate First Class Frank J. Bart and rivate John Joseph Kelly of the 2d Division were awarded Congressional Medals f Honor, the highest award given by the nited States Government for bravery.

Corporal Pruitt of the Marine Brigade ttacked singlehanded two machine guns, cated not far from the site of this monument. He captured them, killed two of he enemy, and then captured 40 prisoners in a dugout near by. This gallant oldier was killed soon afterward by shellre while sniping at the enemy.

Private Bart of the Infantry Brigade vas on duty as a company runner when he advance was held up by machine-gun re not far from Médéah Farm. He voluntarily picked up an automatic rifle, ran ut ahead of the line, and silenced a hosile machine-gun nest, killing the German unners. The advance then continued nd when it was again hindered shortly fterwards by fire from another machineun nest this courageous soldier repeated is bold exploit by putting the second machine gun out of action.

Private Kelly of the Marine Brigade, vhile his unit was attacking a German osition between here and Sommepy, ran hrough the American barrage 100 yards in advance of the front line and attacked an enemy machine-gun nest, killing the gunner with a grenade, shooting another member of the crew with a pistol and returning through the barrage with eight prisoners which he had captured.

The dangerous position of the Infantry Brigade, whose front line about halfway between here and St. Etienne formed a deep salient into the German lines during the night of October 3–4, was somewhat relieved when the Marine Brigade attacked at 6:00 a. m. on October 4 and moved up abreast of it. Early in the morning, however, the Infantry Brigade had withstood fierce German counterattacks against its flanks, launched from the vicinity of Médéah Farm and from St. Etienne.

That afternoon the attack was renewed on the entire front of the division. In front of here the Infantry Brigade advanced at 2:30 p. m. but came under severe machine-gun fire from German positions along the road joining St. Etienne with Orfeuil, seen to the right, and was forced to retire after severe losses.

The Marine Brigade attacked about noon toward St. Etienne and reached the edge of the wood on this side of the town before it was stopped. During the afternoon a counterattack against its left flank was repulsed. The gains made during the afternoon were not held as the advanced troops, after suffering heavily from hostile machine-gun and shell fire, were forced to fall back. Meanwhile, the marine units facing to the left at the end of Blanc Mont Ridge had beaten off two determined German counterattacks.

Men of the 42d Division at a Dugout Near the Second-Line Trenches Northwest of Suippes, July 10, 1918

Most of the German assaults on this day were determined, carefully planned attacks to regain the high ground between here and St. Etienne.   Many of them collided with 2d Division attacks and thus the area became one great maelstrom of violence.   Reports of 2d Division officers speak of this day's fighting as the most severe in their experience.

The line organized by the 2d Division on the night of October 4–5 was about half way from here to St. Etienne.   The left flank of the division was far ahead of the adjoining French unit.

During the day, the French division on the right had advanced about 700 yards beyond Médéah Farm.   On the left the French had moved forward in the 2d Division zone of action and attacked to the west (observer's left) forcing the Germans to evacuate all of the Notre Dame des Champs Ridge, which was recently pointed out to the left rear.

On October 5 the 2d Division ordered an attack which was only to be launched when the French units came up on the flanks.   Due to the withdrawal of the German troops to the left of here, the French advanced during the day and the Marine Brigade attacked in the afternoon, moving forward several hundred yards.   Other local fighting took place in the 2d Division zone of action but no further changes in the front line occurred.

On October 6 the division advanced its lines about 700 yards all along its front, the heaviest fighting taking place just this side of St. Etienne.   During that night, a brigade of the American 36th Division took over all of the 2d Division front line except that held by two of its battalions.   No attacks were made on the 7th by American units.

Early on October 8 an attack, accompanied by tanks and a heavy artillery barrage, was launched on the entire division front.   It was opposed by severe artillery and machine-gun fire, and the fighting waged fiercely in St. Etienne and just beyond the St. Etienne–Orfeuil road during most of the day.   Two strong German counterattacks were repulsed and

by that night St. Etienne had been captured by a marine battalion still in the line, and the division front line had been advanced an average distance of 600 yards.   On the right the French came up alongside the American division.

It was during this fighting near St. Etienne that there occurred the deeds, indicative of the fine spirit and bravery of the 36th Division, for which Corporal Samuel M. Sampler and Private First Class Harold L. Turner were awarded Congressional Medals of Honor.

Corporal Sampler's company having suffered severe casualties from enemy machine-gun fire was finally stopped.   Corporal Sampler discovered the location of the hostile machine guns on an elevation, and armed with German hand grenades which he had picked up, he rushed forward in the face of heavy enemy fire until he was near the guns, where he threw his grenades into the hostile position.   His third grenade landed among the enemy, killing two of them, silencing the machine guns, and causing the surrender of 28 German soldiers, whom he sent to the rear as prisoners.   As a result of his courageous act the company was enabled to resume the advance immediately.

After Private Turner's platoon had started the attack, he assisted in organizing a platoon consisting of the battalion scouts, runners and a detachment of Signal Corps troops.   As second in command of this platoon he fearlessly led them forward through heavy enemy fire, continually encouraging the men.   Later deadly machine-gun fire was encountered which reduced the strength of his command to four men, and forced these to take shelter.   The enemy machine-gun emplacement, 25 yards distant, kept up a continual fire from four machine guns.   After the fire had shifted momentarily, Private Turner rushed forward with fixed bayonet and charged the position alone, capturing the strong point, 50 German soldiers and the four machine guns in it.   His remarkable display of courage and fearlessness was largely instrumental in enabling his company to continue its advance.

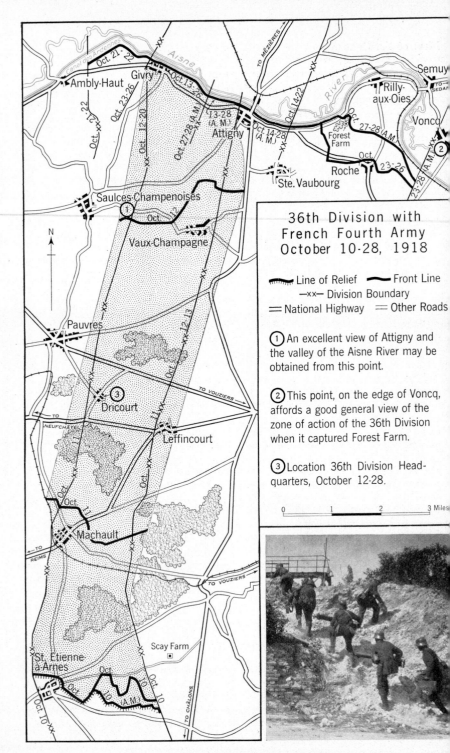

Canal des Ardennes
Oct. 21-22
Oct. 13-26
Aisne
TO MÉZIÈRES
River
Semuy
TO SEDAN
Ambly-Haut
Givry
Oct. 23-26
Oct. 12-20
Oct. 12-22
13-28
(A. M.)
Oct. 27-28 (A.M.)
Oct. 14-22
Rilly-aux-Oies
Attigny
Oct. 14-28
(A. M.)
Vonca
Oct. 27-28 (A.M.)
Oct. 23-28 (A.M.)
2
Forest
Farm
Ste. Vaubourg
Oct.
Roche
Oct. 23-26

Saulces-Champenoises
1
Oct.
Vaux-Champagne

N

Oct. 12-13

Pauvres

TO VOUZIERS

3
Dricourt

TO
NEUFCHÂTEL

Oct. 11

Leffincourt

Oct. 11

Oct.

Oct. 11

Machault

TO
REIMS

TO VOUZIERS

Scay Farm

St. Etienne
a-Arnes
Oct.

Oct. 10

Oct. 10
(A. M.)

Oct. 10

TO CHÂLONS

Oct. 10 xx

36th Division with French Fourth Army October 10-28, 1918

⌒⌒⌒ Line of Relief   ▬▬ Front Line
—xx— Division Boundary
═ National Highway   = Other Roads

① An excellent view of Attigny and the valley of the Aisne River may be obtained from this point.

② This point, on the edge of Voncq, affords a good general view of the zone of action of the 36th Division when it captured Forest Farm.

③ Location 36th Division Head-quarters, October 12-28.

0   1   2   3 Miles

On October 9 some fighting occurred in front of here but no appreciable gains were made. The French were now up with the 2d Division on both flanks.

The 36th Division took command of the zone of action of the 2d Division on October 10. The artillery and engineers of the 2d remained with the 36th Division until that division was relieved.

The importance of the achievements of the 2d Division here can not be overemphasized and too much credit can not be given it. Blanc Mont Ridge was the key to any advance in this region and its capture caused the Germans to start a withdrawal which enabled the entire Fourth Army to move forward.

On the morning of October 10, based on information that the enemy was retreating, the 36th Division was ordered to keep in close contact with the German forces and pursue them vigorously. It attacked that afternoon and reached the road between St. Etienne and Scay Farm, seen to the right front, in the right part of its zone of action. The French were then held up near Scay Farm. The lines near St. Etienne were unchanged.

During the evening of October 10 information was again received that the Germans were withdrawing so the 36th Division ordered its units to start the pursuit at 9:30 a. m. on the following day. Considerable machine-gun resistance was overcome during October 11 but by evening the division was beyond Machault, seen about 5 miles directly ahead.

The pursuit was continued on the 12th when Dricourt and Vaux-Champagne were captured, the division advancing about 7 miles. On the next day the Aisne River, about 14 miles to the right front from here, was reached. The high ground seen on the horizon in that direction is just beyond the river.

After further fighting near the Aisne River the 36th Division was relieved from the line on October 28. Its fine accomplishments in this region are even more creditable when it is considered that the division had been in France but two months, had never served at the front

even in a quiet sector, was separated from its engineer regiment and field artillery brigade, and was critically short of transportation of all kinds.

Before leaving the upper terrace go to the side opposite the stairway leading to this terrace and note the village of Séchault to the right front, 9 miles away. That town and Bellevue Signal Ridge, the wooded nose of land seen to the right of it below the horizon, were the scenes of hard fighting by the infantry regiments of the 93d Division whose zones of action are to be visited later during this tour.

EN ROUTE AMERICAN MONUMENT NORTH OF SOMMEPY TO SOUTHEAST OF ARDEUIL

Continue along road toward the northeast, without retracing route.

This road marked the front line of the 2d Division Infantry Brigade at noon on October 3. On the slopes to the left of it were many German dugouts and shelters built by German troops during the early years of the World War when the battle line was about 5 miles to the right.

At the next road junction was located Médéah Farm. The right of the 2d Division line remained near it from October 3 to 6, in contact with the French.

(34.5 m 55.5 km) **At the road junction near Médéah Farm, turn right.**

(35.5 m 57.2 km) **At the next crest,** the road crosses the eastern end of Blanc Mont Ridge along which the infantry advanced.

(36.4 m 58.6 km) **A short distance beyond the first pronounced right bend in the road,** the tour leaves the zone of action of the 2d Division Infantry Brigade.

(38.1 m 61.3 km) **Upon reaching the next village, Sommepy, turn sharp left toward the village of Manre.**

(39.9 m 64.2 km) **About 1½ miles farther on, to the right** is seen a small monument commemorating two French regiments. A German concrete machine-gun emplacement is located close to it.

(41.9 m 67.5 km) **Beyond the next wood, to the right front on the hillside across the valley** are seen (1937) many traces of German artillery emplacements.

German Infantry Advancing With a Machine Gun, July 1918. © G

(42.1 m 67.8 km) **At the next cross-roads, turn to the right.**

(43.7 m 70.4 km) **Continue through the next village, Manre, toward Séchault.**

There is a fine observation point on the high ridge south of Ardeuil where most of the ground fought over by the regiments of the 93d Division can be seen. For those who are especially interested in that fighting or who wish to enjoy an extensive panorama, turn right at near edge of Ardeuil and follow road toward Gratreuil until top of ridge is reached. Length of detour—2½ miles. Time required—30 minutes.

(45.8 m 73.7 km) **At far side of next village, Ardeuil, turn to the right toward the village of Séchault.**

(46.3 m 74.5 km) **Beyond this turn, about ½ mile farther on along the road, at the first crest, STOP.**

Face down the road, which direction is approximately southeast.

This point is near the middle of the area of operations in the Champagne region of the 369th, 371st and 372d Infantry Regiments of the 93d Division.

The village seen to the left front is Séchault and the high ridge seen ahead to the right of the road is Bellevue Signal Ridge. The direction of advance of the units fighting near here was from the observer's right front to left rear.

If the tourist is not familiar with the account, given earlier in this chapter, of the operations in this region of the regiments of the American 93d Division it should be read at this time.

The near edge of the Argonne Forest is seen on the sky line beyond Séchault.

When the American First Army made its attack on the other side of the Argonne Forest on September 26, the French Fourth Army advanced in this direction from its front line which was then about 4 miles away to the right front.

With this French Army were three infantry regiments of the American 93d Division. These regiments had been incorporated into two French divisions, the 369th being part of the French 161st Division and the 371st and 372d being part of the French 157th Division.

On September 26, when the French 161st Division jumped off, the 369th Infantry was in support. During the day it entered a gap in the front line and captured the town of Ripont, about 3 miles from here, over the ridge to the right front. It continued to advance in this direction until September 28 when, after hard fighting, it established itself on the far side of Bellevue Signal Ridge.

On the 28th the French 157th Division entered the battle line to the right of here and both the 371st and 372d Infantry Regiments were engaged with it in the fighting. Attacking in this direction they advanced about 600 yards to this side of the ridge seen to the right. On that night the 371st was close to the crest of that ridge and the 372d on the near slopes of it. Two companies of the 372d lost direction and became separated from their battalion. Parts of these spent the night just this side of Séchault. Bussy Farm, seen to the right front, was occupied by the 372d Infantry after dark.

The French 161st Division, of which the American 369th Infantry was a part, on the morning of September 29 completed the capture of Bellevue Signal Ridge and the hill, Mont Cuvelet, seen to the left of it. About 2:45 p. m. the 369th Infantry launched an attack from those heights against Séchault and took the town, digging in just beyond it. During this advance the members of the 372d Infantry who had spent the night just this side of town were rescued from their exposed position.

On September 29 the French 157th Division formed at the foot of the slopes seen to the right front for an attack at 10:00 a. m. Part of the 372d Infantry advanced toward Séchault, which was outside the zone of action assigned its division. At 1:00 p.m. patrols of the regiment entered the town but were driven out by hostile machine-gun fire. Later in the day, after the town had been captured by the 369th Infantry, troops of the 372d mopped up part of it. During the evening the 372d was withdrawn from the line and reorganized near Bussy Farm.

The 371st Infantry attacked from near Bussy Farm at 10:00 a. m. on September 29, passed over the ground in rear of here, captured Ardeuil, seen to the rear, and that evening established its front line about 1 mile to the left rear of this point.

On the 30th the 369th attacked in the morning and by afternoon had advanced about ½ mile from

Séchault. During the night it was relieved and moved to Bellevue Signal Ridge where it remained until October 7, when the division to which it was attached was taken out of the front line.

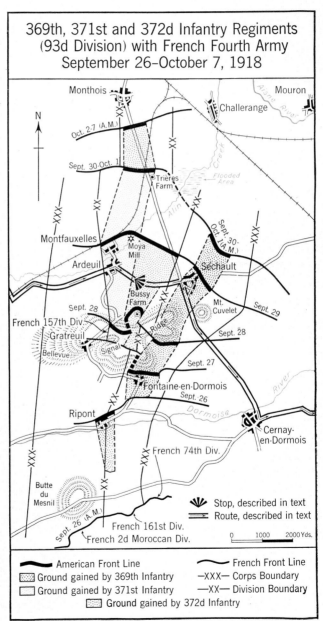

369th, 371st and 372d Infantry Regiments (93d Division) with French Fourth Army September 26–October 7, 1918

remarkable courage and tenacity at critical times, he was the only officer of his battalion who advanced beyond the town, and by clearing out machine-gun and sniping posts he contributed largely to the success of his battalion in holding its objective. His example of bravery and fortitude and his eagerness to continue with his mission despite severe wounds set before the enlisted men of his command an admirable standard of morale and self-sacrifice.

On September 30 the 371st advanced over a mile in the direction to the left rear from here and captured Trières Farm. On October 1 it was relieved by the 372d and reorganized near this point. The 372d advanced about ¾ mile on October 2 and, after repulsing a German attack on the 5th, was relieved from the line on October 7.

On the slopes of the nose of the heights to the right of here is a small

The Balloon Coming Down in F

Observers Dropping From Observation Balloon After Attack by German Aviator

It was during the fighting near Séchault on September 29 and 30 that First Lieutenant George S. Robb of the 369th Infantry performed the deeds for which he was awarded the Congressional Medal of Honor. During the attack he was severely wounded by machine-gun fire while at the head of his platoon. Refusing to go to the dressing station for treatment until ordered to do so, he returned within 45 minutes and remained on duty throughout the day and night, inspecting the lines and establishing outposts. Early the next morning he was again wounded and later that day was struck by fragments of a bursting shell that killed three officers of his company. He at once assumed command and took a leading part in preparing the new position for defense. Displaying

Monument to 371st Infantry Near Ardeuil

nonument, see picture above, to the 371st
nfantry. It is inaccessible by automobile.

EN ROUTE SOUTHEAST OF ARDEUIL TO NORTHEAST OF BINARVILLE

*About 2½ miles north of Séchault along
he main road is located a small monument
o the 372d Infantry. To visit, turn left
oward Monthois at next main crossroads.
Length of detour—5 miles. Amount of
ime required—25 minutes.*

(47.2 m 76.0 km) **At near edge of the
next village, Séchault, turn right.**

(48.3 m 77.8 km) **Beyond next bend in
oad, after passing first crossroad, to the
ight** can be seen the edge of the heights
along which the 369th Infantry fought on
September 27 and 28. The Argonne
Forest can be seen covering the hills on
he sky line to the left front.

(50.3 m 81.0 km) **Just after entering
he next village, Cernay-en-Dormois,
urn to the left.**

(50.9 m 81.9 km) **Beyond the town, at
he first pronounced crest, about 100
yards to the left of the road** are located
(1937) the remains of a number of German concrete battery positions. Although close to the road but little of them

can be seen from it. A visit to these
gun positions will prove most interesting.

(54.8 m 88.2 km) **Continue through
next village, Condé-les-Autry.**

**Beyond town, at first road junction, just
before turning** there is a fine view to the
left rear of the ground recently passed
over on the tour. Bellevue Signal Ridge
can be easily identified.

(55.4 m 89.2 km) **At road junction,
turn to the right.**

(57.2 m 92.1 km) **At next main road
junction, marked by a monument to the
French 9th Cuirassier Regiment, turn
sharply to the left.**

(57.9 m 93.2 km) **Some distance farther on, while descending steep hill, to the
right along the bank** can be seen (1937)
several entrances to former German
shelters and dugouts.

(58.2 m 93.7 km) **At foot of hill, the
pond crossed** is that of Charlevaux Mill.
During the war that part of it to the right
of the road did not exist.

(58.3 m 93.8 km) **Beyond the bridge,
to the right across the valley is soon seen**

Monument to 372d Infantry South of Monthois

the small ravine by means of which the troops of the "Lost Battalion" advanced to this vicinity on October 2.

(58.6 m 94.3 km) **Just beyond the first LEFT bend in the road, at the small stone marked "Lost Battalion", located near the right edge of the road, STOP.**

Face to the right, which direction is approximately south.

This point is in the Argonne Forest. One of the most heroic defenses of the war was made on the steep bank just below where the tourist is now standing.

Road Marker Indicating Site of "Lost Battalion"

If the reader is not familiar with it, he should read the account of the "Lost Battalion", given on page 337 of this chapter. The sketch on the next page should be consulted from time to time.

On October 1 the 77th Division was stopped by a strongly organized German defensive line about ½ mile in front of here and the French troops were held up to the right of here, about ¾ mile northwest of the road junction at which the monument to the French 9th Cuirassier Regiment was recently pointed out.

On the morning of October 2 the 77th Division launched an attack all along its front in an attempt, which proved unsuccessful, to capture the ridge back of here. About noon one of its brigades ordered a second attack with this road as its objective. In that attack the units were directed to push forward without regard to the progress of adjoining units as it had been erroneously reported that the French had made a deep advance north of Binarville and it was believed that the German resistance in front of here was weakening. During the course of this brigade attack, six companies of the 308th Infantry and parts of two companies of the 306th Machine Gun Battalion made a deep advance through an unoccupied portion of the hostile line, the German troops having moved over to repel French attacks on their right. This small American force, meeting little opposition, came into this valley through the ravine, to the right of here, recently pointed out, and about 6:00 p. m. took up a position, which extended from this vicinity about 350 yards to the left, on the slope below the road. This position was immediately organized for all around defense and attempts were made to secure liaison with adjoining troops.

During early evening a battalion of the 307th Infantry attempted to join the force here, but in the darkness the companies lost contact and only one, the leading company, succeeded in advancing through the hostile wire. It took up a position about 300 yards from here, to the right front on the near slope of the hill across the valley, where it remained during the night of October 2 in close communication with the troops on this side.

During the night the enemy troops closed the gap in their line and cut off the American force in this vicinity.

On October 3 all efforts of the 77th Division to relieve its so-called "Lost Battalion" failed. Early that morning the company across the valley moved to this side and took up a position on the left of the force here. Shortly thereafter one company was sent to clear a way back up the ravine which had been followed in reaching this spot. It ran into heavy hostile fire and returned, reporting the gap closed. Shortly thereafter another company crossed the valley to the left of here in an attempt to secure contact with the remainder of its division. This unit was attacked on both flanks with such energy that only with great difficulty was

it able to return. That marked the last attempt of the troops here to fight their way back to the lines of their division.

The position organized by the "Lost Battalion" on the steep slope below here was in the form of an elongated oval more than 350 yards in length, with an average

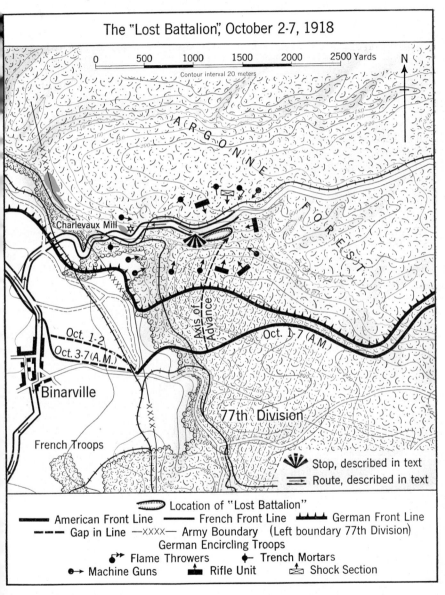

The "Lost Battalion", October 2-7, 1918

width of about 75 yards. The machine gun companies were placed on the flanks. The position had one great advantage in that this slope was so steep that German artillery, located in rear of the observer was unable to fire on the men who occupied it. The force dug in and prepared as best it could to withstand a siege.

During October 3 and 4 homing pigeons were used to send six messages back to division headquarters, giving by map coordinates the exact location of the force and describing its critical situation.

In the meantime, the enemy had completely surrounded the "Lost Battalion". The Germans on the hills to the left and front greeted every movement with rifle fire while heavy machine guns emplaced on the hill to the right front delivered plunging bursts that swept the full length of the American position. Trench mortars, located to the right beyond the mill, and to the rear of the observer, added their fire to the deluge of projectiles which was being poured on the position of this beleagured force.

The food available was equal to but one day's supply for four companies and that was consumed by noon of October 3. There was no medical officer, and medical supplies were scarce. As the starving

Hillside Where the "Lost Battalion" Was Surrounded for Five Days Near Charlevaux Mill

troops were prevented from getting adequate supplies of water by the intense machine-gun fire sweeping the valley, their condition soon became serious.

Airplanes were dispatched with messages and food, but such as were dropped fell each time out of reach. During one of these attempts, Second Lieutenant Harold Ernest Goettler, Air Service, and his observer, Second Lieutenant Erwin R. Bleckley, Field Artillery, were brought down by hostile machine-gun fire from the ground. They were posthumously awarded Congressional Medals of Honor.

For the next four days the 77th Division tried unsuccessfully to break through to its isolated force, which in the meantime was performing prodigies of valor in withstanding the German attacks which were launched against it daily.

On the afternoon of October 7 the Germans sent a captured American soldier to the commander of the "Lost Battalion", with a message advising him to surrender, and stating that a white flag displayed in the American position would be considered as a sign of his intention to do so. This message was answered only by gathering in the white panels which had been used for signalling American airplanes and which lay on the ground at the foot of this slope.

At the time the message was sent, the Germans were on the point of launching a powerful attack, supported by five flame throwers and additional trench mortars. Failing to receive a reply to their message, the Germans placed a terrific trench-mortar bombardment upon the Americans and sprayed them with liquid fire. However, this brave force, summoning all its strength, rose up from its shelters and counterattacked the Germans, killing the operators of the flame throwers and beating off the attack.

This small force of Americans isolated behind the German front line, which refused to surrender and which so persistently avoided capture, was a source of considerable comment among the Germans and in their official communications it was referred to as the "Amerikanernest."

As a result of the successful flank attack by the American I Corps near the edge of the Argonne Forest to the left of here, the Germans were forced on October 7 to withdraw their front line in this vicinity. About 7:00 p. m. troops of the 77th Division, after a sharp fight in overcoming machine-gun resistance, reached this valley and rescued the "Lost Battalion", which in six days had its effective strength reduced from more than 600 to 194 men, all of whom were in a severely weakened condition.

Illustrative of the heroism of this defense are the gallant exploits for which Major Charles W. Whittlesey, the commander of the detachment during the fighting, Captain George G. McMurtry and Captain Nelson M. Holderman were awarded Congressional Medals of Honor.

Major Whittlesey displayed marked ability and indomitable spirit in his conduct of the defense, frequently visiting under fire all parts of the position and encouraging the men by his cool demeanor and calm assurance. On the fifth day he received from the Germans a written demand to surrender which he treated with contempt, although at that time his command was out of rations, had suffered a loss of more than 50 per cent and was entirely surrounded by the enemy.

Captain McMurtry commanded a battalion of this force. Although wounded in the knee by shrapnel on October 4 and suffering great pain, he continued throughout the entire period to encourage his officers and men with an irresistible optimism that contributed largely toward preventing panic and disorder among the troops. On October 4, during a heavy barrage, he personally directed and supervised the moving of the wounded to a protected place before himself seeking shelter. On October 6 he was again wounded in the shoulder by a German grenade, but continued personally to organize and direct the defense against the German attack until it was defeated. After assistance had arrived he refused relief and personally led his men out of the position on October 8 before permitting himself to be evacuated to the hospital.

Captain Holderman commanded one of the companies. He was wounded on October 4, on October 5 and again on October 7, but throughout the entire period, although suffering great pain and subjected to fire of every description, he continued personally to lead and encourage the officers and men under his command with unflinching courage and with distinguished success. On October 6, in a wounded condition, he rushed through enemy machine-gun and shell fire and carried two wounded men to a place of greater safety.

Major Charles W. Whittlesey
77th Division,
October 29, 1918

The individual rifle pits used by the men of the "Lost Battalion" can be seen (1937) by climbing about 30 feet down the steep slope leading from the road.

The tour from here retraces itself to the road fork at the French 9th Cuirassier monument. At that point the zone of action of the 368th Infantry of the 92d Division is entered. Before leaving this stop the tourist should consult the map which appears on the next page and, if not already familiar with it, read the account of the operations of the 368th Infantry given on page 339 of this chapter.

EN ROUTE NORTHEAST OF BINARVILLE TO NORTH OF VIENNE-LE-CHÂTEAU

As the road here is (1937) too narrow to permit turning, proceed to road junction about ½ mile ahead, turn around there and retrace route to the monument to the French 9th Cuirassiers recently passed. (60.8 m 97.9 km) Upon reaching the monument, continue straight ahead.

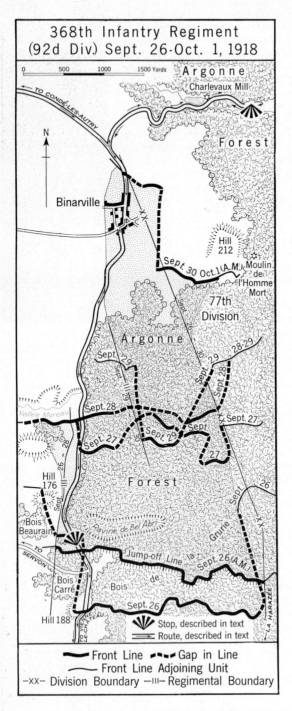

368th Infantry Regiment (92d Div.) Sept. 26-Oct. 1, 1918

0   500   1000   1500 Yards

Argonne

Charlevaux Mill

TO CONDÉ-LES-AUTRY

N

Forest

Binarville

Hill 212

Sept. 30 Oct.1 (A.M.)   Moulin de l'Homme Mort

77th Division

Argonne

Sept. 29

Sept. 29   Sept. 28-29   Sept. 28-29

Sept. 28   Sept. 28   Sept. 27

Vallee Moreau

Sept. 28   Sept. 30

Sept. 27   Sept. 29   Sept.   27

Sept. 26

Hill 176

Forest

Bois Beaurain   Ravine de Bel Abri

Grurie   Sept. 26

Jump-off Line   la   Sept. 26 (A.M.)

LE VIENNE   LA HARAZEE

TO SERVON

Bois Carré   Bois   de

Sept. 26

Hill 188   ☀ Stop, described in text
    ═ Route, described in text

━━ Front Line   ━ ━ Gap in Line
━━ Front Line Adjoining Unit
-xx- Division Boundary ─III─ Regimental Boundary

(60.9 m 98.0 km) **Between monument and next bend in road, immediately to right of road** was located on September 30 the front line held by one company of the 368th Infantry and part of the 9th Cuirassiers after they had captured Binarville, which is seen to the right front.

(61.4 m 98.8 km) **In Binarville, at church, turn left.**

After the capture of this town about 4:00 p.m. on September 30, two companies of the 368th Infantry were heavily shelled in it and withdrew to former German trenches about 300 yards away. An outpost, however, was left northeast of town.

Between here and the next town, Vienne-le-Château, the route goes opposite to the direction of advance of the 368th Infantry. The zone of action of that unit was located almost entirely to the left of this road.

(62.4 m 100.4 km) **Beyond town, at the third crest,** was situated the line from which the French 9th Cuirassiers jumped off on the afternoon of September 30 to attack Binarville. A battalion of the 368th Infantry, which during the morning had reached a position in the woods to the left, joined in this attack, although without orders, and captured the town.

Two days before, on September 28, elements of the 368th Infantry had reached this hill during the afternoon but as the hostile fire was increasing in intensity they withdrew to the far side of the valley ahead.

(62.7 m 100.9 km) **At bottom of next deep valley, on**

the right side of the road, are located a number of German shelters which are (1937) being preserved.

For the next ¾ mile, this road and the area to the left of it were the scene of considerable movement back and forth by the units of the 368th Infantry. Part of the area was taken on September 26 but given up. On the 27th in spite of considerable confusion it remained definitely in the hands of the regiment.

(63.4 m 102.8 km) **Beyond next crest, at far side of wide shallow valley, about halfway up the hill, STOP.**

Face back down the road, which direction is just west of north.

During most of the World War this point was near the French front line. The ground immediately in front was in no man's land and the German trenches were close to the bottom of this slope.

On September 26 the 368th Infantry jumped off from the trenches near this point on a 1½ mile front, mainly to the right of here, with the mission of feeling out the enemy, maintaining contact with the units on its flanks and aggressively following up any retirement of the Germans. The attack was made at 5:25 a. m., with poor artillery support. It finally developed into separate movements by three different groups. The one nearest here had worked its way by dusk into the German trenches in the valley ahead. The other two groups had penetrated the German lines for a considerable distance but later in the day retired to a position about ¼ mile behind the line from which they had started.

On the 27th, the units here attacked and advanced over the next ridge. On that day the whole regimental line moved forward about 1 mile.

Those who desire to return to Reims or spend further time on the battlefields in the Champagne region should turn right at next road junction toward Servon, and follow route to Souain shown by a double black broken line on the map opposite page 368. The region in the vicinity of Hurlus is most interesting as no reconstruction work has been done there and

Gas Mask Drill

the nature of the soil is such that the wartime trenches, dugouts and various other field fortifications are relatively well preserved at this time (1937).

All roads through the French artillery training camp, which is shown enclosed in dotted lines on the map opposite page 368, are blocked at certain times when the artillery of the French Army is firing.

(64.3 m 103.5 km) **A short distance beyond next road junction** are seen a French World War monument and cemetery.

(65.1 m 104.8 km) **In next village, Vienne-le-Château, turn left at church.**

(66.1 m 106.4 km) **While approaching the next village, La Harazée, to the left front across the valley can be seen a** French World War military cemetery.

The left boundary of the American 77th Division on September 26 included the village of La Harazée.

(66.5 m 107.1 km) **In the village, La Harazée, at the road fork near the church, bear to the right toward Le Four de Paris.**

92d Division Soldiers Stringing Wire South of Binarville

(67.0 m 107.8 km) **Beyond town, to the left of road, along the steep bank** can be seen the remains of many French wartime shelters in excellent condition (1937). The battle line for several years was only about ½ mile away to the left but the steep bank here gave these shelters full protection from hostile artillery fire.

(67.9 m 109.3 km) **The next road junction is the one called Le Four de Paris where this tour comes to an end.**

The quickest automobile route to Paris is straight ahead via Le Claon, Ste. Menehould, Châlons-sur-Marne and Montmirail.

The tourist going to the area of the American Meuse-Argonne offensive should turn left here and cross the Argonne Forest. The front line from which the 77th Division jumped off on September 26 is crossed about 300 yards from this road junction. The two most interesting features on side roads off the main road through the forest are the Ossuaire de la Haute Chevauchée (see the reference to Hill 285 on page 322) and Champ Mahaut (see page 316). Both of these are pointed out by signs along the road. Just beyond the forest is located the town of Varennes.

ADDITIONAL PLACES OF INTEREST IN THE CHAMPAGNE REGION

I N addition to the places described in the itinerary, there are several other places in the Champagne region where there now exist features of special interest or which are of sufficient historical importance to warrant special mention in this text. For reference purposes and for the benefit of the tourist who travels in the area, these places have been recorded below.

Camp of Attila. Near the village of La Cheppe, 8 miles northeast of Châlons-sur-Marne, is located a large, oval-shaped embankment, about 40 feet high, enclosing about 60 acres. This is an ancient entrenchment said to have been the site of a Roman camp or Gallic town. Some accounts state that it was constructed by Attila and used by him as a camp after the battle of Châlons in 451 A. D.

Châlons-sur-Marne. Known to the Romans as Catalaunum, this city is mentioned in history as early as the 3d Century. Between here and Troyes, Attila the Hun was defeated by the Romans and their allies in 451 A. D. Since then the city has been the scene of many battles. It was unsuccessfully attacked by the English in 1430 and again in 1434. The town was occupied by the Prussians in 1814 and by the Russians during the following year. The Germans occupied it in 1870 and again in August and September, 1914. It was one of the principal objectives of the German Armies during the offensive of July 15, 1918, but was not taken. In the city is an interesting cathedral dating from the 13th Century and containing fine stained-glass windows.

Rethel. This ancient town of Roman origin was within the German lines from 1914 until the last days of the war. It contains an ancient church, part of which dates from the 13th Century, and several buildings dating from the 17th Century.

Ste. Menehould. This city, picturesquely located at the junction of the Auve and Aisne Rivers, controls one of the passes through the Argonne Forest and has figured in many campaigns in this region. Louis XVI and Marie Antoinette, while fleeing from the French revolutionists in 1791, were recognized here by the postmaster, Drouet, who then rode through the Argonne Forest by an unfrequented road and caused the arrest of the royal fugitives when they stopped at the village of Varennes.

Valmy. This village, about 5 miles west of Ste. Menehould, was the scene of one of the decisive battles of the world when in 1792 the French Revolutionary Army under General Kellermann defeated the Prussians under the Duke of Brunswick. On the battlefield south of the village of Valmy is a statue of Kellermann, Duke of Valmy, who died in 1820.

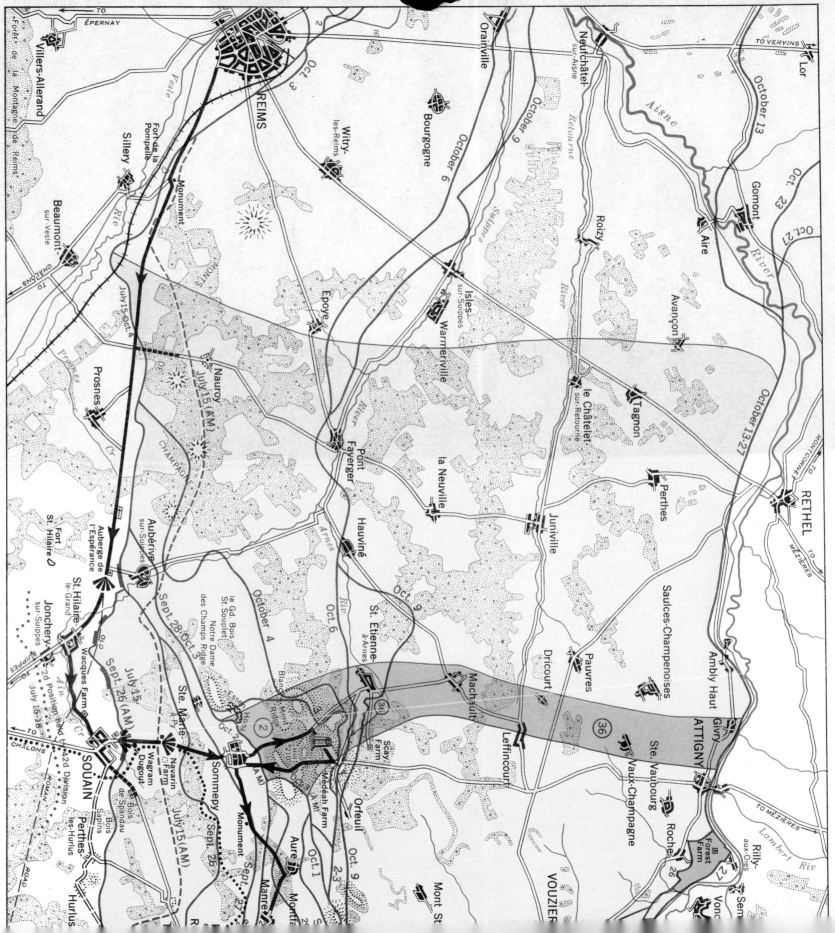

American Battle Operations in the Champagne Region

Scale 1/200000

0   5   10   15 Miles

0   5   10   15 Kilometers

Route, described in text

Return route

Side trip

Stop, described in text

Highway

Front line for date shown

Front line held by 42d Division July 15-18

Front line held July 15 (AM) at start of Champagne-Marne Defensive

2d Position held by 42d Division July 15-18

All front lines are as of midnight for dates shown unless otherwise noted; thus September 26 on a line indicates the line held at midnight September 26/27. The dates September 26-27 on a line indicate that the line was located at the same place at midnight of both September 26 and September 27.

Black dotted line encloses approximate area in which roads are blocked by artillery practice at certain times.

American memorial

French military cemetery

Ruins

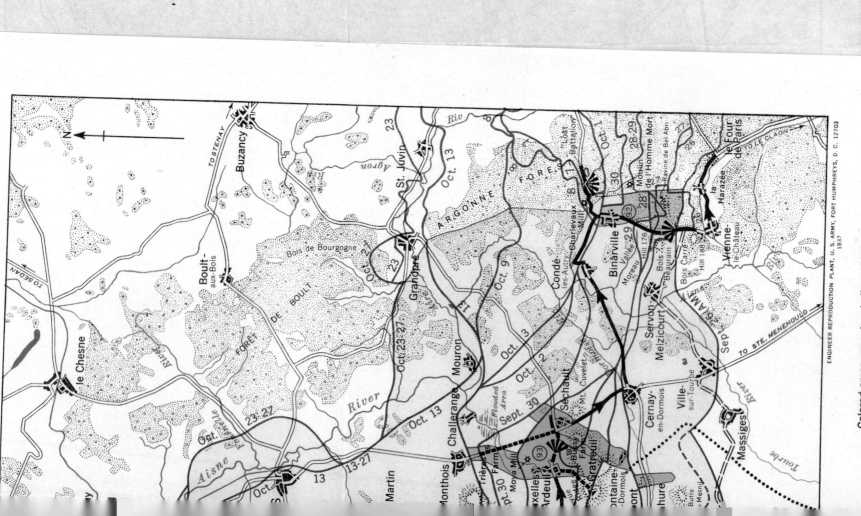

Colored areas except as indicated below show ground gained
by American units with the French Fourth Army
September 26–October 27

Ground gained by French divisions of French Fourth
Army September 26–October 27

② Large circled numeral in a colored area indicates
the American division which fought there

㊱ Small circled numeral indicates part of American
division which fought attached to another division

ENGINEER REPRODUCTION PLANT, U. S. ARMY, FORT HUMPHREYS, D. C. 12703
1937

SUMMARY OF COMBAT SERVICE OF AMERICAN DIVISIONS IN THE CHAMPAGNE REGION

Name of Div.	Period of Service 1918	Character of Service	Location of Service General vicinity of—	Army to which Attached [1]	Corps to which Attached [1]	Casualties [2]
2	Oct. 2–10	Battle	North of Sommepy, Blanc Mont and St. Etienne-à-Arnes.	Fourth	XXI	4,821 (1,506)
36	Oct. 10–28	Battle	Machault, west of Attigny and Forest Farm.	Fourth	XXI until Oct. 18, then XI.	1,009 (50)
42	July 15–18	Battle	Souain and St. Hilaire-le-Grand.	Fourth	XXI	1,590
	July 19	Sector	Souain and St. Hilaire-le-Grand.	Fourth	XXI	11
92 (368th Inf. only)	Sept. 25	Sector	Northeast of Vienne-le-Château.	Fourth	XXXVIII	4
	Sept. 26–Oct. 1	Battle	Binarville and to the south.	Fourth	XXXVIII	266
93 (369th Inf. only)	Apr. 8–July 3	Training in Line and Sector.	Ville-sur-Tourbe	Fourth	VIII	41
	July 15–18	Battle	Massiges	Fourth	VIII	45
	July 19–Aug. 19	Sector	Massiges	Fourth	VIII	82
	Sept. 11–16	Sector	Massiges	Fourth	XXXVIII	10
	Sept. 26–Oct. 1	Battle	Séchault	Fourth	IX	785
93 (371st Inf. only)	Sept. 28–Oct. 1	Battle	Ardeuil	Fourth	IX	882
93 (372d Inf. only)	Sept. 28–Oct. 7	Battle	South of Monthois	Fourth	IX	579

[1] All armies and corps are French.
[2] Casualties are for period in line only. Figures in parentheses give casualties for units temporarily attached. Add figure in parentheses to the one above in order to obtain the total casualties during the entire operation.

42d Division Machine Gun Battalion Headquarters
North of St. Hilaire-le-Grand

91st Division Engineers Repairing Tracks Blown Up by the Germans Near Waereghem, Belgium, November 1, 1918

Bapaume, March 17, 1917. © B

Chapter VI

THE AMERICAN BATTLEFIELDS
NORTH OF PARIS

THIS chapter gives brief accounts of all American fighting which occurred on the battle front north of Paris and complete information concerning the American military cemeteries and monuments in that general region. The military operations which are treated are those of the American 1st, 27th, 30th, [3]d, 37th, 80th and 91st Divisions and [th]e 6th and 11th Engineer Regiments. Because of the great distances apart of

areas and to all of the American cemeteries and monuments. This route is recommended for those who desire to make an extended automobile tour in the region. Starting from Paris, it can be completely covered in four days, allowing plenty of time to stop on the way.

The accounts of the different operations and the descriptions of the American cemeteries and monuments are given in the order they are reached when following

Southern Entrance to the St. Quentin Canal Tunnel, Near Bellicourt, October 1, 1918

[th]e areas where this fighting occurred no [iti]nerary is given. Every operation is [de]scribed, however, by a brief account [ill]ustrated by a sketch. The account and [sk]etch together give sufficient information [to] enable the tourist to plan a trip through [an]y particular American combat area.

The general map on the next page [in]dicates a route which takes the tourist [eit]her into or close to all of these combat

the suggested route. For this reason they do not appear in chronological order.

Many American units other than those mentioned in this chapter, such as aviation, tank, medical, engineer and infantry, served behind this part of the front. Their services have not been recorded, however, as the space limitations of this chapter required that it be limited to those American organizations which actually engaged

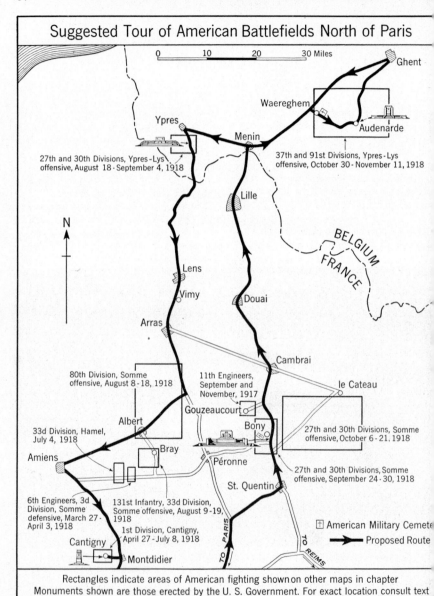

Suggested Tour of American Battlefields North of Paris

0   10   20   30 Miles

Ghent

Waereghem

Audenarde

37th and 91st Divisions, Ypres-Lys
offensive, October 30 - November 11, 1918

Ypres

Menin

27th and 30th Divisions, Ypres-Lys
offensive, August 18 - September 4, 1918

Lille

N

Lens

Vimy

Douai

BELGIUM

FRANCE

Arras

Cambrai

80th Division, Somme
offensive, August 8-18, 1918

11th Engineers,
September and
November, 1917

le Cateau

Gouzeaucourt

Albert

Bony

27th and 30th Divisions, Somme
offensive, October 6-21, 1918

33d Division, Hamel,
July 4, 1918

Bray

Péronne

Amiens

27th and 30th Divisions, Somme
offensive, September 24-30, 1918

St. Quentin

6th Engineers, 3d
Division, Somme
defensive, March 27 -
April 3, 1918

131st Infantry, 33d Division,
Somme offensive, August 9-19,
1918

TO PARIS

TO REIMS

American Military Cemetery

1st Division, Cantigny,
April 27 - July 8, 1918

Proposed Route

Cantigny

Montdidier

Rectangles indicate areas of American fighting shown on other maps in chapter
Monuments shown are those erected by the U. S. Government. For exact location consult text

in physical combat with the enemy during which territory was either lost or gained.

Numerous battles in which American troops took no part were fought north of Paris. No attempt has been made to describe these battles or to indicate on the maps in this chapter more than a few of

the important memorials which have been constructed to commemorate them. The tourists who are interested in these or the historical events which took place the region prior to 1917 should provide themselves with the necessary additional guidebooks before starting on their tour.

THE 27th and 30th Divisions trained and served in line with the British [Ar]my in the summer of 1918, and took [par]t in an operation near Ypres which [end]ed early in September. After that [eng]agement they were sent southward, [cov]ering the battle lines north of St. Quen[tin] with the British Fourth Army.

The terrain in this region is open and [roll]ing, with pronounced ridges and val[ley]s and many sunken roads. There are [pra]ctically no fences or hedges and but [few] trees and isolated houses. It is ex[cel]lent terrain for defensive fighting.

[O]n this section of the front the Ger[ma]ns made use of the St. Quentin Canal [as] the primary feature of their formidable [Hi]ndenburg Line. Between Bellicourt [an]d a point about ½ mile north of Bony, [wh]ere the channel passed through a [tun]nel, they took advantage of this spa[cio]us underground passage, which was [de]ep enough below ground to be safe [fro]m the heaviest bombardment, to in[sta]ll barracks, storehouses and other [acc]ommodations for their troops. Large [ch]ambers dug in the tunnel walls were [equ]ipped as kitchens, offices, dressing [sta]tions and stables, while barges, strand[ed] in the dry channel, were used as living quarters. The tunnel, nearly 4 miles long, was artificially ventilated, heated and electrically lighted; and there, close to the front line, the German troops lived safely and in comparative comfort.

From the tunnel below, underground passages led to the defenses above, which consisted of two separate trench systems. The principal one, the Hindenburg Line, was located in a zone about 1,000 yards wide immediately west of the tunnel. The other, located about a mile away, served as the outpost zone for the Hindenburg Line. These trench systems were connected with each other by numerous communicating trenches and both were protected by many bands of wire entanglements. All in all the defenses here in the autumn of 1918 were among the most formidable on the Western Front.

About the middle of September the British began to attack the outpost zone in order to establish a good line of departure for a general attack on September 29 against the Hindenburg Line. This general attack and the Meuse-Argonne offensive of the American First Army were two of the four great Allied attacks which were either started or continued with increased force late in September.

Interior of St. Quentin Canal Tunnel Near Bellicourt, Showing a Barge Which Was Used as a Barrack by the Germans

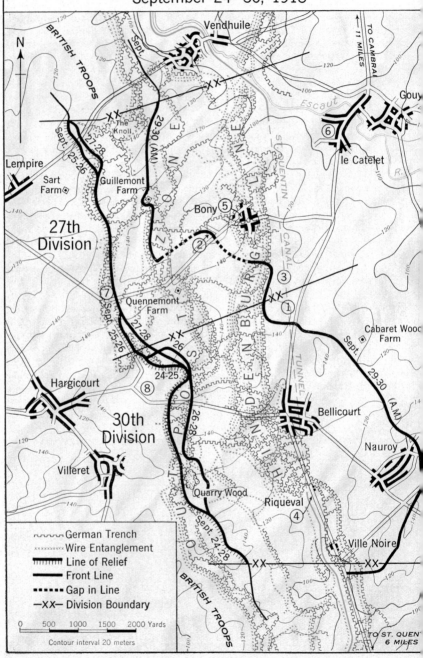

27th and 30th Divisions in Somme Offensive
September 24–30, 1918

Vendhuile

BRITISH TROOPS

N

TO CAMBRAI 11 MILES

Escaut

Gouy

The Knoll

6

le Catelet

Sept. 27-28

Sept. 25-26

Lempire

Sart Farm

Guillemont Farm

27th Division

Bony 5

2

3

1

Cabaret Wood Farm

7

Quennemont Farm

Sept. 25-26

Sept. 27-28

26

24-25

8

Hargicourt

30th Division

Villeret

26-28

Bellicourt

Nauroy

Quarry Wood

Riqueval

4

Ville Noire

Sept. 24-28

BRITISH TROOPS

ᔕᔕᔕ	German Trench
×××××	Wire Entanglement
ᎢᎢᎢᎢ	Line of Relief
▬▬▬	Front Line
▪▪▪▪	Gap in Line
—××—	Division Boundary

0 500 1000 1500 2000 Yards

Contour interval 20 meters

TO ST. QUEN 6 MILES

(374)

The 30th and 27th Divisions went into line in adjoining zones of action on September 24 and 25, respectively, as part of the American II Corps, although under the tactical control of the Australian Corps. They were supported by British artillery, as these two divisions did not have their own artillery brigades with them. The line taken over by the 30th Division was west of Bellicourt and that of the 27th Division was west of Bony. The front was very active at the time that the 30th Division came under heavy

27 during a preliminary attack which the 27th Division had been ordered to make.

In the zone of action taken over by the 27th Division the British in several attempts had been unable to do much more than dent the German outpost position. The principal strong points of that position were Quennemont Farm, Guillemont Farm and The Knoll, which were near the crest of the reverse slope of a ridge and about ½ mile from the American front line.

The 27th Division was ordered to take these strong points on September 27.

Road Near Guillemont Farm. ⓒ B

artillery fire while entering the line. It repulsed a raid on September 25 and on the afternoon of the 26th counterattacked and drove back a German raiding party. In the 30th Division zone of action a large part of the German outpost position had been captured by the British. Most of the remainder was seized on the evening of September 26 when the 30th Division advanced about 300 yards and occupied Quarry Wood and a trench running to the north from it. The left flank of the division was heavily engaged on September

At 5:30 a. m. the regiment designated to make the attack jumped off in a carefully planned assault, supported by tanks and a heavy barrage. The attacking troops, following close behind the barrage, reached the general line of the objective and gained footholds around Quennemont Farm, Guillemont Farm and The Knoll. Severe resistance which developed at these places, together with machine-gun fire from the rear and flanks, and strong counterattacks from the valleys leading to the Hindenburg Line, made it impossible to consoli-

CIRCLED NUMERALS ON MAP INDICATE LOCATION OF THE FOLLOWING

① Monument erected by U.S. Government
② Somme American Cemetery
③ St. Quentin Canal tunnel
④ Monument to 30th Div.

⑤ Town Hall donated by Americans
⑥ Ruins of old château
⑦ Good panorama of 27th Div. battlefield
⑧ Excellent view of 30th Div. battlefield

te the ground gained. Parts of the
:acking line were forced back and others
thdrew, although small parties whose
mbers were unknown remained isolated
shell holes on the ground advanced
er. The close of the day showed practi-
lly no gains except on each flank, where
e front line was advanced a few hundred
rds. The casualties in this regiment
re unusually heavy, all company offi-
rs except two being killed or wounded.
It was at The Knoll during this fighting
at First Lieutenant William B. Turner,
th Division, performed the heroic deeds
r which he was awarded the Congres-
nal Medal of Honor. Under terrific
tillery and machine-gun fire he led a
all group of men in the attack after
ey became separated in the darkness
m their company. Singlehanded he
shed an enemy machine gun that sud-
nly opened fire on his group, and killed
e crew with his pistol. He then pressed
rward to another machine-gun nest,
yards away, and killed one gunner
fore his detachment arrived and put
e gun out of action. With the utmost
avery and disregard for three wounds
had received, he continued to lead
s men over three lines of hostile
nches, killing several of the enemy in
nd-to-hand combat. After his pistol
nmunition had been exhausted, this
llant officer seized the rifle of a dead
ldier, bayoneted several members of a
stile machine gun crew, and shot the
her. Upon reaching the fourth-line
nch, which was his objective, Lieuten-
t Turner, with the nine men remaining in
s group, captured it and resisted a hostile
unterattack until he was finally killed.
Sergeant Reidar Waaler, 27th Division,
so received the Congressional Medal of
onor for his fighting on September 27.
the face of heavy artillery and machine-
n fire near Ronssoy, he crawled for-
ard to a burning British tank, in which
me of the crew were imprisoned, and
cceeded in rescuing two men. Al-
ough the tank was then burning
rcely and contained ammunition likely
explode, he returned to the tank and

made a search for other occupants, remaining until satisfied that there were no
more living men in the vehicle.

On the night of September 27 the brigade designated to make the general
assault took over all of the front line of
the 27th Division. Its orders prohibited
any organized attack on September 28
and the attempts of the brigade on that

Monument Erected by the State of
Tennessee South of Bellicourt

day to push the front line farther forward
by means of patrols were unsuccessful.

The failure of the preliminary operation had a grave effect upon the subsequent general attack because the British,
whose artillery was supporting the 27th
Division, made the error of starting the
artillery barrage in front of the line which
had been set as the objective of the preliminary operation instead of in front of
the actual jump-off line. Consequently,
when the attack was made, British artillery
fire in the intervening zone, which was

German Prisoners Captured by the 27th and 30th Divisions
Near the St. Quentin Canal

about 1,100 yards in depth, was entirely lacking, thus placing upon the assault troops of the 27th Division the impossible task of capturing a strong position without the aid of close-in artillery support.[1] The reason given for this decision, which proved so extremely costly in American lives, was the probable presence of wounded and isolated groups of Americans stranded in the intervening zone.

Meanwhile, in preparation for the main attack, the British heavy artillery had been hammering away for two days at the strong points and other defenses of the Hindenburg Line in this vicinity.

This was the situation at 5:30 a. m. on September 29 when the 27th and 30th Divisions, on a battlefield enveloped by autumn mists and low-hanging clouds, jumped off for the main offensive.

Behind a heavy rolling barrage the 30th Division, accompanied by tanks,

moved forward with great rapidity acro[ss] the main German trench system. [In] spite of the fog the leading waves push[ed] on beyond the Hindenburg Line and t[he] tunnel to near Nauroy, leaving in the[ir] wake many unseen and uncaptured stro[ng] points. The southern mouth of the tu[n]nel was quickly blocked and Bellicou[rt] was captured, but the enemy, who we[re] able to reach their positions above grou[nd] by means of underground passages [of] which the Americans were unawar[e,] desperately remanned machine-gun nes[ts] previously overrun by the 30th Divisio[n.] From these and the strong points pass[ed] by in the fog the Germans opened fire [on] the American reserve units, wire detai[ls,] runners and other groups which we[re] following up the assaulting waves. Th[is] caused much confusion and many isolat[ed] combats continued throughout the mor[n]ing over a large part of the zone of actio[n.] The dash of the American troops, ho[w]ever, finally prevailed and in the end [all] the German soldiers who had been fou[nd]

---

[1] This attack illustrates the serious situations which would have resulted from any permanent amalgamation of American troops with the Allied Armies.

rear of the American front lines after the initial assault were killed or captured. Illustrative of this fighting are the exploits of Sergeant Joseph B. Adkison and Sergeant Milo Lemert of the 30th Division for which they were awarded Congressional Medals of Honor.

When murderous machine-gun fire at a range of 50 yards made it impossible for his platoon to advance, and caused his men to take cover, Sergeant Adkison alone, with the greatest intrepidity, rushed across 50 yards of open ground directly in the face of the hostile machine gun, kicked the gun from the parapet into the enemy trench, and at the point of his bayonet captured the three men manning the gun. The gallantry and quick decision of this soldier enabled his platoon to resume its advance.

Sergeant Lemert, seeing the left of his company held up, located the enemy machine gun which had been causing numerous casualties. In spite of heavy fire he rushed it singlehanded, killing the entire crew with grenades. Continuing along the enemy trench in advance of his company, he charged another machine gun, silencing it with grenades. A third machine gun opened fire upon him from the left and with similar skill and bravery he destroyed this also. Later, in company with another sergeant, he attacked a fourth machine-gun nest, being killed as he reached the parapet of the emplacement. The courageous action of Sergeant Lemert in destroying in turn four enemy machine-gun nests prevented many casualties in his company and materially aided it in achieving its objective.

The 27th Division, with tanks in the lead, left its trenches on schedule time and started across the wide expanse of level ground in the German outpost zone. The British artillery fire supporting the American attack came down beyond the powerful German positions at The Knoll, Guillemont Farm and Quennemont Farm, and their garrisons, unhampered by any Allied artillery bombardment, at once opened a withering machine-gun fire that swept the entire front of the 27th Division. The

After the Battle Near Nauroy
German prisoners are in the foreground, 30th Division troops are on road in rear

American Infantry Hurrying Forward Under Artillery Fire. © B

tanks were soon put out of action, throwing an additional burden on the infantry, which gallantly struggled forward in shattered waves. As the reserves moved forward they encountered the fire of machine-gun nests that the troops preceding them had passed by in the fog. Most of the divisional zone between the jump-off line and the tunnel thus became one vast maelstrom of violence. Around Guillemont Farm and The Knoll, the 107th Infantry Regiment of the 27th Division had 337 men killed and 658 wounded on September 29. No other American regiment suffered such a heavy loss in a single day during the war. In spite of all this, however, the troops attacked boldly and incessantly. By noon, Quennemont Farm, part of the elaborate trench system south of Bony, the ground now occupied by the American cemetery and The Knoll were in the hands of the 27th Division.

As previously planned, Australia troops passed through the America divisions in the early afternoon and con tinued the drive, many Americans joinin the Australians in their attacks. B nightfall these troops had occupied all Nauroy and from there a line that ra generally northwestward to a point abou ½ mile southwest of Vendhuile.

This fighting of the 27th Division wa characterized by many individual feats bravery among which were the exploit of Privates First Class Frank Gaffney an Michael Valente, both of whom wer given the Congressional Medal of Hono.

Private Gaffney, an automatic rifleman pushing forward alone with his gun afte all the other members of his squad ha been killed, discovered several German placing a machine gun in position. H killed the crew, captured the gun, bombe several dugouts and, after killing fou

27th Division Tank Destroyed by a German Mine East of Ronssoy

re of the enemy with his pistol, held position until reinforcements came when 80 prisoners were captured. 'rivate Valente, finding the advance of organization held up by withering my machine-gun fire, volunteered to forward. With utter disregard of his 1 personal danger, accompanied by other soldier, Private Valente rushed ward through intense machine-gun directly upon the enemy nest, killing 9 and capturing five of the enemy and ncing that gun. Discovering another

tinued their assaults and succeeded in breaking the Hindenburg Line, thus opening the way for additional advances.

Following this battle the 27th and 30th Divisions received many commendations for their heroic conduct. General Pershing and Marshal Haig, as well as the Commander of the Australian Corps, were warm in their praise of the splendid fighting qualities of the divisions and of the results they had achieved.

This battlefield may be visited by taking a train to the city of St. Quentin or

Wrecked British Airplane Near Bony, October 3, 1918

chine-gun nest close by, which was aring a deadly fire on the American ces, preventing their advance, he and companion charged this strong point, ing the gunner and putting the chine gun out of action. Without itation they jumped into the enemy's nch, killed two and captured 16 rman soldiers. Private Valente was er wounded and sent to the rear. His npanion, Private Joseph Mastine, was arded the Distinguished Service Cross. The American divisions were relieved ly on September 30 but scme elements he 27th Division remained in line and tinued to attack with the Australians ing September 30 and October 1.

Although the casualties in this operaa had been exceptionally heavy the aerican soldiers had persistently con-

Cambrai and hiring an automobile there.

Locations of Headquarters

The locations of the principal headquarters of the American corps and divisions serving in this region were as follows:

II Corps:
    Sept. 26–Oct. 5__ Bois de Belloy, near Assevillers.
    Oct. 5–12_____ Bois de Buire.[1]
    Oct. 12–25_____ Wiancourt.

27th Division:
    Sept. 24–28_____ Bois de Buire.[1]
    Sept. 28–Oct. 2__ In a quarry west of Ronssoy.
    Oct. 13–21_____ Busigny.

30th Division:
    Sept. 22–28_____ Bois de Buire.[1]
    Sept. 28–Oct. 1__ In a quarry southeast of Roisel.
    Oct. 6–10_____ In a quarry near Templeux-le-Guérard.
    Oct. 10–22_____ Montbrehain.

[1] Located one mile northeast of Tincourt-Boucly.

THE AMERICAN MONUMENT NORTH OF BELLICOURT

BEAUTIFUL and impressive memorial to commemorate all American
ts which served with the British
mies in France during the World War
been constructed by the United States
vernment north of Bellicourt.

This monument is conveniently located
ng the main highway running north
m St. Quentin. It stands in the center
a small park area the landscaping of
ich frames in an admirable manner the
ceful lines of the memorial.

The main decorative feature of the
nument is an imposing sculptured
up consisting of an American eagle
ting on a pedestal of stars and stripes
ked by two allegorical figures repre-
ting Victory and Remembrance.

Below the sculptured group is the
licatory inscription, carved with raised
ters on a gilded background, and
und the monument on a frieze are in-
ibed the names of places which were
minent in the American fighting com-
morated by the memorial.

On the rear face of the monument is a
p illustrating the American operations
the vicinity, and from the terrace
ar it a fine view of the battlefield
ight over by the 27th and 30th Divi-
ns can be obtained. A raised circular
entation table on the terrace indicates
directions and distances to the impor-
it places in the vicinity.

Included among the decorative features
the insignia and names of the II
rps, 27th, 30th, 33d and 80th Divisions,
d 6th and 11th Engineers, all of whose
mbat operations with the British forces
commemorated here.

The monument is constructed directly
er the St. Quentin Canal tunnel which
s built by Napoleon between 1802 and
10. The ridge upon which the monu-
nt stands was formed from the ex-
vated earth hoisted up from below.
e small, round, tower-like structures
ich are seen at regular intervals along
e ridge are the ends of ventilating shafts
at supply air to the tunnel below.

In excavating for the foundation of
this monument several filled-in passages
were found extending into the bank
from the road side, in one case connecting
with the canal tunnel below, and in
others leading to underground rooms at
different levels. These were the remains
of some of the wartime field works which
honeycombed the embankment of the
canal tunnel throughout its entire length.

The battle operations of the 27th and
30th Divisions in this region are described
on pages 373–381. The following will
help to make that description clearer and
to tie it in with the terrain visible from
the terrace of the monument. (Consult
the map which appears on page 374.)

**Go to the center of the orientation table
and face away from the monument.
Most of the places mentioned in the
following description can be identified by
the direction arrows on the table.**

Upon arriving at this front the 27th
Division on September 25 took over a
portion of the front line whose center was
located about ½ mile to the left of Guillemont Farm, the group of buildings plainly
seen to the right front. The 30th Division
took over a sector on September 24 about
½ mile this side of Villeret, whose church
steeple is plainly visible to the left front.
The boundary line between the zones of
action of the two divisions roughly paralleled the directional arrow pointing
toward Hargicourt and passed about 300
yards to the right of this point.

All American attacks in this vicinity
were from the general direction toward
which the observer is now facing.

The strong German defensive position
known as the Hindenburg Line was on
the slopes immediately in front of this
canal tunnel. It comprised a defensive
zone about 1,000 yards wide, consisting
of three lines of trenches heavily protected
by thick masses of barbed-wire entanglements and defended by numerous machi e
guns and other weapons. The town of
Bony, seen to the right, and the town of
Bellicourt, seen to the left along the

tunnel, were included in it. Bony, which had been thoroughly prepared for all-around defense, was about in the center of the zone of action of the 27th Division, and Bellicourt, which was protected by an elaborate trench system, was close to the center of the zone of action that was assigned to the 30th Division.

The ground upon which is now located the Somme American Cemetery, whose flagpole can be seen in the distance to the right front just to the right of Guillemont Farm, was located between the Hindenburg Line and its outpost zone.

The outpost zone of the Hindenburg Line included strong points at The Knoll, the low bare hill which can be faintly seen to the right front on a clear day; Guillemont Farm; Quennemont Farm, invisible from here but just this side of the first wood whose tops are seen to the right of front; and ran just this side of Villeret.

Nauroy, to the left rear, was one of the objectives of the 30th Division in the main attack against the Hindenburg Line. Gouy, to the right rear, was one of the objectives of the 27th Division.

The American front line at the end of September 29, the day of the main attack, did not include the site of this monument, the Germans having held this ground throughout all the severe fighting of that day. It did, however, include Nauroy and

in this direction ran to just this side Cabaret Wood Farm, which can be s around the side of the monument stepping to the left edge of the orien tion table and looking to the rear. Th it changed direction and passed about yards to the left (south) of here. Ab 500 yards in front of this monument, j over the first ridge, it changed direct again and ran toward Bony; about h way there it again changed direction a followed an irregular path passing to observer's left of the town of Vendh which is close to the high smoke stack s in the distance through the trees beyo the left edge of Bony.

Some of the high points of the fight near here are the following: About mile to the right front over the first rid about 200 men of the 27th Division ea on September 29 captured a section the Hindenburg Line after fierce hand-hand fighting. They consolidated th position in the German trenches af capturing many prisoners and four fi guns. Attempts to enter Bony down trenches of the Hindenburg Line were successful. Several German counter tacks launched from Bony against t group of American soldiers were repuls

Other units of the 27th Division reach the ground upon which the Americ cemetery now stands. These units h

West Face of American Memorial Near Bellicourt

30th Division Reserves Digging In Near Molain, October 18, 1918

heir position during the day in spite of plunging fire from near Bony and the intense efforts of the Germans to dislodge hem. Many American casualties were suffered at the site of the cemetery.

Aided by the fog a number of 27th Division soldiers on the morning of September 29 penetrated the German lines as far as the village of Gouy, seen to the ight rear. These men were reported in that town by an Allied airplane but in he end were either killed or captured.

Near the exit of the canal tunnel beyond Bony, a British heavy tank manned by Americans was disabled by a direct hit of a German shell, which killed or wounded all of the crew. Sergeant John C. Latham and Corporals Alan L. Eggers and Thomas E. O'Shea, 27th Division, who had become separated from their platoon by a smoke barrage and had taken cover in a shell hole within the enemy lines, heard a call for help from the tank, whereupon they left their shelter and started toward the tank under heavy fire from German machine guns and trench mortars. In crossing the fire-swept area Corporal O'Shea was mortally wounded and died soon afterwards, but Sergeant Latham and Corporal Eggers, undeterred, continued on to the tank, rescued a wounded officer and assisted two wounded soldiers to a near-by trench. One of the wounded members of the tank crew, Sergeant Frank P. Williams, after having assisted his wounded officer, returned to the tank under heavy fire and continued to operate a 6-pounder against the enemy until driven out by armor-piercing shells. Sergeant

Latham and Corporal Eggers returned to the tank in the face of violent fire, dismounted a machine gun and took it back to where the wounded men were. With this weapon, and assisted by Sergeant Williams, they succeeded in keeping off the enemy all day and later under cover of darkness brought the machine gun and wounded men back to the American lines. Sergeant Latham and Corporals Eggers and O'Shea were awarded Congressional Medals of Honor. Sergeant Williams was awarded the Distinguished Service Cross.

The casualties of the 27th and 30th Divisions on this battlefield totaled more than 7,500 officers and men.

Upon being relieved from the front line in this vicinity, the 27th and 30th Divisions rested in rear areas until October 6, when the 30th Division as part of the American II Corps again entered the battle. Its new zone of action was near Montbrehain, the direction to which is indicated on the orientation table although invisible from this point.

The account, given on pages 389–393, of the operations of the 27th and 30th Divisions in this region after October 1, should be read at this time if the area of that fighting is not to be visited later.

Upon leaving this monument the tourist should visit the Somme American Cemetery which is 2.2 miles away by road. To go there, at exit from monument turn left on the main road and take the first road to the left. After passing through the town of Bony, stop on the road when the cemetery comes in full view and read pages 387–388.

THE SOMME AMERICAN CEMETERY NEAR BONY

IN October 1918 a temporary American cemetery was established on the bare, hell-torn fields about ½ mile southwest of the ruins of the small village of Bony. In that cemetery were buried the men of the 27th and 30th Divisions who lost their lives in the fighting near by for the possession of the Hindenburg Line.

The temporary cemetery with its wooden crosses painted white and arranged in regular rows made a deep impression upon the survivors of the American divisions who had fought in the region and they asked that a permanent cemetery be established there. No more fitting spot could have been found than that gentle slope where they and their fallen comrades had performed such deeds of valor and, in answer to their request, it became the site of a permanent military cemetery.

Among the 1,833 Americans who now sleep there, are soldiers not only from the 27th and 30th Divisions but those of the 1st Division who gave their lives at Cantigny, and of the 33d and 80th Divisions and 6th and 11th Engineers who fell while serving with the British.

By means of architectural features and of trees, flowers and shrubs especially appropriate to the region, this cemetery has been developed into a resting place of outstanding beauty. A splendid view of this American shrine can be obtained while approaching it from Bony.

The cemetery consists of a grave area enclosed by a low stone wall, and an adjoining area where the superintendent's quarters, including a reception room for the convenience of visitors, are located. Inquiries for the location of a particular grave or for other information should be made at the reception room.

A flagpole from which the American flag flies during daylight hours is located at the center of the grave area. The rear wall is high and joins two hangars used for service purposes. This wall is covered with ivy and will ultimately be shaded in year by tall cedars of Lebanon. The

shorter axis of the cemetery is bordered by beds of red roses. The longer axis, flanked by small square-cut box hedges, leads to the chapel at its eastern end.

The chapel, of striking design, stands like a castle guarding the graves of these men who died for their country. Among its exterior decorations are sculptured

Interior of Chapel in American Cemetery
Near Bony

articles of military equipment, including a large field gun, shells, rifles and a tank.

The interior of the chapel is entered through a bronze door, beautiful in its simplicity, and directly across from it, above the altar, is a cross-shaped window with panes of crystal glass. The effect of the sunlight through this window is deeply impressive. The small side windows are purple in tone and include in their designs the insignia of the various divisions, corps and higher units which formed part of the American Expeditionary Forces.

On the interior walls are carved the names of those men who lost their lives in the American operations in France north of Paris and who now sleep in unknown graves. Above, on each side of the altar, are American flags, while opposite them, near the door, are flags of the infantry and field artillery, the combat

startling reality. This was due to singular coincidence by which the carve_ fashioning the figure from a block white stone, came upon a coal-black sp_ which turned out to be exactly the rig_ position and of exactly the right size_ form a lifelike ball for the eye. Th_ spot has now faded to a great extent.

A walk through the peaceful atm_ phere of this cemetery will bring to t_ American visitor a feeling of its fitness_ a resting place for America's heroic dea_

Chapel at American Cemetery Near Bony

branches of the army which sustained the greatest number of casualties during the war. An American flag hangs above the entrance door. The bronze work of the chapel is unusually effective and all features of the interior combine to give an atmosphere of impressive dignity.

On the outside of the chapel, facing the road, are carved two American eagles. When the carving was done one of these, the one nearer Bony, had an eye of

This cemetery can be easily reached _ taking a train to St. Quentin or Cambr_ the nearest large towns, and by hiring _ automobile at either of those places.

The American monument to commem_ rate all American units which served wi_ the British Armies in France is 1 mi_ away to the southeast. (See page 383.)

The accounts of the fighting of the 27_ and 30th Divisions near here are giv_ on pages 373–381 and pages 389–39_

27TH AND 30TH DIVISIONS IN THE SOMME OFFENSIVE
OCTOBER 1—22, 1918

THE *area where this operation occurred is not picturesque and practically no evidences of the fighting remain. The roads are (1937) generally narrow, winding and difficult to follow and many are sunken which makes it difficult to view the landscape.*

After taking a prominent part in breaking the Hindenburg Line north of St.

On October 7 the 30th Division made a preliminary attack to straighten its line. This was partially successful but resulted in severe losses. On the 8th the division, participating in a general offensive of the British Fourth Army, attacked vigorously and captured the towns of Brancourt-le-Grand and Prémont. It gained all objec-

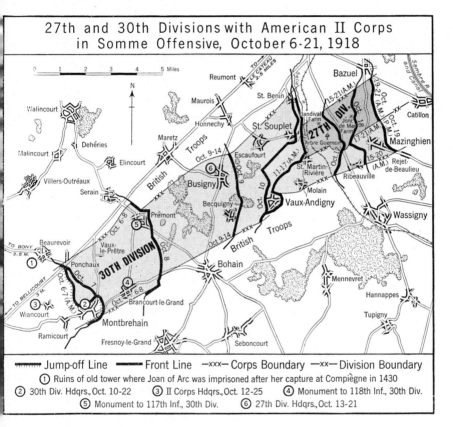

27th and 30th Divisions with American II Corps in Somme Offensive, October 6-21, 1918

⚞⚞⚞ Jump-off Line   ▬▬ Front Line   —xxx— Corps Boundary   —xx— Division Boundary

① Ruins of old tower where Joan of Arc was imprisoned after her capture at Compiègne in 1430
② 30th Div. Hdqrs., Oct. 10-22   ③ II Corps Hdqrs., Oct. 12-25   ④ Monument to 118th Inf., 30th Div.
⑤ Monument to 117th Inf., 30th Div.   ⑥ 27th Div. Hdqrs., Oct. 13-21

Quentin, the American II Corps was withdrawn from the front line on September 30 while the British continued the pressure against the retreating Germans. By October 5 the British had advanced about 3¾ miles, and the next morning the II Corps entered the line, taking command of a zone of action near Montbrehain with the 30th Division in line and the 27th in reserve. (Consult the sketch on this page.)

tives by early afternoon and ended the day well ahead of the divisions on its flanks. The assaults were energetically continued until the 11th, by which time the division had advanced about 10 miles, reaching the Selle River (known also as the Sourcelle River) in the vicinity of St. Souplet. During this fighting the progress of the division was delayed considerably by flanking fire because the British troops

Congested Traffic at Montbrehain in Rear of the American Lines,
October 14, 1918

on its right flank were unable to move forward as rapidly as the 30th Division.

The 27th Division relieved the 30th on October 12 and held the II Corps front while a new general attack was being prepared. During this period constant house-to-house sniping and patrol fighting took place near the eastern edge of St. Souplet. On the night of October 15–16 the 30th Division again entered the line, taking over the right portion of the zone of action of the 27th Division.

At 5:20 a. m. on October 17 the II Corps attacked eastward across the Selle River in conjunction with an attack by the remainder of the British Fourth Army and the French First Army. In a heavy mist the troops waded the small stream, climbed the steep opposite bank and assailed the enemy's trenches on the heights beyond. Although its divisions were seriously depleted in strength as a result of their previous severe fighting, important advances were made.

The 30th Division captured Molain and St. Martin-Rivière in hard fighting on the 17th, making an advance of about 2 miles. The next day it took Ribeauville and on the 19th captured the village of Mazinghien. The division was relieved from the

front line during the night of October 19.

The 27th Division had severe fighting along the railway which crossed its zone of action beyond the Selle River, at Bandival Farm and in the hamlet near Arbre Guernon, all of which were taken on the 17th. The next day Jonc de Mer Farm was captured after a stiff fight and on the 19th the division advanced about 1 mile farther, where it was relieved by a British division on October 21.

When the 27th and 30th Divisions were relieved from the battle line they were approaching the Sambre River, about 19 miles northeast of where they had originally entered the line in September. In their operations after October 5 the 27th Division suffered more than 2,100 casualties and the 30th about 4,000.

During this fighting the Germans were retiring on this front because of the deep advance being made by the American First Army in the Meuse-Argonne region. Much of the combat, especially that of the 30th Division, was in overcoming the resistance of machine gun units left behind in commanding positions. Illustrative of this type of fighting are the brave exploits for which Sergeant Thomas Lee Hall, Sergeant Richmond H. Hilton and Corporal

ames D. Heriot, all noncommissioned
officers with the 30th Division, were
awarded Congressional Medals of Honor.

On October 8, northwest of Brancourt-
e-Grand, Sergeant Hall commanded a
platoon which, after having by his skillful
leadership overcome two machine-gun
ests, was stopped by additional machine-
gun fire of great intensity.   Ordering his
men to take cover in a sunken road, he
advanced alone on the enemy machine-
gun post, killed five members of the crew
with his bayonet and thereby made possible a further advance.   While attacking
another machine-gun nest later in the day
he was mortally wounded.

Sergeant Hilton's company on October
8, while advancing through the village of
Brancourt-le-Grand, was held up by
ntense enfilade fire from a machine gun.
Discovering that this fire came from a
machine-gun nest among shell holes at
the edge of town, Sergeant Hilton, accompanied by a few other soldiers but
well in advance of them, pressed on toward this position, firing with his rifle
until his ammunition was exhausted and
then with his pistol, killing six of the
enemy and capturing ten.   During the
course of this daring exploit he received a
wound from a bursting shell which resulted
in the loss of an arm.

Corporal Heriot on October 11 at
Vaux-Andigny with four other soldiers
organized a combat group and attacked a
German machine-gun nest which had been
inflicting heavy casualties on his company.   In advancing toward it, two of
his men were killed, and because of the
heavy fire from all sides the remaining
two sought shelter.   Unmindful of the
hazard attached to his mission, Corporal

American Troops Awaiting Orders Behind the Front Line Near Prémont,
October 8, 1918.   © B

Heriot, with fixed bayonet, alone charged the machine gun, making his way through the fire for a distance of 30 yards and forcing the enemy to surrender. During this action he received several wounds in the arm, and later in the same day while charging another machine-gun nest this gallant soldier was mortally wounded.

In the operations after October 7, the 30th Division took about 2,400 prisoners, and the 27th Division 1,500. Among their captures were many field guns, machine guns, trench mortars, ammunition

the preceding narrative, the following members of the 27th and 30th Divisions were awarded Medals of Honor for their heroic actions during the advance to the Selle River and just east of it.

Private Edward R. Talley, 30th Division, seeing several comrades killed in attempting to silence a hostile machine-gun nest on October 7 near Ponchaux, attacked the position singlehanded. Armed only with a rifle, he rushed the nest in the face of intense enemy fire, killed or wounded at least six of the crew and put

27th Division Troops Crossing the Selle River on a Temporary Bridge
at St. Souplet, October 19, 1918

dumps, much railroad rolling stock and military property of all kinds. This battle was the last operation of the war in which either the 27th Division or the 30th Division took an active part.

For the locations of headquarters of American corps and divisions while serving in this region turn to page 381.

This battlefield can be visited by going to Cambrai or St. Quentin by rail and from either of those places by automobile.

✦

In addition to the men whose Medal of Honor citations have been included in

the gun out of action. When the enemy attempted to bring forward another gun he drove them back with effective rifle fire.

First Lieutenant James C. Dozier, 30th Division, was painfully wounded near Montbrehain on October 8, but continued to lead his men, displaying the highest type of bravery and skill. When his command was held up by heavy machine-gun fire, he disposed his men in the best cover available and, aided by one soldier, continued forward to attack a machine-gun nest. Creeping up in the face of intense fire, he killed the entire crew with hand

Americans Receiving Coffee From Inhabitant of Becquigny
Soon After Capturing the Town

enades and a pistol and later captured a
umber of Germans in a near-by dugout.
When his company was held up on
:tober 8 near Montbrehain by violent
achine-gun fire from a sunken road,
rgeant Gary Evans Foster, 30th Divi-
on, went forward with an officer to
tack the hostile machine-gun nests.
e officer was wounded, but Sergeant
ıster continued on alone in the face of
avy fire and by the effective use of hand
enades and his pistol killed several of
e enemy and captured 18.
When, during an advance on October
the company of the 30th Division to
ich Corporal James E. Karnes and
ivate Calvin John Ward belonged, was
ld up near Vaux-le-Prêtre by a machine-
n nest which was enfilading their line,
ese two soldiers advanced against it.
ey succeeded in silencing the nest by
lling three of the crew and capturing
e guns and seven of the enemy.
When Private Robert L. Blackwell's
atoon of the 30th Division was almost

surrounded by the enemy near St. Souplet on October 11, and his platoon commander called for volunteers to carry a
message requesting reinforcements, he
volunteered for this mission, well knowing the extreme danger to which he would
be exposed. While attempting to get
through the heavy shell and machine-gun
fire this gallant soldier was killed.

Corporal John C. Villepigue, 30th Division, having been sent out with two
other soldiers on October 11 to scout
through Vaux-Andigny, met with heavy
enemy machine-gun fire which killed one
of his men and wounded the other. Continuing his advance 500 yards in advance
of his platoon he attacked and killed with
a hand grenade four of the enemy in a
dugout. Crawling forward to a point
150 yards in advance of his first encounter,
he rushed a machine-gun nest, killing four
and capturing six of the enemy and taking two light machine guns. After being
joined by his platoon in this advanced position he was severely wounded in the arm.

Salvage Dump of the 30th Division at Montbrehain, October 14, 1918

11TH ENGINEERS AT THE BATTLE OF CAMBRAI
NOVEMBER 20—DECEMBER 3, 1917

THE 11th Engineers was one of nine regiments of engineers organized and sent to France at the request of the Allied Governments, soon after the United States entered the war, to help the Allied troops catch up on emergency railroad work.

From August 1917 until January 1918 the regiment, composed principally of railway specialists, was on duty with the British employed in building and repairing railroads near the front line. While so engaged two enlisted men of the regiment were wounded by shellfire near the village of Gouzeaucourt on September 5, 1917. These were the first American soldiers to be wounded while serving at the front with an American unit.

On November 20, 1917, the British Third Army launched a surprise attack toward Cambrai without the customary artillery preparation, the infantry advancing behind a screen of 380 tanks. These tactics were more successful than expected and the British succeeded in breaking through the Hindenburg Line, almost reaching the outskirts of Cambrai. German reserves were rushed to the area

Explosion of a German Time Bomb in Camb[r]
at the Time of Its Capture, October 8, 1918

and on November 30 the enemy launche[d] a counteroffensive which by its weig[ht] and suddenness surprised the British.

At this time the 11th Engineers w[as] at work building a railroad yard ne[ar] Gouzeaucourt, about 2 miles behind t[he] battle line. The German assault uni[ts] made rapid progress and soon reached t[he] area where the Americans, wh[o] were unarmed, were at wor[k.] Many of the Americans with[-] drew under fire, secured arm[s] and assisted the British in orga[n-] izing new defensive positio[ns] west of Gouzeaucourt. Othe[rs] joined with the British a[nd] helped stop the attack, some [of] them having no weapons at t[he] start except picks and shove[ls.] A number of men were capture[d] but many of these escaped whe[n] the enemy was suddenly cou[n-] terattacked about noon by [a] British division, the America[ns] participating in this a s s a u l[t.] The regiment had 18 casualti[es] in the fighting on November 3[0.]

This locality can be visited [by] taking a train to Cambrai [or] St. Quentin and hiring an aut[o-] mobile at one of those place[s.]

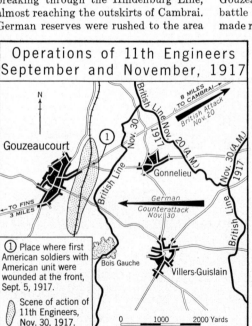

Operations of 11th Engineers
September and November, 1917

N

British Line Nov. 20

8 MILES TO CAMBRAI

British Attack Nov. 20

Gouzeaucourt

British Line Nov. 30

1917

British Line Nov. 20 (A.M.)

Nov. 30 (A.M.)

1917

①

Gonnelieu

German Counterattack Nov. 30

←TO FINS 3 MILES

British Line

Bois Gauche

Villers-Guislain

① Place where first American soldiers with American unit were wounded at the front, Sept. 5, 1917.

Scene of action of 11th Engineers, Nov. 30, 1917.

0   1000   2000 Yards

37TH AND 91ST DIVISIONS IN THE YPRES-LYS OFFENSIVE

OCTOBER 28—NOVEMBER 11, 1918

IN the middle of October, while the American First Army was heavily engaged in the Meuse-Argonne offensive, a request was received from the Allied Commander-in-Chief for two American divisions to be sent to Flanders to give impetus to an offensive there which had been going on since September 28. Urgent as was his own need for troops, the American Commander-in-Chief nevertheless designated two of his best divisions, the 37th and 91st, and these units reported within a few days to the French Army of Belgium, which was then part

30. The 37th Division was in the French XXX Corps and its zone of action was along the railroad northeast of Waereghem, close to the town of Olsene. The 91st was in the French VII Corps and its zone of action was just south of Waereghem. (See the sketch on this page.)

At that time this region, which had been well behind the German front line since the autumn of 1914, was little damaged and was still occupied by most of its civilian population. The terrain where these divisions fought was slightly rolling and broken by numerous houses, patches

37th and 91st Divisions in Ypres-Lys Offensive
October 30 - November 11, 1918

Jump-off Line ▬▬▬ Front Line —xxx— Corps Boundary —xx— Division Boundary
①Flanders Field American Cemetery ②91st Div. Hdqrs., Nov. 1-4 ③37th Div. Hdqrs., Nov. 1-4
④37th Div. Hdqrs., Nov. 9-11 ⑤91st Div. Hdqrs., Nov. 10-11 ⑥37th Div. memorial bridge
A monument has been erected at Audenarde by the United States Government

of the Group of Armies of Flanders commanded by the King of the Belgians.

The two divisions, with a French division between them, went into the front lines near Waereghem on October

of trees, fenced-in small fields and ditches.

The 37th and 91st Divisions took part in a general attack which was launched eastward toward the Escaut River (also known as the Scheldt) at 5:30 a. m. on

October 31. The 37th Division advanced against hostile artillery and machine-gun fire about 2½ miles to the western outskirts of Cruyshautem where it dug in for the night. The 91st drove forward in spite of intense artillery and machine-gun fire and captured the Spitaals Bosschen, a large wooded area a short distance in front of its jump-off line. It

Sergeant Charles R. Reilley, Engineer 91st Division, who voluntarily accom panied a patrol into the city on Novembe 1, while it was still occupied by the enemy He obtained important data regardin destroyed bridges and assisted in a figh with a strong enemy patrol. He als captured a German spy while the latte was attempting to escape, and drove

Waereghem, Belgium, November 1, 1918

was then delayed as the French division on its right had been unable to keep up and this exposed the right flank of the 91st Division to severe hostile enfilade fire which was continued throughout the day.

When the attack was resumed on November 1 it became evident that the Germans were making a retirement and the 37th and 91st Divisions pushed forward rapidly. The 37th Division advanced about 5 miles to the Escaut River, reaching it near Eyne and Heurne. The 91st advanced about the same distance to a position close to Audenarde.

The 91st Division occupied part of Audenarde on November 2 and the remainder of it on the 3d. Before it was relieved on November 4 the division had made reconnaissances of the river and was preparing plans to force a crossing.

Among the first to enter Audenarde was

sniper to cover, thus saving the life his captain who was about to be fire upon. For his gallant actions he wa awarded the Distinguished Service Cros

Early on November 2 the 37th Divisio forced a crossing of the river southea of Heurne under heavy fire, the infantr improvising a bridge from trees felle near the riverbank. The river at th point is canalized and is about 100 fee wide with steep banks about eight fee high. That night the engineers of th division erected footbridges at Heuv and Eyne upon which more troop crossed. A German attack against th bridgehead position launched about 5:0 p. m. on November 4 was repulse The division was relieved from the fron line during the night of November 4–

Both divisions then began prepara tions to take part in another gener offensive. These plans were hastened when the Allied Commander-in-Chief sent word on November 9 that the Germans were withdrawing in disorder along the entire front and directed that they be attacked vigorously. As a result both American divisions were ordered back into the line early on November 10 and directed again to drive forward.

The 37th was assigned a zone of action along the west bank of the Escaut River, about ¾ mile to the northeast of the one it had previously held, in the bend of the river east of Syngem. The division was under the orders of the French XXXIV Corps. The French divisions which were relieved by the 37th had attempted to cross the river unsuccessfully on the 9th.

When the 37th Division took over the sector it was found that the Germans had not withdrawn. The division, however, in spite of hostile shell and machine-gun fire forced a crossing of the river for a second time, the engineers building a foot-bridge just north of the destroyed Hermelgem–Syngem bridge. By the evening of that day the division was established firmly on the far bank.

The 91st Division relieved French troops in the French XXX Corps, about 4 miles east of Audenarde, on November 10.

During the night of November 10 the Germans on this front were badly disorganized and retiring rapidly, their retreat being due largely to the success of the American First Army in the Meuse-Argonne operation which on November 7 had severed, near Sedan, the main German lateral railroad along the Western Front.

37th Division Memorial Bridge at Eyne, Belgium

Troops of the 91st Division in Front of the Hôtel-de-Ville, Audenarde, Belgium, November 12, 1918

On November 11 both the 37th and 91st Divisions advanced practically unopposed. Patrols of the 37th were in the villages of Dickele and Zwartenbroek while those of the 91st were near Elst and in Boucle-St. Blaise by 11:00 a. m. when the Armistice became effective.

During their operations in Flanders deep advances were made by the two American divisions. The total casualties of the 37th Division were almost 1,600 and those of the 91st were about 1,000.

This battlefield can be easily visited by traveling by train to Waereghem, Audenarde or Ghent and hiring an automobile.

✦

Locations of Headquarters

The principal American headquarters during these operations were as follows:

37th Division:
Oct. 29–Nov. 1_____ Denterghem.
Nov. 1–4_____ Cruyshautem.
Nov. 9–11_____ Château de Huysse.

91st Division:
Oct. 30–Nov. 1_____ Desselghem.
Nov. 1–4_____ Stuivenberghe Château.
Nov. 10–11_____ Audenarde.

THE FLANDERS FIELD AMERICAN CEMETERY NEAR
WAEREGHEM, BELGIUM

THE Flanders Field Cemetery, the only American military cemetery in Belgium, has been developed by the United States Government into a beautiful and appropriate resting place for the soldiers who are buried there.

This cemetery is located near Waereghem, 43 miles west of Brussels, upon a battlefield of the 91st Division. It contains the graves of 368 Americans, most of whom are soldier dead from the 37th and 91st Divisions which operated in the vicinity and the 27th and 30th Divisions which served for a considerable time in the front line just south of Ypres.

The enclosing wall of the cemetery and the reception building near the entrance are of red brick. The impressive chapel, built of pure white stone, occupies the center of the cemetery grounds.

Above the entrance to the chapel the following inscription, "GREET THEM EVER WITH GRATEFUL HEARTS", reminds the visitor of the important service rendered the world by the dead buried here.

On its outer walls appears the following inscription in English, French and Flemish:

THIS CHAPEL HAS BEEN ERECTED
BY THE UNITED STATES OF AMERICA
IN MEMORY OF HER SOLDIERS
WHO FOUGHT AND DIED
IN BELGIUM
DURING THE WORLD WAR.
THESE GRAVES ARE THE
PERMANENT AND VISIBLE SYMBOL
OF THE HEROIC DEVOTION
WITH WHICH
THEY GAVE THEIR LIVES
TO THE
COMMON CAUSE OF HUMANITY

Below this inscription, in bas-relief, are small sculptured figures symbolizing Grief, Remembrance and History.

The altar inside the chapel is of black and white marble, upon which rest a cross and two vases for flowers. It bears the inscription: "I WILL RANSOM THEM FROM THE POWER OF THE GRAVE, I WILL REDEEM THEM FROM DEATH." Above, carved on a rose-tinted marble panel, is a Crusader's sword outlined in gold. On each side of the altar are draped flags of the United States, Belgium, France, Great Britain and Italy. On the side walls of the chapel, on marble panels, are listed the names of the American soldiers who lost their lives in Belgium but have no known graves.

The quiet beauty of the interior is enhanced by a mosaic ceiling of striking design and a large ornamental window over the door which lights the room with a subdued yellow light.

The furniture of the chapel consists of four seats and kneeling benches, where those so inclined may rest for meditation and prayer. This furniture is of carved oak, stained a black color with the veining in white, and it harmonizes perfectly with the black and white marble which has been used for the altar.

Each of the four grave blocks is framed by a trimmed hedge and at three of the corners of the cemetery are circular nooks, ornamented by attractive urns, flanked by stone benches and closely surrounded by trees and hedges.

On the bases of the urns are the insignia of the 27th, 30th, 37th and 91st Divisions, the divisions to which belonged most of the men now buried here.

This little cemetery is dear to the hearts of the people of the neighborhood who visit it in large numbers on Sundays and holidays. On the Sunday nearest Memorial Day (May 30) a touching ceremony of praise and thanksgiving is held in memory of the American war dead.

The cemetery may be easily visited by taking a train to Waereghem, or to Ghent, 17 miles away, which is larger and contains much more of historical interest.

If the tourist has not already done so, the account of the operations of the 37th and 91st Divisions, which is given on the preceding pages, should be read.

The monument erected by the United States Government to commemorate the fighting of the American soldiers in this part of Belgium is located at Audenarde, 6½ miles to the east from this cemetery.

Interior of Chapel, American Cemetery Near Waereghem, Belgium

THE AMERICAN MONUMENT AT AUDENARDE, BELGIUM

UNDER the century-old trees of a public square near the west side of the city of Audenarde in Belgium, the United States Government has erected an attractive monument to commemorate the services of the 37th and 91st Divisions and the 53d Field Artillery Brigade of the American Army all of which fought in battle in this region. The monument stands at the end of a small park, which has been improved by the planting of hedges and shrubs and the

French and on the other side in Flemish.

The names of the units commemorated by the memorial are carved on its face above the shield of the United States.

In the center of a round place in the roadway near by is a Belgian monument erected in honor of the Belgian volunteer troops who served in Mexico from 1864 to 1867 and aided in establishing Maximilian on the throne of Mexico.

For an account of the operations of the 37th and 91st Divisions in the general

American Memorial at Audenarde, Belgium

addition of paths and benches. On the front of it, below a shield of the United States and flanked by two American eagles, is the dedicatory inscription which in gilded letters and reads as follows:

ERECTED BY THE
UNITED STATES OF AMERICA
TO COMMEMORATE THE
SERVICES OF AMERICAN TROOPS
WHO FOUGHT IN THIS VICINITY
OCT. 30–NOV. 11, 1918

This inscription is repeated on one side in

vicinity of Audenarde see pages 395–397.

The Flanders Field American Cemetery near the village of Waereghem is approximately 6 miles away to the west.

Audenarde may be easily reached by train and the American monument is not far from the railroad station. The city is on one of the main highways from the North Sea to Brussels and can be easily visited by automobile from Ghent, which is 17 miles to the north, and also from Brussels, which is about 37 miles to the east.

THE 27th and 30th Divisions served with the British Army from the time of their arrival in Europe in May 1918 until the Armistice. During the summer adjoining divisional sectors along the Ly salient just south of Ypres. They wer familiar with this front, as various uni of the 30th Division had been trainir

27th and 30th Divisions in Ypres-Lys Offensive August 18-September 4, 1918

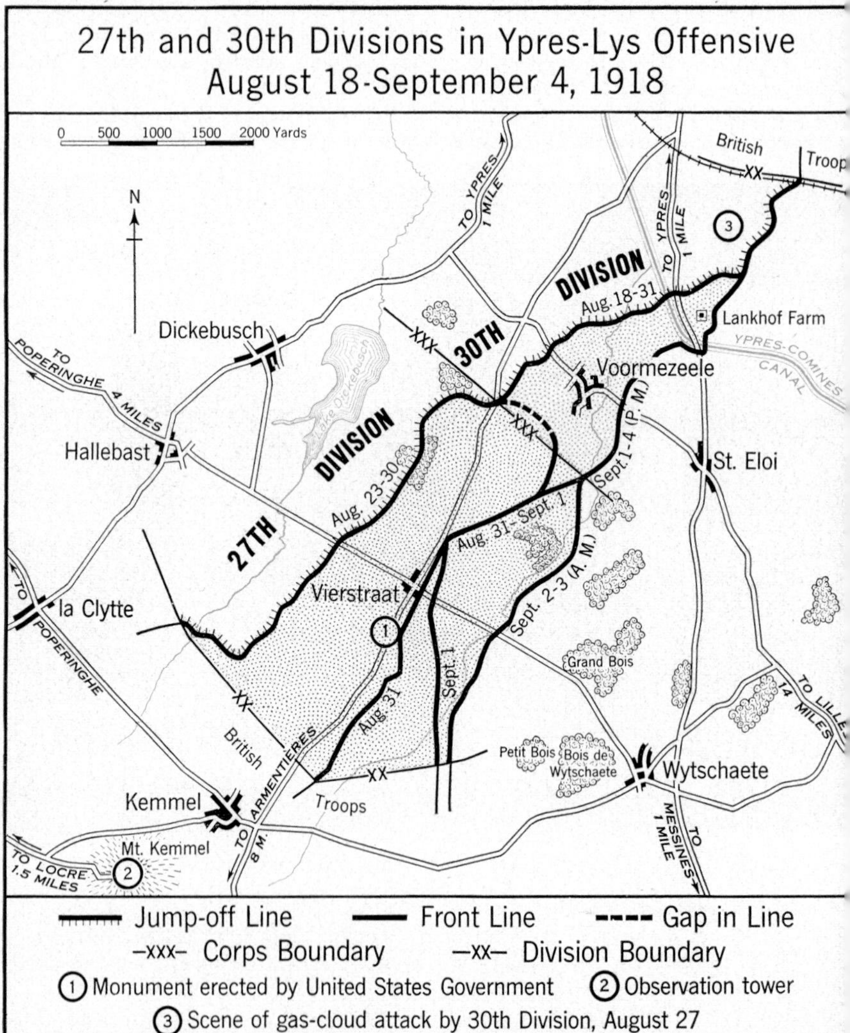

0   500   1000   1500   2000 Yards

N

British Troop

3

TO YPRES 1 MILE

TO YPRES 1 MILE

DIVISION
Aug. 18-31

30TH

Lankhof Farm

YPRES-COMINES CANAL

Dickebusch

Voormezeele

TO POPERINGHE 4 MILES

Hallebast

DIVISION
Aug. 23-30

Sept 1-4 (P. M.)

St. Eloi

27TH

Aug. 31-Sept. 1

Sept. 2-3 (A. M.)

la Clytte

TO POPERINGHE

Vierstraat

1

Grand Bois

Sept. 1

Aug. 31

British

Petit Bois Bois de Wytschaete

Wytschaete

TO LILLE 14 MILES

TO MESSINES 1 MILE

Kemmel

TO ARMENTIÈRES 8 M.

XX

Troops

Mt. Kemmel

2

TO LOCRE 1.5 MILES

┄┄┄ Jump-off Line	━━━ Front Line	┅┅┅ Gap in Line
—xxx— Corps Boundary		—xx— Division Boundary

① Monument erected by United States Government ② Observation tower
③ Scene of gas-cloud attack by 30th Division, August 27

they were trained at the front, under the administrative control of the American II Corps, by attaching small units to British organizations in Picardy and Flanders. In August, while with the British Second Army, they assumed complete charge of on it with the British since July 16, an units of the 27th since July 25. Th 30th Division took command of its sect on August 18 as part of the British I Corps and the 27th Division on Augus 23 as part of the British XIX Corp

It was discovered on August 30 that the Germans were making a general withdrawal from the Lys salient for the purpose of shortening their front line. Conquently the 27th Division was ordered to reconnoiter the situation on its front at night and the 30th Division was expected to send out strong patrols the next morning. According to its instructions if no determined opposition was encountered by the patrols of the 30th Division it was to advance and occupy a new line which included Voormezeele.

with considerable resistance on the morning of August 31 so the division did not attempt to advance during that day.

The 27th Division attacked at 7:00 a. m. on September 1 after a 3½-hour artillery bombardment. Machine-gun nests were overcome and all objectives were taken before noon. Shortly thereafter, having received new orders, the division attacked again but a German counterattack combined with heavy machine-gun fire forced it to withdraw slightly.

Early on September 1 the 30th Division

27th Division Wagon Train Near Cloth Hall, Ypres, Belgium

The 27th Division reconnoitered that night and encountered resistance. However, about 10:00 a. m. on August 31 information was received from the British IX Corps that the enemy had retired from Mont Kemmel. The division was, therefore, ordered to move forward in connection with the British troops on its right. This movement was started promptly and the objectives, which included the village of Vierstraat, were reached about 4:00 o'clock in the afternoon. The patrols of the 30th Division met

moved forward to beyond Voormezeele and by 8:30 a. m. had reached the objectives prescribed by the British II Corps.

The 27th Division did not make a determined attack on September 2 because it was obvious from the stubborn fighting of the previous day that the Germans were no longer retiring but had taken up strong new positions which they were prepared to defend vigorously. The division, however, pushed its units forward until they had contact with the new German line along its entire length.

Captured British Tank Being Used by Germans, September 1918. ⓒ G

Cloth Hall of Ypres, Belgium, in 1935

During September 2 the 30th Divisi
repulsed a small hostile attack in the a
northeast of Lankhof Farm.

The 27th Division was relieved
September 3 and the 30th Division
September 4.   The casualties of the 2'
Division up to the time of its relief h
totaled almost 1,300 officers and m
and those of the 30th about 800.

Both divisions reentered the line ab
three weeks later in the region north
St. Quentin and took part there in
fierce battle for the Hindenburg L
described on pages 373–381.

This battlefield near Ypres can
visited by taking a train to that city a
traveling out from there by automob

✧

Locations of Headquarters

The headquarters of the Ameri
units during the operations here were

II Corps:
    Aug. 30–Sept. 3_ _ Houtkerque.
27th Division:
    Aug. 23–Sept. 3_ _ Douglas Camp, north of Ab
30th Division:
    Aug. 20–Sept. 4_ _ Vogeltje Convent, 2 miles to
        northwest of Poperinghe.

THE AMERICAN MONUMENT NEAR VIERSTRAAT, BELGIUM

MMEDIATELY alongside the road leading south from Ypres toward Mont ‸emmel, near the little hamlet of Vier‸raat, Belgium, is located a monument ‸ected by the United States Government ‸ commemorate the services of the ‸merican troops who fought in that gen‸al region during the World War.

This monument consists of a central ‸ock of white stone in front of which, ‸rved out of stone, is an American ‸lmet resting upon a wreath. The in‸ription which appears on the face of ‸e monument above the helmet is flanked ‸ each side by an American bayonet ‸rved in relief. The inscription reads:

ERECTED BY THE
UNITED STATES OF AMERICA
TO COMMEMORATE THE SERVICES
OF AMERICAN TROOPS
WHO FOUGHT IN THIS VICINITY
AUGUST 18–SEPTEMBER 4, 1918

This inscription is repeated in French ‸d Flemish on the ends of the central ‸ock. On the rear face appear the in‸gnia of the 27th and 30th Divisions, ‸e American units whose fighting is com‸emorated by the memorial.

Surrounding the monument proper is a ‸rrace enclosed by a railing. The ac‸unt of the American operations in the ‸cinity, given on the preceding pages,

should be read from this terrace. By consulting the sketch and reading the following description with his back to the road, the tourist will obtain a good idea of the American fighting near here.

The group of houses seen to the left down the road is the town of Vierstraat.

Just to the right of Vierstraat the church steeple of Voormezeele can be seen through the trees. That town was captured by the 30th Division on September 1.

Mont Kemmel is the highest hill in the region and is seen to the right rear.

The jump-off line of the 27th Division on August 31 was about ½ mile away, just over the ridge sloping up across the road from the monument. The division advanced in this direction on that day and reached a line which included the site of this monument and extended about a mile to the right and left from it, running roughly parallel to this road.

The line held by the 27th Division at the time of its relief on September 3 ran along the bottom of the small valley seen directly ahead. That valley can be traced by the patches of trees which grow on the banks of the small stream in it.

The large town on the sky line directly ahead is Wytschaete. In this particular vicinity the position to which the Germans retired ran along the lower slopes of the ridge upon which that village is located.

American Monument Near Vierstraat, Belgium

80TH DIVISION IN THE SOMME OFFENSIVE
AUGUST 8—18, 1918

UPON its arrival in France in June 1918 the 80th Division was assigned the British First Army. It was under the administrative control of the American Corps and later served with both the British Second and Third Armies.

On July 4 the division joined the Third Army and for training in the front line its regiments were distributed along the British V, IV and ... Corps. These corps were in ... in that order from Albert to ...ras. The 317th Infantry ...giment was with the IV ...rps, the 318th with the V ...rps and the 319th and 320th ...th the VI Corps. Parts of ...se American units first en-...ed the front line on July 23. While elements of the 80th ...vision were occupying por-...ns of the line, the British on ...gust 8 launched the Somme ...ensive south of Albert. The ...tial assault made a deep ...netration into the German ...es and as a direct result the ...emy was soon forced to give ...und at other places.

A battalion of the 317th ...fantry was holding a front-...e sector with the New ...aland Division when the ...rmans began to retire in ...nt of them. Meeting slight ...istance, the American bat-...ion advanced 1½ miles with ... New Zealanders on August ... and occupied the villages of ...re and Puisieux-au-Mont. ...other battalion of the regi-...nt repulsed a German raid ...ich was made against its ...nt lines during the night of August 17–18. The other American regiments did not ...n ground although the 320th Infantry ...essfully repulsed a German raid on ...gust 4, southeast of Boiry-St. Martin, ... again on the night of August 13–14

near the village of Boisleux-St. Marc.

The last units of the 80th Division were relieved from the front line during the night of August 18–19 and on the 19th the 80th Division was relieved from further duty with the British. It immediately started to move to the St. Mihiel region to join the American First Army.

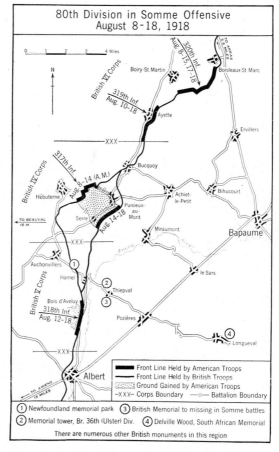

80th Division in Somme Offensive
August 8-18, 1918

Front Line Held by American Troops
Front Line Held by British Troops
Ground Gained by American Troops
—XXX— Corps Boundary   —II— Battalion Boundary

① Newfoundland memorial park ③ British Memorial to missing in Somme battles
② Memorial tower, Br. 36th (Ulster) Div. ④ Delville Wood, South African Memorial
There are numerous other British monuments in this region

While serving with the British the division had 274 casualties. Its headquarters during the period was at Beauval.

The area of this operation can be easily visited by taking a train to the city of Albert and hiring an automobile there.

THE 33d Division upon its arrival in France during the latter part of May 1918 joined the British Fourth Army. Early in July it was serving with that Army near Amiens, its elements being divided for training between the British III Corps and the Australian Corps.

The Australian 4th Division was directed to attack on July 4 with the object of capturing the village of Hamel, which is located at the center of a ba saucer-shaped valley just south of t Somme River and 11 miles east of Amien Companies C and E, 131st Infantr and A and G, 132d Infantry, all of t 33d Division, were attached to the Au tralian 4th Division for the operatio The Americans, totaling about 1,0 men, advanced with the Australians ar promptly secured their objectives. Tv of the American cor panies assisted in r pulsing a Germ counterattack at dus Although the numb of Americans engag on this day was n great, their conduct w such as to receive hi commendation from t British commanders.

It was during t fighting that Corpor Thomas A. Pope pe formed the heroic de for which he w awarded the Congre sional Medal of Hon His company was a vancing when it w halted by hostile m chine-gun fire. Goi forward alone he rush a machine-gun nes killed several of t crew with his bayon and, standing astri the gun, held off t other members of t crew until reinfor ments arrived a captured them.

The four compan were withdrawn duri the night of July 5 and rejoined their vision which was tra ing in the rear are

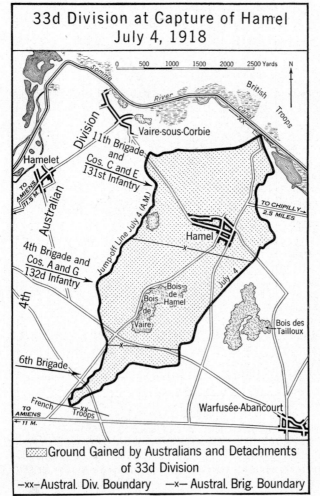

33d Division at Capture of Hamel
July 4, 1918

0   500   1000   1500   2000   2500 Yards   N

Somme River

British Troops

Vaire-sous-Corbie

Canal

Division

11th Brigade and Cos. C and E 131st Infantry

Hamelet

Australian

TO AMIENS 11.5 M.

Jump-off Line July 4 (A.M.)

TO CHIPILLY 2.5 MILES

Hamel

4th Brigade and Cos. A and G 132d Infantry

4th

Bois de Hamel

Bois de

Vaire

July 4

Bois des Tailloux

6th Brigade

French TO AMIENS 11 M.

XX Troops

Warfusée-Abancourt

Ground Gained by Australians and Detachments of 33d Division

—xx— Austral. Div. Boundary   —x— Austral. Brig. Boundary

Street Scene in Amiens, April 25, 1918. © B

American Troops Marching to the Music of a British Band. © B

From July 17 to August 6 elements of the 33d Division trained in line with British units on the front south of Albert.

When the British launched their Somme offensive against the Amiens salient on August 8, the infantry units of the 33d Division were in reserve, attached to the

from the British 58th Division. Fro[m] this ridge the German troops threatene[d] the flank of the Australian Corps on th[e] south bank. (See the sketch below.)

To retake this position the 131st Infantry, 33d Division, was directed t[o] join the British 58th Division imm[e-]

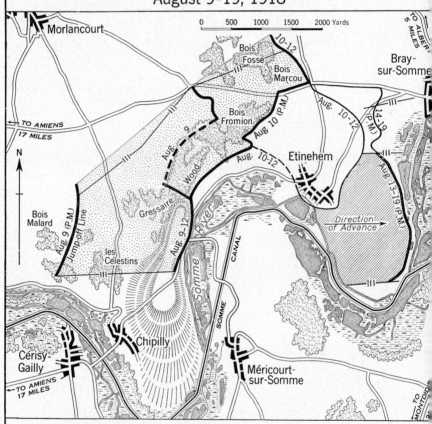

131st Infantry (33d Division) in the Somme Offensive August 9–19, 1918

Morlancourt

Bois Fossé
Bois Marcou

Bray-sur-Somme

TO AMIENS 17 MILES

Bois Fromion

Aug. 10 (P.M.)

Aug. 10–12

Etinehem

N

Aug. 9

Wood

Aug. 10–12

Bois Malard

Aug. 9 (P.M.)

Gressaire

Jump-off Line

les Célestins

Aug. 9–12

Somme River

SOMME CANAL

Direction of Advance

Chipilly

Cérisy-Gailly

TO AMIENS 17 MILES

Méricourt-sur-Somme

0   500   1000   1500   2000 Yards

TO ALBERT 5 MILES

Aug. 14–19 (P.M.)

Aug. 13–19 (P.M.)

TO MONTDID[IER]

— Front Line 131st Infantry — Front Line Australians ▬ ▬ Gap in Line
▦ Ground Gained, 131st Infantry —III— Regimental Boundary
▨ Ground Gained, 131st Infantry and Australians

British III Corps. The offensive made great progress on the first day although Chipilly Ridge, a high bare ridge situated on the north bank of the Somme within a large horseshoe bend of the river, was in German hands, having been recaptured

diately. It moved forward and after difficult night march took part during th[e] afternoon of August 9 in an assault again[st] Chipilly Ridge and Gressaire Wood.

The attack was made at 5:30 p. m[.] the American regiment double-timin[g]

art of the last 4 miles to reach its jump-off line on time. It advanced under hurriedly issued orders with but little reconnaissance; and in spite of heavy machine-gun and artillery fire drove the hostile troops from the northern end of Chipilly Ridge and the southern part of Gressaire Wood. The Australian 4th Division launched an attack from across the river at the same time and as a result of the combined attacks the town of Chipilly and the southern end of Chipilly Ridge were also captured.

Illustrative of the gallant exploits of the American soldiers on this day are the deeds for which Corporal Jake Allex, 33d Division, was awarded the Congressional Medal of Honor. At a critical point when all the officers with his platoon had become casualties, Corporal Allex took command and led the platoon forward until its advance was stopped by fire from a machine-gun nest. He then advanced alone for about 30 yards in the face of intense fire and attacked the nest. With his bayonet he killed five of the enemy and when the bayonet broke he used the butt of his rifle and captured 15 prisoners

On August 10 the Australian Corps was assigned the zone north of the river, and the 131st Infantry was placed under the Australian 4th Division. That day the regiment advanced and occupied the remainder of Gressaire Wood.

As a result of these two days of fighting the regiment had in its possession an important enemy position, 700 prisoners, 10 pieces of artillery, 1 airplane and more than 100 captured machine guns.

On the 13th the 131st Infantry joined the Australians in an attack which captured the ridge east of Etinehem. It stayed in the line until the night of August 19–20 taking part in local attacks and assisting the Australian troops in organizing the positions gained.

During this period other units of the 33d Division served in the front lines or as reserves for various British divisions.

The attack of August 9 and 10 won for the 33d Division the warm praise of the British commanders. On August 12 the

The King of England Decorating Men of the 33d Division, August 12, 1918

King of England visited the division headquarters at Molliens-au-Bois where he personally presented British decorations to the members of the 33d Division who had distinguished themselves in the fighting at Hamel on July 4.

These battlefields of the 33d Division can be visited by going to Amiens by rail and traveling from there by automobile.

The division suffered more than 1,400 casualties while serving on the British Front. On August 23 it was relieved from this front and began its movement to the region of Verdun where it became part of the American First Army.

British, French and American Military Police in Amiens, May 1918. © B

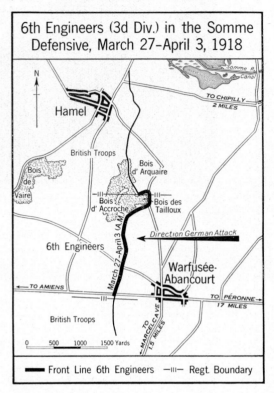

6th Engineers (3d Div.) in the Somme Defensive, March 27–April 3, 1918

N

Somme R.
Canal

TO CHIPILLY
2 MILES

Hamel

British Troops

Bois
d' Arquaire

Bois
de
Vaire

Bois
d' Accroche

Bois des
Tailloux

Direction German Attack

6th Engineers

March 27–April 3 (A.M.)

Warfusée-
Abancourt

TO AMIENS

TO PÉRONNE
17 MILES

British Troops

TO MARCELCAVE
1.5 MILES

0   500   1000   1500 Yards

——— Front Line 6th Engineers   —‖‖— Regt. Boundary

assistance. They were assigned to the British Fifth Army to aid in constructing bridges and other works essential for the defense of the front recently taken over by that Army from the French. These engineers were building heavy steel bridges near Péronne when the German March 2 offensive broke through the British lines in that vicinity. On March 22 this engineering work had to be discontinued due to enemy shellfire, and the American troops were ordered to move farther to the rear.

The German advance toward Amiens was so rapid and the troops opposing it so few in number that the British, as a measure almost of desperation, assembled every available man to occupy the old French trenches, known as the Amiens Defense Line, which extended approximately north and south about 10 miles east of that city. The detachments of troops which were hurriedly collected and put in position, with orders to defend to the last man, included Companies B and D of the 6th Engineers. This combined force was popularly known as "Carey Force" because of General Carey, the British general who commanded them.

EARLY in February 1918 the Headquarters and Companies B and D of the 6th Engineers, 3d Division, were detailed to the British Army in response to an urgent request of the British Commander-in-Chief for American engineer

German Artillery Moving Forward After the Break-Through East of Amiens in March 1918. © G

Amiens–St. Quentin Road. © B

This force, totaling about 2,200 men, held about 8 miles of trenches on the generally flat terrain in the vicinity of the main road leading to Amiens. It was composed of certain British army troops; tunneling, workshop and electrical companies; detachments from five different schools; and the units of the 6th Engineers. It was later reinforced by 00 convalescents from the hospitals and 400 Canadian railroad troops.

The American engineers occupied the right of the Amiens Defense Line, near Marcelcave, on March 26 but on the following day moved by truck to Bois es Tailloux, about 1 mile northwest of Varfusée-Abancourt. There it took over the defense of that wood and of the line s far south as the main Amiens road. On March 27 the retreating British retired behind the Amiens Defense Line. Varfusée-Abancourt was captured by the Germans late in the evening and during that night patrols of the 6th Engineers were engaged with the enemy in town. Heavy fighting took place south of town on March 28, in which the 6th Engineers was not involved, but on both March 29 and 30 the American troops repulsed determined attacks against their position.

No further efforts to advance in force were made by the Germans until after the American detachment was relieved on April 3. On the 8th it resumed engineering work near Amiens and two months later rejoined its division near the village of Château-Thierry.

The area of this 6th Engineer fighting can be easily visited by taking a train to Amiens and hiring an automobile there.

Large German Gun Destroyed East of Chipilly, Near Chuignes

1ST DIVISION AT CANTIGNY

APRIL 27–JULY 8, 1918

DURING the emergency created by the German offensive of March 21, General Pershing placed all American combat troops then in Europe at the disposal of General Foch. Among these units was the 1st Division which on April 5 was moved to the region north of Paris, and on April 27 was given command of a sector west of Montdidier as part of the VI Corps of the French First Army. This marked the first entry into line of an

order to reduce the difficulties of holdin̄ the front line in the vicinity of that plac

The 28th Infantry of the 1st Divisio was selected to carry out the attack ar for several days rehearsed its plans ov similar terrain in the rear area. Durī the attack the regiment was supported American and French artillery, machī gun, Stokes mortar, 37-mm. gun, tan flame-throwing and engineer units ar two companies from the 18th Infantr

1st Division Infantry Going "Over the Top" at Cantigny, May 28, 1918

American division on an active battle front. (See Chapter I, page 27.)

At that time the Germans were in the midst of their series of great offensives and there was a possibility that the next attack might include the 1st Division sector. The activity and firing on this front were so great that it was only with difficulty that any semblance of a defensive position could be prepared.

The most prominent feature of the German lines facing the 1st Division was the high ground on which Cantigny is located. Not only did it furnish excellent positions from which the Germans could observe the American sector, but it also served as a screen for hostile movements and other activities in its rear.

Early in May the command of the division was transferred to the French X Corps and about the middle of the month it was decided to dislodge the Germans from their positions near Cantigny, in

The assault was launched at 6 : 45 a. r on May 28 and in spite of heavy resistan mainly beyond the town and severe art̄ lery and machine-gun fire from the le flank all objectives were soon gaine The construction of trenches, the layin̄ of barbed wire and the preparation strong points on the newly capture ground were promptly started by t̄ American troops concerned.

The German reaction was immedia and unusually violent, indicating a desī to shatter American morale. Counte attack after counterattack was launche against the newly-won positions durī the next two days, and starting abo noon on May 28 the American lin̄ around Cantigny were subjected tō intense 72-hour bombardment from h̄ tile guns of all calibers. At the end that time the Americans still held eve inch of ground they had gained and t̄ Germans were compelled to accept defē

During the defense against the German counter-attacks the two companies the 18th Infantry in serve and one company of e 26th Infantry were aced in the front lines.

The capture of Cantigny as the first large offensive eration by an American vision. It was considered brilliant exploit and was rticularly gratifying to e Allies as it furnished a ncrete example of the ghting ability of American oops, who were then begin- ng to arrive in France in rge numbers. As this gagement occurred the y after the great German fensive of May 27 broke rough the French lines the Chemin des Dames, was a very bright spot r the Allies in an other- ise gloomy situation.

The 1st Division on June took over additional front- e in order to release French oops for service elsewhere. orth of Cantigny the front e was advanced slightly on June 3 to more advantageous location. During ne 9 the division was subjected to a

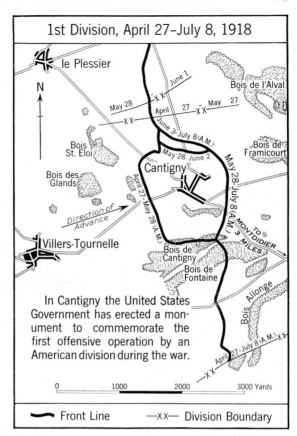

1st Division, April 27–July 8, 1918

In Cantigny the United States Government has erected a monument to commemorate the first offensive operation by an American division during the war.

◂ Front Line   —××— Division Boundary

Germans Leaving Dugout at Cantigny After Flame Thrower Had Been Used in it

severe artillery bombardment, as on that day the Germans launched their great offensive between Montdidier and Noyon, which was just east of the sector occupied by the troops of the 1st Division.

The division remained in line a total of 73 days and suffered almost 5,200 casualties. It was relieved on July 8, and ten days later played an outstand- ing rôle in the counteroffensive south of Soissons against the Aisne-Marne salient.

The Headquarters of the 1st Division was located at the village of Le Mesnil-St. Firmin, April 24–June 4, and at the village of Tartigny, June 4–July 8.

This battlefield of the 1st Division may be conveniently visited by automobile from Paris or by taking a train to Montdi- dier (54 miles from Paris) or to Amiens and hiring an automobile at either place.

THE AMERICAN MONUMENT AT CANTIGNY

THE United States Government has constructed in a public square at Cantigny a small but appropriate monument to commemorate the first large offensive action by an American division which took place during the World War.

The monument consists of a shaft near the upper four corners of which are American eagles. A row of stars encircles the top and on the sides are carved, in French and English, the following inscriptions:

has been developed into a park which landscaped in an attractive manner ar the whole development has proved a we come addition to the village life.

This monument may be convenient visited by automobile from Paris whic is 54 miles to the south or from Amien the nearest large city, which is 25 mil north of the site. For the tourist wh desires the minimum auto trip the tra should be taken to Montdidier, which

THE FIRST DIVISION
UNITED STATES ARMY, OPERATING
UNDER THE X FRENCH CORPS,
CAPTURED THE TOWN OF CANTIGNY
ON MAY 28, 1918, AND HELD IT
AGAINST NUMEROUS COUNTERATTACKS

ERECTED BY THE
UNITED STATES OF AMERICA
TO
COMMEMORATE THE FIRST ATTACK
BY AN AMERICAN DIVISION
IN THE WORLD WAR

---- + ----

Around the monument proper is a paved circular terrace from which a considerable portion of the ground over which the American troops advanced may be seen. Ornamental stone benches have been placed on this terrace and trimmed hedges enclose it. The surrounding area

3 miles away on the railroad and whe taxicabs for a visit to Cantigny and th surrounding battlefields may be hired.

Before leaving the site of the mon ment the description on the precedi pages of the battle operations of the 1 Division in this vicinity should be rea

SUMMARY OF COMBAT SERVICE OF AMERICAN DIVISIONS IN THE OPERATIONS NORTH OF PARIS

Name or Div.	Period of Service 1918	Character of Service	Location of Service General Vicinity of—	Army to Which Attached [1]	Corps to Which Attached [1]	Casualties [2]
1	Apr. 27–June 8.	Sector	Cantigny	Fr. First	Fr. VI until May 5, then Fr. X.	4,111
	June 9–13	Battle	Cantigny	Fr. First	Fr. X	567
	June 14–July 8.	Sector	Cantigny	Fr. First	Fr. X	485
3 (6th Engrs. only)	Mar. 27–Apr. 3.	Battle	Warfusée-Abancourt	Fifth	None	77
27	July 25–Aug. 18.	Training in Line.	South of Ypres	Second	XIX	417
	Aug. 19–Sept. 3.	Battle	Vierstraat	Second	XIX	862
	Sept. 25–30	Battle	West of Bony	Fourth	Am. II	4,508
	Oct. 12–21	Battle	Southeast of Le Cateau.	Fourth	Am. II	2,103
30	July 16–Aug. 18.	Training in Line and Sector.	South of Ypres	Second	II	298
	Aug. 19–Sept. 4.	Battle	Voormezeele	Second	II	466
	Sept. 24–30	Battle	Bellicourt	Fourth	Australian until Sept. 25, then Am. II.	3,018
	Oct. 6–12	Battle	Brancourt - le - Grand and St. Souplet.	Fourth	Am. II	2,480
	Oct. 16–19	Battle	Mazinghien	Fourth	Am. II	1,491
33	June 23	Training in Line.	East of Amiens	Fourth	III	1
	July 2–6	Training in Line.	Hamel	Fourth	III	214
	July 17–Aug. 6.	Training in Line.	West and southwest of Albert.	Fourth	III and Australian.	237
	Aug. 9–20	Battle	Chipilly Ridge	Fourth	III until Aug. 10, then III and Australian.	982
37	Oct. 30–Nov. 4.	Battle	Cruyshautem and Eyne.	Fr. Sixth	Fr. XXX	1,455
	Nov. 10–11	Battle	Dickele	Fr. Sixth	Fr. XXXIV	117
80	July 23–Aug. 7.	Training in Line.	North of Albert	Third	IV, V and VI	129
	Aug. 8–18	Battle	North of Albert	Third	IV, V and VI	145
91	Oct. 30–Nov. 4.	Battle	Southeast of Waereghem and Audenarde.	Fr. Sixth	Fr. VII	963 (54)
	Nov. 10–11	Battle	Boucle-St. Blaise	Fr. Sixth	Fr. XXX	3 (1)

[1] All armies and corps are British unless otherwise indicated. In this table Fr.=French.

[2] Casualties are for period in line only. Figures in parentheses give casualties for units temporarily attached. Add figure in parentheses to the one above in order to obtain the total casualties during the entire operation.

Chapter VII

AMERICAN OPERATIONS ON THE VOSGES FRONT

THE Western Front, extending for more than 400 miles from Switzerland to the North Sea, was so long that neither the Allies nor the Germans could obtain sufficient men to undertake operations on a large scale throughout its entire length. Consequently each massed of Belfort, no great amount of fighting had taken place since 1914 and although the terrain was appropriate for military operations the narrowness of the pass between the mountains and the Swiss border, called the Belfort Gap, made the region not suitable for large-scale operations.

42d Division Troops in Front-Line Trench Near Baccarat, June 3, 1918
Scene is typical of the trenches and terrain in the Vosges region

troops most heavily near those places where there existed a strong likelihood that the other might attack or where the terrain or other strategic factors were such that an offensive would have good chances to bring about decisive results.

The rugged terrain in the Vosges Mountains, north of the Swiss border, was a serious obstacle to major operations in that region because of the difficulty of maneuvering and supplying any considerable number of troops during an advance. South of these mountains near the town

The battle line between the Vosges Mountains and the Moselle River followed roughly the former frontier between France and Germany. The French had prepared before the World War to meet a German attack on that particular front and one of the main reasons Germany violated the neutrality of Belgium was to avoid a major offensive there. Severe fighting, however, occurred in the region early in the war when the Germans attempted to take Nancy, but after 1914 it became inactive as both sides

An American Division on the March, Winter of 1917–1918

realized that offensive operations on other parts of the battle line which were not as strong offered more possibility of success.

When the American troops arrived in France the entire stretch southeastward from the Moselle River to the Swiss border was a quiet or inactive front held by comparatively few troops. This front, commonly known to the Americans as the "Vosges Front", was used by many American divisions for training purposes. It was admirably suited for the purpose as it was conveniently located with respect to the St. Mihiel salient, which was early selected as the scene of the first offensive operation by the American Army, and with respect to the American line of communications, which was being developed to supply troops on the St. Mihiel front.

The normal program of training pre-scribed for an American division after arrival in France was first to carry o intensive training in an area in rear of t front lines, then to serve in quiet sect for a time with French or British troo and finally to complete its training battle in a sector of its own. This ro tine procedure was broken in emergenci and some American divisions, such as t 3d, 4th, 36th, 78th and 91st, went direct from training areas into battle witho sector service, while the 79th, 89th a 90th Divisions took command of sect without any period of affiliation wi troops of the Allied Armies.

The 1st, 5th, 6th, 29th, 32d, 35th, 37 42d, 77th, 81st, 88th and 92d Divisions the American Army had their first sect service at the front in the Vosges regi Elsewhere on the Western Front t

Delousing Machine in Operation at Saacy, August 10, 1918

American Patrol Starting on a Raid Near Badonviller, March 17, 1918

4, 26th, 28th, 82d and 93d Divisions had their first front-line training with the French; the 27th, 30th, 33d and 80th with the British, and the 7th Division mainly with the American Second Army.

Service in quiet sectors varied widely character. For considerable periods the daily life of the front-line troops would be comparatively uneventful, disturbed only by routine patrolling and desultory shelling. At intervals, however, this comparative quiet was shattered by hard-fought local operations and raids. The natural enthusiasm of the American troops and their inherent desire to start active operations as quickly as possible usually produced a marked increase in the fighting in these normally quiet sectors. While this had no immediate effect on the general military situation it did result in

giving valuable combat experience to the American soldiers who later served so creditably on the Marne, at St. Mihiel, along the Meuse and in the Argonne.

Sections of the front line assigned to divisions were called "division sectors". A particular sector was often changed in both size and name as the military situation changed. However, those of the Vosges Front were not radically changed while the American divisions served in the region and, consequently, it has been possible on the following pages to give a general description of the sectors as they were known to the American troops who occupied them. The division sectors of the Vosges region are graphically shown on the sketch which appears on the next page. In the text which follows the sketch they are discussed in order from south to north.

Mail Call at Rolampont, February 1918

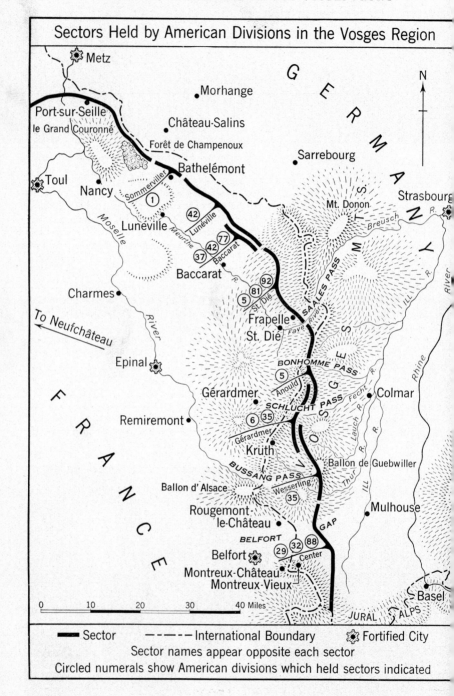

Sectors Held by American Divisions in the Vosges Region

Scale: 0   10   20   30   40 Miles

━━━━━ Sector   ---------- International Boundary   ✺ Fortified City

Sector names appear opposite each sector

Circled numerals show American divisions which held sectors indicated

The Center Sector lay wholly in German territory. It extended north from the Swiss border and controlled the important Belfort Gap. The American 32d, 87th and 88th Divisions served in that order at different times in this sector.

The Wesserling Sector, also on German soil, secured for the Allies the Bussang Pass and the greater part of the mountain pass called the Ballon de Guebwiller. The 35th Division trained in this sector and the 369th Infantry of the 93d Division served here just prior to the Armistice, as part of a French division.

The Gérardmer Sector covered the Schlucht Pass and lay entirely in German territory. It was held by the 35th and 5th Divisions at different times.

The Anould Sector was astride the principal range of the Vosges Mountains, its southern portion being on German soil. It covered the Bonhomme Pass. The 5th Division gained front-line experience here and the 371st and 372d Infantry Regiments of the 93d Division served in this same sector as part of a French division just before the Armistice.

The St. Dié Sector, north of St. Dié, controlled the southern exit of the Saales Pass. It was held at various times by the 5th, 92d and 81st Divisions.

A corps front extended from the western slopes of the Vosges Mountains toward the northwest. It was known to the 42d Division, which trained on it, as the Lunéville Sector. The corps front was divided into three divisional sectors, the one nearest the Vosges being called the Baccarat Sector. This last-named division sector was held at different times by the 42d, 77th and 37th Divisions.

Farther to the northwest was the Sommerviller Sector. Units of the 1st Division entered the front lines in this sector for training with the French on October 23, 1917. This marked the first time that elements of an American division held a section of the front-line trenches.

The following incidents in the history of the American divisions which served in the Vosges region will give an idea of the more active part of the American occupation of the so-called quiet sectors there.

While the 1st Division was in the Sommerviller Sector training with the French it took the first German prisoner captured by the A.E.F. The first Americans to be captured were taken by the Germans in a raid at Bathelémont on November 3, 1917, and in the same raid the first American soldiers were killed in action, three men losing their lives. These three men are now commemorated by a monument which the French erected in 1918 over their graves near Bathelémont.

When the 5th Division took command of the St. Dié Sector, the German position near Frapelle formed a salient projecting into the American lines. The division decided to seize this salient and on August 17 captured it in a small but well-executed attack. Consolidation of the new position was begun in spite of a violent hostile artillery bombardment which continued almost without interruption for three days. The division, however, clung grimly to its gains, repulsing a German counterattack on August 18. By the 20th the new position was completely organized and securely in American hands. The 5th Division lost approximately 400 men in this fighting.

On October 4 about 60 men of the 6th Division near Sondernach, east of Gérardmer, were attacked by a party of 300 Germans, equipped with machine guns and flame throwers. Although cut off by a barrage and greatly outnumbered, the Americans repulsed the attack and captured five prisoners.

While occupying the Center Sector, elements of the 29th Division raided the German lines on August 31 and on September 7, inflicting many casualties.

The front lines of the 32d Division were raided on July 19, while the division was in the Center Sector. The raiding party in this operation was repulsed, leaving two prisoners in American hands.

While training with a French division in the Wesserling Sector, troops of the 35th Division raided a German position on July 6, inflicting losses upon the enemy troops and capturing seven prisoners.

Outpost in the Forest of Parroy, Northeast of
Lunéville, March 5, 1918
Position destroyed by shellfire soon after
picture was taken

On September 11, while in the Baccarat
Sector, a party of the 37th Division penetrated the German lines and captured two
prisoners without any losses.

While with the French in the Lunéville
Sector, units of the 42d Division participated in three raids on March 9.

The Germans raided the 77th Division
in the Baccarat Sector on June 24. They
were repulsed after a sharp fight.

A post of the 81st Division in the St.
Dié Sector was attacked by German troops
on October 9. The enemy was promptly
driven back, leaving a number of dead
and one prisoner in American hands.

During October the 88th Division
holding the Center Sector encountered
strong resistance when it attempted to

Firing a Trench Mortar During Sector
Occupation Near Baccarat, June 3, 1918

improve the position of its front lin

On September 4 the Germans raid
the lines of the 92d Division, at th
time serving in the St. Dié Sector. T
raid was repulsed after a brisk fight.

While the American First Army w
preparing for the St. Mihiel offensive, a
American corps commander and a grou
of staff officers were sent to Belfort o
August 28 with orders to prepare pla
for a major offensive in the direction
Mulhouse and the heights southeast
that place. No American divisions we
moved, nor did General Pershing actual
contemplate such an attack, but the Ge
mans instantly became aware of the i
creased activity in the vicinity and we
led to bring more divisions to the Vosg
region, thus decreasing their availabili
for use on the St. Mihiel front where t
attack was actually made. This succes
ful maneuver which deceived the enem
has become known as the Belfort ruse.

If the war had continued beyond N
vember 11 that part of this region nort
west of the Vosges Mountains would hav
seen greater activity as the Allied Con
mander-in-Chief had decided to launc
an offensive east of the Moselle Rive
This attack was to be participated in b
six American divisions of the America
Second Army, which was to advance in
northeasterly direction from the vicinit
of Port-sur-Seille, and by a French arm
group adjoining it on the east. The da
for this offensive was fixed as Novemb
14, and the movement of the divisions an
other troops which were to take part i
the attack had already begun when th
Armistice was signed. (See map page 114

The Vosges region holds vivid memori
for many American soldiers as it was the
that so many of them, after arduo
months of training in the rear areas, ha
their first experience with trench life an
their first contact with the enemy. On
division, the 6th, had its only front-li
experience in the Vosges Mountain
Deeds of individual bravery were nu
merous and the Distinguished Servi
Cross was awarded to 85 members of th
A.E.F. for their heroism on this fron

ADDITIONAL PLACES OF INTEREST
IN THE VOSGES REGION

Baccarat. Location of 42d Div. Hdqrs., ⟨Ma⟩r. 30–June 21; 77th Div. Hdqrs., ⟨Ju⟩ne 19–Aug. 4; and 37th Div. Hdqrs., ⟨Jul⟩y 23–Sept. 17.

Ballon d'Alsace. Southernmost moun⟨tai⟩n mass of the Vosges. It rises to a ⟨hei⟩ght of over 4,000 feet and dominates ⟨th⟩e northern side of the Belfort Gap.

Ballon de Guebwiller. Southeastern ⟨sho⟩ulder of the Vosges. Lying between ⟨th⟩e Thur and Lauch Rivers, this rugged ⟨are⟩a reaches a height in excess of 4,600

monument located in front of the castle.

Belfort Gap. A rolling valley about 15 miles wide between the Vosges Mountains and the Jural Alps. It is of strategic importance and on the French side is controlled by the fortress of Belfort.

Bonhomme Pass. A pass through the Vosges northeast of Gérardmer.

Bussang Pass. An important pass in the eastern part of the Vosges Mountains which gives access to the valley of the Thur River and that of the upper Rhine.

Street in Badonviller on April 29, 1918
Note entrances to dugouts and cellars

⟨fee⟩t. It dominates the eastern exit of the ⟨Be⟩lfort Gap and the valley of the Rhine ⟨Ri⟩ver to the north of Mulhouse.

Belfort. An important fortified town ⟨for⟩ming the southern element of the ⟨Fr⟩ench frontier defenses in 1914. The ⟨to⟩wn was fortified late in the 17th Cen⟨tu⟩ry by the famous military engineer, ⟨Va⟩uban. It successfully withstood siege ⟨by⟩ the Prussians in the War of 1870. ⟨Th⟩is successful defense is commemorated ⟨by⟩ the great Lion of Belfort, a memorial

Charmes Gap. Between the fortifications of Epinal and Toul lies the relatively open Lorraine plain, in the center of which stands the town of Charmes. Before August 1914 this area had been left without permanent fortifications so that in the event of war the stream of German invasion would be canalized to this definite course. It became known as Charmes Gap and it was through this gap that the Germans attempted during 1914 to turn the French position near Nancy.

Epinal. An important fortified town situated at a strategic point on the Moselle River about 38 miles south of Nancy. In 1914, at the beginning of the war, it was one of the principal elements of the French frontier defenses.

Gérardmer. Location of 5th Div. Hdqrs., June 7–July 15; 35th Div. Hdqrs., Aug. 14–Sept. 2; 6th Div. Hdqrs., Sept. 3–23 and Sept. 25–Oct. 26.

This village, situated on a beautiful lake, is a summer resort in a setting of forests and mountains.

Krüth. The 35th Div. Hdqrs. was located here July 27–Aug. 14.

Le Grand Couronné. The name given by the French to the bastionlike heights north and east of Nancy. It was from these heights that the French forces hurled back many powerful assaults by the German Army in the Battle of Nancy during August and September, 1914.

Mont Donon. The most northern mountain mass of the Vosges. It dominates the valley of the Breusch River to the north of the Saales Pass.

Montreux-Château. Location of 29th Div. Hdqrs., Sept. 14–22, and 88th Div. Hdqrs., Oct. 7–Nov. 4.

Montreux-Vieux. Location of 29th Div. Hdqrs., Aug. 9–Sept. 14.

Neufchâteau. I Corps Hdqrs., Jan. 20–June 18; IV Corps Hdqrs., June 20–Aug. 13; and VI Corps Hdqrs., Aug. 1–12. These corps headquarters while at Neufchâteau exercised administrative but not tactical control over the American divisions assigned to them.

Remiremont. III Corps Hdqrs., June 10–July 12; V Corps Hdqrs., July 10–Aug. 18; and VII Corps Hdqrs., Aug. 20–Nov. 8. While at Remiremont, these headquarters exercised administrative but not tactical control over the American divisions assigned to them.

Rougemont-le-Château. Location of 32d Div. Hdqrs., June 9–July 20.

Saales Pass. This pass, in the northern Vosges, is second in importance to Belfort Gap. It gives access to the upper part of the Breusch River valley and thence to the Rhine River valley near Strasbourg.

St. Dié. Location of 5th Div. Hdqr July 15–Aug. 23; 92d Div. Hdqrs., A 24–Sept. 20; and 81st Div. Hdqrs., duri the period Sept. 21–Oct. 20.

This ancient town grew up about monastery established in the 7th Centu One of the earliest printing presses w located at this place in the 15th Centur

Schlucht Pass. An important openi in the eastern Vosges which gives acc to the valley of the Fecht River and t

Front-Line Trench of the 32d Division, Alsa
June 14, 1918

upper Rhine. This pass was taken I the French in August 1914 during the invasion of upper Alsace and was held I them throughout the war.

Strasbourg. Location of an old Cel city which was captured by the Roma It is situated at the junction of the and Breusch Rivers, 2 miles west of t Rhine, and has long been a point of gre strategic importance. It was ceded Germany in 1871 but returned to Fran at the conclusion of the World War. T city contains many interesting featur

SUMMARY OF COMBAT SERVICE OF AMERICAN DIVISIONS

ON THE VOSGES FRONT

me Div.	Period of Service 1918 Unless Otherwise Indicated	Character of Service	Location of Service General Vicinity of—	Army to Which Attached [1]	Corps to Which Attached [1]	Casualties [2]
1	Oct. 23–Nov. 20, 1917.	Training in Line.	Bathelémont	Eighth	IX	45
5	June 14–July 16.	Training in Line.	Northeast of Gérardmer.	Seventh	XXXIII	149
	July 19–Aug. 23.	Sector	North of St. Dié	Seventh	XXXIII	580
6	Aug. 31–Oct. 12.	Training in Line and Sector.	Southeast of Gérardmer.	Seventh	XXXIII until Oct. 4, then I.	311
29	July 27–Sept. 23.	Training in Line and Sector.	East of Belfort	Seventh	XL	744
32	May 20–July 19.	Training in Line and Sector.	East of Belfort	Seventh	XL	365 (2)
35	June 20–Sept. 2.	Training in Line and Sector.	Southeast of Krüth and southeast of Gérardmer.	Seventh	XXXIII	360
37	July 28–Sept. 16.	Training in Line and Sector.	Northeast of Baccarat	Eighth	VI	174
42	Feb. 21–Mar. 23.	Training in Line.	East of Lunéville and northeast of Baccarat.	Eighth	VII	893
	Mar. 31–June 21.	Sector	Northeast of Baccarat	Eighth	VII until May 12, then VI.	1,104
77	June 21–Aug. 4.	Training in Line and Sector.	Northeast of Baccarat	Eighth	VI	375
81	Sept. 18–Oct. 19.	Training in Line and Sector.	North of St. Dié	Seventh	XXXIII until Oct. 1, then X.	116
88	Sept. 23–Nov. 4	Training in Line and Sector.	East of Belfort	Seventh	XL	72
92	Aug. 23–Sept. 20.	Training in Line and Sector.	North of St. Dié	Seventh	XXXIII	355
93 (9th Inf.ly)	Oct. 17–Nov. 11.	Sector	Southeast of Krüth	Seventh	I	23
93 (71st Inf.ly)	Oct. 16–Nov. 11.	Sector	Northeast of Gérardmer.	Seventh	X	9
93 (72d Inf.ly)	Oct. 14–Nov. 11.	Sector	Northeast of Gérardmer.	Seventh	X	33

[1] All armies and corps are French.

[2] Casualties are for period in line only. Figures in parentheses give casualties for units temporarily attached. d figure in parentheses to the one above in order to obtain the total casualties during the entire operation.

Chapter VIII

AMERICAN OPERATIONS IN
ITALY AND NORTHERN RUSSIA

XCEPT for small forces sent to Italy and Northern Russia, all American military operations in Europe during the World War were con- to dissipating its strength by sending troops to other theaters of operations, as often proposed by Allied governments. In two cases, however, this was ordered

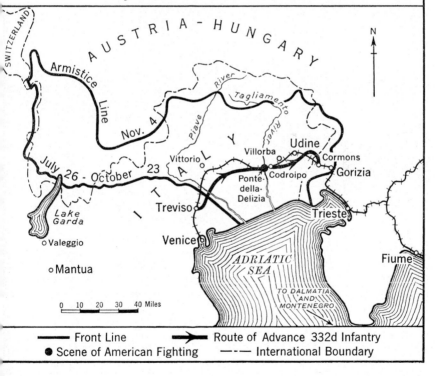

The 332d Infantry (83d Division) with the Italian Army July 26, 1918–March 29, 1919

——— Front Line ➡ Route of Advance 332d Infantry
● Scene of American Fighting —·— International Boundary

ned to the Western Front. The High Command of the A.E.F. realized that the decision in the war would depend upon victory or defeat on the Western Front and, consequently, was decidedly opposed by higher authority and the operations of these American forces, in Italy and Russia, form the subject of this chapter.[1]

[1] An American expedition, not under the A.E.F., was sent to Siberia. It is mentioned in Chapter XIV.

AMERICAN TROOPS IN ITALY

JULY 26, 1918—APRIL 7, 1919

THE 332d Infantry Regiment, 83d Division, with attached medical and supply units, was sent to the Italian front in July 1918 in response to urgent requests from the Italian Government. Its principal missions were to build up Italian morale and to depress that of the enemy by creating the impression that a large force of Americans had reached that front

different articles of uniform and equipment, left the city by a separate road circulated during daylight hours in exposed positions for both the Italian and Austrians to see, and returned after nightfall to its station at Treviso in a inconspicuous a manner as possible.

On October 24, the opening day o the Italian Vittorio-Veneto offensive, th

Scene in Codroipo, Italy, a Short Time After Its Capture by the 332d Infantry
on November 4, 1918

and was preparing to enter the battle line and to take an active part in the fighting.

The regiment was first stationed near Lake Garda, where it trained in methods of warfare suitable for the difficult mountain terrain which comprised the greater part of the Italian theater of operations. Early in October it moved to Treviso, behind the Piave River Front, where it was assigned to the Italian 31st Division. From there, for purposes of deceiving the enemy, it staged a series of marches in which each battalion, with

Italian 31st Division, with the 332d In fantry attached, was in reserve. It joined in the pursuit of the fleeing Austrians o October 29 as part of the British XI Corps of the Italian Tenth Army, th American regiment forming the advanc guard of the corps. On November 3 after several hard marches, the 332d In fantry established contact with an enem rear-guard battalion which was defendin the crossings of the Tagliamento Rive near the village of Ponte-della-Delizia.

Early on November 4 the 2d Battalion

The 332d Infantry Crossing the Piave River on a Ponton Bridge
in Pursuit of the Austrians

rossed the river on a narrow footbridge nd after a brief fight captured the Austrian position on the far side. Continuing o move forward along the Treviso–Udine ailroad, the 2d Battalion occupied the own of Codroipo where it took possession f large stores of munitions and supplies. t 3:00 p. m., November 4, when the rmistice between Italy and Austria-Iungary became effective, the leading merican elements were at Villorba.

After this Armistice the American troops ormed part of the Allied forces stationed 1 Austria and along the Dalmatian coast. he 1st and 3d Battalions were at Cor- ions near Gorizia, Austria. Later in Tovember the 1st Battalion was ordered to go to Treviso and the 3d Battalion to Fiume, Austria. The 2d Battalion was stationed at Cattaro, Dalmatia, and a detachment from it was sent to Cetinje, Montenegro. In March 1919 the regiment was assembled in Genoa and on April 3 its last elements embarked from that seaport for the United States.

In addition to this American infantry force, 30 American ambulance sections, a base hospital and 54 airplane pilots also served with the Italian Army. The American pilots, as members of Italian bombardment squadrons, engaged in bombing raids behind the Austrian lines, being especially active during the progress of the Vittorio-Veneto offensive.

Detachment of the 332d Infantry Near the Front Lines
Northeast of Treviso, Italy, October 5, 1918

AMERICAN TROOPS IN NORTHERN RUSSIA

SEPTEMBER 4, 1918—AUGUST 5, 1919

PRIOR to the collapse of Russia in 1917, vast quantities of military supplies had been assembled in the northern part of that country at the ports of Archangel and Murmansk, the latter being an

there. Consequently an Allied for under British command was dispatche by sea and on August 3, 1918, seized th city of Archangel and drove the Bolshe vik troops to the south of that plac

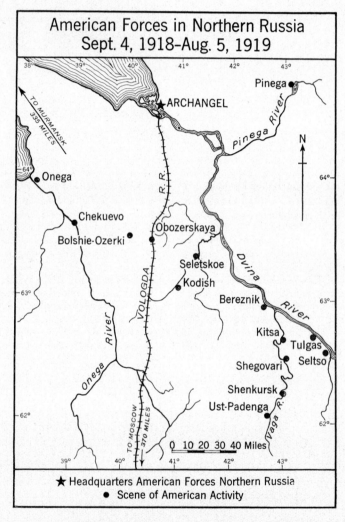

American Forces in Northern Russia
Sept. 4, 1918–Aug. 5, 1919

★ Headquarters American Forces Northern Russia
● Scene of American Activity

open port the year round though north of the Arctic Circle. The Supreme War Council believed that Allied troops should be sent to secure these ports for the use of the Allies and to save the supplies located

The British Government, through i Ambassador at Washington, urged Amer can participation in the undertaking. A a result the War Department on July 2 directed the Commander-in-Chief of th merican Expeditionary Forces to send ree battalions of infantry and three mpanies of engineers to join this Allied enture. The 339th Infantry, 1st Battal- n of the 310th Engineers, 337th Field ospital and 337th Ambulance Company, I of the 85th Division, were designated. hey sailed from England, and arrived Northern Russia on September 4. Operating under British command, this places were as great a distance as 200 miles from their main base at Archangel.

The American soldiers soon partici- pated in the fighting, their first casualties occurring on September 16 in the general area to the south of Obczerskaya.

During their service in Russia the Amer- ican troops conducted many small opera- tions under arduous conditions, the normal hardships of warfare being intensified by

An Advanced Outpost of the 339th Infantry in Northern Russia,
February 21, 1919

1all American contingent was soon split) in isolated detachments protecting, th Allied troops and Russian volunteers, e vital points on the railroads and rivers nich were the main avenues of approach the coast.   The Americans were spread t over a front of 450 miles and in some the deep snow, intense cold, darkness of winter in the Arctic Zone and the long lines of communication, which were in con- stant danger of being cut by the enemy.

During January 1919 the Bolsheviki launched an offensive northward between the Dvina River and the railroad, forcing

American Soldiers in Archangel, Russia, October 25, 1918

Convoy En Route from Archangel to Bereznik, Russia
Typical view of the terrain of the region

American Blockhouse at Tulgas, on the Dvina River, Russia
Two patrols are in front of the blockhouse, one returning, the other just starting

evacuation of Ust-Padenga, Shenkursk Shegovari after heavy fighting. This sed the Allies to establish a new line of ense, and in garrisoning it the American es became more widely dispersed than ore. In March severe fighting devel-d around Bolshie-Ozerki and on May 1 ng-threatened attack in the vicinity of Vaga River, 18 miles southeast of town of Bereznik, was beaten off. During April 1919 the American 167th 168th Railroad Transportation Com-ies joined the expedition, operating nly in the Murmansk region. After forming valuable service they were rned to France three months later. he American soldiers began to be with-wn from the forward positions late in

May 1919. They were assembled at Arch-angel and soon thereafter sailed for France, being replaced by British troops newly arrived from England and by Rus-sian soldiers. On August 5 the headquar-ters of the American force in Northern Russia was officially closed.

In the opinion of the senior American officer the expedition was not particularly well managed and his troops were sub-jected to needless hardships.

More than 400 casualties were suffered by this small American force, most of them occurring after the fighting had ceased on the Western Front. In spite of this, how-ever, and the trying nature of their serv-ice, the American units performed their duties with great fortitude and bravery.

Outpost of the 339th Infantry at Ust-Padenga, Russia
This was the most distant post from the base at Archangel

American Docks at Nantes, November 3, 1918
Third largest port of the A.E.F.

Chapter IX

THE SERVICES OF SUPPLY

ᴵN rear of the area actually occupied by the fighting elements of a modern army, a great organization is required keep the combat units constantly supplied with the men and means necessary operations against the enemy. Replacements of men and animals, great quantities of rations, ammunition, weapons, equipment and supplies of all kinds must be obtained and delivered to

The building up of this organization was one of the most difficult problems which faced the Commander-in-Chief of the A.E.F. upon his arrival in France. It was imperative that the essential supply services be ready to operate when the first combat troops arrived and that their facilities be expanded progressively to supply the needs of the vast forces soon to come. In spite of the handicaps of

Locomotive Repair Shop at Nevers Under Construction by American Engineers
Nevers was an important railroad and storage center

e front. To accomplish this, complete transportation facilities must be provided, d these must not only be adequate to handle the enormous volumes of freight t also to move organizations from one int to another and to evacuate the wounded to the rear. In the A.E.F. these and other tasks, which involved the construction and operation of transportation systems, telephone and telegraph lines, hospitals, depots, docks, mills, repair shops and factories of various kinds, were performed by an organization known successively as the "Line of Communications", the "Service of the Rear" and the Services of Supply" or briefly "S.O.S."

emergency pressure, the great distance from America, a foreign language and foreign customs, and an already over-burdened railroad system in France, the organization was developed steadily so that when the crisis came at the time of the Meuse-Argonne offensive it was able to handle with great success the enormous demands made by the First Army upon it.

The "Line of Communications" was formed on July 5, 1917, shortly after General Pershing arrived in France. At that time it was given no definite boundaries but consisted mainly of the port of St. Nazaire and the city of Nevers, the latter being the Headquarters of the Advance

Section. Its active area was gradually extended, however, and on February 16, 1918, the "Line of Communications" was reorganized and called the "Service of the Rear". This designation was changed

communication began within the Unite States and extended across the sea 1 France. They entered France main at ports along its western coast from Bre southward, as those farther north we.

Services of Supply of the American Expeditionary Forces

⊗ General Headquarters A. E. F.   ⊙ Headquarters S. O. S.   • Port used by S. O. S.
O Important Town   ▬▬▬ Line of Jan. 1918   +–+–+ Railroad
------- Section Boundary   Numbers indicate base sections

on March 13, 1918, and throughout the remainder of its existence the organization was known as the "Services of Supply" or more generally as the "S.O.S." The American lines of supply and

already heavily burdened with Briti and French traffic. The railway lin which ran northeastward from the southern ports to the main areas of Ame can operations were selected for the u the A.E.F., thus avoiding the con-ested region near Paris where the greater art of the French war factories and large apply depots were located.

For purposes of administration the O.S. was divided into several base sec-ans, located around the ports of debarka-on, and one intermediate and one ad-ance section located ogressively n e a r e r e front lines. Even-ally there were nine ase sections, including e in England, one in aly and one compris-g Antwerp and Rot-rdam. The extent of e S.O.S. and its terri-rial organization at e time of the Armi-ice are shown on the eceding sketch.

The C o m m a n d i n g eneral of the S.O.S. as responsible directly the Commander-in-hief of the A.E.F. e was in charge of all tivities of the Serv-es of Supply and of all rsonnel and matériel om the moment they rived at the ports til they r e a c h e d ints in the forward eas designated by .H.Q. He coordinated e work of the differ-t supply branches, ch as the quarter-aster, e n g i n e e r, dnance, signal, trans-ortation, aviation, emical warfare and edical, and so planned that, as far as ossible, there would be on hand at all mes sufficient supplies to meet every quirement of the forces at the front.

The scarcity of vessels made it im-erative that as many articles as possible e purchased in Europe, so an agency of e S.O.S., called the General Purchasing

Major General James G. Harbord
Commanding General of the Services of
Supply from July 29, 1918,
to May 26, 1919

Board, was created to supervise and coordinate such purchases. The effi-ciency of this agency as well as its great value is illustrated by the fact that from June 1917 to December 1918 approxi-mately 10,193,000 ship tons of material were acquired in Europe for the use of the American Army, while shipments from the United States to the A.E.F. during that same period amounted to a p p r o x i m a t e l y 7,675,000 ship tons.

A further saving in tonnage was made by the f o r m a t i o n of a salvage service, which collected, repaired and r e i s s u e d discarded shoes, hats, clothing and other articles of equip-ment. T h i s s e r v i c e, besides saving much raw material, reclaimed for use supplies valued at $126,367,322.

The construction of the many establish-ments and f a c i l i t i e s necessary to the proper functioning of the sup-ply service was per-f o r m e d c h i e f l y by American e n g i n e e r troops. Nearly 1,000 miles of standard-gauge railway tracks; 4 docks, with 23 berths, includ-ing the necessary equip-ment for u n l o a d i n g ships; about 25,000,000 square feet of covered storage space; 16,000 b a r r a c k s, which, if placed end to end, would have reached 303 miles, or from Washington, D. C., to Albany, New York; bakeries; several enormous hospitals; refrigeration plants; and many other structures were built by the American Army in France. The base hospital center at Mars consisted of 700 buildings, with a floor space of 33 acres.

One of the refrigerating plants could store 6,500 tons of meat and produce 500 tons of ice per day; and one of the mechanical bakeries had a daily capacity of 800,000 pounds of bread, enough to fill about 50 standard American freight cars. Forestry operations, which produced more than 200,000,000 feet of lumber and about 4,000,000 railway ties, were carried on to assist in providing the materials needed in the construction program, the size of

motives and 56,000 cars for the Alli

The supplies collected were stored different points between the base por and the combat zone. It was inadvisat to place large quantities too close to t front because of the enormous losses a consequent scarcity of supplies whi would result if the Germans made a su stantial advance. On the other hand, stored near the base ports they would too far from the battle front and an inte

American Lumber Mill Near Eclaron
At the time of the Armistice 81 of these mills were in operation

which is indicated by the examples that have just been given in this paragraph.

The transportation of supplies required a great amount of rolling stock. As only a part of this could be procured from the French, assembly plants were erected in which more than 1,500 locomotives and 18,000 cars were constructed from parts received from the United States. American railroad repair shops in France also reconditioned approximately 2,000 loco-

ruption of the lines of communicati would interfere with sending them fc ward and thus seriously embarrass t troops in contact with the enemy. D pots were therefore established in the bas intermediate and advance sections, tho in the advance section containing rel tively small reserves and being located near to the combat areas as practicabl It was originally planned that sufficie reserve stocks should be kept in Fran

View of Yards at La Rochelle
Shows 80 cars, representing one day's assembling at this American plant

supply the army for three months, thus providing an ample factor of safety in case ocean traffic were interrupted. In August 1918, however, it was considered safe to reduce this reserve requirement to 5 days. From the advance depots supplies were distributed regularly to the troops through great combination depots and railway yards known as regulating stations, which operated directly under General Headquarters, A.E.F.

The growth and development of the Services of Supply, which kept pace with those of the combat forces, and the successful carrying out of its innumerable, important and complicated tasks form an outstanding achievement of the A.E.F. It actually supplied successfully an army of 2,000,000 men and, at the time of the armistice, plans for the necessary expansion to care for the needs of an army of 4,000,000 men were well under way. By that date this huge organization had reached a strength of 644,540 men, not including 23,772 civilian employees carried on its rolls, and comprised about one third of the American soldiers in Europe.

The vital importance of the S.O.S. and its value to the fighting troops are indicated by the following telegram which was sent on September 23, 1918, after the successful attack of the American First Army in the St. Mihiel region, to the Commanding General of the Services of Supply by the Commander-in-Chief of the A.E.F., who at the time was also directly in command of the First Army:

"I want the officers and men of the S.O.S., under your command, to know how much the First Army appreciates the prompt response made to every demand for men, equipment, supplies and transportation necessary to carry out the recent operations. Please extend to all our hearty congratulations and say that they share the success with us."

Supplies in Storage at Montoir

LOCATIONS IN FRANCE OF ACTIVITIES
OF THE SERVICES OF SUPPLY

THE following list gives some of the places in France where establishments were created or operated by the Services of Supply. This list although incomplete will give an idea of the magnitude of the work performed by that organization.

HEADQUARTERS, S.O.S.

Tours. Also aviation instruction center and base depot; refrigeration plant.

A beautiful fountain at Tours erected by the United States Government commemorates the services of the S.O.S. It is located on the Quai d'Orléans at the southern end of the Pont Wilson. For a description of this memorial see page 479.

ADVANCE SECTION *

Bazoilles-sur-Meuse. Hospital center; salvage plant; storage depot; cold-storage and ice-making plant; medical school.

Beaune. A university, established here by the A.E.F. after the Armistice, was attended by about 9,000 Americans; hospital center; general storage depot.

Belfort. Motor transport repair shops.

Besançon. Location of a forestry district headquarters and remount depot.

Bourbonne-les-Bains. Remount depot and veterinary hospital; medical supply depot; advance motor transport center.

Châtillon-sur-Seine. Location of II Corps schools; air service school in gunnery and observation; gasoline storage depot; field and mechanical bakeries.

* See map, page 438, for location of these Sections.

Colombey-les-Belles. Air service pot for advance section of the S.O

Commercy. Remount depot and v erinary hospital; motor transport cen

Contrexéville. Hospital center.

Corbeil. Coffee roasting plant.

Dijon. Advance quartermaster dep motor transport shops; camouflage pla air service depot; forestry district hdc

Donjeux. Tractor artillery repair sho motor transport service park.

Doulaincourt. Ordnance shops.

Eclaron. Location of a forestry d trict headquarters.

Epinal. Motor transport overhaul and repair shop; forestry district hdqrs

Gondrecourt. I Corps schools.

Hanlon Field, 1 mile east of Chaumo Location of A.E.F. gas defense school.

Haussimont. Artillery observati school; training center for railway ar lery; ordnance training center and rep shop for artillery on railway mounts.

Is-sur-Tille. Headquarters of Adva Section of S.O.S., Sept. 17–Nov. 1, 19 regulating station, from which more th 1,000,000 men were supplied at one tin largest bakery in the A.E.F.; ordna school and shops; air service intermedi depot; artillery camp; important cen of railroad construction in this area.

Jonchery. Advance quartermaster pot; advance ammunition storage dep center of railroad construction; ordnar school; advance motor transport cent

New Cars and Trucks Assembled at Bassens, October 1, 1918

Horses for the American Forces Just Unloaded at Bordeaux

Langres. Army schools, which in-
ded 17 separate schools; motor trans-
rt repair and supply center; hospital
ter; Headquarters of the Advance Sec-
n, Services of Supply, during the period
m January 20 to June 28, 1918.

Léonval. Advance miscellaneous stor-
e depot; chemical warfare ammunition
ot and repair shops.

Le Valdahon. Aerial observation school
artillery; field artillery school and
ining camp; ordnance repair shop;
ation of veterinary hospital.

Liffol-le-Grand. Regulating station;
ot camp; railroad repair shop and
gine terminal; mechanical bakery; scene
many large general activities.

Lux. Location of a remount depot and
erinary hospital.

Mailly. Heavy artillery school before
noval to Angers; artillery camp.

Montiers-sur-Saulx. Location of a
nount depot and veterinary hospital.

Nancy. Location of a remount depot.

Neufchâteau. Headquarters of the
vance Section, S.O.S., Nov. 1, 1917–Jan.
and after Oct. 23, 1918; motor trans-
t overhaul park; veterinary hospital.

Nogent-en-Bassigny. Headquarters of
the Advance Section, S.O.S., during the
period, June 28 to October 23, 1918.

Rimaucourt. Hospital center.

St. Dizier. Regulating station.

Sampigny. Location of a large motor
transport park and repair center.

Toul. Important hospital center; refrigeration plant; veterinary hospital.

Vaucouleurs. Advance storage depot.

Vitrey. Trench artillery school center.

Vitry-le-François. Motor transport repair center; important railroad junction.

INTERMEDIATE SECTION

Aix-les-Bains. Central point of the
principal leave area for the A.E.F.

Allerey. Hospital center; storage depot;
ice-making and cold-storage plant.

Autun. Military police school.

Blois. Reclassification camp for officers; concentration and reclassification
point for enlisted casuals discharged from
hospitals in the A.E.F.

Bourges. Location of the central records office for all personnel of the A.E.F.;
ordnance school, shops and depot; forestry district headquarters; field bakery.

Sorting Salvaged Shoes

Châteauroux. Gas mask salvage depot; forestry district headquarters.

Chinon. Location of the Chemical Warfare Service training center.

Clamecy. III Corps schools.

Clermont-Ferrand. Training center for heavy tractor artillery; aviation instruction center; ordnance training center and repair shops; hospital center; quartermaster depot; location of a field bakery.

Decize. Motor transport school.

Gien. Heavy artillery tractor school; forestry district headquarters.

Gièvres. General intermediate storage depot, the largest depot in the A.E.F. It reached a strength of about 700 officers and 25,000 soldiers. Included in this depot were the largest refrigeration and ice-making plant in the A.E.F.; coffee roasting plant and field bakery; coal and gasoline storage; central baggage office; remount depot and veterinary hospital. Center of railroad construction.

Grenoble. One of the leave areas.

Issoudun. Aviation instruction center comprising 12 flying fields; intermediate quartermaster depot; ammunition storage depot; site of prisoner of war enclosu:

La Cluze. Location of a forestry d trict headquarters.

Le Blanc. Field artillery motor tra? ing center and ordnance repair shop.

Le Mans. Replacement depot; ri range with 775 targets; motor transpc repair shop; chaplains' school. Aft the Armistice this was the principal ar in which troops were assembled, inspect and equipped preparatory to embarki for the United States. Its maximu capacity was 230,000 men.

Le Puy. Forestry district headquarte

Mars. Location of a hospital cent

Mehun-sur-Yèvre. Location of larg ordnance repair shop in A.E.F., whe rifles, machine guns and cannon were i conditioned; storage depot.

Mesves-sur-Loire. One of the larg hospital centers of the A.E.F.

Montierchaume. General intermed ate storage depot, similar to the one Gièvres but only half completed at t time the hostilities ceased.

Montlouis. Potato storage depot.

Neuvy-Pailloux. Tank center.

Nevers. Headquarters of the Advan Section, S.O.S., July 10–Sept. 17, 191 Headquarters of the Intermediate Se tion, S.O.S., after Sept. 17, 1917; also : important railroad and storage cente principal locomotive repair shops of t: Expeditionary Forces; veterinary hospit*

Drafting an Operation Map

Pont-de-Claix. Gas cylinder filling plant ᵾn by the Chemical Warfare Service.

Pouilly. Location of a supply depot.

Richelieu. Camp for officer prisoners war, more than 800 being confined.

Romorantin. Aviation production ᵾnter and base depot; motor transport ᵾair shop and storage depot.

St. Aignan. Replacement depot. After ᵾe Armistice it became a clearing point ᵾ troops returning to the United States.

St. Pierre-des-Corps. Central camp ᵾ prisoners of war; supply depot; salvage ᵾnt; postal and statistical bureaus.

Selles-sur-Cher. Remount depot.

Sougy. Location of a remount depot ᵾd veterinary hospital.

Valbonne. Infantry school for officer ᵾndidates; location of a field bakery.

Verneuil. Motor transport reconstruc-ᵾn shop of the A.E.F.; motor transport ᵾpply depot; prisoner of war enclosure.

Vichy. Location of a hospital center.

DISTRICT OF PARIS

Arnouville-les-Gonesse. Artillery sec-ᵾn of the Army anti-aircraft school.

Clichy-la-Garenne. Air base depot.

Le Bourget. Temporary regulating sta-ᵾn which included Noisy-le-Sec and was ᵾd in conjunction with the French.

BASE SECTION NO. 1

Angers. Heavy artillery school; engi-ᵾer training base; ordnance training ᵾnter and repair shops; railroad trans-ᵾrtation officers' school; hospital center; ᵾation of a cold-storage plant.

Baugé. Forestry district headquarters.

Coëtquidan. Artillery training camp; ᵾial observation school; veterinary hos-ᵾal; ordnance repair shop; storage depot.

Donges. Ammunition depot.

Les Sables-d'Olonne. Secondary port ᵾ entry, principally used for coal.

Meucon. Field artillery training camp; ᵾillery aerial observation school; ord-ᵾnce repair shop for mobile artillery.

Montoir. Large storage depot and ᵾlroad yards; engine terminal and rail-ᵾad repair shop; coal storage yards. A ᵾge new dock to accommodate eight ships

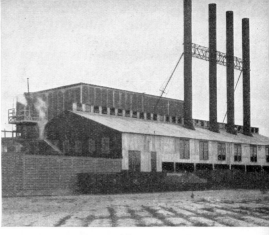

Ice Plant at Gièvres
Third largest in the world, constructed by A. E. F.

was unfinished at the time of the Armistice. This was the main depot for supplies received at the port of St. Nazaire.

Nantes. Port of entry; motor assembly and repair shop; hospital center.

St. Jean-de-Monts. Location of an aerial gunnery and an ordnance school.

St. Nazaire. Headquarters of Base Section No. 1; principal freight port, about 2,552,000 tons of freight were received here before May 1, 1919; remount depot and veterinary hospital; ice-making and refrigeration plant; center of railroad construction; locomotive erecting shops; camps.

Saumur. Artillery school for officers and candidates for commission; bakery.

Savenay. Hospital center for wounded being returned to the United States.

BASE SECTION NO. 2

Angoulême. Ordnance training center and repair shops; training center for personnel of artillery ammunition trains.

Bassens. Large American docks; storage warehouses and cold-storage plant; machine repair shop for the transport service; engine terminal; center of railroad construction and many other activities.

Bayonne. One of the smaller ports used by the A.E.F.; remount depot.

Beau Désert. Hospital center; small storage depot; prisoner of war enclosure.

Bordeaux. Headquarters of Base Section No. 2. At the time of the Armistice this port was rapidly becoming the principal freight port of the A.E.F. and by May 1, 1919, it had received about 2,197,000

Railway Yards and Warehouses at St. Sulpice
Constructed by American Engineers

tons. In its vicinity were a large number of sawmills, hospitals and warehouses.

Carbon-Blanc. Location of a remount depot and veterinary hospital.

Cazaux. Aerial gunnery school.

Dax. Forestry district headquarters.

Hendaye. Remount depot.

Labrit. Forestry district headquarters.

La Courtine. Field artillery training camp; miscellaneous storage depot.

Le Courneau. Field artillery training camp; miscellaneous storage depot.

Libourne. Heavy tractor artillery training center; ordnance training center and shops; miscellaneous storage depot.

Limoges. Heavy tractor artillery training center; ordnance training center and shops; storage depot; hospital center.

Mérignac. Remount depot.

Mimizan. Location of a forestry district headquarters.

Pauillac. Naval air station; port of entry and port of embarkation for troops

Assembling an American Locomotive at the St. Nazaire Shops of the S.O.S.

returning to the United States after hostilities had ceased; small storage yard.

Perigueux. Hospital center.

Pontenx-les-Forges. Forestry district headquarters; location of a field bakery

St. Loubès. Large base depot; ordnance storage depot; oil storage tank center of railroad construction.

St. Sulpice. Large storage depot; coffee-roasting plant; field bakery; coal storage yard; center of railroad construction

Sougé-Champ-de-Tir. Artillery concentration and training camp; balloon aerial gunnery and observation school ordnance repair shop and remount depot

BASE SECTION NO. 4

Calais. One of the ports used by American troops arriving by way of England.

Le Havre. Headquarters of Base Section No. 4; auxiliary port for American shipping; most of the men trans-shipped from England landed here; storage depot refrigeration plant; location of a motor transport service and reception parks.

Rouen. Port of entry for gasoline, coal and other supplies; motor transport shop

BASE SECTION NO. 5

Brest. Headquarters of Base Section No. 5; principal port for debarkation and embarkation of troops. A lighterage wharf, warehouses and refrigeration plant were constructed by Americans there.

A beautiful monument to commemorate the achievements of the United States Navy during the World War has been erected by the American Government

ent on an old fortification wall over-
oking the harbor. See page 475 for a
neral description of this memorial.

Cherbourg. Port of debarkation for
oops arriving by way of England.

Granville. Port of entry for coal.

Pontanézen Barracks. Largest Amer-
an camp in France; rest camp for troops
ebarking or embarking at Brest.

Rennes. Locomotive terminal; repair
op for railroad cars and locomotives.

Miramas. Storage depot for the port
of Marseille; prisoner of war enclosure.

Nice. Main town in Riviera leave area.

BASE SECTION NO. 7

Aigrefeuille. Location of a base depot;
classification yards and coal storage depot.

La Pallice. Headquarters of Base Section No. 7 for a time; port of entry for oil
and other freight; gasoline storage depot;
refrigeration plant and remount depot.

Loading Cars at Quartermaster Depot No. 1, Nevers
Note women laborers employed for this work

St. Malo. Leave center in Brittany;
econdary port of entry, mainly for coal.

BASE SECTION NO. 6

Marseille. Headquarters of Base Sec-
ion No. 6; motor reception park; remount
epot. Due to submarine activities in the
Mediterranean and the greater distance
rom America this port was not used exten-
ively by the American Expeditionary
Forces during the war. After the Armistice
t was a secondary port of embarkation
or troops returning to the United States.

La Rochelle. Headquarters of Base
Section No. 7 after removal from La Pallice;
operated as a port in conjunction with
La Pallice; railroad car erection center;
remount depot and veterinary hospital.

Marans. Location of a secondary coal
port and coal storage depot.

Mortagne. Cement plant, leased from
the French, was operated by the S.O.S.

Rochefort. Port for coal and general
cargo; site of prisoner of war enclosure.

Tonnay-Charente. Coal port and coal
storage depot, operating with Rochefort.

Chapter X

OPERATIONS OF THE UNITED STATES NAVY
IN THE WORLD WAR

HE information given in this chapter is based upon data furnished officially by the Secretary of the Navy.
When the United States entered the war the Allied Navies appeared to be lacking in effective means for combating the German submarines which had started a campaign of unrestricted warfare two months previously. It was extremely important, therefore, that immediate

of shipping a month, which was much greater than the rate of replacement.

The task facing the American Navy was one of tremendous difficulty. It had to assist as soon as possible in counteracting the submarine menace and in addition had to organize means of providing passage across the Atlantic for hundreds of thousands of American troops and enormous quantities of supplies.

German Submarine *U-58* Surrendering to
United States Destroyers *Fanning* and *Nicholson*, November 1917

American naval assistance be furnished to aid them in meeting the crisis.

Admiral William S. Sims, who was to become Commander-in-Chief of the United States Naval Forces in European waters, landed in England shortly after America's entry into the war and established his headquarters at London. He was at once informed by the British authorities that if losses due to hostile submarines were not checked quickly the Allies would probably be defeated, as they were then losing about 800,000 tons

Action against submarines was initiated at once by dispatching to Europe the limited number of destroyers then available. These were augmented by converted yachts, gunboats, small cruisers and revenue cutters, and immediate steps were taken to build additional destroyers.

The first fighting unit of the American Navy to arrive in European waters was a detachment of six destroyers which, on May 4, 1917, steamed into the harbor at Queenstown, Ireland, where a main base was established. This force was soon increased to 34 destroyers. A main base was later established at Brest, and the force operating from there gradually grew in size until it approximated that of Queenstown. A third main base

the war the Cruiser and Transport Fo was organized to carry American troe overseas. The few suitable vessels ava able were taken over by the Governme at once and the German liners intern

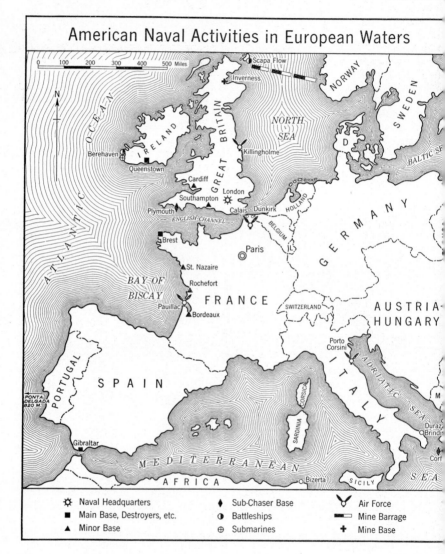

American Naval Activities in European Waters

Legend:

- ☼ Naval Headquarters
- ■ Main Base, Destroyers, etc.
- ▲ Minor Base
- ◗ Sub-Chaser Base
- ◐ Battleships
- ⊕ Submarines
- ⋎ Air Force
- ▬ Mine Barrage
- ✚ Mine Base

was established at Gibraltar. Secondary bases were established along the Bay of Biscay and at various other places along the European and Mediterranean coast.

Soon after the United States entered

in American ports were later added t this fleet. Every effort was mad throughout the war to obtain additiona ships for this service, which carried total of 911,000 men to Europe, or a littl

ss than half of the number sent. Most
the remainder were transported in
ips under British control.

To guard against submarine attack,
merican transports making the trip to
urope were, as far as practicable,
thered into groups and escorted through
e danger zone by destroyers and other
med vessels. This method of combat-
g the submarine menace was most suc-
ssful and the results obtained were re-
arkable. Not a single vessel of the
ruiser and Transport Force was lost
the eastward voyage, although three
ips returning to the United States were
nk out of a total of five torpedoed.

Nearly all the troops who crossed the
tlantic in American and French ships
nded at French ports, while those going
other vessels landed in England. This
cessitated the establishment of a small
ansport force of American ships at
uthampton, the chief port used for
embarkation to France, in order to aug-
ent the British cross-channel service.

As the number of troops overseas in-
eased, the task of supplying them be-
me more difficult. This problem was
et by the formation of the Naval Over-
as Transportation Service, which was
force distinct from the troop transport
ganization. It developed into a fleet
more than 400 vessels, manned by ap-
oximately 4,500 officers and 29,000 men.
o form this great organization it was
cessary to take vessels from every
ailable source, and included in it were
ips taken over from the Shipping
oard, new tonnage resulting from the
tensive building program of the Emer-
ncy Fleet Corporation, and a number
ships which were brought from the
reat Lakes under considerable difficul-
s. The convoy system was also used
sofar as possible in the operation of this
et, and only seven vessels were lost by
emy action. This was considered an
ceptionally fine record.

As soon as the safety of the transports
d supply ships had been reasonably
sured, aggressive steps were taken
ainst enemy submarines. This was

(451)

Stern of Destroyer Showing 4-Inch Gun and
Depth Bombs Used Against Submarines

Explosion of a 300-Pound Depth Bomb Dropped
by a United States Destroyer, May 18, 1918

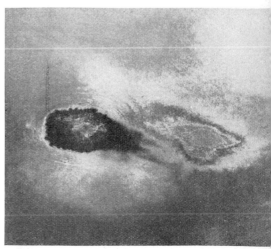

Oil Patch Indicating a "Hit" With a Depth Bomb

United States Naval Vessels With Captive Balloon in Tow
The balloon was used in searching for German submarines

done by the laying of mine barrages, the employment of a hunting force of small ships, supplemented by aircraft, and the use of submarines.

Before America's entry into the war the British had considered closing the northern entrance to the North Sea by placing a mine barrage from Scotland to Norway, but had given up this idea as impracticable. The American naval authorities felt, however, that with a new type of mine which had been developed in the United States this scheme could be undertaken successfully. In October 1917 it was decided to make the attempt, in conjunction with the British, and the construction of mines was begun in the United States. The total length of the mine barrage to be put down was 270 miles, and the estimated number of mines required was about 75,000. Bases were established on the eastern coast of Scotland, necessary vessels were procured and equipped, and in March 1918 operations were begun by the British and in June by the United States. By the time hostilities ceased the British had placed approximately 14,000 mines and the Americans 56,000, as a result of which 12 enemy submarines are known definitely to

have been put out of action either being sunk or considerably damaged.

Plans were also made for placing mi barrages in other areas, and a mine ba was planned at Bizerta, Tunis, from whe operations were to be conducted in t Adriatic and Aegean Seas, but the signi of the Armistice halted the undertaki

In order to establish a large and eff tive hunting force of surface vessels, cc struction was undertaken in America several hundred boats called "submari chasers". These were small wooden ve sels, 110 feet long, powered by gasoli motors, and equipped with sound-dete ing devices. A force of 135 of these ve sels was sent to Europe. Most of the based at Plymouth, England, Queer town, Ireland, and Corfu, Greece, a were very effective in the protection merchant shipping. During the peri of operation of the Plymouth detachme between Start Point and Lizard Head n a single merchant vessel was lost in area as a result of German submari attacks. A detachment from the Co group sailed from Brindisi, Italy, w the Allied fleet and participated with in the attack on the Austrian port Durazzo, doing especially valuable wc screening the larger vessels of the fleet m attack by Austrian submarines. In June 1917 a small detachment of the ival Air Service arrived in Europe and in thereafter the establishment of avian bases was begun along the French, iglish and Italian coasts in order to ist in the escort of shipping. At the ining of the Armistice this force had veloped into an organization of approxately 19,000 officers and enlisted men, erating from 27 bases.

The operations of this force against stile craft at sea were very successful. ith its growth, plans were made for ensive action against the submarines their bases, and eight squadrons, based ar Calais and Dunkirk, frequently mbed the Belgian ports of Zeebruge, tend and Bruges until they were freed the autumn of 1918 by the attacks of e Allied Armies. Until the cessation of stilities the American naval air units o helped the Royal Air Force by operatg against objectives which aided the vance of the northern British Armies. The Allied naval authorities having cided to employ some of their own bmarines as an additional means of mbating similar hostile craft, two ups of American submarines were distched to European waters. One group erated from Ponta Delgada, Azores, d the other from Berehaven, Bantry y, Ireland, and effectively covered e areas in the vicinity of these places.

During the early days of America's effort there appeared to be no necessity for dispatching any great portion of her battle fleet to European waters. Therefore, except for two divisions, it remained on the American side of the Atlantic, where it was engaged principally in training the large numbers of recruits taken into the Navy during the war.

Of the two divisions of battleships sent to Europe, one, comprising four vessels later increased to five, joined the British at Scapa Flow in December 1917, thereafter participating in operations of the Grand Fleet. The other division of three battleships took station in 1918 at Berehaven, from where it was to operate against any enemy raiding cruisers that might break through the cordon drawn around the German coast.

Aside from the foregoing purely naval operations, a brigade of marines served as part of the 2d Division, and five 14-inch naval guns on railroad mounts, manned by naval personnel, operated along the battle front firing against distant targets. These naval railroad batteries arrived in France during July and August, 1918, and were all in action during October. They continued in service taking part in the fighting until the Armistice.

To commemorate the achievements of the Navy, memorials have been erected at Brest and Gibraltar by the United States Government. Information concerning these memorials may be found in Chapter XII.

An American Convoy Nearing the English Coast

Bordeaux. The Naval District Headquarters, located here, directed the operations of vessels engaged in convoy work and submarine hunting in this vicinity. Near the city the construction of a high-powered naval radio station was undertaken for communication with the United States, but this was still under construction at the time the Armistice was signed.

Cardiff, Wales. American Naval Hea quarters for the administration of 1 coal transport service, which carried c for the Army from this port to France

Gibraltar. A naval force operat from here made many attacks upon st marines, and during July and Augu 1918, escorted 25 per cent of all Medit ranean convoys to French ports, as w

United States Transport *George Washington*, Battleship *Pennsylvania*
and a Submarine Chaser at Brest

Brest. American Naval Headquarters in France and main port of debarkation for troops carried on American naval transports. A force of over 30 destroyers and many yachts which based here operated as escorts for troop and supply convoys. During July and August, 1918, over 3,000,000 tons of shipping were convoyed in and out of French ports by vessels from this base with a loss of less than one-tenth of 1 per cent of this shipping.

as 70 per cent of all convoys to Engl ports from the vicinity of Gibraltar.

Inverness, Scotland. The main b for American mining operations in t North Sea was established at this p in the autumn of 1917.

Killingholme, England. An Ameri naval air base was located here. Pla operating from it flew approximat 57,000 sea miles while escorting ab 6,000 vessels through the submarine zo

American Submarine Off the Coast of Ireland

'auillac. An assembly plant for all
/al planes shipped to the Continent
s located here. A force of about 5,000
cers and men built and operated it.

'orto Corsini, Italy. American naval
'rs from this base, which was taken
'r from the Italians in July 1918, par-
pated in raids upon the Austrian port
Pola and carried out 5,500 flights while
rolling and reconnoitering.

Queenstown, Ireland. First American
/al base in Europe. The U. S. S.
cholson and *Fanning*, based here, sank
' German *U–58* and captured its crew
November 1917. During July and
gust, 1918, destroyers operating
efly from this port furnished 75 per

cent of escorting vessels for approximately
2,700,000 tons of shipping into British
harbors, steaming a total of 260,000 miles
and accomplishing the task without the
loss of a single ship.

Rochefort. Eight naval vessels, including five converted yachts, operated
from this port during the war and escorted
a total of 182 convoys.

St. Nazaire. Naval District Headquarters and principal port for army supplies. First detachment of American
troops landed here June 26, 1917. A
force consisting principally of converted
yachts was concentrated at this port and
performed the duties of mine sweeping,
submarine hunting and convoy escorting.

United States Naval Air Station at Pauillac

Flagpole at the Somme American Cemetery

Chapter XI

AMERICAN MILITARY CEMETERIES
IN EUROPE

THERE are eight permanent American military cemeteries in Europe. These have been developed by the United States Government into places of distinguished beauty and no American Cemetery. The other American cemeteries are located on the battlefields of France and Belgium and have been included in the tours described in this book. The cemeteries were originally estab-

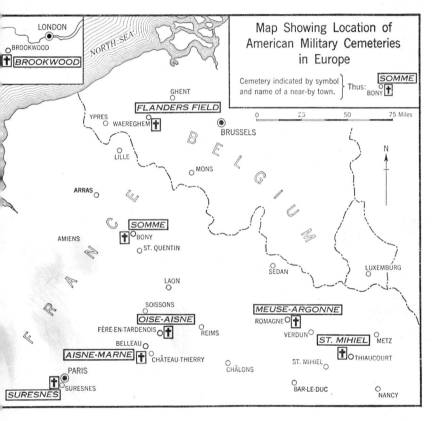

Map Showing Location of
American Military Cemeteries
in Europe

Cemetery indicated by symbol and name of a near-by town. } Thus: SOMME BONY

LONDON
BROOKWOOD
BROOKWOOD
NORTH SEA
GHENT
FLANDERS FIELD
YPRES
WAEREGHEM
BRUSSELS
LILLE
MONS
ARRAS
SOMME
BONY
AMIENS
ST. QUENTIN
LAON
SEDAN
LUXEMBURG
SOISSONS
MEUSE-ARGONNE
ROMAGNE
OISE-AISNE
FÈRE-EN-TARDENOIS
REIMS
VERDUN
ST. MIHIEL
METZ
BELLEAU
THIAUCOURT
AISNE-MARNE
CHÂTEAU-THIERRY
ST. MIHIEL
PARIS
CHÂLONS
SURESNES
SURESNES
BAR-LE-DUC
NANCY

FRANCE
BELGIUM

0   25   50   75 Miles

who travels in Europe should fail to visit as many of them as his time will permit. The cemeteries are conveniently located with respect to the routes which travelers normally follow. From the center of Paris it is only 5 miles to the cemetery at Suresnes, and from London it is less than an hour by train to the Brookwood lished by the War Department. They are now (1937) under the jurisdiction of the American Battle Monuments Commission, which has erected in each one an appropriate memorial chapel and has added the additional architectural and landscape features necessary to make all of them outstanding in beauty and dignity.

General View of the Headstones at the Meuse-Argonne Cemetery

The development of each cemetery is formal in character and this formality is emphasized by the regular rows of white marble headstones which mark the graves of the soldiers buried there. The headstones are of two designs, a cross for those of the Christian faith and a six-pointed star for those of the Jewish faith.

Every soldier now buried in an American military cemetery who lost his life during the World War and whose body has been identified has his name, rank, organization, state and date of death carved on the headstone over his grave. These men are called the "known dead" to distinguish them from the "unknown dead" whose bodies have not been found or, if found, have not been identified.

With one exception, all "unknown dead" whose bodies have been found are now buried in the cemeteries in Europe, each resting in a separate grave marked with a headstone bearing the following inscription: "HERE RESTS IN HONORED GLORY AN AMERICAN SOLDIER KNOWN BUT TO GOD". The single exception is that of the "Unknown Soldier" who was buried in a superb tomb bearing the same inscription at the Arlington National Cemetery near Washington, D. C. This soldier, selected from the unidentified dead of the A. E. F., was returned to America and buried with full military honors

at this national shrine, where, as th representative of his comrades, he receive daily the homage of a grateful people.

The "unknown dead" whose bodie were not found consist mainly of soldier who were buried hurriedly during batt without suitable markers on their grave or with markers which were obliterate by shellfire, men who were blown t pieces by high-explosive shells, an prisoners who died without their identit being recorded. Through the misfo tunes of war these men have thus bee denied the honored burial which ha been given to their comrades in deatl

Others who have no identified grave are the soldiers and sailors whose restin place is the sea. This group includ men who died at sea and were burie there, as well as those who lost their live at sea due to the action of the enemy.

The Commission early decided tha each of these "unknown dead" shoul have his name, rank, organization, stat and date of death inscribed in one of th chapels in the American cemeteries i Europe. As a result, in the chapel each battlefield cemetery are inscribe the names of the "unknown" soldier who lost their lives in that region. I addition, on panels of the chapel in th Meuse-Argonne Cemetery are recorde the names of the "unknown dead" of th rvices of Supply and of the American ;pedition to Northern Russia. The Jnknown Soldier" who is buried at the lington National Cemetery is therefore iong the soldiers whose names appear the walls of one of the chapels in the nerican military cemeteries in Europe. The names of the "unknown" soldiers d sailors whose bodies were lost or ried in European waters are recorded in e chapels at Suresnes and Brookwood. Of the 81,067 American soldiers, sailors d marines who gave their lives in irope and European waters during the ir, the number who still remain "un-own" is 4,431. This number includes i43 who are buried in unidentified aves in the permanent American ceme-ries in Europe, 1,537 whose grave is the a, 1,250 whose remains have never been und, and the "Unknown Soldier" who buried at the Arlington National metery.

At the time of the Armistice there were proximately 2,400 places in Europe in iich American dead were temporarily ried. After hostilities ceased, provi-n was made for the permanent burial these bodies in accordance with the pressed wishes of the nearest relatives ncerned, and the eight permanent nerican cemeteries in Europe were es-blished. These cemeteries, with their ,902 burials, now contain the graves of all members of the American forces whose bodies remain in Europe except as follows: 42 men whose bodies were left in their original graves outside the cemeteries at the request of relatives; 18 who are buried beneath the Lafayette Escadrille monument at Garches, near Paris, where 21 of their former comrades of the Escadrille are also buried; those whose bodies were released to relatives for private interment, and those whose remains have not been found.

A brief description of each of the American cemeteries is given on the following pages. The photographs accompanying them will give a good idea of the appearance of the different cemeteries and the small maps will be found useful by the tourist in locating a cemetery after he arrives in its general neighborhood.

An information bureau is maintained at the European Office of the American Battle Monuments Commission, located in the American Government Office Building, 2 Avenue Gabriel, Place de la Concorde, Paris, where locations of particular graves and information concerning the cemeteries may be obtained.

An American superintendent is on duty at each cemetery to give information and other assistance to visitors. Reception rooms are available at the cemeteries for the comfort and convenience of tourists.

All distances in this chapter are air line.

Airplane View of the St. Mihiel Cemetery

MEUSE-ARGONNE CEMETERY NEAR
ROMAGNE-SOUS-MONTFAUCON

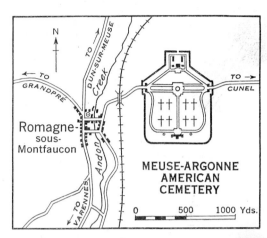

THIS is the largest and most impressive American cemetery Europe. It contains 14,240 ves. Most of those buried here ve their lives during the Meuse-gonne offensive, the greatest tle in all American history.

The cemetery is located just in r of the Hindenburg Line in a all valley between Romagne d Cunel. Its size and the rmony of its architectural development make it rank high ong the beautiful cemeteries of world. The immense field of ite marble crosses arranged long regular rows on the slop-; hillside, with the chapel silhouetted the crest above, is a sight which, once is seen, will not quickly be forgotten. A more complete description of this netery is given on pages 247–248.

A hostess house, which has facilities to ovide rooms and meals for a limited mber of visitors during the summer onths, is now maintained at the ceme-y for the convenience of the relatives of the men who are buried in the cemetery.

The cemetery is about 18 miles northwest of Verdun, which is a tourist center and easily reached by train. Good hotel accommodations are available in the city and automobiles can be hired there. Both the cemetery and the Meuse-Argonne American memorial on Montfaucon are included in most of the regular tours of the battlefields which start from Verdun.

Romagne Entrance, Meuse-Argonne Cemetery

OISE-AISNE CEMETERY NEAR FÈRE-EN-TARDENOIS

ON a battlefield where many of America's bravest sons met their death, near Fère-en-Tardenois, is located the Oise-Aisne Cemetery, the second largest American cemetery in Europe. It contains 6,012 graves. The majority of the battle dead who sleep there are from divisions which fought in the vicinity and to the north as far as the Oise River. In 1922 a considerable number of bodies were moved to this cemetery from the general area to the southwest of Paris.

The quiet surroundings now give no indication of the conflict that raged in this region while American soldiers were fighting here for the Ourcq River heights.

The cemetery itself is a peaceful harmony of landscaping and architecture.

The pink and gray sandstone chapel a walls give color at all times but perfect is reached in the spring when the ro and flowering shrubs are in full bloom

The cemetery is about 14 miles fr Château-Thierry and Soissons and sligh more from Reims. Good train servic available to each of those places, wh hotel accommodations can be obtair and automobiles hired. The main railr line between Paris and Reims passes cl to the village of Fère-en-Tardenois.

For further information concerning t cemetery and its features see pages 75–

The American cemetery near Bell and the American memorial on Hill just outside cf Château-Thierry are e about 14 miles away to the southwe

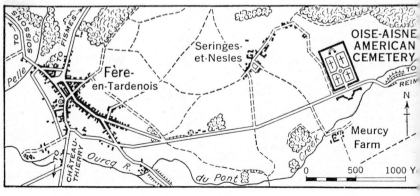

ST. MIHIEL CEMETERY NEAR THIAUCOURT

HIS is the third largest of the American military cemeteries in Europe and ...ains 4,152 graves. It is located on ...nd restored to France, after more than ... years of German occupation, by the ...t offensive of the American ...t Army which resulted in ...cing the St. Mihiel salient. ...he cemetery contains many ...ks of art and architecture ...ommemoration of those who ... on this field of honor. ... interior decorations of the ...pel and museum, which ...ude an inlaid marble map ...uring the American fighting ...the vicinity, are of special ...rest. For a more complete ...cription of this cemetery and the ...ures located in it, see pages 147–149. ...he American memorial on Montsec, ...memorating the St. Mihiel operation ...other American fighting in the region, ... miles to the southwest and can be

seen from the cemetery on a clear day.

The cemetery is less than 26 miles from Nancy, Verdun and Metz. There is good train service to these places, and at each of them hotel accommodations are

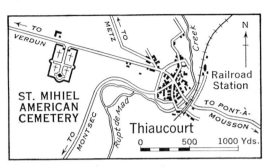

available and automobiles may be hired. Thiaucourt is on the main railroad line between Paris and Metz and a few of the trains stop there. The town is four hours by train from Paris. There are, however, no good hotels at Thiaucourt.

St. Mihiel Cemetery Near Thiaucourt

AISNE-MARNE CEMETERY NEAR BELLEAU

THIS cemetery lies at the foot of the hill upon which stands Belleau Wood. It contains 2,288 graves, mainly those of American soldiers who fought in the near vicinity or in the Marne River valley. The imposing chapel standing against

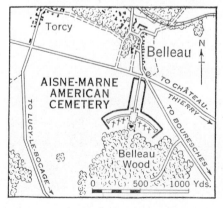

the hillside is of French Romanesc style of architecture. The natural s ting of the cemetery and chapel, and t perfection of detail of the architectu and landscape development, all comb to give this historic spot an atmosph of exceptional beauty and dignity.

The cemetery is 45 miles from Pa and about 5 miles northwest of Châtea Thierry, which is on a main railroad l running east from Paris. Fair hotel commodations are available at Châtea Thierry and automobiles for a visit to t battlefields may be hired there.

A more detailed description of t cemetery is given on pages 49–52.

A visit to the cemetery will give t tourist an opportunity to see Belle Wood, which adjoins the cemetery, a the Aisne-Marne American memor which is on a hill above Château-Thier:

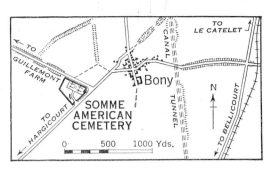

⌐HIS cemetery, located about halfway on the road between Quentin and Cambrai, is just ithwest of Bony and contains 33 graves. Its style of architure expresses the spirit of rged determination which in-red the American soldiers their repeated assaults across a neighboring fields while advancing to attack the Hindenrg Line in front of Bony.

The men buried here are mainly those o lost their lives while serving with e British Armies in France or in the erations of the 1st Division with the ench Army near the town of Cantigny. The chapel is remarkable for its cross-aped window of crystal glass above the ar, the harmony of its interior decora-ns, the beauty of its bronze doors and interesting carved exterior decorations. The cemetery is about 9 miles north of St. Quentin, which can be reached by train from Paris in two hours. Hotel accommodations are available and motor transportation may be hired there.

For a more complete description of this cemetery consult pages 387–388.

The American monument north of Bellicourt which commemorates the services of all American troops who fought with the British Armies in Europe during the World War is one mile away to the southeast.

Chapel at the Somme American Cemetery Near Bony

SURESNES AMERICAN CEMETERY NEAR PARIS

ON the slopes of Mont Valérien, 5 miles from the heart of Paris, is located the Suresnes Cemetery containing 1,541 graves. The men buried there are mainly those who died during the World War in hospitals located in Paris or at other places in the Services of Supply.

The cemetery is entered through an ornamental, wrought-iron gateway, and paths lead from it directly to the impressive chapel of an early colonial design. From its site against the steep wooded hillside, the chapel looks out over the fields of white marble headstones, a[nd] from its terrace a fine panorama of [a] large part of the city of Paris is obtaine[d]

Inside the chapel is an artistic marb[le] altar flanked by large marble urns co[n]taining green shrubbery. The effect [of] these is heightened by the beautif[ul] mosaic above them depicting the An[gel] of Victory laying a tribute upon t[he] tombs of the soldier dead. The interi[or] of the chapel is illuminated by a subdu[ed] light from six attractive stained-gla[ss] windows and on the walls are bron[ze] tablets giving the names of Americ[an] soldiers and sailors whose grave is t[he] sea.[1] Carved benches have been pr[o]vided for meditation and prayer.

Nature has aided with a generous ha[nd] the careful planning which created th[is] peaceful resting place and a visit to hon[or] these soldier dead is recommended wh[en] the trees and shrubs are in flower.

The reception building which contai[ns] facilities for visitors is located at t[he] southern end of the cemetery.

The town of Suresnes can be easi[ly] reached from Paris by train, autobus [or] automobile. The cemetery is only abo[ut] 200 yards from the main railroad statio[n]

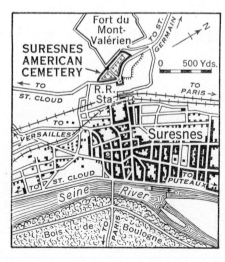

[1] Additional names of those men who have no gra[ve] except the sea are given in the Brookwood chap[el]

FLANDERS FIELD CEMETERY NEAR
WAEREGHEM, BELGIUM

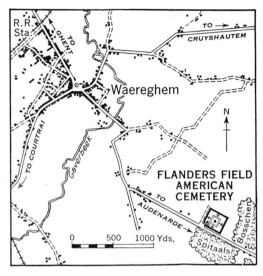

THIS cemetery, located about halfway between Brussels and Ypres, contains 368 graves. The men who rest here are mainly those who gave their lives during the American fighting in Belgium. The beautiful chapel at the center of the cemetery is surrounded on four sides by the fields of white marble headstones. The landscaping gives an impression of quiet harmony and the whole development forms a fitting resting place for the American heroes who are buried at this place.

Additional information concerning this cemetery and the features in it is given on page 399. The American monument in the town of Audenarde is 7 miles away on the direct road to Brussels. The cemetery is 17 miles southwest of Ghent, 24 miles northeast of Lille and 39 miles west of Brussels. The nearest railroad station, which is in the village of Waereghem, can be reached by fast train from Paris in approximately five hours.

Flanders Field American Cemetery Near Waereghem, Belgium

American Cemetery Near Brookwood, England

BROOKWOOD CEMETERY NEAR BROOKWOOD, ENGLAND

HIS cemetery, located near the village
of Brookwood about 25 miles south-
 of London, contains 468 graves.
ining it is a British World War cem-
y in which are buried many of the
I from their colonial forces. Both of
e burial areas form part of a very
e and beautiful British cemetery that
established privately many years ago.
he American soldiers who rest in the
okwood Cemetery were brought there
r the Armistice, from various places
ughout England, Scotland and Ire-
, and comprise those members of the
rican Expeditionary Forces who lost
r lives in Great Britain or its sur-
ding waters during the war. They
de many of the victims of the S. S.

evergreens which form a perfect setting
for the chapel, a graceful building of
classic design decorated with features of
both religious and patriotic interest.

The interior of the chapel is of brown
stone, soft in coloring. Small stained-
glass windows, remarkable for the beauty
of their designs, light the altar and the
carved cross above it. On the walls are
inscribed the names of American soldiers
and sailors whose grave is the sea.[1] Inlaid in the floor is a large bronze coat of
arms of the United States; and high above
the altar, carved in relief on the wall, is
an eagle with the inscription below it,

WITH GOD IS THEIR REWARD

A visit to the cemetery can not fail to
bring a feeling of satisfaction to the

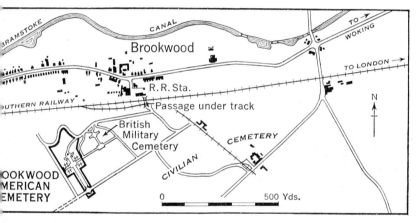

ania which was sunk by a German
marine on February 5, 1918, not far
y from the west coast of Scotland.
n the southwest side of the cemetery,
ss from the British military burial
nd, is situated a reception building
h contains facilities for the comfort
isitors. The office of the superin-
ent is in that building and inquiries
ld be made there for the location of a
icular grave or for other information.
 the center of the cemetery is an
mental flagpole from which the
rican flag flies, each day of the year,
the soldier dead buried here.
he regular rows of white marble
stones are shaded by thick masses of

American visitor that these soldiers who
died in Great Britain and who still remain
there are sleeping in such beautiful, dignified and peaceful surroundings.

It is a pleasant drive by automobile
from London to Brookwood, through an
interesting part of England, and a round
trip to the cemetery in this way can be
made comfortably in half a day. Brookwood can also be reached by train in
less than an hour from London. The
railroad service is exceptionally good,
trains running about every hour, and the
American cemetery is only about 300 yards
to the southwest of the railroad station.

[1] Additional names of those men who have no grave
except the sea are recorded at the Suresnes Cemetery.

Entrance, Aisne-Marne Cemetery

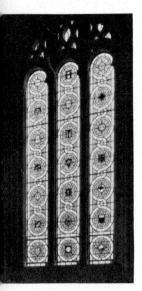

Chapel Window in the
Meuse-Argonne Cemetery

Altar of Chapel
in the Somme Cemetery

Altar of Chapel
in the Brookwood Cem

Line of Crosses in the Brookwood Cemetery

Bronze Gates at the Somme Cemetery

Entrance, Brookwood Cemetery

saic and Altar of Chapel
the St. Mihiel Cemetery

Altar of Chapel
in the Meuse-Argonne Cemetery

Monument in the
St. Mihiel Cemetery

saic and Altar of Chapel at the Suresnes Cemetery

A Corner of the Flanders Field Cemetery

Meuse-Argonne Memorial at Montfaucon

Chapter XII

AMERICAN WORLD WAR MEMORIALS IN EUROPE
ERECTED BY
THE UNITED STATES GOVERNMENT

WHEN the American Battle Monuments Commission was created in 1923 one of the most important duties given it was to erect memorials in Europe to commemorate the services of the American forces there during the World War. This work has now been completed and the eleven memorials and two bronze tablets erected by the Commission commemorate these services in a complete yet dignified and modest way. The memorials vary in size from three large ones, which commemorate the American fighting in the three areas of France where the American combat forces were engaged in greatest numbers, to smaller ones recording the wartime services of American units outside of these areas. No two of them are alike, as each was designed to fit its particular site and to give a comparative degree of commemoration with respect to the others. The architects were carefully selected from Americans of prominence in their profession and all concerned bent every effort to make the results reflect the pride of America in the historic events which the memorials commemorate.

The completed project has been the subject of much favorable comment and the larger monuments are now visited each year by many thousands of travelers from American and European countries. The map on page 477 shows the locations of the memorials, and the photographs in this chapter will give a good idea of their appearance. Those on the battlefields have been described in connection with the tours and in the following pages references are given to the pages upon which these descriptions are to be found. *All distances in this chapter are air line.*

MEUSE-ARGONNE MEMORIAL AT MONTFAUCON

This is the most imposing American monument in Europe. It commemorates the brilliant victory of the American First Army in the Meuse-Argonne offensive, September 26–November 11, 1918, and pays tribute to the previous heroic services of the Armies of France on the important battle front upon which the memorial has been constructed.

The massive shaft rises from the ruins of the hilltop village of Montfaucon and dominates the surrounding country. From the observation platforms high above the ground an extended view is obtained of a large part of the territory over which the soldiers of the American First Army advanced during the autumn of 1918.

Consult pages 203–204 for additional information concerning this memorial.

A caretaker is at the memorial during daylight hours. While he is on duty visitors are permitted to ascend the tower.

The Meuse-Argonne American Cemetery is 5 miles to the north. The nearest large town is Verdun, 14 miles to the southeast, which is easily reached by train. At that place good hotel accommodations are available and automobiles for visits to the battlefields may be hired in front of the railroad station.

ST. MIHIEL MEMORIAL ON MONTSEC

This memorial stands on the high isolated hill of Montsec. It commemorates the capture of the St. Mihiel salient by the American First Army, the operations of the American Second Army on November 9–11, 1918, and the other combat services of the American divisions both in this region and in Alsace and Lorraine.

St. Mihiel Memorial at Montsec

It consists of a large circular colonnade, the center of which on a raised plat-m is a bronze relief map of the St. ihiel salient. The size of the memorial, commanding site and the perfection of proportions all combine to make it one the most impressive in the world. See pages 123–127 for a more complete scriptive account of this monument. The memorial is about 24 miles from rdun, Nancy and Metz. Good hotel commodations exist at those places and tomobiles for a visit to the site may be red there. The St. Mihiel American metery near Thiaucourt is 8 miles away the northeast. Thiaucourt is also the arest main-line railroad station to the onument and automobiles for a trip to e battlefields may be hired at that place.

AISNE-MARNE MEMORIAL NEAR CHÂTEAU-THIERRY

An impressive memorial, overlooking âteau-Thierry and the Marne River, s been erected on Hill 204 to com-emorate the services of the American d French soldiers who participated in e important operations in the Aisne-arne region during 1918, and to me-orialize the friendship and cooperation iich existed between the French and nerican Armies during the World War. The monument proper is a long double lonnade ornamented on the west face ⹉ heroic figures representing France and e United States and on the east face by large symbolic eagle. Appropriate in-riptions give details of the fighting. ie architecture is outstanding in ap-arance and has been made even more ective by the beautiful landscaping. For a more complete description of this onument and its features see page 57. This is the closest to Paris of any of the nerican memorials and it is but 4 miles ⹉ay from Belleau Wood and the nerican cemetery near Belleau. The se-Aisne American Cemetery is 14 iles to the northeast, near Fère-en-ardenois. Hotel accommodations may ⹉ had (1937) at Château-Thierry, which on a main railroad line running east om Paris, and automobiles for trips to e battlefields may easily be hired there.

NAVAL MEMORIAL AT BREST

In recognition of the heroic work of the American Navy in convoying troops and supplies to Europe, a large memorial has been erected on an old fortification wall of the city. The site overlooks the harbor of Brest, which was a base of operations for American naval vessels during the war as well as a large port of debarkation and embarkation for the American troops.

The memorial consists of a tall shaft from the top of which is obtained a fine view of the harbor. It is constructed of Brittany granite with decorative features of nautical interest. The surrounding area has been improved with planting and forms an attractive park, much appreciated by the inhabitants of the town.

Brest is in Brittany near the most western point of France. It is 315 miles from Paris and may be reached by train from that city in less than eight hours.

MEMORIAL NEAR SOMMEPY

On the crest of Blanc Mont Ridge, 3 miles north of Sommepy, has been erected a memorial to commemorate the achievements of the American and French soldiers who fought in the Champagne region of France during the World War. The American 2d, 36th, 42d and 93d Divisions saw battle service in the vicinity and their names and divisional insignia appear on the monument, which is located on ground captured by the 2d Division. The memorial consists of a tower notable for the beauty and simplicity of its lines. A flight of steps leads to an observation platform on top where a fine view may be obtained and where direction arrows point out prominent places on the landscape. A good view, however, may also be had from the lower terrace.

At the present time (1937) the tower is open to visitors only on Sundays. See page 350 for additional information of this monument and its surroundings.

The nearest cities are Reims, 22 miles to the west, and Châlons-sur-Marne, 23 miles to the south. Good hotel accommodations are available at both of those places. The village of Sommepy may be reached by railroad from Paris in four hours and automobiles may be hired there.

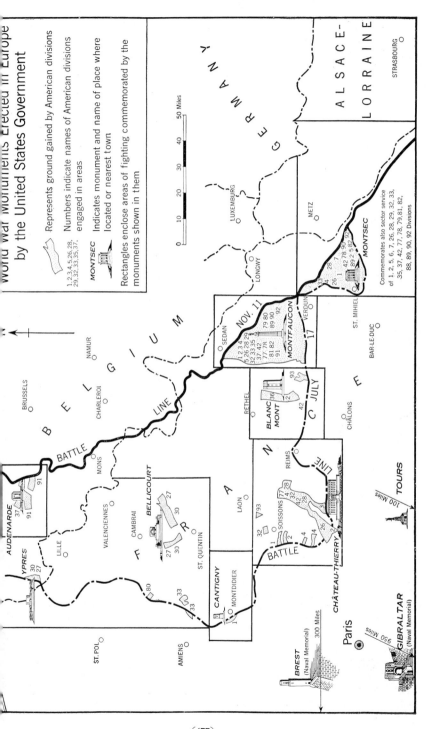

World War Monuments Erected in Europe by the United States Government

American Naval Memorial at Brest

MEMORIAL NEAR BELLICOURT

A memorial near Bellicourt commemo-
tes the American units, totaling ap-
oximately 90,000 men, which fought
th the British Armies in France during
e World War. It is on a battlefield of
e 27th and 30th Divisions, being pic-
resquely located on the ridge over the
. Quentin Canal tunnel which was such
strong feature of the Hindenburg Line.
A detailed description of the monument
d its features is given on page 383.
The Somme American Cemetery near
ony is 1 mile away to the northwest.
The Bellicourt memorial is 9 miles
rth of St. Quentin and 13 miles south
Cambrai. Hotel accommodations are
ailable at those places and automobiles
r a visit to the site may be hired there.

MEMORIAL AT TOURS

A beautiful fountain has been construct-
at Tours by the United States Govern-
ent in grateful recognition of the
hievements of the more than 640,000
embers of the American Expeditionary
orces who served in the Services of Sup-
y and whose work behind the battle
es made possible the brilliant accom-
ishments of the armies in the field.
The fountain is of outstanding beauty
d is worthy of a high place among the
any architectural gems of that historic
rt of France. It stands in the heart of
ours near the southern end of the Pont
ilson, the main bridge which crosses the
ire River within the city boundaries.
On the lower circular basin is carved the
dicatory inscription. Below the upper
sin appear the coats of arms of Tours,
est, St. Nazaire, Le Mans, Is-sur-Tille,
evers, Neufchâteau and Bordeaux;
ench cities where important installa-
ons of the Services of Supply were lo-
ted. Above the upper basin are four
autiful figures representing Adminis-
ation, Construction, Procurement and
istribution, the four principal divisions
the Services of Supply organization.
e crowning feature is a bronze Ameri-
n Indian releasing an American eagle.
model of this figure won a gold medal

during a recent American competition.
The small adjoining park area is part
of the memorial and is being maintained
by the United States Government.

Tours was the headquarters of the
Services of Supply during the war. It is
in the center of the famous château region
of France and is three hours south of
Paris by train. It may be visited from
that place by automobile or autobus.
The trip is interesting as the main roads
pass by or near many famous châteaux.

NAVAL MEMORIAL AT GIBRALTAR

At Gibraltar, the gateway to the Mediterranean, the United States Government
has constructed a memorial archway of
stone from the neighboring mountain to
commemorate the achievements and com-
radeship of the American and British
Navies in that vicinity during the World
War. Many American vessels used the
harbor as a base for naval operations.

The memorial serves a useful purpose
as it includes a flight of steps which con-
nects the town of Gibraltar with the large
British naval establishments below.

Gibraltar is a port of call for most passenger vessels using the Mediterranean
and a visit to the monument may be
made from the pier in about half an hour.

BELLEAU WOOD

Belleau Wood, 5 miles northwest of
Château-Thierry, was given to the
United States Government by an American association which had acquired it soon
after the World War. It is now being
maintained as a memorial to all American
soldiers who fought in the war. The remains of trenches, shell holes and many
relics of the war, including weapons salvaged in the vicinity, may be seen there.

For further information concerning the
wood and the American fighting in the vicinity, consult pages 45–49 of Chapter II.

The Aisne-Marne American Cemetery
adjoins Belleau Wood on its north side.

The wood is easily reached from Paris,
45 miles away, either directly by automobile or by train to Château-Thierry and
then by automobile from that place.

American Monument Near Bellicourt

American Memorial at Tours to the Services of Supply, A.E.F.

American Memorial Near Sommepy

American Naval Memorial Arch at Gibraltar

American Memorial at Vierstraat

MEMORIAL AT AUDENARDE, BELGIUM

In the historic town of Audenarde, Belgium, a small memorial has been erected in a public park to commemorate the services of the approximately 40,000 American soldiers who fought in that vicinity toward the end of the World War.

A more complete description of this memorial and its location with respect to the nearest large cities in the surrounding country may be found on page 401.

The Flanders Field American Cemetery near Waereghem, where many of the soldiers who died during the American operations in this immediate vicinity are buried, is about 7 miles away to the west.

American Monument at Cantigny

MEMORIAL NEAR VIERSTRAAT, BELGIUM

About 4 miles south of Ypres, Belgium near the hamlet of Vierstraat and not fa from the base of Mont Kemmel, a sma monument has been erected to commeme rate the services of the 27th and 30t Divisions which participated with th British in the Ypres-Lys offensive in tha region in August and September, 1918.

See page 405 for a more complete de scription of this memorial and its feature

The Flanders Field American Cemeter near Waereghem, Belgium, where a con siderable number of the men who died i the operations near Vierstraat are burie is approximately 27 miles away to the eas

American Monument at Audenarde

MEMORIAL AT CANTIGNY

In the center of the little village of Ca tigny a small park has been develope into an attractive memorial to commeme rate the capture of that village by th American 1st Division in the first offer sive operation carried out by a lar{ American unit during the World War.

A more detailed description of th memorial and directions for reaching have been given on page 416 of this boo

BRONZE TABLET AT CHAUMONT

An attractive bronze tablet has bee placed at the entrance to the Damrémon Barracks at Chaumont and upon it is th

Bronze Tablet at Chaumont

owing inscription which has been
cribed both in English and in French:

GENERAL HEADQUARTERS
OF THE
AMERICAN EXPEDITIONARY FORCES
IN EUROPE
DURING THE WORLD WAR
OCCUPIED THE BUILDINGS
OF THE CASERNE DAMRÉMONT FROM
SEPTEMBER 1, 1917, TO JULY 11, 1919,
AND FROM HERE DIRECTED
THE ACTIVITIES OF MORE THAN
TWO MILLION AMERICAN SOLDIERS

✦

BRONZE TABLET AT SOUILLY

An ornamental bronze tablet has been
ced on the outside of the town hall at
uilly and upon it is the following
cription both in English and French:

HEADQUARTERS
OF THE AMERICAN FIRST ARMY
OCCUPIED THIS BUILDING FROM
SEPTEMBER 21, 1918,
TO THE END OF HOSTILITIES
AND FROM HERE CONDUCTED
THE MEUSE-ARGONNE OFFENSIVE,
ONE OF THE GREAT OPERATIONS
OF THE WORLD WAR

✦

The memorials described above, except
for Belleau Wood, were constructed by
the United States Government and all of
them are now being maintained by it.

*A table giving information concerning
the principal American World War memorials in Europe erected by agencies other
than the United States Government has
been included in this book in Chapter XV.*

Bronze Tablet at Souilly

View of the Aisne-Marne Memorial From Across the Marne River

Upper Part of Naval
Memorial at Brest

Symbolic Figures, Aisne-Marne Memorial

Lower Terrace, Naval
Memorial at Brest

Memorial Near Bellicourt

Aisne-Marne Memorial

Looking Southeast Toward the Hill, Monument and Village of Montfaucon

Details of the S.O.S.
Memorial Fountain at Tours

Meuse-Argonne Memorial

Terrace of the St. Mihiel
Memorial

Porcelain Map at the St. Mihiel Memorial

Orientation Table at the St. Mihiel Memorial

Chapter XIII

AFTER THE ARMISTICE

THE Armistice was signed at 5:00 o'clock in the morning of November 11, 1918, on Marshall Foch's [tr]ain in the Forest of Compiègne, and [to]ok effect at 11:00 a. m. on the same day. Its terms, which are summarized on [pa]ges 507–509, required Germany to evac[ua]te all invaded and occupied territory in [Be]lgium, Luxemburg and France (in[clu]ding Alsace-Lorraine), and to with-draw her armies across the Rhine River. They also provided that the Allied forces should be permitted peaceably to occupy bridgeheads, 18 miles in radius, east of the Rhine at Mayence, Coblenz and Cologne, and that a neutral zone 6 miles wide in which neither the Allies nor Germany could maintain troops would be established along the east bank of the Rhine and around each of the bridgeheads.

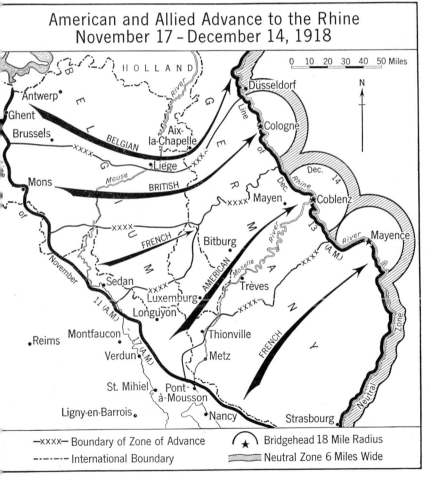

American and Allied Advance to the Rhine
November 17 - December 14, 1918

0   10   20   30   40   50 Miles

N

HOLLAND

Antwerp
Ghent
Brussels
Mons
Düsseldorf
Cologne
Aix-la-Chapelle
Liège
Mayen
Coblenz
Mayence
Bitburg
Trèves
Sedan
Luxemburg
Longuyon
Thionville
Metz
Reims
Montfaucon
Verdun
St. Mihiel
Pont-à-Mousson
Ligny-en-Barrois
Nancy
Strasbourg

BELGIAN
BRITISH
FRENCH
AMERICAN
FRENCH

Meuse
Moselle River
Rhine River
Rhine River

Dec. 14
Dec. 13

November 11 (A.M.)

Line of Dec.

Neutral Zone

—xxxx— Boundary of Zone of Advance
--------- International Boundary
Bridgehead 18 Mile Radius
Neutral Zone 6 Miles Wide

The advance of the American and Allied Armies was so regulated that they occupied all territory evacuated by the Germans within a short time after the German troops withdrew. The plans for the advance prescribed that the French should move through Alsace-Lorraine to Mayence, the Americans through Luxemburg and the Moselle valley to Coblenz, the British to Cologne, and the Belgians by way of Aix-la-Chapelle to the lower Rhine River.

On November 7 the Commander-in-Chief of the American Expeditionary Forces had directed that an American Third Army be organized and on November 14 this Army, with Major General Joseph T. Dickman as commander, was designated as the Army of Occupation. It was composed initially of the III Corps, containing the 2d, 32d and 42d Divisions; and the IV Corps, comprising the 1st, 3d and 4th Divisions. To these were added on November 22 the VII Corps, containing the 5th, 89th and 90th Divisions. On that same day the Third Army detached the 5th Division from the VII Corps and gave it the duty of guarding the extended lines of communication of the Army.

The advance to the Rhine was begun by the Americans and Allies on November 17 along the entire Western Front. Although active operations against a hostile enemy were not involved, there were nevertheless many difficult problems to be met. For the Americans, these included the creation in a limited time of a staff and serv-

Major General Joseph T. Dickman
Commanding General of the
Third Army from November
15, 1918, to April 28, 1919

ices for the supply and rapid moveme of more than 200,000 men through count where transportation lines in many plac were completely destroyed and whe food was scarce. Moreover, the weath was cold and rainy and in many places t roads were nearly impassable. Althou the troops had been hastily assembled a had been allowed no opportunity to re and refit after the tryi period of the Meus Argonne offensive, th cheerfully met every c mand made upon the: The advance elemer of the Third Arn passed through the ci of Luxemburg on N vember 21 and arriv two days later at t German frontier. The they rested until Decer ber 1 when all of t Armies of Occupati pushed on into German

Through the liberat districts of France ai Luxemburg the Ame: cans were received wi wild demonstrations joy, but upon enterir Germany they were r garded with a mixture curiosity and suspicio However, the fine co duct of the Army and tl firmness and justice the American comman ers quickly quieted ai apprehensions the civ population may ha' had and no incidents hostility took place.

The leading troops the Third Army reache the Rhine River on December 9. On tl 13th, American, French and British infa try divisions crossed the river, having bee preceded in some cases by advance el ments the day before. In the America Third Army, the III Corps, whose con position had been changed to include tl

2d and 32d Divisions, was designated occupy the northern portion of the ⅰgehead at Coblenz, the southern por- ⅰ having been transferred to French trol. The American bridgehead in- ⅰed the fortress of Ehrenbreitstein ⅰated immediately across the Rhine ⁻er from Coblenz and dominating it. ⁻he III Corps crossed on four bridges— ⁻ at Coblenz, and one each at Engers

remained west of the Rhine. Luxemburg was occupied by the 5th and 33d Divisions, both of which were under command of the American Second Army, and not under control of the Army of Occupation.

To the south of Coblenz the French occupied a bridgehead with headquarters at Mayence, while to the north, the British occupied a bridgehead with head- quarters at Cologne. Although the Bel-

Zone of American Army of Occupation, December 21, 1918

0   10   20   30   40   50 Miles

N

Rhine

British Troops

Ahrweiler • (42)   2 Rengsdorf
Heddesdorf (32)   1
Andernach Neuwied Montabaur
(4) (3) Coblenz

Cochem R. Wiesbaden

(89) (90)
Kylburg •   Bad Bertrich
Wittlich •   Berncastel
THIRD

BELGIUM

LUXEMBURG

Moselle
• Trèves ARMY

French Troops

dan

SECOND

ARMY

Verdun •

Line of November 11 (AM)

• Metz

-xxxxx- Boundary of American Zone
-xxxx- Boundary between American Armies
------- Division Boundary
★ Headquarters Third Army
▨ Neutral Zone
▬ ▬ ★ Bridgehead

ⅰ Remagen below Coblenz—and by the ht of December 14 had completed ⅰ occupation of the American part of ⅰ bridgehead. The remainder of the ⅰerican Army of Occupation, consisting ⅰthe IV Corps, comprising the 3d, 4th ⅰ 42d Divisions, and the VII Corps, ⅰtaining the 89th and 90th Divisions,

gians advanced to the Rhine and occupied jointly with the French a zone in the Rhineland to the north of the British, with headquarters at Aix-la-Chapelle, they had no force across the river.

An additional bridgehead at Kehl across the Rhine from Strasbourg and including the ring of forts of that place,

1st Division Marching Into Luxemburg, November 21, 1918

German Army Leaving Luxemburg
A Signal Corps photographer of the American Army arrived in time to take this picture

Fort Ehrenbreitstein, as Seen From Across the Rhine River at Coblenz

Captured German Guns on the Place de la Concorde, Paris, November 1918

was established on February 4, 1919, by the French on their own responsibility.

When finally located on December 21, 1918, the headquarters of the principal units of the American Army of Occupation in Germany were placed as follows:

Third Army	Coblenz
III Corps	Neuwied
IV Corps	Cochem
VII Corps	Wittlich
1st Division	Montabaur
2d Division	Heddesdorf
3d Division	Andernach
4th Division	Bad Bertrich
32d Division	Rengsdorf
42d Division	Ahrweiler
89th Division	Kylburg
90th Division	Berncastel

Immediately after the Armistice the American Commander-in-Chief started preparations for moving his forces back to the United States with the least possible delay. The Services of Supply was promptly reorganized to carry out the intricate details connected with this work, and approximately 25,500 men of the American forces actually sailed from France, homeward bound, in November. Before the end of the year this number had been increased to about 124,000.

Upon the cessation of hostilities practically every man of the 2,000,000 in the A.E.F. wanted to return to the United States at once; but with the limited number of ships available this was, of course, impossible. While military train-

ing was continued after the Armis against the remote possibility that op tions might be resumed, the hig commanders realized that this was a m trying period for the soldiers and un took measures to make life for them interesting as possible commensurate v the maintenance of a satisfactory sta ard of discipline and military cond

Men were allowed regular leaves to v leave areas established at various sum and winter resorts in France and in occupied portion of Germany, and rangements were made whereby t could visit several other countries s as Great Britain, Belgium and Italy.

A vast school system was establis in which more than 230,000 men enro Wherever troops were quartered in number, classes were organized and struction given in practically every s ject taught in the public schools of United States, as well as in trade business subjects. At Beaune a h university was established for advar instruction and approximately 9,000 diers registered to take the course.

An Education Corps Commission formed to direct all lecturers, schools extension courses in the A.E.F. men selected as instructors for the sch were competent educators with previ experience. This often resulted in cla for officers being conducted by priv from the ranks. The educational sys

28th Division En Route to St. Nazaire, April 22, 1919, for Embarkation to the United Stat

American Soldiers Embarking at St. Nazaire, December 6, 1918

the whole was democratic, well planned
d produced very substantial results.
Horse shows were held by nearly every
vision, and many of the units organized
eatrical troupes, which traveled through-
t the A. E. F. giving performances.
1ese activities were encouraged and
led in every way by the army officials,
d to a large extent contributed to the
easure and contentment of the troops.
The men were also encouraged to par-
•ipate in sports and games, and a great
hletic program was carried out which
lminated in the Inter-Allied Games
ld near Paris in June and July, 1919.
Don the invitation of the American
•mmander-in-Chief, eighteen of the
lied and associated nations sent con-
stants to this meet, which was a re-
arkable success from every standpoint.
1e Pershing Stadium, where it took
ace, was built mainly by engineers from
e American Army. The funds were
nated by the Young Men's Christian
sociation, which presented the structure
General Pershing. It was later turned
er by him to the French people.
In the spring of 1919 a composite
giment of selected officers and men was
rmed from the Third Army. Selection
s based on appearance, soldierly
alities and war record. It was used
an escort of honor to the American
•mmander-in-Chief, and paraded in
ris, London and other places, includ-

ing New York and Washington, D. C.,
when the regiment returned to America.
In the meantime the transfer of troops
to the United States had been progressing
rapidly. Marshal Foch wished to retain
a large force, at least 15 divisions, in
Europe, but was told that the American
Army would be withdrawn as soon as
possible. President Wilson finally agreed
that American representation in the
occupied territory would be a small
detachment only, to be known as the
"American Forces in Germany", which
would serve, as the French said, merely
to keep the American flag on the Rhine.
By May 19, 1919, all American combat
divisions, except five in occupied German
territory, had received their embarkation
orders to sail for American ports.
The units of the Army of Occupation
were relieved as fast as practicable
during the summer of 1919, and the 1st
Division, the last large organization to
leave for home, began its movement on
August 15. With the dissolution of the
Third Army on July 2, 1919, the "American Forces in Germany" consisting of
about 6,800 men came into being and remained on the Rhine for more than three
years. The American flag on Fort
Ehrenbreitstein was finally lowered on
January 24, 1923, when the last of the
American troops in Germany entrained.
The American zone was formally turned
over to the French three days later on.

Chapter XIV

INTERESTING FACTS AND GENERAL INFORMATION CONCERNING THE AMERICAN EXPEDITIONARY FORCES

ocation of General Headquarters:
Paris—June 13, 1917–Sept. 1, 1917.
Chaumont-en-Bassigny—Sept. 1, 1917–
ly 11, 1919.
Paris—July 12, 1919–Sept. 1, 1919.

ocation of First Army Headquarters:
La Ferté-sous-Jouarre—August 10, 18–August 13, 1918.
Neufchâteau—August 13, 1918–August 3, 1918.
Ligny-en-Barrois—August 28, 1918–ptember 21, 1918.
Souilly—Sept. 21, 1918–Nov. 25, 1918.
Bar-sur-Aube—November 25, 1918–pril 20, 1919.

ocation of Second Army Hdqrs.:
Toul—Oct. 12, 1918–April 15, 1919.

ocation of Headquarters, S. O. S.:
Paris—July 5, 1917–January 13, 1918.
Tours—Jan. 13, 1918–Aug. 31, 1919.

he United States and the Allies:
When the United States entered the ᵗorld War it did not unite itself to any ᶜher nation by a treaty of alliance but ᵉrely associated itself with the Allies in ᵉir effort to defeat the Central Powers. ᵘch being the case, the United States as not one of the "Allies" and is not ᶜluded when that term is used alone.

he Supreme War Council:
The Supreme War Council was com-ᵒsed of the heads of the Governments of ᵉ United States, Great Britain, France ᶰd Italy, each with a civilian assistant ᶰd a military adviser. It was essentially ᵃ civilian agency and did not command ᵉ armies in the field. Its function was ᵒ establish unity of purpose among the ᵉat powers in the prosecution of the ᵃr. Consequently, it dealt principally ith the general policies affecting the ᵢlitary situation, the character of opera-

tions to be undertaken in the various theaters of war and the allotment of man power, equipment, supplies and shipping to the various fronts upon which the Allied Armies were carrying on fighting.

Military Representatives who served on the Supreme War Council, November 7, 1917, to November 11, 1918:

UNITED STATES
General Tasker H. Bliss.

GREAT BRITAIN
Lieutenant General Sir Henry H. Wilson to February 18, 1918.
General Sir Henry Rawlinson to March 27, 1918.
Major General C. J. Sackville-West to after the Armistice.

FRANCE
General Ferdinand Foch to November 29, 1917.
General Maxime Weygand to April 10, 1918.
General Emile Eugène Belin to after the Armistice.

ITALY
Lieutenant General Luigi Cadorna to February 7, 1918.
Lieutenant General Gaetano Giardino to April 16, 1918.
Lieutenant General Mario Nicolis di Robilant to after the Armistice.

Important governmental officials of nations engaged on the Western Front, April 6, 1917, to November 11, 1918:

UNITED STATES
President—Woodrow Wilson.
Secretary of State—Robert Lansing.
Secretary of War—Newton D. Baker.
Ambassador to Great Britain—Walter H. Page.
Ambassador to France—Wm. G. Sharp.

Painting of the Permanent Military Representatives
by Captain Dana Pond, February 14, 1919
Left to right: General di Robilant, Italy; General Tasker H. Bliss, U. S.;
General Belin, France; General Sackville-West, Great Britain

Ambassador to Italy—Thomas N. Page.
Minister to Belgium—Brand Whitlock.

GREAT BRITAIN

Reigning Sovereign—King George V.
Prime Minister—David Lloyd George.
Secretary of State for Foreign Affairs—
Arthur J. Balfour.
Secretary of State for War—
The Earl of Derby to Apr. 20, 1918.
Viscount Milner to after the Armistice.
Ambassador to United States—
Sir Cecil A. Spring-Rice.

FRANCE

President—
Raymond Poincaré.
Premier—
Alexandre Ribot to September 13, 1917.
Paul Painlevé to November 17, 1917.
Georges Clemenceau from November
17, 1917, to after the Armistice.
Minister of Foreign Affairs—
Alexandre Ribot to November 17, 1917.
Stephen Pichon to after the Armistice.

Minister of War—
Paul Painlevé to November 17, 19
Georges Clemenceau from Novemb
17, 1917, to after the Armistice.
Ambassador to the United States—Jean
Jusserand.
Ambassador to Great Britain—Pa
Cambon.

ITALY

Reigning Sovereign—
King Victor Emmanuel III.
Prime Minister—
Paolo Boselli to October 20, 1917.
Vittorio Orlando from October 2
1917, until after the Armistice.
Minister of Foreign Affairs—
Baron Sidney Sonnino.
Minister of War—
General Paolo Motrone to June 1
1917.
General Gaetano Giardino from Ju
16, 1917, to October 29, 1917.
General Vittorio Alfieri to Mar. 20,191
General Vittorio Zupelli from Mar
20, 1918, until after the Armistic

bassador to the United States—
ount Vincenzo Macchi di Cellere.

BELGIUM

mporary seat of government at Le
    Havre, France]
gning Sovereign of the Kingdom—
.ing Albert I.
mier—
ount de Broqueville to May 31, 1918.
·. Cooreman to after the Armistice.
iister of Foreign Affairs—
.aron Beyens to August 4, 1917.
ount de Broqueville to Oct. 17, 1917.
'. Hymans until after the Armistice.
iister of War—
'ount de Broqueville to Aug. 4, 1917.
ieneral de Ceuninck from August 4,
    1917, until after the Armistice.
iister to United States—
mmanuel Havenith to Apr. 12, 1917.
.mile E. de Cartier de Marchienne
    until after the Armistice.

GERMANY

gning Sovereign—Emperor William II.

Chancellor—
    Theobald von Bethmann-Hollweg to
        July 14, 1917.
    Dr. George Michaelis to Nov. 1, 1917.
    Count von Hertling to Sept. 29, 1918.
    Prince Max von Baden from October 3,
        1918, to after the Armistice.
Secretary of Foreign Affairs—
    Arthur Zimmermann to Aug. 7, 1917.
    Dr. Richard von Kühlmann from
        August 7, 1917, to July 9, 1918.
    Paul von Hintze to October 3, 1918.
    Dr. Wilhelm Solf to after the Armistice.
Minister of War—
    Hermann von Stein to Oct. 9, 1918.
    General Heinrich Scheüch from October
        9, 1918, until after the Armistice.

AUSTRIA-HUNGARY

Reigning Sovereign—Emperor Charles I.
Prime Minister—
    Count Heinrich Clam-Martinic to
        June 21, 1917.
    Dr. Ernst von Feuchtenegg from June
        23, 1917, to July 22, 1918.
    Dr. Maximilian von Heinlein from
        July 25, 1918, to October 27, 1918.
    Dr. Heinrich Lammasch to Oct. 30, 1918.

Field Marshal von Hindenburg with General von Ludendorff
and Members of His Staff

VON LUDENDORFF   VON HINDENBURG

Minister of Foreign Affairs—Count Ottokar Czernin to April 14, 1918.

Baron Stephan von Rajecz from April 16, 1918, to October 24, 1918.

Count Julius Andrassy to Nov. 2, 1918.

Dr. Ludwig von Flotow from November 2, 1918, to after the Armistice.

Minister of War—
General Alexander von Krobatin to April 8, 1917.
General Rudolf von Steinstätten from April 12, 1917, to October 30, 1918.

General-in-Chief of the Allied Armies:
On March 26, 1918, Marshal Ferdinand Foch of the French Army was designated to coordinate the action of the French and British Armies on the Western Front and on April 3 he was given strategic direction of the French, British and American Armies on that front. On April 14 he was given the official title of "General-in-Chief of the Allied Armies in France", and on May 2 Italy agreed that he would exercise strategic direction of her armies. For ease of reference Marshal Foch's position has been called in this book that of "Allied Commander-in-Chief".

Important military commanders in rope, Apr. 6, 1917, to Nov. 11, 1
Commander-in-Chief, A. E. F.—
eral John J. Pershing.

Commander-in-Chief, B. E. F.—
Marshal Sir Douglas Haig.

Commander-in-Chief, French Arn
General Robert George Nivelle, to 17, 1917. General Henri Philippe P from May 17, 1917, to after the Armis

Commander-in-Chief, Italian Arm
General Luigi Cadorna, to Novemb 1917. General Armando Diaz November 8, 1917, to after the Armis

Commander-in-Chief, Belgian Arr
King Albert I.

Commander-in-Chief, German Arr
Although Emperor William II nominally in command of the Ger Army, Field Marshal Paul von Hir burg, as Chief of the General Staff o Field Army, was actually in comman

Commander-in-Chief, Austro-Hu
rian Army—Emperor Charles I was inally in command but General Arz Straussenburg, who held the positio Chief of Staff, was actually in comm

————— ✦ —————

Members of Supreme War Council, November 7, 1917, to November 11, 19

Country	Permanent Representative	Civilian Assista
United States	President Woodrow Wilson	Edward M. Hous
Great Britain	Prime Minister David Lloyd George	Viscount Milner
France	Premier Georges Clemenceau	Stephen Pichon
Italy	Prime Minister Vittorio Orlando	Baron Sidney Son

————— ✦ —————

American Army Commanders [1]

Name of Army	Commander	Period (19
First	General John J. Pershing	Aug. 10–Oct
	Maj. Gen. Hunter Liggett [2]	Oct. 16–No
Second	Maj. Gen. Robert L. Bullard [2]	Oct. 12–No

————— ✦ —————

American Corps Commanders [1]

Name of Corps	Commander	Period (19
I	Maj. Gen. Hunter Liggett	Jan. 20–Oct
	Maj. Gen. Joseph T. Dickman	Oct. 12–No
II	Position vacant	Feb. 24–Jun
	Maj. Gen. George W. Read	June 15–No

[1] From date of organization until the Armistice.   [2] Appointed Lieutenant General on Nov. 1, 1918

. . . . . . Position vacant . . . . Mar. 30–June 17
Maj. Gen. William M. Wright . . . . June 17–July 12
Maj. Gen. John E. McMahon [3] . . . . July 12–July 14
Maj. Gen. Robert L. Bullard . . . . July 14–Oct. 12
Maj. Gen. John L. Hines . . . . Oct. 12–Nov. 11
. . . . . . Position vacant . . . . June 19–Aug. 18
Maj. Gen. Joseph T. Dickman . . . . Aug. 18–Oct. 12
Maj. Gen. Charles H. Muir . . . . Oct. 12–Nov. 11
. . . . . . Maj. Gen. William M. Wright . . . . July 12–Aug. 18
Maj. Gen. George H. Cameron . . . . Aug. 18–Oct. 12
Maj. Gen. Charles P. Summerall . . . . . . Oct. 12–Nov. 11
. . . . . . Position vacant . . . . Aug. 1–Aug. 26
Maj. Gen. Omar Bundy . . . . Aug. 26–Sept. 13
Position vacant . . . . Sept. 13–Oct. 23
Maj. Gen. Charles C. Ballou . . . . Oct. 23–Nov. 10
Maj. Gen. Charles T. Menoher . . . . Nov. 10–Nov. 11
. . . . . . Maj. Gen. William M. Wright . . . . Aug. 19–Sept. 6
Position vacant . . . . Sept. 6–Sept. 13
Maj. Gen. Omar Bundy . . . . Sept. 13–Oct. 25
Position vacant . . . . Oct. 25–Nov. 11

——————— ✦ ———————

American Division Commanders

me of Div.	*Commander*	*Period* [1]
. . . . . .	Maj. Gen. William L. Sibert	Oct. 23, 1917 [2]– Dec. 14, 1917
	Maj. Gen. Robert L. Bullard	Dec. 14, 1917– Apr. 5, 1918
	Brig. Gen. Beaumont B. Buck [3]	Apr. 5–Apr. 13
	Maj. Gen. Robert L. Bullard	Apr. 13–July 15
	Maj. Gen. Charles P. Summerall	July 15–Oct. 12
	Brig. Gen. Frank E. Bamford [3]	Oct. 12–Oct. 18
	Brig. Gen. Frank Parker	Oct. 18–Nov. 11
. . . . . .	Maj. Gen. Omar Bundy	Mar. 17–July 15
	Maj. Gen. James G. Harbord	July 15–July 26
	Brig. Gen. John A. Lejeune, USMC [3]	July 26–July 27
	Maj. Gen. James G. Harbord	July 27–July 28
	Brig. Gen. John A. Lejeune, USMC [4]	July 28–Nov. 11
. . . . . .	Maj. Gen. Joseph T. Dickman	May 31–Aug. 18
	Brig. Gen. Fred W. Sladen [3]	Aug. 18–Aug. 27
	Maj. Gen. Beaumont B. Buck	Aug. 27–Oct. 18
	Brig. Gen. Preston Brown	Oct. 18–Nov. 11
. . . . . .	Maj. Gen. George H. Cameron	July 18–Aug. 14
	Brig. Gen. Benjamin A. Poore [3]	Aug. 14–Aug. 27
	Maj. Gen. John L. Hines	Aug. 27–Oct. 11
	Maj. Gen. George H. Cameron	Oct. 11–Oct. 22
	Brig. Gen. Benjamin A. Poore [3]	Oct. 22–Oct. 31
	Maj. Gen. Mark L. Hersey	Oct. 31–Nov. 11

918 unless otherwise indicated.   Other reference numerals used above are explained on the next page.

American Division Commanders—Continued

Name of Div.	Division Commander	Period
5	Maj. Gen. John E. McMahon	June 14²–Oct.
	Maj. Gen. Hanson E. Ely	Oct. 18–Nov
6	Maj. Gen. Walter H. Gordon	Aug. 31–Nov
7	Brig. Gen. Charles H. Barth	Oct. 10–Oct.
	Brig. Gen. Lutz Wahl ³	Oct. 24–Oct.
	Maj. Gen. Edmund Wittenmyer	Oct. 28–Nov
26	Maj. Gen. Clarence R. Edwards	Feb. 6–Oct.
	Brig. Gen. Frank E. Bamford	Oct. 25–Nov
27	Maj. Gen. John F. O'Ryan	July 25–Nov
28	Maj. Gen. Charles H. Muir	July 1–Oct.
	Brig. Gen. Frank H. Albright ³	Oct. 23–Oct.
	Maj. Gen. William H. Hay	Oct. 25–Nov
29	Maj. Gen. Charles G. Morton	July 27–Nov
30	Brig. Gen. Samson L. Faison ³	July 16–July
	Maj. Gen. Edward M. Lewis	July 18–Nov
32	Maj. Gen. William G. Haan	May 20–Nov
33	Maj. Gen. George Bell, Jr.	June 23–Nov
35	Brig. Gen. Nathaniel F. McClure	June 20–July
	Maj. Gen. Peter E. Traub	July 20–Nov
	Brig. Gen. Thomas B. Dugan ³	Nov. 1–Nov
	Maj. Gen. Peter E. Traub	Nov. 2–Nov
36	Maj. Gen. William R. Smith	Oct. 10–Nov
37	Maj. Gen. Charles S. Farnsworth	July 28–Nov
42	Maj. Gen. Charles T. Menoher	Feb. 21–Nov
	Brig. Gen. Douglas MacArthur	Nov. 10–Nov
77	Maj. Gen. George B. Duncan	June 21–July
	Brig. Gen. Evan M. Johnson ³	July 20–July
	Maj. Gen. George B. Duncan	July 28–Aug
	Brig. Gen. Evan M. Johnson ³	Aug. 19–Aug
	Maj. Gen. Robert Alexander	Aug. 27–Nov
78	Maj. Gen. James H. McRae	Sept. 16–Nov
79	Maj. Gen. Joseph E. Kuhn	Sept. 16–Nov
80	Maj. Gen. Adelbert Cronkhite	July 23–Nov
81	Maj. Gen. Charles J. Bailey	Sept. 18–Nov
82	Maj. Gen. William P. Burnham	June 25–Oct.
	Maj. Gen. George B. Duncan	Oct. 4–Nov
88	Maj. Gen. William Weigel	Sept. 23–Nov
89	Brig. Gen. Frank L. Winn	Aug. 10–Sept
	Maj. Gen. William M. Wright	Sept. 6–Nov
90	Maj. Gen. Henry T. Allen	Aug. 24–Nov
91	Maj. Gen. William H. Johnston	Sept. 22–Nov
92	Maj. Gen. Charles C. Ballou	Aug. 23–Nov

² The first date which appears opposite each division is that of its first entry into line. It is not the dat division commander was appointed.   ³ Temporarily in command.   ⁴ Promoted to Maj. Gen. on Aug. 1,

mmanders of the Services of Supply:
Colonel David S. Stanley (temporary),
ly 5, 1917–July 24, 1917.
Major General Richard M. Blatchford,
ly 25, 1917–November 1, 1917.
Brigadier General Mason M. Patrick
mporary) from November 1, 1917, to
vember 27, 1917.
Major General Francis J. Kernan,
)vember 27, 1917–July 29, 1918.
Major General James G. Harbord,
ly 29, 1918–May 26, 1919.
Brigadier General William D. Connor,
ay 26, 1919–August 31, 1919.

Insignia used by units of the A. E. F.:
Various American units during the
World War adopted colored insignia which
after approval by G. H. Q. were used as
the distinctive emblem of the unit. Cloth
reproductions of these insignia were worn
by the officers and men on the upper part
of the left sleeve of their uniforms. The
insignia were also often painted on the
various pieces of transportation. The
distinctive insignia used by the divisions
and various other units of the American
Expeditionary Forces are shown on the
colored charts on the following pages.

───── ✦ ─────

Miles of Western Front occupied by American and Allied forces in 1918

te (1918)	American	British	French [1]	Belgian	Total
n. 31	6	116	323	23	468
ar. 20	17	116	312	23	468
ar. 30	19	92	353	23	487
)r. 10	31	92	348	23	494
)r. 30	34	83	358	23	498
ay 30	23	83	393	23	522
ne 10	36	83	389	23	531
ne 20	65	83	360	23	531
ly 10	62	92	354	23	531
ly 20	55	92	362	23	532
ly 30	68	92	318	23	501
g. 10	79	93	277	23	472
1g. 20	85	93	276	23	477
1g. 30	90	87	262	23	462
pt. 10	98	87	241	23	449
pt. 30	82	83	258	28	451
t. 10	101	83	244	15	443
t. 30	79	68	248	15	410
)v. 11	83	70	214	25	392

The sections of the front which were held by Italian and Portuguese divisions are included with French.

───── ✦ ─────

aximum number of miles of front line
held at one time by American units:
101 miles on October 10, 1918.

tal length of the Western Front:

Oct. 1914—468 miles.
July 17, 1918—532 miles.

aximum number of American divisions
that saw action during any one week:
29 during second week of October 1918.

Approximate average actual strength of
the various combat divisions on the
Western Front during the year 1918:

American 25,500
British 11,800
French 11,400
German 12,300

Greatest number of Americans that arrived
in Europe during any single month:
313,410 during the month of July 1918.

Cumulative arrivals in Europe of American military personnel for the A. E. F.:

By May 31, 1917 1,308
By June 30, 1917 16,220
By July 31, 1917 20,120
By Aug. 31, 1917 39,383
By Sept. 30, 1917 61,927
By Oct. 31, 1917 92,265
By Nov. 30, 1917 129,623
By Dec. 31, 1917 183,896
By Jan. 31, 1918 224,655
By Feb. 28, 1918 254,378
By Mar. 31, 1918 329,005
By Apr. 30, 1918 434,081
By May 31, 1918 667,119
By June 30, 1918 897,293
By July 31, 1918 1,210,703
By Aug. 31, 1918 1,473,190
By Sept. 30, 1918 1,783,955
By Oct. 30, 1918 1,986,618
By Nov. 11, 1918 2,057,675

Actual combat strength of the A. E. F.:

Mar. 21, 1918 162,482
May 27, 1918 406,844
Aug. 10, 1918 822,358
Sept. 12, 1918 999,602
Oct. 12, 1918 1,078,190
Nov. 11, 1918 1,078,222

These figures include only combat troops and exclude the troops in the S. O. S., headquarters, schools, hospitals, liaison service and other special services.

Combat strength of A. E. F. by branch of service at the time of the Armistice:

Infantry and M. G. Battalions. 646,000
Engineers 81,600
Signal Corps 21,300
Air Service 34,800
Artillery 278,500
Tank Corps 10,200
Amm. Trains, Q. M., etc. . . 70,800
Medical Department . . . . [1] 152,300
Cavalry 6,000
Ordnance . . . . [1] 22,900

---

[1] Including those on duty in the Services of Supply.

Total strength of A. E. F. on Nov. 1

Its total strength was 1,981,701, which were included 32,385 marin‹

Percentage of total strength in vario‹ branches of the A. E. F., Nov. 191‹

	Officers; % of total	Enlist‹ Mer % ‹ tota
Infantry	23.83	32.
Engineers	8.69	12.
Field Artillery	10.91	11.
Casuals (all branches) . .	3.39	10.
Medical Dept. (Army) . .	18.46	7.
Quartermaster Corps . .	6.33	7.
Coast Artillery Corps . .	4.00	3.
Air Service	7.30	3.
Ammunition Trains . . .	1.47	2.
Signal Corps	1.63	1.
Supply Trains	1.02	1.
Ordnance Department . .	1.53	1.
Marines	0.75	0.
Headquarters Troops . .	0.21	0.
Military Police	0.49	0.
Hdqrs. Detachments. . .	0.00	0.
Tank Corps	0.91	0.
Cavalry	0.25	0.
Postal Express Service . .	0.15	0.
Medical Dept. (Navy) . .	0.07	0.
G.H.Q. and General Staff	8.49	0.

Number of civilians employed by A. E. ‹

42,644 at the time of the Armisti‹

Greatest number of American soldiers hospitals in Europe at any one time:

190,564 men on November 7, 1918.

Provisions for hospitalization in A. E. ‹

On November 11, 1918, there we
192,844 normal beds, which could ha‹
been increased in an emergency to 2‹
547. There were 153 base hospitals,
camp hospitals, 12 convalescent camp
21 hospital trains and 6,875 ambulanc‹

First casualty of A. E. F.:

First Lieutenant Louis J. Genel‹
Medical Corps, suffered a shell wound
July 14, 1917, while serving with t‹
British at the front southwest of Arr‹

DISTINCTIVE INSIGNIA
AMERICAN EXPEDITIONARY FORCES

GENERAL HEADQUARTERS

ARMIES

FIRST ARMY　　SECOND ARMY　　THIRD ARMY

CORPS

I CORPS　　　　II CORPS

III CORPS　　IV CORPS　　V CORPS

VI CORPS　　VII CORPS　　VIII CORPS　　IX CORPS

DIVISIONS

1ST DIVISION   2D DIVISION   3D DIVISION

4TH DIVISION   5TH DIVISION   6TH DIVISION   7TH DIVISION

8TH DIVISION   26TH DIVISION   27TH DIVISION

28TH DIVISION   29TH DIVISION   30TH DIVISION   31ST DIVISION

32D DIVISION   33D DIVISION   34TH DIVISION

DIVISIONS

35TH DIVISION

36TH DIVISION

37TH DIVISION

38TH DIVISION

40TH DIVISION

41ST DIVISION

42D DIVISION

76TH DIVISION

77TH DIVISION

78TH DIVISION

79TH DIVISION

80TH DIVISION

81ST DIVISION

82D DIVISION

83D DIVISION

84TH DIVISION

85TH DIVISION

DIVISIONS

86TH DIVISION   87TH DIVISION   88TH DIVISION   89TH DIVISION

90TH DIVISION   91ST DIVISION   92D DIVISION   93D DIVISION

SPECIAL UNITS

SERVICES   ADVANCE SECTION   CHEMICAL
OF SUPPLY   S. O. S.   WARFARE SERVICE

DISTRICT   AMBULANCE   RESERVE   TANK
OF PARIS   SERVICE   MALLET   CORPS

RAILHEAD   A. E. F.
NORTH   REGULATING STATION
RUSSIA

st soldiers of A. E. F. killed by enemy:
First Lieutenant William T. Fitzsim-
ins and Privates First Class Rudolph
ibino, Jr., Oscar C. Tugo and Leslie G.
ools, all of United States Base Hos-
al No. 5, lost their lives at 10 : 55 p. m.,
otember 4, 1917, when the Germans
inbed a British hospital with which
ey were on duty near Dannes-Camiers.

**st battle casualties of an American unit
while it was serving at the front:**
Sergeant Matthew R. Calderwood and
ivate William F. Branigan, both of Com-
iny F, 11th Engineers, were wounded
shellfire on September 5, 1917, while
rking on a railway near Gouzeaucourt.
ie 11th Engineers served with the
itish from August 1917 to June 13, 1918.

st American soldiers killed in action:
Corporal James B. Gresham and
ivates Thomas F. Enright and Merle
Hay, all of the 16th Infantry, 1st
vision, lost their lives when the Ger-
in troops raided the American trenches
Bathelémont on November 2, 1917.

nerican Expedition to Siberia:
On August 15, 1918, the 27th Infantry
iived at Vladivostok, Siberia, from the
ilippine Islands, followed one week
er by the 31st Infantry from the same
ice. To these regiments were added
edical, ordnance, transportation and
her auxiliary units. The purposes of
e expedition were threefold: to help the
echo-Slovaks (who had been held as
isoners of war in Russia and were then
Siberia, liberated and partially organ-
d) consolidate their forces and get in
uch with their Slavic kinsmen; to steady
y efforts at self-government or self-
fense in which the Russians themselves
ght be willing to accept assistance; and
guard military stores which might sub-
juently be needed by any Russian forces
iich might be organized again to fight
ainst the Central Powers. The expedi-
n was withdrawn on April 1, 1920. As
is book is concerned mainly with the
nerican military operations and bat-
fields in Europe, the Siberian Expedi-
n will not be described in more detail.

Lafayette Escadrille:
This organization was composed of
Americans who volunteered to become
aviators in the French Army before the
United States entered the war. After
the American forces reached France,
90 of these early volunteers were finally
commissioned in the American Army.

American Field Service:
This Service consisted of a group of
American volunteer ambulance sections
which joined the French forces early in
the World War and a similar group of
truck sections, known as the "Réserve
Mallet", organized immediately after the
United States entered the war. By the
time the first elements of the American
Expeditionary Forces reached France, the
American Field Service had grown to a
strength of about 2,000 men, and in the
fall of 1917 most of its personnel were
enlisted or commissioned in the American
Army. The Service was later increased
to 81 ambulance sections and 24 truck
sections. It did not serve with American
troops but remained with the French
Army until the termination of hostilities.

Trench Maps Used by the A. E. F.:
Opposite pages 136 and 220 there appear sections of the 1/20,000 (about 3″ = 1
mile) trench map, called "plan direc-
teur", which was the principal map used
by the Americans and French for battle
operations during the war. These sections show terrain in the vicinity of
Remenauville and Vauquois. Information concerning the Allies is shown in red
and that of the Germans in blue. The
full lines are trenches, the small squares
are dugout entrances, the lines of small
crosses represent bands of barbed wire,
and the short, isolated, heavy lines with
small projections on them are artillery
positions. The horizontal and vertical
lines form a grid which was the basis for
a system of coordinates used to designate
points on the map. These maps existed
for almost the entire area of the Western
Front and were constantly being revised
as new information concerning the field
fortifications of the enemy was obtained.

All maps which showed the Allied trenches were secret. These were printed only in comparatively small numbers and had a limited distribution. The 1/20,000 map without the Allied trenches was the one mainly used by front-line units. Maps of this type of a scale 1/10,000 and 1/5,000 were also in quite common use.

Air Service of the A. E. F.:

In April 1918 the Air Service had three squadrons at the front. This number increased rapidly until the Armistice, when 45 American squadrons with 740 planes were operating. 12 of these squadrons had been equipped with American-built planes. In November 1918 the Air Service reached a total strength of 7,726 officers and 70,769 men; of these, 446 officers and 6,365 men constituted the balloon section. 23 American balloon companies served at the front. American aviators brought down 753 enemy planes and 71 balloons which were officially confirmed. American losses to enemy aviators were 357 planes and 35 balloons.

Largest concentration of aviation for an offensive during the war:

The concentration of American and Allied aviation for the St. Mihiel offensive in September 1918 was the largest during the war, consisting of 21 balloon companies and 701 pursuit planes, 366 observation planes, 323 day-bombers and 91 night-bombers, a grand total of 1,481 planes.

No American-made cannon or shell was used by the American First Army:

Except for four 14-inch naval guns, the First Army throughout its entire service at the front did not fire a single cannon or shell which was made in America.

No tank of American manufacture was ever used on the Western Front:

All tanks operated by the American Army in the war were of French or British make. American manufacturers were just beginning to produce tanks in quantity when the Armistice became effective.

Munitions which were provided by t Ordnance Department of the A. E. I

An idea of the munitions furnished f the A. E. F. by its Ordnance Departme is given by the following figures, whi indicate the total number of articles f nished but do not include the equipme and supplies brought with the Americ units when they disembarked in Franc

600,000 rifles.
93,326 machine guns.
75,000 automatic rifles.
4,000 cannon.
10,000,000 rounds of art. ammuniti

Partial list of munitions which were pu chased in France by the A. E. F.:

514 tanks.
1,190 155-millimeter howitzers.
3,035 75-millimeter guns.
9,592 Hotchkiss machine guns.
40,000 Chauchat automatic rifles.
2,909,200 trench-mortar shells.
3,000,000 bombs.
5,011,000 75-millimeter shells.

Partial list of munitions purchased fro the British by the A. E. F.

122 9.2-inch howitzers.
212 8-inch howitzers.
865 6-inch Newton mortars.
2,550 3-inch Stokes mortars.

Ammunition expended by the A. E. F. actual combat with the enemy:

181,391,341 rounds, caliber .30 (rifl
120,901,102 rounds, caliber 8-mil meter (automatic rifle).
21,385,164 rounds, caliber .45 (pisto
2,274,229 rounds, caliber 37-millimete
7,550,835 rounds, caliber 75-millimete
1,983,937 rounds, calibers greater tha 75-millimeter.
2,724,067 grenades, all types.
362,911 bombs (Stokes mortar, etc

Record movement of mail in the A. E. I

In December 1918, the record mont a total of 131,900 sacks of mail we received by the A. E. F. and 25,532 ba of mail were sent to the United State

ocurement of animals for the A. E. F.:
The procurement of horses and mules
s a major problem and a shortage
vays existed. The following informa-
n gives the source, number purchased
d average delivered cost of the animals
ich were secured for use of the A. E. F.:

ited States. . . .	67,825	$487.00
ance.	135,722	379.81
eat Britain. . . .	21,030	411.26
ain	18,462	435.00
Total	243,039	$416.63
tal cost of animals.	$101,259,342.48	

Merchant shipping lost during the war:
12,946,000 gross tons of world merchant shipping were lost through hostile
acts. This is almost one third of the
world total as of July 1914. More than
3,250,000 tons of Allied shipping were
destroyed during the five-month period
from February 1 to June 30, 1917.

American troops landing in England:
Of all American troops which arrived
in France, about 49 per cent were landed
in England, mainly at Liverpool, then
moved by train to the English Channel
and by boat across it to northern France.

Mail Call

tes paid the British Government for
transporting American soldiers to
Europe in vessels under its control:

Under the Reading-Hines Agreement
de after the Armistice on February 11,
19, the United States agreed to pay the
itish Government the following rates
r the American soldiers which it had
eviously transported to Europe:

t class.	$176.30
class	$128.65
class	$76.24

Cost of war to the United States:
For the 25 months from April 1917 to
May 1919 the war cost the United States
more than $1,000,000 per hour. Its total
expenditure, excluding loans to the Allies,
was $22,000,000,000. At the time of the
Armistice the cost was about $2,000,000
per hour. The pay of officers and men
amounted to only about 13 per cent
of this amount. The total expenditure
of 22 billions was practically equal to the
entire cost of running the United States
Government from 1791 to 1914, inclusive.

Foreign loans made by the United States during and after the war:

The following table gives the status in 1937 of the foreign loans made by the United States during and after the World War. The last loan made was in 1929.

Country	Pre-Armistice cash loans	Post-Armistice		Total loans	Total payments received to Nov. 1, 1937
		Cash loans	War supplies and relief supplies		
Armenia			$11,959,917.49	$11,959,917.49	
Austria			24,055,708.92	24,055,708.92	$862,668
Belgium	$171,780,000	$177,434,467.89	29,872,732.54	379,087,200.43	52,191,273
Cuba	10,000,000			10,000,000.00	12,286,751
Czecho-Slovakia		61,974,041.10	29,905,629.93	91,879,671.03	20,134,092
Estonia			13,999,145.60	13,999,145.60	1,248,432
Finland			8,281,926.17	8,281,926.17	4,868,891
France	1,970,000,000	1,027,477,800.00	407,341,145.01	3,404,818,945.01	486,075,891
Great Britain	3,696,000,000	581,000,000.00		4,277,000,000.00	2,024,848,817
Greece		[1] 27,167,000.00		27,167,000.00	3,778,384
Hungary			1,685,835.61	1,685,835.61	468,466
Italy	1,031,000,000	617,034,050.90		1,648,034,050.90	100,829,880
Latvia			5,132,287.14	5,132,287.14	761,549
Liberia		26,000.00		26,000.00	36,471
Lithuania			4,981,628.03	4,981,628.03	1,237,956
Nicaragua			431,849.14	431,849.14	168,575
Poland			[2] 159,666,972.39	159,666,972.39	22,646,297
Rumania		25,000,000.00	12,911,152.92	37,911,152.92	4,791,007
Russia	[3] 187,729,750		4,871,547.37	192,601,297.37	8,750,311
Yugoslavia	10,605,000	16,175,465.56	24,978,020.99	51,758,486.55	2,588,771
Total	7,077,114,750	2,533,288,825.45	740,075,499.25	10,350,479,074.70	2,748,574,488

[1] Includes $12,167,000 authorized under act of Feb. 14, 1929.
[2] Includes $3,736,628.42 acquired by U. S. Shipping Board Emergency Fleet Corp. for services rendered
[3] Exclusive of $5,000,000 conditional advance not availed of and returned.

✦

United States Liquidation Commission:

The United States Liquidation Commission was created on February 11, 1919, to dispose of America's surplus war stocks in Europe and to settle all claims against the United States. Supplies and equipment of the estimated value of $672,000,000 were returned to America. The balance of the stocks was sold in Europe for the sum of $822,923,225.82.

Sales were made as follows:
$108,700,000 for cash on delivery.
$532,500,000 to France.
$29,000,000 to Belgium.
$140,100,000 to Poland, Czecho-Slovakia and other countries of Central and Southern Europe and the Near East.

The most important sale consummated was what is known as the "Bulk Sale France" of surplus war stocks in France which remained unsold on August 1, 1919, for the following considerations:

(a) $400,000,000 in 10-year 5% bonds
(b) The assumption by France of all rent for installations accruing after August 1919, and the agreement of France to hold the United States harmless against all claims arising out of American occupation and use of such installations.
(c) The waiver by France of all claims (estimated at $150,000,000) for taxes and customs duties on properties imported into France and sold after April 6, 1917

rman Debt to the United States:
Germany is indebted to the United
ates for the costs of the American Army
Occupation and the awards of the
ixed Claims Commission (United States
d Germany). This indebtedness was
iginally funded at 3,169,700,000 reichs-
irks, which at the present (1937) rate
exchange, 40.33 cents to the reichs-
ark, is more than $1,250,000,000. The
tal payments of principal and interest
:eived from Germany on this debt to
)vember 1, 1937, was $33,587,809.69.

Welfare Organizations with the A. E. F.:
There were seven welfare organizations operating officially in the A. E. F.
Their names and the maximum number
of workers who served in each are given
below. The total of the list is 12,585.

Young Men's Christian Assn. . 5,861
American Red Cross 5,500
Knights of Columbus 800
Salvation Army 200
Young Women's Christian Assn. . 136
Jewish Welfare Board 68
American Library Association . 20

The Y. M. C. A. Was Always Ready to Lead a Song,
Château-Thierry, August 13, 1918

he Stars and Stripes":
This was the service newspaper of the
nerican Expeditionary Forces, written,
.ted and published by men from the
aks. The first number was issued in
ris on February 8, 1918. The paper
peared weekly thereafter until June 13,
19. It was one of the greatest aids in
eping up the spirit and morale of the
n overseas, and at the height of its
pularity had a circulation of 522,000.

The Armistice with Germany:
The Armistice with Germany was
signed at 5:00 a. m. on November 11,
1918. It originally covered a period of
36 days, with provisions for extension,
and in the event of noncompliance with
its terms was subject to being terminated
by either party on 48 hours' notice. It
was extended and modified several times
after it became effective on November 11.
The articles of the Armistice provided

First Edition of "The Stars and Stripes"

for the cessation of hostilities six hours after signature; evacuation within a prescribed time of all invaded and occupied territory in Belgium, Luxemburg and France (including Alsace-Lorraine); withdrawal of German Armies then operating in Russia, Austria-Hungary, Rumania, Turkey and East Africa; retirement across the Rhine, within 31 days after signature, of the German Armies on the Western Front to a line in rear of a neutral zone 6 miles wide, parallel to the right bank of the Rhine River from the Dutch to the Swiss border; occupation by American and Allied Armies, at the expense of the German Government, of German territory up to the Rhine and including bridgeheads at Mayence, Coblenz and Cologne; the evacuations and withdrawals to be attended by no destruction of property or injury to inhabitants; non-reciprocal return of prisoners, whether military, naval or civilian, including hostages and sentenced persons; restitution of all seized property and payment of damages; surrender in good

condition of the following equipme 2,500 pieces of heavy artillery and equal number of field artillery, 25,(machine guns, 3,000 trench morta 1,700 planes including all night-bomba ment planes, 5,000 locomotives, 15,(railroad cars and 5,000 trucks.

In addition Germany agreed imme ately to disarm and, within seven da intern 10 battleships, 6 battle cruisers light cruisers and 50 destroyers. All ot. naval vessels were to be assembled a disarmed, submarines in particular w to proceed intact within 14 days to des nated ports for surrender. Location a movements of all ships at sea, naval merchant marine, were to be report while all merchant ships that had be seized were to be returned without re procity and in good condition. All bo and naval supplies along the Belgian co were to be abandoned to the Alli Moreover, the Germans were to surr der all Russian vessels of war or co merce and all naval supplies that h been seized in the Black Sea. Germa

to cease all requisitioning, seizures or
rcive measures to procure supplies in
mania and Russia for use at home.
e Allies were to have free access to
cuated areas of the Eastern Front
Danzig and the Vistula River to
ble them to supply food to the popula-
is and maintain order among them.

nistices with Bulgaria, Turkey and
Austria-Hungary:

The armistices with these countries in
8 were effective at the following times:
Bulgaria—12:00 noon, September 29.
Turkey—12:00 noon, October 31.
Austria-Hungary—3:00 p. m., Nov. 4.
The United States had never declared
r on Bulgaria or Turkey and conse-
ntly was not a party when the armies with these two countries were made.

icial termination of the World War:

The war with Germany and Austria-
ngary was officially terminated by a
it resolution of Congress approved
y 2, 1921. Later, separate treaties of
ce were concluded between the United
tes on the one hand and Germany,
stria and Hungary on the other. The
eaty of Berlin, with Germany, became
ctive on November 11, 1921; the

Treaty of Vienna, with Austria, on November 8, 1921; and the Treaty of Buda-
pest, with Hungary, on Dec. 17, 1921.

Treaty of Versailles:

On account of the complicated problems involved, the Allied and Associated
Powers were obliged to abandon the
original plan of a general treaty with all
of the enemy states and to treat with each
one of these states separately.

The treaty of peace terminating the
war with Germany was signed at
Versailles, June 28, 1919, by the representatives of 26 Allied and Associated
Powers on the one hand and Germany
on the other. China refused to sign the
treaty. In ratifications of this treaty exchanged on January 10, 1920, the United
States was not a participating party.

Important among the provisions of
the treaty was the Covenant of the
League of Nations. The League was to
function at Geneva under a Council and
an Assembly, with a permanent Secre-
tariat. The Covenant provided for the
placing under various powers as manda-
tories the administration of the former
German colonies. Provision was made
for guaranteeing the territorial integrity
and political independence of all League

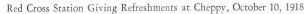

Red Cross Station Giving Refreshments at Cheppy, October 10, 1918

members, including Germany, against external aggression. Reduction and limitation of national armaments were planned and members agreed to take common action against any nation threatening peace, to submit serious disputes to arbitration and mutually to apply financial, economic and military sanctions against any member resorting to war in disregard of its covenants.

The boundaries of Germany were determined, her political status with reference to other European states, both old and new, particularly Poland and Czecho-Slovakia, was established, Alsace-Lorraine was restored to French sovereignty as from November 11, 1918, and the coal mines of the Saar basin were ceded to France as compensation for German damage to French mines and as part payment toward the total reparation due. The government of the Saar basin was to pass from Germany to an international commission representing the League and a plebiscite of the inhabitants after 15 years was to determine their eventual political status. Germany acknowledged the independence of Austria and pledged herself strictly to respect it.

Germany was forbidden to maintain or construct any fortifications either on the left bank of the Rhine or on the right bank to the west of a line about 30 miles to the east of that river, or to maintain or assemble any armed force in that area, under penalty of being regarded as having committed a hostile act calculated to disturb the peace of the world. Her army, reduced to 100,000 and not more than seven infantry and three cavalry divisions, was to be devoted exclusively to maintenance of domestic order and frontier control. Conscription was abolished and strict limitations were imposed on the manufacture or importation of armament, ammunition and equipment; military and naval aviation were forbidden and the acquisition or construction of submarines was prohibited. The military and naval establishments were fixed so low in personnel and matériel as effectively to prevent an offensive war.

The treaty publicly arraigned th former German Emperor William II for supreme offence against internation morality and the sanctity of treaties, ar arranged for the constituting of a speci tribunal for his trial and punishment.

It further placed upon Germany a her allies responsibility for reparati for all losses and damages sustained the Allied and Associated Powers a their nationals as a consequence of t aggression of the enemy. The amount such reparation was to be determined an Inter-Allied Reparation Commissio

German ports and inland waterway including the Kiel Canal, were opened the nationals of all Allied and Associat Powers on a footing of complete equali with the citizens of Germany.

There were other provisions of political, financial, economic and soc character too numerous to enumera here which with the foregoing made th treaty of 440 articles the most volumino document of its kind in modern time

Decorations and Medals:

The United States Governme awarded various decorations and o service medal for service during the Wor War. These decorations and the med are shown on the chart on the followi page and are described below. Decor tions which could be awarded for servi in either peace or war, for acts n directly incident to the war, have n been reproduced on the chart.

Decorations which were awarded throu the War Department:

Medal of Honor, presented by t President, in the name of Congress, persons who, while members of the Arm distinguished themselves conspicuous by gallantry and intrepidity at the risk life above and beyond the call of du while in action involving actual confli with an armed enemy.

Distinguished Service Cross, present to persons serving with the Army w distinguished themselves by extraordina heroism in connection with milita operations against an armed enem

DECORATIONS
UNITED STATES OF AMERICA

MEDAL OF HONOR
UNITED STATES NAVY

MEDAL OF HONOR
UNITED STATES ARMY

DISTINGUISHED SERVICE CROSS
UNITED STATES ARMY

DISTINGUISHED SERVICE MEDAL
UNITED STATES NAVY

DISTINGUISHED SERVICE MEDAL
UNITED STATES ARMY

NAVY CROSS
WITH GOLD STAR

PURPLE HEART

SILVER STAR
WITH OAK-LEAF CLUSTER

VICTORY MEDAL

FOREIGN DECORATIONS

DISTINGUISHED CONDUCT MEDAL
GREAT BRITAIN

MILITARY CROSS
GREAT BRITAIN

MILITARY MEDAL
GREAT BRITAIN

MEDAILLE MILITAIRE
FRANCE

LEGION OF HONOR
FRANCE

CROIX DE GUERRE
FRANCE

CROIX DE GUERRE
BELGIUM

ORDER OF LEOPOLD
BELGIUM

WAR CROSS
ITALY

Distinguished Service Medal, awarded) persons serving with the Army who istinguished themseives by exceptionally eritorious service to the Government in position of great responsibility.

Silver Star, awarded to persons who ere cited for gallantry in action in rders issued from the headquarters of a rce normally commanded by a general fficer, or issued by the War Department, hich citation does not warrant the ward of a Medal of Honor or Distinuished Service Cross. This decoration as originally a small silver star worn on ie ribbon of a service medal, but in 1932 was replaced by a separate medal.

Purple Heart, awarded to persons who erformed singularly meritorious acts of traordinary fidelity or essential service. wound which necessitated treatment by medical officer and which was received action is considered as resulting from singularly meritorious act of essential rvice. This decoration was established y General George Washington in 1782 it was subsequently allowed to lapse. was reinstituted in 1932 on the 200th niversary of Washington's birth.

Oak-Leaf Cluster. Not more than one each of the decorations named above uld be awarded to any one person, but r each succeeding act or achievement fficient to justify the award of the coration, a bronze Oak-Leaf Cluster as presented to be worn on the ribbon ' the medal previously awarded.

ecorations which were awarded through the Navy Department:

Medal of Honor (new), presented by e President, in the name of Congress, persons who distinguished themselves nspicuously by gallantry and intredity at the risk of life above and beyond e call of duty and without detriment to e mission of their commands, while in tion involving conflict with the enemy.

Distinguished Service Medal, prented to persons in the naval service ho distinguished themselves by excepnally meritorious service to the Govnment in duty of great responsibility.

Navy Cross, presented to persons who distinguished themselves by extraordinary heroism or distinguished service in the line of their profession, such heroism or service not being sufficient to justify the award of either a Medal of Honor or a Distinguished Service Medal.

Gold Star, awarded by the Navy Department under conditions identical to those for which the War Department awards the Oak-Leaf Cluster and worn similarly on the ribbons of the medals.

Victory Medal:

Awarded to all persons in the military and naval services who were on active duty at any time between April 6, 1917, and November 11, 1918, or who were members of the American Expedition to Siberia or Northern Russia after November 11, 1918. Clasps are worn on the ribbon of this service medal to indicate the major operations, defensive sectors, country or type of naval duty in which the World War service was performed.

Foreign decorations which were awarded to a number of American soldiers:

Many Americans received decorations from the Allied Governments during the World War. The foreign decorations most commonly awarded to Americans are shown on the chart facing this page. These were given to Americans for the same general reasons that they were given to the individuals of the Allied country concerned. The particular medals shown on the chart were awarded as follows:

Great Britain:

Military Cross—To army officers of junior rank for heroism in action.

Distinguished Conduct Medal—To enlisted men of the army for conspicuous gallantry on the field of battle.

Military Medal—To enlisted men of the army for meritorious action under fire.

France:

Legion of Honor—For extraordinary and distinguished service, civil or military. Awards are made in various grades.

Médaille Militaire—To enlisted men and generals of the army for signal acts of valor or especially meritorious service.

Officers and Men Being Presented with Medal of Honor at Chaumont, February 9, 1919

Left to right: Captains Edward C. Allworth, George H. Mallon, George G. McMurtry, 1st Lieutenants Samuel Woodfill, Harold A. Furlong, 2d Lieutenant Donald M. Call, 1st Sergeants Johannes S. Anderson, Sydney G. Gumpertz, Sergeants Willie Sandlin, Archie A. Peck, Harold I. Johnston,

Croix de Guerre—To officers and en-
ted men of the army for meritorious
ts performed in the theater of operations.
elgium:
Order of Leopold—For extraordinary
d distinguished service, civil or military.
wards are made in various grades.
Croix de Guerre—To officers and en-
ted men of the army for meritorious
ts performed in the theater of operations.
aly:
War Cross—For war deeds of heroism.

The Constitution of the United States
rbids the acceptance of foreign decora-
ons by the members of its government
of its armed forces without the con-
nt of Congress. This authorization
as granted by Congress through one
neral law in the case of all Allied deco-
tions presented to members of the
ilitary forces of the United States during
within one year after the World War.

merican units which were awarded
French decorations during the war:
The French Government awarded
corations for especially meritorious
nduct in action during the war to 156
merican units varying in size from a
ction to a brigade. These decorations
ere the fourragère and the Croix de
uerre with various combinations of
alms and gilt, silver and bronze stars.
he American unit to which such an
ward has been made is authorized by
e American Government to place on its
ag a silk streamer 2¾ inches wide and
ot less than 3 feet nor more than 4 feet
ng, or on its guidon a smaller streamer,
hich is attached to the staff near the
earhead. One streamer is used for
ch award and on each streamer, which
in the colors of the decoration, are em-
oidered the names commemorating the
tions for which the unit was cited.
Under French regulations, an organiza-
on twice decorated with a Croix de
uerre with palm was entitled, upon
suance of orders by the French Ministry
War, to a braided and knotted cord,
lled a fourragère, in the green and red
lors of the Croix de Guerre. An or-

ganization which received the Croix de
Guerre with four palms was likewise entitled to a fourragère in the yellow and
green colors of the Médaille Militaire.
American units so decorated are authorized by the American Government to
wear the fourragère. In these units the
fourragère is placed with the streamers on
the flag or guidon and all members of the
organization wear the fourragère on the
left shoulder of the uniform as long as
they remain members of the organization.
Individuals are also awarded the fourragère as a personal decoration under conditions similar to those pertaining to an
organization. At ceremonies the decoration itself may be placed on the streamer
of the flag or guidon of an organization to
which the award has been made.

For each citation after the award of a
Croix de Guerre, a palm or a gilt, silver
or bronze star was awarded instead of
another Croix de Guerre medal.

The following list shows the awards
received by all American units decorated
by the French for service during the
World War. These are arranged in order
of the relative rank of the award.

**Fourragère and Croix de Guerre with
4 Palms, 1 Gilt Star and 1 Silver Star:**
Amb. Serv. Sec. No. 646.[1]

**Fourragère and Croix de Guerre with
2 Palms, 1 Gilt Star and 1 Bronze Star:**
Amb. Serv. Sec. No. 625.

**Fourragère and Croix de Guerre with
2 Palms and 1 Gilt Star:** 5th Marines,
6th Marines, 2d M. G. Bn., 3d M. G.
Bn., 2d Field Signal Bn.
**Fourragère and Croix de Guerre with
2 Palms:** 9th Inf., 16th Inf., 18th Inf.,
23d Inf., 26th Inf., 28th Inf., 1st M. G.
Bn., 4th M. G. Bn., 5th M. G. Bn.,
6th M. G. Bn. (Marines), 5th F. A.,
6th F. A., 7th F. A., 12th F. A., 15th
F. A., 17th F. A., 2d Trench Mortar
Battery, 1st Engrs., 2d Engrs., 1st

---

[1] Partial list of the abbreviations which are used:

Amb.—Ambulance	M. G.—Machine Gun
Bn.—Battalion	Plat.—Platoon
Det.—Detachment	Sec.—Section
F. A.—Field Artillery	Serv.—Service
Hdqrs.—Headquarters	Tn.—Train

Field Signal Bn., Hdqrs. and Hdqrs. Det. 2d Division, Hdqrs. and Hdqrs. Det. 3d Inf. Brig., Hdqrs. and Hdqrs. Det. 4th Brig. (Marines), Hdqrs. and Hdqrs. Det. 2d F. A. Brig., Hdqrs. Troop 2d Division, 2d Military Police Co., 2d Tn. Hdqrs., 2d Ammunition Tn., 2d Engr. Tn., 2d Supply Tn., 2d Sanitary Tn., 2d Mobile Ordnance Repair Shop, Mobile Veterinary Sec. No. 2, 103d Aero Squadron (formerly Lafayette Escadrille), Ambulance Service Section No. 539, Services attached to 2d Division: Foden Disinfecting Squad No. 17, Machine Shop Truck Units No. 303 and 363, Military Postal Express Serv. Det., Mobile Surgical Unit No. 3, Railhead Detachment, Sales Commissary Unit No. 1, Salvage Squad No. 2, Veterinary Field Units Numbers 1, 2 and 3.

Croix de Guerre with 2 Palms: Ambulance Service Section No. 567.

Croix de Guerre with 1 Palm and 1 Gilt Star: Ambulance Service Section No. 523.

Croix de Guerre with 1 Palm and 2 Silver Stars: Ambulance Service Sections No. 626, 629 and 633.

Croix de Guerre with 1 Palm and 1 Silver Star: Ambulance Service Sections No. 621 and 622.

Croix de Guerre with 1 Palm: 3d Inf. Brig., 4th Brig. (Marines), 63d Inf. Brig., 64th Inf. Brig., 30th Inf., 38th Inf., 125th Inf., 126th Inf., 127th Inf., 128th Inf., 353d Inf., 371st Inf., 372d Inf., 1st Bn. 102d Inf., Co. I 9th Inf., Co. L 9th Inf., Co. F 167th Inf., Co. C 370th Inf., a composite Plat. Co. A 111th Inf., 2d Plat. Co. B 111th Inf., 7th M. G. Bn., 9th M. G. Bn., 119th M. G. Bn., 120th M. G. Bn.,

121st M. G. Bn., Battery H 53d Coast Artillery, 6th Engrs., 302d Engrs., Co. 56th Engrs., 91st Aero Squadron, 94 Aero Squadron, Amb. Serv. Secs. No. 5{ 525, 544, 546, 583, 631 and 648.

Croix de Guerre with 1 Gilt Star a 1 Silver Star: Ambulance Service Sectio No. 516, 534 and 635.

Croix de Guerre with 1 Gilt Star: 4 Inf., 7th Inf., 39th Inf., 104th Inf., C F 9th Inf., Co. G 9th Inf., 4th Plat. C K 9th Inf., 2d Plat. Co. C 308th In Stokes Mortar Sec. Hdqrs. Co. 102d In 10th F. A., 18th F. A., 76th F. A., 147 F. A., Battery D 17th F. A., 308 Trench Mortar Battery, 1st Anti-Aircr M. G. Bn., Ambulance Service Sectio No. 7, 585, 638 and 642.

Croix de Guerre with 2 Silver Stars a 3 Bronze Stars: Ambulance Service S tion No. 628.

Croix de Guerre with 2 Silver Star Amb. Serv. Sections No. 591 and 636.

Croix de Guerre with 1 Silver Star a 1 Bronze Star: Ambulance Service S tions No. 553 and 623.

Croix de Guerre with 1 Silver St: 369th Inf., 1st and 2d Plats. Co. B 168 Inf., Stokes Mortar Sec. Hdqrs. C 168th Inf., 8th M. G. Bn., 119th F. 120th F. A., 121st F. A., 5th Field Sig Bn., Mobile Hospital No. 1, Evacuati Hospital No. 7, Ambulance Service S tions No. 503, 510, 533, 535, 558, 5 580, 586, 627, 632, 634, 637, 639, 6 641, 643, 644 and 645.

Croix de Guerre with 1 Bronze St: Headquarters and Supply Co. 1st B talion Anti-Aircraft Artillery, Ambulan Service Sections Numbers 593 and 5!

United States Steamships *George Washington, America* and *De Kalb* in Convoy, May 18, 1918

AMERICAN DIVISIONS SENT TO EUROPE

THEIR DATES OF ARRIVAL, CASUALTIES AND LOCALITIES
FROM WHICH ORIGINALLY RAISED

REGULAR ARMY DIVISIONS

	Date Div. Hdqrs. arrived in France	Battle deaths and died of wounds	Wounded	Locality from which division was originally raised (Many divisions were reorganized prior to sailing for Europe)
1	June 26, 1917	4, 996	17, 324	At large.
2	. . . . . .	[1] 5, 155	[2] 18, 080	At large. (Included one brigade of marines.) Division formed in France in 1917.
3	Apr. 4, 1918	3, 401	12, 000	At large.
4	May 17, 1918	2, 903	9, 917	Do.
5	May 1, 1918	2, 120	6, 996	Do.
6	July 22, 1918	68	318	Do.
7	Aug. 11, 1918	287	1, 422	Do.
8	Nov. 9, 1918	. . . .	. . . .	At large. (Part arrived in France just prior to Armistice.)

NATIONAL GUARD DIVISIONS

6	Oct. 28, 1917	2, 281	11, 383	New England.
7	May 31, 1918	1, 829	6, 505	New York.
8	May 18, 1918	2, 874	11, 265	Pennsylvania.
9	June 28, 1918	1, 053	4, 517	New Jersey, Virginia, Maryland, Delaware, District of Columbia.
0	May 24, 1918	1, 641	6, 774	Tennessee, North Carolina and South Carolina.
1	Oct. 15, 1918	. . . .	. . . .	Georgia, Alabama and Florida. (Became 7th Depot Division.)
2	Feb. 20, 1918	3, 028	10, 233	Michigan and Wisconsin.
3	May 24, 1918	993	5, 871	Illinois.
4	Oct. 3, 1918	. . . .	. . . .	Nebraska, Iowa, North Dakota, South Dakota and Minnesota. (Personnel used as replacements.)
5	May 11, 1918	1, 298	5, 998	Missouri and Kansas.
6	July 30, 1918	591	1, 993	Texas and Oklahoma.
7	June 23, 1918	1, 066	4, 321	Ohio.
8	Oct. 4, 1918	. . . .	. . . .	Indiana, Kentucky and West Virginia. (Personnel used as replacements.)
9	Aug. 27, 1918	. . . .	. . . .	Arkansas, Mississippi and Louisiana. (Became 5th Depot Division.)
0	Aug. 24, 1918	. . . .	. . . .	California, Colorado, Utah, Arizona and New Mexico. (Became 6th Depot Division.)
1	Dec. 31, 1917	93	315	Washington, Oregon, Montana, Idaho, Wyoming, Colorado, North Dakota, South Dakota, New Mexico and District of Columbia. (Became 1st Depot Division.)
2	Nov. 1, 1917	2, 810	11, 873	Composite division from 26 States and District of Columbia.

NATIONAL ARMY DIVISIONS

6	July 16, 1918	4	22	New England and New York. (Became 3d Depot Division.)
7	Apr. 13, 1918	2, 110	8, 084	New York City and vicinity.
8	June 8, 1918	1, 530	5, 614	New York, New Jersey and Delaware.
9	July 16, 1918	1, 517	5, 357	Pennsylvania, Maryland and District of Columbia.
0	May 30, 1918	1, 241	4, 788	Virginia, West Virginia and Pennsylvania.
1	Aug. 16, 1918	248	856	North Carolina, South Carolina and Florida.
2	May 13, 1918	1, 413	6, 664	Georgia, Alabama and Tennessee.
3	June 17, 1918	67	257	Ohio and Pennsylvania. (Became 2d Depot Division.)
4	Sept. 25, 1918	. . . . . .	. . . .	Kentucky, Indiana, Illinois. (Personnel used as replacements.)
5	Aug. 10, 1918	145	281	Michigan and Wisconsin. (Became 4th Depot Division.)
6	Sept. 23, 1918	. . . . . .	. . . .	Illinois and Wisconsin. (Personnel used as replacements.)
7	Sept. 9, 1918	. . . . . .	. . . .	Arkansas, Louisiana, Mississippi and Alabama.
8	Sept. 4, 1918	20	58	North Dakota, Minnesota, Iowa and Illinois.
9	June 21, 1918	1, 466	5, 625	Kansas, Missouri, South Dakota, Nebraska, Arizona, Colorado and New Mexico.
0	July 7, 1918	1, 496	6, 053	Texas and Oklahoma.
1	July 23, 1918	1, 454	4, 654	Montana, Nevada, Wyoming, Utah, Washington, Oregon, California and Idaho.
2	June 19, 1918	182	1, 465	Colored troops (various states).
3	Mar. 5, 1918	591	2, 943	Colored National Guard and other troops (various states) four infantry regiments only.
er troops_____		976	2, 802	
		52, 947	202, 628	

[1] Includes 2454 Marine Corps and 18 Navy serving with the Marine Corps.
[2] Includes 8894 Marine Corps and 123 Navy serving with the Marine Corps.
[3] 332d Infantry of this division went to Italy in July 1918 and saw active service.
[4] 339th Infantry of this division served at Archangel, Russia, for a time.

Div.	Popular Nickname	Numeral Designation of Units in Division			
		Inf. Brigades	Inf. Regiments	F. A. Brig.	F. A. Regts.
1	None	1, 2	16, 18, 26, 28	1	5, 6, 7
2	None	3, 4	9, 23, **5, 6**	2	12, 15, 17
3	Marne	5, 6	4, 7, 30, 38	3	10, 18, 76
4	Ivy	7, 8	39, 47, 58, 59	4	13, 16, 77
5	Red Diamond	9, 10	60, 61, 6, 11	5	19, 20, 21
6	None	11, 12	51, 52, 53, 54	6	3, 11, 78
7	None	13, 14	55, 56, 34, 64	7	8, 79, 80
8	Pathfinder	15, 16	12, 62, 8, 13	8	2, 81, 83
26	Yankee	51, 52	101, 102, 103, 104	51	101, 102, 103
27	New York	53, 54	105, 106, 107, 108	52	104, 105, 106
28	Keystone	55, 56	109, 110, 111, 112	53	107, 108, 109
29	Blue and Gray	57, 58	113, 114, 115, 116	54	110, 111, 112
30	Old Hickory	59, 60	117, 118, 119, 120	55	113, 114, 115
31	Dixie	61, 62	121, 122, 123, 124	56	116, 117, 118
32	Iron Jaws	63, 64	125, 126, 127, 128	57	119, 120, 121
33	Prairie	65, 66	129, 130, 131, 132	58	122, 123, 124
34	Sandstorm	67, 68	133, 134, 135, 136	59	125, 126, 127
35	None	69, 70	137, 138, 139, 140	60	128, 129, 130
36	Lone Star	71, 72	141, 142, 143, 144	61	131, 132, 133
37	Buckeye	73, 74	145, 146, 147, 148	62	134, 135, 136
38	Cyclone	75, 76	149, 150, 151, 152	63	137, 138, 139
39	Delta	77, 78	153, 154, 155, 156	64	140, 141, 142
40	Sunshine	79, 80	157, 158, 159, 160	65	143, 144, 145
41	Sunset	81, 82	161, 162, 163, 164	66	146, 147, 148
42	Rainbow	83, 84	165, 166, 167, 168	67	149, 150, 151
76	None	151, 152	301, 302, 303, 304	151	301, 302, 303
77	Metropolitan	153, 154	305, 306, 307, 308	152	304, 305, 306
78	Lightning	155, 156	309, 310, 311, 312	153	307, 308, 309
79	Liberty	157, 158	313, 314, 315, 316	154	310, 311, 312
80	Blue Ridge	159, 160	317, 318, 319, 320	155	313, 314, 315
81	Stonewall	161, 162	321, 322, 323, 324	156	316, 317, 318
82	All American	163, 164	325, 326, 327, 328	157	319, 320, 321
83	Ohio	165, 166	329, 330, 331, 332	158	322, 323, 324
84	Lincoln	167, 168	333, 334, 335, 336	159	325, 326, 327
85	Custer	169, 170	337, 338, 339, 340	160	328, 329, 330
86	Black Hawk	171, 172	341, 342, 343, 344	161	331, 332, 333
87	Acorn	173, 174	345, 346, 347, 348	162	334, 335, 336
88	Cloverleaf	175, 176	349, 350, 351, 352	163	337, 338, 339
89	Middle West	177, 178	353, 354, 355, 356	164	340, 341, 342
90	Alamo	179, 180	357, 358, 359, 360	165	343, 344, 345
91	Wild West	181, 182	361, 362, 363, 364	166	346, 347, 348
92	Buffalo	183, 184	365, 366, 367, 368	167	349, 350, 351
93	None [1]	185, 186	369, 370, 371, 372		

Marine units, all in 2nd Division, in bold face type.   [1] Never operated as a division.

Numeral Designation of Units in Division			Days in Front Line				Approximate Number of Miles Advanced	Prisoners Captured	Prisoners Lost	Replacements Received	Div.
ngr. gt.	M. G. Bns.	Training in line	Sector	Battle	Total					
1	1, 2, 3	47	148	28	223	32	6, 469	152	30, 206	1
2	4, 5, 6	58	48	33	139	37	12, 026	157	35, 343	2
6	7, 8, 9	0	39	50	89	25	2, 240	314	24, 033	3
4	10, 11, 12	0	11	36	47	15	2, 756	72	19, 559	4
7	13, 14, 15	33	39	32	104	18	2, 356	100	12, 611	5
318	16, 17, 18	6	37	0	43	0	12	3	2, 784	6
5	19, 20, 21	0	33	0	33	1	69	20	4, 112	7
319	22, 23, 24							1		8
101	101, 102, 103	42	118	45	205	23	3, 148	457	14, 411	26
102	104, 105, 106	25	0	32	57	7	2, 357	229	5, 255	27
103	107, 108, 109	14	44	44	102	6	921	732	21, 717	28
104	110, 111, 112	13	46	23	82	4	2, 187	68	4, 977	29
105	113, 114, 115	33	1	35	69	18	3, 848	75	2, 384	30
106	116, 117, 118							2		31
107	119, 120, 121	25	37	38	100	22	2, 153	161	20, 140	32
108	122, 123, 124	27	33	38	98	22	3, 987	127	5, 415	33
109	125, 126, 127							1		34
110	128, 129, 130	37	43	30	110	7	781	167	10, 605	35
111	131, 132, 133	0	0	19	19	13	549	24	3, 397	36
112	134, 135, 136	7	57	13	77	19	1, 495	23	6, 282	37
113	137, 138, 139							2		38
114	140, 141, 142							2		39
115	143, 144, 145							3		40
116	146, 147, 148							4		41
117	149, 150, 151	31	100	45	176	34	1, 317	112	17, 253	42
301	301, 302, 303							3		76
302	304, 305, 306	25	31	63	119	44	750	403	12, 728	77
303	307, 308, 309	0	18	22	40	13	432	123	3, 190	78
304	310, 311, 312	0	29	18	47	12	1, 077	80	6, 246	79
305	313, 314, 315	16	0	31	47	24	1, 813	100	4, 495	80
306	316, 317, 318	11	18	5	37	3	101	51	1, 984	81
307	319, 320, 321	17	58	30	105	11	845	240	8, 402	82
308	322, 323, 324							3		83
309	325, 326, 327							1		84
310	328, 329, 330							18		85
311	331, 332, 333									86
312	334, 335, 336									87
313	337, 338, 339	22	21	0	43	0	3	9	734	88
314	340, 341, 342	0	54	28	82	30	5, 061	25	7, 669	89
315	343, 344, 345	0	43	26	69	17	1, 876	81	4, 437	90
316	346, 347, 348	0	6	17	23	21	2, 412	28	12, 530	91
317	349, 350, 351	7	56	0	63	5	38	17	2, 920	92
								4		93

Impromptu Service at Exermont Soon After Its Capture

Chapter XV

MISCELLANEOUS

◀HE American Battle Monuments Commission was created by Con- gress in 1923. In carrying out its ⟨ of commemorating the services of the erican forces in Europe during the rld War the Commission erected appro- ate memorials abroad, improved the ht military cemeteries there and in this ume records the vital part American iers and sailors played in bringing the ; to an early and successful conclusion. ll dates which appear in this book are usive. For instance, when a period stated as November 7–9 it includes three days, i. e., November 7, 8 and 9. ⁻he date given for the relief in the nt line of one division by another is t when the command of the sector sed to the division entering the line. the few instances where no date of sage of command could be found it s assumed that command passed as ected in the field orders and when the d orders did not specify the time it s assumed that the command passed n the completion of the relief of the front-line unit of the division. When units of a division entered the ⁻ for training, the date of entry into line is that when the first unit went ɔ the front line; the date used for the mination of this service is that when last unit of the division left the line.)n the maps and sketches all dates on battle lines refer to midnight of the ⁻ in question unless otherwise indicated. ⁻ example, if the date September 26 ⟩ears on a battle line, it means the line ₃ there at midnight of September 26. ⁻he unit boundaries shown on the small tches are those prescribed in official d orders. On all maps which use ɔred areas or stippling to show ground ned, the field order boundaries are dis- arded and each color or type of stippling ws the ground actually passed over by troops of the organization concerned.

The size or type of the map illustrating any particular operation in no way indi- cates the importance of the operation; clearness was the only governing factor. The 1/200,000 maps at the ends of Chapters II, III, IV and V have been placed there with the idea that while the tourist is reading the text or following the tour of a chapter he will keep the map at the end unfolded, available for reference.

As a general rule, only the locations of headquarters of corps and divisions from which active operations were directed more than three days are mentioned in the text. Those who desire more com- plete information on the subject can find it in the two volumes published officially by the Historical Section, Army War College, entitled "Order of Battle of the United States Land Forces in the World War, American Expeditionary Forces".

All casualty figures are derived from official records of the War Department and include only the killed and wounded in action and those who died of wounds re- ceived in action. They exclude all missing in action, captured and sick. In all cases, except on page 515, casualties are given only for the periods units actually served in the front line. In the tables at the ends of the various chapters, the casualties of units which served temporarily attached to the different divisions are given by separate figures. The casualties which appear on page 515 are from the Report of the Secretary of War for 1926, with the addition of the Marine Corps and the Navy casualties. These figures do not include the casualties of the attached units.

This text embodies the results of a very exhaustive study made by the Commis- sion, using data from German and other sources concerning the location of the Hindenburg Line in the Meuse-Argonne region. Unless otherwise indicated the part of that position described in the text and on the maps is its main line of resistance.

Typical 2d Division Battlefield Marker

Medal of Honor citations have been used freely because these citations give a vivid picture of the hardest part of the fighting. At one place or another in the book information is given concerning the citations of each of the 94 men awarded the Army Congressional Medal of Honor. As the majority of these men were in the infantry, the branch of service has been indicated in the text only in case the soldier was in some other branch of the army.

The classification in this text of the front-line service of American divisions into battle and sector service is the same as given in General Order No. 16, War Department, 1921, and its amendments.

French maps and guidebooks:

There are on sale in France and Belgium excellent road maps and inexpensive guidebooks, written in English, giving complete, up-to-date information concerning roads, hotels, restaurants and objects of some historical interest. These books and maps will be found of great value while making a tour of the battlefields.

Information concerning French roads

The roads in France are numbe[r] National highways are the best roads are designated by the letter "N" follo[w] by a numeral; for example, N–3 is National Highway No. 3. Departme[n] roads, corresponding to state roads in United States, are designated by letters "G. C." or "G. C. D." and a n[u] ber; for example, G. C. 6 or G. C. D These also are good roads and rank below the national highways. The let[ters] "I. C." and "V. O." indicate local ro[a] The main difference in all these road in width rather than in the characte[r] the surface. National roads are wide, comparatively straight, and are mar[ked] so they are easy to follow, whereas l[ocal] roads are narrow, very winding, and general have not many road signs.

All roads except poor ones have alc[ng] side them a stone post at each kilome[ter] That part of the post facing the r[oad] bears a number and the designation the road, such as N–3 or G. C. 6. sides of the posts generally give the n[ame] of the next large village or town and distance to it. Small posts about inches high usually mark each tent[h] a kilometer between successive p[osts] Roads change the numbering of t[he] kilometer posts, given on the side fa[cing] the road, at each departmental bound[ary]

Conversion of meters and kilometers

1 kilometer	=	0.62137 mile
1 mile	=	1.6093 kilometers
1 meter	=	39.37 inches
	=	1.09 yards
1 yard	=	0.9144 meter

A simple rule for roughly conver[ting] kilometers to miles is to multiply number of kilometers by 0.6. To cha[nge] from miles to kilometers do the oppo[site] and divide the number of miles by

The graphic scales below can be u[sed] for conversion purposes where dista[nces] shorter than 20 kilometers are invol[ved]

```
0  1  2  3  4  5  6  7  8  9  10  11  12  13  14  15  16  17  18  19
                              Kilometers
0     1     2     3     4     5     6     7     8     9    10    11    12
                              Miles
```

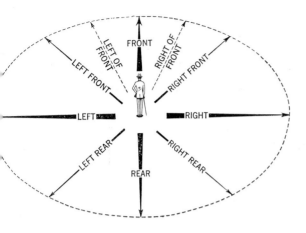

ormation for use on described tours:
On the described tours road direc-
ns have been given where there is a
ssibility that the tourist might go
ray. At junctions where no road
tructions are given the tourist should,
course, continue straight ahead.

The speedometer distances recorded by
tomobiles vary greatly and those re-
ded by the same car under different
nditions, such as wet and dry weather,
: not the same. These points are men-
ned so that too much reliance will not
placed on speedometer readings.

At the stops the tourist is told to face
a certain direction and the account of
: operations is given with respect to
it facing. The meanings of the various
pressions used to indicate the different
ections are illustrated by the sketch
ated on the upper part of this page.

edals issued by the cities of Verdun,
St. Mihiel and Château-Thierry:

The cities of Verdun, St. Mihiel and
âteau-Thierry have issued special med-
which are available to all American
erans who served in the general vicinity
these cities during the war. These
dals may be obtained by writing and
ding some proof of service in the Amer-
n Army and in the region to the mayors
the cities concerned, who will place
: letter in the proper hands. A small
: is charged for the cost of the medal.

The requirements
for these medals are
not always strictly en-
forced. In general, all
those who served in
the area bounded by
the following (all towns
are inclusive) are eli-
gible for the Verdun
medal: Conflans-en-
Jarnisy, Thiaucourt,
Montsec, St. Mihiel,
Noyers, Ste. Mene-
hould and to the north
as far as the Armistice
line. The area pre-
scribed for the St.
Mihiel medal is roughly as follows: Pont-à-
Mousson, Ménil-la-Tour, Ligny-en-Barrois, Souilly, Les Eparges and Vandières.
No general area has been prescribed for
eligibility for the Château-Thierry medal.

Typical 1st Division Battlefield Monument

AMERICAN WORLD WAR MEMORIALS IN EUROPE
ERECTED BY AGENCIES OTHER THAN
THE UNITED STATES GOVERNMENT

IN addition to the memorials erected by the United States Government there are a number of other American World War memorials in Europe. Some of these were in existence before the American Battle Monuments Commission was created and others are useful memorials constructed with the Commission's approval. A few are memorials to American units which served with the French Army before the United States entered the war and concerning the erection of which the Commission was without jurisdiction.

For the benefit of those interested there is given below a tabulation of American World War commemorative memorials in Europe of which the American Battle Monuments Commission has a record and which were erected by agencies other th[an] those of the United States Governme[nt].

This table does not include monume[nts] to units smaller than a regiment, mark[ers] now falling to pieces, French village m[onu]ments which commemorate Americ[an] units in addition to their own dead, a[nd] monuments to foreign armies erected [by] Americans or from American sources.

In this connection it may be stated th[at] the Commission feels that the memor[ial] project of the United States Governme[nt] described in Chapter XII, adequat[ely] commemorates all units of the Americ[an] forces in Europe during the World W[ar] and that the erection of any additio[nal] American monuments abroad would r[not] be in good taste and should be prohibit[ed].

Unit or event commemorated	Number	Location	Character	Date erected	Remarks
V Corps	1	3 miles southeast of Mouzon (Ardennes) on the main road.	Small marker built of field stones.	Soon after the Armistice.	Erected by member[s of] unit to mark V C[orps] line at the Armist[ice.] See picture, page
1st Division	5	(a) Along road ½ mile southeast of Cantigny (Somme). (b) On main highway west of Buzancy (Aisne). (c) At road junction east of Vigneulles (Meuse). (d) Along main road ½ mile east of St. Juvin (Ardennes). (e) Along road south of Wadelincourt (Ardennes).	Small concrete shaft, surmounted by a carved eagle of stone.	1919	Erected by the 1st [Div.] Names of dead [in] vicinity given [on] bronze plates. picture on page
2d Division	22	On all of the battlefields where the division had fighting.	Concrete boulder about 3 feet in diameter, with 2d Div. insignia in bronze upon it.	Soon after the Armistice.	Erected by men f[rom] the division. picture on page
3d Division	1	Château-Thierry (Aisne), northwest of the main bridge.	Stone monument of medium size.	1923	Erected by divis[ion] to its deeds and de[ad]. See picture, page

Unit or event commemorated	Number	Location	Character	Date erected	Remarks
Division	3	(a) About 1 mile west of Fismes (Marne). (b) At the eastern exit of Manheulles (Meuse). (c) About 1 mile west of town of Brieulles-sur-Meuse.	Small stone obelisk.	Soon after the Armistice.	Erected by the division. See the picture appearing on page 80.
Division	28	On all of the battle-fields where the division had fighting.	Small obelisk of concrete.	Soon after the Armistice.	Erected by men of the division. Inscriptions give details of fighting. See picture on page 525.
Division	1	Dun-sur-Meuse	An ornamental wrought-iron railing on a bridge.	1932	Erected by the 5th Div. Assn. to commemorate crossing of the Meuse River.
Division	1	Belleau (Aisne)	Reconstruction of village church.	1929	Erected by the 26th Div. Assn. in memory of division's dead. See picture, page 53.
Division	1	Fismes (Marne)	Ornamental stone bridge.	1927	Erected by the State of Pennsylvania. See picture, page 525.
Division	1	Along the main road south of town of Bellicourt (Aisne).	Small monument of cut stone.	1923	Erected by the State of Tennessee to her troops of the 59th and 60th Brigades. See picture, page 377.
Division	1	Montfaucon (Meuse).	Substantial stone building, donated for use as an almshouse.	1929	Erected by the State of Ohio. See picture of building on page 214.
Division	1	Eyne, Belgium	A large bridge, stucco finish.	1929	Erected by the State of Ohio to commemorate crossing of Escaut River by 37th Division. See the picture on page 397.
Division	1	Nantillois (Meuse)	Medium-size stone fountain.	1927	Erected by the State of Pennsylvania. See picture on page 525.
Infantry (Division.)	1	Seicheprey (Meurthe-et-Moselle).	Small granite fountain (no water).	1923	Presented by men and women of the State of Connecticut. See picture on page 128.
Infantry (Division.)	1	Southwest edge of Prémont (Aisne).	Small monument of cut stone.	1923	Erected by private subscription. Same design as 30th Div. monument. See picture on page 377.

Memorial at St. Nazaire Commemorating First
American Troops to Land in France

Memorial Near Islay, Scotland, to Th
Lost Their Lives on the S. S. *Tusc*

Lafayette Escadrille Monument Erected Near
Garches by Members of the Unit

3d Aviation Center Monument
at Issoudun

Monument on the Borne de Cornouiller to
American Troops Who Fought Near By

U. S. Naval Ai
Monument, Mout

n in Nantillois Erected by State of
Pennsylvania

Monument in Paris to American Volunteers
Who Died for France

Memorial Bridge at Fismes Erected by
State of Pennsylvania

th Division
ld Marker

315th Infantry, 79th Division, Memorial
Building in Nantillois

French Monument
at Bathelémont

Unit or event commemorated	Number	Location	Character	Date erected	Remarks
118th Infantry (30th Division.)	1	In the northern part of town of Brancourt-le-Grand (Aisne).	Small monument of cut stone.	1923	Erected by pri subscription. S design as 30th monument. picture on page
310th Infantry (78th Division.)	1	In church at town of Semur-en-Auxois (Côte-d'Or).	Stained-glass church window.	1927	In memory of the c of the regiment.
313th Infantry (79th Division.)	1	Alongside the road in old town of Montfaucon (Meuse).	Bronze tablet on a fence post.	Soon after the Armistice.	Tablet states that town was captr by the regiment.
315th Infantry (79th Division.)	1	Nantillois (Meuse)	Building given to the village as a recreation center.	1930	Erected by the ment in memor its dead. See pic appearing on page
362d Infantry (91st Division.)	1	Gesnes-en-Argonne (Meuse).	Concrete post, about 4 feet high.	Soon after the Armistice.	A small bronze p describes fightin regiment in vici
371st Infantry (93d Division.)	1	On hill in open field about ½ mile south of town of Ardeuil (Ardennes). (Difficult of access.)	Small granite monument, which lists names of the dead.	About 1924	In memory of the ment's dead in v ity. See the pic appearing on page
372d Infantry (93d Division.)	1	Along main road, ¼ mile south of Monthois (Ardennes).	Small obelisk of cut granite.	1920	In memory of n bers of the regin killed in action, S 26–Oct. 7, 1918. picture on page
6th Engineers	1	Cathedral at Amiens (Somme).	Tablet	1919	Erected by the citi of Amiens to c memorate the dea 6th Engineers lo defense of that pl
23d Engineers	1	In village of Varennes-en-Argonne (Meuse) across from the church.	Concrete marker, about 5 feet high.	Soon after the Armistice.	Erected by the me the regiment.
The American Field Service.	1	At Pont-à-Mousson (Meurthe-et-Moselle).	Large Renaissance fountain.	1931	Erected by mem of unit to those American Fi Service who diec France. See pic appearing on page
The Lafayette Escadrille.	1	At Garches (Seine-et-Oise), near Paris.	Imposing memorial of cut stone.	1928	Erected by unit. C tains bodies of n bers. See the ture appearing page 524.
All Pennsylvania troops who served in the World War.	1	At Varennes-en-Argonne (Meuse).	Development of a public park.	1927	Erected by the Sta Pennsylvania. picture on page

t or event memorated	Num-ber	Location	Character	Date erected	Remarks
of Missouri ● gave their s during the ·ld War.	1	At the road junction, south of the town of Cheppy (Meuse).	Stone shaft surmounted by a bronze figure.	1922...........	Erected by the State of Missouri. See the picture on page 216.
hose of the 3. Naval Air ation at utchic-La-au who lost r lives.	1	Moutchic (Gironde) west of Bordeaux.	Stone obelisk.......	Soon after the Armistice.	Erected by subscription from officers and men of naval air station. See the picture on page 524.
ose who were ed at Third ation Center.	1	11 kilometers from Issoudun (Indre), on road to Vatan, about 40 yards off from the road.	Stone, of medium size, surrounded by an iron chain on stone posts.	Soon after the Armistice.	Erected by subscription from officers who were on duty at the Aviation Center at the time. See the picture on page 524.
ican soldiers ● were killed he village of ·emont.	1	Apremont (Meuse), near Montsec.	Building with a fountain outside.	1922...........	Erected with funds donated by the city of Holyoke, Massachusetts.
ican soldiers ● were killed r Seicheprey.	1	On outside of church in Seicheprey (Meurthe-et-Moselle), near door.	Small ornamental plaque of bronze.	1929...........	Funds were supplied by an American.
●vements of ●erican troops ● fought in the nity of Sivry-·Meuse.	1	On the Borne de Cornouiller near Sivry-sur-Meuse. (Difficult of access.)	Stone obelisk.......	1925...........	See picture, page 524.
ne American nteers who ● for France.	1	In Place des Etats-Unis at Paris.	Stone, sculptured group on front.	1923...........	Erected by the French. American dead of the Foreign Legion, Lafayette Escadrille and American Field Service are listed. Picture on page 525.
●e first Ameritroops to ● in France.	1	St. Nazaire-sur-Loire (Loire Inférieure).	Stone shaft surmounted by a bronze soldier on an eagle's back.	1926...........	Erected by public subscription from Americans. See the picture appearing on page 524.
first three ●ericans killed front during World War.	1	In Bathelémont (Meurthe-et-Moselle) 12 kilometers north of Lunéville.	Stone shaft, about 18 feet high.	1918...........	Erected by the French. See picture page 525.
●e who lost ir lives as a ●lt of the king of S. S. scania during b. 5, 1918.	1	Near Islay, Scotland.	Stone tower on a rocky headland.	1920...........	Constructed by the American Red Cross not long after the war. See the picture appearing on page 524.

The Consulting Architect of the American Battle Monuments Commission:

Dr. Paul P. Cret of Philadelphia has been the Consulting Architect of the Commission throughout its entire existence.

Architects who designed the memorials constructed by the Commission:

The chapels and monuments erected in Europe by the American Battle Monuments Commission were designed by the following named American architects:

John Russell Pope, New York.
Meuse-Argonne memorial, Montfaucon.

York & Sawyer, New York.
The chapel and other architectural features in Meuse-Argonne cemetery.

Egerton Swartwout, New York.
St. Mihiel monument, on Montsec.
The chapel, entrance and flagpole in the Brookwood cemetery in England.

Paul P. Cret, Philadelphia.
Aisne-Marne memorial, on Hill 204.
The chapel in Flanders Field cemetery.
Monument located north of Bellicourt.
Memorial archway located at Gibraltar.
Bronze tablet on building at Chaumont.
Bronze tablet on building at Souilly.

Cram & Ferguson, Boston.
Chapels and other features in Aisne-Marne and Oise-Aisne cemeteries.

Ralph Milman and the Howard Shaw Associates, Chicago.
Monument on old fortification at Brest.

Arthur Loomis Harmon, New York.
Memorial fountain at city of Tours.
Monument near village of Sommepy.
Monument in the village of Cantigny.

George Howe, Philadelphia.
Chapel and other architectural features in the Somme cemetery near Bony.
Vierstraat monument, south of Ypres.

Thomas Harlan Ellett, New York.
The chapel and other architectural features in the St. Mihiel cemetery.

Charles A. Platt, New York.
The chapel and main entrance gate at the Suresnes cemetery, near Paris.

Harry Sternfeld, Philadelphia.
Monument and park development in the village of Audenarde in Belgium.

Sculptors and artists who did outstand works of art for the Commission

The work of the following sculptors artists in connection with the chapels memorials erected by the Commissio Europe is worthy of special recognit

C. P. Jennewein, Sculptor, New York
All sculpturing for Tours fountain.

Adolph Weinman, Sculptor, New Yor
Meuse-Argonne memorial, Montfau

Paul Manship, Sculptor, New York.
Soldier monument and urn at chap the St. Mihiel cemetery, Thiauco

John Bradley Storr, Sculptor, Chicag
All sculpturing for Brest monumen

A. Bottiau, Sculptor, Paris.
Features for Aisne-Marne monum
All sculpturing on Bellicourt monum
Flanders Field chapel near Waeregh

Marcel Loyau, Sculptor, Paris.
Sculpturing for Somme cemetery cha

Barry Faulkner, Painter, New York.
Mosaics on the interior walls of St. Mihiel and Suresnes chapels.

Reginald Hallward, London.
All stained-glass windows in both Brookwood and Suresnes chapels

Officials of European Office, Amer Battle Monuments Commission, supervised construction:

The following officials who served ir European Office of the Commission w the memorials and chapels were b constructed had important duties in nection with the construction work. officers are in the Regular Army and listed in order of reporting for duty.

Lt. Col. X. H. Price, C. E. (In chai
Capt. Thomas North, F. A.
Lt. Col. Harris Jones, C. E.
Maj. George A. Horkan, Q. M. C.
Maj. Hubert W. Beyette, Q. M. C.
Lt. Col. Wilhelm D. Styer, C. E.
Capt. Robert A. Schow, Inf.
Maj. Willis E. Teale, C. E.
Lt. Col. Raymond G. Moses, C. E
Maj. George F. Hobson, Q. M. C.
Capt. Louis J. Rumaggi, C. E.
Mr. Henry R. Brown.

GLOSSARY OF MILITARY TERMS USED IN THIS BOOK

id Station. A medical establishment, near the
nt, for emergency treatment and further disposi-
n of combat casualties.

Artillery Preparation. Scheduled artillery fire de-
red before an attack to destroy or neutralize the
my defenses, matériel and personnel.

Barrage. A curtain formed by fire from artillery
other weapons firing from fixed mounts. A
anding barrage" is one usually placed across a
bable avenue of enemy approach. A "rolling
rage" is one that precedes the attacking infantry
a prescribed rate in order to assist its advance. A
x barrage" is a continuous standing barrage,
ering the rear and flanks of an area in order to
vent the escape or reinforcement of the enemy
hin the area.

Base Section. A rear area or subdivision of the
vices of Supply.

Battalion (Infantry, American). A tactical unit
sisting of a headquarters and four rifle companies.
normal command of a major. Total World War
ngth 1,027 officers and men.

Battery (American). An artillery unit consisting
a specified number of guns, usually four, and the
sonnel to man them. Commanded by a captain.

Bridgehead. A position covering a bridge, located
the side toward the enemy.

Brigade (Field Artillery, American). An organiza-
a comprising a headquarters, two regiments of
mm. guns, one regiment of 155-mm. howitzers,
one 6-inch trench mortar battery. The normal
mand of a brigadier general. World War
ngth 4,908 combatants and 48 guns, 24 how-
rs and 12 trench mortars.

Brigade (Infantry, American). An organization
sisting of a headquarters, two infantry regiments
a machine gun battalion. The normal command
a brigadier general. World War strength 8,324
batants; 6,459 rifles.

Camouflage. Means employed to conceal from
tile observation, both ground and air, troops and
tériel located in exposed areas.

Captive Balloon. A balloon, held by cables, used
observation purposes. Some of these, because of
ir shape, were called "sausage balloons."

Casualties. The dead, wounded, captured, missing
action and sick in campaign and battle. Those
from disease are not included in the heading
ttle casualties."

Command Post. The place from which a com-
nder directs the operations of his unit. Often
ed during the World War a "P. C." meaning a
t of command. Now generally abbreviated in
United States Army and called a "C. P."

Company (Infantry, American). The authorized
mand of a captain. World War strength 256
cers and men.

Concentration Camp. A camp in which troops are
mbled preparatory to service against an enemy or
transportation to the theater of war. A camp or
tonment where prisoners or refugees are interned.

Consolidate (a position). To prepare a captured
position for defense by erecting field fortifications, etc.

Convoy. A group of vehicles or vessels, the escort
and the matériel or personnel being transported.

Corps (American). A tactical unit normally
made up of a headquarters, two or more divisions and
auxiliary troops. The normal command of a major
general or lieutenant general.

Defile. Any narrow space or place which can be
passed only when troops are in column, such as a ford,
bridge or mountain pass.

Depot. A place where military supplies are collected for distribution.

Detachment. A group separated from its organization for a special purpose.

Division (American). Two brigades of infantry and
one brigade of artillery. It contained also engineer,
machine gun, signal, medical and transportation
units and a headquarters. World War strength
28,105 officers and men; 16,193 rifles. The normal
command of a major general.

Doughboy. Name applied to an American infan-
tryman. A colloquialism.

Dressing Station. Place established during combat for the reception of casualties and treatment of
minor wounds. Also known as an aid station. See
under "Aid Station."

Dump. A place where supplies are temporarily
stored for distribution in the field.

Emplacement. A prepared gun position.

Enfilade. A firing in the direction of the length of
a trench, line or column of troops. This is also known
as "flanking fire".

Evacuate. To withdraw from a position. To
remove sick, wounded, prisoners or the civil population to the rear.

Field Fortifications. All field works, shelters and
obstacles constructed to increase the powers of
resistance of a force.

Flame Thrower. A device for projecting flame.
Carried on the back and operated by gas pressure, it
threw a flame of burning oil about 20 yards and was
capable of two minutes continuous operation.

Flank. The right or left of a command or position.
To pass around or turn a flank. To threaten a flank.

Fox Hole. Individual shelter or rifle pit, usually
dug during combat.

French Colonial Division. A division composed of
troops from a French colony. During the war it was
abbreviated to D. I. C.

Front. Zone of active operations. Any section of
the battle line. The lateral space occupied by a unit.

Front Line. The most advanced line which would
be defended in case of attack.

Gas. A chemical agent for producing a poisonous
or irritant atmosphere. In general, gases were persistent (mustard) or non-persistent (chlorine or phos-
gene), depending on how long the area upon which
they were used would remain contaminated. Placed
upon hostile areas by guns, mortars and projectors.
The gas was sometimes released from cylinders to be

carried by wind currents toward the enemy position.

Grenade. A small bomb. One type could be thrown by hand and another was projected from a rifle by means of a grenade discharger.

Hindenburg Line. Name given originally by the British to a powerful defensive position of great strength constructed by the Germans between Soissons and Cambrai to which they conducted a strategic retirement in February 1917. The name was later applied by the Allies and Americans to strong German defensive positions on other parts of the front.

Howitzer. A rifled, breech-loading cannon with comparatively short barrel and low muzzle velocity, fired at ranges and elevations intermediate between field guns and mortars.

Infiltrate. To pass troops in relatively small numbers through gaps or weakly held portions of the hostile lines. To move troops into or nearer a hostile position by sending forward single men, small groups or thin lines at widely separated intervals.

Intelligence Service. The organization in an army whose duty it is to collect, study, interpret and distribute information of the enemy and to prevent the enemy from obtaining information.

Liaison. Close touch maintained between units, by agents or officers, for the purpose of exchanging information and insuring cooperation.

Lines of Communication. All routes, land, water and air, which connect a military force in the field with its base of operations, and along which supplies and reinforcements are sent to the front and wounded are moved to the rear.

Machine Gun. A gun firing on the automatic principle from a fixed mount. During the war such guns were usually water cooled.

Machine-Gun Nest. One or more machine guns emplaced or concealed in a firing position. Usually organized so that two or more guns could be mutually supporting and could deliver crossing bands of fire.

Matériel. All material things necessary for war purposes. Used in contradistinction to personnel.

Mine Barrage. A line or network of sea mines to prevent the passage of ships. A mine layer is a boat equipped for placing mines, and a mine sweeper is one used in removing them from the water.

Minenwerfer. A German bomb-throwing weapon designed for trench use. It was muzzle-loading and rifled, and had a curved trajectory. A small mortar.

Mobilization. The organizing and assembling of troops and all resources of a nation for war.

Mopping Up. To clear an area or position that has been advanced over in an attack, by killing or capturing the enemy soldiers remaining in it.

Morale. The mental state of an individual or body of troops, especially in relation to performance of duty; also applies to the civilian population.

Mortar. A cannon with a comparatively short barrel and a low muzzle velocity which is fired at high angles to shell areas behind steep ridges.

Munitions. Military stores of all kinds.

No Man's Land. The strip of ground between opposing front lines. On the Western Front it varied in width from a few yards to several hundred.

Order of Battle. The general disposition of troops or their arrangement when participating in battle.

Outflank. To pass around or turn the flank of enemy so as to be able to threaten his flank or r

Patrols. Small detachments used for a numbe purposes, such as raiding and reconnoitering enemy and protection.

Pillbox. A covered concrete emplacement for or more machine guns.

Pioneer Troops. Military laborers employed building roads, digging trenches, etc.

Platoon (American). One of the elements o company, World War strength about 50 men. normal command of a lieutenant.

Ponton. A boat used to hold part of the road of a floating bridge.

Raid. A sudden and rapid invasion of a ho position, usually carried out by a small force for purpose of returning with prisoners and informa

Railhead. A point on a railway where ammuni and supplies are transferred to dumps or vehicles delivery to the troops.

Reclassification Camp. A camp to which indi uals are sent for examination in order to determine duty for which they are best suited.

Reconnaissance. The examination of a localit of a hostile force in order to gather informatio military value.

Regiment (Infantry, American). An organiza composed, during the World War, of a headquar three battalions, a headquarters company, a su company and a machine gun company. Stren 3,770 combatants. The normal command of officer of the rank of colonel.

Regulating Stations. Large railway yards f which supplies were forwarded to the railheads.

Remount Depot. Replacement depot for ani casualties. A remount is the replacement furnis

Salient. A part of a battle line which proj pointedly into opposing territory.

Sector. An area occupied by a unit in defe the frontage of such an area.

Sortie. A sudden offensive movement made f a fortified base.

Squad (American). A basic unit of organizat consisting normally of a corporal and seven priva A general term for various small groups.

Strategic Center. A region which because of commanding position, harbor facilities, lines of c munication, natural resources, bases of supply s ated there, or other reasons is of great advantag the holder in the conduct of operations, and the of which would seriously cripple him.

Strong Point. A compact area strongly organ and garrisoned for a protracted defense.

Tank. An armored self-propelled vehicle of track-laying type (caterpillar tractor), combi fire-power, mobility and shock action.

Western Front. The name applied to the ba front in France and Belgium extending from North Sea to the Swiss border.

Zone of Action. The area between certain def limits or boundaries, generally at right angles to front, assigned to a unit in offensive action o a withdrawal from a certain locality.

Zone of Operations. The region within which army operates between its base and its object

Page

E